Information-Based Complexity

This is a volume in
COMPUTER SCIENCE AND SCIENTIFIC COMPUTING

Werner Rheinboldt and Daniel Siewiorek, editors

Information-Based Complexity

J. F. Traub
Department of Computer Science
Columbia University
New York, New York

G. W. Wasilkowski
Department of Computer Science
University of Kentucky
Lexington, Kentucky

H. Woźniakowski
Institute of Informatics
University of Warsaw
Warsaw, Poland
and
Department of Computer Science
Columbia University
New York, New York

ACADEMIC PRESS, INC.
Harcourt Brace Jovanovich, Publishers
Boston   San Diego   New York
Berkeley   London   Sydney
Tokyo   Toronto

ACADEMIC PRESS, INC.
1250 Sixth Avenue, San Diego, CA 92101

United Kingdom Edition published by
ACADEMIC PRESS INC. (LONDON) LTD.
24–28 Oval Road, London NW1 7DX

Sections 5–7 of Chapter 5, Section 4 of Chapter 7, and part of Section 7 of
Chapter 8 were written by **A. G. Werschulz**, Division of Science and
Mathematics, Fordham University, and Department of Computer Science,
Columbia University.

Section 4 of Chapter 5 was written by **T. Boult**, Department of Computer
Science, Columbia University.

Library of Congress Cataloging-in-Publication Data

Traub, J. F. (Joseph Frederick), 1932–
        Information-based complexity / J. F. Traub, G. W. Wasilkowski, H.
    Wozniakowski.
            p.   cm. – (Computer science and scientific computing)
        Bibliography: p.
        Includes indexes.
        ISBN 0-12-697545-0
        1. Computational complexity.   I. Wasilkowski, G. W.
    II. Wozniakowski, H. III. Title.   IV. Series.
    QA267.T73 1988
    511.3–dc19   87-28918
                                                                        CIP

88 89 90 91   9 8 7 6 5 4 3 2 1
Printed in the United States of America

To our children:

Claudia and Hillary Traub,

Bartek and Kubuś Wasilkowski,

Artur Woźniakowski,

and to my mother:

Jadwiga Wasilkowska.

Table of Contents

Preface

The purpose of this book is to provide a comprehensive treatment of information-based complexity. We present theory and applications. In addition to integrating the work of many researchers, new results are also developed.

In two earlier books, we analyzed the worst case setting. Here we study the worst case, average case, probabilistic, random, and asymptotic settings. The effect of noisy information is briefly discussed. Some open problems are also indicated.

We wish to acknowledge many debts. Our special thanks are to A. G. Werschulz who authored several sections, as indicated on the front page, suggested many improvements to the whole book and was of invaluable help in preparing the TeX version of the book and in preparing the two indices. We thank T. Boult who wrote the computer vision section. We are pleased to thank S. Kwapień for useful remarks and guidance concerning measure theory.

We appreciate valuable suggestions from M. A. Kowalski and K. Sikorski, and comments from M. A. Kon, D. Lee, E. W. Packel, and L. Plaskota. We also thank T. Orowan who superbly typed a number of the chapters in TeX.

We are pleased to thank the National Science Foundation (Grant ICT-85-17289 and DCR-86-03674) and the Advanced Research Projects Agency (Contract N00039-84-C-0165) for supporting the work reported here.

J. F. Traub
G. W. Wasilkowski
H. Woźniakowski

xiii

Chapter 1

Overview

The *computational complexity* of a problem is its intrinsic difficulty as measured by the minimal computational resources, such as time or memory, required for its solution. Equivalently, the computational complexity is the minimal cost among all algorithms that solve the problem. Such a minimal cost algorithm is said to be *optimal*. The computational complexity is a *problem invariant*; it is independent of any particular algorithm. The notion of an invariant is important in many scientific fields. We believe that computational complexity is a fundamental invariant of computer science.

Computational complexity sets intrinsic limits on which problems can be solved. Problems that cannot be solved because limitations dictate that the requisite computational resources can never be achieved are said to be *intractable*. Having provided a benchmark for the intrinsic difficulty of a problem, one may compare its computational complexity with the cost of any algorithm that solves the problem to tell how well the given algorithm measures up.

The reader will note from our usage above that the term *computational complexity* serves double duty, both as the name of a scientific field, as well as a crucial problem invariant within that field.

A central notion in the theory which is developed in this book is *information*. We do not mean information in the sense of Claude Shannon and information theory. For present purposes, information is what we know about the problem to be solved. Information will be defined in the general formulation of Chapter 3.

Most problems arising in the sciences or engineering have the characteristic that information relevant to their solution is either partial or noisy. For such problems, only approximate solutions are possible.

As a digital computer can only manipulate a finite set of numbers, any problem whose domain of possible problem elements is infinite will necessarily have only partial information. In particular, this is true of continuous problems defined on an infinite dimensional function space.

We emphasize that information-based complexity is not restricted to infinite dimensional problems. For instance, it can be used to study finite dimensional problems with complete but noisy information. Also, it can be used if the complexity of computing an exact solution is prohibitively large and one is willing to settle for an approximate solution to reduce the complexity.

As a simple example of partial and noisy information consider the computation of a definite integral. For most integrands we cannot compute the integral utilizing the fundamental theorem of the calculus since there is no closed form expression for the antiderivative. We have to approximate the integral numerically. Usually, the integrand is evaluated at a finite number of points. The information is the values of the integrand at these points. In general, an infinite number of integrands have the same values at these points, and therefore the information is partial. In addition, there will be round-off error in evaluating the integrand, and so the information is noisy. The integral is estimated by combining the integrand values. Since the information we are using does not uniquely identify the integrand, we can compute only an approximate solution. There is intrinsic uncertainty in the answer.

For problems arising in science and engineering the information has another characteristic; it is *priced*. For instance, in the integration example we should be charged for the evaluations of the integrand.

The branch of computational complexity that deals with the intrinsic difficulty of the approximate solution of problems for which the information is partial, noisy, and priced is called *information-based complexity*.

Problems with partial, noisy, and priced information arise in many areas. These include economics, numerical analysis, physics, human and robotic vision, scientific and engineering computation, geophysics, decision theory, signal processing, and control theory.

On the other hand, there are problems for which the information is *complete, exact*, and *free*. The branch of computational complexity that deals with such problems is known as *combinatorial complexity*. An example is provided by the traveling salesman problem. In this problem the information is a set of cities along with the distances between all pairs of cities. Since the information specifies the problem uniquely, the information is complete. Furthermore, this information is exact and free. These assumptions are typical for many other important problems, for example, for NP-complete problems.

In both combinatorial complexity and information-based complexity we seek to solve a problem using an algorithm with minimal cost. Since problems of information-based complexity can only be solved approximately, the notion of *error* is important. We require that the problem be solved with error no greater than a threshold ε. The ε-*complexity* is then defined as the minimal cost among all algorithms which solve the problem with error at most ε.

The cost and error of algorithms can be variously defined, leading to different settings. In the *worst case* setting, the cost and error are defined by their worst performance. In the *average case* setting, the cost and error are defined by their average performance. In the *probabilistic* setting, errors on sets of small measure are ignored. Mixed settings, where the cost is defined in one sense and the error in a different sense, are also of interest.

An error criterion must be specified. Absolute and relative criteria are among those studied. Since results are sensitive to the error criteria, this further enriches the subject.

The purpose of this book is to provide a comprehensive treatment of information-based complexity. We shall sometimes refer to two earlier books. Both of these deal with the worst case setting:

- *A General Theory of Optimal Algorithms*, J. F. Traub and H. Woźniakowski, Academic Press, 1980. We will refer to this book as GTOA.
- *Information, Uncertainty, Complexity*, J. F. Traub, G. W. Wasilkowski, and H. Woźniakowski, Addison-Wesley, 1983. We will refer to this book as IUC.

We briefly indicate the contents of this book. In Chapter 2 we use the example of continuous binary search to illustrate the main issues and concepts of information-based complexity. Results are obtained for the major settings and error criteria. In the following chapter we present an abstract formulation of information-based complexity and rigorously define such concepts as information, ε-complexity, optimal information, and optimal algorithm. The major settings are also defined.

The theory of the worst case setting is given in Chapter 4. Twelve applications for the worst case setting are discussed in Chapter 5.

Chapters 6 and 7 develop theory and applications for the average case setting, while Chapter 8 deals with theory and applications for the probabilistic setting.

In Chapter 9 we take a different cut through the subject. We fix the problem and compare the ε-complexities for varying settings and error criteria. We do this for the integration and function approximation problems.

In Chapter 10 we study the asymptotic setting which is extensively used in numerical analysis. The objective in this setting is to achieve the best possible speed of convergence. Relations are obtained between the asymptotic and worst case settings, and between the asymptotic and average case settings.

Up to this point, the book is restricted to deterministic information and algorithms. In Chapter 11 we study random information and random algorithms.

Chapter 12 deals with the important but technically difficult case of noisy information. The worst case and average cases are discussed.

For the reader's benefit, concepts and results from functional analysis and measure theory used in this book are summarized in the appendix. The bibliography contains over 440 entries.

Typically, a chapter and its sections are followed by Notes and Remarks which include commentary on the text, extensions to the results, and bibliographical discussion. In Notes and Remarks we also give reference to papers with original results as well as papers which serve as a basis of the chapter or section. The lack of such a reference indicates that the analysis is new. Sections sometimes conclude with exercises for the reader.

We end this overview by describing our system for referring to material within the text. Theorems, equations, remarks, etc. are separately numbered for each section. A reference to material within the same section does not name the section. A reference to material within a different section of the same chapter names the section, and a reference to material within a different chapter names the chapter and the section.

Notes and Remarks as well as Exercises are also separately numbered for each section. For instance, **NR 5.4:3** denotes the third entry in Notes and Remarks in Section 5.4 of a given chapter, and **E 2:1** denotes the first exercise in Section 2 of a given chapter.

Notes and Remarks

NR 1:1 For work on information-based complexity up to 1980 see GTOA. It deals with partial information and the worst case setting. A brief history and an annotated bibliography of 325 books and papers is included.

IUC deals with partial or noisy information in the worst case setting. It utilizes a more general framework than that used in most of this book, see Remark 2.1 of Chapter 3.

A number of surveys have been written for certain audiences or emphasizing particular viewpoints. These include Traub and Woźniakowski [84a], Wasilkowski [85], Woźniakowski [85, 86a], Packel and Traub [87], Packel, Traub, and Woźniakowski [87], and Packel and Woźniakowski [87].

Chapter 2

Example: Continuous Binary Search

1. Introduction

We use the simple example of continuous binary search, which is a generalization of the 20 questions game, to illustrate major issues and concepts of information-based complexity. The statement of the continuous binary search problem consists, as does the statement of any problem studied in this book, of three parts:

- problem formulation,
- information,
- model of computation.

The concepts of *error* and *cost* of an algorithm, as well as *ε-complexity* are defined. The ε-complexity is understood as the minimal cost required to compute approximations to within ε. For brevity, ε-complexity will be also called *complexity*. Depending on how the error and cost are defined, we consider three basic settings:

- worst case,
- average case,
- probabilistic.

We discuss continuous binary search in the three settings for two error criteria: absolute and relative. We shall see how the complexity depends on the setting and on the error criterion. We end this chapter with several remarks concerning further settings and noisy information.

In many formulas of this book we use the Ω, Θ, O, and o notations, see Knuth [76]. For two functions f and g defined on $\mathbb{R}_+$ and taking nonnegative values, we write $f(\varepsilon) = \Omega(g(\varepsilon))$ if there exist positive constants c_1 and c_2 such that $f(\varepsilon) \geq c_1 g(\varepsilon)$ for all $\varepsilon \in [0, c_2]$. By $f(\varepsilon) = \Theta(g(\varepsilon))$ we mean that $f(\varepsilon) = \Omega(g(\varepsilon))$ and $g(\varepsilon) = \Omega(f(\varepsilon))$, i.e., there exist positive constants c_1, c_2, and c_3 such that $c_1 g(\varepsilon) \leq f(\varepsilon) \leq c_2 g(\varepsilon)$ for $\varepsilon \in [0, c_3]$. By $f(\varepsilon) = O(g(\varepsilon))$ we mean that $g(\varepsilon) = \Omega(f(\varepsilon))$, and by $f(\varepsilon) = o(g(\varepsilon))$ we mean that $\lim_{\varepsilon \to 0} f(\varepsilon)/g(\varepsilon) = 0$. In particular, $f(\varepsilon) = g(\varepsilon)(1 + o(1))$ means that $\lim_{\varepsilon \to 0} f(\varepsilon)/g(\varepsilon) = 1$. Analogous definitions apply when the parameter $n \to +\infty$ replaces $\varepsilon \to 0$.

We are ready to define and analyze continuous binary search.

1.1. Problem Formulation

Let f be a real number from the interval $F = (0,1)$. Our aim is to compute the number f to within a prescribed accuracy ε, where ε belongs to the interval $[0,1)$.

1.2. Information

In order to compute an approximation, we ask *"true or false"* questions about the number f. We assume that *any* question is allowed, i.e., for an arbitrary subset T of the interval F and any $f \in F$, we can evaluate $Q(f;T)$,

$$Q(f;T) = \begin{cases} 1 & \text{if } f \in T, \\ 0 & \text{if } f \notin T. \end{cases}$$

1.3. Model of Computation

We assume that each question has a fixed cost c, where $c > 0$. Additionally, we assume that we can perform arithmetic operations and comparisons of real numbers. It is assumed that each such operation costs unity and is performed exactly. That is, we use the real number model of computation.

Notes and Remarks

NR 1.3:1 We assume that each question costs the same. This is quite a restrictive assumption. In an alternative model of computation the cost of a question depends on the question. Under such a model of computation, it is much harder to obtain tight complexity bounds.

2. Complexity

What is the complexity of continuous binary search, i.e., what is the minimal cost of finding an ε-approximation? Which questions should be asked, and how should the answers be combined in order to find an ε-approximation with minimal cost?

We now formalize these issues. The information about the number f from $F = (0,1)$ is gathered by asking questions. More precisely, our information about f is provided by

$$N(f) = [Q(f;T_1), Q(f;T_2), \ldots, Q(f;T_{n(f)})].$$

Here the choice of T_i, as well as the number $n(f)$ of questions, may depend on the previous answers.

Knowing $N(f)$, we compute an approximation to f by an algorithm ϕ, where $\phi : N(F) \to F$. That is, $U(f) = \phi(N(f))$ serves as an approximation to f, and $|f - U(f)|$ is the *absolute* error. Formally, U is a pair, $U = (\phi, N)$.

The cost of computing $U(f)$ consists of two parts. First we compute $y = N(f)$ with the cost denoted by $\mathrm{cost}(N, f)$. We are charged for the computation of $Q(f;T_i)$, $i = 1, 2, \ldots, n(f)$, and for the selection of T_i. In our model of computation, $\mathrm{cost}(N, f) \geq c\,n(f)$. Next, given y, we compute $\phi(y)$. Let $\mathrm{cost}(\phi, y)$ denote the cost of computing the value $\phi(y)$, i.e., the total number of arithmetic operations and comparisons needed to compute $\phi(y)$.

We now define the error, $e(U)$, and the cost, $\mathrm{cost}(U)$, of $U = (\phi, N)$. They depend on the setting.

In the *worst case* setting, the error and cost are defined by the worst performance,

$$e(U) = \sup_{f \in F} |f - \phi(N(f))|,$$

$$\mathrm{cost}(U) = \sup_{f \in F} \{\mathrm{cost}(N, f) + \mathrm{cost}(\phi, N(f))\}.$$

In the *average case* setting, the error and cost are defined by the average performance. That is, assuming that F is equipped with a probability measure μ, we let

$$e(U) = \int_F |f - \phi(N(f))|\, \mu(df),$$

$$\mathrm{cost}(U) = \int_F \big(\mathrm{cost}(N, f) + \mathrm{cost}(\phi, N(f))\big)\, \mu(df).$$

In the *probabilistic* setting, the error is defined as in the worst case setting, but disregarding a set of measure at most δ, where $\delta \in [0,1]$, and the cost is given as in the worst case setting,

$$e(U) = \inf\left\{ \sup_{f \in F-A} |f - \phi(N(f))| : A \subset F \text{ and } \mu(A) \leq \delta \right\},$$

$$\text{cost}(U) = \sup_{f \in F}\left\{ \text{cost}(N,f) + \text{cost}\left(\phi, N(f)\right) \right\}.$$

Different ways of defining the cost in the probabilistic setting are mentioned in **NR 2:2**.

We are ready to define the ε-complexity of continuous binary search. As always, complexity is the minimal cost of computing approximations with a prescribed accuracy. That is,

$$\text{comp}(\varepsilon) = \inf\left\{ \text{cost}(U) : U \text{ such that } e(U) \leq \varepsilon \right\}$$

with the convention that the infimum of the empty set is taken as $+\infty$.

We stress that $\text{cost}(U)$ and $e(U)$ depend on the setting. Therefore, $\text{comp}(\varepsilon)$ is the worst case, average case, or probabilistic complexity depending on which definitions of the cost and error are used. Sometimes we write $\text{comp}^{\text{wor}}(\varepsilon)$, $\text{comp}^{\text{avg}}(\varepsilon)$, or $\text{comp}^{\text{prob}}(\varepsilon, \delta)$ to emphasize the setting and the dependence on the parameter δ in the probabilistic setting. In the following sections, we present the complexity of continuous binary search in all three settings.

Notes and Remarks

NR 2:1 It is possible to define the error and cost of an algorithm in the $\mathcal{L}_p$ sense, $p \geq 1$. That is, in the average case setting the error and cost are defined by

$$e(U) = \left(\int_F |f - U(f)|^p \, \mu(df) \right)^{1/p},$$

$$\text{cost}(U) = \left(\int_F \left(\text{cost}(N,f) + \text{cost}(\phi, N(f)) \right)^p \mu(df) \right)^{1/p}.$$

NR 2:2 In the probabilistic setting, the cost can be also defined on the average. One can also disregard a set A of measure at most δ for which we do not control the error.

3. Worst Case Setting

We prove that the worst case complexity is given by

$$\text{comp}^{\text{wor}}(\varepsilon) = c \left\lceil \log_2 \frac{1}{\varepsilon} - 1 \right\rceil.$$

(Here and elsewhere, by $\lceil x \rceil$ we mean the smallest integer no smaller than x, and by $\lfloor x \rfloor$ the largest integer no greater than x.)

We first establish a lower bound on $\mathrm{comp}^{\mathrm{wor}}(\varepsilon)$. Take a pair $U = (\phi, N)$ such that $e(U) \le \varepsilon$. Since the cost is defined by a worst performance, one can assume without loss of generality that $n(f) \equiv n$; that is, the number of questions is independent of f. Observe that $N(f)$ can take at most 2^n different values. Thus, the interval $F = (0, 1)$ can be partitioned into p disjoint subsets A_i, $i = 1, 2, \ldots, p$ with $p \le 2^n$, such that $U(\cdot) = \phi(N(\cdot))$ is constant on each of these sets. There exists a subset A_j with diameter at least 2^{-n}. That is, for $a = \inf\{f : f \in A_j\}$ and $b = \sup\{f : f \in A_j\}$, we have $b - a \ge 2^{-n}$. Then

$$\varepsilon \ge e(U) \ge \sup_{f \in A_j} |f - U(f)| \ge \inf_{u \in F} \sup_{f \in A_j} |f - u|$$

$$= \inf_{u \in F} \max\{|a - u|, |b - u|\} = \frac{b - a}{2} \ge 2^{-(n+1)}.$$

So, $n \ge \lceil \log_2 \varepsilon^{-1} - 1 \rceil$. Since $\mathrm{cost}(U) \ge cn$, we conclude that $\mathrm{cost}^{\mathrm{wor}}(U) \ge c \lceil \log_2 \varepsilon^{-1} - 1 \rceil$ for *any* $U = (\phi, N)$, unless $e(U) > \varepsilon$. Therefore, $\mathrm{comp}^{\mathrm{wor}}(\varepsilon) \ge c \lceil \log_2 \varepsilon^{-1} - 1 \rceil$, as claimed.

We now show that the bound $c \lceil \log_2 \varepsilon^{-1} - 1 \rceil$ can be achieved by asking bisection questions, i.e., by asking whether f is less than the midpoint α of an interval of uncertainty. For the first question $\alpha = 1/2$ and for the second α is either $1/4$ or $3/4$, depending on the answer to the first question. Note that to pose the ith bisection question, we have to know the answers to the $(i-1)$ previous questions. Suppose that $k = \lceil \log_2 \varepsilon^{-1} - 1 \rceil$ bisection questions are asked and that f_ε is the midpoint of the last interval of uncertainty. Then

$$|f - f_\varepsilon| \le 2^{-(k+1)} \le \varepsilon.$$

The same information may be gathered by asking k simultaneously posed questions in such a way that the cost of computing f_ε is zero. The ith question is given by: "Is the ith bit of f zero?", $i = 1, 2, \ldots, k$ (or equivalently: Does f belong to Q_i, where Q_i is the set of f whose ith bit is zero?). Then we set

$$f_\varepsilon = \sum_{i=1}^{k} b_i 2^{-i} + 2^{-(k+1)}.$$

Here $b_i = 0$ if the ith question is answered affirmatively, and $b_i = 1$ otherwise. When all b_i, $i = 1, 2, \ldots, k$, are known, the number f_ε can be obtained with no extra cost. Indeed, b_i is the ith bit of f_ε, and $f_\varepsilon = 0.b_1 b_2 \ldots b_k 1$ in binary notation. Thus, the cost of computing f_ε is equal to $c\,k = c \lceil \log_2 \varepsilon^{-1} - 1 \rceil$, which is just the lower bound established before. Thus, the worst case complexity is $c\lceil \log_2 \varepsilon^{-1} - 1\rceil$, and questions about successive bits of f and the algorithm for combining them given by $f_\varepsilon = 0.b_1 b_2 \ldots b_k 1$ are optimal (in the sense of minimizing the cost).

Exercises

E 3:1 Analyze the worst case setting with $F = (a, b)$, where $a < b$.

4. Average Case Setting

We study complexity in the average case setting assuming that the elements f are uniformly distributed. This means that the probability measure μ is the Lebesgue measure, $\mu(A) = \int_A dx$ for any Borel set $A \subset F$. In order for the error and cost to be well defined, we assume that the sets T_i in the definition of N and the algorithm ϕ are Borel measurable.

We prove that the average case ε-complexity for uniform distribution is essentially the same as in the worst case. Roughly, they differ only by the cost of one question.

We first show that for $\varepsilon \in [0.25, 1)$ we have $\mathrm{comp}^{\mathrm{avg}}(\varepsilon) = 0$, and for $\varepsilon < 0.25$ we have

$$\mathrm{comp}^{\mathrm{avg}}(\varepsilon) \le c \left\lceil \log_2 \frac{1}{\varepsilon} - 2 \right\rceil. \tag{1}$$

Indeed, if $\varepsilon \ge 0.25$ then set $f_\varepsilon = 0.5$. The average error is then equal to $\int_0^1 |f - 0.5|\, df = 0.25 \le \varepsilon$. Thus, we can solve the problem with zero cost.

Let now $\varepsilon < 0.25$. Consider the same information N_k as in the worst case with $k = \lceil \log_2 \varepsilon^{-1} - 2 \rceil$. That is, the ith question is given by: "Is the ith bit of f zero?", $i = 1, 2, \ldots, k$. Then

$$f_\varepsilon = U_k(f) = \phi_k(N_k(f)) = 0.b_1 b_2 \ldots b_k 1,$$

where $b_i = 0$, if the ith answer is yes, and $b_i = 1$, otherwise.

The information $N_k(f)$ takes 2^k different values and partitions the interval $F = (0, 1)$ into disjoint sets $A_1 = (0, 2^{-k})$ and $A_i = [(i - 1)2^{-k}, i2^{-k})$ for $i = 2, 3, \ldots, 2^k$. Furthermore, $U_k(f) = (i - 0.5)2^{-k}$ for any $f \in A_i$. From this, we can find the average error of U_k,

$$e(U_k) = \int_0^1 |f - U_k(f)|\, df = \sum_{i=1}^{2^k} \int_{A_i} |f - (i - \tfrac{1}{2})2^{-k}|\, df$$

$$= \tfrac{1}{4} \sum_{i=1}^{2^k} 2^{-2k} = \tfrac{1}{4} 2^{-k} = 2^{-(k+2)} \le \varepsilon.$$

Therefore, $\text{comp}^{\text{avg}}(\varepsilon) \leq \text{cost}(U_k) \leq c\lceil\log_2 \varepsilon^{-1} - 2\rceil$, as claimed.

We now show that the bound $c\lceil\log_2 \varepsilon^{-1} - 2\rceil$ cannot be substantially improved. First note that

$$\inf_u \int_A |f - u|\, df \geq \tfrac{1}{4}\mu^2(A) \tag{2}$$

for any Borel set A. Indeed, this can be easily verified if A is an interval. Then using simple geometrical arguments, (2) can be verified for A being a countable union of disjoint intervals. But this is enough to conclude that (2) holds for any Borel set.

Take an arbitrary pair $U = (\phi, N)$ such that $e(U) \leq \varepsilon$. Recall that, in general, N has varying cardinality $n(f)$. Let B_i denote the subset of F for which $n(f) = i$. Then

$$e(U) = \sum_{i=1}^{\infty} \int_{B_i} |f - U(f)|\, df.$$

For $f \in B_i$, $\phi(N(f))$ takes p_i different values for some $p_i \leq 2^i$. Let B_i be the union of disjoint sets $A_{i,j}$, $j = 1, \ldots, p_i$, for which $\phi(N(f)) \equiv u_{i,j}$ $\forall f \in A_{i,j}$. Then (2) yields

$$e(U) = \sum_{i=1}^{\infty}\sum_{j=1}^{p_i} \int_{A_{i,j}} |f - u_{i,j}|\, dx \geq \tfrac{1}{4}\sum_{i=1}^{\infty}\sum_{j=1}^{p_i} \mu^2(A_{i,j})$$

$$\geq \sum_{i=1}^{\infty} \frac{1}{4p_i}\left(\sum_{j=1}^{p_i} \mu(A_{i,j})\right)^2 \geq \sum_{i=1}^{\infty} 2^{-(i+2)}\mu^2(B_i).$$

On the other hand, the average cost is estimated by

$$\text{cost}(U) \geq c\int_0^1 n(f)\, df = c\sum_{i=1}^{\infty} i\,\mu(B_i) \geq c\,h(\varepsilon),$$

where the function h is given by

$$h(\varepsilon) = \inf\left\{\sum_{i=1}^{\infty} iz_i \;:\; z_i \geq 0,\; \sum_{i=1}^{\infty} z_i = 1,\; \sum_{i=1}^{\infty} 2^{-(i+2)}z_i^2 \leq \varepsilon\right\}.$$

For a positive z define

$$g(z) = \inf\left\{\sum_{i=1}^{\infty} 2^{-(i+2)}z_i^2 \;:\; z_i \geq 0,\; \sum_{i=1}^{\infty} z_i = 1,\; \sum_{i=1}^{\infty} iz_i = z\right\}.$$

The value of $g(z)$ can be found using a standard technique, and $g(z) \sim 2^{-(z+2)}$ for large z. Since $h(\varepsilon) = g^{-1}(\varepsilon)$, we have

$$h(\varepsilon) = \left(\log_2 \frac{1}{\varepsilon} - 2 \right) (1 + o(1)) \quad \text{as} \quad \varepsilon \to 0.$$

This and (1) prove that

$$\mathrm{comp}^{\mathrm{avg}}(\varepsilon) = c \left\lceil \log_2 \frac{1}{\varepsilon} - 2 \right\rceil (1 + o(1)) \quad \text{as} \quad \varepsilon \to 0.$$

This also proves that $k = \lceil \log_2 \varepsilon^{-1} - 2 \rceil$ questions about successive bits of f and the algorithm of combining them given by $f_\varepsilon = 0.b_1 b_2 \ldots b_k 1$ are almost optimal in the average case setting.

Notes and Remarks

NR 4:1 This section is based on Woźniakowski [85].

Exercises

E 4:1 Analyze the average case setting with $F = (a, b)$ and $\mu(A) = \int_A p(x)\,dx$, where p is a density function. Prove that the existence of a subinterval (a_1, b_1) such that $p(x) \geq p_0 > 0$ for $x \in (a_1, b_1)$ yields

$$\mathrm{comp}^{\mathrm{avg}}(\varepsilon) = c \log_2 \frac{1}{\varepsilon} (1 + o(1)) \quad \text{as} \quad \varepsilon \to 0.$$

This means that the leading term of the complexity does not depend on the measure. The dependence on the measure is only through the $o(1)$ term.

E 4:2 Analyze the average case setting with $F = (-\infty, +\infty)$ and with Gaussian measure, $\mu(A) = (2\pi\sigma)^{-1/2} \int_A e^{-x^2/(2\sigma)}\,dx$ for some positive σ. Prove that again $\mathrm{comp}^{\mathrm{avg}}(\varepsilon) = c \log_2 \varepsilon^{-1} (1 + o(1))$. As in **E 4:1** the dependence on the variance σ is only through the $o(1)$ term.

5. Probabilistic Setting

We remind the reader that in the probabilistic setting the error of an algorithm is given as in the worst case modulo a set of measure at most δ. Let $\mathrm{comp}^{\mathrm{prob}}(\varepsilon, \delta)$ denote the probabilistic complexity.

If $1 - \delta \leq 2\varepsilon$ then $\mathrm{comp}^{\mathrm{prob}}(\varepsilon, \delta) = 0$. Indeed, take $A = [1-\delta, 1)$ and $f_\varepsilon = (1 - \delta)/2$. Then $\mu(A) = \delta$ and $\sup\{|f - f_\varepsilon| : f \in F - A\} = (1 - \delta)/2 \leq \varepsilon$. Thus, we can solve the problem with zero cost since f_ε can be precomputed.

Assume now that $1 - \delta > 2\varepsilon$. We show that

$$c \left\lceil \log_2 \frac{1}{\varepsilon} - \log_2 \frac{1}{1 - \delta} - 1 \right\rceil \leq \text{comp}^{\text{prob}}(\varepsilon, \delta)$$

$$\leq c \left(\left\lceil \log_2 \frac{1}{\varepsilon} \right\rceil - \left\lfloor \log_2 \frac{1}{1 - \delta} \right\rfloor - 1 \right). \tag{1}$$

Take a pair $U = (\phi, N)$ such that $e(U) \leq \varepsilon$. Since the cost is defined as in the worst case setting, we can assume, without loss of generality, that $n(f) \equiv n$. From the definition of the error of U we know that

$$\sup_{f \in F - A} |f - U(f)| \leq \varepsilon$$

for some set A of measure at most δ. As in the worst case setting, it is easy to see that the above supremum is no less than $2^{-(n+1)} \operatorname{diam}(F - A)$. The diameter of $F - A$ is at least $1 - \delta$, and therefore $n \geq \log_2((1 - \delta)/\varepsilon) - 1$. This proves the left-hand side of (1).

To prove the right-hand side of (1), take $A = [1 - \delta, 1)$ and $p = \lfloor \log_2(1/(1 - \delta)) \rfloor$. Hence $2^{-p} \geq 1 - \delta$. Then for any $f \in F - A$, the first p bits of f are zero, since $f < 1 - \delta$ implies $f 2^p < (1 - \delta) 2^p \leq 1$. This means that we do not have to ask about the first p bits of $f \in F - A$. Asking only the last $k - p$ questions from N_k, $k = \lceil \log_2 \varepsilon^{-1} - 1 \rceil$, and setting $f_\varepsilon = 0.0 \ldots 0 b_{p+1} \ldots b_k 1$, we have that $|f - f_\varepsilon| \leq \varepsilon$ for any $f \in F - A$. Therefore,

$$\text{comp}^{\text{prob}}(\varepsilon, \delta) \leq c \left(\left\lceil \log_2 \frac{1}{\varepsilon} \right\rceil - \left\lfloor \log_2 \frac{1}{1 - \delta} \right\rfloor - 1 \right),$$

as claimed.

Similarly to the results of the worst and average case settings, $k = \lceil \log_2 \varepsilon^{-1} - 1 \rceil$ questions about successive bits of f and the algorithm of combining them given by $f_\varepsilon = 0.0 \ldots 0 b_{p+1} \ldots b_k 1$ are almost optimal in the probabilistic setting.

Exercises

E 5:1 Prove that the lower bound in (1) can be always achieved, i.e., $\text{comp}^{\text{prob}}(\varepsilon, \delta) = c \lceil \log((1 - \delta)/\varepsilon) - 1 \rceil$.

E 5:2 Analyze the probabilistic setting with cost defined in the average sense.

6. Relative Error

We have analyzed continuous binary search in three settings for the absolute error criterion. That is, the distance between the number f and its approximation $U(f) = \phi(N(f))$ has been defined by $|f - U(f)|$.

There are many other ways of defining the error between f and $U(f)$. One of them is the relative error, where the distance between f and $U(f)$ is given by $|f - U(f)|/|f|$.

How does the complexity depend on the error criterion? This is one of the basic issues studied in this book. Here, we find the complexity of continuous binary search in three settings for the relative error and compare it to the complexity for the absolute error.

The definition of complexity for relative error is as before, with the only difference that the absolute error is replaced by the relative one in the definition of the algorithm error. To emphasize the error criterion, we shall write $\text{comp}(\varepsilon; \text{REL})$ to indicate that relative error is used.

6.1. Worst Case Setting

We shall prove that it is impossible to find an ε-approximation with finite cost, i.e.,

$$\text{comp}^{\text{wor}}(\varepsilon; \text{REL}) = +\infty, \quad \forall \varepsilon \in [0, 1).$$

Thus, the change in the error criterion makes the problem unsolvable. For the absolute error, the ε-complexity is $c\lceil \log_2 \varepsilon^{-1} - 1 \rceil$, whereas for the relative error it is infinite, even if ε is very close to one.

To prove this, let N consist of n questions and let $A_1, \ldots, A_p$, $p \le 2^n$, be a partition of $F = (0, 1)$ such that $U(\cdot) = \phi(N(\cdot))$ is constant on each of these sets.

Let $a_i = \inf\{f : f \in A_i\}$ and $b_i = \sup\{f : f \in A_i\}$. Then

$$\inf_{u \in F} \sup_{f \in A_i} \frac{|f - u|}{|f|} = \inf_{u \in F} \max\left\{ \left| 1 - \frac{u}{a_i} \right|, \left| 1 - \frac{u}{b_i} \right| \right\} = \frac{b_i - a_i}{b_i + a_i},$$

and the infimum is attained for $u = 2a_i b_i / (a_i + b_i)$, the harmonic mean of a_i and b_i.

There exists a set A_i such that $b_i > 0$ and $a_i = 0$. For such a set, we have $\inf_u \sup_{f \in A_i} |f - u|/|f| = 1$. Thus, the error of U is bounded from below by

$$e(U) = \sup_{f \in F} \frac{|f - U(f)|}{|f|} \ge \max_{1 \le i \le p} \inf_u \sup_{f \in A_i} \frac{|f - u|}{|f|} = 1 > \varepsilon,$$

and the pair $U = (\phi, N)$ does not solve the problem. Since this holds for any ϕ and N, the ε-complexity is infinite, as claimed.

Exercises

E 6.1:1 Analyze the worst case setting for the modified relative error criterion, i.e., when the distance between f and $U(f)$ is given by $|f - U(f)|/(|f| + \eta)$, where η is a given positive number. Prove that for ε small relative to η, the ε-complexity is roughly $c \log_2(1/\varepsilon)$.

E 6.1:2 Analyze the worst case setting for the error criterion in which the distance between f and $U(f)$ is given by $|f - U(f)|/\max(|f|, |U(f)|)$.

6.2. Average Case Setting

We shall prove that the average case complexity for relative error is essentially the same as for absolute error,

$$\text{comp}^{\text{avg}}(\varepsilon; \text{REL}) = c \log_2 \frac{1}{\varepsilon} \left(1 + o(1)\right) \quad \text{as} \quad \varepsilon \to 0.$$

However, the optimal information and algorithm are quite different from the optimal information and algorithm for absolute error.

We start with a lower bound. Since $|f - U(f)|/|f| \geq |f - U(f)|$ for all $f \in F$, the complexity for relative error is no less than the complexity for absolute error. That is,

$$\text{comp}^{\text{avg}}(\varepsilon; \text{REL}) \geq \text{comp}^{\text{avg}}(\varepsilon) = c \log_2 \frac{1}{\varepsilon} \left(1 + o(1)\right) \quad \text{as} \quad \varepsilon \to 0. \quad (1)$$

Thus, it is enough to establish an upper bound of the form $c \log_2 \varepsilon^{-1}(1 + o(1))$. We first show that the information and algorithm which are almost optimal for absolute error are *not* optimal for relative error.

As in Section 4, let N_k be information about the first k bits of f. Let $A_1 = (0, 2^{-k})$ and $A_i = [(i-1)2^{-k}, i2^{-k})$, $i = 2, 3, \ldots, 2^k$, be a partition of F. Let $U_k(f) = \phi_k(N_k(f)) = (i - 1/2)2^{-k}$ for $f \in A_i$. What is the error of U_k for the relative error criterion? We have

$$e(U_k) = \int_0^1 \frac{|f - U_k(f)|}{|f|} \, df \geq \int_0^{2^{-k}} \frac{|f - 2^{-(k+1)}|}{|f|} \, df = +\infty.$$

Thus, no matter how large k is, the error of U_k is infinite. The reason for this negative result could be either that the information N_k is poor or that the algorithm ϕ_k makes very poor use of the information N_k. We show that the latter is true. Indeed, for $0 < a < b$, we have

$$\inf_u \int_a^b \frac{|f - u|}{|f|} \, df = \inf_{u \in (a,b)} \int_a^b \left|1 - \frac{u}{f}\right| \, df$$

$$= \inf_{u \in (a,b)} \left(\int_a^u \left(\frac{u}{f} - 1\right) df + \int_u^b \left(1 - \frac{u}{f}\right) df\right)$$

$$= \inf_{u \in (a,b)} \left(u \ln \left(\frac{u^2}{ab}\right) + b + a - 2u\right) = \left(\sqrt{b} - \sqrt{a}\right)^2,$$

and the infimum is attained for $u = \sqrt{ab}$, the geometric mean of a and b. From this we conclude that the algorithm ϕ_k^* minimizes the error if

$$U_k^*(f) = \phi_k^*(N_k(f)) = 2^{-k}\sqrt{i(i-1)} \quad \text{for } f \in A_i.$$

Observe that $U_k^*(f) = 0$ for $f \in A_1$, whereas $U_k(f) = 2^{-(k+1)}$ for $f \in A_1$. The error of U_k^* is given by

$$e(U_k^*) = 2^{-k}\sum_{i=1}^{2^k}\left(\sqrt{i} - \sqrt{i-1}\right)^2 = 2^{-k}\sum_{i=1}^{2^k}\frac{1}{\left(\sqrt{i}+\sqrt{i-1}\right)^2}$$
$$= 2^{-(k+2)}\ln 2^k \left(1 + o(1)\right) = \frac{k}{2^{k+2}}\left(1 + o(1)\right) \quad \text{as } k \to +\infty.$$

Can we do better? That is, can we find information N_k^* consisting of k questions for which there exists an algorithm with error essentially less than $k2^{-(k+2)}$?

The answer is affirmative. We find k questions for which the error will be 2^{-k}, i.e., $k/4$ times better than for bit questions. Observe that k questions are equivalent to partitioning of $F = (0, 1)$ into 2^k disjoint subsets A_i. Let $A_1 = (0, x_1)$ and $A_i = [x_{i-1}, x_i)$, $i = 2, 3, \ldots, 2^k$, with $x_0 = 0 < x_1 < x_2 < \cdots < x_{2^k} = 1$. By asking k questions, we can identify a subset A_i with the number f. Then the best algorithm is to take the geometric mean $\sqrt{x_{i-1}x_i}$. This yields the error $\sum_{i=1}^{2^k}\left(\sqrt{x_i} - \sqrt{x_{i-1}}\right)^2$. This error is minimized for $x_i = i^2 2^{-2k}$ and is equal to 2^{-k}, as claimed.

Let $k = \lceil \log_2 \varepsilon^{-1} \rceil$ and let N_k^* be information corresponding to the sets A_i with $x_i = i^2 2^{-2k}$. This information consists of the following questions. The first one is: "Is f less than $1/4$?" Suppose that after i questions we conclude that f belongs to $[x_j, x_{j+2^{k-i}}]$ for some j. Then the $(i + 1)$st question is: "Is f less than $x_{j+2^{k-i-1}}$?" Knowing the answer, we conclude that f belongs to $[x_j, x_{j+2^{k-i-1}}]$ or to $[x_{j'}, x_{j'+2^{k-i-1}}]$ with $j' = j + 2^{k-i-1}$. After k answers, we identify the interval $[x_j, x_{j+1}]$ with the number f. The algorithm ϕ_k^* using N_k^* is then defined by

$$\phi_k^*(N_k^*(f)) = \sqrt{x_j x_{j+1}} = x_j + j2^{-2k}.$$

The cost of (ϕ_k^*, N_k^*) does not exceed ck since $x_j + j2^{-2k}$ can be precomputed. Therefore,

$$\text{comp}^{\text{avg}}(\varepsilon; \text{REL}) \le c\left\lceil \log_2 \frac{1}{\varepsilon} \right\rceil.$$

This and (1) proves that

$$\text{comp}^{\text{avg}}(\varepsilon; \text{REL}) = c \, \log_2 \frac{1}{\varepsilon} \left(1 + o(1) \right) \quad \text{as} \ \varepsilon \to 0.$$

We conclude that the information N_k^* and the algorithm ϕ_k^* with $k = \lceil \log_2 \varepsilon^{-1} \rceil$ are almost optimal on the average for the relative error.

Notes and Remarks

NR 6.2:1 We showed that the information N_k about successive bits led to the error $k2^{-(k+2)}$ and that it could be improved $k/4$ times. This seems like a big improvement with respect to error. However, if information N_k is used with $k = (\log_2(4\varepsilon)^{-1} + \log_2 \log_2(4\varepsilon)^{-1})(1 + o(1))$ then the error of the algorithm ϕ_k^* is no greater than ε. Thus, with an extra $\log_2 \log_2(4\varepsilon)^{-1}$ questions, we can solve the problem by asking about successive bits instead of optimally chosen questions.

Exercises

E 6.2:1 Analyze the average case setting for the relative error in the $\mathcal{L}_p$ sense, i.e.,

$$e(U) = \left(\int_0^1 |f - (U(f))|^p / |f|^p \, df \right)^{1/p}.$$

6.3. Probabilistic Setting

We shall prove that the probabilistic complexity for the relative error satisfies

$$\text{comp}^{\text{prob}}(\varepsilon, \delta; \text{REL}) = c \left\lceil \log_2 \frac{\log_2 \frac{1}{\delta}}{\log_2 \frac{1+\varepsilon}{1-\varepsilon}} \right\rceil. \tag{2}$$

For small ε, we have

$$\text{comp}^{\text{prob}}(\varepsilon, \delta; \text{REL}) = c \, \log_2 \left(\frac{1}{2\varepsilon} \log_2 \frac{1}{\delta} \right) \left(1 + o(1) \right).$$

We sketch the proof of (2). For any $A \subset F$, let $a = \inf\{f : f \in A\}$ and $b = \sup\{f : f \in A\}$. As observed before,

$$\inf_u \max_{f \in A} \left| \frac{f - u}{f} \right| = \frac{b - a}{b + a},$$

and the infimum is attained for $u = 2ab/(a + b)$, the harmonic mean of a and b.

Take an arbitrary pair $U = (\phi, N)$ such that $e(U) \le \varepsilon$ and N consists of k questions. There exists a set A such that $|f - U(f)| \le \varepsilon |f|$ for $f \in F - A$

and $\mu(F-A) \geq 1-\delta$. Information N partitions $F-A$ into disjoint subsets $A_1, A_2, \ldots, A_p$, $p \leq 2^k$, and $\sum_{i=1}^{p} \mu(A_i) \geq 1-\delta$. Let $a_i = \inf\{f : f \in A_i\}$ and $b_i = \sup\{f : f \in A_i\}$. Since

$$\varepsilon \geq e(U) = \max_{1 \leq i \leq p} \max_{f \in A_i} \frac{|f - U(f)|}{|f|} \geq \max_{1 \leq i \leq p} \frac{b_i - a_i}{b_i + a_i},$$

we can assume without loss of generality that $A = (0, \delta]$ and $A_i = (a_i, a_{i+1}]$ with $a_1 = \delta$ and $a_{p+1} = 1$. Hence $b_i = a_{i+1}$ and

$$a_{i+1} \leq \frac{1+\varepsilon}{1-\varepsilon}\, a_i, \quad i = 1, 2, \ldots, p.$$

Thus, $1 \leq a_p(1+\varepsilon)/(1-\varepsilon) \leq \delta\big((1+\varepsilon)/(1-\varepsilon)\big)^p$ and therefore $2^k \geq p \geq \log_2 \delta^{-1}/\log_2\big((1+\varepsilon)/(1-\varepsilon)\big)$. This yields

$$\text{cost}(\phi, N) \geq ck \geq c\left\lceil \log_2 \frac{\log_2 \frac{1}{\delta}}{\log_2 \frac{1+\varepsilon}{1-\varepsilon}} \right\rceil,$$

and proves the lower bound on the probabilistic complexity.

To prove the upper bound we proceed as follows. Let $x_i = \delta\big((1+\varepsilon)/(1-\varepsilon)\big)^i$ for $i = 0, 1, \ldots, 2^k$, with $k = \big\lceil \log_2\big(\log_2 \delta^{-1}/\log_2[(1+\varepsilon)/(1-\varepsilon)]\big)\big\rceil$. Then information N_k^* is defined as in Section 6.2, with the $(i+1)$st question: "Is f less than $x_{j+2^{k-i-1}}$?", where $f \in [x_j, x_{j+2^{k-i}}]$. After k answers we identify the interval $[x_j, x_{j+1}]$ with the number f and approximate it by

$$\phi_k(N_k(f)) = \frac{2x_j x_{j+1}}{x_j + x_{j+1}} = x_j(1+\varepsilon).$$

The error of (ϕ_k, N_k^*) does not exceed ε on $[\delta, 1]$, and its cost is ck since $x_j(1+\varepsilon)$ can be precomputed. This proves (2). Hence, information N_k^* and the algorithm ϕ_k are optimal in the probabilistic setting for the relative error.

Exercises

E 6.3:1 Analyze the probabilistic setting for the relative error criterion with cost defined in the average sense.

7. Comparison of Complexity

The results of Sections 3–6 enable us to compare the complexity for the continuous binary search problem in the three settings for the absolute and relative error criteria. The ε-complexity is of the form

$$\text{comp}(\varepsilon) = c\, Z(\varepsilon)\big(1 + o(1)\big) \quad \text{as } \varepsilon \to 0,$$

where the function Z is given in the following table.

	Absolute	Relative
Worst	$\log_2 \dfrac{1}{\varepsilon}$	$+\infty$
Average	$\log_2 \dfrac{1}{\varepsilon}$	$\log_2 \dfrac{1}{\varepsilon}$
Probabilistic	$\log_2 \dfrac{1-\delta}{\varepsilon}$	$\log_2 \left(\dfrac{1}{2\varepsilon} \log_2 \dfrac{1}{\delta} \right)$

For absolute error, the ε-complexity is achieved by bit questions and by the arithmetic mean of the last uncertainty interval. For small ε and δ, the ε-complexity is essentially the same in the three settings.

For relative error, the worst case complexity is infinite. For the average case and probabilistic settings, the complexity is achieved by asking different questions than for the absolute error. The algorithm used to achieve the complexity is the geometric mean of the last uncertainty interval for the average case setting and the harmonic mean of the last uncertainty interval for the probabilistic setting.

The probabilistic case is harder than the average case; it requires roughly $\log_2 \log_2(1/\delta)$ more questions. If δ goes to zero, the probabilistic complexity goes (very slowly) to infinity. This agrees with the infinite complexity for the worst case.

8. Mixed Settings

A setting depends on how the error and cost of algorithms are defined. The error and cost can be defined in a worst, average, or probabilistic sense. Additional settings will be studied in Chapters 10 and 11.

For some problems, it is quite natural to use a mixed setting, where the error of an algorithm is defined in one sense and the cost in a different sense. In this way, one can have nine different settings. The choice of error criterion may enlarge this number.

For example, consider the worst-average case. That is, the error of an algorithm is defined in a worst case sense and the cost in an average one. This setting is especially appropriate for problems where we have to guarantee a small error for every f and we seek to minimize the cost on the average.

Let us briefly consider continuous binary search in this worst-average setting for the relative error criterion. We show that the ε-complexity is now given by

$$\text{comp}^{\text{wor-avg}}(\varepsilon; \text{REL}) = c \, \log_2 \frac{1}{\varepsilon} \left(1 + o(1) \right) \quad \text{as} \quad \varepsilon \to 0.$$

An upper bound can be obtained by asking bit questions. More precisely, for $f \in F = (0,1)$ we ask k questions about successive bits, where k is the smallest number for which $(b_i - a_i)/(b_i + a_i) \le \varepsilon$. Here $[a_i, b_i]$ is the uncertainty interval after the first i answers have been obtained. It is easy to see that $k = k(f) \le \log_2(\varepsilon f)^{-1}$. Furthermore, the number $k(f)$ of questions goes to infinity as f goes to zero.

Knowing k answers, the number f is approximated by the harmonic mean $2a_k b_k / (a_k + b_k)$. The error is then no greater than ε for *any* f. The average cost can be estimated by

$$c \int_0^1 \log_2 \frac{1}{\varepsilon f} \, df + 4 = c \left(\log_2 \frac{1}{\varepsilon} + \frac{1}{\ln 2} \right) + 4 = c \left(\log_2 \frac{1}{\varepsilon} + 1.446451... \right) + 4.$$

Observe that the worst case cost of this algorithm is infinite (because $k(f) \to \infty$ for $f \to 0$). Its average cost is finite since $\int_0^1 \log_2 f^{-1} \, df < \infty$.

To get a lower bound on the ε-complexity, it is enough to notice that it is no less than the average case ε-complexity for the absolute error, i.e., that $\text{comp}^{\text{wor-avg}}(\varepsilon; \text{REL}) \ge \text{comp}^{\text{avg}}(\varepsilon)$, which form is given in Section 4.

Notes and Remarks

NR 8:1 Continuous binary search in the worst-average setting provides an example, where *varying* cardinality of information is crucial. That is, it is important that the number of questions varies with f. If we restrict ourselves to always using information with the same number of questions, then it can be shown that the complexity is infinite.

NR 8:2 As already mentioned in **NR 2:2**, the probabilistic-average setting is also interesting.

Exercises

E 8:1 Find the ε-complexity of continuous binary search in the nine mixed settings for absolute and relative error criteria.

9. Noisy Information

We have considered continuous binary search for *exact* information. That is, we have assumed that each question is answered correctly. It is interesting to study the same problem with *noisy* information, where some questions may receive erroneous answers. There are various ways of measuring noise, some of which are discussed in Chapter 12. In the worst case, one may assume that up to p questions receive erroneous answers, where p is a given constant. In the average case, one may assume that errors in answers are random variables with a known distribution. Finally, in the probabilistic case, one may assume that k questions are erroneously answered with a given probability p_k for $k = 1, 2, \ldots$ and $\sum_{k=1}^{\infty} p_k = 1$.

What is the ε-complexity of continuous binary search for noisy information? We do not know and leave this as an open question to the reader. We remark that noisy information should be analyzed for different settings. Since error, cost, and noise may be defined in three different ways, one can generate up to 27 settings. Furthermore, the choice of error criterion will enlarge the number of different settings.

Notes and Remarks

NR 9:1 Continuous binary search with noisy information is studied by Rivest, Meyer, Kleitman, Winklmann, and Spencer [80]. They seek a subset A of $F = (0, 1)$ such that $f \in A$ and the Lebesgue measure of A does not exceed ε. They assume that up to p of the questions receive erroneous answers. The result is that for small ε, roughly $\log_2 \varepsilon^{-1} + p \log_2 \log_2 \varepsilon^{-1}$ questions are needed for the solution.

Exercises

E 9:1 Consider worst case noise, i.e., up to p questions receive erroneous answers. Repeating each question $(2p + 1)$ times, one can obtain the true answer. Thus, the ε-complexity with such noisy information cannot be larger than $(2p + 1)$ times the ε-complexity for exact information. Can we do better?

10. Final Comments

We have used continuous binary search to illustrate basic concepts of information-based complexity. Now we relate this example to general problems studied in this book.

In the continuous binary search problem we approximate a number f. In general, we may want to approximate $S(f)$, where f is an element of a given set F and S is a given operator. For many important examples, f is a function of one or many variables and F is a set of functions with common properties such as smoothness, convexity, or boundedness in some norm.

Examples which have been studied in literature include linear and nonlinear operators S. They model problems in applied mathematics, computer vision, image understanding, numerical analysis, optimization, and prediction and estimation.

In the continuous binary search, information is provided by answers to a number of questions. We stress that this type of information is *atypical*. For many problems information is usually provided by a finite number of evaluations of $L(f)$ for some functionals $L : F \to \mathbb{R}$. If f is a function, then $L(f)$ is often the value of f or of one of its derivatives at some point. Sometimes we can assume that L's can be arbitrary linear functionals or even continuous nonlinear functionals.

In the continuous binary search, we assume the real number model of computation. This model is used extensively throughout the book. Despite its obvious limitation, the real number model is a useful mathematical abstraction closely related to the floating point computations almost universally used for scientific computation. This point will be discussed in the next chapter.

We have analyzed continuous binary search in the worst case, average case, and probabilistic settings. These three settings will be extensively studied in general and then applied to a number of specific problems.

The importance of the error criterion was shown for continuous binary search by analyzing the absolute and relative error criteria. Different error criteria, including the absolute and relative ones, will be analyzed. We shall see how the complexity and the optimal choice of information and algorithm depend on the error criterion.

Most of the book is devoted to exact information. Only Chapter 12 deals with noisy information. We realize the need and importance of studying noisy information. We expect it will be one of the research directions for the future.

Chapter 3

General Formulation

1. Introduction

In this chapter we present an abstract formulation of information-based complexity. We shall carefully define a problem *formulation*, specification of the *information*, and a *model* of computation.

The problem formulation states what we want to approximate, for which problem elements we seek this approximation, and what error criterion is used.

Specification of the information states what kind of computation about problem elements is allowed. A basic assumption is that we do *not* generally have full knowledge of a problem element.

Specification of the model of computation states what operations are permissible and how much they cost. We shall use the real number model of computation in which all evaluations are performed exactly at finite unit cost.

The complexity is then defined as the minimal cost of computing an approximation with error not exceeding a preassigned threshold. The complexity depends on how cost and error are defined. In this book we shall concentrate primarily on three settings:

(i) worst case: cost and error are defined by a hardest problem element,
(ii) average case: cost and error are defined on the average with respect
     to a probability measure on the class of problem elements,

(iii) probabilistic: cost and error are defined as in the worst case, but error is modified by disregarding a set of problem elements of pre-assigned measure.

Depending on which of these three settings is used, we have worst case, average case, or probabilistic complexity.

We then discuss an asymptotic setting. In this setting, the best possible speed of convergence is analyzed. Finally we discuss randomization, where the choice of information and algorithms is random. This is in contrast to the previous settings, where information and algorithms are chosen deterministically.

Notes and Remarks

NR 1:1 The chapter is based on Wasilkowski [86a] and Woźniakowski [85, 86a]. Some parts are similar to corresponding parts of GTOA, IUC, and Nemirovsky and Yudin [83].

2. Formulation

2.1. Problem Formulation

Let F be a set and G be a normed linear space over the scalar field of real or complex numbers. Our problem is defined in terms of an operator $S : F \rightarrow G$, called the *solution operator*. Elements f from F are called *problem elements*, and elements $S(f)$ are called *solution elements*. For each f from F, we wish to compute an approximation of $S(f)$. Let $U(f)$ be the computed approximation. The distance between $S(f)$ and $U(f)$ will be measured according to a given error criterion. The most basic error criterion studied in this book is the *absolute* error, $\|S(f) - U(f)\|$.

To simplify the presentation, the effect of varying the error criterion is isolated from the mainstream of this book and is presented in the concluding sections of several chapters. Examples of such error criteria include the relative error, $\|S(f) - U(f)\|/\|S(f)\|$, and the normalized error, $\|S(f) - U(f)\|/\|f\|$, under the assumption that the set F is equipped with a norm.

Let $\varepsilon \geq 0$. We shall say that $U(f)$ is an *ε-approximation* of f iff $\|S(f) - U(f)\| \leq \varepsilon$. Our goal is to compute elements $U(f)$ such that they are ε-approximations

(i) for all elements f from F or *
(ii) on the average or
(iii) for a subset of F with preassigned measure.

In cases (ii) and (iii), we assume that F is equipped with a probability measure μ. Then (ii) means that $(\int_F \|S(f) - U(f)\|^p \, \mu(df))^{1/p} \leq \varepsilon$ for some $p \in [1, +\infty)$, and (iii) means that $\|S(f) - U(f)\| \leq \varepsilon$ for $f \in B$, where $\mu(B) \geq 1 - \delta$ for some $\delta \in [0, 1]$.

We illustrate problem formulation by an example.

EXAMPLE 2.1.1. INTEGRATION Let F be a class of r times continuously differentiable functions $f : [0, 1] \rightarrow \mathbb{R}$ such that $f(0) = f'(0) = \cdots = f^{(r)}(0) = 0$ and $\|f\|_F = \max_{0 \leq t \leq 1} |f^{(r)}(t)|$. We assume that $\|f\|_F \leq q$, where q is a known positive number. Here r is a nonnegative integer. Let $G = \mathbb{R}$ with $\|g\| = |g|$ for $g \in G$. Let $S(f) = \int_0^1 f(t) \, dt$ be the integration operator. An element $U(f)$ is an ε-approximation of f iff $U(f)$ is a real number such that $|S(f) - U(f)| \leq \varepsilon$. An example of the kind of probability measure which we will use in (ii) and (iii) is provided by the truncated Wiener measure placed on the rth derivatives. That is, for a Borel set A of F we have $\mu(A) = w(D^r(A))/w(D^r(F))$, where D^r denotes the differentiation operator of order r, $D^r f = f^{(r)}$, and w is the classical Wiener measure, see Section 2.9 of the appendix.

REMARK 2.1.1. We stress that many (but not all) problems can be formulated by the solution operator S defined as a mapping from a set F into a normed linear space G. This is obviously not true if the range of S is not a normed linear space. It is also not true for certain other problems, including the following one.

Consider functions $f : [0, 1] \rightarrow \mathbb{R}$ which satisfy a Lipschitz condition with constant 1, $|f(x) - f(y)| \leq |x - y| \; \forall x, y \in [0, 1]$, for which $f(0)f(1) < 0$. Suppose we wish to compute a number x such that $|f(x)| \leq \varepsilon$. This problem cannot be formulated using the above definition of solution operator. However, this problem can be formulated with a more general definition as follows. Let F and G be given sets and let W be a given mapping,

$$W : F \times \mathbb{R}_+ \rightarrow 2^G.$$

Here, $\mathbb{R}_+ = [0, +\infty)$ and 2^G is the class of all subsets of G. Thus, $W(f, \varepsilon)$ is a subset of G. We assume that $W(f, \varepsilon)$ is nonempty and grows as ε increases. Thus, the mapping W has two properties

(i) $W(f, 0) \neq \emptyset, \quad \forall f \in F$,
(ii) $\varepsilon_1 \leq \varepsilon_2$ implies $W(f, \varepsilon_1) \subset W(f, \varepsilon_2), \forall \varepsilon_1, \varepsilon_2 \in \mathbb{R}_+, \forall f \in F$.

These two properties of W enable us to define an ε-approximation of f as an element x_ε of G such that

$$x_\varepsilon \in W(f, \varepsilon).$$

How restrictive are the assumptions (i) and (ii)? The first one states that there is something to find. With the interpretation that ε measures uncertainty, the second assumption states that as the required uncertainty decreases, the set of elements that satisfy that criterion does not increase. Thus, one may view these two assumptions as natural.

The mapping W is called a *generalized solution operator*. It clearly generalizes the previous definition since $W(f, \varepsilon) = \{g \in G : \|S(f) - g\| \le \varepsilon\}$ satisfies (i) and (ii). For the problem presented at the beginning of this remark, we have

$$W(f, \varepsilon) = \{x \in [0, 1] : |f(x)| \le \varepsilon\}.$$

For some problems analyzed in this book, the solution operator will be of such a generalized form. We shall indicate when this generalized solution operator is used.

Notes and Remarks

NR 2.1:1 Generalized solution operators have been analyzed in IUC. Werschulz [83] has shown that, roughly speaking, the two properties of a generalized solution operator induce a family of pseudometrics on G. Furthermore, he has shown that a *family* is necessary. That is, there exists a problem that cannot be represented using a single pseudometric, see **E 2.1:1**.

NR 2.1:2 Throughout this book we assume that the uncertainty is measured by a nonnegative real number ε. In fact, the generalized solution operator can be defined for ε being an element of a partially ordered set. For some applications, it is natural to assume that ε is a vector or a function. Such problems have been studied in Appendices F and G of IUC. For instance, consider the pointwise approximation problem for functions $f : [0, b] \to \mathbb{R}$ which satisfy a Lipschitz condition with constant one. One wants to compute a function g such that $|f(x) - g(x)| \le \varepsilon(x)$ for $x \in [0, b]$. For particular choices of the uncertainty function $\varepsilon(\cdot)$, one obtains an absolute, $\varepsilon(x) \equiv \varepsilon$, or relative, $\varepsilon(x) = a_1 x + a_2$ for positive a_1 and a_2, error criterion. It is shown in Appendix G of IUC that the absolute error criterion requires, in terms of the interval length b, exponentially more function evaluations than the relative error criterion.

Exercises

E 2.1:1 (Werschulz [83]) Let F be the class of functions $f : [0, 1] \to G = \mathbb{R}$ which satisfy a Lipschitz condition with a constant K, $|f(x) - f(y)| \le K|x - y|$, and have at least one zero. Let $W(f, \varepsilon) = \{x \in [0, 1] : |f(x)| \le \varepsilon\}$. Prove that this generalized solution operator cannot be represented as the solution operator $S : F \to G$, where G is now equipped with a pseudometric rather than a norm.

E 2.1:2 Let F and G be as in **E 2.1:1**. Suppose we are interested in approximating a zero of a function $f \in F$ with the absolute error criterion. (i) Prove that this problem cannot be formulated by any solution operator $S : F \to G$. (ii) Define a generalized solution operator W corresponding to this problem.

2.2. Information

To compute an ε-approximation, we need to know something about f. A basic assumption is that we do not necessarily have full knowledge of a problem element f. Instead, it is assumed that we can gather knowledge about f by computations of the form $L(f)$, where $L : F \to H$ for some set H.

Let Λ denote a class of permissible information operations L. That is, $L \in \Lambda$ iff $L(f)$ can be computed for each f from F. In theoretical computer science, the information operation L is sometimes called an *oracle*.

For example, for the continuous binary search problem of Chapter 2, $H = \{0, 1\}$ and Λ consists of questions, i.e., $L(f)$ is the answer to the question: "Is f an element of T?" For the integration problem of Example 2.1.1, it is natural to assume that we can compute function or derivative values. That is, $L(f) = f^{(i)}(x)$, where $0 \le i \le r$ and $x \in [0, 1]$. Here $H = \mathbb{R}$. A collection of such L forms Λ.

For some other problems with F contained in a linear space, we may assume that an arbitrary linear functional can be computed. Sometimes, but rather for purely theoretical reasons, we may assume that an arbitrary (possibly nonlinear) continuous functional can be computed. In each case, Λ is a corresponding collection of permissible functionals.

For each problem element f we can compute a number of permissible information operations which constitute the information about f. We now discuss two classes of information. The first one is the class of *nonadaptive* information, where the same information operations are computed for each f. Namely, information N is called *nonadaptive* iff there exist $L_1, \ldots, L_n \in \Lambda$ such that

$$N(f) = [L_1(f), L_2(f), \ldots, L_n(f)], \quad \forall f \in F.$$

The number n of information operations, called the *cardinality* of N, is denoted by $\mathrm{card}(N)$. Sometimes we write $N = N^{\mathrm{non}}$ to underline that N is nonadaptive.

We stress that the computation of nonadaptive information can be done in parallel very efficiently with linear speedup. To see this, suppose one has k processors, $k \le n$. Since $L_1, L_2, \ldots, L_n$ are given simultaneously, each processor can evaluate $\lceil n/k \rceil$ of them. Hence, the total time needed to compute $N(f)$ is proportional to $\lceil n/k \rceil$, which is roughly k times smaller than n, and n is proportional to the time of computing $N(f)$ in a sequential environment. That is why nonadaptive information is sometimes called *parallel* information.

The second class of information is called *adaptive*. Now the information operations L_i as well as the total number of them may vary with f. More precisely, information N is called *adaptive* iff

$$N(f) = [L_1(f), L_2(f; y_1), \ldots, L_{n(f)}(f; y_1, \ldots, y_{n(f)-1})],$$

where $y_1 = L_1(f)$ and $y_i = L_i(f; y_1, y_2, \ldots, y_{i-1})$ for $i = 2, 3, \ldots, n(f)$. Here y_i is the value of the ith information operation, and the choice of the ith operation $L_i(\cdot; y_1, \ldots, y_{i-1})$ may depend on previously computed values $y_1, \ldots, y_{i-1}$. Since only permissible operations can be performed, we assume that $L_i(\cdot; y_1, \ldots, y_{i-1})$ belongs to the class Λ for every fixed $y_1, \ldots, y_{i-1}$.

The number $n(f)$ denotes the total number of information operations on the problem element f and is called the *cardinality* of N at f. It is determined dynamically during the process of computing successive values y_i. More precisely, suppose that we have already computed $y_1 = L_1(f), y_2 = L_2(f; y_1), \ldots, y_i = L_i(f; y_i, \ldots, y_{i-1})$. Based on these values, we decide whether another, $(i+1)$st, evaluation is needed. If the decision is "NO", $n(f)$ becomes i and $y_1, \ldots, y_i$ constitute the final information about f, $N(f) = [y_1, \ldots, y_i]$. Otherwise, if the decision is "YES", we choose L_{i+1} and evaluate $L_{i+1}(f) = L_{i+1}(f; y_1, \ldots, y_i)$, and the whole process is repeated. As mentioned above, the decision is made based on available knowledge about f. That is, we have Boolean functions $\text{ter}_i : H^i \to \{0, 1\}$, called *termination functions*, and in the ith step our termination decision is "YES" iff $\text{ter}_i(y_1, y_2, \ldots, y_i) = 1$. Thus, the cardinality $n(f)$ at f is equal to

$$n(f) = \min\{i : \text{ter}_i(y_1, y_2, \ldots, y_i) = 1\},$$

with the convention that $\min \emptyset = +\infty$. Although we do not need to assume that $n(f)$ is finite, we usually choose termination functions in such a way that it is. This can be done, for instance, by taking $\text{ter}_k(y_1, \ldots, y_k) \equiv 1$ for a large k. Sometimes we write $N = N^a$ to stress that N is adaptive.

We illustrate the computation of $N(f)$ in a pseudo-Pascal notation:

```
begin
    i := 0;
    repeat
        i := i + 1;
        compute yᵢ = Lᵢ(f)
    until terᵢ(y₁, . . . , yᵢ) = 1;
    N(f) := [y₁, y₂, . . . , yᵢ]
end
```

Adaptive information requires sequential computation. We have to wait until y_i is computed to decide whether another information operation is needed and, if so, what it should be. That is why adaptive information is sometimes called *sequential* information.

We illustrate nonadaptive and adaptive information by assuming that f is a function and $N(f) = [f(t_1), f(t_2), \ldots, f(t_{n(f)})]$. If $n(f) \equiv n$ and the points t_i are given *a priori* (simultaneously) then N is nonadaptive. If either $n(f)$ varies or the choice of the point t_i depends on $f(t_1), f(t_2), \ldots, f(t_{i-1})$ then N is adaptive.

The total information about the problem elements is given by

- *a priori* knowledge that they belong to a given set, $f \in F$, and
- computed information expressed by the values of certain information operations on them, $y = N(f)$.

In general, an information operator N is many-to-one. Therefore, knowing that $f \in F$ and $y = N(f)$, we are unable to identify f uniquely, since there exist many problem elements sharing the same information with f. This is why N is called *partial*.

REMARK 2.2.1. We are now in a position to contrast problems studied in information-based complexity with problems encountered in combinatorial complexity such as in combinatorial optimization or graph theory. This may be summed up simply as:

Information-based Complexity: Compute an approximation to $S(f)$ given $N(f)$,

Combinatorial Complexity: Compute an approximation to (or the exact value of) $S(f)$ given f.

As we see, the difference is in the information. In information-based complexity, the information is partial; in combinatorial complexity, the information is complete.

REMARK 2.2.2. Throughout most of this book we assume that information operations are computed exactly. This is, of course, a simplification since in practice there are observation errors and/or computational rounding errors. That is, information is *noisy* and $y = N(f)$ is computed with some error. Examples of noisy information include erroneous answers to some questions in the continuous binary search problem of Chapter 2 or noisy function values in the integration problem of Example 2.1.1. The analysis of noisy information is much harder than the analysis of exact information. Therefore, there are, so far, relatively few results for noisy information. Some of them are presented in Chapter 12.

There is one more important property of the information N. As will be precisely defined in the next section, information is *priced*. That is, we are charged for each information operation on a problem element. The cost of the computation of $N(f)$ depends on the cardinality $n(f)$. That is why we would like to minimize the number $n(f)$ of information operations which are necessary to compute an ε-approximation.

Notes and Remarks

NR 2.2:1 The presentation of this section is taken from Wasilkowski [86a].

NR 2.2:2 Consider information with fixed cardinality, $n(f) \equiv n$. Then the notions of adaption and nonadaption depend on the class Λ. If the class Λ is "too big" then they coincide. Indeed, let $N(f) = [L_1(f), L_2(f; L_1(f)), \ldots, L_n(f; L_1(f), \ldots)]$. If $L_i(\cdot; L_1(\cdot), \ldots, L_{i-1}(\cdot; L_1(\cdot), \ldots)) \in \Lambda$ then N is nonadaptive. For example, consider the continuous binary search problem of Chapter 2. The class Λ consists of *all* questions and therefore each information N with fixed cardinality is nonadaptive. In particular, n bisection questions form nonadaptive information. For such a general class Λ, the only difference between adaptive and nonadaptive information is through varying cardinality $n(f)$.

On the other hand, consider the same problem with a restricted class Λ consisting of the questions: "Is $f \leq x$?" for a real x. Then n bisection questions form adaptive information, and bit questions are not allowed. Thus, adaptive information with fixed cardinality can be different from nonadaptive information, if there are some restrictions on the class Λ. As mentioned in Section 2.2, this is the case when we can compute only function evaluations. The same is true if we can compute only linear and/or continuous nonlinear functionals. On the other hand, if one theoretically considers Λ consisting of all functionals (linear or nonlinear) then any information with fixed cardinality is nonadaptive.

Exercises

E 2.2:1 Let F be a class of functions $f : [0,1] \to \mathbb{R}$. Consider two classes of permissible information operations. The first one Λ_1 is the class of function evaluations such that $L \in \Lambda_1$ iff there exists $x \in [0,1]$ so that $L(f) = f(x), \forall f \in F$. The second class Λ_2 consists of function evaluations such that $L \in \Lambda_2$ iff for each $f \in F$ there exists x so that $L(f) = f(x)$. For which class are the notions of adaptive information with fixed cardinality and nonadaptive information the same and for which are they different?

2.3. Model of Computation

Our model of computation is defined by two postulates:

(i) We assume that we are charged for each information operation. That is, we assume that for every $L \in \Lambda$ and $f \in F$, the computation of $L(f)$ costs c, where $c > 0$.

(ii) Let Ω denote the set of permissible combinatory operations including the addition of two elements in G, multiplication by a scalar in G, arithmetic operations and comparison of real numbers, and evaluations of certain elementary functions. We assume that each combinatory operation is performed exactly with unit cost.

We now discuss points (i) and (ii). We assume in (i) that the cost of information operations is fixed and does not depend on a specific operation nor on a problem element. For instance, if function evaluations are permitted then the cost of computing $f(x)$ is fixed and independent of f

and x. This means that we are really charged for the use of a subroutine call independently of the body of the subroutine and its input. In actual computation, the cost of computing $f(x)$ may depend on f and x.

Obviously, (i) is a simplifying assumption. A model of computation with costs depending on information operations or on f should be studied. The analysis of such a model is harder and often leads to less sharp bounds on the complexity. Furthermore, the results may be quite different than those presented in this book, as indicated in **NR 2.3:4**.

We assume in (ii) that the cost of combinatory operations is fixed and scaled to unity. For example, the cost of addition or multiplication of two real numbers is assumed to be the same. This assumption is made for simplicity. It is straightforward to translate the results presented in this book to the case where various combinatory operations are priced differently.

We assume that information and combinatory operations are performed with infinite precision and at finite cost. This formally corresponds to the real (complex) number model of computation, where real (complex) numbers are used, and all combinatory operations are performed with infinite precision. Although infinite precision does not exist in actual computation, we believe it is a very useful mathematical abstraction. For scientific computations, fixed precision floating point arithmetic is almost universally used. In the fixed precision model, we have an additional source of error due to roundoff, and numerical stability becomes an important issue.

We use the real (complex) number model, rather than the fixed precision floating point model, to avoid being distracted by roundoff issues. The numerical stability of algorithms which are optimal in the sense of complexity should be studied. For some such algorithms stability properties are known and are discussed in the corresponding parts of the book.

We also assume a *sequential* model of computation. That is one operation is allowed at a time and the total cost of operations is the sum of the operation costs. *Parallel* or *distributed* models are also of interest. In such a model one can perform a number of operations simultaneously with the total cost measured by the number of parallel steps, and not by the total number of operations as in the sequential model.

The study of information-based complexity with different models of computation is a rich area for future research. Such models may also include various formal models of discrete theoretical computer science. Models which should be studied include those with one or more of the following characteristics:

- computation is parallel or distributed
- cost of information operations depends on the specific operation, problem element, or precision

- cost of combinatory operations depends on the operation or precision.

Notes and Remarks

NR 2.3:1 Different models of computation have been analyzed for some problems studied in this book. We mention two of them.

The first one is a model based on recursive function theory. There is a very interesting stream of work of Ker-I Ko and others who study complexity of numerical computation in this model. Examples include such problems as integration, ordinary differential equations, and finding the maximum value of a function. The reader is referred to a recent overview of Ko [86] and the papers cited therein.

The second model is a bit model of computation, where it is assumed that one can get a rational binary approximation of a real number to within any accuracy with the cost depending on the number of bit operations. This interesting stream of research is well represented by the work of A. Schönhage for such problems as factorizing polynomials, finding roots of polynomials, or multiplication and division over different fields of numbers. The reader is referred to a recent overview of Schönhage [86] presented at the International Congress of Mathematicians in 1986.

NR 2.3:2 The real number model of computation is also used in algebraic complexity, where computation is performed by straight-line programs and we are charged for the total number of arithmetic operations. Probably the most well-known problem of algebraic complexity is multiplication of two $n \times n$ matrices A and B. It is assumed that all coefficients of A and B are known. That is, we have complete information about the problem and that's why we can find the exact solution $C = AB$. We wish to minimize the total number of arithmetic operations needed to compute all coefficients of C. There is an important stream of work due to Strassen, Pan, Bini, Capovani, Lotti and Romani, Schönhage, Coppersmith and Winograd, who reduced the cost of finding C from $\Theta(n^3)$ to $\Theta(n^{2.376\cdots})$. As of June 1987, the best exponent known is due to Coppersmith and Winograd [87]. The complexity of this problem is still unknown. The reader is referred to the book of Pan [84], who surveys the field of fast matrix multiplication as of 1984.

NR 2.3:3 As mentioned in Section 2.3, the transition from the real number model to floating point arithmetic requires numerical stability of algorithms. Roughly speaking, an algorithm is numerically stable if the output of the algorithm in floating point arithmetic is the exact solution for slightly perturbed data. For instance, consider the solution of a system of linear equations $Ax = b$, where A is an $n \times n$ matrix from a given class $\mathcal{A}$ and b is an $n \times 1$ vector. Then the algorithm is numerically stable for the class $\mathcal{A}$ iff for every A from $\mathcal{A}$ the computed vector z is the exact solution of $(A + E)z = b$, where $\|E\|$ is small relative to $\|A\|$, $\|E\| = O(2^{-t}\|A\|)$, with the constant in the O notation independent of A. Here t denotes the number of mantissa bits in floating point arithmetic.

The problem of solving linear equations is equivalent to the matrix multiplication problem. That is, it is possible to translate a fast algorithm for matrix multiplication to solve linear equations preserving the order of cost. Thus, we can solve linear equations with $O(n^{2.376\cdots})$ arithmetic operations, although the constant in the O notation is enormous.

Are such algorithms numerically stable? Are there optimality-stability trade-offs? For the problem of solving linear systems, we have a trade-off. Miller [75] proved that any numerically stable algorithm must take $\Theta(n^3)$ arithmetic operations. Thus, if we insist on numerical stability then we have to perform of order n^3 arithmetic operations. This can be achieved by standard algorithms such as Gaussian elimination, Householder, and Gram-Schmidt orthogonalization methods.

The algorithms which solve linear equations using $O(n^p)$ arithmetic operations with $p < 3$ cannot be numerically stable. However, if one weakens the definition of numerical stability, then it is possible to reduce the bound $O(n^3)$. We know one such case for symmetric and positive definite matrices, where Strassen's algorithm, Strassen [69], implemented in floating point arithmetic computes the vector z with the relative error $\|z - A^{-1}b\|/\|A^{-1}b\| = O(2^{-t}\|A\|\|A^{-1}\|)$.

We stress that optimality-stability trade-offs depend on a particular problem. For some problems, an algorithm which is optimal in the sense of complexity is also numerically stable. This is the case, for instance, for the approximate solution of large linear systems with a symmetric and positive definite matrix. Then the Chebyshev algorithm with iterative refinement is optimal and stable, as will be discussed in Section 9 of Chapter 5. The second example is provided for integration of smooth periodic functions, for which the trapezoid algorithm is optimal and stable, see Section 2.1 of Chapter 5.

We believe that optimality-stability trade-offs are an important research direction. We know very little about these trade-offs and progress in this direction will be very welcome.

NR 2.3:4 We now discuss a model of computation where the cost of each information operation $L(f)$ may be different. Let $c(L, f)$ denote the cost of computing $L(f)$. Assume that for permissible L, $c(L, \cdot)$ is a one-to-one mapping. Suppose that we compute $L(f)$ and we know the cost $a = c(L, f)$ needed for this computation. Then we can recover f exactly since $f = c^{-1}(L, a)$. Hence, only one evaluation is needed to gather enough information to solve the problem exactly. In fact, we do not need the value of $L(f)$; what matters is the cost $a = c(L, f)$. On the other hand, if $c(L, f) \equiv c$, as assumed in Section 2.3., the knowledge of c does not help. All problem elements f and all information evaluations are indistinguishable with respect to the information cost. This implies that we need to compute more information operations and the values of $L_i(f)$ are needed in order to get enough information about f to compute an ε-approximation.

2.4. How Can We Compute Approximations?

Let us summarize the formulation presented in Sections 2.1–2.3.

Problem Formulation.

Compute ε-approximations $U(f)$, i.e., $U(f)$ such that $\|S(f)-U(f)\| \le \varepsilon$, for *all* elements f from F, or on the average, or for a subset of F with preassigned measure.

Information.

(i) We know *a priori* the sets F and G, the norm in G, the solution operator S, the absolute error demand ε, and possibly an *a priori* probability measure μ on F.

(ii) We can compute $L(f)$ for any $L \in \Lambda$ and any $f \in F$.

Model of Computation.

(i) Each information operation $L(f)$ costs c, $c > 0$.

(ii) Each combinatory operation from Ω costs unity.

How can we compute approximations $U(f)$? First we gather enough knowledge about a problem element f. As explained in Section 2.2, we can perform a number of permissible information operations. Let $y = N(f)$ be the computed information,

$$N(f) = [L_1(f), L_2(f; y_1), \ldots, L_{n(f)}(f; y_1, \ldots, y_{n(f)-1})].$$

Let $\mathrm{cost}(N, f)$ denote the information cost of computing $y = N(f)$. Since we are charged for each computation of $L_i(\cdot; y_1, y_2, \ldots, y_{i-1})$,

$$\mathrm{cost}(N, f) \geq c\,n(f).$$

If N is nonadaptive, the operations $L_i(\cdot; y_1, \ldots, y_{i-1}) \equiv L_i$ are given a priori, $n(f) \equiv n$ and then $\mathrm{cost}(N, f) = c\,n$. If N is adaptive, we are also charged for the selection of $L_i(\cdot; y_1, \ldots, y_{i-1})$ as well as for the computation of cardinality $n(f)$. Usually, in such a case, $\mathrm{cost}(N, f) > c\,n(f)$.

Knowing $y = N(f)$, the approximation $U(f)$ is computed by combining the information to produce an element of G which approximates $S(f)$. That is, $U(f) = \phi(N(f))$, where ϕ is a mapping,

$$\phi : N(F) \to G.$$

We call ϕ an (idealized) algorithm. The algorithm ϕ combines the known information (input) and produces an approximation (output) to $S(f)$. An idealized algorithm is any rule using the information $y = N(f)$. We stress that this is a very general notion of algorithm. For some complicated mappings ϕ, implementation of $\phi(y)$ may be very expensive or even impossible. Our model of computation tells us what can be computed and how much it costs. Our goal will be to compute $\phi(y)$ with minimal cost. If the cost of $\phi(y)$ is high, ϕ will be automatically eliminated.

Of course, we sometimes want to guarantee that an algorithm ϕ has some additional properties such as being on-line or enjoying numerical stability. Then we should restrict the class of idealized algorithms to a class of "realizable" algorithms. We emphasize that restricting the notion of algorithm cannot decrease the error.

Let $\mathrm{cost}(\phi, y)$, $y = N(f)$, denote the combinatory cost of computing $\phi(y)$. That is, if the computation of $\phi(y)$ requires the evaluation of k combinatory operations from Ω then $\mathrm{cost}(\phi, y) = k$ and if $\phi(y)$ requires at least one operation not in Ω then $\mathrm{cost}(\phi, y) = +\infty$. The total cost of computing $U(f) = \phi(N(f))$ is given then by

$$\mathrm{cost}(U, f) = \mathrm{cost}(N, f) + \mathrm{cost}(\phi, N(f)).$$

3. Complexity in Three Settings

We are ready to precisely define the notion of ε-complexity. For brevity, we shall sometimes say complexity instead of ε-complexity. This notion plays a crucial role in our study. As always, complexity is understood as the minimal cost of computing approximations with error not exceeding ε.

The complexity depends on how the error and cost of approximation are defined. As in Section 2.4, let $U(f) = \phi(N(f))$ be an approximation to the solution element $S(f)$ and let $\text{cost}(U, f)$ denote the cost of computation of $U(f)$. We consider three definitions of error and cost that lead to the three major settings.

(i) **Worst Case Setting:** The *worst case error* and *worst case cost* of U are defined by

$$e(U) = \sup_{f \in F} \|S(f) - U(f)\|,$$

$$\text{cost}(U) = \sup_{f \in F} \text{cost}(U, f).$$

(ii) **Average Case Setting:** Let μ be a probability measure defined on F. The *average case error* and *average case cost* of U are defined by

$$e(U) = \sqrt{\int_F \|S(f) - U(f)\|^2 \, \mu(df)},$$

$$\text{cost}(U) = \int_F \text{cost}(U, f) \, \mu(df).$$

(iii) **Probabilistic Setting:** Let $\delta \in [0, 1]$. The *probabilistic error* of U is defined by

$$e(U) = \inf \left\{ \sup_{f \in F - A} \|S(f) - U(f)\| \; : \; A \text{ such that } \mu(A) \leq \delta \right\},$$

and the *probabilistic cost* as in the worst case setting, i.e.,

$$\text{cost}(U) = \sup_{f \in F} \text{cost}(U, f).$$

The ε-*complexity* is then defined as the minimal cost among all U with error at most ε,

$$\text{comp}(\varepsilon) = \inf\{\text{cost}(U) : U \text{ such that } e(U) \leq \varepsilon\},$$

with the convention that inf $\emptyset = +\infty$.

Information N and an algorithm ϕ that uses N are called *optimal information* and *optimal algorithm*, respectively, iff $U = (\phi, N)$ satisfies

$$\text{cost}(U) = \text{comp}(\varepsilon) \quad \text{and} \quad e(U) \leq \varepsilon.$$

Formally, N should be called optimal ε-complexity information and ϕ an optimal ε-complexity algorithm. Since ε is regarded as fixed, we simplify the terminology by omitting the reference to ε. Thus, an optimal algorithm using optimal information computes an ε-approximation with minimal cost.

Observe that $\text{comp}(\varepsilon)$ is the *worst case complexity* if both $e(U)$ and $\text{cost}(U)$ are defined as in (i). Similarly, $\text{comp}(\varepsilon)$ is the *average case complexity* if $e(U)$ and $\text{cost}(U)$ are defined as in (ii). Observe that the average case error is defined in the $\mathcal{L}_2$ sense, whereas the average case cost is defined in the $\mathcal{L}_1$ sense. One may chose $p, p' \in [1, +\infty)$ and redefine them as

$$e(U) = \left(\int_F \|S(f) - U(f)\|^p \, \mu(df) \right)^{1/p},$$

$$\text{cost}(U) = \left(\int_F \text{cost}^{p'}(U, f) \, \mu(df) \right)^{1/p'}.$$

We choose $p = 2$ for the error and $p' = 1$ for the cost to simplify the analysis. We indicate in a few places how the results for these p and p' generalize for arbitrary p and p' from $[1, +\infty)$ or even for more general definitions.

The complexity $\text{comp}(\varepsilon)$ is the *probabilistic complexity* if both $e(U)$ and $\text{cost}(U)$ are defined as in (iii). Hence, $\text{comp}(\varepsilon)$ is the minimal cost (in the worst case) provided that the error exceeds ε with probability at most δ. Although the cost of U is defined by the worst case, other definitions also seem reasonable. One may define the cost following the probabilistic error,

$$\text{cost}(U) = \inf \left\{ \sup_{f \in F - A} \text{cost}(U, f) \; : \; A \text{ such that } \mu(A) \leq \delta \right\}$$

or

$$\text{cost}(U) = \sup\{\text{cost}(U, f) \; : \; f \in F \text{ and } \|S(f) - U(f)\| \leq e(U)\}.$$

In these two definitions, the $\text{cost}(U, f)$ is not controlled on a set of measure δ, and the computations can sometimes take an arbitrary amount of time. One may also consider the cost as in the average case setting and disregard a set A for which the error is not controlled. The results reported in this book are essentially the same no matter which definition of the probabilistic cost is used.

Sometimes we write $\text{comp}^{\text{wor}}(\varepsilon)$, $\text{comp}^{\text{avg}}(\varepsilon)$, and $\text{comp}^{\text{prob}}(\varepsilon, \delta)$ instead of $\text{comp}(\varepsilon)$, to emphasize the setting and the dependence on the parameter δ in the probabilistic setting.

We stress that complexity depends on the solution operator S, the space F, and the class Λ of permissible information operations. In the average case and probabilistic settings, it also depends on the *a priori* measure μ. For brevity, we do not list all of them as arguments of complexity. Instead we stress dependence on ε and sometimes on the setting and the parameter δ. The reader should keep this abbreviation in notation in mind.

REMARK 3.1. We indicate how ε-complexity is defined for generalized solution operators given as in Remark 2.1.1. We only need to define the error of an approximation U since the notion of cost is unchanged.

Let $U(f) = \phi(N(f))$ be an approximation for the generalized solution operator W. The local error of U for f is defined by

$$e(U, f) = \inf\{\eta : U(f) \in W(f, \eta)\}.$$

Thus, $e(U, f)$ is the smallest η for which $U(f)$ is an η-approximation of f. The error of U is then defined by taking $e(U, f)$ instead of $\|S(f) - U(f)\|$ in (i), (ii) or (iii). For example, in the average case setting we have $e(U) = \left(\int_F e(U, f)^2 \, \mu(df) \right)^{1/2}$. Observe that if

$$W(f, \varepsilon) = \{g \in G : \|S(f) - g\| \le \varepsilon\}$$

then $e(U, f) = \|S(f) - U(f)\|$, and the two definitions of the error coincide.

We end this section with a remark about mixed settings. One may consider the error of an approximation in one sense and the cost in another sense. For instance, for problems which model high risk phenomena, one would prefer to analyze the error in a worst sense, whereas the cost could be defined in an average sense. This leads to a mixed setting. The corresponding complexity can then be denoted by $\text{comp}^{\text{wor}-\text{avg}}(\varepsilon)$ to indicate which definitions of error and cost are used. Although the major stream of the book is devoted to worst case, average case, and probabilistic settings, ocasionally we shall also discuss mixed settings.

Notes and Remarks

NR 3:1 We have taken the view that the error parameter ε is fixed, and we seek an ε-approximation of minimal cost. It may be often interesting to fix the cost, say at most k, and to seek the best approximation which can be computed at that cost. That is, we seek information N and an algorithm ϕ using N such that the cost of $U(f) = \phi(N(f))$ is at most k and the error of U is as small as possible. Let $e(k) = \inf\{e(U) : U$ such that $\text{cost}(U) \leq k\}$. This is just the inverse of the determination of ε-complexity. Clearly, since $\text{comp}(\varepsilon)$ is a nonincreasing function of ε, we may define its inverse as $\text{comp}^{-1}(k) = \inf\{\varepsilon : \text{comp}(\varepsilon) \leq k\}$. Then $e(k) = \text{comp}^{-1}(k)$. The best approximation computed at cost at most k is given by $U = (\phi, N)$, which is an optimal ε-complexity algorithm and optimal ε-complexity information for $\varepsilon = \text{comp}^{-1}(k)$.

NR 3:2 Suppose the average case error and cost are defined in the $\mathcal{L}_p$ sense. In particular, $e(U) = \left(\int_F \|S(f) - U(f)\|^p \, \mu(df)\right)^{1/p}$. If p goes to infinity then

$$e(U) = \inf\{ \sup_{f \in F - A} \|S(f) - U(f)\| : A \text{ such that } \mu(A) = 0\}.$$

This corresponds to the worst case error modulo a set of measure zero which is the same as the probabilistic error with $\delta = 0$. How is the average complexity for $p \in [1, +\infty]$ related to the worst case complexity for $p = 2$? This and similar questions will be studied in the subsequent chapters.

4. Asymptotic Setting

We briefly discuss an asymptotic setting which is commonly used in numerical analysis. In this setting, we approximate the solution element $S(f)$ by a sequence $\{U_n(f)\}$ where $U_n(f) = \phi_n(N_n(f))$ and information N_n consists of n, possibly adaptive, evaluations about f. In the asymptotic setting, we are not so much interested in the complexity as in achieving the best possible speed of convergence. To illustrate this, assume for simplicity that $\|S(f) - U_n(f)\| = \Theta(n^{-p})$ with $p = p(f)$. Then we wish to find information $\{N_n\}$ and algorithms $\{\phi_n\}$ such that the number p, which measures the speed of convergence, is maximized. We may be interested in maximizing p

  (i) for all f from F, or
  (ii) for all f except a set of measure zero.

The asymptotic setting is analyzed in Chapter 10. We show, in particular, relations between the worst case and asymptotic settings whenever (i) is used and between the average case and asymptotic settings whenever (ii) is used.

5. Randomization

We briefly mention how randomization can be used in one of the settings of information-based complexity. It can be used at both the information and algorithm levels. Randomization lies at the core of Monte Carlo methods which are used, for instance, in approximate integration of multivariate functions. Randomization has also been useful for a variety of computer science problems including primality testing and combinatorial problems.

To explain the concept of random information and random algorithms, consider information consisting of n function evaluations

$$N(f;t) = [f(t_1), f(t_2), \ldots, f(t_n)],$$

where $t = [t_1, t_2, \ldots, t_n]$.

In the worst case, average case or probabilistic setting, we assume that the points $t_1, t_2, \ldots, t_n$ are given *deterministically*. Here, the points t_i are chosen *randomly* according to some distribution λ which may depend adaptively on f. Knowing t and $N(f;t)$, we may *randomly* choose an algorithm ϕ according to a distribution γ defined on the class Φ. Then the error and cost of the approximation $U(f) = \phi(N(f;t), t)$ can be defined by

$$e(U, f) = \int_\Phi \int_{\mathbb{R}^n} \|S(f) - \phi(N(f;t), t)\| \, \lambda(dt) \, \gamma(d\phi),$$

$$\text{cost}(U, f) = \int_\Phi \int_{\mathbb{R}^n} \{\text{cost}(N(f, t), t) + \text{cost}(\phi, N(f;t), t)\} \, \lambda(dt) \, \gamma(d\phi).$$

Thus, $e(U, f)$ and $\text{cost}(U, f)$ are defined as the average error and cost with respect to random choice of information points and algorithms.

The error $e(U)$ and the cost $\text{cost}(U)$ can then be defined as in one of three settings of Section 3. This leads then to ε-complexity with randomization.

We end this section by an example of random information for the multivariate integration problem. Let $B = [0, 1]^d$ be the d dimensional cube. Let F consist of functions $f : B \to \mathbb{R}$ such that $\int_B f^2(t) \, dt \le 1$. The solution operator is given by

$$S(f) = \int_B f(t) \, dt.$$

Assume that only function values can be computed. Then the classic Monte Carlo algorithm

$$U(f) = \frac{1}{n} \sum_{i=1}^n f(t_i),$$

with uniformly distributed points t_i, is an example of an algorithm which uses random information. The error of the Monte Carlo algorithm is given by

$$e(U, f) \le \frac{1}{\sqrt{n}} \sqrt{\int_B f^2(t) \, dt - \left(\int_B f(t) \, dt \right)^2} \le \frac{1}{\sqrt{n}},$$

and the above inequalities are sharp. If $n = \lceil \varepsilon^{-2} \rceil$, then the Monte Carlo algorithm provides ε-approximations for *all* f from F with cost at most $\lceil \varepsilon^{-2} \rceil (c+1)$. We stress that the cost of the Monte Carlo algorithm does not depend on the dimension d. Can we do better? What is the ε-complexity of the multivariate integration problem with randomization? These and related questions are studied in Chapter 11.

Chapter 4

Worst Case Setting: Theory

1. Introduction

In this chapter we analyze the worst case setting, where the error and cost are defined by the worst performance. We present theoretical results which enable us to obtain complexity bounds. In Chapter 5 these results will be specialized for 12 problems of practical interest.

The complexity bounds obtained in this chapter are derived as follows. First we present the radius and diameter of information which play an important role in our analysis. The radius of information is a sharp lower bound on the error of any algorithm using this information. Thus, it is possible to compute an ε-approximation only if the radius of the information is no greater than ε.

The minimal cardinality of information with radius at most ε is called the ε-*cardinality number* and is denoted by $m(\varepsilon)$. To compute an ε-approximation we have to compute at least $m(\varepsilon)$ information operations. Therefore, $c\,m(\varepsilon)$ is a lower bound on the complexity, where c is the cost of one information operation.

We present conditions under which this bound is almost sharp. They hold if for some information N with radius at most ε and information cost $c\,m(\varepsilon)$, there exists an algorithm that uses N whose error is minimal and whose combinatory cost is negligible compared to $c\,m(\varepsilon)$.

These assumptions hold for many (but not for all) problems. Probably the most important class of problems for which the complexity is roughly

$c\,m(\varepsilon)$ is the class of those *linear* problems for which linear optimal error algorithms exist. By a linear problem we mean the approximation of a *linear* operator on a *balanced and convex* set with the class of permissible information operations consisting of *linear functionals*. An *optimal error algorithm* is an algorithm whose error is equal to the radius of information. The major part of this chapter is devoted to the study of linear problems.

For linear problems we show that adaptive information does not significantly help. More precisely, it is shown that the radius of adaptive information N^a cannot be smaller than one half of the radius of correspondingly chosen nonadaptive information N^{non}, i.e., $r(N^a) \geq r(N^{non})/2$, with the cardinality of N^{non} not greater than that of N^a and with the structure of N^{non} the same or simpler than that of N^a. Furthermore, for many cases, the constant $1/2$ can be dropped and $r(N^a) \geq r(N^{non})$. Special cases of this result date back to Kiefer [57] and Bakhvalov [71], see **NR 5.2:1** for more information.

We are aware that the statement "adaption does not help" is counterintuitive. It seems to contradict the practitioner's experience as well as many papers where, for a number of specific problems, adaption is reported to be much more effective than nonadaption.

We stress that the result "adaption does not help in the worst case setting" holds under the three assumptions which define the linearity of a problem. If one of these three assumptions is violated, adaption may be much more powerful, as illustrated by three examples in Section 5.2.

One can also argue that adaption does not help because the worst case setting is used. In particular, this means that the power of adaption is measured by the worst performance. Thus, it may be that adaption fails just for a few problem elements and still is much more efficient than nonadaption for a majority of problem elements. The power of adaptive information for linear problems in average case or probabilistic settings is studied in Chapters 6 and 8.

Let us return to how complexity bounds are obtained. Knowing that adaption does not help (or helps by a factor of at most two), we can restrict ourselves to nonadaptive information and to look for nonadaptive information of cardinality n that minimizes the radius. Such information is called *nth optimal* information. We then choose the smallest n for which the radius of nth optimal information does not exceed ε, and that is how lower bounds on the ε-cardinality number as well as on the complexity are obtained.

As we shall see, the radii of nth optimal information are closely related to the Gelfand n-widths of the solution set. Relations to linear Kolmogorov n-widths will be also discussed. These relations are of practical interest since many deep and difficult-to-prove results in approximation theory may be used to establish optimality of information.

To obtain a complexity upper bound proportional to $c\,m(\varepsilon)$, we study the class of linear algorithms. This class consists of algorithms whose combinatory cost is often negligible as compared to the information cost. When do linear optimal error algorithms exist? This subject has a rich history and started with the pioneering work of Sard [49] and Nikolskij [50], see **NR 5:1**.

Linear optimal error algorithms are known to exist for a number of linear problems. Smolyak [65] proved their existence assuming that the solution operator is a linear functional.

Such algorithms exist under a number of other assumptions. On the other hand, for some linear problems no linear optimal error algorithm exists. In fact, we present a problem for which the error of any linear algorithm is infinite, whereas the radius of information is finite and can be made arbitrarily small if appropriate information is used. We also indicate that the minimal error of a linear algorithm is related to the linear Kolmogorov width of the solution set.

For linear problems the complexity is roughly $c\,m(\varepsilon)$ if linear optimal error algorithms exist. We exhibit linear problems for which $m(\varepsilon)$ can be arbitrary large. Thus, there exist linear problems with arbitrarily large complexity.

In this chapter, we also analyze nonlinear algorithms which are optimal or nearly optimal error algorithms. This is done for either nonlinear or linear problems. For nonlinear problems, we discuss central and interpolatory algorithms. For linear problems, we also discuss spline algorithms. Spline algorithms play an important role in the study of linear problems. Here, we discuss spline algorithms for the worst case setting, while in Chapters 6 and 8 we discuss them for the average case and probabilistic settings.

The analysis for the worst case setting is done mostly for the absolute error criterion. In the final section we briefly analyze the relative, normalized, and convex and symmetric error criteria. We indicate which results for the absolute error criterion also hold for different error criteria.

2. Radius and Diameter of Information

Let $N : F \to H$ be information defined as in Section 2.2 of Chapter 3. Let $y = N(f)$ be the information computed about f. In general, N is *partial*, i.e., N is a many-to-one operator. Therefore knowing y we cannot identify the problem element f uniquely. Let

$$N^{-1}(y) = \{\tilde{f} \in F : N(\tilde{f}) = y\}$$

be the set of indistinguishable problem elements, and let

$$SN^{-1}(y) = \{S(\tilde{f}) \in G : \tilde{f} \in N^{-1}(y)\}$$

be the set of indistinguishable solution elements. This can be schematized as in Figure 2.1:

$$\boxed{N^{-1}(y)} \quad \xrightarrow{\;S\;} \quad \boxed{SN^{-1}(y)}$$

$$N^{-1} \Big\uparrow$$

$$y$$

Figure 2.1

We want to compute an approximation $U(f)$ based on $y = N(f)$. That is, $U(f) = \phi(N(f))$ for some mapping ϕ. The element $U(f)$ should therefore approximate $S(f)$ as well as all elements $S(\tilde{f})$ from the set $SN^{-1}(y)$. It is intuitively obvious that we can guarantee that $U(f)$ is a good approximation iff the set $SN^{-1}(y)$ is "small". The smallness of the set $SN^{-1}(y)$ is measured by its radius.

Let us recall that the *radius* of a set A in a normed linear space G is defined by

$$\mathrm{rad}(A) = \inf_{x \in G} \; \sup_{a \in A} \|x - a\|.$$

Roughly speaking, it is the radius of the smallest ball which contains the set A.

Observe that $\mathrm{rad}(SN^{-1}(y))$ is the radius of the set of indistinguishable solution elements. It is clear that we can find an ε-approximation for $y = N(f)$ iff $\mathrm{rad}(SN^{-1}(y)) \le \varepsilon$ (modulo a technical assumption that the infimum is attained).

To simplify the notation, while stressing the importance of information N, we shall denote the radius of $SN^{-1}(y)$ by $r(N, y)$ and call it the *local radius of information N at y*,

$$r(N, y) = \mathrm{rad}\,(SN^{-1}(y)).$$

The (*global*) *radius of information* is defined as the local radius for a worst y, i.e.,

$$r(N) = \sup_{y \in N(F)} r(N, y).$$

Thus, the radius of information is the radius of the smallest ball which contains $SN^{-1}(y)$ for a worst y. It is clear that we can find an ε-approximation for all f from F iff $r(N) \leq \varepsilon$ (once more, modulo a technical assumption that the corresponding infimum is attained).

The radius of information plays a major role in information-based complexity. It measures the intrinsic uncertainty caused by partial information. Observe that $r(N)$ depends on the information N and on the problem formulation, i.e., on S, F, and G. It does not depend on how approximations $U(f)$ are constructed.

Another useful way of measuring intrinsic uncertainty of information N is the diameter of information. As we shall see, for some problems it is much easier to find the diameter of information than to find the radius, and therefore certain results are more easily developed in terms of the diameter.

We begin by recalling the definition of the *diameter* of a set A in a normed linear space G, which is given by

$$\text{diam}(A) = \sup_{a_1, a_2 \in A} \|a_1 - a_2\|.$$

That is, roughly speaking, the diameter is the largest distance between any two elements of the set A. Obviously, $\text{rad}(A) \leq \text{diam}(A) \leq 2\,\text{rad}(A)$. It can happen that $\text{diam}(A)$ takes any value from the interval $[\text{rad}(A), 2\,\text{rad}(A)]$ even for a finite nonzero $\text{rad}(A)$, see **E 2:1**.

The *local diameter of information* is defined by

$$d(N, y) = \text{diam}(SN^{-1}(y)),$$

and the (*global*) *diameter of information* by

$$d(N) = \sup_{y \in N(F)} d(N, y).$$

Combining the last two equalities we have

$$d(N) = \sup \left\{ \|S(f_1) - S(f_2)\| : f_1, f_2 \in F \quad \text{and} \quad N(f_1) = N(f_2) \right\}.$$

Thus, the diameter of information is, roughly speaking, the largest distance between two solution elements which are indistinguishable with respect to information N. Obviously,

$$r(N) \leq d(N) \leq 2\,r(N).$$

It can happen that $d(N)$ takes any value from the interval $[r(N), 2r(N)]$ even for a finite nonzero $r(N)$, see **E 2:2**.

Notes and Remarks

NR 2:1 This section is based on GTOA, Chapter 1. The concept of radius (and diameter) of information relies on the *adversary principle*, i.e., on finding problem elements f_1 and f_2 which share the same information and whose solution elements $S(f_1)$ and $S(f_2)$ are as far away as possible. Many papers are, at least implicitly, based on the adversary principle, see GTOA, p. 16 for a list of such papers. The general significance of the adversary principle was pointed out by Winograd [76] and Woźniakowski [75]. Winograd [76] introduced a general "fooling" technique and showed its importance for a number of problems. Some of these ideas were already used in Brent, Winograd, and Wolfe [73], where the optimality of nonstationary one-point iterations with memory for the solution of scalar nonlinear equations was analyzed. Woźniakowski [75] studied the solution of nonlinear operator equations and introduced the concept of order of information. Order of information plays a role similar to radius of information and is useful for establishing the optimality of stationary iterations for solving nonlinear equations.

NR 2:2 An example of a linear solution operator and linear information N with $d(N) < 2\,r(N)$ may be found in Micchelli and Rivlin [77, p. 9].

NR 2:3 (IUC, Chapter 1) We indicate how the radius of information is defined for a generalized solution operator, see Remark 2.1.1 of Chapter 3. As before, we first define a local radius of information. Knowing $y = N(f)$ we want to find an element $U(f)$ which belongs to $W(\tilde{f}, \delta)$ for all $\tilde{f}$ indistinguishable from f, $\tilde{f} \in N^{-1}(y)$, for δ as small as possible. We can do this iff the intersection of the sets $W(\tilde{f}, \delta)$ is not empty. This leads to the definition of the local radius $r(N, y)$ as

$$r(N, y) = \inf \left\{ \delta : \bigcap_{\tilde{f} \in N^{-1}(y)} W(\tilde{f}, \delta) \neq \emptyset \right\},$$

with the convention that $\inf \emptyset = +\infty$. Then the global radius is defined as the local radius for a worst y,

$$r(N) = \sup_{y \in N(F)} r(N, y).$$

It is easy to check that for $W(f, \varepsilon) = \{g \in G : \|S(f) - g\| \leq \varepsilon\}$, the local and global radii for a generalized solution operator are identical with the corresponding radii for a solution operator.

NR 2:4 (IUC, Appendix C) The diameter of information for a generalized solution operator is defined as follows. We define the distance between two elements f_1 and f_2 from F by

$$\text{dist}(f_1, f_2) = \inf\{\delta_1 + \delta_2 : W(f_1, \delta_1) \cap W(f_2, \delta_2) \neq \emptyset\}.$$

Then

$$d(N, y) = \sup_{f_1, f_2 \in N^{-1}(y)} \text{dist}(f_1, f_2)$$

is the local diameter, and

$$d(N) = \sup_{y \in N(F)} d(N, y)$$

is the (global) diameter of information N. We have

$$d(N, y) \leq 2\,r(N, y), \quad \forall y \in N(F), \qquad \text{and} \qquad d(N) \leq 2\,r(N).$$

Indeed, suppose that $r(N, y)$ is finite. Then for $\delta > r(N, y)$ we have $W(f_1, \delta) \cap W(f_2, \delta) \neq \emptyset$, $\forall f_1, f_2 \in N^{-1}(y)$. This yields that $\text{dist}(f_1, f_2) \leq 2\delta$. Thus, $d(N, y) \leq 2\delta$. Letting δ tend to $r(N, y)$ we get $d(N, y) \leq 2r(N, y)$ and $d(N) \leq 2r(N)$, as claimed.

In general, it is not true that $r(N, y) \leq d(N, y)$. In fact, it can happen that $r(N, y) = +\infty$ and $d(N, y) = 0$, see **E 2:3**. This means that, in general, $d(N, y)$ is not a good estimate of $r(N, y)$. However, for "regular" problems we still have

$$r(N, y) \leq d(N, y), \quad \forall y \in N(f), \qquad \text{and} \qquad r(N) \leq d(N).$$

The generalized solution operator W is *regular* iff for every f_1 and f_2 from F we have

$$W(f_1, 0) \subset W(f_2, \text{dist}(f_1, f_2) + \delta), \quad \forall \delta > 0.$$

Indeed, suppose that $d(N, y)$ is finite. Take $\delta > d(N, y)$. Then for every f_1 and f_2 from $N^{-1}(y)$, $\text{dist}(f_1, f_2) < \delta$. Regularity of W yields $\emptyset \neq W(f_1, 0) \subset W(f_2, \delta)$. Thus, $W(f_1, \delta) \cap W(f_2, \delta)$ is nonempty, which implies that $r(N, y) \leq \delta$. Letting δ tend to $d(N, y)$, we get $r(N, y) \leq d(N, y)$ and $r(N) \leq d(N)$, as claimed.

We now check that for $W(f, \varepsilon) = \{g \in G : \|S(f) - g\| \leq \varepsilon\}$, the local diameters of a generalized solution operator are identical with the local diameters of a solution operator. To do this, it is enough to prove that

$$\text{dist}(f_1, f_2) = \|S(f_1) - S(f_2)\|.$$

To this end, take any δ_1 and δ_2 such that $W(f_1, \delta_1) \cap W(f_2, \delta_2) \neq \emptyset$. Let g be an element of $W(f_1, \delta_1) \cap W(f_2, \delta_2)$. Then $\|S(f_1) - S(f_2)\| \leq \|S(f_1) - g\| + \|S(f_2) - g\| \leq \delta_1 + \delta_2$. Hence, $\|S(f_1) - S(f_2)\| \leq \text{dist}(f_1, f_2)$. Taking $\delta_1 = 0$ and $\delta_2 = \|S(f_1) - S(f_2)\|$ we conclude that $S(f_1) \in W(f_1, 0) \cap W(f_2, \delta_2)$. Thus, $\text{dist}(f_1, f_2) \leq \|S(f_1) - S(f_2)\|$. This implies $\text{dist}(f_1, f_2) = \|S(f_1) - S(f_2)\|$, as claimed.

Exercises

E 2:1 Let G be a linear space of continuous functions $f : [0,1] \to \mathbb{R}$ equipped with the sup norm, $\|f\| = \max_{0 \leq t \leq 1} |f(t)|$, such that $f(0) = 0$. Let $\alpha \in [1,2]$. Define the set $A = \{f \in G : -1 \leq f(t) \leq \alpha - 1, \forall t \in [0,1]\}$. Show that $\text{diam}(A) = \alpha \, \text{rad}(A)$ and $\text{rad}(A) = 1$.

E 2:2 Consider the solution operator $S(f) = f$ with $F = A$ and G defined as in **E 2:1**. Let $N(f) = [f(t_1), f(t_2), \ldots, f(t_n)]$ for some distinct points t_i from $[0,1]$. Show that $d(N, y) = \alpha \, r(N, y)$ and $r(N, y) = 1$ for all y from $N(F)$.

E 2:3 (IUC, Appendix C) Let $F = G = \{1, 2, 3\}$. Define W as follows: $W(1, \varepsilon) = \{1, 2\}$, $W(2, \varepsilon) = \{2, 3\}$ and $W(3, \varepsilon) = \{1, 3\}$. Show that W is not regular. For $N(f) \equiv 0$, prove that $r(N, y) = +\infty$ and $d(N, y) = 0$.

E 2:4 (GTOA p. 151)
(i) Consider two information operators N_1 and N_2. We say that N_1 is *contained* in N_2, $N_1 \subset N_2$, iff $N_2^{-1}(N_2(f)) \subset N_1^{-1}(N_1(f))$ for all f from F. We say that N_1 is *equivalent* to N_2, $N_1 \asymp N_2$, iff $N_2^{-1}(N_2(f)) = N_1^{-1}(N_1(f))$ for all f from F. Show that $N_1 \subset N_2$ implies $r(N_2) \leq r(N_1)$ and $d(N_2) \leq d(N_1)$. Show that $N_1 \asymp N_2$ implies $r(N_2) = r(N_2)$ and $d(N_2) = d(N_1)$.

(ii) Assume that information operators N_1 and N_2 are linear over a linear space F_1. Let F be an absorbing set of F_1, i.e., for any $f_1 \in F_1$ there exists a positive number b such that $bf_1 \in F$. Prove

$$N_1 \subset N_2 \quad \Leftrightarrow \quad \ker N_2 \subset \ker N_1 \qquad \text{and} \qquad N_1 \asymp N_2 \quad \Leftrightarrow \quad \ker N_2 = \ker N_1.$$

3. Algorithms

In this section we discuss two classes of algorithms which enjoy strong optimal error properties. They are called central and interpolatory algorithms, respectively.

Notes and Remarks

NR 3:1 This section is based on GTOA, Chapter 1.

3.1. Local and Global Errors

An approximation $U(f)$ is computed as $\phi(N(f))$, where N is an information operator and ϕ is an algorithm which maps $N(F)$ into G. For a given N, we want to find an algorithm ϕ which minimizes the error. Recall that the (worst case) error of U is given by

$$e(U) = \sup_{f \in F} \|S(f) - U(f)\| = \sup_{f \in F} \|S(f) - \phi(N(f))\|.$$

Since $U = (\phi, N)$, it is convenient to denote $e(U)$ by $e(\phi, N)$ to stress the role of the information N and of the algorithm ϕ. The error $e(\phi, N)$ will be called the (*global*) error of an algorithm ϕ that uses information N.

We now discuss the local error of ϕ. Given $y = N(f)$, the element $\phi(y)$ has to approximate all elements $S(\tilde{f})$ from the set $SN^{-1}(y)$. Let

$$e(\phi, N, y) = \sup_{\tilde{f} \in N^{-1}(y)} \|S(\tilde{f}) - \phi(y)\|$$

denote the *local error* of ϕ. Obviously, the *global error* of ϕ is equal to the local error for a worst y,

$$e(\phi, N) = \sup_{y \in N(F)} e(\phi, y).$$

We are interested in algorithms with minimal error. We say that ϕ^* is an *optimal error algorithm* iff

$$e(\phi^*, N) = \inf_{\phi} e(\phi, N).$$

From the definition of local and global radii we have

$$e(\phi^*, N, y) \geq r(N, y), \quad \forall y \in N(F), \quad \text{and} \quad e(\phi^*, N) \geq r(N).$$

We show in Section 3.2 that these bounds are sharp.

Notes and Remarks

NR 3.1:1 (IUC, Chapter 1) For a generalized solution operator W, the local error of an algorithm ϕ is defined by

$$e(\phi, N, y) = \inf \left\{ \delta : \phi(N(f)) \in \bigcap_{\tilde{f} \in N^{-1}(y)} W(\tilde{f}, \delta) \right\},$$

and the (global) error by $e(\phi, N) = \sup_{y \in N(F)} e(\phi, N, y)$. From **NR 2:3**, it follows that

$$e(\phi, N, y) \geq r(N, y), \quad \forall y \in N(F), \quad \text{and} \quad e(\phi, N) \geq r(N).$$

3.2. Central Algorithms

We can select an algorithm ϕ in such a way that the local error of ϕ is equal or arbitrarily close to the local radius $r(N, y)$.

To do this, recall the notion of a (Chebyshev) *center* of a set A in a normed linear space G. It is a center m of a ball of minimal radius which contains A,

$$\sup_{a \in A} \|m - a\| = \text{rad}(A).$$

The center need not exist, be unique, nor be an element of A, see **E 3.2:1**.

Assume for a moment that the set $SN^{-1}(y)$ has a center $m = m(y)$ for all $y \in N(F)$. Then the algorithm ϕ^c defined by

$$\phi^c(y) = m(y)$$

is called *central*. The central algorithm minimizes the local error for all y since

$$e(\phi^c, N, y) = r(N, y).$$

Obviously, the (global) error of the central algorithm is also minimal and equal to the radius of information,

$$e(\phi^c, N) = r(N).$$

Thus, ϕ^c is an optimal error algorithm, but obviously not every optimal error algorithm is central.

If the set $SN^{-1}(y)$ has no center for at least one $y \in N(F)$ then a central algorithm does not exist. In this case, take an arbitrary positive δ. Then there exists $m = m(y, \delta)$ such that $\sup_{a \in SN^{-1}(y)} \|m - a\| \leq r(N, y) + \delta$. Define the algorithm $\phi_\delta(y) = m(y, \delta)$. Its local error is at most $r(N, y) + \delta$, and its global error is at most $r(N) + \delta$. Since δ is arbitrary, this shows that we can find algorithms whose local and global errors are arbitrarily close to $r(N, y)$ and $r(N)$. We summarize this in

THEOREM 3.2.1. *The local and global radii of information N are sharp lower bounds on the local and global errors of any algorithm using N, i.e.,*

$$r(N, y) = \inf_\phi e(\phi, N, y), \quad \forall y \in N(F), \qquad \text{and} \qquad r(N) = \inf_\phi e(\phi, N).$$

A central algorithm ϕ^c, if it exists, minimizes the global and local errors for all y.

We now turn to the question of how to construct a central algorithm. Let $A = SN^{-1}(y)$. We remark that if the closure of A is symmetric with respect to some element p (i.e., $h + p \in \overline{A}$ implies $-h + p \in \overline{A}$) then p is the center of A. Indeed, assume that for some u from G, $\sup_{a \in A} \|a - u\| < \sup_{a \in A} \|a - p\|$. Take $x \in A$ such that $\|a - u\| < \|x - p\|$, $\forall a \in \overline{A}$. Let $x = p + h$. Then $p - h \in \overline{A}$ and

$$2\|h\| = \|(p + h) - u - (p - h) + u\|$$
$$\leq \|(p + h) - u\| + \|(p - h) - u\| < 2\|x - p\| = 2\|h\|,$$

which is a contradiction. Thus, $p = m$ is a center of A. In this case, we also have $d(N, y) = 2r(N, y)$. Indeed, let $r(N, y) < +\infty$ and choose u from A such that $\|m - u\| \geq r(N, y) - \delta$ for a positive δ. Let $h = u - m$. Define $u_1 = m + h$ and $u_2 = m - h$. Then u_i belongs to $\overline{A}$ and $\|u_1 - u_2\| = 2\|u - m\| \geq 2(r(N, y) - \delta)$. Thus, $d(N, y) \geq 2(r(N, y) - \delta)$. Letting δ tend to zero, we get $d(N, y) \geq 2r(N, y)$. Since the opposite inequality is always true, we get $d(N, y) = 2r(N, y)$, as claimed.

In general, it is hard to find a center of a set, and so it is hard to obtain a central algorithm. In Section 5 we shall study conditions on the problem formulation under which centers can be easily found.

Notes and Remarks

NR 3.2:1 (IUC, Chapter 1) For the generalized solution operator, a central algorithm ϕ^c is defined by $\phi^c(y) = m(y)$ for an arbitrary $m(y) \in \bigcap_{f \in N^{-1}(y)} W(f, r(N, y))$. If this intersection is empty then there is no central algorithm. But, in this case, one can find an algorithm whose local error is arbitrarily close to $r(N, y)$. So, Theorem 3.2.1 is valid also for generalized solution operators.

Exercises

E 3.2:1 Let G be the linear space of functions $f : [0,1] \to \mathbb{R}$ which are continuously differentiable. Consider the set

$$A = \{f \in G : |f(x) - f(y)| \le |x - y|, \forall x, y \in [0,1], \text{ and } f(0) = 0, f(1) = 1/2\}.$$

Show that A has no center if G is equipped with the $\mathcal{L}_2$ norm, $\|f\| = \sqrt{\int_0^1 f^2(t)\,dt}$, and has infinitely many centers (some of them outside A) if G is equipped with the sup norm, $\|f\| = \max_{0 \le t \le 1} |f(t)|$.

3.3. Interpolatory Algorithms

We now consider a second class of algorithms which are, at least conceptually, easier to obtain than central algorithms. This is the class of interpolatory algorithms defined as follows.

Let $y = N(f)$ be the computed information. Knowing y, choose an element $\tilde{f}$ from F such that $\tilde{f}$ *interpolates* the data, that is, $N(\tilde{f}) = y$. Then the algorithm ϕ^I defined by

$$\phi^I(y) = S(\tilde{f})$$

is called *interpolatory*. Thus, $\phi^I(y)$ is the exact solution for some problem element which is indistinguishable from f. Usually, the element $\tilde{f}$ is chosen in such a way that $S(\tilde{f})$ is "simple" to calculate. Examples of interpolatory algorithms can be found in many applications. For example, a standard way of integration or approximation of a function f is to compute n function values at some points, $N(f) = [f(t_1), f(t_2), \dots, f(t_n)]$, replace the function f by an appropriate interpolating polynomial (or piecewise polynomial) $\tilde{f}, N(\tilde{f}) = N(f)$, and then solve the problem $S(\tilde{f})$ exactly for $\tilde{f}$.

The error of an interpolatory algorithm can be easily analyzed. Observe that $\phi^I(y)$ belongs to $SN^{-1}(y)$. Therefore, the local error of ϕ^I does not exceed the local diameter of information,

$$e(\phi^I, N, y) \le d(N, y) \le 2\,r(N, y).$$

As shown is Section 3.2, the local error of any algorithm is at least $r(N, y)$. Thus, an interpolatory algorithm minimizes the local error to within a factor of 2. Similarly, the global error of any interpolatory algorithm is bounded by the (global) diameter of information

$$e(\phi^I, N) \le d(N) \le 2\,r(N).$$

Hence $e(\phi^I, N) = \alpha\, r(N)$ for some $\alpha \in [1, 2]$. This means that an interpolatory algorithm also minimizes the global error within a factor of at most 2.

How are central and interpolatory algorithms related? It is easy to verify that if for each y from $N(F)$, all centers of the set $SN^{-1}(y)$ belong to this set, then any central algorithm is interpolatory. On the other hand, if for some y, all centers of $SN^{-1}(y)$ are outside this set then no central algorithm is interpolatory, see **E 3.3:1** and **E 3.3:2**. In terms of the radius of information, we have the following. If $r(N) > 0$ then there exists an interpolatory algorithm which is not central. If $r(N) = 0$ then there is only one central and interpolatory algorithm, $\phi^c(N(f)) = \phi^I(N(f)) = S(f)$.

Notes and Remarks

NR 3.3:1 (IUC, Appendix A) We discuss interpolatory algorithms for generalized solution operators. An algorithm ϕ^I is called interpolatory iff for every f from F

$$\phi^I(N(f)) \in W(\tilde{f}, 0)$$

for some element $\tilde{f} \in N^{-1}(y)$, $y = N(f)$. Hence, $\phi^I(N(f))$ is a 0-approximation of $\tilde{f}$. If $W(f, \varepsilon) = \{g \in G : \|S(f) - g\| \le \varepsilon\}$ then $\phi^I(N(f)) = S(\tilde{f})$, which coincides with the previous definition.

What can we say about the local error of an interpolatory algorithm? Is it still true that $e(\phi^I, N, y) \le 2r(N, y)$? As we shall see, the situation is now more complex, and it can happen that $e(\phi^I, N, y)$ is much larger than $r(N, y)$. Let $y = N(f)$. Recall that the local radius $r(N, y)$ is given by $r(N, y) = \inf\{\delta : A(N, y, \delta) \ne \emptyset\}$, where

$$A(N, y, \delta) = \bigcap_{\tilde{f} \in N^{-1}(y)} W(\tilde{f}, \delta).$$

Define the set $B(N, y)$ as the set of all possible values of interpolatory algorithms at y,

$$B(N, y) = \bigcup_{\tilde{f} \in N^{-1}(y)} W(\tilde{f}, 0).$$

We are interested in the ratio of the smallest δ for which the set $B(N, y)$ becomes a subset of $A(N, y, \delta)$, and the local radius,

$$k(N, y) = \frac{\inf\{\delta : B(N, y) \subset A(N, y, \delta)\}}{r(N, y)} = \frac{\inf\{\delta : B(N, y) \subset A(N, y, \delta)\}}{\inf\{\delta : \emptyset \ne A(N, y, \delta)\}}.$$

Obviously, $k(N, y) \in [1, +\infty]$. The local errors of interpolatory algorithms then satisfy the following relation,

$$\sup_{\phi^I} e(\phi^I, N, y) = k(N, y)\, r(N, y).$$

Here we adopt the convention that $(+\infty)/(+\infty) = 0/0 = 1$ and $+\infty \cdot 0 = +\infty$.

Indeed, let $\delta^* = \inf\{\delta : B(N, y) \subset A(N, y, \delta)\}$. Take an arbitrary δ less than δ^*. Then there exists an element b of the set $B(N, y)$ which does not belong to $A(N, y, \delta)$. The local error of the interpolatory algorithm $\phi^I(y) = b$ is $k(N, y) \, r(N, y)$. If $k(N, y) = +\infty$ then the relation holds.

Assume thus that $k(N, y)$ is finite. Then δ^* is also finite. Take an arbitrary interpolatory algorithm ϕ^I. Then $\phi^I(y) \in B(N, y)$ and $\phi^I(y) \in W(\tilde{f}, \delta)$, $\forall \tilde{f} \in N^{-1}(y)$, and $\forall \delta > \delta^*$. Thus, $e(\phi^I, N, y) \leq \delta$. Letting δ tend to δ^* we have $e(\phi^I, N, y) \leq \delta^* = k(N, y) \, r(N, y)$, as claimed.

Observe that for $W(f, \varepsilon) = \{g \in G : \|S(f) - g\| \leq \varepsilon\}$ we have $k(N, y) = d(N, y)/r(N, y) \leq 2$. This is the previous result that the local error of any interpolatory algorithm does not exceed the local diameter.

For general W, the value of $k(N, y)$ can be arbitrarily large. It can even happen that $r(N, y) = r(N) = 1$ and $k(N, y) = +\infty, \forall y$, see **E 3.3:2**.

Exercises

E 3.3:1 Let $F = \{-1, 1\}$ and $F_1 = G = \mathbb{R}$. Let $S(f) = f$ and $N = 0$. Show that
(i) There exists one central algorithm, which is not interpolatory, with error $r(N) = 1$.
(ii) There exist two interpolatory algorithms with error $d(N) = 2$.

E 3.3:2 (IUC, Appendix A) Let $k \in [1, +\infty]$. For $F = \{0, 2\}$ and $G = \mathbb{R}$, define $\rho(a, b) = |a - b|$ if $|a - b| \leq 1$, and $\rho(a, b) = k$ if $|a - b| > 1$, $a, b \in G$. Consider the generalized solution operator W given by

$$W(f, 0) = \{f\}, \quad W(f, \varepsilon) = \{g : \rho(f, g) < \varepsilon\}, \; \varepsilon > 0.$$

Let $N(f) = 0$. Show that $r(N, 0) = r(N) = 1$ and $e(\phi^I, N, 0) = k$ for any interpolatory algorithm ϕ^I.

4. Cardinality Number and Complexity

In this section we show how bounds on the complexity can be derived using the notion of radius of information. Recall that the radius $r(N)$ measures the intrinsic uncertainty of information N. In particular, we can compute ε-approximations only if $r(N) \leq \varepsilon$.

Let N be adaptive information as in Section 2.2 of Chapter 3. Let $\text{card}(N)$ denote the (worst case) cardinality of information, i.e., the total number of information operations in $N(f)$ for a worst f,

$$\text{card}(N) = \sup_{f \in F} n(f).$$

By the ε-cardinality number $m(\varepsilon)$ we mean the minimal cardinality of information whose radius does not exceed ε,

$$m(\varepsilon) = \min\{\text{card}(N) : N \text{ such that } r(N) \leq \varepsilon\}.$$

Obviously, to compute an ε-approximation for all f we have to use information N whose cardinality is at least $m(\varepsilon)$.

For arbitrary N, the computation of $U(f)$ costs at least $c\,n(f)$, where c is the cost of one information operation. Therefore, the worst case cost of U is bounded from below by $c\,\mathrm{card}(N)$. Since this holds for arbitrary U, we have the following lower bound on the complexity

THEOREM 4.1.

$$\mathrm{comp}(\varepsilon) \geq c\,m(\varepsilon).$$

We now discuss assumptions for which the bound in Theorem 4.1 is almost sharp. Suppose that N is information of cardinality $m(\varepsilon)$ such that

(i) its information cost is $c\,m(\varepsilon)$,
(ii) its radius is at most ε.

Let ϕ be an algorithm that uses N and whose error $e(\phi, N)$ is equal to $r(N)$. That is, $U(f) = \phi(N(f))$ is an ε-approximation for all f from F. Assume that the combinatory cost of ϕ is dominated by the information cost,

$$\mathrm{cost}(\phi, N(f)) << c\,m(\varepsilon), \quad \forall f \in F.$$

Then we have

$$\mathrm{cost}(U) = \mathrm{cost}(\phi, N) \simeq c\,m(\varepsilon).$$

From Theorem 4.1 we conclude that N and ϕ are *almost optimal* information and algorithm, and $\mathrm{comp}(\varepsilon) \simeq c\,m(\varepsilon)$. Thus, we have found the ε-complexity in terms of the ε-cardinality number. We summarize this in

THEOREM 4.2. *If there exists information N of cardinality $m(\varepsilon)$ satisfying assumptions (i) and (ii) whose cost dominates the combinatory cost of an optimal error algorithm ϕ, then*

$$\mathrm{comp}(\varepsilon) \simeq c\,m(\varepsilon)$$

and (ϕ, N) are almost optimal.

How restrictive are the assumptions of Theorem 4.2? These assumptions hold for many important problems including linear problems discussed in the next section. They also hold for the continuous binary search problem of Chapter 1 and for some nonlinear problems analyzed in Chapter 5. There are some counterexamples as well. One is due to Papadimitriou and Tsitsiklis [86]. They present a nonlinear problem of decentralized control theory with $m(\varepsilon) = \Theta(\varepsilon^{-4})$ for which the combinatory cost of any optimal error algorithm is non-polynomial in $1/\varepsilon$ iff the famous conjecture $\mathrm{P} \neq \mathrm{NP}$ holds. Thus, it is very likely that for this problem the combinatory cost dominates information cost, and therefore $\mathrm{comp}(\varepsilon)$ may be much greater than the ε-cardinality, see **NR 4:1**.

Also Nemirovsky and Yudin [83] indicate a number of optimization problems for which the combinatory cost of almost optimal error algorithms is much larger than the information cost. This will be discussed in Section 8 of Chapter 5.

Notes and Remarks

NR 4:1 Papadimitriou and Tsitsiklis [86] consider the following problem

$$F = \{f : [0,1]^4 \to [0,1] : \|f(x_1, \ldots, x_4) - f(y_1, \ldots, y_4)\|_{\sup} \leq \max_{1 \leq i \leq 4} |x_i - y_i|\},$$

$$S(f) = \inf_{\gamma_1, \gamma_2} \int_0^1 \int_0^1 f(x_1, x_2, \gamma_1(x_1), \gamma_2(x_2)) \, dx_1 \, dx_2.$$

For Λ consisting of function evaluations, they prove that the ε-cardinality number is proportional to ε^{-4}. Hence $m(\varepsilon)$ is a polynomial in $1/\varepsilon$. This should be contrasted with their second result which states that the complexity of this problem is not polynomially bounded iff P$\neq$NP holds. Since P$\neq$NP is very likely to be true, we see that there is a big difference between $m(\varepsilon)$ and comp(ε). This shows that, in general, $c\, m(\varepsilon)$ need not be a sharp lower bound for comp(ε).

Exercises

E 4:1 (GTOA p. 29) Let F be a class of k-times differentiable functions $f : \mathbb{R}^d \to \mathbb{R}^d$. Let $N(f) = [f(x_1), f'(x_1), \ldots, f^{(p)}(x_1), \ldots, f(x_n), f'(x_n), \ldots, f^{(p)}(x_n)]$ for distinct points x_i and $p \leq k$. Show that $\dim N(F) = n\, d \binom{d+p}{p}$, which is the cardinality of N if the class Λ consists of linear functionals.

5. Linear Problems

In this section we present the theory of linear problems in the worst case setting. While this narrows our scope significantly, many important problems are linear and the results of this section may be applied to them. Examples of linear problems include scalar or multivariate integration, function approximation, the solution of linear partial differential equations, and linear integral equations. See Chapter 5, where the general results are applied to these specific linear problems.

The theory of the worst case setting for nonlinear problems is very much dependent on a particular problem. Results for such nonlinear problems as optimization, large linear systems, eigenpairs, nonlinear equations, ordinary differential equations, and topological degree can also be found in Chapter 5.

We will obtain tight complexity bounds for linear problems in the worst case setting. First we prove that adaption does *not* significantly help. This result simplifies the search for *optimal* information, i.e., for information of fixed cardinality whose intrinsic uncertainty is minimal. In this way, we will obtain tight estimates on the ε-cardinality number which, as we know from Section 4, when multiplied by c bounds the complexity from below. Finally, we exhibit relations between optimal information and n-widths.

We then turn our interest to algorithms which are, at least conceptually, easy to obtain. We discuss the existence of linear algorithms with error equal to the radius of information. We also discuss spline algorithms, which are specific examples of interpolatory algorithms, and examine their optimal error properties.

Notes and Remarks

NR 5:1 We give a brief historical note on the study of linear problems, citing only the most important references. Sard [49], see also Sard [63], studied linear algorithms using function evaluations at fixed points for the integration problem. Independently, Nikolskij [50], see also Nikolskij [79], posed the same problem and permitted the evaluation points to be optimally chosen. Golomb and Weinberger [59] performed the first systematic study of algorithms with minimal error for the approximation of a linear functional. As already mentioned, Smolyak [65] proved the existence of linear optimal algorithms for the approximation of a linear functional over a convex and balanced set. Micchelli and Rivlin [77], see also Micchelli and Rivlin [85], studied algorithms with minimal errors for linear operators using linear noisy information. The study of complexity with partial, noisy and priced information can be found in GTOA and IUC. Substantial portions of these two books are devoted to the complexity of linear problems.

5.1. Definition of Linear Problems

A *linear problem* is defined by the following three assumptions:

(i) The set F of problem elements is a nonempty convex balanced subset of a linear space F_1 over the field of real numbers. That is, $f_1, f_2 \in F$ implies $tf_1 + (1-t)f_2 \in F \ \forall t \in [0,1]$, and $f \in F$ implies $-f \in F$. When convenient, we shall assume that F is generated by a linear *restriction* operator $T : F_1 \to X$, where X is a normed linear space and $F = \{f \in F_1 : \|Tf\| \leq 1\}$. The requirement that F is convex and balanced is essentially equivalent to the condition that F is generated by a linear restriction operator, see **NR 5.1:1**.

(ii) The solution operator is a *linear* operator $S : F_1 \to G$. Observe that while we are only interested in problem elements from F, it is convenient to be able to work within the whole linear space F_1.

(iii) The class Λ of permissible information operations is a subset of the class of *linear* functionals $L : F_1 \to \mathbb{R}$.

We illustrate the above conditions by the integration example from Chapter 3. The set F is convex and balanced. The restriction operator T is given by $Tf = f^{(r)}$ with the sup norm in the space $X = C([0,1])$. The solution operator is clearly linear. The class Λ consists of functionals of the form $L(f) = f(x)$ for some x from $[0,1]$. Thus, L is linear in f and therefore Λ satisfies (iii).

On the other hand, the continuous binary search problem from Chapter 2 is *not* a linear problem since the class Λ consisting of questions does not satisfy (iii).

Notes and Remarks

NR 5.1:1 (GTOA p. 32) We show that modulo a technical detail, the assumption that F is convex and balanced is equivalent to F being generated by a linear restriction operator. Assume first that $F = \{f \in F_1 : \|Tf\| \leq 1\}$. Obviously, F is convex and balanced. Assume now that F is a convex balanced subset of a linear space F_1. Without loss of generality, we assume that $F_1 = \text{span}(F)$, i.e., F_1 consists of linear combinations of elements from F. Recall the definition of the Minkowski functional (gauge) $q : f_1 \rightarrow \mathbb{R}$,

$$q(f) = \inf\{\alpha^{-1} : \alpha f \in F, \alpha > 0\}.$$

Then q is a seminorm and $\{f \in F_1 : q(f) < 1\} \subset F \subset \{f \in F_1 : q(f) \leq 1\}$, see for instance Wilansky [78].

Let $A = \{f \in F : q(f) = 0\}$. If $f_1, f_2 \in A$ then for any constants c_1 and c_2 we have $q(c_1 f_1 + c_2 f_2) \leq |c_1| q(f_1) + |c_2| q(f_2) = 0$, which shows that $c_1 f_1 + c_2 f_2 \in A$. Thus, A is a linear subspace of F_1. Decompose F_1 as $F_1 = A \oplus A^\perp$, where $A^\perp$ is a linear subspace of F_1, see for instance Edwards [65]. Then $f = f_1 + f_2$, where $f_1 \in A$ and $f_2 \in A^\perp$. Define $X = A^\perp$ and $\|f_2\| = q(f_2)$. Since $q(f_2) = 0$ implies that $f_2 \in A$, $f_2 = 0$ and the seminorm q becomes a norm on X. Thus, X is a linear normed space. Define a linear operator $Tf = f_2$. Since $\|Tf\| = \|f_2\| = q(f_2) = q(f)$, we have

$$\underline{F} = \{f \in F_1 : \|Tf\| < 1\} \subset F \subset \overline{F} = \{f \subset F_1 : \|Tf\| \leq 1\}.$$

Observe that it can happen that F is neither $\underline{F}$ nor $\overline{F}$. It is, however, obvious that the solution operators $\underline{S} = S|_{\underline{F}}$ and $\overline{S} = S|_{\overline{F}}$ have the same radii and diameters for any information. This shows that the problems $\underline{S}$, S, and $\overline{S}$ are only insignificantly different.

5.2. Adaption versus Nonadaption

In this section we study whether adaptive information is more powerful than nonadaptive information for linear problems. Our interest in the power of nonadaptive information is motivated by the following reasons:

(i) Nonadaptive information is much simpler (and therefore much easier to analyze) than adaptive information. If we know that nothing can be gained by using adaptive information, we significantly cut the search space when seeking which information should be used to minimize the cost of computing an ε-approximation.

(ii) For nonadaptive information we have a natural decomposition for parallel computation. Because nonadaptive information minimizes communication requirements, it is also desirable for distributed computation.

Let us first analyze nonadaptive information N of cardinality n,

$$N(f) = [L_1(f), L_2(f), \ldots, L_n(f)]$$

for linear functionals from the class Λ. As we know from Section 2, the radius of information measures the intrinsic uncertainty caused by N. Motivated by the fact that $d(N)/2 \le r(N) \le d(N)$, we now find the diameter $d(N)$ of information.

LEMMA 5.2.1. *For any linear problem and any nonadaptive information* N,

$$d(N) = d(N,0) = 2 \sup_{h \in F \cap \ker N} \|S(h)\|.$$

PROOF: Let $y \in N(F)$. Take two problem elements $f_1, f_2 \in N^{-1}(y) \cap F$. Then $\|S(f_1) - S(f_2)\| = \|S(h)\|$, where $h = f_1 - f_2 \in \ker N$. Since F is balanced, $-f_2 \in F$. Since F is convex,

$$\tfrac{1}{2}h = \tfrac{1}{2}(f_1 - f_2) \in F.$$

Thus, $\|S(f_1) - S(f_2)\| = 2\|S(0.5\,h)\| \le a := 2\sup_{h \in F \cap \ker N} \|S(h)\|$. Since this holds for arbitrary $f_1, f_2 \in N^{-1}(y) \cap F$ and arbitrary $y \in N(F)$, we conclude that $d(N,y) \le d(N) \le a$.

To prove the opposite inequality note that $f = 0$ belongs to F. Take $y = N(0) = 0$. Obviously, $N^{-1}(0) = \ker N$. For an arbitrary $h \in N^{-1}(0)$, define $f_1 = -f_2 = h$. Then $f_i \in N^{-1}(0) \cap F$ and $d(N,0) \ge \|S(f_1) - S(f_2)\| = 2\|S(h)\|$. Taking the supremum with respect to h we get $d(N) \ge d(N,0) \ge a$. This completes the proof. ∎

The essence of Lemma 5.2.1 is that the diameter of arbitrary nonadaptive information is achieved for $y = 0$. This means that the zero information data, $y = N(f) = 0$, is worst for any nonadaptive information N as far as local diameters are considered. This property is the key to proving that the diameter of adaptive information cannot be smaller than the diameter of correspondingly chosen nonadaptive information. More precisely, let N^{a} be adaptive information. That is,

$$N^{\mathrm{a}}(f) = [L_1(f), L_2(f;y_1), \ldots, L_{n(f)}(f;y_1, \ldots, y_{n(f)-1})],$$

where $y_1 = L_1(f)$, $y_i = L_i(f;y_1, \ldots, y_{i-1})$. The cardinality at f is given by

$$n(f) = \min\{i : \mathrm{ter}_i(y_1, \ldots, y_i) = 1\}$$

for some Boolean functions $\mathrm{ter}_i : \mathbb{R}^i \to \{0,1\}$. Since the information operations must be permissible, $L_i(\cdot;y_1, \ldots, y_{i-1})$ are linear functionals from the class Λ for every fixed $y_1, \ldots, y_{i-1}$. We define very special nonadaptive information N^{non} of cardinality $n(0)$ by fixing all the values y_i to be zero. That is, for every $f \in F$

$$N^{\text{non}}(f) = [L_i(f), L_2(f; 0), \ldots, L_{n(0)}(f; 0, \ldots, 0)].$$

Note that $n(0)$ and $L_i(\cdot; 0, \ldots, 0) \in \Lambda$ are well defined since $f = 0$ belongs to F. Information N^{non} is nonadaptive and, clearly, $\text{card}(N^{\text{non}}) \le \text{card}(N^{\text{a}})$. Observe that the form of N^{non} is, in general, simpler than the form of N^{a}.

We compare the power of adaptive information N^{a} with the power of nonadaptive information N^{non} by relating their diameters.

THEOREM 5.2.1. *For any linear problem we have*

$$d(N^{\text{non}}) \le d(N^{\text{a}}).$$

PROOF: Observe that N^{a} restricted to $\ker N^{\text{non}}$ is equal to N^{non}. Indeed, $f \in \ker N^{\text{non}}$ implies that $L_1(f) = 0$ and therefore $y_1 = 0$. Then $y_2 = L_2(f; 0) = 0$, and similarly all y_i are zero and $N^{\text{a}}(f) = N^{\text{non}}(f) = 0$, as claimed. Therefore $(N^{\text{non}})^{-1}(0) = (N^{\text{a}})^{-1}(0)$, which implies that $d(N^{\text{non}}, 0) = d(N^{\text{a}}, 0) \le d(N^{\text{a}})$. Due to Lemma 5.2.1, we have $d(N^{\text{non}}) = d(N^{\text{non}}, 0) \le d(N^{\text{a}})$, as claimed. ∎

Theorem 5.2.1 states that as far as the diameter of information is concerned, we cannot gain by using adaptive information for linear problems. This and the fact that $r(N) \le d(N) \le 2 r(N)$ for any information N yields

$$r(N^{\text{non}}) \le 2 r(N^{\text{a}}).$$

Thus, the far more general structure of adaptive information cannot decrease the uncertainty by more than a factor of two as compared to nonadaptive information. We stress that the inequality above can be strengthened to

$$r(N^{\text{non}}) \le r(N^{\text{a}})$$

whenever $r(N^{\text{non}}) = d(N^{\text{non}})/2$. This holds for a number of cases. For instance, if S is a linear functional, $G = \mathbb{R}$, then $S(N^{\text{non}})^{-1}(y)$ is an interval, and therefore $r(N^{\text{non}}, y) = d(N^{\text{non}}, y)/2$, $\forall y \in N(F)$. Similarly, $r(N^{\text{non}}) = d(N^{\text{non}})/2$ holds if S is a finite dimensional operator and its range space G is equipped with the $\mathcal{L}_\infty$ norm. This is also true if F is generated by a restriction operator T whose range is a Hilbert space, as will be discussed in Section 5.6. We summarize this discussion in

COROLLARY 5.2.1. *For any linear problem, adaption is at most twice as powerful as nonadaption,*

$$r(N^{\text{non}}) \leq 2\,r(N^{\text{a}}).$$

If $r(N^{\text{non}}) = d(N^{\text{non}})/2$ then adaption is no more powerful than nonadaption,

$$r(N^{\text{non}}) \leq r(N^{\text{a}}).$$

While the radius of information is not always equal to half of its diameter, no linear problem has yet been found for which the radius of adaptive information is less than the radius of corresponding nonadaptive information. It would be interesting to prove that $r(N^{\text{non}}) \leq r(N^{\text{a}})$ for all linear problems or to find a linear problem for which $r(N^{\text{non}}) > r(N^{\text{a}})$. (Note added in the proof: Novak [87b] has presented a linear problem for which adaption helps a little.)

We stress that adaption does not help (or helps by a factor of at most two) under the assumption that the problem is *linear*, i.e., when the following three assumptions hold:

  (i) the solution operator is *linear*,
  (ii) the class F of problem elements is *balanced* and *convex*,
  (iii) information consists of *linear* functionals.

If one of the assumptions above does not hold, adaption can help significantly, as illustrated by the following three examples.

EXAMPLE 5.2.1. NONLINEAR SOLUTION OPERATOR   Let F be the class of Lipschitz functions, $f : [-1,1] \to [-1,1]$ and $|f(x) - f(y)| \leq \rho\,|x - y|$, $\forall\, x, y \in [-1,1]$, where $\rho \in [0,1)$. Observe that F is balanced and convex. The nonlinear equation $x = f(x)$ has a unique fixed point $\alpha(f)$ in $[-1,1]$ for any $f \in F$. Define the nonlinear solution operator as $S(f) = \alpha(f)$. Let the class Λ consist of function evaluations.

Sikorski and Woźniakowski [87] showed that the minimal radius of *nonadaptive* information of cardinality n is equal to $\rho/\big(2(n + \rho)\big)$, whereas the minimal radius of *adaptive* information of cardinality n is equal to $\big(\rho/(\rho + 1)\big)^n/2$. Thus, adaption is exponentially more powerful than nonadaption.

For the relative error criterion, $|\alpha(f) - U(f)|/|\alpha(f)| \leq \varepsilon$, where $\varepsilon \leq 1$, we have an even more drastic difference between adaption and nonadaption. Namely, the minimal radius of nonadaptive information of cardinality n is ρ, no matter how large n. Thus, it is impossible to compute an ε-approximation with $\varepsilon < \rho$ by using nonadaptive information. On the other hand, the sequence of the minimal radii of adaptive information goes exponentially fast to zero. Even for ρ close to one, it is enough to compute roughly $\log_2 \varepsilon^{-1} + \log_2 \log_2 (1 - \rho)^{-1}$ function evaluations to get an ε-approximation.

This shows that adaption is infinitely more powerful than nonadaption for the fixed point problem with the relative error criterion. The reader may find a more detailed discussion on this problem in Section 12 of Chapter 5.

EXAMPLE 5.2.2. NONCONVEX AND UNBALANCED CLASSES F We present three problems defined on nonconvex and/or unbalanced classes F for which adaption helps.

The first one is the function approximation problem defined as follows. Let F_1 be the linear space of piecewise constant functions $f : [0, 1] \to \mathbb{R}$ with $f(0) = 0$. Define F as the class of functions from F_1 which take at most two values from $\{0, 1\}$, and which have exactly one discontinuity point. Let $G = L_2([0, 1])$ and $S(f) = f$. Thus, S is linear whereas the class F in neither balanced nor convex. The class Λ consists of function evaluations. From Traub, Wasilkowski, and Woźniakowski [84b] we know that the radius of nonadaptive information N^{non} of cardinality n is bounded by $r(N^{\text{non}}) \geq (2\sqrt{n+1})^{-1}$. This bound is achieved by equally spaced evaluations, i.e., for $N^{\text{non}}(f) = \left[f(1/(n+1)), f(2/(n+1)), \ldots, f(n/(n+1)) \right]$ we have $r(N^{\text{non}}) = (2\sqrt{n+1})^{-1}$. For adaptive information N^{a} of cardinality n we can have $r(N^{\text{a}}) = 2^{-(n+2)/2}$. This is achieved by bisection information. That is, by evaluating f at $x_1 = 1/2$ first. Then x_i is chosen as the midpoint of the subinterval on which f is unknown. For instance, $x_2 = 3/4$ if $f(x_1) = 0$, and $x_2 = 1/4$ if $f(x_1) = 1$. In this case, adaptive information is exponentially better than nonadaptive information.

The second and third examples are from a recent paper of Huerta [86]. He considers the integration problem, $S(f) = \int_0^1 f(t) \, dt$, for nonconvex classes F with information consisting of function evaluations.

The first class F is the class of piecewise constant functions $f : [0, 1] \to \mathbb{R}$ with discontinuities at $x_i(f)$, $i = 1, 2, \ldots, s = s(f)$, where $0 < x_1(f) < x_2(f) < \cdots < x_s(f)$ and $x_{i+1}(f) - x_i(f) > \delta > 0$, and $\|f\|_\infty \leq M$. Here δ and M are given parameters. He proves that the minimal radius of nonadaptive information of cardinality n is $\Theta(n^{-1})$, whereas the minimal radius of adaptive information of cardinality n is $\Theta(2^{-bn})$ for some $b \in \left[\delta/(\delta + 1), 1 \right]$. Thus, once more adaption is exponentially better than nonadaption.

The second class F consists of functions which are piecewise twice continuously differentiable with jump discontinuities at $x_i = x_i(f)$, $i = 1, 2, \ldots, s = s(f)$, such that $0 = x_0 < x_1 < \cdots < x_s < x_{s+1} = 1$ and $x_{i+1} - x_i > \delta_1$. It is also assumed that $f(x_i) = f(x_i^-)$ or $f(x_i) = f(x_i^+)$ with $|\text{Jump } f(x_i)| := |f(x_i^+) - f(x_i^-)| > \delta_2$, $\|f\|_\infty \leq M_1$ and $|f^{(2)}(x)| \leq M_2$ for all $x \notin \{x_1, x_2, \ldots, x_s\}$. Here M_1, M_2, δ_1, and δ_2 are given parameters. Then Huerta proves that the minimal radius of nonadaptive information of cardinality n is $\Theta(n^{-1})$, whereas for adaptive information we have $\Theta(n^{-2})$. Thus, adaption is quadratically better than nonadaption.

We stress that these three problems are rather academic. In practice it is hard, if not impossible, to know the parameters of the classes considered. Nevertheless, these classes illustrate the kind of assumptions sufficient to prove that adaption helps significantly.

EXAMPLE 5.2.3. NONLINEAR INFORMATION   We now consider a variant of the continuous binary search problem, see Chapter 2, with a restricted class of questions. More precisely, let $F = [-1, +1]$ and $S(f) = f$. Thus, S is linear and F is balanced and convex in $F_1 = \mathbb{R}$.

Assume that information can consist only of questions: "Is f less than x ?" for any x from F. That is, Λ consists of $Q(\cdot; x)$ for $x \in F$, where $Q(f; x) = 1$ if $f < x$, and $Q(f; x) = 0$ otherwise.

Observe first that the questions about bits of f, which formed optimal information for unrestricted class of information operations, are now not permissible.

Take nonadaptive information N^{non} of cardinality n,

$$N^{\mathrm{non}}(f) = [Q(f; x_1), Q(f; x_2), \ldots, Q(f; x_n)].$$

Without loss of generality, we can assume that $-1 = x_0 < x_1 < \cdots < x_n < x_{n+1} = 1$. It is easy to verify that $r(N^{\mathrm{non}}) = \max_{0 \le i \le n}(x_{i+1} - x_i)/2 \ge 1/(n+1)$, with equality for $x_i = -1 + 2i/(n+1)$. Thus, the minimal radius of nonadaptive information of cardinality n is $(n+1)^{-1}$.

On the other hand, bisection information consisting of the questions: "Is f less than the midpoint x_i of the uncertainty interval?" is permissible and adaptive. As we know, the radius of the bisection information with n questions is 2^{-n}. Thus, adaption is exponentially better than nonadaption.

We showed that adaption does not help significantly for linear problems. We stress that this result holds in the *worst case* setting. This means that arbitrary adaptive information N^{a} does not provide more information than appropriately chosen nonadaptive information N^{non} for problem elements yielding the zero data, $y = N^{\mathrm{a}}(f) = 0$. However, for some other problem elements with $y = N^{\mathrm{a}}(f) \ne 0$, adaptive information can be more efficient. This is illustrated by the following example.

EXAMPLE 5.2.4.   Consider the approximation problem for the class F of functions defined on $[0,1]$ and satisfying a Lipschitz condition with constant 1. Suppose that for $x_1 < x_2$ and for some $f \in F_1$, we compute $f(x_1)$ and $f(x_2)$ and we observe that $f(x_2) = f(x_1) + x_2 - x_1$. Then $f(x) =$

$f(x_1) + x - x_1$ for $x \in [x_1, x_2]$, and there is no need to compute $f(x)$ for any $x \in (x_1, x_2)$. The rest of computations should sample f outside the interval $[x_1, x_2]$. This can be done by using adaptive information.

This observation led Sukharev [72, 87] to analyze the optimal choice of $(n-i)$ information operations after computing the first i of them. Although such a choice of information operations does not decrease the global radius of information, it may significantly lower the local radius for some y. For further discussion see **NR 5.2:2**.

An alternative approach is to turn to a different setting such as, for instance, the average case or probabilistic setting. We study whether adaption is more powerful than nonadaption in Chapter 6 for the average case setting and in Chapter 8 for the probabilistic setting. Adaption versus nonadaption is also discussed in Chapters 10, 11, and 12, where the asymptotic setting, randomization, and noisy information are analyzed.

Notes and Remarks

NR 5.2:1 The result that adaption does not help (or helps by a factor of at most two) has an interesting history. The first evidence that adaption may not help is due to Kiefer [57]. He considered the integration problem for monotonic and bounded functions and proved that the trapezoid rule with equidistant nodes has minimal error among all adaptive rules using the same number of function evaluations, see also **NR 5.2:2**. Observe that the class of monotonic and bounded functions is not balanced. Therefore, in our terminology, Kiefer's problem is not linear.

The first result that adaption does not help for linear problems was established by Bakhvalov [71]. He considered an arbitrary convex and balanced set F, a solution operator which is a linear functional, and adaptive information consisting of $n(f) \equiv n$ linear functionals. It was generalized to arbitrary linear solution operators by Gal and Micchelli [80] and Traub and Woźniakowski [80a, p. 49], independently. The general case with varying cardinality $n(f)$ was studied by Wasilkowski [86a].

The same result also holds for *some* nonlinear solution operators and for different classes of permissible information operations, see, e.g., papers cited in GTOA and IUC.

NR 5.2:2 Sukharev [72, 87] proposes finding n information operations L_i from the class Λ in such a way that for every $z_i = N_i(f) = [L_1(f), L_2(f; y_1), \ldots, L_i(f; y_1, \ldots, y_{i-1})]$ the information $[L_{i+1}, \ldots, L_n]$ has minimal radius for the approximation of the solution operator S on the set $N_i^{-1}(z_i)$. Such optimal information operations have been obtained for a number of problems, see Sukharev [88] for relevant references. Here we report optimal information operation for the integration of monotonic functions, see Glinkin [81], Glinkin and Sukharev [85] and Sukharev [79b, 87] for proofs.

Let $F = \{f : [a, b] \to \mathbb{R} : f \text{ is nondecreasing and } f(a) = f_a, f(b) = f_b\}$, with fixed f_a and f_b. We wish to approximate $S(f) = \int_a^b f(x)\,dx$ for f from F. It is known, Kiefer [57], that adaption is not more powerful than nonadaption for this problem. Furthermore, the radius of information of cardinality n is minimized if we evaluate the function at equidistant nodes $x_i = a + i(b-a)/(n+1)$, $i = 1, 2, \ldots, n$, and approximate the integral by the trapezoid rule $(b-a)/(2(n+1)) \sum_{i=1}^{n+1} (f(x_i) + f(x_{i-1}))$, with $x_0 = a$ and $x_{n+1} = b$. Then the radius is equal to $(f_b - f_a)(b-a)/(2(n+1))$.

In the papers cited above the following optimal evaluations $f(x_i^*)$ are obtained. The first point x_1^* is any point from the set $\{x_1, x_2, \ldots, x_n\}$. Suppose that $x_1^*, x_2^*, \ldots, x_i^*$ are given. Assume without loss of generality that $x_1^* < x_2^* < \cdots < x_i^*$. Then the next point x_{i+1} is any point of $\bigcup_{j=1}^{i+1} T_j$, where T_j is defined as the lattice of n_j^* equidistant points in $[x_{j-1}^*, x_j^*]$, $T_j = \{x_{j-1}^* + k(x_j^* - x_{j-1}^*)/(n_j^* + 1) : k = 1, 2, \ldots, n_j^*\}$, and the integer parameters n_j^* are the solution of the following minimization problem $\min\{\sum_{j=1}^{i+1} A_j/(2(n_j+1)) : \sum_{j=1}^{i+1} n_j = n-i\}$, with $A_j = (f(x_j^*) - f(x_{j-1}^*))/(x_j^* - x_{j-1}^*)$. Glinkin and Sukharev [85] report numerical comparisons on stochastically generated monotonic piecewise analytic functions and conclude that the trapezoid rule using optimal information evaluations $f(x_i^*)$ is better than the trapezoid rule using the evaluations $f(x_i)$.

NR 5.2:3 The notion of optimal information operations suggest the following questions. Assume that the values of information $y = N(f) \in \mathbb{R}^n$ are distributed according to a given probability measure λ on $\mathbb{R}^n$. Then it seems natural to ask: What is the expected value $\int_{\mathbb{R}^n} r(N, y)\, \lambda(dy)$? How much smaller is it than $r(N)$? For a given b, what is the probability of the data y for which $r(N, y)$ is b times smaller than $r(N)$, i.e., what is $\lambda(\{y : r(N, y) \le b\, r(N)\})$?

We now comment on the assumption about distribution of the data. If, as in the average case or probabilistic settings, problem elements are distributed according to a probability measure μ, then λ should be taken as μN^{-1}. In this case, however, the knowledge of μ can also be used to select information as well as an algorithm. Then the (worst case) radius $r(N)$ of information should be replaced by the average radius $r^{\mathrm{avg}}(N)$ of information, see Chapter 6. This implies that the expected value of the worst case local radius is bounded by

$$\int_{\mathbb{R}^n} r(N, y)\, \lambda(dy) \ge \int_{\mathbb{R}^n} r^{\mathrm{avg}}(N, y)\, \lambda(dy) = r^{\mathrm{avg}}(N, y).$$

Thus, it cannot be better than the error of a central algorithm in the average case setting. On the other hand, the measure μ on the problem elements may not be known, especially for problems defined on infinite dimensional spaces. The measure λ is defined on $\mathbb{R}^n$ no matter what the dimension of the set F is, and therefore it may be easier to obtain than the measure μ. In such a case, the expected value of the worst case local radii can still be computed. Average case analysis, where a probability measure μ on problem elements is replaced by a measure λ on the range of information, has been proposed by Novak [86b,c, 87a], who studies problems such as integration, approximation and optimization.

Exercises

E 5.2:1 (GTOA p. 30) Consider a linear problem defined by a linear operator S, a convex balanced $F = \{f \in F_1 : \|Tf\| \le 1\}$, and nonadaptive information N. Prove that $r(N) < +\infty$ implies $\ker N \cap \ker T \subset \ker S$.

E 5.2:2 (GTOA p. 31) Consider a linear problem as in **E 5.2:1**. Define the index n^* of the linear problem (S, T) as the dimension of an algebraic complement of $\ker T \cap \ker S$ in the space $\ker T$. Thus, $n^* = \dim(\ker T) - \dim(\ker T \cap \ker S)$ whenever $\dim(\ker T \cap \ker S)$ is finite. Prove that $\mathrm{card}(N) < n^*$ implies $r(N) = +\infty$.

E 5.2:3 (GTOA p. 32) Consider a linear problem as in **E 5.2:1**. Let $T = 0$. Thus, $F = F_1$. Show that $r(N)$ is either zero or infinity. More precisely, for nonadaptive information we have $r(N) = 0$ if $\ker N \subset \ker S$, and $r(N) = +\infty$ otherwise.

E 5.2:4 Consider a convex set F which is not necessarily balanced. Instead, assume that F is symmetric with respect to an element f^*, so that $f \in F$ implies $2f^* - f \in F$. For a linear solution operator S and nonadaptive information N prove that

$$d(N) = d(N, f^*) = 2\,r(N, f^*) = 2 \sup_{h \in N^{-1}(N(f^*)) \cap F} \|S(f^* - h)\|.$$

Let $N^{\mathrm{a}}(f) = [L_1(f), L_2(f; y_1), \ldots, L_{n(f)}(f; y_1, \ldots, y_{n(f)-1})]$ be adaptive information. For $i \leq n(f^*)$, let $y_i^* = L_i(f^*; y_1^*, \ldots, y_{i-1}^*)$. Prove that $d(N^{\mathrm{a}}) \geq d(N^{\mathrm{non}})$ for nonadaptive N^{non} defined by

$$N^{\mathrm{non}}(f) = [L_1(f), L_2(f; y_1^*), \ldots, L_{n(f^*)}(f; y_1^*, \ldots, y_{n(f^*)-1}^*)].$$

E 5.2:5 Consider the continuous binary search problem as in Example 5.2.3. That is, $F = [-1, +1]$ and $S(f) = f$. Assume that information is provided by questions of the form "Does f belong to the interval $[a, b]$?" for any a and b from $[-1, +1]$. What is the minimal radius of nonadaptive information of cardinality n?

5.3. Optimal Information

In this section we study information consisting of optimally chosen information operations. From Section 5.2 we know that adaption does not help (or helps by a factor of at most two) and therefore we restrict our attention to nonadaptive information. Since the radius of information measures the intrinsic uncertainty, we wish to choose information operations that minimize the radius. More precisely, let Λ_n consist of permissible nonadaptive information N of cardinality at most n, i.e., $N = [L_1, \ldots, L_k]$ with $L_i \in \Lambda$ and $k \leq n$. Then

$$r(n, \Lambda) = \inf_{N \in \Lambda_n} r(N)$$

is called the *nth minimal radius of (nonadaptive) information* in the class Λ, and $N_n^* = [L_1^*, \ldots, L_n^*]$ is called *nth optimal (nonadaptive) information* in the class Λ iff $L_i^* \in \Lambda$ and $r(N_n^*) = r(n, \Lambda)$.

REMARK 5.3.1. The *nth minimal diameter of (nonadaptive) information* in the class Λ is defined by

$$d(n, \Lambda) = \inf_{N \in \Lambda_n} d(N).$$

Clearly, $r(n, \Lambda) \leq d(n, \Lambda) \leq 2r(n, \Lambda)$. Sometimes it is easier to find the nth minimal diameters than the nth minimal radii. This allows us to estimate the nth minimal radii to within a factor of two.

Let Λ^* be the class of *all* linear functionals L, $L : F_1 \to \mathbb{R}$. Observe that for any class Λ we have $\Lambda \subset \Lambda^*$, and therefore $r(n, \Lambda) \geq r(n, \Lambda^*)$. For brevity we sometimes write $r(n)$ instead of $r(n, \Lambda^*)$.

Without loss of generality assume that the set F is generated by a linear restriction operator $T : F_1 \rightarrow X$, where $X = T(F_1)$. That is, $F = \{f \in F_1 : \|Tf\| \leq 1\}$. For simplicity we assume that T is one-to-one, leaving the general case of many-to-one T to **NR 5.3:1**. Define the linear operator $K = ST^{-1} : X \rightarrow G$. Let B be a linear subspace of X. Denote

$$\|K\|_B = \sup \{ \|Kz\| : z \in B \text{ and } \|z\| \leq 1 \}$$

as the norm of the operator K restricted to the subspace B. The nth minimal norm of K is defined by

$$b(n) = \inf \{ \|K\|_B : B \subset X \text{ and } \operatorname{codim} B \leq n \},$$

where $\operatorname{codim} B$ is the codimension of B. We show a relation between $r(n, \Lambda)$ and $b(n)$.

LEMMA 5.3.1. *The nth minimal radius $r(n, \Lambda)$ is no less than the nth minimal norm of the operator K,*

$$r(n, \Lambda) \geq b(n).$$

PROOF: Let N be nonadaptive information of cardinality at most n from the class Λ_n. Then $r(N) \geq d(N)/2 = \sup\{\|S(h)\| : h \in \ker N \text{ and } \|Th\| \leq 1\}$, due to Lemma 5.2.1. Let $z = Th$. Then

$$r(N) \geq \sup \{ \|ST^{-1}z\| : z \in T(\ker N) \text{ and } \|z\| \leq 1 \} = \|K\|_{T(\ker N)}.$$

Since $\operatorname{codim} T(\ker N) \leq \operatorname{codim} \ker N = \dim N(F_1) \leq n$, we conclude that $r(N) \geq b(n)$. This holds for arbitrary N, and therefore Lemma 5.3.1 follows. ∎

We now turn to an upper bound on the nth minimal radius for the class Λ^*. We show that $r(n) = r(n, \Lambda^*) \leq 2b(n)$. In order to do this, assume, without loss of generality, that $b(n)$ is attained for a linear subspace B_n, $b(n) = \|K\|_{B_n}$. Such a subspace is called the *nth minimal subspace of K*. Decompose X as the direct sum of B_n and its algebraic complement $B_n^{\perp}$, see for instance Edwards [65], $X = B_n \oplus B_n^{\perp}$, where $\operatorname{codim} B_n = \dim B_n^{\perp} \leq n$. That is, $z \in B_n^{\perp}$ iff $z = \sum_{i=1}^{n} L_{i,n}(z) \eta_{i,n}$ for some linear functionals $L_{i,n}$, $L_{i,n} : X \rightarrow \mathbb{R}$, and some elements $\eta_{i,n} \in X$. Define the nonadaptive information

$$N_n(f) = [L_{1,n}(Tf), L_{2,n}(Tf), \ldots, L_{n,n}(Tf)].$$

Obviously, $N_n \in \Lambda_n^*$ since there are *no* restrictions on information operations. We are ready to prove that the radius of N_n is almost minimal.

THEOREM 5.3.1.

(i) *The radius of information N_n is not greater than twice the nth minimal radius of information,*

$$r(N_n) \leq d(N_n) = 2\,b(n) \leq 2\,r(n).$$

(ii) *If $r(N_n) = d(N_n)/2$ then N_n is nth optimal nonadaptive information in the class Λ^* of all linear functionals, and*
$$r(N_n) = r(n) = b(n).$$

PROOF: We begin with (i). It is enough to prove that $d(N_n) = 2b(n)$. We have $d(N_n) = 2\sup\{\|S(h)\| : h \in \ker N_n, \|Th\| \leq 1\} = 2\sup\{\|S(h)\| : L_{i,n}(Th) = 0, i = 1, 2, \ldots, n$ and $\|Th\| \leq 1\} = 2\sup\{\|Kz\| : z \in B_n, \|z\| \leq 1\} = 2\|K\|_{B_n} = 2b(n)$, as claimed.

From Lemma 5.3.1 and (i) we have $b(n) \leq r(n) \leq r(N_n) = d(N_n)/2 \leq b(n)$. Thus, $r(n) = r(N_n) = b(n)$, as claimed. ∎

Information N_n is generated by the nth minimal subspace of the linear operator K, where $K : X \to G$. We specialize the form of information N_n assuming that X and G are separable Hilbert spaces and that the operator K is compact. Further extensions can be found in **NR 5.3:2**. Let K^* be the adjoint operator of K, $K^* : G \to X$. Define a self-adjoint operator

$$K_1 = K^* K : X \to X.$$

Obviously, K_1 is also compact. Let (λ_i, ζ_i) be the eigenpairs of the operator K_1 such that $K_1 \zeta_i = \lambda_i \zeta_i$, $\lambda_1 \geq \lambda_2 \geq \cdots \geq 0$, and $\langle \zeta_i, \zeta_j \rangle = \delta_{i,j}$. Here, $\langle \cdot, \cdot \rangle$ is the inner product of X and $i, j = 1, 2, \ldots, \dim X$. If $\dim X$ is finite then we formally set $\lambda_i = 0$ and $\zeta_i = 0$ for $i > \dim X$.

Define the number k as follows. If $\lambda_1 = 0$ then $k = 0$. If $\lambda_n > 0$ then $k = n$. Otherwise, if $\lambda_1 > 0$ and $\lambda_n = 0$, then $k = \max\{i : \lambda_i > 0\}$. The information N_n is given by $N_n = 0$ if $k = 0$, and

$$N_n(f) = [\langle Tf, \zeta_1 \rangle, \langle Tf, \zeta_2 \rangle, \ldots, \langle Tf, \zeta_k \rangle]$$

for $k \geq 1$. Clearly, $\mathrm{card}(N_n) = k \leq n$.

THEOREM 5.3.2. *Let X and G be separable Hilbert spaces and let K be compact. Then information N_n is nth optimal in the class Λ^* of all linear functionals and*
$$r(N_n) = r(n) = b(n) = \sqrt{\lambda_{n+1}}.$$

PROOF: For $k = 0$ we have $K_1 = 0$ and all $\lambda_i = 0$. Thus, $r(n) = r(N_k) = b(n) = 0$. Assume then that $k \geq 1$. We first show that $B_k = (\ker K_1) \oplus$

span$(\zeta_{k+1}, \zeta_{k+2}, \dots)$ is an nth minimal subspace of the operator K. Indeed, codim $B_k = \dim \text{span}(\zeta_1, \zeta_2, \dots, \zeta_k) = k \leq n$. For $x \in B_k$, we have $x = x_0 + \sum_{i \geq k+1} \langle x, \zeta_i \rangle \zeta_i$, where $x_0 \in \ker K_1$. Then $\|Kx\|^2 = \langle K_1 x, x \rangle = \sum_{i \geq k+1} \lambda_i \langle x, \zeta_i \rangle^2 \leq \lambda_{k+1} \|x\|^2$. Since this bound is sharp, we get $\|K\|_{B_k} = \sqrt{\lambda_{k+1}}$. If $\lambda_{k+1} = 0$ then the proof is complete. If $\lambda_{k+1} > 0$ then $k = n$ and we proceed as follows.

Take any linear subspace B of codimension at most n. Consider $x = \sum_{i=1}^{n+1} c_i \zeta_i$. Then $x \in B$ iff $L_i(x) = 0$ for certain linear functionals $L_i :$ $X \to \mathbb{R}$, $i = 1, 2, \dots, n$. Hence, we have n linear equaions with $n+1$ unknown coefficients c_i. Since ζ_i are orthonormal, we can find a nonzero vector $(c_1^*, c_2^*, \dots, c_{n+1}^*)$ for which $0 \neq x = \sum_{i=1}^{n+1} c_i^* \zeta_i \in B$. Then $\|Kx\|^2 = \langle K_1 x, x \rangle = \sum_{i=1}^{n+1} (c_i^*)^2 \lambda_i \geq \lambda_{n+1} \|x\|^2$. Thus, $\|K\|_B \geq \sqrt{\lambda_{n+1}}$. This completes the proof that B_k is an nth minimal subspace of K.

From Theorem 5.3.1 we then conclude that $r(N_k) \leq d(N_k) = 2b(n)$. Thus, it is enough to show that $r(N_k) = d(N_k)/2$. Consider $y \in N_n(F)$ and the set $N_n^{-1}(y) = \{f \in F_1 : \|Tf\| \leq 1 \text{ and } \langle Tf, \zeta_i \rangle = y_i \text{ for } i = 1, 2, \dots, k\}$. Observe that $f_0 = \sum_{i=1}^{n} y_i \, T^{-1} \zeta_i$ belongs to $N_n^{-1}(y)$. Furthermore, $h + f_0 \in N_n^{-1}(y)$ implies that $-h + f_0 \in N_n^{-1}(y)$. Thus, f_0 is a center of $N_n^{-1}(y)$, and therefore $r(N_n, y) = d(N_n)/2$, as explained in Section 3.2. Since this holds for arbitrary $y \in N_n^{-1}(F)$, $r(N_n) = d(N_n)/2$, as claimed. $\blacksquare$

Theorem 5.3.2 states that the inner products $\langle Tf, \zeta_i \rangle$ supply the best possible information in the class of all linear functionals, provided the spaces X and G are separable Hilbert spaces. Note that the evaluation of $\langle Tf, \zeta_i \rangle$ corresponds to computing the ith Fourier coefficient of Tf in the eigenvalue decomposition of the operator $K_1 = \left(ST^{-1}\right)^* ST^{-1}$.

More general classes of information has been also studied. The reader is referred to **NR 5.3:3** where continuous nonlinear and discontinuous nonlinear information are discussed.

Notes and Remarks

NR 5.3:1 Section 5.3 as well as this note are based on GTOA p. 33-41. If the restriction operator T is many-to-one, the operator K is defined as follows. First, define $T^{-1} : X \to F_1$ as $T^{-1}x = f_2$, where $x = Tf$ and $f = f_1 + f_2$ with $f_1 \in \ker T$ and $f_2 \in (\ker T)^{\perp}$. It is easy to check that T^{-1} is well defined. In particular, if $T = 0$ then $X = T(F_1) = \{0\}$ and $0^{-1} = 0$. The operator K is defined as $K = ST^{-1} : X \to G$. Lemma 5.3.1 is generalized as follows. Define the *index* n^* of the linear problem (S, T) as the dimension of an algebraic complement of $\ker T \cap \ker S$ in the space $\ker T$, see **E 5.2:2**. Then $r(n) = +\infty$ for $n < n^*$. For $n \geq n^*$, we have $r(n) \geq b(n - n^*)$. Theorem 5.3.1 is generalized as follows. Let $\ker T = (\ker T \cap \ker S) \oplus A(T, S)$, where $A(T, S)$ is of dimension n^*. Then $f \in A(T, S)$ iff $f = \sum_{i=1}^{n^*} L_i^*(f) \zeta_i^*$ for some linear functionals L_i^*, $L_i^* : F_1 \to \mathbb{R}$, and some linearly independent elements ζ_i^* from F_1. Then information N_k is defined by

$$N_k(f) = [L_1^*(f), \dots, L_{n^*}^*(f), L_{1,n-n^*}(Tf), \dots, L_{k,n-n^*}(Tf)],$$

where $L_{i,n-n^*}$ are derived as in Section 5.3 from the $(n - n^*)$th minimal subspace B_{n-n^*} of the operator K and $k = k(n - n^*) = \text{codim}\, B_{n-n^*} \le n - n^*$. We have

$$r(N_k) \le d(N_k) = 2\, b(n - n^*) \le 2\, r(n),$$

and if $r(N_k) = d(N_k)/2$ then

$$r(N_k) = r(n) = b(n - n^*).$$

For separable Hilbert spaces X and G, and compact operator K, we have

$$r(N_k) = r(n) = b(n - n^*) = \sqrt{\lambda_{n-n^*+1}},$$

where $\{\lambda_i\}$ is a nonincreasing sequence of the eigenvalues of the operator $K_1 = K^*K$.

NR 5.3:2 Assume now that X and G are separable Hilbert spaces, but the operator K is not necessarily compact. As we shall show in Section 7 of Chapter 5, if K is unbounded then $r(n) = b(n) = +\infty$ for all n. Assume then that K is bounded. Define $K_1 = K^*K : X \to X$. Then K_1 is bounded, self-adjoint and nonnegative definite, but not necessarily compact. Kacewicz and Wasilkowski [86] analyzed this case and proved the following. Let $\text{sp}(K_1)$ denote the spectrum of K_1. Then $\text{sp}(K_1) = \text{p}(K_1) \cup \text{c}(K_1)$, where $\text{p}(K_1)$ is the point spectrum of K_1 and $\text{c}(K_1)$ is the continuous spectrum of K_1. That is, $\text{p}(K_1)$ is the set of all eigenvalues, and an eigenvalue of multiplicity k is counted k-times, and $\text{c}(K_1)$ is the set of all positive numbers x for which $(K_1 - xI)^{-1}$ is well defined on a dense subspace of X but is unbounded, see Dunford and Schwartz [63, p. 907] and Section 1.6.4 of the appendix. Let

$$\lambda_{n+1} = \inf\Big\{ \sup_{\lambda \in \text{sp}(K_1) - B} \lambda : B \subset \text{sp}(K_1) \text{ and } B \text{ has at most } n \text{ elements}\Big\}$$

with the convention that $\sup \emptyset = 0$. Thus, λ_{n+1} is the $(n + 1)$st maximal element from the spectrum of K_1, if such an element exists. Otherwise, λ_{n+1} is the maximal attraction point from $\text{sp}(K_1)$, and in this case $\lambda_k = \lambda_{n+1}, \forall k \ge n + 1$. Then we have

$$r(n) = \sqrt{\lambda_{n-n^*+1}},$$

where n^* is the index of the linear problem (S, T), see **NR 5.3:1**. The nth optimal information is derived similarly as in **NR 5.3:1**.

NR 5.3:3 Kacewicz and Wasilkowski [86] also studied finitely continuous nonlinear information for approximation of $S(f)$, where $S : F_1 \to G$ is a continuous linear operator and F_1, G are real separable Hilbert spaces. Here $f \in F$, where F is the unit ball of F_1. Information is provided by a (nonlinear) mapping $N : F_1 \to \mathbb{R}^n$ which is finitely continuous. By finite continuity of N they mean that N restricted to any finite dimensional space is a continuous operator. Let C_n denote the class of such information. Using the classic Borsuk-Ulam theorem they prove that

$$\inf_{N \in C_n} r(N) = r(n) = \sqrt{\lambda_{n+1}},$$

where λ_{n+1} is defined as in **NR 5.3:2**. Thus, finitely continuous nonlinear information is not more powerful than linear information in the worst case setting. As in **NR 5.3:1**, this result can be generalized for F given by a many-to-one T.

They also consider the same problem in the average case setting and prove that finitely continuous nonlinear information can be much more powerful than linear information. This is reported in **NR 5.5:2** of Chapter 6.

NR 5.3:4 (GTOA p. 152) We briefly discuss nonlinear information $N : F_1 \to \mathbb{R}^n$ without assuming that N is finitely continuous. Let $r(n) = \inf\{r(N) : N : F_1 \to \mathbb{R}^n\}$ denote the nth minimal radius of such information. Then $r(n) = r(1)$ for all n, and $r(1) = 0$ iff the set $S(F)$ has power, at most, of the continuum. This is true for arbitrary nonlinear solution operators S, $S : F \to G$, and arbitrary F and separable G. This shows that nonlinear information (even one nonlinear functional), supplies enough knowledge to solve the problem with arbitrarily small error whenever $S(F)$ has power, at most, of the real numbers. Usually such a nonlinear functional cannot be computed in practice. Therefore, the above result is of only theoretical interest.

Exercises

E 5.3:1 (GTOA p. 38) For a given number $a \in [0, +\infty]$ find a linear problem such that $r(n) = a$ for all n.

E 5.3:2 (GTOA p. 39) Let X and G be separable Hilbert spaces and let $K = ST^{-1} :$ $X \to G$ be bounded. Prove that $r(n) \to 0$ iff K is compact.

5.4. Relations between nth Minimal Radii and Gelfand n-Widths

This is the first of two sections in which we show that some basic concepts in approximation theory can be helpful for estimating the complexity of approximately solved problems. In this section we show a relation between the nth minimal radius of nonadaptive information and the Gelfand n-width of the set $S(F)$. Further relations are exhibited in Section 5.6.

We now remind the reader of the definition of the Gelfand n-width of a balanced subset A of a linear normed space G, which is

$$d^n(A, G) = \inf_{A^n} \sup_{g \in A \cap A^n} \|g\|,$$

where A^n is a subspace of G of codimension at most n. That is, $A^n = \{g \in G : R_i(g) = 0, i = 1, 2, \ldots, n\}$ for some linear functionals R_i, $R_i : G \to \mathbb{R}$. Roughly speaking, the Gelfand n-width is the maximal norm of an element from A subject to n properly chosen linear constraints. Let

$$d^n = d^n(S(F), G)$$

be the Gelfand n-width of the range of the solution operator in G.

We show a relation between the nth minimal radii and diameters of nonadaptive information and the Gelfand n-widths. This will be done for linear problems and the class Λ^* of all linear functionals. As in Section 5.3, we use the abbreviated notation $r(n) = r(n, \Lambda^*)$ and $d(n) = d(n, \Lambda^*)$.

Without loss of generality assume that $F_1 = \text{span}(F)$, i.e., F_1 consists of linear combinations of elements from F. Let $F_1 = (\ker S) \oplus (\ker S)^{\perp}$. Each f from F_1 has a unique decomposition $f = f_1 + f_2$, where $f_1 \in \ker S$ and $f_2 \in (\ker S)^{\perp}$. Define

$$q = q(S, F) = \inf_{f \in F} \sup_{\alpha f_2 \in F} \alpha.$$

Observe that q is well defined since the set F is absorbing, i.e., for each $f_2 \in F_1$ there exists a positive α for which $\alpha f_2 \in F$. Furthermore, q is either infinite or no greater than one. Indeed, if $(\ker S)^{\perp} \subset F$ then, obviously, $q = +\infty$. Otherwise, if $(\ker S)^{\perp}$ is not a subset of F then $q \leq 1$. To show this, take $f_2 \in (\ker S)^{\perp} - F$ and any α for which $\alpha f_2 \in F$. If $\alpha > 1$ then for $t = \alpha^{-1}$ we have $f_2 = t(\alpha f_2) + (1 - t)0 \in F$ since $0 \in F$ and F is convex. This contradicts that $f_2 \notin F$.

As an example, observe that $q = 1$ if $(\ker S)^{\perp}$ is not a subset of F and $f \in F$ implies that $f_2 \in F$. The last implication holds if, for instance, S is one-to-one or F_1 is a Hilbert space, $(\ker S)^{\perp}$ is the orthogonal complement of the closed kernel of S, and F is the unit ball in F_1.

THEOREM 5.4.1. *We have the following bounds*

$$2q\, d^n \leq d(n) \leq 2\, d^n, \quad \forall n,$$

with the convention that $+\infty \cdot 0 = 0$. *If* $q = 1$ *and* $r(n) = d(n)/2$ *then*

$$r(n) = d^n.$$

PROOF: We first prove that $d(n) \leq 2d^n$. Let A be a linear subspace of G whose codimension is at most n. Then $A = \{g \in G : R_i(g) = 0, i = 1, 2, \ldots, n\}$ for some linear functionals R_i, $R_i : G \to \mathbb{R}$. Define the nonadaptive information operator $N(f) = [R_1(S(f)), \ldots, R_n(S(f))]$. Then $\ker N = \{f \in F_1 : S(f) \in A\}$ and $S(\ker N) = A$. From Lemma 5.2.1 we have

$$d(N) = 2 \sup_{h \in F \cap \ker N} \|S(h)\| = 2 \sup_{g \in S(F) \cap A} \|g\|.$$

Taking the infimum with respect to A, we get $d(n) \leq 2d^n$.

We now prove that $2qd^n \leq d(n)$. This is trivially true if $q = 0$. Assume next that $q \in (0, 1]$. Let $N = [L_1, L_2, \ldots, L_n]$. Then $d(N) = 2 \sup\{\|S(h)\| : h \in F$ and $L_i(h) = 0, i = 1, 2, \ldots, n\}$. Assume without essential loss of generality that $G = S(F_1)$, see **E 5.4:2**. For $g \in G = S(F_1)$ we have $g = S(f_2)$, where $f_2 \in (\ker S)^{\perp}$. Define linear functionals R_i, $R_i : G \to \mathbb{R}$, by letting $R_i(g) = L_i(f_2)$, $i = 1, 2, \ldots, n$. Let $A = \{g \in G : R_i(g) = 0, i = 1, 2, \ldots, n\}$. Then codim $A \leq n$ and

$$d^n \leq \sup_{g \in S(F) \cap A} \|g\| \leq \sup \{\|S(f_2)\| : f_2 \in (\ker S)^{\perp}, S(f_2) \in S(F),$$

$$R_i(S(f_2)) = L_i(f_2) = 0, i = 1, 2, \ldots, n\}.$$

Let $\delta \in (0, q)$. Since $S(f_2) \in S(F_1)$, there exists $f \in F_1$ such that $S(f) = S(f_2)$. From the definition of q it follows that there exists a constant $\alpha = \alpha(f) \geq q - \delta$ such that $\alpha f_2 \in F$. Since F is convex, $(q - \delta)f_2$ also belongs to F. Thus,

$$d^n \leq \frac{1}{q - \delta} \sup \{\|S((q - \delta)f_2)\| : (q - \delta)f_2 \in F \cap \ker N\} = \frac{1}{2(q - \delta)} d(N).$$

Taking the infimum with respect to N, we get $2(q - \delta)d^n \leq d(n)$. Since δ is arbitrary, we get $2qd^n \leq d(n)$, as claimed.

It remains to consider the case $q = +\infty$. If $\dim G \leq n$, then $A = \{0\}$ has codimension at most n and therefore $d^n = 0$. Then $d(n) \geq +\infty \cdot 0 = 0$ trivially holds. Consider thus the case $\dim G > n$. We show that $d(n) = +\infty$. Indeed, there exist linearly independent elements $S(f_1), S(f_2), \ldots, S(f_{n+1})$ such that $f_i \in (\ker S)^{\perp}$. Obviously, $f_1, f_2, \ldots, f_{n+1}$ are also linearly independent. Since $q = +\infty$, $(\ker S)^{\perp} \subset F$. Thus, F contains the linear subspace $\text{span}\{f_1, f_2, \ldots, f_{n+1}\}$ of dimension $n + 1$. As before, consider nonadaptive information $N = [L_1, L_2, \ldots, L_n]$. Then there exists a nonzero element $f = \sum_{i=1}^{n+1} c_i f_i \in F \cap \ker N$. Furthermore $S(f) \neq 0$. Then $\alpha f \in F \cap \ker N$ and $\|S(\alpha f)\| = |\alpha| \|S(f)\| \to +\infty$ as $|\alpha| \to +\infty$. This implies that $d(N) = +\infty$. Since this holds for all N, we obtain $d(n) = +\infty$. As established before, $d(n) \leq 2d^n$, and hence $d^n = +\infty$. Thus, $qd^n \leq d(n)$ also holds in this case.

The second part of Theorem 5.4.1 trivially follows from the first part. ∎

Theorem 5.4.1 bounds the nth minimal radii of information through the Gelfand n-widths. This is important since the Gelfand n-widths have been obtained for many sets $S(F)$ and this allows us to obtain estimates of the nth minimal radii. As we shall see in Section 5.8, these estimates will be useful in obtaining bounds on the complexity. The reader is referred to the recent book of Pinkus [85], where the Gelfand n-widths can be found for many sets.

Theorem 5.4.1 also enables us to find nth optimal (or nearly nth optimal) information for the class Λ^*. This is done as follows. Take an *nth extremal subspace* A^n of the set $S(F)$, i.e., a linear subspace A^n of codimension at most n for which

$$d^n = \sup_{g \in S(F) \cap A^n} \|g\|.$$

Then $A^n = \{g \in G : R_i^*(g) = 0, i = 1, 2, \ldots, n\}$ for some linear functionals $R_i^* : G \to \mathbb{R}$. Define the information

$$N_n(f) = [R_1^*(S(f)), R_2^*(S(f)), \ldots, R_n^*(S(f))].$$

From the proof of Theorem 5.4.1 we conclude that $d(N_n) = 2d^n$, and Theorem 5.4.1 yields $d(N_n) \le d(n)/q$. This implies the following corollary.

COROLLARY 5.4.1.

(i) Information N_n has the radius no greater than $2/q$ times the nth minimal radius,

$$r(N_n) \le d(N_n) \le \frac{2}{q} r(n).$$

(ii) If $r(N_n) = d(N_n)/2$ and $q = 1$ then N_n is nth optimal information in the class Λ^* of all linear functionals,

$$r(N_n) = r(n) = d^n.$$

These estimates show a close relation between the Gelfand n-widths and the nth minimal radii of nonadaptive information especially if $q = 1$. We note, however, that it may happen that q is arbitrarily small and that the left-hand estimate of Theorem 5.4.1 can be achieved, i.e., $d(n) = 2qd^n$, as shown in **NR 5.4:2**. We also stress that two-sided estimates between d^n and $r(n)$ hold only for the class Λ^* of all linear functionals. For classes Λ different than Λ^*, the situation becomes more complicated, as explained in **NR 5.4:3**.

Notes and Remarks

NR 5.4:1 This section is based on GTOA p. 41–47. The Gelfand widths and extremal subspaces for sets of practical interest may be found in many papers in approximation theory. The reader is referred to a recent book of Pinkus [85] and the long list of papers cited there.

NR 5.4:2 (GTOA p. 44) We now exhibit a linear problem for which $d(1) = 2qd^1$ with an arbitrarily small positive q. Let $F_1 = \mathbb{R}^3$ and $F = \{f = [f_1, f_2, f_3] : |f_1| \le 1, |f_2 - f_1| \le a, |f_3 - f_1| \le a\}$, where a is a positive constant. Let $S(f) = [0, f_2, f_3]$ and $G = S(F_1) = \{[0, f_2, f_3] : f_i \in \mathbb{R}, i = 2, 3\}$ with the $\mathcal{L}_\infty$ norm. Then $\ker S = \{[f_1, 0, 0] : f_1 \in \mathbb{R}\}$ and $(\ker S)^\perp = G$. Note that $f \in F$ implies $|f_i| \le a + 1, i = 2, 3$, which easily yields

$$q = q(S, F) = \frac{a}{a + 1}.$$

Thus, for small a, q is also small. To find the Gelfand 1-width, observe that

$$d^1 = \inf_L \sup\{\|S(f)\| : S(f) \in S(F) \text{ and } L(S(f)) = 0\},$$

where L is a linear functional and $S(F) = \{[0, f_2, f_3] : \exists f_1, |f_1| \leq 1 \text{ such that } |f_2 - f_1| \leq a, |f_3 - f_1| \leq a\}$. Since $L([0, f_2, f_3]) = f_2 c_2 + f_3 c_3$ for some constants c_2 and c_3, we get

$$d^1 = \inf_{c_2, c_3} \sup\{\max(|f_2|, |f_3|) : [0, f_2, f_3] \in S(F) \text{ and } f_2 c_2 + f_3 c_3 = 0\} = a + 1.$$

To find $d(1)$, observe that the information operator $N(f) = f_2 + f_3 - f_1$ has cardinality one, and the algorithm $\phi(y) = [0, y, y]$ satisfies $\|S(f) - \phi(N(f))\| = \|[0, f_1 - f_3, f_1 - f_2]\| \leq a, \quad \forall f \in F$. Thus, $d(1) \leq d(N) \leq 2\, e(\phi, N) \leq 2\, a$. From Theorem 5.4.1, we get $d(1) \geq (2a/(a + 1))(a + 1) = 2a$. This yields

$$d(1) = 2\, q\, d^1 = 2\, a.$$

Note that $2d^1/d(1) = (a + 1)/a$ can be arbitrarily large for small a. Of course, $d(n) = d^n = 0, \forall n \geq 2$.

NR 5.4:3 (GTOA p. 45) We presented relations between Gelfand widths and minimal radii for the class Λ^* of all linear functionals. For restricted classes Λ of information operations such relations do not hold in general. For instance, consider the integration solution operator $S(f) = \int_{-1}^{+1} f(t)\, dt$ for the class F_1 of absolutely continuous functions such that $\|f'\|_\infty < +\infty$. Let $F = \{f \in F_1 : \|f'\|_\infty \leq 1\}$ and let the class Λ consist of function evaluations. It is known that $r(n, \Lambda) = \Theta(n^{-1})$. On the other hand, $G = \mathbb{R}$ and therefore $d^n = 0, \forall n \geq 1$.

The same situation occurs for finite dimensional operators, $k = \dim S(F_1) < +\infty$. Then $d^n = 0, \forall n \geq k$, whereas for practical classes Λ the nth minimal radius $r(n, \Lambda)$ is positive for all n.

Although Theorem 5.4.1 does not seem applicable for such problems, we show how it can be used. Suppose there exists a linear operator $S_1 : F_1 \to G_1$, where G_1 is a linear normed space such that

$$r(n, \Lambda) = r(n, \Lambda; S_1).$$

Here $r(n, \Lambda; S_1)$ is the nth minimal radius of information for the linear problem (S_1, F) with the class Λ.

The essence of this assumption is that S_1 can be an infinite-dimensional operator (even if S is finite-dimensional) and nonzero Gelfand n-width of $S_1(F)$ provides a lower bound on $r(n, \Lambda)$. To illustrate this, consider once more the integration example presented above. For $N = [f(t_1), f(t_2), \ldots, f(t_n)]$ we have $r(N) = \sup\{\int_{-1}^{+1} |h(x)|\, dx : h(t_i) = 0, i = 1, \ldots, n \text{ and } h \in F\}$. Define the function approximation problem $S_1 f = f$ with the space G_1 of functions from F_1 equipped with the $\mathcal{L}_1$ norm. Then $r(N) = r(N, S_1)$, where $r(N, S_1)$ stands for the radius of N for the function approximation problem. Of course, $q(S_1, F) = 1$. It is known that $d^n(S_1(F), \mathcal{L}_1) = n^{-1}$ and the set $A^n = \{f : f(z_i) = 0, z_1 = -1 + h, z_i = -1 + 2(i - 1)h, i = 2, 3, \ldots, n\}$, with $h = n^{-1}$, is an nth extremal subspace of $S_1(F)$. From this we conclude that $r(n, \Lambda) = n^{-1}$ and $N(f) = [f(z_1), \ldots, f(z_n)]$ is nth optimal information for the integration problem in the class Λ.

This example suggests how the integration problem can be studied in terms of the approximation problem, see Korotkov [77] and also GTOA p. 118–120, where related issues are studied.

Exercises

E 5.4:1 Prove that $d^n = n^{-1}$ for the approximation problem from **NR 5.4:3**.

E 5.4:2 Extend the proof of Theorem 5.4.1 to include the case where $G \neq S(F_1)$.

5.5. Linear Algorithms

In this section we analyze the existence of an optimal error algorithm that is easy to implement. Probably the most common class of easily implementable algorithms is the class of linear algorithms. This explains the practical importance of results establishing the existence of a linear algorithm with almost minimal error.

One might hope that such linear algorithms exist for all linear problems. There is a vast literature on this subject in which linear optimal error algorithms are found for a number of practical linear problems, see **NR 5.5:1**.

We shall show that linear algorithms with minimal error exist for three cases of linear problems:

(i) the range of a solution operator is $\mathbb{R}$,
(ii) the range of a solution operator is suitably extended,
(iii) the range of a restriction operator is a Hilbert space, and the image of the kernel of the information operator is closed.

We also exhibit some counterexamples, that is, linear problems for which there exists no linear optimal error algorithm. In fact, for one linear problem we show that the error of any linear algorithm is infinite whereas the radius of information can be arbitrary small. One might expect that the linear problem for which this holds is artificially constructed. This is not the case, since this linear problem is the inversion of a finite Laplace transform, an issue arising in remote sensing, see Twomey [77].

We first discuss positive results. Due to results of Section 5.2, we restrict ourselves to nonadaptive information,

$$N(f) = [L_1(f), L_2(f), \ldots, L_n(f)],$$

with L_i from a given class Λ of permissible information operations. A *linear algorithm* ϕ^L that uses N is a mapping of the form

$$\phi^L(N(f)) = \sum_{i=1}^{n} L_i(f)q_i, \quad q_i \in G.$$

Since q_i are independent of f, they can be computed in advance. Then the actual computation of $\phi^L(N(f))$, given $N(f)$, requires at most n multiplications and $(n-1)$ additions in the space G. If $G = \mathbb{R}$ then at most n scalar multiplications and $(n-1)$ additions of real numbers are performed. Using the model of computation of Section 2.3 of Chapter 3, the combinatory cost, $\text{cost}(\phi, N(f))$, is at most $2n - 1$. On the other hand, the information cost, $\text{cost}(N, f)$, is cn, where c denotes the cost of the evaluation of one information operation. If $c \gg 1$ then $\text{cost}(\phi, N(f)) \ll \text{cost}(N, f)$. In this sense, linear algorithms are easy to implement.

We now discuss the three cases.

Case (i): The solution operator is a real linear functional.

The following result is due to Smolyak [65].

THEOREM 5.5.1. *Let S be a real linear functional and let F be a balanced convex set. Then there exist numbers q_i such that*

$$\phi^L(N(f)) = \sum_{i=1}^{n} L_i(f) q_i$$

is an optimal error algorithm and

$$e(\phi^L, N) = r(N) = \sup_{h \in F \cap \ker N} S(h).$$

PROOF: Note first that $r(N) = \sup_{h \in F \cap \ker N} S(h)$. Indeed, since $SN^{-1}(y)$ is an interval, we have $r(N, y) = d(N, y)/2$ for all $y \in N(F)$. Thus, $r(N) = d(N)/2 = \sup_{h \in F \cap \ker N} |S(h)|$ due to Lemma 5.2.1. Since F is balanced and S is a real linear functional, the absolute value sign can be omitted in the formula of $r(N)$.

We now prove optimality of ϕ^L. Consider first the case $r(N) = +\infty$. Then every algorithm is optimal and Theorem 5.5.1 holds trivially for arbitrary q_i. Assume thus that $r = r(N) < +\infty$. Let

$$Y = \{(S(f), L_1(f), \dots, L_n(f)) : f \in F\} \subset \mathbb{R}^{n+1}.$$

The set Y is balanced and convex. Consider the boundary point $(r, 0, \dots, 0)$ of the set Y. It is known from convex analysis that Y has a supporting hyperplane passing through the boundary point $(r, 0, \dots, 0)$. That is, there exist a vector $(c_0, c_1, \dots, c_n) \neq (0, 0, \dots, 0)$ such that the hyperplane $c_0(y_0 - r) + \sum_{j=1}^{n} c_j y_j = 0$ passes through $(r, 0, \dots, 0)$ and

$$c_0(S(f) - r) + \sum_{j=1}^{n} c_j L_j(f) \leq 0, \quad \forall f \in F.$$

Without loss of generality we can assume that $L_1, \dots, L_n$ are linearly independent on F, i.e., $\sum_{j=1}^{n} d_j L_j(f) = 0$ for all $f \in F$ implies $d_1 = d_2 =$

$\cdots = d_n = 0$. Then the coefficient c_0 of the supporting plane is nonzero. Indeed, $c_0 = 0$ and the fact that F is balanced yield $\sum_{j=1}^{n} c_j L_j(f) = 0$, $\forall f \in F$, and therefore $c_j = 0$, $j = 1, \ldots, n$, which is a contradiction. Hence $c_0 \neq 0$. Since Y is balanced, the hyperplane $c_0(y_0 + r) + \sum_{j=1}^{n} c_j y_j = 0$ passes through the boundary point $(-r, 0, \ldots, 0)$ and is supporting to the set Y, i.e.,

$$c_0(S(f) + r) + \sum_{j=1}^{n} c_j L_j(f) \geq 0, \quad \forall f \in F.$$

Define $q_j = -c_j/c_0$. Then the last two inequalities yield

$$\left| S(f) - \sum_{j=1}^{n} L_j(f) q_j \right| \leq r = r(N).$$

This proves that the linear algorithm $\phi^L(N(f)) = \sum_{j=1}^{n} L_j(f) q_j$ is an optimal error algorithm. ∎

Theorem 5.5.1 guarantees the existence of a linear optimal error algorithm. The numbers q_i of this algorithm are related to coefficients of a supporting hyperplane of the set Y. In general, they are not unique. For some problems, uniqueness of q_i can be proven and then q_i can be obtained analytically as explained in **NR 5.5:2**. Generalizations of Theorem 5.5.1 for the complex case, noisy information, and/or information with arbitrary cardinality are discussed in **NR 5.5:3**.

We now indicate the importance of Smolyak's theorem. In a classic paper, Sard [49] studied optimal algorithms for integration. He *assumed* that the algorithms are linear and integrate exactly all polynomials up to a certain degree. His information was the values of a function at n *fixed* points. Nikolskij [50] studied optimal algorithms for integration with *optimally* chosen *nonadaptive* points at which a function is evaluated. He also *assumed* linear algorithms. There are many papers which followed the ideas of Sard and Nikolskij. Smolyak's theorem shows that the assumption that algorithms are linear is *not* needed. In fact, nothing is lost by considering linear algorithms, since nonlinear algorithms cannot have smaller error than an appropriately chosen linear algorithm. We stress that this holds if the range of a solution operator is $\mathbb{R}$. Further discussion may be found in **NR 5.5:4**.

Case (ii): The range of a solution operator can be suitably extended.

To motivate this approach we look once more at the proof of Theorem 5.5.1, which suggests how to construct linear optimal error algorithms for certain linear *operators* S. Namely, it is enough to assume that the range space G of the linear solution operator S is such that:

(1) G is a space of bounded real valued functions g defined on a set D,
(2) the norm of G is the sup norm, i.e., $\|g\| = \sup_{x \in D} |g(x)|$.

Indeed, let $f \in F$ and denote $g = S(f)$. Given $N(f) = [L_1(f), \ldots, L_n(f)]$, we approximate $g(x)$ for $x \in D$ using Smolyak's theorem. That is, for every $x \in D$ there exists $q_i = q_i(x), i = 1, 2, \ldots, n$ such that the linear algorithm

$$\phi^L(N(f))(x) = \sum_{i=1}^{n} L_i(f) q_i(x)$$

is an optimal error algorithm for approximating $g(x)$. This means that for every $x \in D$,

$$
\begin{aligned}
\left| (S(f))(x) - \phi^L(N(f))(x) \right| &= \sup_{h \in F \cap \ker N} (S(h))(x) \\
&\leq \sup_{h \in F \cap \ker N} \|S(h)\| = \tfrac{1}{2} d(N) = r(N).
\end{aligned}
$$

To prove that ϕ^L is a linear optimal error algorithm we must show that $\phi^L(N(f)) \in G \; \forall f \in F$, i.e., $\phi^L(N(f))$ is a bounded function for any f in F. Obviously, we can assume that $r(N)$ is finite and that $L_1, L_2, \ldots, L_n$ are linearly independent on F. Then there exist elements $f_1, f_2, \ldots, f_n$ from F and a positive number d such that $L_i(f_j) = 0$ for $i \neq j$ and $|L_j(f_j)| \geq d$. For such elements f_j we have $\|S(f_j) - L_j(f_j) q_j\| \leq r(N)$. Thus, $\|q_j\| \leq d^{-1}(r(N) + \max_{1 \leq i \leq n} \|S(f_i)\|)$. This implies that $\phi^L(Nf)$ is bounded.

This observation enabled Packel [86] to prove that a linear optimal error algorithm exists for an *arbitrary* linear problem if the range of a solution operator is extended to the bounded scalar-valued functions $B(D)$ defined on a suitable chosen topological space D. More precisely he proved

THEOREM 5.5.2. *Given a linear solution operator* $S : F \to G$, *there exist a compact Hausdorff space* D *and elements* $q_i \in B(D)$ *such that*

(i) G *is isometrically isomorphic to a subspace of* $B(D)$,
(ii) $\phi^L(N(f)) = \sum_{i=1}^{n} L_i(f) q_i$ *is a linear optimal error algorithm for the solution operator* $\widehat{S} : F \to B(D)$, *where* $\widehat{S}(f) = \widehat{S(f)}$ *is the isometric image of* $S(f)$ *in* $B(D)$,

$$e(\phi^L, N) = \sup_{f \in F} \|\widehat{S(f)} - \phi^L(N(f))\| = r(N) = \sup_{h \in F \cap \ker N} \|\widehat{S(h)}\|.$$

PROOF: We sketch the proof; details can be found in Packel [86]. Part (i) follows from a standard corollary to the Banach-Alaoglu theorem stating that any normed linear space is isometrically isomorphic to a subspace of $C(D)$, where $C(D)$ is the space of bounded continuous functions on D. In our case, D is the unit ball in the conjugate space of G endowed with the weak* topology, and the isometric action is provided by the Gelfand map which embeds G in its second conjugate space. The linear optimal error algorithm in part (ii) is obtained by applying Smolyak's theorem for each $x \in D$ and showing that the mapping that results when x is varied is bounded on D for each $N(f)$. ∎

Observe that the algorithm ϕ^L from Theorem 5.5.2 takes on values (instead of the space G) in the vastly larger space $B(D)$ containing a copy of G as a subspace. Thus, in this rather impractical sense, linear problems do have linear optimal error algorithms.

We stress that elements of $B(D)$ other than the isometric images from G may have no meaningful connection with elements of G. Nevertheless, one interpretation is that a linear problem does have linear optimal error algorithm if the solution operator is given in an "appropriate" range. Theorems 5.5.1 and 5.5.2 state that the two extreme cases of ranges $\mathbb{R}$ and $B(D)$ are appropriate. We shall see later that even the range $\mathbb{R}^2$ destroys the guarantee of a linear optimal error algorithm.

Theorem 5.5.2 uses the rather extreme case of $B(D)$ as the extended domain. It may be the case that linear optimal error algorithms exist for less drastic extensions of the range of S. In particular, it seems plausible to conjecture, perhaps with additional conditions on the solution operator S, that linear optimal error algorithms exist with range restricted to the space $C(D)$.

Case (iii): The range of a restriction operator is a Hilbert space.

More precisely, we assume that $F = \{f \in F_1 : \|Tf\| \leq 1\}$, where a linear restriction operator T maps F_1 into a Hilbert space X and $T(\ker N)$ is a closed set of X.

In this case, a linear optimal error algorithm is derived as follows. As before we can assume without loss of generality that $N = [L_1, L_2, \ldots, L_n]$ consists of linearly independent functionals L_i. We claim that there exists an element σ_i of F_1 such that

$$N(\sigma_i) = [0, \ldots, \underset{i}{1}, \ldots, 0] \quad \text{and} \quad T\sigma_i \perp T(\ker N).$$

Indeed, since $L_1, L_2, \ldots, L_n$ are linearly independent, the set

$$A = \{f \in F_1 : N(f) = [0, \ldots, \underset{i}{1}, \ldots, 0]\}$$

is nonempty. Let f^* belong to A. Then $f^* - f \in \ker N$ for any $f \in A$, and $\inf_{f \in A} \|Tf\| = \inf_{x \in T(\ker N)} \|Tf^* - x\|$. Since $T(\ker N)$ is closed, the Hilbert space X can be decomposed as $X = T(\ker N) \oplus T(\ker N)^\perp$, where $T(\ker N)^\perp$ is the orthogonal complement of $T(\ker N)$. Thus, $Tf^* = (Tf^*)_1 + (Tf^*)_2$, where $(Tf^*)_1 \in T(\ker N)$, and $(Tf^*)_1$ is orthogonal to $(Tf^*)_2$. Therefore the last infimum is equal to $\|(Tf^*)_2\|$ and is achieved for $x = (Tf^*)_1 = Th$ for some h from $\ker N$. Define $\sigma_i = f^* - h$. Then $\sigma_i \in A$ and $T\sigma_i = (Tf^*)_2$ is orthogonal to $T(\ker N)$, as claimed.

We now present a theorem which is a modified version of Theorem 5 from Micchelli and Rivlin [77], see also **NR 5.7:4**.

THEOREM 5.5.3. *If X is a Hilbert space and $T(\ker N)$ is closed then for arbitrary linear operator S,*

$$\phi^L\big(N(f)\big) = \sum_{i=1}^{n} L_i(f)\, S\sigma_i$$

is an optimal error algorithm and

$$e(\phi^L, N) = r(N) = \sup\big\{\|S(h)\| : h \in \ker N,\ \|Th\| \le 1\big\}.$$

PROOF: For $f \in F$, let $\sigma = \sum_{i=1}^{n} L_i(f)\sigma_i$ and $h = f - \sigma$. Then $Tf = Th + T\sigma$. Since $Th \in T(\ker N)$ and $T\sigma$ is orthogonal to $T(\ker N)$, we conclude that $(Tf)_2 = T\sigma$. Thus, $\|Th\| \le \|Tf\| \le 1$. Observe that Lemma 5.2.1 implies $\|S(f) - \phi^L(N(f))\| = \|S(h)\| \le \sup\{\|S(h)\| : h \in \ker N, \|Th\| \le 1\} = d(N)/2 \le r(N)$. This proves that ϕ^L is a linear optimal error algorithm and $r(N) = d(N)/2$. ∎

The algorithm ϕ^L of Theorem 5.5.3 is called a *spline algorithm* and enjoys many more optimal error properties. Section 5.7 is devoted to analysis of spline algorithms.

So far we have presented positive results. We now exhibit examples of linear problems with no linear optimal error algorithms. The first such example is due to Micchelli and is presented in **NR 5.5:5**.

Here we present two other examples which will be also used later to analyze different error criteria and different settings. In the first one, the space G is the Euclidean space $\mathbb{R}^2$. This shows that Smolyak's theorem cannot be generalized even for such ranges as $\mathbb{R}^k$ with $k \ge 2$. In the second example, we exhibit a linear problem with a small radius of information for which the error of a linear algorithm is infinite. This indicates the need to use nonlinear algorithms for at least some linear problems.

We begin with the first example which is due to Packel [86]. Let $\lambda \in \big(0, 1/\sqrt{2}\big)$ and let $F = \{f \in F_1 : \lambda|f_2| + |f_3| \le 1, |f_1| \le 1\}$, where $f = [f_1, f_2, f_3]$ and $F_1 = \mathbb{R}^3$. Let $S : F_1 \to G = \mathbb{R}^2$ be defined by $S(f) = [f_2, f_3]$

and G be equipped with the Euclidean norm. Consider the information $N(f) = f_2 + \lambda f_1$. Clearly, the problem given by S, F, and N is linear.

We first find that the radius of N is equal to $\sqrt{1 + \lambda^6}$. Indeed, consider the set $SN^{-1}(y) = \{[f_2, f_3] : f_2 + \lambda f_1 = y, \lambda|f_2| + |f_3| \leq 1, |f_1| \leq 1\}$. It can be checked that the set $SN^{-1}(y)$ has maximal radius for $y = \lambda$ and $r(N) = r(N, \lambda) = \sqrt{1 + \lambda^6}$. (Note that for $y = 0$ we have $r(N, 0) = 1$.)

Consider now an arbitrary linear algorithm $\phi^L(y) = [c_1 y, c_2 y]$. We wish to choose ϕ^L with the minimal error. Due to the vertical symmetry, $c_2 = 0$. The optimal c_1 is the solution of

$$\inf_{c_1} \sup_{f \in F} \left\{ (f_2 - c_1(f_2 + \lambda f_1))^2 + f_3^2 \right\}$$

$$= \inf_{c_1} \sup_{0 \leq x \leq 1} \left\{ \left(\frac{|1 - c_1|}{\lambda}(1 - x) + \lambda|c_1| \right)^2 + x^2 \right\}$$

$$= \inf_{0 \leq c_1 \leq 1} \max \left\{ \left(\frac{1 - c_1}{\lambda} + \lambda c_1 \right)^2, 1 + \lambda^2 c_1^2 \right\}.$$

The optimal c_1 satisfies the quadratic equation $(\lambda^2 c_1 - c_1 + 1)^2 = \lambda^4 c_1^2 + \lambda^2$. Thus, $c_1 = \sqrt{1 - \lambda^2}/(\sqrt{1 - \lambda^2} + \lambda)$ and $c_1 > \lambda^2$. Therefore, $e(\phi^L, N) \geq \sqrt{1 + \lambda^2 c_1^2} > r(N) = \sqrt{1 + \lambda^6}$. This proves that there exists no linear optimal error algorithm.

We now turn to the second example which is due to Werschulz and Woźniakowski [86]. This is a linear problem for which the error of any linear algorithm is infinite, whereas the radius of information can be arbitrarily small.

Let X_1 be a real Hilbert space. Consider a bounded linear injection $M : X_1 \to X_1$ such that

$$M(X_1) \neq X_1 \quad \text{and} \quad \overline{M(X_1)} = X_1.$$

Here $\overline{M(X_1)}$ denotes the closure of $M(X_1)$. This holds, for example, when M is a compact operator with dense range in an infinite dimensional Hilbert space.

Let $F_1 = M(X_1)$ and let X_2 be a real normed linear space such that X_1 is continuously embedded in X_2, i.e., there exists a positive constant a such that

$$X_1 \subset X_2 \quad \text{and} \quad \|\cdot\|_{X_2} \leq a\|\cdot\|_{X_1}.$$

Define the space G as X_1 equipped with the norm

$$\|g\|_G = \|Mg\|_{X_2}, \quad \forall g \in X_1.$$

The solution operator S, $S : F_1 \rightarrow G$, is defined by

$$S(f) = g \quad \Leftrightarrow \quad Mg = f.$$

Then S is linear and injective with $MS(f) = f$ and $\|S(f)\|_G = \|f\|_{X_2}$. Observe that S is unbounded in the norm of X_1, i.e., there is no constant b such that $\|S(f)\|_{X_1} \leq b\|f\|_{X_1}$ for every $f \in X_1$.

We now define the set F. Since $F_1 \neq X_1$, there exists an element f_1 from X_1 such that $f_1 \notin F_1$. Since F_1 is a linear subspace of X_1, we can assume without loss of generality that $\|f_1\|_{X_1} = 1$. Consider the orthogonal projection T on X_1 given by

$$Tf = f - \langle f, f_1 \rangle f_1, \quad \forall f \in X_1.$$

Here, $\langle \cdot, \cdot \rangle$ denotes the inner product of X_1. The set F is defined by

$$F = \{ f \in F_1 : \|Tf\|_{X_1} \leq 1 \}.$$

Obviously, F is balanced and convex. The crucial property of F is that the element f_1 does not belong to F, whereas a multiple αf_α of a good approximation f_α to f_1 *does* belong to F. Indeed, for every positive α, the denseness of F_1 in X_1 implies that there exists an element f_α from F_1 such that $\|f_\alpha - f_1\|_{X_1} \leq \alpha^{-1}$. Since $Tf_1 = 0$, we have

$$\|T(\alpha f_\alpha)\|_{X_1} = \alpha \|T(f_\alpha - f_1)\|_{X_1} \leq \alpha \|f_\alpha - f_1\|_{X_1} \leq 1.$$

Thus, $\alpha f_\alpha \in F$, as claimed.

Let $N = [L_1, L_2, \ldots, L_n]$ be nonadaptive information, where L_i are linear functionals. Thus, the problem S, F, and N is linear.

We now show that for any linear algorithm $\phi^L(N(f)) = \sum_{i=1}^{n} L_i(f) q_i$, $q_i \in G$, we have

$$e(\phi^L, N) = +\infty.$$

Indeed, $e(\phi^L, N) = \sup_{f \in F} \|f - \sum_{i=1}^{n} L_i(f) M q_i\|_{X_2}$. Take elements αf_α from F, $\|f_\alpha - f_1\|_{X_1} \leq \alpha^{-1}$. Then

$$e(\phi^L, N) \geq \alpha \left\| f_\alpha - \sum_{i=1}^{n} L_i(f_\alpha) M q_i \right\|_{X_2}$$

$$\geq \alpha \left\| f_1 - \sum_{i=1}^{n} L_i(f_\alpha) M q_i \right\|_{X_2} - \alpha \|f_\alpha - f_1\|_{X_2}$$

$$\geq \alpha \inf_{x \in A} \|f_1 - x\|_{X_2} - 1,$$

where $A = \text{span}(Mq_1, Mq_2, \ldots, Mq_n) \subset F_1$. Since A is finite dimensional and $f_1 \notin F_1$, the last infimum is positive. Let α tend to infinity. Then the last inequality yields $e(\phi^L, N) = +\infty$, as claimed.

We now exhibit a nonlinear algorithm with finite error that uses N. We assume that the functionals L_i that form N are of the form $L_i(f) = \langle f, f_i \rangle$ with orthonormalized f_i, $\langle f_i, f_j \rangle = \delta_{i,j}$, and that $f_2, f_3, \ldots, f_n$ belong to F_1. (Recall that f_1 does *not* belong to F_1.) Let

$$\rho(N) = \sup_{h \in X_1 \cap \ker N} \frac{\|h\|_{X_2}}{\|h\|_{X_1}}.$$

Since X_1 is continuously embedded in X_2, $\rho(N)$ is finite and nonzero.

The nonlinear algorithm ϕ^* with finite error is defined as follows. Choose a positive number δ. For a given $N(f)$, the denseness of F_1 in X_1 implies that there exists an element $u_1 = u_1(N(f))$ from F_1 such that

$$\|Mu_1 - f_1\|_{X_2} \leq \frac{\delta \rho(N)}{|\langle f, f_1 \rangle|}.$$

Since $f_2, \ldots, f_n \in M(X_1)$, there exist $u_2, \ldots, u_n$ such that $Mu_i = f_i$ for $i = 2, \ldots, n$. Define the algorithm

$$\phi^*(N(f)) = \langle f, f_1 \rangle u_1(N(f)) + \sum_{i=2}^{n} \langle f, f_i \rangle u_i.$$

The algorithm ϕ^* is indeed nonlinear, since $u_1(N(f))$ depends nonlinearly on $\langle f, f_1 \rangle$. On the other hand, the algorithm ϕ^* is only "mildly" nonlinear, since for fixed $\langle f, f_1 \rangle$, it is an affine mapping in $\langle f, f_2 \rangle, \ldots, \langle f, f_n \rangle$. We now show that

$$e(\phi^*, N) \leq (1 + \delta) \rho(N).$$

For $f \in F$, set

$$d = \|S(f) - \phi^*(N(f))\|_G = \left\| f - \langle f, f_1 \rangle Mu_1 - \sum_{i=2}^{n} \langle f, f_i \rangle f_i \right\|_{X_2}.$$

Write $f = \langle f, f_1 \rangle f_1 + g$, where $g = Tf$. Then $\langle g, f_1 \rangle = 0$. Since $\langle f_1, f_i \rangle = 0$, we have $\langle f, f_i \rangle = \langle g, f_i \rangle$ for $i = 2, \ldots, n$. Setting $h = g - \sum_{i=2}^{n} \langle g, f_i \rangle f_i$, we then find that

$$d \leq |\langle f, f_1 \rangle| \, \|f_1 - Mu_1\|_{X_2} + \left\| g - \sum_{i=2}^{n} \langle g, f_i \rangle f_i \right\|_{X_2} \leq \delta\rho(N) + \|h\|_{X_2}.$$

Since $\langle f_i, f_j \rangle = \delta_{i,j}$, we have $\langle h, f_j \rangle = 0$ for $j = 1, \ldots, n$. Thus $h \in \ker N$. Moreover, we have

$$\|h\|_{X_1}^2 = \|g\|_{X_1}^2 - 2\sum_{i=1}^{n}\langle g, f_i \rangle^2 + \sum_{i=2}^{n}\langle g, f_i \rangle^2 \leq \|g\|_{X_1}^2 = \|Tf\|_{X_1}^2 \leq 1.$$

Hence, $\|h\|_{X_2} \leq \rho(N)$ and $d \leq (1 + \delta)\rho(N)$. Since this holds for all f from F, $e(\phi^*, N) \leq (1 + \delta)\rho(N)$, as claimed.

The radius of information $r(N)$ is equal to $\rho(N)$. Indeed,

$$r(N) \geq \tfrac{1}{2}d(N) = \sup\{\|S(h)\|_G : h \in F \cap \ker N\}$$
$$= \sup\{\|h\|_{X_2} : h \in F_1 \cap \ker N, \ \|Th\|_{X_1} = \|h\|_{X_1} \leq 1\}$$
$$= \sup\{\|h\|_{X_2}/\|h\|_{X_1} : h \in X_1 \cap \ker N\} = \rho(N).$$

On the other hand, $r(N) \leq e(\phi^*, N) \leq (1 + \delta)\rho(N)$. Since δ is arbitrary, $r(N) = \rho(N)$, as claimed. This also shows that for small δ, the algorithm ϕ^* has almost minimal error.

Finally we show that the radius $r(N)$ can be arbitrarily small. Indeed, let $E : X_1 \to X_2$ be the embedding $Eh = h$. Then $r(N) = \|E\|_{\ker N}$. If E is compact, then one can choose $f_2, f_3, \ldots, f_n$, forming the information N such that $r(N)$ goes to zero as n tends to infinity, see Section 5.3. In this case, the error of the nonlinear algorithm ϕ^* can be arbitrarily small.

We illustrate the above construction of a linear problem by the inversion of a finite Laplace transform. That is, let $X_1 = H^1([0, 1])$ be the Sobolev space of real functions u defined on $[0, 1]$ such that

$$\|g\|_{X_1} = \sqrt{\int_0^1 ((g(t))^2 + (g'(t))^2)\, dt} = \sqrt{\|g\|_{\mathcal{L}_2}^2 + \|g'\|_{\mathcal{L}_2}^2}$$

is finite. Define $M : X_1 \to X_1$ as the finite Laplace transform

$$(Mg)(s) = \int_0^1 \exp(-st)\, g(t)\, dt, \quad \forall\, s \in [0, 1].$$

To show that the linear subspace $F_1 = M(X_1)$ is dense in X_1 it suffices to prove that $\ker M^* = \{0\}$, where M^* is the adjoint of M in the Hilbert space X_1. This can be done directly.

Let $X_2 = \mathcal{L}_2([0, 1])$. Obviously, $\|g\|_{X_2} \leq \|g\|_{X_1}$. For $f \in F_1 = M(X_1)$ we have

$$Mg = f \quad \Leftrightarrow \quad (S(f))(t) = \frac{1}{2\pi i}\int_{\text{Re}\, s = 0} \exp(st)\, f(s)\, ds, \quad \forall\, t \in [0, 1],$$

with $i = \sqrt{-1}$. Let $f_1 \equiv 1$. Observe that f_1 does not belong to the range of M since the last integral is divergent for $f(s) \equiv 1$. The balanced and convex set F is now of the form

$$F = \left\{ f \in F_1 : \int_0^1 (f(s))^2 \, ds - \left(\int_0^1 f(s) \, ds \right)^2 + \int_0^1 (f'(s))^2 \, ds \le 1 \right\}.$$

For the information $N(f) = [\langle f, f_1 \rangle, \langle f, f_2 \rangle, \ldots, \langle f, f_n \rangle]$ with orthonormalized f_i, $\langle f_i, f_j \rangle = \delta_{i,j}$ and $f_2, \ldots, f_n \in F_1$, the radius of information is given by

$$r(N) = \rho(N) = \sup_{h \in H^1([0,1]) \cap \ker N} \frac{\|h\|_{\mathcal{L}_2}}{\sqrt{\|h\|_{\mathcal{L}_2}^2 + \|h'\|_{\mathcal{L}_2}^2}}.$$

One can show that the nth minimal radius, see Section 5.3, is now equal to

$$r(n) = \Theta(n^{-1}).$$

Hence, the problem of inverting a finite Laplace transform is an example of a linear problem for which there exists no linear algorithm with finite error, but yet there is a sequence of (mildly) nonlinear algorithms using information consisting of n inner products whose errors go to zero as n^{-1}.

Notes and Remarks

NR 5.5:1 Linear algorithms have been considered in many papers. The reader may find well over 100 such papers referenced in GTOA for different linear problems including interpolation, approximation, integration, and linear partial differential equations. Usually, the assumption of linearity of an algorithm is made implicitly, and it is not clear how much is lost by such a restriction. We illustrate this point by an example. Consider the integration problem $S(f) = \int_0^1 f(t) \, dt$ for functions from a class F. Assume that the values of f at n distinct points, $f(t_1), f(t_2), \ldots, f(t_n)$, are given. The classic approach to approximate the integral of f is to consider quadrature formulas $Q(f) = \sum_{i=1}^n a_i f(t_i)$. The weights a_i are chosen to guarantee some good error properties.

Note that the quadrature formula Q depends linearly on the information consisting of $f(t_1), f(t_2), \ldots, f(t_n)$. Thus, in our terminology, Q is a linear algorithm. Since restricting the class of algorithms to a specific form may result in enlarging the error, it is not clear why only such algorithms should be considered. Smolyak's theorem states that fortunately this restriction is not harmful as long as the class F is balanced and convex.

NR 5.5:2 The proof of Theorem 5.5.1 is based on Bakhvalov [71].

The numbers q_i which specify a linear optimal error algorithm can be sometimes found analytically as follows, see Smolyak [65] and Bakhvalov [71]. Without loss of generality assume that $L_1, L_2, \ldots, L_n$ are linearly independent on F. Then

$$r_i(x) = \sup\{S(f) : f \in F, L_i(f) = x, L_j(f) = 0 \text{ for } j \ne i\}$$

is well defined for small x, $i = 1, 2, \ldots, n$. Assume that $r_i'(0)$ exists for all i. Then $\phi^L(N(f)) = \sum_{i=1}^n L_i(f) r_i'(0)$ is a unique linear optimal error algorithm. Indeed, let $\phi^L(N(f)) = \sum_{i=1}^n L_i(f) q_i$ be an optimal error algorithm. For small x choose $f \in F$ such that $L_i(f) = x$ and $L_j(f) = 0$ for $j \neq i$. Then

$$|S(f) - x\,q_i| \leq e(\phi, N) = r(N).$$

Observe that $r(N) = r_i(0)$, which implies that $r(N)$ is finite. Since $S(f)$ can be arbitrarily close to $r_i(x)$, we get $r_i(x) - r_i(0) \leq x\,q_i$. Dividing by x, we have

$$\frac{r_i(|x|) - r_i(0)}{|x|} \leq q_i \leq \frac{r_i(-|x|) - r_i(0)}{-|x|}.$$

Since $r_i'(0)$ exists, letting x tend to zero we get $q_i = r_i'(0)$, as claimed.

NR 5.5:3 Smolyak's theorem has been generalized in several directions. Marchuk and Osipenko [75] dealt with noisy information, i.e., where instead of $N(f)$ we know y such that $\|y - N(f)\| \leq \delta$ for a given parameter δ. Osipenko [76] proved the existence of a linear optimal error algorithm for the complex case, i.e., for complex linear functionals $S, L_1, L_2, \ldots, L_n$. Micchelli and Rivlin [77], see also Micchelli and Rivlin [85], dealt with noisy information with arbitrary cardinality, i.e., card(N) can be infinite. Sukharev [86] proved the existence of an *affine* optimal error algorithm without assuming that the set F is balanced. A survey on linear optimal error algorithms may be found in Packel [87a].

NR 5.5:4 (GTOA p. 56-60) We now relate optimal error algorithms to the optimal algorithms in the sense of Sard and Nikolskij for the integration problem.

Sard [49], see also Sard [63], considers integration $S(f) = \int_a^b f(t)\,dt$ for a class of scalar functions $f : [a, b] \to \mathbb{R}$. The information is the values of f at n *fixed* points $t_1, t_2, \ldots, t_n$. For a fixed nonnegative integer r, $r \leq n$, let $\Phi = \Phi(n, r)$ be a class of algorithms ϕ that use $N(f) = [f(t_1), f(t_2), \ldots, f(t_n)]$ such that
   (i) ϕ is linear, $\phi(N(f)) = \sum_{i=1}^n f(t_i) k_i$ for some k_i,
   (ii) ϕ is exact for the class of polynomials of degree at most $r - 1$.
Assuming that $f^{(r-1)}$ is absolutely continuous, Peano's kernel theorem yields

$$S(f) - \phi(N(f)) = \int_a^b f^{(r)}(t)\, k(t)\, dt,$$

where the function k is given by

$$k(t) = \frac{1}{r!}\,(b - t)^r - \sum_{i=1}^n \frac{(t_i - t)_+^{r-1}}{(r-1)!}\, k_i$$

with $t_+ = \max\{t, 0\}$. Sard calls ϕ, $\phi \in \Phi(n, r)$, a *best* (*optimal*) quadrature formula iff $\int_a^b k^2(t)\, dt$ is minimized with respect to all possible k_i's. That is, ϕ is optimal iff its weights k_i minimize $\int_a^b k^2(t)\, dt$.

Optimality in the sense of Sard may seem to be restrictive. It is not clear why an algorithm has to be linear or to be exact for the class of polynomials of degree at most $r - 1$. One might hope that the error of a more general algorithm is smaller than the error of an optimal algorithm in the sense of Sard.

Using Smolyak's theorem it is easy to see that this is not the case. Indeed, let $F = \{f : [a, b] \to \mathbf{R} : f^{(r-1)}$ is abs. cont. and $\|Tf\|_{\mathcal{L}_2} \le 1\}$, where $Tf = f^{(r)}$ and $X = \mathcal{L}_2$. Since F is convex and balanced, there exists a linear optimal error algorithm ϕ^L. The algorithm ϕ^L is exact for elements from ker T, i.e., polynomials of degree at most $r - 1$, see E 5.5:11. Thus, ϕ^L belongs to the class of algorithms considered by Sard and it is also optimal in the sense of Sard.

Optimal algorithms in the sense of Sard for other linear functionals are defined in a similar way. They are also optimal error algorithms for suitably chosen F.

We now discuss optimal algorithms in the sense of Nikolskij also for the integration problem, see Nikolskij [50] as well as the third edition of the book of Nikolskij [79] with the supplement written by Kornejčuk (We have been told that this problem was suggested to Nikolskij by Kolmogorov.) He defines

$$E_n(F; p_i, t_i) = \sup_{f \in F} \left| \int_a^b f(t) \, dt - \sum_{i=1}^n p_i \, f(t_i) \right|$$

$$E_n(F; a, b) = \inf_{p_i, t_i} E_n(F; p_i, t_i).$$

An algorithm $\phi^L(N(f)) = \sum_{i=1}^n p_i \, f(t_i)$ is called optimal in the sense of Nikolskij iff $E_n(F; p_i, t_i) = E_n(F; a, b)$. Thus, Nikolskij considers linear algorithms with optimally chosen points at which f is evaluated. If F is convex and balanced, the assumption on linearity of algorithms is not restrictive, and $E_n(F; p_i, t_i)$ is equal to the radius of information $N(f) = [f(t_1), f(t_2), \ldots, f(t_n)]$. Nikolskij's problem is equivalent to the minimization of the radius of information with respect to the points t_i. Thus, $E_n(F; a, b) = r(n, \Lambda)$ for the class Λ consisting of function evaluations. An optimal algorithm in the sense of Nikolskij is a linear optimal error algorithm using nth optimal information.

Papers dealing with optimal algorithms in the sense of Sard and Nikolskij may be found in GTOA p. 58–59.

NR 5.5:5 (GTOA p. 60) The first example of a linear problem for which there exists no linear optimal error algorithm is due to Micchelli and is based on the papers of Melkman and Micchelli [79] and Micchelli and Rivlin [77]. This example is defined as follows. Let $F_1 = \mathbf{R}^3$ and $G = \mathbf{R}^2$ with the norm $\|g\| = \sqrt[4]{\lambda_1 g_1^4 + \lambda_2 g_2^4}$, where $\lambda_1 > \lambda_2 > 0$. Let $S(f_1, f_2, f_3) = (f_1, f_2)$, and let $T : F_1 \to X = \mathbf{R}^3$ be an embedding, $Tf = f$, with the norm in X given by $\|x\| = \max\{\sqrt{x_1^2 + x_2^2}, |x_3|\}$. Finally, set $N(f) = f_1 + a f_3$, where $0 < a \le 3^{-1}\sqrt{2\lambda_2/(\lambda_1 + \lambda_2)}$. Observe that $d(N) = 2\sqrt[4]{\lambda_2}$. Indeed, $d(N) = 2 \sup_{h \in F \cap \ker N} \|S(h)\| = 2 \sup\{\sqrt[4]{\lambda_1 f_1^4 + \lambda_2 f_2^4} : f_1 + a f_3 = 0, f_1^2 + f_2^2 \le 1, |f_3| \le 1\} = 2\sqrt[4]{\max\{\lambda_2, \lambda_1 a^4 + \lambda_2(1 - a^2)^2\}}$. Define the nonlinear algorithm

$$\phi(y) = \begin{cases} (0, 0) & \text{if } |y| \le 2a, \\ (y, 0) & \text{otherwise.} \end{cases}$$

It can be checked that $e(\phi, N) = \sqrt[4]{\lambda_2}$. This yields that $r(N) = d(N)/2 = \sqrt[4]{\lambda_2}$. Consider now an arbitrary linear algorithm $\phi^L(y) = (c_1 y, c_2 y)$ for some c_1 and c_2. Setting $f_1 = 1$, $f_2 = f_3 = 0$, and $f_1 = 0$, $f_2 = 1$, $f_3 = \pm 1$, we get

$$e^4(\phi^L, N) \ge \max\{\lambda_1(1 - c_1)^4 + \lambda_2 c_2^4, \lambda_1(c_1 a)^4 + \lambda_2(1 \pm a c_2)^4\}.$$

If $c_2 \neq 0$ or $c_2 = 0$ and $c_1 \neq 0$, the second term in the maximum yields $e^4(\phi^L, N) > \lambda_2$. If $c_1 = c_2 = 0$, the first term yields $e^4(\phi^L, N) > \lambda_1 > \lambda_2$. Thus, there exists no linear optimal error algorithm.

NR 5.5:6 The inverse of the finite Laplace transform is used in remote sensing, see Twomey [77]. In fact, this example motivated the paper of Werschulz and Woźniakowski [86].

NR 5.5:7 Consider a linear problem with nonadaptive information $N = [L_1, L_2, \ldots, L_n]$ and the restriction operator $T = I$ for a normed linear F_1. Assume that there exists a linear optimal error algorithm. Then the radius of information can be expressed as

$$r(N) = \inf_{g_i \in G} \left\| S - \sum_{i=1}^{n} g_i L_i \right\|.$$

That is, the radius of information is equal to the error of the approximation of the operator S by $\mathrm{span}(L_1, L_2, \ldots, L_n)$ with respect to the norm $\|\cdot\|$ of the space G.

As we shall see in Chapter 6, and especially Corollary 5.3.1, the average case radius of information has a similar characteristic with the norm $\|\cdot\|$ of G replaced by a norm generated by a probability measure.

Exercises

E 5.5:1 Consider a linear problem whose solution operator is a linear functional. Let N be nth optimal information and let ϕ^L be a linear optimal error algorithm using N. Let $r(n, \Lambda) < r(n-1, \Lambda)$. Assume that the only permissible combinatory operations are additions and multiplications of real numbers. Prove that the combinatory cost of ϕ^L has to be at least $n - 1$.

E 5.5:2 Show that the bound $n - 1$ in **E 5.5:1** can be achieved for some linear problem. Hint: Consider integration for smooth periodic functions as in Section 5.8.

E 5.5:3 (GTOA p. 91-99). Let $F_1 = W_p^r$ be the class of functions $f : [-1, 1] \to \mathbb{R}$ with absolutely continuous $(r-1)$st derivative such that $f^{(r)} \in \mathcal{L}_p$, $p \in [1, +\infty]$. Define $Tf = f^{(r)}$ with $X = \mathcal{L}_p$. That is, $\|Tf\| = \left(\int_{-1}^{+1} |f^{(r)}(x)|^p \, dx \right)^{1/p}$. Let $F = \{f \in F_1 : \|Tf\| \leq 1\}$. Consider the linear problem given by a linear functional S, $S : F \to \mathbb{R}$, and nonadaptive information,

$$N_n(f) = [f(x_1), \ldots, f^{(k_1)}(x_1), \ldots, f(x_s), \ldots, f^{(k_s)}(x_s)],$$

where $n = k_1 + k_2 + \cdots + k_s + s$, $k_i \leq r - 1$, and $x_1, x_2, \ldots, x_s$ are distinct points from [-1,1]. Let w be the Hermite interpolatory polynomial of degree at most $n - 1$ using this information. Prove that for $n \leq r$, the algorithm Sw is a linear optimal error algorithm. Prove that it is also central.

E 5.5:4 Specialize the linear problem from **E 5.5:3** by taking the interpolation solution operator $S(f) = f(x_0)$, $x_0 \in [-1, 1]$, and $x_0 \neq x_i$, $i = 1, 2, \ldots, s$. Prove that

$$r(N_n) = +\infty \quad \text{for } n < r,$$

$$r(N_n) = \prod_{i=1}^{s} |x_0 - x_i|^{k_i+1} / r! \quad \text{for } n = r \text{ and } p = +\infty,$$

$$r(N_n) = |x_1 - x_0|^{r-1/p} / ((r-1)!((r-1)q + 1)^{1/q}) \quad \text{for } n = r \text{ and } s = 1,$$

where $1/q + 1/p = 1$ for arbitrary p.

E 5.5:5 Specialize the linear problem from **E 5.5:3** by taking the differentiation solution operator $S(f) = f'(0)$, see also Werschulz [79b]. Assume also that $k_i = 0$, $n = 2k + 1$ is an odd number, and $x_{2i} = ih$, $i = 0, 1, \ldots, k$, $x_{2i-1} = -ih$, $i = 1, 2, \ldots, k$. Here the parameter $h \in (0, k^{-1})$. Prove that for $n = r$ and $p = +\infty$, $r(N_n) = (h^{r-1}/r!)\left(\lfloor r/2 \rfloor\right)^2$ and the algorithm Sw takes the form

$$\frac{(k!)^2}{h} \sum_{j=1}^{k} \frac{(-1)^{j+1}}{j(k+j)!(k-j)!} [f(jh) - f(-jh)].$$

E 5.5:6 Specialize the linear problem from **E 5.5:3** by taking the integration solution operator $S(f) = \int_{-1}^{+1} \rho(x)f(x)\,dx$, where ρ is a weight function. Let $k_i = 0$. Define $q_i(x) = \prod_{j=1}^{i}(x - x_j)$, $i = 0, 1, \ldots, n$, and the inner product $\langle f, g \rangle = \int_{-1}^{+1} \rho(x)f(x)g(x)\,dx$ for $f, g \in F_1$. Prove that $r(N_n) = +\infty$ for $n < r/2$, and for $n \geq r/2$ we have

$$r(N_n) < +\infty \quad \Leftrightarrow \quad n = r \text{ or } \langle q_n, q_i \rangle = 0, i = 0, 1, \ldots, r - 1 - n.$$

For $p = +\infty$, and $n = r$ or $\langle q_n, q_i \rangle = 0$, $i = 0, 1, \ldots, r - 1 - n$, prove that $r(N_n) = r!^{-1} \int_{-1}^{+1} \rho(x)|q_n(x)|\,dx$.

E 5.5:7 Consider the interpolation problem $S(f) = f(x_0)$ with information

$$N_n(f) = [f(x_1), f'(x_1), \ldots, f^{(n-1)}(x_1)].$$

Prove that
(i) the Taylor interpolation formula

$$\phi^L(N_n(f)) = \sum_{i=0}^{n-1} \frac{f^{(i)}(x_1)}{i!}(x_0 - x_1)^i$$

is a linear optimal error algorithm for the class $F = \{f \in W_p^n : \|f^{(n)}\|_p \leq 1\}$, see **E 5.5:4** and Bojanov [75],
(ii) for $x_1 = 0$ the algorithm

$$\phi^L(N_n(f)) = \sum_{i=0}^{n-1} \frac{f^{(i)}(0)}{i!}\left(1 - x_0^{2(n-i+1)}\right)x_0^i$$

is a unique linear optimal error algorithm for the class F of analytic functions defined and bounded in modulus by unity on the unit disk, see Osipenko [72, 76].

E 5.5:8 Consider a linear problem with a solution operator $S : F_1 \to G$, where $G = \mathbb{R}^k$ is equipped with the $\mathcal{L}_2$ norm. Prove that there exists a linear algorithm ϕ^L such that $e(\phi^L, N) \leq \sqrt{k}\, r(N)$.

E 5.5:9 Similarly to **E 5.5:8**, consider a solution operator $S : F_1 \to G$, where $G = \mathbb{R}^k$ is equipped with an arbitrary norm $\|\cdot\|$. Define d_1 and d_2 such that $d_1\|g\|_{\mathcal{L}_\infty} \leq \|g\| \leq$

$d_2\|g\|_{\mathcal{L}_\infty}, \forall\, g \in \mathbb{R}^k$. Prove that there exists a linear algorithm ϕ^L such that $e(\phi^L, N) \leq (d_2/d_1)\, r(N)$ for arbitrary information N.

E 5.5:10 (GTOA p. 61-63) Consider a linear problem with a linear solution operator and $F = \{f \in F_1 : \|Tf\| \leq 1\}$, where $T : F_1 \to X = T(F_1)$. For nonadaptive information N, assume that $T(\ker N)$ is closed and decompose $X = T(\ker N) \oplus T(\ker N)^\perp$. Define

$$\beta = \sup\left\{ \frac{\|g_1\|}{\|g_1 + g_2\|} : g_1 \in T(\ker N), g_2 \in T(\ker N)^\perp \right\}.$$

Prove that there exists a linear algorithm ϕ^L using N such that $e(\phi^L, N) \leq \beta\, r(N)$.

E 5.5:11 (GTOA p. 53) Consider a linear problem with $F = \{f \in F_1 : \|Tf\| \leq 1\}$. Prove that for any homogeneous algorithm ϕ with finite error

$$\phi(N(f)) = S(f), \quad \forall\, f \in \ker T.$$

E 5.5:12 (GTOA p. 53) Consider a linear problem with $F = \{f \in F_1 : \|Tf\| \leq 1\}$ and nonadaptive information $N = [L_1, L_2, \ldots, L_n]$. Suppose there exist elements $f_1, f_2, \ldots, f_n$ from F such that $L_i(f_j) = \delta_{i,j}$ and $f_j \in \ker T$ for all $i, j = 1, 2, \ldots, n$. Prove that the linear algorithm $\phi^L(N(f)) = \sum_{i=1}^n L_i(f)\, S(f_i)$ is central and

$$e(\phi^L, N) = r(N) = \sup_{h \in \ker N} \frac{\|S(h)\|}{\|Th\|}.$$

E 5.5:13 Find a central algorithm for the linear problem of Packel [86].

E 5.5:14 Consider the linear problem from the last part of Section 5.5 for which the error of an arbitrary linear algorithm is infinity. Prove that the error of an arbitrary homogeneous algorithm is also infinity. Hint: As in Section 5.5, take f_α from F_1 such that $\|f_\alpha - f_1\|_{X_1} \leq 1/\alpha$ and $N(f_\alpha)$ does not depend on α. Then consider αf_α and show that $\|\alpha f_\alpha - M\phi(N(f_\alpha))\|_{X_2}$ goes to infinity with $|\alpha|$.

E 5.5:15 (Werschulz and Woźniakowski [86]) Consider the linear problem from the last part of Section 5.5. Let $N : X_1 \to X_3$, where X_3 is a linear space. Prove that

(i) if N and ϕ are homogeneous and $\phi(N(F))$ lies in a finite dimensional space, then $e(\phi, N) = +\infty$,

(ii) if X_3 is normed and N and ϕ are homogeneous and continuous in the norm of X_1, then $e(\phi, N) = +\infty$. Let $N(f) = f$ and $\phi(N(f)) = S(f)$. Why does $e(\phi, N) = 0$ not contradict (ii)?

E 5.5:16 (Werschulz [87c]) Consider the inversion of a finite Laplace transform for a simpler (and perhaps more natural) set

$$F = \{f \in M(X_1) : \|f'\|_{\mathcal{L}_2} \leq 1\}$$

than the one considered in Section 5.5. Prove that the error of a linear algorithm is again infinity, whereas the nth minimal radius of information is proportional to n^{-1}.

E 5.5:17 (Werschulz [87c]) Consider the inversion of a finite Laplace transform for the set

$$F = \{f \in M(X_1) : \|f\|_{\mathcal{L}_2}^2 + \|f'\|_{\mathcal{L}_2}^2 \leq 1\}.$$

Thus, now an *a priori* bound is given on the *norm* of problem elements, rather than on their *seminorm*. Prove that linear optimal error algorithms *exist* for arbitrary information and the nth minimal radius is proportional to n^{-1}.

E 5.5:18 Consider two linear problems from Section 5.5 for which there exists no linear optimal error algorithm. What linear optimal error algorithms are obtained if the range of the solution operator is extended as in Theorem 5.5.2?

5.6. Optimal Linear Algorithms and Linear Kolmogorov n-Widths

This is the second section in which we show that approximation theory can be helpful in determining complexity of approximately solved problems. (The first section was Section 5.4, where relations between nth radii and Gelfand n-widths were discussed.)

Consider a linear problem S, F, and N. That is, S is a linear operator, $S : F_1 \to G$, F is a balanced convex set of F_1, and $N = [L_1, L_2, \ldots, L_n]$ is nonadaptive information. As in Section 5.4 assume that $F_1 = \text{span}(F)$ and consider the class Λ^* of all linear functionals as permissible information operations.

As in Section 5.5 we are interested in linear algorithms that use N. Let $\Phi^L(n)$ denote the class of linear algorithms that use nonadaptive information of cardinality at most n. That is, $\phi^L \in \Phi^L(n)$ means that there exists $N = [L_1, L_2, \ldots, L_n]$, $L_i \in \Lambda^*$ and $q_i \in G$ such that $\phi^L(N(f)) = \sum_{i=1}^{n} L_i(f) q_i$. Let $e(\phi^L) = e(\phi^L, N)$ denote its error. Define

$$\lambda(n) = \inf_{\phi^L \in \Phi^L(n)} e(\phi^L)$$

as the nth *minimal error of linear algorithms*. An algorithm ϕ^L from the class $\Phi^L(n)$ is called an nth *optimal linear algorithm* iff $e(\phi^L) = \lambda(n)$.

We remind the reader that $\lambda(n)$ is no less than the nth minimal nonadaptive radius of information, $\lambda(n) \geq r(n)$. As shown in Section 5.5, it can happen that for some linear problem, $\lambda(n) = +\infty, \forall n$, whereas $r(n)$ goes to zero as n goes to infinity. On the other hand, in Section 5.5 we provided conditions under which there exists a linear optimal error algorithm. For such problems $\lambda(n) = r(n)$.

We now relate the nth minimal error $\lambda(n)$ of linear algorithms to the *linear Kolmogorov n-width* of the set $S(F)$. We remind the reader of the definition of the linear Kolmogorov n-width of a balanced set B of the linear normed space G, which is

$$\lambda_n(B, G) = \inf_{A_n} \inf_{A: A(B) \subset A_n} \sup_{g \in B} \|g - Ag\|,$$

where A is a linear operator with range $A(B)$ in a linear subspace A_n of dimension at most n. The essence of this definition is that the identity operator restricted to B is approximated by n dimensional linear operators. The linear Kolmogorov n-width is the minimal error of such approximations. Further discussion may be found in **NR 5.6:1**. Let

$$\lambda_n = \lambda_n(S(F), G)$$

be the linear Kolmogorov n-width for the solution set $S(F)$.

We now present relations between $\lambda(n)$ and λ_n, see also **NR 5.6:2**. This will be done analogously to Theorem 5.4.1. Recall that $q = q(S, F)$ is defined in Section 5.4.

THEOREM 5.6.1. *We have the following bounds*

$$q\,\lambda_n \leq \lambda(n) \leq \lambda_n, \quad \forall\, n,$$

with the convention that $+\infty \cdot 0 = 0$.

PROOF: We first prove that $\lambda(n) \leq \lambda_n$. Let A be a linear operator with $A(S(F))$ in an n-dimensional subspace of G. Then there exist linear functionals R_i, $R_i : G \to \mathbb{R}$, and elements ζ_i from G such that $A(S(f)) = \sum_{i=1}^n R_i(S(f))\zeta_i$. Define the information $N = [R_1 S, R_2 S, \ldots, R_n S]$ and the linear algorithm $\phi^L(N(f)) = A(S(f))$. Then $\phi^L \in \Phi^L(n)$ and $e(\phi^L) = \sup_{f \in F} \|S(f) - \phi^L(N(f))\| = \sup_{g \in S(F)} \|g - Ag\|$. Taking the infimum with respect to A, we get $\lambda(n) \leq \lambda_n$, as claimed.

We now prove that $q\,\lambda_n \leq \lambda(n)$. As in Section 5.4 we can assume that $G = S(F_1)$. Recall that $q \in [0, 1]$ or $q = +\infty$. If $q = 0$, it is trivially true. Assume first that $q \in (0, 1]$. Let $\phi^L(N(f)) = \sum_{i=1}^n L_i(f)\,\zeta_i$ belong to $\Phi^L(n)$. Define the linear operator $A : G \to G$, as $Ag = \sum_{i=1}^n L_i(f_2)\,\zeta_i$, where $g = S(f_2)$ with $f_2 \in (\ker S)^\perp$. The operator A is well defined and $A(S(F)) \subset \text{span}(\zeta_1, \zeta_2, \ldots, \zeta_n)$. Consider

$$S(f) - A(S(f)) = S(f_2) - \sum_{i=1}^n L_i(f_2)\,\zeta_i, \quad \forall\, f \in F.$$

Let $\delta \in (0, q)$. From the definition of $q = q(S, F)$ it follows that for every $f \in F$ there exists a constant $\alpha = \alpha(f) \geq q - \delta$ such that αf_2 belongs to F. Thus,

$$\|S(f) - A(S(f))\| = \alpha^{-1}\|S(\alpha f_2) - \phi^L(N(\alpha f_2))\| \leq \frac{e(\phi^L)}{q - \delta}.$$

Since ϕ^L and δ are arbitrary, we get $\lambda_n \leq q^{-1}\lambda(n)$.

It remains to consider the case $q = +\infty$. If $G = S(F_1)$ has dimension at most n, then clearly $\lambda_n = 0$, and $q\,\lambda_n = +\infty \cdot 0 = 0 \leq \lambda(n)$ trivially holds. Assume then that $\dim G > n$. Then the proof of Theorem 5.4.1 implies that $r(n) = +\infty$. Since $\lambda(n) \geq r(n)$, we conclude that $\lambda(n) = +\infty$ and $q\lambda_n \leq \lambda(n)$ also holds in this case. The proof is complete. ∎

Theorem 5.6.1 allows us to find an nth optimal linear (or nearly nth optimal linear) algorithm. Indeed, take a linear subspace A_n and a linear operator A, $A(S(F)) \subset A_n$, such that

$$\lambda_n = \sup_{g \in S(F)} \|g - A_g\|.$$

That is, $A(S(f)) = \sum_{i=1}^{n} R_i^*(S(f))\,\zeta_i^*$ for some linear functionals R_i^*, $R_i^* : G \to \mathbb{R}$, and elements ζ_i^* from G.

Define the information $N^* = [R_1^* S, R_2^*, \ldots, R_n^* S]$ and the linear algorithm $\phi^*(N^*(f)) = A(S(f))$. Then we have

COROLLARY 5.6.1.

(i) *The algorithm ϕ^* has error no greater than $1/q$ times the nth minimal error of linear algorithms,*

$$e(\phi^*) \leq \frac{1}{q}\lambda(n).$$

(ii) *If $q = 1$ then ϕ^* is an nth linear optimal error algorithm.*

(iii) *If $q = 1$ and $\lambda(n) = r(n)$ then ϕ^* is a linear optimal error algorithm using nth optimal information. If, in addition, $r(N^*) = d(N^*)/2$ then the Gelfand n-width and the linear Kolmogorov n-width of the set $S(F)$ are equal,*

$$\lambda_n = d^n = r(n).$$

The linear Kolmogorov n-widths have been found for many important sets. Theorem 5.6.1 enables us to use these results to ascertain the behavior of the nth minimal error of linear algorithms. As in Section 5.4, it can happen that the left-hand side of Theorem 5.6.1 can be achieved for any q, see **NR 5.6:3**.

We now characterize minimal error of linear algorithms using relations between Gelfand and linear Kolmogorov n-widths. Consider a linear problem for which F_1 is a normed linear space, S is continuous and linear, F is the unit ball of F_1, and $\Lambda = \Lambda^*$ is the class of all linear functionals. Assume also that $q = q(S, F)$ is finite. For such a linear problem Gelfand and linear Kolmogorov n-widths satisfy the following inequality,

$$\lambda_n \leq (1 + \sqrt{n})\,d^n,$$

see Pinkus [85, p. 33] and papers cited there. From Theorems 5.4.1 and 5.6.1, we then conclude

$$r(n) \leq \lambda(n) \leq \frac{1 + \sqrt{n}}{q} \, r(n).$$

That is, there exists a linear algorithm using nonadaptive information of cardinality n whose error exceeds the nth minimal radius at most $(1+\sqrt{n})/q$ times. This bound is essentially sharp, i.e., it can happen that the minimal error of linear algorithms from the class $\Phi^L(n)$ is proportional to $\sqrt{n}\,r(n)$. Indeed, take $F_1 = W_1^r$ as the Sobolev space of functions $f : [0,1] \to \mathbb{R}$ whose $f^{(r-1)}$ is absolutely continuous and $f^{(r)} \in \mathcal{L}_1(0,1)$. Let $G = \mathcal{L}_2$ and consider the approximation problem $S(f) = f$. It is known, see Pinkus [85, p. 232] and papers cited there, that

$$\lambda_n = \Theta\left(n^{-r+1/2}\right) \quad \text{and} \quad d^n = \Theta\left(n^{-r}\right).$$

Since now $q = 1$, we have

$$\lambda(n) = \Theta\left(n^{-r+1/2}\right) \quad \text{and} \quad r(n) = \Theta\left(n^{-r}\right).$$

Thus, we have $\lambda(n) = \Theta\left(\sqrt{n}\,r(n)\right)$, as claimed.

Notes and Remarks

NR 5.6:1 This section is based on GTOA p. 64–67. It is known that the Gelfand n-width is no greater than the linear Kolmogorov n-width, $d^n(B,G) \leq \lambda_n(B,G)$, $\forall n$. For some sets, the inequality is strict.

The Kolmogorov n-width $d_n(B,G)$ is defined similarly to the linear Kolmogorov n-width by dropping the assumption that A is a linear operator, i.e.,

$$d_n(B,G) = \inf_{A_n} \sup_{g \in B} \inf_{x \in A_n} \|g - x\|.$$

Clearly, $d_n(B,G) \leq \lambda_n(B,G)$ and for some sets the inequality is strict. For many sets of practical importance, $d_n(B,G) = \lambda_n(B,G)$, see Tikhomirov [76] and Pinkus [85].

NR 5.6:2 Relations between the errors of linear algorithms and the Kolmogorov n-widths of the solution sets have been discussed in several papers. See among others Babuška and Sobolev [65], Bakhvalov [62, 68], Chzhan Guan-Tszyuan [62], Golomb [77], Melkman [77], Melkman and Micchelli [79], Micchelli and Pinkus [77], Micchelli and Rivlin [77], Novak [86a, 87a], and Schulz [74].

NR 5.6:3 Consider the problem described in **NR 5.4:2**. It is easy to show that for this problem we have $\lambda_1 = a + 1$. Consider the linear algorithm $\phi^L(y) = [0, y, y]$, where $y = N(f) = f_2 + f_3 - 1$. Its error $e(\phi^L) = a$. Since $q = a/(a+1)$, we conclude from

Theorem 5.6.1 that $\lambda(1) = a$. Thus, $\lambda(1) = q\,\lambda_1$ and q is small for small a. Equivalently, $\lambda_1/\lambda(1) = (a+1)/a$ can be arbitrarily large for small a. Of course, $\lambda(n) = \lambda_n = 0$, for all $n \geq 2$.

Exercises

E 5.6:1 Explain why the estimate $\lambda_n \leq (1+\sqrt{n}\,)d^n$ cannot be used for the second example of the linear problem from Section 5.5 with no linear optimal error algorithm.

5.7. Spline Algorithms

In Section 5.5 we discuss the existence of optimal error algorithms which are easy to implement for the approximation of linear problems. The (global) error of such an algorithm is equal to the radius of information. For an optimal error algorithm ϕ and some information value $y = N(f)$, the local error $e(\phi, N, y) = \sup_{f \in N^{-1}(y) \cap F} \|S(f) - \phi(y)\|$ might be much greater than the local radius of information $r(N, y)$. This happens if $e(\phi, N, y) \simeq r(N)$ and $r(N, y) << r(N)$.

This is undesirable since the user may want to solve the problem just for the data y with the error comparable to the smallest possible one. This explains our interest in algorithms whose local errors are always comparable to the local radii of information. Let

$$\operatorname{dev}(\phi, N) = \sup_{y \in N(F)} \frac{e(\phi, N, y)}{r(N, y)}$$

be the *deviation* of ϕ, with $0/0 = 1$ by convention. Thus, the deviation of an algorithm is always at least one and measures the ratio between the local errors and radii for a worst data y.

We seek algorithms with small deviation. Obviously, central algorithms have deviation equal to one, but as mentioned earlier, they are often difficult to obtain or might even not exist. On the other hand, linear algorithms are easy to implement. Therefore we shall study the following question: When do linear algorithms have small deviation?

The answer to this question will be provided by *spline algorithms*, see **NR 5.7:1**. In order to define them we proceed as follows. First we remind the reader of the definition and some basic properties of splines in normed linear spaces, see among others Anselone and Laurent [68], Atteia [65], and Holmes [72].

Let $N : F_1 \to \mathbb{R}^n$ and $T : F_1 \to X$ be the two linear operators, where F_1 is a linear space and X is a normed linear space both over the real field.

Let $y \in N(F_1)$. An element $\sigma = \sigma(y)$ is called a *spline interpolating y* (briefly a *spline*) iff

(i) $N(\sigma) = y$,

(ii) $\|T\sigma\| = \min\{\|Tf\| : f \in F_1, N(f) = y\}$.

Thus, σ is an element which interpolates the data y and has a minimal T-norm among all elements interpolating y, see **NR 5.7:2**.

Let $x \in X$. Define

$$P(x) = \left\{ h \in \ker N : \|x - Th\| = \inf_{z \in T(\ker N)} \|x - z\| \right\}$$

as the set of elements h for which Th is a best approximation of x from the set $T(\ker N)$. Then the following relations hold:

   (i) there exists a spline $\sigma(y)$ interpolating y iff the set $P(Tf)$ is nonempty for some f from F_1 such that $N(f) = y$,
  (ii) an element $\sigma, N(\sigma) = y$, is a spline iff $f - \sigma \in P(Tf)$ for every f from F_1 such that $N(f) = y$,
 (iii) there exists a unique spline $\sigma(y)$ interpolating y iff $\ker N \cap \ker T = \{0\}$ and $P(Tf)$ has exactly one element for every f from F_1 such that $N(f) = y$.

Splines are homogeneous, i.e., if $\sigma(y)$ is a spline interpolating y then $\alpha\,\sigma(y)$ is a spline interpolating αy for any constant α. This means that $\sigma(\alpha y) = \alpha\,\sigma(y)$ whenever the spline $\sigma(y)$ is unique.

The set of splines interpolating y is convex. That is, if σ_1 and σ_2 are splines interpolating y then $t\sigma_1 + (1 - t)\sigma_2$ is also a spline interpolating y, $\forall\,t \in [0, 1]$.

If $\ker N \cap \ker T = \{0\}$ and X is a strictly convex space then there exists at most one spline interpolating y. Indeed, suppose there exist two splines, σ_1 and σ_2, interpolating y. We have $\|T\sigma_1\| = \|T\sigma_2\|$. If one of them is zero then $T\sigma_1 = T\sigma_2 = 0$ and $\sigma_i \in \ker N \cap \ker T$. Then $\sigma_1 = \sigma_2 = 0$. Assume thus that $T\sigma_i \neq 0$ for $i = 1, 2$. Then $(\sigma_1 + \sigma_2)/2$ is also a spline and

$$\|T\sigma_1 + T\sigma_2\| = \|T\sigma_1\| + \|T\sigma_2\|.$$

Since X is strictly convex, there exists a positive α such that $T\sigma_1 = \alpha\,T\sigma_2$. Then $\|T\sigma_1\| = \|T\sigma_2\| \neq 0$ implies that $\alpha = 1$. Thus, $\sigma_1 - \sigma_2 \in \ker T \cap \ker N$ and therefore $\sigma_1 = \sigma_2$, as claimed.

Suppose that X is a Hilbert space with the inner product $\langle \cdot, \cdot \rangle$, and $T(\ker N)$ is closed. Then a spline exists since the set $P(x)$ is nonempty. Furthermore, σ is a spline interpolating y iff $N(\sigma) = y$ and $\langle T\sigma, Th \rangle = 0$, $\forall\,h \in \ker N$. Indeed, if σ is a spline then for $h \in \ker N$ we have $N(\sigma + \alpha h) = y$ and $\|T\sigma\| \leq \|T(\sigma + \alpha h)\|$, $\forall\,\alpha \in \mathbb{R}$. The last inequality implies that $0 \leq \alpha^2 \|Th\|^2 + 2\alpha\langle T\sigma, Th \rangle$, which can be true for small $|\alpha|$ only if $\langle T\sigma, Th \rangle = 0$. On the other hand, if $N(\sigma) = y$ and $T\sigma$ is orthogonal to $T(\ker N)$ then for $N(f) = y$ we have $h = f - \sigma \in \ker N$, and $\|Tf\| = \|T\sigma + Th\| =$

$\sqrt{\|T\sigma\|^2 + \|Th\|^2} \geq \|T\sigma\|$, as claimed. Moreover, the set $N^{-1}(y) = \{f \in F_1 : N(f) = y, \|Tf\| \leq 1\}$ is a hypercircle and the spline $\sigma = \sigma(y)$ is a center of this set, i.e., $f \in N^{-1}(y)$ implies that $2\,\sigma(y) - f \in N^{-1}(y)$. Indeed, this follows from the fact that $N(2\sigma - f) = y$ and for $h = \sigma - f \in \ker N$ we have $\|T(2\sigma - f)\| = \|T\sigma + Th\| = \sqrt{\|T\sigma\|^2 + \|Th\|^2} = \|Tf\| \leq 1$. A spline depends linearly on y, i.e., if splines $\sigma(y_1)$ and $\sigma(y_2)$ interpolate y_1 and y_2, respectively, then $\alpha_1\sigma(y_1) + \alpha_2\sigma(y_2)$ is a spline interpolating $\alpha_1 y_1 + \alpha_2 y_2$ for any constants α_1 and α_2. The splines $\sigma(y)$ are uniquely defined iff $\ker N \cap \ker T = \{0\}$.

We now define a *spline algorithm* ϕ^s by

$$\phi^s(y) = S\sigma(y), \quad \forall y \in N(F),$$

where $\sigma(y)$ is a spline interpolating y, and $F = \{f \in F_1 : \|Tf\| \leq 1\}$, see **NR 5.7:1**. To guarantee the existence of a spline algorithm we have to assume that the set $P(Tf)$ is nonempty for any $f \in F$. Observe that the spline algorithm is *interpolatory*, see Section 3.3. Indeed, for $y \in N(F)$ we have $y = N(f)$ for some $f \in F$, and $\|T\sigma(y)\| \leq \|Tf\| \leq 1$. Thus, $\sigma(y) \in F$, $\sigma(y) \in N^{-1}(y)$ and therefore ϕ^s is interpolatory. Hence $e(\phi^s, N, y) \leq 2\,r(N, y)$ and the deviation of the spline algorithm is at most two.

The spline algorithm is *homogeneous*, but not necessarily linear. The spline algorithm is uniquely defined iff the set $SP(Tf)$ is a singleton for all f from F. Indeed, let $y = N(f)$ for $f \in F$. Consider the splines σ_1 and σ_2 interpolating y. Then $f - \sigma_i = h_i \in P(Tf)$ and $S\sigma_1 - S\sigma_2 = S(h_2) - S(h_1)$. Thus, $SP(Tf)$ is a singleton iff $S\sigma_1 = S\sigma_2$, as claimed.

We now address the question posed in the first part of this section about linear algorithms with small deviation. As we shall see, the answer depends on whether a spline algorithm is linear.

THEOREM 5.7.1. *Let $SP(Tf)$ be a singleton set for any $f \in F$ and let the radius $r(N)$ of information be finite. If the spline algorithm is linear then the class of linear algorithms that use N and have finite deviation consists of exactly one element, namely the spline algorithm. If the spline algorithm is not linear then the class of linear algorithms that use N and have finite deviation is empty.*

PROOF: In fact, we prove a slightly stronger statement that the deviation of any homogeneous nonspline algorithm ϕ is infinite.

If $e(\phi, N) = +\infty$ then $r(N) < +\infty$ implies that $\text{dev}(\phi, N) = +\infty$. Assume then that $e(\phi, N) < +\infty$. Since $SP(Tf)$ is a singleton, there exists a unique spline algorithm $S\sigma(y)$. We first show that $\sigma(y) \in \ker T$ implies $\phi(y) = S\sigma(y)$. Indeed, for any α we have $\alpha\,\sigma(y) \in F$ and $\|\phi(\alpha y) - S(\alpha\sigma(y))\| = |\alpha|\,\|\phi(y) - S\sigma(y)\| \leq e(\phi, N) < +\infty, \forall \alpha \in \mathbb{R}$. This implies $\phi(y) = S\sigma(y)$. Since ϕ is a nonspline algorithm, there exists y

such that $\phi(y) \neq S\sigma(y)$ and $T\sigma(y) \neq 0$. Define $\bar{y} = y/\|T\sigma(y)\|$ and consider the set $SN^{-1}(\bar{y})$. This set is a singleton with the only element $S\sigma(\bar{y})$. Obviously, $r(N, \bar{y}) = 0$. Since ϕ is homogeneous, $\phi(\bar{y}) = \phi(y)/\|T\sigma(y)\| \neq S\sigma(y)/\|T\sigma(y)\| = S\sigma(\bar{y})$. Thus, $e(\phi, N, \bar{y}) \neq 0$ and $\mathrm{dev}(\phi, N) \geq e(\phi, N, \bar{y})/r(N, \bar{y}) = +\infty$. Hence, there exists no nonspline algorithm with finite deviation which is homogeneous. From this, Theorem 5.7.1 follows. ∎

The assumption in Theorem 5.7.1 that $SP(Tf)$ is a singleton for any $f \in F$ is essential as shown in **NR 5.7:3**.

Theorem 5.7.1 states that to find a linear algorithm with small deviation, we have to guarantee linearity of a spline algorithm. In particular, this is the case if X is a Hilbert space and $T(\ker N)$ is a closed subspace in X. To show this, consider $N = [L_1, L_2, \ldots, L_n]$ with linearly independent linear functionals L_i. Then the algorithm

$$\phi^s(N(f)) = \sum_{i=1}^{n} L_i(f) S\,\sigma_i$$

presented in Theorem 5.5.3 is the unique spline algorithm if the radius $r(N)$ of information is finite. Indeed, for σ_i such that $N(\sigma_i) = e_i = [0, \ldots, \underset{i}{1}, \ldots, 0]$ and $T\sigma_i$ orthogonal to $T(\ker N)$, σ_i is a spline interpolating e_i. Consequently, $\sigma = \sum_{i=1}^{n} L_i(f)\,\sigma_i$ interpolates $N(f)$ and is also orthogonal to $T(\ker N)$. Thus, σ is a spline interpolating $N(f)$ and ϕ^s is a spline algorithm. It is the unique spline algorithm, since $SP(Tf)$ is a singleton for any $f \in F_1$. Indeed, let σ_1 and σ_2 be splines interpolating $y = N(f)$. Then $T\sigma_i$ is orthogonal to $T(\ker N)$ and $h = \sigma_1 - \sigma_2$ belongs to $\ker N$. Then $\|T\sigma_1\| = \|T\sigma_2\| = \|T\sigma_1 - Th\| = \sqrt{\|T\sigma_1\|^2 + \|Th\|^2}$. This implies that $Th = 0$. Thus, $h \in \ker N \cap \ker T \subset \ker S$, see **E 5.2:1**. Hence $h \in \ker S$, i.e., $S\sigma_1 = S\sigma_2$, as claimed.

From Theorem 5.5.3 we know that ϕ^s is a linear optimal error algorithm. We now prove that ϕ^s is central, see **NR 5.7:4**.

THEOREM 5.7.2. *Let X be a Hilbert space, let $T(\ker N)$ be closed and let $r(N)$ be finite. Then the spline algorithm $\phi^s(N(f)) = \sum_{i=1}^{n} L_i(f)\,S\sigma_i$ is a linear central algorithm, i.e., $\mathrm{dev}(\phi^s, N) = 1$, and*

$$e(\phi^s, N, y) = r(N, y) = \sqrt{1 - \|T\sigma(y)\|^2}\, r(N),$$

where $r(N) = \sup_{h \in \ker N} \|S(h)\|/\|Th\|$.

PROOF: Since $N^{-1}(y) \cap F$ is symmetric with respect to $\sigma(y)$, $S\big(N^{-1}(y) \cap F\big)$ is symmetric with respect to $\phi^s(y) = S\sigma(y)$. As we know from Section

3.2, this implies that ϕ^s is a central algorithm. Its local error is given by

$$e(\phi^s, N, y) = r(N, y)$$
$$= \sup\left\{\|S(\sigma(y) + h) - S\sigma(y)\| : \sigma(y) + h \in N^{-1}(y) \cap F\right\}$$
$$= \sup\left\{\|S(h)\| : h \in \ker N, \|Th\| \leq \sqrt{1 - \|T\sigma(y)\|^2}\right\}$$
$$= \sqrt{1 - \|T\sigma(y)\|^2} \sup_{h \in \ker N} \frac{\|S(h)\|}{\|Th\|}.$$

Since $r(N) = \sup_{h \in \ker N} \|S(h)\| / \|Th\|$, the proof is completed. ∎

It is natural to ask whether there are more general conditions than these presented in Theorem 5.7.2 under which a spline algorithm is linear. This problem has been investigated by Kon and Tempo [87] who proved that for arbitrary S the assumptions that X is a Hilbert space and $T(\ker N)$ is closed are necessary, see **NR 5.7:5**.

We end this section by a remark about spline and linear optimal error algorithms assuming that S is a linear functional, $T(\ker N)$ is closed in a Hilbert space X, and $r(N) < +\infty$. We show that the spline algorithm ϕ^s is a unique linear optimal error algorithm that uses information $N(f) = [L_1(f), L_2(f), \ldots, L_n(f)]$ for linearly independent L_i. Indeed, as in **NR 5.5:2** consider

$$r_i(x) = \sup\{S(f) : f \in A_i\},$$

where $A_i = \{f \in F : L_i(f) = x, L_j(f) = 0 \text{ for } j \neq i\}$.

Observe that for $f \in A$ we have $f = x\sigma_i + h$, where $h \in \ker N$ and $\|Tf\|^2 = x^2\|T\sigma_i\|^2 + \|Th\|^2 \leq 1$. Thus,

$$r_i(x) = \sup\left\{xS(\sigma_i) + S(h) : h \in \ker N, \|Th\| \leq \sqrt{1 - x^2\|T\sigma_i\|^2}\right\}.$$

As in the proof of Theorem 5.7.2, we conclude that

$$r_i(x) = x\, S(\sigma_i) + \sqrt{1 - x^2\|T\sigma_i\|^2}\, r(N).$$

This yields that $r_i'(0) = S(\sigma_i)$. From **NR 5.5:2** we have that there exists a unique linear optimal error algorithm $\phi^L(N(f)) = \sum_{i=1}^n L_i(f)g_i$, with $g_i = r_i'(0) = S(\sigma_i)$. This means that ϕ^L is a spline algorithm. We summarize this in

COROLLARY 5.7.1. *Consider a linear problem for which S is a linear functional, $T(\ker N)$ is closed in a Hilbert space X, and $r(N) < +\infty$. Then the spline algorithm is a unique linear optimal error algorithm.*

Thus, under assumptions of Corollary 5.7.1 we see that the construction of a linear optimal error algorithm presented in the proof of Smolyak's theorem coincides with the construction of a spline algorithm. Furthermore, linearity of an optimal error algorithm implies that such an algorithm is central.

Notes and Remarks

NR 5.7:1 This section is based on the paper of Wasilkowski and Woźniakowski [78] which appeared as Chapter 4 in GTOA. Splines are extensively used in numerical mathematics and in approximation theory. Many optimality properties of splines are known. Schoenberg [64a,b] was apparently the first to realize the close connection between splines and algorithms optimal in the sense of Sard. The first implicit use of optimal properties of splines can be traced back to a classic paper of Golomb and Weinberger [59] who studied approximation of linear functionals. Papers dealing with optimality of splines can be found in GTOA p. 69. As we shall see in the following chapters of this book, spline algorithms will also play a major role in the average case, probabilistic, and asymptotic settings.

NR 5.7:2 The primary example of splines is a piecewise smooth polynomial. This agrees with a general definition of splines in normed linear spaces by taking suitable spaces F_1 and X, and linear operators N and T. Indeed, let $F_1 = W_2^k[0,1]$ be the Sobolev space of real functions f defined on $[0,1]$ whose $(k-1)$st derivative is absolutely continuous and the kth derivative belongs to $X = \mathcal{L}_2[0,1]$. Let $Tf = f^{(k)}$ and

$$N(f) = [f(x_1), f(x_2), \ldots, f(x_n)]$$

for distinct x_i from $[0,1]$, $n \geq k$. It is well known that the function σ which interpolates the data and whose kth derivative has the minimal $\mathcal{L}_2$ norm is the natural spline of degree $2k-1$.

NR 5.7:3 (GTOA p. 73) We show an example in which $SP(Tf)$ is not a singleton set and there exists a nonspline linear algorithm with finite deviation. Let $F_1 = G = X = C[0,1]$ be the class of continuous functions on $[0,1]$ with the sup norm, $\|f\| = \max_{0 \leq t \leq 1} |f(t)|$. Let $S = T = I$ be the identity operator and $y = N(f) = [f(t_1), f(t_2), \ldots, f(t_n)]$ for some distinct $t_i \in [0,1]$. It is easy to show that $r(N, y) = 1$, $\forall y \in N(F)$, and the unique center of $SN^{-1}(y)$ is the zero function. Observe, however, that the center does not belong to $SN^{-1}(y)$. Furthermore, every function σ, $\sigma \in F_1$, which agrees with f at t_i, $\sigma(t_i) = f(t_i)$, $i = 1, 2, \ldots, n$, and $\|\sigma\| \leq \max_{1 \leq i \leq n} |f(t_i)| = \|y\|_\infty$, is a spline. Thus, for $y = N(f) \neq 0$ there exist infinitely many splines interpolating y, and of course

$$SP(Tf) = P(f) = \{h \in \ker N : \|f - h\| \leq \|y\|_\infty\}$$

is not a singleton set.

Consider the central linear algorithm $\phi(y) \equiv 0$. Of course, $\mathrm{dev}(\phi, N) = 1$. Since ϕ is not interpolatory, it is not a spline algorithm. It can be shown that any interpolatory algorithm ϕ has the local error $e(\phi, N, y) = 2$, $\forall y \in N(F), \|y\|_\infty = 1$, and therefore $\mathrm{dev}(\phi, N) = 2$. It is also easy to show that there exists a linear spline algorithm of deviation 2.

NR 5.7:4 Optimality of spline algorithms in a Hilbert space has been established by a number of people for particular cases. Micchelli and Rivlin [77] studied the general case with $F_1 = X$ and the restriction operator $T = I$. Their proof techniques can be also used for an arbitrary linear operator T as it was done in Theorem 5.7.2.

NR 5.7:5 Kon and Tempo [87] assumed that F_1 is a reflexive strictly convex Banach space of dimension at least 3 and T is the indentity operator, $X = F_1$. They proved that the following statements are equivalent
1. F_1 is a Hilbert space.
For any continuous linear information and any linear solution operator there exists
2. a linear interpolatory algorithm
3. a linear spline algorithm
4. a linear algorithm with finite deviation
5. a linear central algorithm.
The equivalence of these statements is proved by the use of the result of Rudin and Smith [61] which states that linearity of projection operators can only happen if F_1 is a Hilbert space.

For a general linear bijective operator T, $T : F_1 \to X$, the result of Kon and Tempo [87] can be stated as follows. Let X be a reflexive strictly convex Banach space. Then the following statements are equivalent
1. X is a Hilbert space
For any linear information N for which $T(\ker N)$ is closed and any linear solution operator there exists
2. a linear interpolatory algorithm
3. a linear spline algorithm
4. a linear algorithm with finite deviation
5. a linear central algorithm.
Thus, linearity of a spline algorithm for general N and S can only happen if X is a Hilbert space.

Exercises

E 5.7:1 (GTOA p. 75) Consider $F_1 = G = X$ as the space of scalar polynomials of degree $\le n$. Let $\|f\| = \max_{0 \le t \le 1} |f(t)|$ and let $S = T = I$. Information is given by $y = N(f) = [f'(0), f''(0)/2!, \ldots, f^{(n)}(0)/n!]$. Define $g(y,t) = \sum_{i=1}^{n} y_i\, t^i$, $y_i = f^{(i)}(0)/i!$, and let $\overline{g}(y) = \max_{0 \le t \le 1} g(y,t)$, $\underline{g}(y) = \min_{0 \le t \le 1} g(y,t)$. Prove that

$$\phi^s(y)(t) = g(y,t) - \tfrac{1}{2}\big(\overline{g}(y) + \underline{g}(y)\big)$$

is a unique spline algorithm which is central and nonlinear, and

$$e(\phi^s, N, y) = 1 - \tfrac{1}{2}\big(\overline{g}(y) - \underline{g}(y)\big) \le r(N) = 1.$$

5.8. Complexity

We provide complexity bounds for linear problems using results of Sections 4 and 5. Recall our assumptions. The solution operator $S : F_1 \to G$ is linear, $F = \{f \in F_1 : \|Tf\| \le 1\}$ with a linear restriction operator $T : F_1 \to X$, and Λ is a class of permissible linear functionals $L : F_1 \to \mathbb{R}$.

The ε-complexity is estimated in terms of the ε-cardinality number $m(\varepsilon)$ which is the smallest cardinality of information with radius at most ε, see Section 4. Since adaptive information cannot help much, see Section 5.2, we can estimate the ε-cardinality number in terms of the nth minimal radii $r(n, \Lambda)$, see Section 5.3, as follows

$$\min\{n : r(n, \Lambda) \leq 2\varepsilon\} \leq m(\varepsilon) \leq \min\{n : r(n, \Lambda) \leq \varepsilon\}.$$

Furthermore, if the nth minimal diameter $d(n, \Lambda) = 2\,r(n, \Lambda)$ then

$$m(\varepsilon) = \min\{n : r(n, \Lambda) \leq \varepsilon\}.$$

Observe that the relation $d(n, \Lambda) = 2\,r(n, \Lambda)$ holds if, for example, the range of the solution operator is $\mathbb{R}$ or the range of the restriction operator is a Hilbert space and $T(\ker N)$ is closed.

In Section 5.5 we presented general assumptions under which there exists a linear optimal error algorithm ϕ^L. If this is the case, its combinatory cost is at most $2n - 1$, where n is the cardinality of information used. The information cost is cn, where c is the cost of one information operation. For $c \gg 1$, the combinatory cost is much less than the information cost. This discussion and Theorems 4.1 and 4.2 yield the following.

THEOREM 5.8.1. *The ε-complexity of a linear problem is bounded from below by*

$$\mathrm{comp}(\varepsilon) \geq c \min\{n : r(n, \Lambda) \leq 2\varepsilon\}.$$

Let $d(n, \Lambda) = 2\,r(n, \Lambda)$ and let N_n be nth optimal information in the class Λ, $r(N_n) = r(n, \Lambda)$. Suppose there exists a linear optimal error algorithm ϕ^L that uses N_n. Then

$$c\,m(\varepsilon) \leq \mathrm{comp}(\varepsilon) \leq \mathrm{cost}(\phi^L, N_n) \leq (c + 2)\,m(\varepsilon) - 1,$$

where $m(\varepsilon) = \min\{n : r(n, \Lambda) \leq \varepsilon\}$. For $c \gg 1$, the information $N_{m(\varepsilon)}$ and the algorithm ϕ^L are almost optimal.

We illustrate Theorem 5.8.1 by two examples. In the first example, assume that the solution operator S is a linear functional. Then the assumptions of Theorem 5.8.1 hold and

$$c\,m(\varepsilon) \leq \mathrm{comp}(\varepsilon) \leq (c + 2)\,m(\varepsilon) - 1.$$

We now specialize this example by assuming that $F_1 = \widetilde{W}_\infty^r[0, 2\pi]$ is the class of 2π-periodic functions $f : [0, 2\pi] \rightarrow \mathbb{R}$, whose $(r - 1)$st derivative is absolutely continuous and whose rth derivative belongs to $\mathcal{L}_\infty[0, 2\pi]$. Define $Tf = f^{(r)}$ and $X = \mathcal{L}_\infty[0, 2\pi]$. Let $S(f) = \int_0^{2\pi} f(t)\, dt$ and let Λ consist of function evaluations, see Section 2.1 of Chapter 5 where this problem is discussed in more detail. The nth minimal radius $r(n, \Lambda)$ was found by Motornyj [73],

$$r(n, \Lambda) = \frac{2\pi K_r}{n^r},$$

where $K_r = (4/\pi) \sum_{i=0}^{\infty} (-1)^{i(r+1)}/(2i+1)^{r+1}$ is the Favard constant, and $K_r \in [1, \pi/2]$.

The nth optimal information N_n is given by the evaluation of f at n equally spaced points $x_i = 2\pi(i-1)/n$, $i = 1, 2, \ldots, n$, and the well known rectangle (or trapezoid in this case) quadrature formula

$$\phi^L(N_n(f)) = \frac{2\pi}{n} \sum_{i=1}^{n} f\left(2\pi \frac{i-1}{n}\right)$$

is a linear optimal error algorithm, see also **NR 5.8:2**. Note that the combinatory cost of ϕ^L is now only n, since all the weights in ϕ^L are equal.

The ε-cardinality number is equal to

$$m(\varepsilon) = \left\lceil \left(\frac{2\pi K_r}{\varepsilon}\right)^{1/r} \right\rceil,$$

and Theorem 5.8.1 yields that the complexity is bounded by

$$c\left\lceil \left(\frac{2\pi K_r}{\varepsilon}\right)^{1/r} \right\rceil \leq \mathrm{comp}(\varepsilon) \leq (c+1)\left\lceil \left(\frac{2\pi K_r}{\varepsilon}\right)^{1/r} \right\rceil.$$

The lower bound can be slightly improved by observing that any algorithm that computes an ε-approximation must use at least $m(\varepsilon)$ function values and therefore must perform at least $m(\varepsilon)-1$ combinatory operations. Thus,

$$\mathrm{comp}(\varepsilon) = (c+1)\left\lceil \left(\frac{2\pi K_r}{\varepsilon}\right)^{1/r} \right\rceil + a,$$

where $a = -1$ or $a = 0$.

We now illustrate Theorem 5.8.1 by the second example for which $\Lambda = \Lambda^*$, X and G are separable Hilbert spaces, T is an bijective linear operator, and the linear operator $K = ST^{-1} : X \to G$ is compact. From Section 5.3 we conclude that $d(n, \Lambda^*) = 2\,r(n, \Lambda^*)$ and the ε-cardinality number is given by

$$m(\varepsilon) = \min\left\{n : \lambda_{n+1} \leq \varepsilon^2\right\},$$

where $\{\lambda_i\}$ is a nonincreasing sequence of the eigenvalues of the self-adjoint operator $K_1 = K^*K : X \to X$, $K_1 \zeta_i = \lambda_i \zeta_i$, $\langle \zeta_i, \zeta_j \rangle = \delta_{i,j}$ and $\langle \cdot, \cdot \rangle$ is the inner product of X.

The nth optimal information N_n is of the form

$$N_n(f) = [\langle Tf, \zeta_1 \rangle, \langle Tf, \zeta_2 \rangle, \ldots, \langle Tf, \zeta_n \rangle] .$$

From Sections 5.5 and 5.7 we conclude that the algorithm

$$\phi^s(N_n(f)) = \sum_{i=1}^{n} \langle Tf, \zeta_i \rangle \, ST^{-1} \zeta_i$$

is a linear optimal error, spline, and central algorithm.

Based on the last example, we now show that the complexity of a linear problem can go to infinity arbitrarily fast as ε goes to zero. Furthermore, there are no "gaps" in the complexity functions. More precisely, we have

THEOREM 5.8.2. *Let* $g : [0, +\infty) \rightarrow \mathbb{R}_+$ *be an arbitrary increasing continuous function such that* $\lim_{x \to +\infty} g(x) = +\infty$. *Then there exists a linear problem such that*

$$m(\varepsilon) = \lceil g(\varepsilon^{-1}) \rceil, \quad \forall \varepsilon \le \varepsilon_0 := 1/g^{-1}(\lfloor g(0) \rfloor + 1).$$

Thus, for $c \gg 1$ *and small* ε, *we have*

$$\text{comp}(\varepsilon) \simeq c \lceil g(\varepsilon^{-1}) \rceil.$$

PROOF: Let $X = G$ be an infinite dimensional Hilbert space with an orthonormal system $\{\zeta_i\}$, $\langle \zeta_i, \zeta_j \rangle = \delta_{i,j}$. Define $Tf = f$ and $S(f) = \sum_{i=1}^{\infty} \beta_i \langle f, \zeta_i \rangle \zeta_i$. Here $\beta_i = 1/g^{-1}(i - 1)$ for $i - 1 \ge n^* = \lfloor g(0) \rfloor + 1$ and $\beta_i = \beta_{n^*+1}$ for $i \le n^*$. Note that $i - 1 \ge n^*$ implies that $i - 1 > g(0)$ and $g^{-1}(i - 1) > 0$. Thus β_i is well defined and $\beta_1 \ge \beta_2 \ge \cdots \ge 0$, $\lim_{i \to \infty} \beta_i = 0$. The operator S is self-adjoint and compact. We have $K_1 = S^2$ and $\lambda_i = \beta_i^2$. The ε-cardinality number is now equal to $m(\varepsilon) = \min\{n : \beta_{n+1} \le \varepsilon\}$. Note that $\beta_{n^*+1} \ge \varepsilon$ for $\varepsilon \le \varepsilon_0$. Thus, $\beta_{n+1} \le \varepsilon$ implies that $g^{-1}(n) > 1/\varepsilon$. This leads $g(\varepsilon^{-1}) \le m(\varepsilon) < g(\varepsilon^{-1}) + 1$. Thus, $m(\varepsilon) = \lceil g(\varepsilon^{-1}) \rceil$, as claimed. The rest follows from the second part of Theorem 5.8.1. ∎

Theorem 5.8.2 states that essentially any increasing function can be the complexity of a linear problem. This may be contrasted with the theory of recursively computable functions in which complexity gaps are known to occur, see Borodin [72].

Notes and Remarks

NR 5.8:1 This section is based on GTOA, Chapter 5.

NR 5.8:2 The rectangle quadrature formula is also an optimal error algorithm for the space $F_1 = \widetilde{W}_p^r[0, 2\pi]$ which consists of 2π-periodic functions whose $(r-1)$st derivative is absolutely continuous and whose rth derivative belongs to $X = \mathcal{L}_p[0, 2\pi]$, as proven by Ligun [76] for $p = 1$ and by Žensykbaev [76,77a] for all p.

Exercises

E 5.8:1 Let comp(ε) be the ε-complexity for a linear problem with $F = \{f \in F_1 : \|Tf\| \le 1\}$. Consider the linear problem with $F(\lambda) = \{f \in F_1 : \|Tf\| \le \lambda\}$ for some positive λ. Show that the ε-complexity with $F(\lambda)$ is equal to comp(ε/λ).

6. Different Error Criteria

We have discussed so far the absolute error criterion. That is, the error between the exact value, $S(f)$, and the computed one, $U(f) = \phi(N(f))$, was measured by $\|S(f) - U(f)\|$. Other error criteria are also of interest. For instance, one may want to compute an element $U(f)$ such that the *relative error*

$$\frac{\|S(f) - U(f)\|}{\|S(f)\|}$$

does not exceed a given threshold ε. To avoid troubles with $S(f) = 0$ or small $\|S(f)\|$, one can study the *modified relative error* in which

$$\frac{\|S(f) - U(f)\|}{\|S(f)\| + \eta}$$

is considered for some (small) positive η. One can also consider the *normalized error*, where

$$\frac{\|S(f) - U(f)\|}{\|f\|}$$

is analyzed under the assumption that F_1 is equipped with a norm.

These and more general error criteria will be discussed throughout this book. In this section we discuss various error criteria in the worst case setting. The average case and probabilistic settings will be analyzed in Sections 6 of Chapters 6 and 8.

6.1. Relative Error

In this section we analyze the relative error criterion. We seek an ε-approximation with $\varepsilon < 1$. If $\varepsilon \ge 1$ then the problem is trivial since the zero algorithm has relative error equal to one for any f.

Let N be adaptive information and let ϕ be an algorithm that uses N. The error of an algorithm ϕ is now defined by

$$e^{\text{rel}}(\phi, N) = \sup_{f \in F} \frac{\|S(f) - \phi(N(f))\|}{\|S(f)\|},$$

with the convention that $0/0 = 0$. As always, the radius of information is the minimal error of algorithms using N,

$$r^{\text{rel}}(N) = \inf_{\phi} e^{\text{rel}}(\phi, N).$$

We show that this does not lead to interesting results, at least for linear problems, i.e., for a linear operator S defined on a balanced and convex F, and for information consisting of linear functionals. Namely, for arbitrary adaptive information N we have

$$r^{\text{rel}}(N) = 1$$

whenever the local radius $r(N, 0)$ for the absolute error is positive. Indeed, proceeding as in Lemma 5.2.1, one can show that

$$r(N, 0) = \sup_{h \in F \cap \ker N} \|S(h)\|$$

with $\ker N = N^{-1}(0)$. Thus, there exists an element h from $F \cap \ker N$ such that $S(h) \neq 0$. Then $-h$ also belongs to $F \cap \ker N$. For an arbitrary algorithm ϕ using N we have

$$e^{\text{rel}}(\phi, N) \geq \sup_{f \in F \cap \ker N} \frac{\|S(f) - \phi(0)\|}{\|S(f)\|}$$

$$\geq \frac{1}{2}\left(\frac{\|S(h) - \phi(0)\|}{\|S(h)\|} + \frac{\|S(h) + \phi(0)\|}{\|S(h)\|}\right) \geq 1.$$

Hence $r^{\text{rel}}(N) = 1$, as claimed.

Observe that $r(N, 0) > 0$ iff $r(N^{\text{non}}) > 0$, where N^{non} is nonadaptive information derived from N as in Theorem 5.2.1. Thus, except for the trivial case of $r(N^{\text{non}}) = 0$, we cannot find an approximation with relative error less than one no matter what kind of information is used.

REMARK 6.1.1. One can also consider a relative error criterion in which the roles of $S(f)$ and $\phi(N(f))$ are interchanged. Then

$$e^{\text{rel}}(\phi, N) = \sup_{f \in F} \frac{\|S(f) - \phi(N(f))\|}{\|\phi(N(f))\|}$$

with the convention that $0/0 = 0$.

As before, this does not lead to interesting results at least for linear problems since $e^{\mathrm{rel}}(\phi, N) \geq 1$ whenever $r(N,0) > 0$. Indeed, taking the element h from the last proof we have

$$e^{\mathrm{rel}}(\phi, N) \geq \max_{f \in \{0,h\}} \frac{\|S(f) - \phi(0)\|}{\|\phi(0)\|} = \max\left\{ \frac{\|\phi(0)\|}{\|\phi(0)\|}, \frac{\|S(h) - \phi(0)\|}{\|\phi(0)\|} \right\} \geq 1,$$

as claimed.

These two relative error criteria are studied in the average case setting. For linear problems, the average complexity under the first relative error criterion is finite if the dimension of the range of S is at least three. The average complexity under the second relative error criterion is finite no matter what is the dimension of the range of S. This is reported in Section 6 of Chapter 6.

One may argue that $\|S(f) - \phi(N(f))\|/\|S(f)\|$ is not always a reasonable measure of error, since it requires small relative error even for elements f with $\|S(f)\|$ extremely small. Therefore, it seems reasonable to modify the definition of the relative error by adding a small positive number to the denominator. This leads to the *modified relative error* in which the error of an algorithm ϕ is defined by

$$e^{\mathrm{rel}}(\phi, N; \eta) = \sup_{f \in F} \frac{\|S(f) - \phi(N(f))\|}{\|S(f)\| + \eta}$$

for some (presumably small) number η. Note that if $\|S(f)\|$ is large compared to η then we are close to the relative error, whereas if $\|S(f)\|$ is small compared to η then we are close to the absolute error divided by η. Define

$$r^{\mathrm{rel}}(N; \eta) = \inf_{\phi} e^{\mathrm{rel}}(\phi, N; \eta).$$

For linear problems we have the following relations between $r^{\mathrm{rel}}(N; \eta)$, the radius $r(N)$, and the local radius $r(N,0)$, the last two for the absolute error criterion,

$$\frac{r(N,0)}{r(N,0) + \eta} \leq r^{\mathrm{rel}}(N; \eta) \leq \min\left\{ 1, \frac{r(N)}{\eta} \right\}.$$

Indeed, taking $\phi(N(f)) \equiv 0$, we get $r^{\mathrm{rel}}(N; \eta) \leq 1$. For an arbitrary positive δ, take an algorithm ϕ such that $e(\phi, N) \leq r(N) + \delta$. Then

$e^{\text{rel}}(\phi, N; \eta) \leq (r(N) + \delta)/\eta$, which proves the right-hand side. To prove the left-hand side, choose f from $F \cap \ker N$ such that

$$\|S(f)\| \geq r(N, 0) - \delta = \sup_{h \in F \cap \ker N} \|S(h)\| - \delta.$$

Such an element exists due to Lemma 5.2.1 and Theorem 5.2.1, and due to the fact that $F \cap \ker N$ is symmetric with respect to zero. For any algorithm ϕ, we have $2\|S(f)\| \leq \|S(f) - \phi(0)\| + \|S(-f) - \phi(0)\|$. This yields

$$\|S(\alpha f) - \phi(0)\| \geq \|S(f)\|,$$

where $\alpha = -1$ or $\alpha = +1$. From this, we get

$$e^{\text{rel}}(\phi, N; \eta) \geq \frac{\|S(\alpha f) - \phi(0)\|}{\|S(\alpha f)\| + \eta} \geq \frac{r(N, 0) - \delta}{r(N, 0) + \eta},$$

which completes the proof.

These estimates can be summarized as follows.

  (i) If $\eta << r(N, 0)$ then $r^{\text{rel}}(N; \eta) \simeq 1$.
  (ii) If $\eta \leq r(N, 0)$ then $r^{\text{rel}}(N; \eta) \in [1/2, 1]$.
  (iii) If $\eta >> r(N, 0)$ and $r(N) = r(N, 0)$ then $r^{\text{rel}}(N; \eta) = (1 - \alpha) r(N)/\eta$, where $\alpha \in [0, r(N)/\eta]$.

Observe that for nonadaptive information N we have $2 r(N, 0) = d(N, 0) = d(N)$ and the relation $r(N) = d(N)/2 = r(N, 0)$ holds for many linear problems. If so, the ε-complexity, $\text{comp}^{\text{rel}}(\varepsilon; \eta)$, for the relative error is related to the ε-complexity for the absolute error by

$$\text{comp}^{\text{rel}}(\varepsilon; \eta) = \text{comp}\left(\varepsilon \eta (1 + o(1))\right) \quad \text{as } \varepsilon \to 0.$$

The information and algorithm which are $\varepsilon\eta$-complexity optimal for the absolute error are also ε-complexity almost optimal for the relative error with η.

Notes and Remarks

NR 6.1:1 This section is based on GTOA p. 196.

Exercises

E 6.1:1 Consider the error criterion $\|S(f) - U(f)\|/(\|U(f)\| + \eta)$ for a positive η. Show that for small ε this error criterion is essentially the same as the error criterion considered in Section 6.1, i.e., $\|S(f) - U(f)\|/(\|S(f)\| + \eta)$.

E 6.1:2 Consider the error criterion $\|S(f) - U(f)\|/(\max\{\|S(f)\|, \|U(f)\|\})$. Show that for linear problems, this error criterion is equivalent to the standard relative error criterion.

E 6.1:3 Consider the error criterion $\|S(f) - U(f)\|/(\max\{\|S(f)\|, \|U(f)\|\} + \eta)$ for a positive η. Show that for small ε this error criterion is essentially the same as the one in **E 6.1:1**.

6.2. Normalized Error

We have assumed so far that $f \in F$. In many cases the set F is of the form $F = \{f \in F_1 : \|Tf\| \leq 1\}$, where $T : F_1 \to X$ is a linear (restriction) operator. Sometimes it is difficult to verify whether $\|Tf\| \leq 1$. One may resolve this by switching to the *normalized* error, where the distance between $S(f)$ and $U(f) = \phi(N(f))$ is measured by

$$\frac{\|S(f) - U(f)\|}{\|Tf\|}.$$

Here f can be an arbitrary element of F_1, and $0/0 = 0$ by the convention.

The normalized error is often, although sometimes implicitly, used in computational practice. This is the case when one estimates $\|S(f) - U(f)\|$ by $\kappa(n)\|Tf\|$ for some function $\kappa(\cdot)$ with n denoting the cardinality of N. Usually the norms in F_1 and X are different and for many problems Tf denotes some derivative of f. Obviously, one wants to find the smallest possible $\kappa(n)$, which is a subject of many papers.

For the normalized error criterion, the error of an algorithm ϕ that uses N is defined by

$$e^{\mathrm{nor}}(\phi, N) = \sup_{f \in F_1} \frac{\|S(f) - U(f)\|}{\|Tf\|},$$

and the radius of information is given by

$$r^{\mathrm{nor}}(N) = \inf_{\phi} e^{\mathrm{nor}}(\phi, N).$$

As we shall see, for many linear problems the radius $r^{\mathrm{nor}}(N)$ of information for the normalized error criterion is equal to the radius $r(N)$ of information for the absolute error criterion with $F = \{f \in F_1 : \|Tf\| \leq 1\}$. Indeed, this holds if there exists a homogeneous optimal error algorithm ϕ^* for the absolute error and

$$e(\phi^*, N) = r(N) = \sup_{h \in \ker N} \frac{\|S(h)\|}{\|Th\|},$$

where S, T, and N are linear operators. Although the algorithm $\phi^*(y)$ is defined only for $y = N(f)$ with $\|Tf\| \le 1$, due to its homogeneity, it can be easily extended for all $y \in N(F_1)$. Then the normalized error of ϕ^* is estimated by

$$\frac{\|S(f) - \phi^*(N(f))\|}{\|Tf\|} = \left\| S\left(\frac{f}{\|Tf\|}\right) - \phi^*\left(N\left(\frac{f}{\|Tf\|}\right)\right) \right\| \le r(n).$$

Thus, $r^{\mathrm{nor}}(N) \le r(N)$. Take now arbitrary ϕ and $h \in \ker N$. Then $-h \in \ker N$ and

$$e^{\mathrm{nor}}(\phi, N) \ge \frac{1}{2}\left(\frac{\|S(h) - \phi(0)\|}{\|Th\|} + \frac{\|S(h) + \phi(0)\|}{\|Th\|}\right) \ge \frac{\|S(h)\|}{\|Th\|}.$$

Taking the supremum with respect to $h \in \ker N$, we get $e^{\mathrm{nor}}(\phi, N) \ge r(N)$. Since ϕ is arbitrary, $r^{\mathrm{nor}}(N) \ge r(N)$.

Thus, we have proven that the same algorithm ϕ^* is optimal for both the absolute and normalized error criteria and

$$r^{\mathrm{nor}}(N) = r(N).$$

We now strengthen this result by assuming that the range of the operator T is a Hilbert space and $T(\ker N)$ is closed. In this case, the spline algorithm $\phi^s(y) = S\sigma(y)$ from Section 5.7 minimizes the local errors also for the normalized error criterion. More precisely, the local error of an algorithm ϕ that uses N is now given by

$$e^{\mathrm{nor}}(\phi, N, y) = \sup_{f \in F_1 : N(f) = y} \frac{\|S(f) - \phi(y)\|}{\|Tf\|}.$$

We prove that for the local radius of information, which is, as always, given by

$$r^{\mathrm{nor}}(N, y) = \inf_{\phi} e^{\mathrm{nor}}(\phi, N, y),$$

we have

$$e^{\mathrm{nor}}(\phi^s, N, y) = r^{\mathrm{nor}}(N, y) = \sup_{h \in \ker N} \frac{\|S(h)\|}{\sqrt{\|T\sigma(y)\|^2 + \|Th\|^2}}.$$

Indeed, let $f \in N^{-1}(y) = \{f \in F_1 : N(f) = y\}$. Since $\sigma = \sigma(y)$ is a spline interpolating y, we have $f_1 = 2\sigma - f \in N^{-1}(y)$ and $\|Tf\| = \|Tf_1\| = \sqrt{\|T\sigma\|^2 + \|Th\|^2}$ with $h = \sigma - f \in \ker N$. Thus,

$$e^{\mathrm{nor}}(\phi, N, y) \ge \frac{1}{2}\left(\frac{\|S(f) - \phi(y)\|}{\|Tf\|} + \frac{\|S(f_1) - \phi(y)\|}{\|Tf_1\|}\right) \ge \frac{1}{2}\frac{\|S(f) - S(f_1)\|}{\|Tf\|}$$

$$= \frac{\|S(f) - \phi^s(y)\|}{\|Tf\|} = \frac{\|S(h)\|}{\sqrt{\|T\sigma\|^2 + \|Th\|^2}}.$$

Since the supremum with respect to $f \in N^{-1}(y)$ is the same as the supremum with respect to $h \in \ker N$, we have $e^{\mathrm{nor}}(\phi, N, y) \geq e^{\mathrm{nor}}(\phi^s, N, y)$, as claimed.

Observe that for the global radius and error we have

$$r^{\mathrm{nor}}(N) = e^{\mathrm{nor}}(\phi^s, N) = \sup_{h \in \ker N} \frac{\|S(h)\|}{\|Th\|}.$$

From Theorem 5.7.2 we conclude that

$$r^{\mathrm{nor}}(N) = r(N).$$

We now comment on adaptive information. Let

$$N^{\mathrm{a}}(f) = [L_1(f), L_2(f; y_1), \ldots, L_{n(f)}(f; y_1, \ldots, y_{n(f)-1})].$$

As for nonadaptive information, it is easy to show that

$$r^{\mathrm{nor}}(N^{\mathrm{a}}) \geq \sup_{h \in (N^{\mathrm{a}})^{-1}(0)} \frac{\|S(h)\|}{\|Th\|}.$$

Define nonadaptive information $N^{\mathrm{non}} = [L_1, L_2(\cdot, 0), \ldots, L_{n(0)}(\cdot, 0, \ldots, 0)]$. As before, assume that there exists a homogeneous optimal error algorithm ϕ^* that uses N^{non} such that $e(\phi^*, N^{\mathrm{non}}) = \sup\{\|S(h)\|/\|Th\| : h \in \ker N^{\mathrm{non}}\}$. Then $r^{\mathrm{nor}}(N^{\mathrm{a}}) \geq r^{\mathrm{nor}}(N^{\mathrm{non}})$. Thus, adaption does not help for linear problems.

We now discuss the complexity for the normalized error criterion. If for arbitrary nonadaptive information N there exists a homogeneous optimal error algorithm ϕ^* and $e(\phi^*, N) = \sup\{\|S(h)\|/\|Th\| : h \in \ker N\}$ then the ε-cardinality numbers $m(\varepsilon)$ for both the absolute and normalized error criteria are the same. If the cost of computing $\phi^*(y)$ is negligible with respect to the information cost, then the complexities for both error criteria are essentially the same and equal to $c\,m(\varepsilon)$, c is the cost of one information operation.

We stress that the close relation between the normalized and absolute error criteria holds under the assumption that homogeneous optimal error algorithms exist. If this assumption is violated then these error criteria are not related, as illustrated by the following example.

Consider the linear problem of the last part of Section 5.5. For this problem, the error of any homogeneous algorithm is infinite, see **E 5.5:14**, although the radius of information is finite and can be arbitrarily small. We now show that for the normalized error criterion, $e^{\mathrm{nor}}(\phi, N) = +\infty$ for arbitrary ϕ and N. Indeed, as in Section 5.5, take f_α from F_1 such that $N(f_\alpha) = y$ for all α and $\lim_{\alpha \to \infty} f_\alpha = f_1$. Then

$$\frac{\|S(f)_\alpha - \phi(N(f_\alpha))\|}{\|Tf_\alpha\|} = \frac{\|f_\alpha - M\phi(y)\|_{X_2}}{\|f_\alpha - \langle f_\alpha, f_1 \rangle f_1\|_{X_1}} \to +\infty$$

since the numerator goes to $\|f_1 - M\phi(y)\|_{X_2} \neq 0$ and the denominator goes to zero as α tends to $+\infty$. Thus, $r^{\mathrm{nor}}(N) = +\infty$, which means that it is impossible to solve this particular linear problem with the normalized error criterion.

Further generalizations may be found in **NR 6.2:1**.

Notes and Remarks

NR 6.2:1 (IUC, Appendix E) The normalized error is an example of the error criterion defined as follows. Let $\rho : \mathbf{R}_+ \to \mathbf{R}_+$ be a given function. Define the distance between $S(f)$ and $U(f) = \phi(N(f))$ by

$$\|S(f) - U(f)\| \rho(\|Tf\|).$$

Thus, for $\rho(x) = 1/x$ we obtain the normalized error. Formally speaking, this corresponds to the generalized solution operator W given by

$$W(f, \varepsilon) = \{g \in G : \|S(f) - g\| \rho(\|Tf\|) \leq \varepsilon\}.$$

For linear S, N, and T, the diameter of information, see **NR 2:4**, is equal to

$$d(N; \rho) = \sup \left\{ \|S(f_1 - f_2)\| \min\{\rho(\|Tf_1\|), \rho(\|Tf_2\|)\} : f_1, f_2 \in F_1, N(f_1 - f_2) = 0 \right\}.$$

Furthermore, if $\ker T \cap \ker N \subset \ker S$ then

$$d(N; \rho) = d(N) \sup_{x > 0} x \, \rho(x),$$

with the convention that $0 \cdot \infty = 0$. Here $d(N)$ is the diameter of information for the absolute error with $F = \{f \in F_1 : \|Tf\| \leq 1\}$. If $\ker T \cap \ker N \not\subset \ker S$ then

$$d(N; \rho) = \begin{cases} +\infty & \text{if } \rho(0) \neq 0 \text{ or } (\rho \not\equiv 0 \text{ and } T \not\equiv 0), \\ 0 & \text{otherwise.} \end{cases}$$

As indicated in **NR 2:4**, the radius $r(N; \rho)$ of information is always at least $d(N; \rho)/2$. If $\sup_{x \geq 0} \rho(x) < +\infty$ then $r(N; \rho) \leq d(N; \rho)$.

From these relations one can also conclude that the ε-complexity for the error criterion ρ corresponds to the $(\varepsilon / \sup_{x > 0} x\rho(x))$- complexity for the absolute error with $\|Tf\| \leq 1$. Corresponding relations hold for optimal information and algorithms.

NR 6.2:2 (Micchelli [84]) The error criterion from **NR 6.2:1** can be generalized as follows. Let $\Delta : \mathbf{R}_+ \times \mathbf{R}_+ \to \mathbf{R}_+$. Assume that for every $t \in \mathbf{R}_+$, $\Delta(\cdot, t)$ is nondecreasing and convex, and $\Delta(0, t) = 0$. Consider the error criterion for which the distance between $S(f)$ and $U(f) = \phi(N(f))$ is given by

$$\Delta\left(\|S(f) - U(f)\|, \|Tf\|\right).$$

For $\Delta(s, t) = s\rho(t)$ we obtain the error criteria of **NR 6.2:1**. For $\Delta(s, t) = s/t$ we obtain the normalized error. The error criterion Δ corresponds formally to the generalized solution operator W given by

$$W(f; \varepsilon) = \{g \in G : \Delta(\|S(f) - U(f)\|, \|Tf\|) \le \varepsilon\}.$$

For linear S, N, and T whose range X is Hilbert and $T(\ker N)$ is closed, the spline algorithm $\phi^s(y) = S\sigma(y)$ is central and its error is equal to $\sup_{h \in \ker N} \Delta(\|S(h)\|, \|Th\|)$.

Exercises

E 6.2:1 Prove that for a linear problem, $r^{\mathrm{nor}}(N)$ is finite if there exists a homogeneous algorithm whose error under the absolute error criterion is finite.

E 6.2:2 Analyze the error criterion $\|S(f) - U(f)\|/(\|Tf\| + \eta)$. Hint: See **NR 6.2:1**. Compute the radius of information for the linear problem of the last part of Section 6.2 for which $r^{\mathrm{nor}}(N) = \infty$. Explain why the assumption $\eta > 0$ is essential.

6.3. Convex and Symmetric Error

In this section we study a general error criterion, which is defined through a functional $\mathrm{ER} : G \to \mathbb{R}_+$. That is, for $f \in F$ the distance between $S(f)$ and $U(f) = \phi(N(f))$ is given by

$$\mathrm{ER}\left(S(f) - U(f)\right).$$

The error of U is then defined by

$$e(U) = \sup_{f \in F} \mathrm{ER}\left(S(f) - U(f)\right).$$

We assume that ER is convex and symmetric, ie., $\mathrm{ER}\left(tg_1 + (1-t)g_2\right) \le t\,\mathrm{ER}(g_1) + (1-t)\,\mathrm{ER}(g_2)$ and $\mathrm{ER}(g_1) = \mathrm{ER}(-g_1)$ for $t \in [0, 1]$ and $g_1, g_2 \in G$. Examples of such ER include $\mathrm{ER}(g) = \|g\|^p$ for $p \ge 1$. For $p = 1$ we get the absolute error. Observe that the definition of ER requires G to be a linear space, but not necessarily normed.

Recall that for the absolute error criterion, the algorithm $\phi^c(y) = m(y)$ is central whenever the set $S(N^{-1}(y) \cap F)$ is symmetric with respect to $m(y)$, see Section 3.2. It is easy to see that the algorithm ϕ^c remains central for the convex and symmetric ER error criterion. Indeed, $g \in A = S(N^{-1}(y) \cap F)$ implies that $g_1 = 2m - g \in A$, where $m = m(y)$. For any algorithm

ϕ we have $\mathrm{ER}\,(g - \phi(y)) \leq e(\phi, N, y) = \sup_{h \in A} \mathrm{ER}\,(S(h) - \phi(y))$ and $\mathrm{ER}\,(g_1 - \phi(y)) \leq e(\phi, N, y)$. Note that

$$g - \phi^c(y) = \tfrac{1}{2}(g - \phi(y)) + \tfrac{1}{2}(\phi(y) - g_1),$$

and convexity and symmetry of ER yield

$$\mathrm{ER}\,(g - \phi^c(y)) \leq \tfrac{1}{2}\mathrm{ER}\,(g - \phi(y)) + \tfrac{1}{2}\mathrm{ER}\,(g_1 - \phi(y)) \leq e(\phi, N, y).$$

Thus, ϕ^c is central, as claimed. We stress that centrality of ϕ^c holds under the assumption that the set $\overline{S(N^{-1}(y) \cap F)}$ is symmetric, which sometimes happens even for nonlinear S or N.

On the other hand, if S is linear, N nonadaptive linear, and F balanced and convex, and the set $N^{-1}(y) \cap F$ is symmetric with respect to $\eta(y)$, then $m(y) = S\eta(y)$ and the radius of information $r^{\mathrm{ER}}(N)$ is bounded by

$$\sup_{h \in F \cap \ker N} \mathrm{ER}(S(h)) \leq r^{\mathrm{ER}}(N) \leq \sup_{h \in F \cap \ker N} \mathrm{ER}(2S(h)).$$

If $F = \{f : \|Tf\| \leq 1\}$ with a linear T whose range is a Hilbert space and $T(\ker N)$ is closed, then the central algorithm ϕ^c is equal to the spline algorithm $\phi^s(y) = S\sigma(y)$ and

$$r^{\mathrm{ER}}(N) = \sup_{h \in F \cap \ker N} \mathrm{ER}(S(h)).$$

Assume now that G is equipped with a norm and that $\mathrm{ER}(g) = H(\|g\|)$ with $H : \mathbb{R}_+ \to \mathbb{R}_+$ convex and nondecreasing. Then

$$r^{\mathrm{ER}}(N) = H\big(r(N)\big).$$

This implies that the complexity for the error functional $\mathrm{ER}(g) = H(\|g\|)$ is related to the complexity for the absolute error by

$$\mathrm{comp}^{\mathrm{ER}}(\varepsilon) = \mathrm{comp}\,\big(H^{-1}(\varepsilon)\big).$$

The information and algorithm which are $H^{-1}(\varepsilon)$-complexity optimal for the absolute error are also ε-complexity optimal for the error functional $\mathrm{ER}(g) = H(\|g\|)$.

Further generalizations may be found in **NR 6.3:1**.

REMARK 6.3.1 Consider the error functional $\mathrm{ER} : G \to \mathbb{R}$ defined by

$$\mathrm{ER}(g) = \log_2 \frac{1}{\|g\|}.$$

Then ER $(S(f) - U(f))$ is the number of significant bits of $S(f)$ recovered by $U(f)$. We call ER the *precision* error functional. Note that ER is a symmetric function which is neither convex nor concave. Also the values of ER(g) take different signs.

For given information N, let $U(f) = \phi(N(f))$ for some algorithm ϕ. Let

$$e^{\text{pre}}(\phi, N) = \inf_{f \in F} \text{ER}\left(S(f) - \phi(N(f))\right)$$

be the number of significant bits of $S(f)$ recovered by $\phi(N(f))$ for a worst f. Let $\text{comp}^{\text{pre}}(k)$ denote the complexity under the precision error criterion of computing k bits of the solution elements $S(f)$,

$$\text{comp}^{\text{pre}}(k) = \inf\left\{ \text{cost}(\phi, N) : \phi, N \text{ such that } e^{\text{pre}}(\phi, N) \geq k\right\}.$$

Since $e^{\text{pre}}(\phi, N) \geq k$ iff $\sup_{f \in F} \|S(f) - \phi(N(f))\| \leq 2^{-k}$, we immediately conclude that $\text{comp}^{\text{pre}}(k)$ is equal to the complexity under the absolute error criterion with $\varepsilon = 2^{-k}$,

$$\text{comp}^{\text{pre}}(k) = \text{comp}\left(2^{-k}\right).$$

A more interesting situation occurs when the precision error criterion is considered in the average case setting. This is done in Section 6.4 of Chapter 6.

Notes and Remarks

NR 6.3:1 Consider the error functional ER : $G \times \mathbb{R}_+ \to \mathbb{R}_+$ such that ER$(\cdot, x)$ is convex and symmetric for all $x \in \mathbb{R}_+$. This error criterion generalizes the previous ones. Indeed, if ER does not depend on x, then it coincides with the error functional of Section 6.3. If ER$(g, x) = \Delta(\|g\|, x)$ then we get the error functional of **NR 6.2:2**.

The error criterion ER corresponds formally to the generalized solution operator W given by

$$W(f, \varepsilon) = \{g \in G : \text{ER}(S(f) - U(f), \|Tf\|) \leq \varepsilon\}.$$

Once more, the spline algorithm $\phi^s(y) = S\sigma(y)$ is a central algorithm for linear S, N, and T with a Hilbert range and closed $T(\ker N)$. Indeed, as in Section 6.2, take $f \in N^{-1}(y)$. Then $f_1 = 2\sigma - f \in N^{-1}(y)$, $\sigma = \sigma(y)$, and $\|Tf\| = \|Tf_1\|$. For any algorithm ϕ we have

$$S(f) - \phi^s(y) = \tfrac{1}{2}(S(f) - \phi(y)) + \tfrac{1}{2}(\phi(y) - S(f_1)).$$

Convexity and symmetry of ER yield

$$\text{ER}\left(S(f) - \phi^s(y), \|Tf\|\right) \leq \tfrac{1}{2}\text{ER}\left(S(f) - \phi(y), \|Tf\|\right) + \tfrac{1}{2}\text{ER}\left(S(f_1) - \phi(y), \|Tf_1\|\right)$$
$$\leq e^{\text{ER}}(\phi, N, y).$$

Taking the supremum with respect to $f \in N^{-1}(y)$, we conclude that the spline algorithm is central. Its local error is equal to the local radius of information,

$$r^{\mathrm{ER}}(N, y) = \sup_{h \in \ker N} \mathrm{ER}\left(S(h), \sqrt{\|T\sigma(y)\|^2 + \|Th\|^2}\right).$$

Exercises

E 6.3:1 Analyze the error criterion with $\mathrm{ER}(g) = \max\{0, \log_2(1/\|g\|)\}$.

Chapter 5

Worst Case Setting: Applications

1. Introduction

In this chapter we apply the results of Chapter 4 to twelve problems. The first six are the following linear problems: integration, function approximation, computer vision, linear partial differential equations, integral equations, and ill-posed problems. We exhibit tight complexity bounds and (almost) optimal information and algorithms.

The next six problems are nonlinear and include optimization, large linear systems, eigenvalues and eigenvectors, ordinary differential equations, nonlinear equations, and topological degree. Since there is no general theory for nonlinear problems, each of these nonlinear problems is analyzed using a different proof technique which utilizes the specific properties of that nonlinear problem.

The complexity analysis of each problem is usually based on the work of many people, as cited in the various sections as well as in Notes and Remarks. We report many results needed for our complexity analysis without proofs. The reader interested in the detailed analysis should consult the references cited.

2. Integration

In this section we study the integration problem. As indicated in Chapter 4, research on optimal algorithms for integration was initiated by Sard [49] and Nikolskij [50]. There is a huge literature on this subject. The reader may find in GTOA a partial list of over 100 papers written before 1979. Also the third edition of the book of Nikolskij [79], with a supplement written by Kornejčuk, contains a long list of relevant papers. The reader may consult the papers of Bojanov [86], Novak [87a], and Žensykbaev [81], where the integration problem is thoroughly studied and long lists of relevant papers may be found.

Here we confine ourselves to the integration problem for three classes of scalar smooth functions, for other classes see **NR 2:1** and **2:2**. The first class consists of smooth periodic functions, the second class consists of smooth nonperiodic functions, and the third one of functions belonging to a reproducing kernel Hilbert space. Here we analyze the worst case setting, whereas the average case and probabilistic settings are analyzed in Section 2 of Chapter 7 and Section 7 of Chapter 8, respectively.

Notes and Remarks

NR 2:1 We indicate some of the work on optimal algorithms for multivariate integration. A partial list includes Babenko [76], Bakhvalov [59, 61, 64, 70, 72], Besov [80, 81], Keast [73], Kornejčuk [68], Korobov [63], Korotkov [77], Novak [83, 87a], Polovinkin [74], Sharygin [63, 77], Smolyak [60], Sobol [69], Sobolev [65], and Sukharev [79a, 88]. A typical result is that the ε-complexity is proportional to $\varepsilon^{-d/r}$, where d is the number of variables of the integrand functions and r measures their smoothness. Observe that the ε-complexity is exponential in the dimension d. If d is large relative to r then for even modest ε, the ε-complexity is huge. The problem of finding an ε-approximation then becomes intractable.

To illustrate this, consider the integration problem $S(f) = \int_{[0,1]^d} f(t)\,dt$ for two classes

$$C_d^{r,\alpha} = \{f : [0,1]^d \to \mathbf{R} : |D^{(i)}f(x) - D^{(i)}f(y)| \le \|x - y\|_\infty^\alpha$$
$$\text{for all partial derivatives } D^{(i)}, |i| \le r\}$$

and

$$W_p^{r,d} = \{f : [0,1]^d \to \mathbf{R} : \sum_{|i|=r} \|f^{(i)}\|_p \le 1\}.$$

Here $r \ge 1$, $\alpha \in (0,1]$, $p \in [1, +\infty]$, $i = [i_1, \ldots, i_d]$ is a multiindex with $|i| = \sum_{j=1}^d i_j$, and $f^{(i)}$ denotes the operator derivative in $\mathcal{L}_p$.

If Λ consists of function evaluations, the nth minimal radii are: $r(n) = \Theta(n^{-(r+\alpha)/d})$ for the class $C_d^{r,\alpha}$, see Bakhvalov [59], and $r(n) = \Theta(n^{-r/d})$ for the class $W_p^{r,d}$ if $r\,p > d$ or $p = 1$ and $r = d$, see Sobolev [65] for $p = 2$, Polovinkin [74] for $1 < p < +\infty$, and Novak [87a] for general p. This implies that the ε-complexity is proportional to $c\varepsilon^{-d/(r+\alpha)}$ for the class $C_d^{r,\alpha}$, and to $c\varepsilon^{-d/r}$ for the class $W_p^{r,d}$, where c is the cost of one function evaluation. As claimed, the ε-complexity is exponential in d.

NR 2:2 We briefly discuss the integration problem $S(f) = \int_{-1}^{+1} f(x)\,dx$ for analytic functions. Papers dealing with optimal algorithms for this problem include Andersson

[80], Andersson and Bojanov [84], Bakhvalov [67], Barnhill [67, 68], Barnhill and Wixom [67, 68], Barrar, Loeb, and Werner [74], Bojanov [73, 74, 86], Chawla [68], Chawla and Jain [68a, 68b], Chawla and Kaul [73], Dyn, Micchelli, and Rivlin [86], Gautschi and Varga [83], Haber [71], Kowalski, Werschulz, and Woźniakowski [85], Larkin [70], Loeb [74], Loeb and Werner [74], Micchelli and Rivlin [85], Newman [79], Osipenko [76], Paulik [77], Pinkus [75], Schwing, Sikorski, and Stenger [84], Sikorski [82b], Sikorski and Stenger [84], Stenger [66, 78], Stetter [69], Werschulz [79a, 80, 81a], and Wilf [64].

We illustrate the results for two classes. Consider first the Hardy space H^p of analytic functions in the unit disc such that $\|f\|_p \leq 1$, where $1 < p < +\infty$. The information consists of function and derivative evaluations. The behavior of the nth minimal radius $r(n)$ of information has been studied in a number of papers. In particular, Bojanov [73] showed that $r(n)$ is of order $\exp\left(-\alpha\sqrt{n}\right)$ for a positive α. Andersson [80] improved this bound by showing that $\alpha_1 \leq r(n)n^{-1/(2p')}\exp\left(\pi\sqrt{n/p'}\right) \leq \alpha_2\sqrt{np'}$, where $1/p + 1/p' = 1$, and α_1, α_2 are positive. Finally, Andersson and Bojanov [84] proved that

$$r(n) = \Theta\left(n^{1/(2p')}\exp\left(-\pi\sqrt{n/p'}\right)\right).$$

From the form of $r(n)$, one can easily conclude that the ε-complexity is given by

$$\text{comp}(\varepsilon) = (c+a)\,\frac{p'}{\pi^2}\,\ln^2\frac{1}{\varepsilon}\,(1+o(1)) \quad \text{as } \varepsilon \to 0,$$

where c is the cost of one function evaluation and $a \in [1,2]$. Fortran subroutines of almost optimal algorithms for integration of analytic functions from the class H^p may be found in Schwing, Sikorski, and Stenger [84], Sikorski and Stenger [84], and their theoretical properties in Sikorski [82b].

Consider now the class of functions $f : [-1, +1] \to \mathbb{R}$ which have an analytic extension in an open disc $D_r = \{z \in C : |z| < r\}$ whose modulus is bounded by unity on $\overline{D_r}$. Here we assume that $r \geq 1$. The ε-complexity is proportional to $\ln^2(1/\varepsilon)$ for $r = 1$ and to $\ln(1/\varepsilon)$ for $r > 1$. On the other hand, Gauss quadrature finds an ε-approximation with cost proportional to $\varepsilon^{-1/2}$ for $r = 1$ and proportional to $\ln(1/\varepsilon)$ for $r > 1$. Thus, for $r = 1$ Gauss quadrature is exponentially more expensive than the optimal algorithm, see Kowalski, Werschulz, and Woźniakowski[85]. The reader is also referred to Dyn, Micchelli, and Rivlin [86], where the weighted integration problem in H^∞ is studied.

2.1. Smooth Periodic Functions

In this section we consider integration of (2π)-periodic functions $f : \mathbb{R} \to \mathbb{R}$ whose $(r-1)$st derivative is absolutely continuous, and rth derivative belongs to the space $\mathcal{L}_p(0, 2\pi)$, $r \geq 1$ and $p \in [1, +\infty]$. Let $F_1 = \widetilde{W}_p^r(0, 2\pi)$ denote the space of such functions. Let $X = \mathcal{L}_p(0, 2\pi)$ and $Tf = f^{(r)}$. Thus, $\|Tf\|_p = (\int_0^{2\pi} |f^{(r)}(t)|^p dt)^{1/p}$.

We approximate $S(f) = \int_0^{2\pi} f(t)\, dt$ for f from

$$F = \{f \in F_1 : \|Tf\|_p \leq q\}, \quad \text{where } q > 0.$$

Assume that function values and their derivatives up to order $r - 1$ can be computed. That is, Λ consists of linear functionals of the form $L(f) = f^{(j)}(x)$ for some $x \in [0, 2\pi]$ and $j \in [0, r-1]$.

This problem is linear. Therefore adaption does not help, and there exists a linear optimal error algorithm for arbitrary nonadaptive information.

Nonadaptive information N of cardinality $n, n \geq 1$, has now the form

$$N(f) = \left[f^{(j_1)}(t_1), f^{(j_2)}(t_2), \ldots, f^{(j_n)}(t_n) \right]$$

for some $t_i \in [0, 2\pi]$, and $j_i \in [0, r-1]$. That is, we have Birkhoff information on f. The problem of nth optimal nonadaptive information relies on finding t_i and j_i for which the radius of information N is minimized.

This problem has been completely solved and the nth optimal nonadaptive information is of the form

$$N_n^*(f) = \left[f(0), f\left(\frac{2\pi}{n} \right), \ldots, f\left(\frac{2\pi}{n}(n-1) \right) \right].$$

Optimality of N_n^* in the class of function evaluations was proved by Motornyj [73, 74] for $p = +\infty$ and arbitrary r and for $p = 1$ with even r, by Žensykbaev [76, 77a] for $p \in (1, +\infty)$ and arbitrary r, and by Ligun [76] for $p = 1$ and odd r. Optimality of N_n^* was extended to the class Λ of function and derivative evaluations by Ligun [78] for $p = 1$ and by Žensykbaev [82] for arbitrary p.

For $p > 1$, nth optimal information is unique up to an arbitrary shift, i.e., the information $N_n(f) = \left[f(a), f((2\pi/n) + a), \ldots, f((2\pi/n)(n-1) + a) \right]$ is also nth optimal, where a is an arbitrary real number.

It is also known that the rectangle formula (or trapezoid formula),

$$\phi^*\left(N_n^*(f) \right) = \frac{2\pi}{n} \sum_{i=1}^{n} f\left(\frac{2\pi}{n}(i-1) \right),$$

is a linear optimal error algorithm. From Corollary 5.7.1 of Chapter 4 it follows that ϕ^* is also the spline algorithm for $p = 2$, see also **NR 2.1:1**. The error of (ϕ^*, N_n^*) is given by

$$r(n, \Lambda) = r(N_n^*) = e(\phi^*, N_n^*) = \frac{2q}{n^r} \| \overline{D}_r \|_{p'}.$$

Here

$$\overline{D}_r(t) = \gamma_{r,p} + \sum_{k=1}^{\infty} \frac{\cos(kt - \pi r/2)}{k^r}.$$

with the constant $\gamma_{r,p}$ chosen to minimize the norm $\|\overline{D}_r\|_{p'}$, where $1/p' + 1/p = 1$. For some values of p, $\|\overline{D}_r\|_{p'}$ is known.

For $p = 2$ we have

$$\|\overline{D}_r\|_2 = \sqrt{\pi \, \zeta(2r)},$$

where ζ is Riemann's zeta function. Hence $\zeta(2r) = \sum_{k=1}^{\infty} k^{-2r}, 1 \leq \zeta(2r) \leq 1 + 1/(2r - 1)$, and $\zeta(2r) = 2^{2r-1}\pi^{2r}|B_{2r}|/(2r)!$, where B_{2r} are Bernoulli numbers, $B_2 = 1/6$, $B_4 = -1/30$, $B_6 = 1/42$, $B_8 = -1/30, B_{10} = 5/66,\ldots$, see e.g., Gradshteyn and Ryzhik [80, pp. 1074–1080].

For $p = +\infty$ we have

$$\|\overline{D}_r\|_1 = \pi \, K_r, \quad \text{where} \quad K_r = \frac{4}{\pi} \sum_{k=0}^{\infty} \frac{(-1)^{k(r+1)}}{(2k+1)^{r+1}}$$

is the Favard constant. We have $K_0 = 1$, $K_1 = \pi/2$, $K_2 = \pi^2/8$, $K_3 = \pi^3/24$, and $1 = K_0 < K_2 < \cdots < 4/\pi < \cdots < K_3 < K_1 = \pi/2$.

For $p = 1$ and even r we have

$$\|\overline{D}_r\|_\infty = \frac{\pi}{4} \, K_{r-1}.$$

We now turn to the ε-cardinality number. From the formula for $r(n, \Lambda)$ we have

$$m(\varepsilon) = \min\left\{n : r(n, \Lambda) \leq \varepsilon\right\} = \left\lceil \left(\frac{2q\|\overline{D}_r\|_{p'}}{\varepsilon}\right)^{1/r} \right\rceil.$$

The ε-complexity is bounded by $c\,m(\varepsilon) \leq \text{comp}(\varepsilon) \leq (c+1)\,m(\varepsilon)$. Observe that the upper bound is of the form $(c+1)\,m(\varepsilon)$ instead of the typical bound $(c+2)\,m(\varepsilon) - 1$. This is due to the fact that the rectangle formula requires only $n = m(\varepsilon)$ arithmetic operations. As in Section 5.8 of Chapter 4, one can slightly improve the lower bound by noticing that at least $m(\varepsilon) - 1$ arithmetic operations have to be performed. Thus,

$$\text{comp}(\varepsilon) = (c+1)\,m(\varepsilon) + a \quad \text{with } a = -1 \text{ or } a = 0.$$

For $c \gg 1$, we have $\text{comp}(\varepsilon) \simeq c\,m(\varepsilon)$ and the information N_n^* consisting of $n = m(\varepsilon)$ function values at equally spaced points and the rectangle formula ϕ_n^* are almost optimal.

For $p = 2$, the formulas for $r(n, \Lambda)$ and $m(\varepsilon)$ simplify to

$$r(n, \Lambda) = q(2\pi)^{r+1/2}\sqrt{\frac{|B_{2r}|}{(2r)!}}\frac{1}{n^r} \quad \text{and} \quad m(\varepsilon) = \left\lceil 2\pi\left(\frac{q}{\varepsilon}\sqrt{\frac{2\pi|B_{2r}|}{(2r)!}}\right)^{1/r} \right\rceil.$$

Numerical stability of (ϕ_n^*, N_n^*) in t digit floating point binary arithmetic is discussed in **NR 2.1:2**. Under natural assumptions, it is shown that roundoff errors do not destroy optimality properties of (ϕ_n^*, N_n^*) whenever ε is larger than 2^{-t}.

Notes and Remarks

NR 2.1:1 For $p = 2$, it is easy to derive the explicit form of the spline algorithm ϕ^s that uses information N_n^*. Indeed, as in Section 5.5 of Chapter 4, let σ_i be a spline interpolating the ith unit vector $e_i = [0, \ldots, 1, 0, \ldots, 0] \in \mathbb{R}^n$. Observe that σ_i is now the periodic natural spline of degree $2r - 1$ whose rth derivative is orthogonal to $T(\ker N_n^*)$, i.e., $\langle \sigma_i^{(r)}, h^{(r)} \rangle_{\mathcal{L}_2} = 0$ for all $h \in \widetilde{W_2^r}$ with $h(t_i) = 0$, where $t_i = 2\pi(i-1)/n$, $i = 1, 2, \ldots, n$. Periodicity of σ_i and constant distance between two consecutive t_j's imply that

$$\sigma_i(t) = \sigma_1(t - t_i).$$

The spline algorithm ϕ^s is given by $\phi^s(y) = \sum_{i=1}^n f(t_i) g_i$, where $g_i = \int_0^{2\pi} \sigma_i(t)\,dt = \int_0^{2\pi} \sigma_1(t - t_i)\,dt = \int_0^{2\pi} \sigma_1(t)\,dt = g_1$. Thus, the weights g_i of the spline algorithm are all equal. Since $f \equiv 1 \in \ker T \cap \widetilde{W_2^r}$, see **E 5.5:11** of Chapter 4, we get $\int_0^1 1\,dt = 2\pi = \phi^s(1, \ldots, 1) = ng_1$. Hence $g_1 = 2\pi/n$ and the spline algorithm

$$\phi^s(N_n^*(f)) = \frac{2\pi}{n} \sum_{i=1}^n f\left(\frac{2\pi}{n}(i-1)\right)$$

coincides with the rectangle formula. In particular, this means that the rectangle formula is a central algorithm whose local error at y is equal to $\sqrt{q^2 - \|\sigma^{(r)}(y)\|_2^2}\, r(N_n^*)$, where $\sigma(y) = \sum_{i=1}^n y_i\, \sigma_1(t - t_i)$ is the periodic natural spline of degree $2r - 1$ which interpolates the data y, see Theorem 5.7.2 of Chapter 4.

NR 2.1:2 Consider the rectangle formula $u = \phi_n^*(N_n^*(f)) = h \sum_{i=1}^n f(t_i)$, where $h = 2\pi/n$, $t_i = h(i-1)$, and $n = m(\varepsilon) = \lceil (2q\|\overline{D_r}\|_{p'}/\varepsilon)^{1/r} \rceil = \Theta((1/\varepsilon)^{1/r})$. Suppose that the rectangle formula is implemented in t digit floating point binary arithmetic fl, see Wilkinson [63]. Let $fl(f(t_i))$ denote the computed values of $f(t_i)$ in fl. We assume that they are computed with high relative precision,

$$fl(f(t_i)) = f(t_i)(1 + \delta f_i), \quad |\delta f_i| \le A_1 2^{-t},$$

for some constant $A_1 = A_1(f)$. To compute u, apply the standard algorithm for summing n numbers

```
s_0 := 0;
for i := 1 step 1 until n do
s_i := s_{i-1} + f(t_i);
u := h * s_n
```

Then the computed $\overline{u} = fl(u)$ is given by

$$\overline{u} = \frac{2\pi}{n} \sum_{i=1}^n f(t_i)(1 + \delta f_i)(1 + \varepsilon_i),$$

where $|\varepsilon_i| \leq 1.06 \, (n + 2 - i) \, 2^{-t}$ whenever $(n+1)2^{-t} \leq 0.1$, see Wilkinson [63]. We have

$$|\bar{u} - u| \leq A_2 \, n \, 2^{-t} \int_0^{2\pi} |f(t)| \, dt,$$

where $A_2 = (1.06 + A_1/n) \, (1 + o(1))$ as $t \to +\infty$. Comparing the computed value $\bar{u}$ to the exact value $S(f)$ we get

$$|\bar{u} - S(f)| \leq |u - S(f)| + |\bar{u} - u| \leq \varepsilon + A_2 \, n \, 2^{-t} \int_0^{2\pi} |f(t)| \, dt \leq \varepsilon + A_3 \, 2^{-t} \, \varepsilon^{-1/r},$$

where $A_3 = A_2 \, (2q\|\overline{D}_r\|_{p'})^{1/r} \int_0^{2\pi} |f(t)| \, dt \, (1 + o(1))$ as $\varepsilon \to 0$.

The error $|\bar{u} - S(f)|$ is roughly at most ε if ε is essentially larger than $(A_3 2^{-t})^{r/(r+1)}$. This often holds in practice, since $2^{-tr/(r+1)}$ is very small. Indeed, if $t = 48$ then even for $r = 1$ we have $2^{-tr/(r+1)} = 2^{-24} < 10^{-7}$.

Furthermore, there exist summation algorithms for computing u for which a better bound on $|\bar{u} - u|$ is available. Let

$$|\bar{u} - u| \leq A_2 \, h(n) \, 2^{-t} \int_0^{2\pi} |f(t)| \, dt.$$

Then for the "log-in" algorithm we have $h(n) = \log_2 n$, for the Gill-Møller algorithm we have $h(n) = 3 + n^2 \, 2^{-t}$, and for the repetitive Gill-Møller algorithm we have $h(n) = 2.23 \, k$, where k is an integer for which $n^{2/k} \, 2^{-t} \leq 0.1$ and $2.1 \, k \, 2^{-t} \leq 0.1$. The reader may find these estimates in Møller [65], Kiełbasiński [73], and Jankowski, Smoktunowicz, and Woźniakowski [83].

Suppose now that the Gill-Møller algorithm is used for computing the value of u. Then

$$\bar{u} - S(f) = O(\varepsilon + 2^{-t} + \varepsilon^{-2/r} \, 2^{-2t}).$$

The error $|\bar{u} - S(f)|$ is roughly at most ε if ε is essentially larger than $2^{-2t/(1+2/r)}$ and 2^{-t}. For $t = 48$ and $r = 1$, $\max\left\{2^{-2t/(1+2/r)}, 2^{-t}\right\} = 2^{-32} < 10^{-9}$.

A more detailed roundoff error analysis for the integration problem may be found in Jankowski and Woźniakowski [85].

Exercises

E 2.1:1 For the integration problem of Section 2.1 consider the information $N(f) = [f(t_1 + a), f(t_2 + a), \ldots, f(t_n + a)]$ for $t_i, a \in \mathbb{R}$. Show that the radius of such information does not depend on a.

E 2.1:2 Let F_1 be a linear space of periodic functions. Consider $F = \{f \in F_1 : \|Tf\| \leq 1\}$, where $T : F_1 \to X$ is linear and X is a Hilbert space. Let $N(f) = [f(t_1), f(t_2), \ldots, f(t_n)]$ with $t_{i+1} - t_i \equiv \text{const}$. Assume that $f \equiv 1 \in \ker T$, $g \in F$ implies that $g(\cdot - a) \in F$ for arbitrary a, and $T(\ker N)$ is closed. Prove that the rectangle formula for the information N is an optimal error algorithm.

2.2. Smooth Nonperiodic Functions

In this section we consider integration of nonperiodic functions from the class $F_1 = W_p^r = W_p^r(0, 1)$. This class consists of functions $f : [0, 1] \to \mathbb{R}$ for which $f^{(r-1)}$ is absolutely continuous and $f^{(r)}$ belongs to $\mathcal{L}_p(0, 1)$, $r \geq 1$ and $p \in [1, +\infty]$. Let $X = \mathcal{L}_p(0, 1)$ and $Tf = f^{(r)}$ with norm $\|Tf\|_p = \left(\int_0^1 |f(t)|^p \, dt \right)^{1/p}$.

We approximate $S(f) = \int_0^1 f(t) \, dt$ for f from

$$F = \{ f \in F_1 : \|Tf\|_p \leq q \}, \quad \text{where } q > 0.$$

As in Section 2.1, let Λ consist of linear functionals of the form $L(f) = f^{(j)}(x)$ for some $x \in [0, 1]$ and $j \in [0, r-1]$.

Since this is a linear problem, adaption does not help and there exists a linear optimal error algorithm for any nonadaptive information.

For nonadaptive Birkhoff information, $N(f) = [f^{(j_1)}(t_1), \ldots, f^{(j_n)}(t_n)]$, $n \geq r$, consider a linear algorithm $\phi(N(f)) = \sum_{i=1}^n g_i f^{(j_i)}(t_i)$, where $g_i \in G = \mathbb{R}$. Then Peano's kernel theorem yields

$$\int_0^1 f(t) dt - \phi(N(f)) = \int_0^1 f^{(r)}(t) \, G_r(t) \, dt,$$

where G_r is a monospline (up to a factor $(-1)^r/r!$) of the form,

$$G_r(t) = \frac{(1-t)^r}{r!} - \sum_{i=1}^n g_i \frac{(t_i - t)_+^{r-1-j_i}}{(r-1-j_i)!}.$$

The error of the algorithm ϕ is given by

$$e(\phi, N) = q \, \|G_r\|_{p'}, \quad 1/p' + 1/p = 1.$$

The radius of information is equal to the error of an optimal linear algorithm and therefore

$$r(N) = q \inf_{g_i \in \mathbb{R}} \left\| \frac{(1-\cdot)^r}{r!} - \sum_{i=1}^n g_i \frac{(t_i - \cdot)_+^{r-1-j_i}}{(r-1-j_i)!} \right\|_{p'}.$$

Thus, the radius of information N corresponds to the minimal norm among all monosplines G_r with fixed points t_i and indices j_i.

For nth optimal information, points t_i and indices j_i are chosen to minimize $r(N)$. Therefore

$$r(n, \Lambda) = q \inf \left\{ \left\| \frac{(1 - \cdot)^r}{r!} - \sum_{i=1}^{n} g_i \frac{(t_i - \cdot)_+^{r-1-j_i}}{(r-1-j_i)!} \right\|_{p'} : \right.$$

$$\left. g_i \in \mathbb{R}, t_i \in [0, 1], j_i \le r - 1 \right\}. \quad (1)$$

Thus, the nth minimal radius corresponds to the minimal norm of the monospline G_r for optimally chosen points t_i and indices j_i.

Žensykbaev [82] proved that nth optimal information consists of n function values, i.e., $j_i \equiv 0$. Thus, as for the periodic case, function values supply more information than derivatives. The existence of nth optimal information was proved by Bojanov [77, 78]. Its uniqueness for $p > 1$ was proved by Žensykbaev [77b, 78]. The explicit form of points t_i^* and weights g_i^* which form the nth optimal information $N_n^*(f) = [f(t_1^*), f(t_2^*), \ldots, f(t_n^*)]$ and the linear optimal error algorithm $\phi_n^*(N_n^*(f)) = \sum_{i=1}^{n} g_i^* f(t_i^*)$ is not known for $r > 3$.

Žensykbaev [77b, 78] showed that the optimal t_i^* and g_i^* satisfy the following system of nonlinear equations

$$\int_0^1 |G_r(t)|^{p'-1}(t_j^* - t)_+^{r-1} \operatorname{sign}(G_r(t)) \, dt + \sum_{k=0}^{r-1} (t_j^*)^k \lambda_k = 0$$

$$g_j^* \int_0^1 |G_r(t)|^{p'-1}(t_j^* - t)_+^{r-2} \operatorname{sign}(G_r(t)) \, dt + \sum_{k=1}^{r-1} \frac{k}{r-1} (t_j^*)^{k-1} \lambda_k = 0$$

for $j = 1, 2, \ldots, n$, and

$$\sum_{k=1}^{n} (t_k^*)^i g_k^* = \frac{1}{i+1}$$

for $i = 0, 1, \ldots, r - 1$ with the smallest possible g_1^* (or equivalently with the smallest possible t_1^*). Here λ_k are Lagrange multipliers. Furthermore

$$r(n, \Lambda) = r(N_n^*) = e(\phi^*, N_n^*) = \frac{q}{(r!)^{1/p}} \left(\frac{r \, p' \, \lambda_0}{1 + r \, p'} \right)^{1/p'},$$

where, as before, $1/p' + 1/p = 1$, and λ_0 is the zeroth Lagrange multiplier which depends on n. For any $p \in [1, +\infty]$, we have $r(n, \Lambda) = \Theta(n^{-r})$.

Although the exact value of $r(n, \Lambda)$ is not known, it is easy to obtain quite sharp bounds on $r(n, \Lambda)$ in terms of the minimal radii $r^{\text{per}}(\cdot, \Lambda)$ for the periodic case of Section 2.1. Namely, we have

$$r^{\text{per}}(n, \Lambda) \le (2\pi)^{r+1-1/p} \, r(n, \Lambda) \le r^{\text{per}}(n - 1 - 2\lfloor r/2 \rfloor, \Lambda). \quad (2)$$

To show this recall from Chapter 4 that

$$r^{\text{per}}(n, \Lambda) = \inf_{0 \leq t_i \leq 2\pi} \sup \left\{ \int_0^{2\pi} f(t)\, dt : f \in \widetilde{W}_p^r, \|f^{(r)}\|_{[0,2\pi]} \leq q, \right.$$

$$\left. f(t_i) = 0, \ i \leq n \right\},$$

where $\|f^{(r)}\|_{[a,b]} = \left(\int_a^b |f^{(r)}(t)|^p\, dt \right)^{1/p}$. Changing variables we get 1-periodic functions and

$$r^{\text{per}}(n, \Lambda) = 2\pi \inf_{0 \leq t_i \leq 1} \sup \left\{ \int_0^1 f(t)\, dt : f \in \widetilde{W}_p^r(0,1), \right.$$

$$\left. \|f^{(r)}\|_{[0,1]} \leq (2\pi)^{r-1/p}\, q, \ f(t_i) = 0, \ i \leq n \right\}$$

$$= (2\pi)^{r+1-1/p} \inf_{0 \leq t_i \leq 1} \sup \left\{ \int_0^1 f(t)\, dt : f \in \widetilde{W}_p^r(0,1), \right.$$

$$\left. \|f^{(r)}\|_{[0,1]} \leq q, \ f(t_i) = 0, \ i \leq n \right\}$$

$$\leq (2\pi)^{r+1-1/p}\, r(n, \Lambda).$$

The last inequality follows from the fact that the set of 1-periodic functions with $\|f^{(r)}\|_{[0,1]} \leq q$ is a subset of F. This proves the lower bound on $r(n, \Lambda)$.

To get an upper bound consider the nonadaptive information of cardinality $k = m + 2r - 1$, $m \geq 1$, of the form

$$N_k(f) = \left[f(0), \ldots, f^{(r-1)}(0), f(1), \ldots, f^{(r-1)}(1), \right.$$

$$\left. f\left(\frac{1}{m}\right), f\left(\frac{2}{m}\right), \ldots, f\left(\frac{m-1}{m}\right) \right].$$

This information has been studied by Johnson [60] for $p = 1$, Karlin [69], Barrar, and Loeb [76], Jetter and Lange [78] for $p = 2$, Žensykbaev [79] and Girschovich [78] for arbitrary p. It is known that the radius of information N_k is given by

$$r(N_k) = (2\pi)^{-(r+1-1/p)}\, r^{\text{per}}(m, \Lambda),$$

and that the Euler-Maclaurin type-quadrature formula,

$$\phi^*(N_k(f)) = \frac{f(0) + f(1)}{2m} + \frac{1}{m} \sum_{i=1}^{m-1} f\left(\frac{i}{m}\right) + \sum_{i=1}^{r-1} a_i \left(f^{(i)}(1) - f^{(i)}(0) \right),$$

is an optimal error algorithm. Here $a_i = -m^{-(i+1)}B_{i+1}/(i+1)!$, $i = 1, 2, \ldots, r-2$, and $a_{r-1} = -m^{-r}(B_r - \gamma_{r,p'})/r!$, where B_j are the classical Bernoulli numbers and $\gamma_{r,p'}$ is the best constant of approximation of the Bernoulli polynomial $B_r(\cdot)$ in the class $\mathcal{L}_{p'}(0,1)$, $1/p' + 1/p = 1$, i.e., $\|B_r(\cdot) - \gamma_{r,p'}\|_{p'} = \min_\gamma \|B_r(\cdot) - \gamma\|_{p'}$. For $p = p' = 2$, $\gamma_{r,2} = 0$. Since $B_i = 0$ for odd i, we have $a_{2i} = 0$. Therefore the algorithm ϕ^* really uses the information

$$\overline{N}_n(f) = [f(0), f(\tfrac{1}{m}), \ldots, f(1), f'(0), f'(1), f^{(3)}(0), f^{(3)}(1), \\ \ldots, f^{(s)}(0), f^{(s)}(1)], \tag{3}$$

where $n = m + 1 + 2\lfloor r/2 \rfloor$, $s = 0$ if $r = 1$, and $s = 2\lfloor r/2 \rfloor - 1$ otherwise. Then

$$\phi^*\left(\overline{N}_n(f)\right) \tag{4}$$

$$= \frac{f(0) + f(1)}{2m} + \frac{1}{m}\sum_{i=1}^{m-1} f\left(\frac{i}{m}\right) + \sum_{i=1}^{\lfloor r/2 \rfloor} a_{2i-1}\left(f^{(2i-1)}(1) - f^{(2i-1)}(0)\right).$$

The coefficients a_{2i-1} can be precomputed since Bernoulli numbers are readily available, see e.g., Gradshteyn and Ryzhik [80, p. 1079-1080]. Then $\phi^*(\overline{N}_n(f))$ can be computed in time $c\,(n+1) + \lfloor r/2 \rfloor + 1$, where c, as always, is the cost of one information evaluation.

The error of the algorithm ϕ^* that uses $\overline{N}_n$ is given by

$$e(\phi^*, \overline{N}_n) = r(\overline{N}_n) = r(N_k) = (2\pi)^{-(r+1-1/p)}\, r^{\mathrm{per}}(m, \Lambda).$$

Since $r(n, \Lambda) \le r(\overline{N}_n) = (2\pi)^{-(r+1-1/p)}\, r^{\mathrm{per}}(n - 1 - 2\lfloor r/2 \rfloor, \Lambda)$, the upper bound of (2) is proven.

In particular, for $p = 2$ we have

$$q\sqrt{\frac{|B_{2r}|}{(2r)!}}\,\frac{1}{n^r} \le r(n, \Lambda) \le q\sqrt{\frac{|B_{2r}|}{(2r)!}}\,\frac{1}{(n - 1 - 2\lfloor r/2 \rfloor)^r}\,. \tag{5}$$

For arbitrary p, we conclude from the formula for $r^{\mathrm{per}}(n, \Lambda)$ that

$$r(n, \Lambda) = \frac{2q\,\|\overline{D}_r\|_{p'}}{(2\pi)^{r+1-1/p}}\,\frac{1}{n^r}\,(1 + o(1)) \quad \text{as } n \to +\infty, \tag{6}$$

where $\overline{D}_r$ is given in Section 2.1 and $\|\overline{D}_r\|_{p'} = \left(\int_0^{2\pi} |\overline{D}_r(t)|^{p'}\,dt\right)^{1/p'}$ with $1/p' + 1/p = 1$.

From (6) it also follows that the information (3) is almost nth optimal since

$$r(n, \Lambda) \leq r(\overline{N}_n) \leq r(n - 1 - 2\lfloor r/2 \rfloor, \Lambda)$$

and

$$\frac{r(\overline{N}_n)}{r(n, \Lambda)} = 1 + o(1) \quad \text{as } n \to +\infty.$$

We now briefly discuss the ε-cardinality number. From (2) we conclude that

$$m^{\mathrm{per}}\left((2\pi)^{r+1-1/p}\,\varepsilon\right) \leq m(\varepsilon) \leq m^{\mathrm{per}}\left((2\pi)^{r+1-1/p}\,\varepsilon\right) + 1 + 2\lfloor r/2 \rfloor,$$

where $m^{\mathrm{per}}(\varepsilon)$ is the ε-cardinality number for the periodic case and is given in Section 2.1. From (6) we conclude that

$$m(\varepsilon) = \left(\frac{q}{\varepsilon}\,\frac{2\,\|\overline{D}_r\|_{p'}}{(2\pi)^{r+1-1/p}}\right)^{1/r}\left(1 + o(1)\right).$$

In particular, for $p = 2$ we have

$$m(\varepsilon) = \left(\frac{q}{\varepsilon}\,\sqrt{\frac{|B_{2r}|}{(2r)!}}\right)^{1/r}\left(1 + o(1)\right).$$

For the ε-complexity we have

$$c\,m(\varepsilon) \leq \mathrm{comp}(\varepsilon) \leq (c + 2)\,m(\varepsilon) - 1.$$

For $c \gg 1$, the information $\overline{N}_n$ and the algorithm ϕ_n given by (3) and (4) for $n = m(\varepsilon)$ are almost optimal.

Notes and Remarks

NR 2.2:1 Sections 2.1 and 2.2 are based on a supplement written by Kornejčuk which is a part of the third edition of the book of Nikolskij [79] and on a recent survey of Bojanov [86]. Many relevant papers on optimal integration may be found in these two papers.

NR 2.2:2 Many problems in approximation theory are reduced to the approximation of the function $(1 - \cdot)^r/r!$ by functions of the form $(t_i - \cdot)_+^{r-1-j_i}$, (or equivalently to the minimal norm of a monospline of degree r). For example, consider Hermitian information

$$N(f) = [f(t_1), f'(t_1), \ldots, f^{(j_1)}(t_1), \ldots, f(t_k), f'(t_k), \ldots, f^{(j_k)}(t_k)]$$

for the integration problem in the class $F_1 = W_p^r$. Then the problem of nth optimal information reduces to the approximation of $(1 - \cdot)^r/r!$ by

$$\mathrm{span}\{(t_1 - \cdot)_+^{r-1}, \ldots, (t_1 - \cdot)_+^{r-1-j_1}, \ldots, (t_k - \cdot)_+^{r-1}, \ldots, (t_k - \cdot)_+^{r-1-j_k}\}$$

in the space $\mathcal{L}_{p'}(0,1)$ for optimally chosen points t_i. The solution for $j_i \equiv r - 1$ and for $j_i \equiv r - 2$ for even r has been found by Ibragimov and Aliev [65] for $p = 1, 2$ or $+\infty$, by Aksen and Tureckij [66] for any p and $j_i \equiv r - 2$ with even r, and by Lušpaj [66] for $j_i \equiv r - 1$, as well as by Kautsky [70].

There is also an interesting stream of work in statistical literature, where optimal design problems are shown to be reducible to the approximation of functions including $(1 - \cdot)^r/r!$, see Sacks and Ylvisaker [66, 68, 70a,b] and Wahba [71]. We comment on these papers in Section 2.3 of Chapter 5 and Section 2.1 of Chapter 7.

NR 2.2:3 There is a number of papers where Hermitian information is studied for the integration problem of Section 2.2,

$$N(f) = [f(t_1), f'(t_1), \ldots, f^{(j_1)}(t_1), \ldots, f(t_k), f'(t_k), \ldots, f^{(j_k)}(t_k)]$$

with fixed distinct $t_i \in [0,1]$ and $j_i \leq r - 1$. Let $n = (j_1 + 1) + (j_2 + 1) + \cdots + (j_k + 1)$ denote the total number of evaluations. Then there exist points $\tau_1, \tau_2, \ldots, \tau_n \in [0,1]$ such that for the information $N_n^*(f) = [f(\tau_1), f(\tau_2), \ldots, f(\tau_n)]$ we have

$$r(N_n^*) \leq r(N).$$

This means that the evaluation of derivatives cannot supply more information than the evaluation of function values. This was proved by Powell [68] for $p = 2$, and by Barrar and Loeb [76] for general p.

This result was strengthened by Bojanov [80] by showing that the cardinality of information N_n^* can be reduced to $m = \lceil \sum_{i=1}^{k} (j_i + 2)/2 \rceil$. That is, there exist points $\tau_1, \tau_2, \ldots, \tau_m$ such that for $N_m^*(f) = [f(\tau_1), f(\tau_2), \ldots, f(\tau_m)]$ we have $r(N_m^*) \leq r(N)$. Note that if one of j_i is positive then $m < n$. This means that derivatives supply less information than function values.

The same inequality, $r(N_m^*) \leq r(N)$, is also true for Hardy spaces of analytic functions, see Bojanov [78] and Andersson and Bojanov [84], and for Hilbert spaces with reproducing kernels, see Bojanov [77].

NR 2.2:4 As already mentioned, Žensykbaev [82] proved that n function values provide no less information than arbitrary Birkhoff information. Actually his result is even stronger. For the class W_p^r, consider information

$$N(f) = [L_1(f), \ldots, L_k(f), f^{(j_1)}(t_1), \ldots, f^{(j_n)}(t_n)],$$

where $L_i(f) = f^{(k_i)}(0)$ or $f^{(k_i)}(1)$ for some k_i and $j_i \in [0, r - 1]$. Then there exist points $x_1, \ldots, x_n$ such that for the information

$$N^*(f) = [L_1(f), \ldots, L_k(f), f(x_1), \ldots, f(x_n)]$$

we have $r(N^*) \leq r(N)$. This means that function evaluations provide no less information than derivative evaluations even if some Birkhoff information at boundary points is used. The same is true for the class $\widetilde{W}_p^r$.

NR 2.2:5 For $r \geq 2$, the algorithm ϕ^* defined by (4) uses odd derivatives of f at the boundary points 0 and 1. Sometimes the evaluation of derivatives is hard or even impossible, and the only permissible information operations are given by function values. In this case, the algorithm ϕ^* should be modified. It can be done by computing additionally $4\lfloor r/2 \rfloor - 2$ function values at the points h, $2h$, ..., $(2\lfloor r/2 \rfloor - 1)h$, $1 - h$, $1 - 2h$, ..., $1 - (2\lfloor r/2 \rfloor - 1)h$ for small h. Then the divided difference algorithm supplies approximations to all needed derivatives with error tending to zero with h. Thus, we have an algorithm which uses $m + 1 + 4\lfloor r/2 \rfloor - 2 = n + 2\lfloor r/2 \rfloor$ function values with error arbitrary close to the error of the algorithm ϕ^*. Note, however, that round off error analysis indicates that h should not be too small as compared to the relative precision of floating point arithmetic.

NR 2.2:6 Consider a modification of the class of functions studied in Section 2.2,

$$F_1 = \{f : [0,1] \to \mathbb{R}, \ f^{(r)} \text{ is continuous}, \ f(0) = f'(0) = \cdots = f^{(r)}(0) = 0\}.$$

Let $Tf = f^{(r)}$ and let $X = C(0,1)$ or $X = \mathcal{L}_2(0,1)$. That is, $\|Tf\| = \max_{0 \le t \le 1} |f^{(r)}(t)|$ or $\|Tf\| = (\int_0^1 f^{(r)}(t)\,dt)^{1/2}$. We approximate $S(f) = \int_0^1 f(t)\,dt$ for f from $F = \{f \in F_1 : \|Tf\| \le q\}$. As before let Λ consist of $L(f) = f^{(j)}(x)$, $x \in [0,1]$, and $0 \le j \le r$. This class of functions will be used to analyze the average case and probabilistic settings for the integration problem.

For $X = C(0,1)$, F is a subclass of W_∞^r. It is clear that the change of the norm from $\mathcal{L}_\infty$ to C does not essentially change the results of Section 2.2. For $X = \mathcal{L}_2(0,1)$, F is a subclass of W_2^r. Using the results of Section 2.2 as well as **NR 2.2:3** and **2.2:4** one can verify that the nth minimal radius $r(n,\Lambda)$ is bounded by

$$r^{\mathrm{per}}(n + \lceil r/2 \rceil, \Lambda) \le (2\pi)^{r+1-1/p} r(n, \Lambda) \le r^{\mathrm{per}}(n - \lfloor r/2 \rfloor, \Lambda),$$

where $p = +\infty$ if $X = C(0,1)$, and $p = 1/2$ if $X = \mathcal{L}_2(0,1)$. From Section 2.1 we thus conclude that

$$r(n, \Lambda) = \begin{cases} \dfrac{q\,K_r}{(2\pi)^r\,n^r}\,(1 + o(1)) & \text{as } n \to +\infty, \quad \text{if } X = C(0,1), \\[3ex] \dfrac{q}{n^r}\sqrt{\dfrac{|B_{2r}|}{(2\pi)!}}\,(1 + o(1)) & \text{as } n \to +\infty, \quad \text{if } X = C(0,1), \end{cases}$$

with the Favard constant K_r and the Bernoulli number B_{2r}, respectively.

Consider the information

$$N_n(f) = [f(1), f'(1), f^{(3)}(1), \ldots, f^{(s)}(1), f(\tfrac{1}{m}), f(\tfrac{2}{m}), \ldots, f(\tfrac{m-1}{m})]$$

with $s = 0$ if $r = 1$, and $s = 2\lfloor r/2 \rfloor - 1$ otherwise. Here $n = m + \lfloor r/2 \rfloor$. The radius of information N_n is bounded by

$$r(n, \Lambda) \le r(N_n) \le r(n - \lfloor r/2 \rfloor, \Lambda)$$

Therefore,

$$\frac{r(N_n)}{r(n, \Lambda)} = 1 + o(1) \quad \text{as } n \to \infty.$$

Thus, N_n is nearly nth optimal information. The algorithm

$$\phi_n^*(N_n(f)) = \frac{f(1)}{2m} + \frac{1}{m}\sum_{i=1}^{m-1} f\left(\frac{i}{m}\right) + \sum_{i=1}^{\lfloor r/2 \rfloor} a_{2i-1}\, f^{(2i-1)}(1)$$

is a linear optimal error algorithm, $e(\phi^*, N_n) = r(N_n)$, where a_{2i-1} are defined as in Section 2.2. The ε-cardinality number, $m(\varepsilon) = \min\{n : r(n, \Lambda) \leq \varepsilon\}$, is given by

$$
m(\varepsilon) = \begin{cases}
\dfrac{1}{2\pi} \left(\dfrac{q K_r}{\varepsilon} \right)^{1/r} (1 + o(1)) & \text{as } \varepsilon \to 0, \quad \text{if } X = C(0,1), \\[3ex]
\left(\dfrac{q}{\varepsilon} \sqrt{\dfrac{|B_{2r}|}{(2r)!}} \right)^{1/r} (1 + o(1)) & \text{as } \varepsilon \to 0, \quad \text{if } X = \mathcal{L}_2(0,1).
\end{cases}
$$

The ε-complexity is bounded by $c\, m(\varepsilon) \leq \text{comp}(\varepsilon) \leq (c + 2)\, m(\varepsilon) - 1$. For small ε and large c, the information N_n and the linear optimal error algorithm ϕ_n^* that uses N_n with $n = m(\varepsilon)$ are close to optimal,

$$
\text{comp}(\varepsilon) \simeq \text{cost}(\phi_n^*, N_n) \simeq c\, m(\varepsilon).
$$

Exercises

E 2.2:1 Consider the integration problem as in Section 2.2 for the space $W_p^r(a,b)$. Let $m(\varepsilon; a, b)$ denote its ε-cardinality number. Show that $m(\varepsilon; a, b) = m(\varepsilon/(b-a)^{r+1-1/p})$, where $m(\varepsilon)$ is the ε-cardinality number for the space $W_p^r(0,1)$.

E 2.2:2 Consider the integration problem of Section 2.2 with $p = 2$. For the information N_n consisting of $f^{(i)}(0)$, $f^{(i)}(1)$ for $i = 0, 1, \ldots, r-1$, and $f(i/m)$ for $i = 1, 2, \ldots, m-1$, $n = m + 2r - 1$, define a polynomial $\sigma = \sigma(N_n(t))$ of degree at most $2r - 1$ which interpolates the boundary values,

$$
\sigma^{(i)}(0) = f^{(i)}(0), \quad \sigma^{(i)}(1) = f^{(i)}(1), \quad i = 0, 1, \ldots, r - 1
$$

Define the algorithm $\phi(N_n(f)) = m^{-1} \sum_{i=1}^{m-1} \left(f(i/m) - \sigma(i/m) \right) + \int_0^1 \sigma(t)\, dt$. Show that ϕ is a spline algorithm and that $e(\phi, N_n) = r(N_n)$.

2.3. Weighted Integration in a Reproducing Kernel Hilbert Space

We briefly discuss the weighted integration problem for functions $f : [a, b] \to \mathbb{R}$ which belong to a reproducing kernel Hilbert space F_1. That is, there exists $k : [a, b] \times [a, b] \to \mathbb{R}$, called a *reproducing kernel*, such that $k(\cdot, x) \in F_1$ for every $x \in [a, b]$ and

$$
f(x) = \langle f, k(\cdot, x) \rangle, \quad \forall f \in F_1, \ \forall x \in [a, b],
$$

where $\langle \cdot, \cdot \rangle$ is the inner product in F_1. We assume that F_1 is a subset of $\mathcal{L}_2(a, b)$.

Let $F = \{ f \in F_1 : \|f\| = \sqrt{\langle f, f \rangle} \leq q \}$ be the ball of F_1 with radius q. Consider the following solution operator,

$$
S(f) = \int_a^b f(x)\, \rho(x)\, dx, \quad \forall f \in F_1,
$$

where ρ is a known function from $\mathcal{L}_2(a, b)$. Let Λ consist of function values.

This is a linear problem (with $G = \mathbb{R}$, $T = I$, and $X = F_1$). Therefore, adaption does not help and there exists a linear optimal error algorithm for arbitrary nonadaptive information.

Let $N_n(f) = [f(t_1), f(t_2), \ldots, f(t_n)]$ for distinct points t_i from $[a, b]$. Consider the function

$$\sigma(\cdot) = \sum_{j=1}^{n} g_j \, k(\cdot, t_j), \quad g_j \in \mathbb{R},$$

with g_j such that $\sigma(t_j) = f(t_j)$. There always exists such a unique σ, since $k(\cdot, t_1), \ldots, k(\cdot, t_n)$ are linearly independent and the Gram matrix $\left(k(t_i, t_j)\right)_{i,j}$ is nonsingular.

We now show that σ is a spline. Indeed, let $h \in F_1$ and $h(t_j) = 0$. Then

$$\langle h, \sigma \rangle = \sum_{j=1}^{n} g_j \, \langle h, k(\cdot, t_j) \rangle = \sum_{j=1}^{n} g_j \, h(t_j) = 0,$$

i.e., σ is orthogonal to $\ker N$. Hence σ is the spline, as claimed. The spline algorithm now takes the form

$$\phi^s\left(N_n(f)\right) = \sum_{j=1}^{n} g_j \int_a^b k(x, t_j) \, \rho(x) \, dx, \quad g_j = g_j\left(N_n(f)\right).$$

Since g_j depends linearly on $N_n(f)$, it can be written as $g_j = \sum_{i=1}^{n} a_{i,j} f(t_i)$ for some $a_{i,j}$ independent of f. As a matter of fact, $a_{i,j}$'s are the entries of the inverse of the Gram matrix. Hence

$$\phi^s\left(N_n(f)\right) = \sum_{i=1}^{n} f(t_i) \, g_i^*, \quad g_i^* = \sum_{j=1}^{n} a_{i,j} \int_a^b k(x, t_j) \, \rho(x) \, dx.$$

Consider now the error of the spline algorithm ϕ^s. For arbitrary $f \in F_1$ we have

$$\left| S(f) - \sum_{i=1}^{n} f(t_i) \, g_i^* \right| = \left| \int_a^b \rho(x) \, \langle f, k(\cdot, x) \rangle \, dx - \sum_{i=1}^{n} g_i^* \, \langle f, k(\cdot, t_i) \rangle \right|$$

$$= \left| \left\langle f, \int_a^b \rho(x) \, k(\cdot, x) \, dx - \sum_{i=1}^{n} g_i^* \, k(\cdot, t_i) \right\rangle \right|$$

$$\leq \|f\| \, \left\| f^* - \sum_{i=1}^{n} g_i^* \, k(\cdot, t_i) \right\|.$$

Here the function f^* is given by

$$f^*(t) = \int_a^b \rho(x)\, k(t, x)\, dx, \qquad \forall t \in [a, b]. \tag{1}$$

Obviously, f^* belongs to F_1. Since the last inequality is sharp, the supremum with respect to $\|f\| \leq q$ yields

$$e(\phi^s, N_n) = q \left\| f^* - \sum_{i=1}^n g_i^*\, k(\cdot, t_i) \right\|.$$

Since the spline algorithm has minimal error among all algorithms, and in particular among all linear algorithms, we conclude that

$$r(N_n) = q \inf_{a_i \in \mathbb{R}} \left\| f^* - \sum_{i=1}^n a_i\, k(\cdot, t_i) \right\|. \tag{2}$$

That is, the radius of information is equal to the error of approximating the function f^* by $\mathrm{span}\{k(\cdot, t_1), k(\cdot, t_2), \ldots, k(\cdot, t_n)\}$, see also **NR 5.5:7** of Chapter 4.

We now turn to nth optimal nonadaptive information. Due to (2), we need to find points t_i, or equivalently basis functions $k(\cdot, t_1), \ldots, k(\cdot, t_n)$ for which the error of approximating f^* is minimized,

$$r(n, \Lambda) = q \inf_{a \leq t_i \leq b} \inf_{a_i \in \mathbb{R}} \left\| f^* - \sum_{i=1}^n a_i\, k(\cdot, t_i) \right\|. \tag{3}$$

The information $N_n(f) = [f(t_1^*), \ldots, f(t_n^*)]$ and the spline algorithm ϕ^s that uses N_n are almost optimal if $n = m(\varepsilon) = \min\{k : r(n, \Lambda) \leq \varepsilon\}$ and t_i^* are chosen as points for which the infimum in (3) is attained. As usual, $\mathrm{comp}(\varepsilon) = (c + b)\, m(\varepsilon)$ for $b \in [0, 2]$.

This shows that the complexity analysis of the weighted integration problem in a reproducing kernel Hilbert space reduces to the approximation of the function f^* by linear combinations of functions of the form $k(\cdot, t_1), \ldots, k(\cdot, t_n)$. This is important since the latter problem has been solved for many functions f^*. For such functions f^* we have tight complexity bounds. We illustrate this point by two examples.

EXAMPLE 2.3.1. For $r \geq 1$, define $F_1 = \{f \in W_2^r(0, 1) : f(0) = \cdots = f^{(r-1)}(0) = 0\}$. The inner product in F_1 is given by

$$\langle f, g \rangle = \int_0^1 f^{(r)}(t)\, g^{(r)}(t)\, dt.$$

The space F_1 is a Hilbert space with the reproducing kernel

$$k(x,t) = \int_0^1 \frac{(x-u)_+^{r-1}(t-u)_+^{r-1}}{((r-1)!)^2}\, du.$$

In this case, the function f^* given by (1) takes the form

$$f^*(t) = \int_0^1 \int_0^1 \rho(x)\frac{(x-u)_+^{r-1}(t-u)_+^{r-1}}{((r-1)!)^2}\, du\, dx.$$

Its rth derivative is equal to

$$(f^*)^{(r)}(t) = \int_0^1 \rho(x)\frac{(x-t)_+^{r-1}}{(r-1)!}\, dx.$$

Then (3) takes the form

$$r(n,\Lambda) = q \inf_{0 \le t_i \le 1}\ \inf_{a_i \in \mathbb{R}} \left\| \int_0^1 \rho(x)\frac{(x-\cdot)^{r-1}}{(r-1)!}\, dx - \sum_{i=1}^n a_i \frac{(t_i-\cdot)_+^{r-1}}{(r-1)!} \right\|_2.$$

For $\rho(x) \equiv 1$, $(f^*)^{(r)}(t) = (1-t)^r/r!$ and this is exactly the same problem as we discussed in Section 2.2 for $p = 2$ and $j_i \equiv 0$. From (5) of Section 2.2 it follows that

$$r(n,\Lambda) = q\sqrt{\frac{|B_{2r}|}{(2r)!}}\frac{1}{n^r}(1+o(1)) \quad \text{as } n \to +\infty.$$

For large c and small ε, we have

$$\mathrm{comp}(\varepsilon) \simeq c\, m(\varepsilon) \simeq c\left(\frac{q}{\varepsilon}\sqrt{\frac{|B_{2r}|}{(2r)!}}\right)^{1/r}.$$

We finally comment on the optimal information and algorithm. Consider the information N_n and the algorithm ϕ_n^* introduced in **NR 2.2:6**. The information N_n is now not permissible since it consists of a few derivative evaluations. We can, however, approximate them by function values as explained in **NR 2.2:5**. After such a modification the pair (ϕ_n^*, N_n) with $n = m(\varepsilon)$ becomes almost optimal.

EXAMPLE 2.3.2. For $r \ge 1$, define $F_1 = \{f \in \widetilde{W_2^r} = \widetilde{W_2^r}(0,2\pi) : f(0) = 0\}$. The inner product in F_1 is given by

$$\langle f,g\rangle = \int_0^{2\pi} f^{(r)}(t)\, g^{(r)}(t)\, dt.$$

It is known that for $f \in F_1$ we have

$$f(x) = \pi^{-1} \int_0^{2\pi} \left(D_r(x - t) - D_r(-t) \right) f^{(r)}(t)\, dt.$$

Here $D_j(u) = \sum_{k=1}^{\infty} \left(\cos(ku - \pi j/2) \right) k^{-j}$ is a (2π)-periodic function, $j \geq 1$. The functions D_j are related to Bernoulli polynomials $B_j(\cdot)$. Namely, $D_1(u) = -\pi B_1(u/(2\pi))$ if $u \in (0, 2\pi)$, and $D_j(u) = -2^{j-1}\pi^j B_j(u/(2\pi))/j!$ if $u \in [0, 2\pi]$ for $j \geq 2$. Observe that $D_j' = D_{j-1}$ and $\int_0^{2\pi} D_j(x - t)\, dt = 0$, $\forall x \in [0, 2\pi]$.

The formula for $f(x)$ can be rewritten as $f(x) = \langle f, k(\cdot, x) \rangle$, where

$$k_t^{(r)}(t, x) = \frac{1}{\pi} \left(D_r(x - t) - D_r(-t) \right).$$

From this and the fact that $k(\cdot, x) \in F_1$ we get

$$k(t, x) = \frac{(-1)^r}{\pi} \left(D_{2r}(x - t) - D_{2r}(-t) - D_{2r}(x) + D_{2r}(0) \right)$$

$$= \pi^{-1} \sum_{k=1}^{\infty} k^{-2r} \left(\cos k(x - t) - \cos kt - \cos kx + 1 \right).$$

Thus, F_1 is a Hilbert space with reproducing kernel k.

The function f^* given by (1) is now of the form

$$f^*(t) = \frac{(-1)^r}{\pi} \int_0^{2\pi} \rho(x) \left(D_{2r}(x - t) - D_{2r}(-t) - D_{2r}(x) + D_{2r}(0) \right) dx,$$

$$(f^*)^{(r)}(t) = \frac{1}{\pi} \int_0^{2\pi} \rho(x) \left(D_r(x - t) - D_r(-t) \right) dx.$$

Then (3) takes the form

$$r(n, \Lambda) = q \inf_{0 \leq t_i \leq 2\pi} \inf_{a_i \in \mathbb{R}} \left\| \frac{1}{\pi} \int_0^{2\pi} \rho(x) \left(D_r(x - \cdot) - D_r(-\cdot) \right) dx \right.$$

$$\left. - \sum_{i=1}^{n} \frac{a_i}{\pi} \left(D_r(t_i - \cdot) - D_r(-\cdot) \right) \right\|_2.$$

For $\rho(x) \equiv 1$, this simplifies to $(f^*)^{(r)}(t) = -2D_r(-t)$ and

$$r(n, \Lambda) = q \inf_{0 \leq t_i \leq 2\pi} \inf_{a_i \in \mathbb{R}} \left\| 2D_r - \sum_{i=1}^{n} \frac{a_i}{\pi} \left(D_r(\cdot - t_i) - D_r \right) \right\|_2.$$

Thus, $r(n, \Lambda)$ is the error of approximating the function $2D_r$ by span $\big(D_r(\cdot - t_1) - D_r, \ldots, D_r(\cdot - t_n) - D_r\big)$ for optimally chosen t_i.

On the other hand, we know that

$$r(n, \Lambda) = q \inf_{0 \le t_i \le 2\pi} \sup \left\{ \left| \int_0^{2\pi} f(t)\, dt \right| : f \in \widetilde{W_2^r}, \; \|f^{(r)}\|_2 \le 1, \right.$$

$$\left. f(0) = f(t_1) = \ldots = f(t_n) = 0 \right\}.$$

From Section 2.1 we conclude that $r(n, \Lambda)$ is equal to the $(n+1)$st minimal radius of information for the class $\widetilde{W_2^r}$ and without the initial condition $f(0) = 0$. Therefore

$$r(n, \Lambda) = q\, (2\pi)^{r+1/2} \sqrt{\frac{|B_{2r}|}{(2r)!}} \frac{1}{(n+1)^r}.$$

The optimal points t_i are given by $t_i = 2\pi i/(n+1)$, $i = 1, 2, \ldots, n$. The ε-cardinality number is given by

$$m(\varepsilon) = \left\lceil 2\pi \left(\frac{q}{\varepsilon} \sqrt{\frac{2\pi |B_{2r}|}{(2r)!}} \right)^{1/r} \right\rceil - 1,$$

and the ε-complexity is bounded by

$$(c + 1)\, m(\varepsilon) - 1 \le \mathrm{comp}(\varepsilon) \le (c + 1)\, m(\varepsilon).$$

The information $N_n^*(f) = \big[f(2\pi/(n+1)), \ldots, f(2\pi n/(n+1))\big]$ and the rectangle (or trapezoid) formula $\phi_n^* \big(N_n^*(f)\big) = \big(2\pi/(n+1)\big) \sum_{i=1}^n f(2\pi i/(n+1))$ with $n = m(\varepsilon)$ are almost optimal.

Notes and Remarks

NR 2.3:1 The approach of this section follows Sacks and Ylvisaker [70b]. They motivated the approximation of the function $f^*(t) = \int_0^1 \rho(x)\, k(t, x)\, dx$, $t \in [0, 1]$, by linear combinations of $k(\cdot, t_1), \ldots, k(\cdot, t_n)$ by statistical considerations including the regression design problem, see also Section 2.2 of Chapter 7.

In a series of papers, Sacks and Ylvisaker [66, 68, 70a,b] and Wahba [71] proved, in particular, the following. Assume that for some $m \ge 1$, we have

$$\lim_{x \searrow t} \frac{\partial^{2m-1}}{\partial x^{2m-1}} k(x, t) - \lim_{x \nearrow t} \frac{\partial^{2m-1}}{\partial x^{2m-1}} k(x, t) = (-1)^m\, \alpha(t), \quad \text{where} \quad \alpha(t) > 0.$$

Suppose that ρ is strictly positive and has a bounded first derivative on $[0, 1]$. Define the points $t_{i,n}^*$ by

$$\int_0^{t_{i,n}^*} (\rho^2(u)\, \alpha(u))^{1/(2m+1)}\, du = \frac{i}{n} \int_0^1 (\rho^2(u)\, \alpha(u))^{1/(2m+1)}\, du$$

for $i = 1, 2, \ldots, n$, where $n = 1, 2, \ldots$ and $t_{0,n}^* = 0$.

The function f^* is approximated by a combination of $k(\cdot, t_i), k'(\cdot, t_i), \ldots, k^{(m-1)}(\cdot, t_i)$, $i \in [1, n]$, where $k^{(j)}(x, t) = (\partial^j/\partial t^j)k(x, t)$ denotes differentiation with respect to the second argument. Let

$$
e_{n,m}(f^*, \{t_i\}) = \inf_{a_{i,j} \in \mathbb{R}} \left\| f^* - \sum_{i=0}^{n} \sum_{j=0}^{m-1} a_{i,j}\, k^{(j)}(\cdot, t_i) \right\|
$$

denote the minimal error of such approximation. Let $e_{n,m}(f^*)$ be the error for optimally chosen points t_i,

$$
e_{n,m}(f^*) = \inf_{0 \le t_i \le 1} e_{n,m}(f^*, \{t_i\}).
$$

Then

$$
e_{n,m}(f^*) = e_{n,m}(f^*, \{t_{i,n}^*\})\,(1 + o(1))
$$

$$
= \frac{1}{n^m}\, \frac{m!}{\sqrt{(2m)!(2m-1)!}} \left(\int_0^1 \rho^2(u)\, \alpha(u)^{(2m+1)^{-1}}\, du \right)^{(2m+1)/2} (1 + o(1)),
$$

as $n \to 0$. This means that the points $t_{i,n}^*$ are almost optimal and the error of approximation is of order n^{-m}.

This was proven by Sacks and Ylvisaker for $\alpha(t) \equiv \text{const} > 0$, and generalized by Wahba for $\alpha(t) > 0$. As mentioned in **NR 2.2:2**, this problem has been also studied for some specific functions f^* in the papers devoted to optimal integration. In this case, the exact value of $e_{m,r}$ as well as the optimal points $t_{i,n}^*$ are known, for a survey see the supplement of Kornejčuk in Nikolskij [79].

We now relate $e_{n,m}(f^*)$ to the nth minimal radius $r(n, \Lambda)$ of information. Recall that Λ consists of only function evaluations and $\langle f, k^{(j)}(\cdot, t_i) \rangle = f^{(j)}(t_i)$ is not a permissible evaluation for $j > 0$. Nevertheless, we have the following bounds

$$
q\, e_{n,m}(f^*) \le r(n, \Lambda) \le q\, e_{nm,m}(f^*).
$$

The left bound is obvious and the right one follows from the fact that we can approximate derivatives by additional function evaluations. From the formula for $e_{n,m}(f^*)$, we thus have $r(n, \Lambda) = \Theta(n^{-m})$.

Exercises

E 2.3:1 Consider the problem from Example 2.3.1 with $\rho(t) = 1$. Let $\alpha(\cdot)$ be defined as in **NR 2.3:1**. Show that $m = r$ and $\alpha(t) \equiv 1$.

E 2.3:2 Consider the problem from Example 2.3.2 with $\rho(t) = 1$. Let $\alpha(\cdot)$ be defined as in **NR 2.3:1**. Show that $m = r$ and $\alpha(t) \equiv 1$.

3. Function Approximation

In this section we deal with the *function approximation* problem, i.e., the problem for which the solution operator is given by $S(f) = f$ and F is a class of functions. The approximation problem has been studied in many papers especially for classes of scalar functions. The reader may consult Chapter 6 of GTOA and a forthcoming book of Šukharev [88] for a partial list of relevant papers.

Here we focus on the approximation problem for functions of several variables. We restrict ourselves to two classes of multivariate smooth functions, for other classes see **NR 3:1**.

These two classes are studied in the three settings. The worst case setting is analyzed in this section whereas the average case and probabilistic settings are analyzed in Section 3 of Chapter 7 and Section 7 of Chapter 8, respectively.

Notes and Remarks

NR 3:1 Consider the approximation problem for the classes $C_d^{r,\alpha}$ and $W_p^{r,d}$ defined in **NR 2:1** with $G = \mathcal{L}_\infty$ for two classes of information evaluations, Λ_1 consisting of all linear functionals and Λ_2 consisting of only function values. Let $r(n, \Lambda_i)$ denote the nth minimal radius of information of cardinality n in the class Λ_i, $i = 1, 2$.

From Sections 5.4 and 5.6 of Chapter 4 we know that for the class Λ_1 the nth minimal radius is equal to the Gelfand and linear Kolmogorov n-width. For the class $C_d^{r,\alpha}$, the nth width was estimated by Tikhomirov [60] and therefore we have $r(n, \Lambda_1) = \Theta(n^{(r+\alpha)/d})$. For $d = 1$ and $\alpha = 0$, the nth width (and the nth minimal radius) is equal to $K_r(\pi n)^{-r}(1 + o(1))$, see Tikhomirov [69], with the Favard constant K_r.

The same bounds hold for the class Λ_2, see Novak [87a], which shows that function values are nearly optimal in the class of all linear functionals. This and linearity of an optimal error algorithm yield that the ε-complexity for $C_d^{r,\alpha}$ in both classes Λ_i is proportional to $c\varepsilon^{-d/(r+\alpha)}$, where c is the cost of one information evaluation. Thus, the complexity is exponential in d.

For the class $W_p^{r,d}$, linear Kolmogorov n-widths are analyzed in Kashin [77, 80], Höllig [79, 80], Novak [87a], and Pinkus [85]. For $2r > d$, we have $r(n, \Lambda_1) = \Theta(n^{-r/d+a})$, where $a = 1/p$ for $p \geq 2$ and $a = 1/2$ for $1 \leq p < 2$. The ε-complexity is thus proportional to $c\varepsilon^{-d/(r-a\,d)}$. For the class Λ_2 with $p\,r > d$, we have $r(n, \Lambda_2) = \Theta(n^{-r/d+1/p})$, see Novak [87a], and the ε-complexity is proportional to $c\varepsilon^{-d/(r-d/p)}$. Observe that function values are now non-optimal in the class of all linear functionals if $p \in [1, 2)$. For both classes Λ_i, the complexity is exponential in d.

3.1. Smooth Periodic Functions

Consider the approximation problem for functions $f : \mathbb{R}^d \to \mathcal{C}$ which are (2π)-periodic with respect to all variables x_j, and which are r_j times differentiable with respect to x_j almost everywhere with $\partial^{r_j} f/\partial x_j^{r_j}$ belonging to the space $\mathcal{L}_2 = \mathcal{L}_2(D)$, $D = [0, 2\pi]^d$. Here $\mathcal{C}$ denotes the set of complex numbers. For simplicity, and reasons explained later, we also assume that functions f are orthogonal to unity, $\langle f, 1 \rangle = \int_D f(t)\, dt = 0$. Let $F_1 = F_1(r, \mathcal{L}_2)$ denote the space of such functions, $r = [r_1, r_2, \ldots, r_d]$.

For given real coefficients $a = [a_1, a_2, \ldots, a_d]$, define the differential operator $T : F_1 \to \mathcal{L}_2$ by

$$Tf = \sum_{j=1}^{d} a_j \frac{\partial^{r_j}}{\partial x_j^{r_j}} f.$$

The operator T serves as a linear restriction operator and the set F is given by

$$F = \{f \in F_1 : \|Tf\| \le 1\}.$$

We wish to approximate $S(f) = f$, $S : F_1 \to G = \mathcal{L}_2$, assuming that the class Λ of permissible information operations consists of *all* linear functionals $L : F_1 \to \mathbb{C}$.

In the first part of this section we assume that the vectors $r = [r_1, \ldots, r_d]$ and $a = [a_1, \ldots, a_d]$ satisfy the following condition:

$$r \text{ contains at most one odd component}, \tag{i}$$

$$\operatorname{sign} a_j \begin{cases} \ne 0 & \text{if } r_j \text{ is odd}, \\ = u & \text{if } r_j \text{ is multiple of 4}, \\ = -u & \text{otherwise}, \end{cases} \quad \forall j, \tag{ii}$$

where $u = \pm 1$. As we shall see later these conditions are sufficient and "almost" necessary for the ε-complexity to be finite.

As we know from Chapter 4, the ε-complexity depends on the eigenvalues of the operator K_1. To find them, we first consider the eigenpairs of the operator T. Given a vector $t = [t_1, t_2, \ldots, t_d]$ with integers t_j, define the function

$$e_t(x) = (2\pi)^{-d/2} \exp\left(i \langle x, t \rangle\right),$$

where $i = \sqrt{-1}$, $x = [x_1, x_2, \ldots, x_d] \in \mathbb{R}^d$, and $\langle x, t \rangle = \sum_{j=1}^{d} x_j t_j$.

The set $\{e_t\}$ forms an orthonormal system of $\mathcal{L}_2$. Note that $e_t \in F_1$ for $t \ne 0$ and e_t is an eigenfunction of the operator T, $T e_t = b_t e_t$, where the eigenvalue b_t is given by

$$b_t = \sum_{j=1}^{d} a_j (i t_j)^{r_j}.$$

Since r and a satisfy (i) and (ii), it is easy to check that

$$|b_t| = \begin{cases} \sum_{j=1}^{d} |a_j| \, t_j^{r_j} & \text{if } r \text{ has no odd component}, \\ \left(\left(\sum_{j=1}^{d} |a_j| \, t_j^{r_j} \right)^2 + \left(|a_s| \, t_s^{r_s} \right)^2 \right)^{1/2} & \text{otherwise}, \end{cases}$$

with r_s being the odd component of r. Note that $|a_j| > 0$ and this implies that $b_t \neq 0$ for $t \neq 0$.

Observe that $e_0(x) \equiv (2\pi)^{-d/2} \notin F_1$ and $F_1 = \overline{\mathrm{span}\{e_t : t \neq 0\}}$. Therefore, the operator T is one-to-one on F_1 and we can apply the results of Section 5.3 of Chapter 4 to find the ε-complexity, and optimal information and algorithm.

Observe that without the assumption $\langle f, 1 \rangle = 0$, the operator T would have the zero eigenvalue with e_0 as its eigenfunction. It would be still possible to apply the results of Section 5.3 of Chapter 4, as explained in **NR 5.3:1**, but the situation would be slightly more complicated. Opting for simplicity, we impose the condition $\langle f, 1 \rangle = 0$ instead. See **NR 3.1:2**, where the approximation problem is discussed without assuming that $\langle f, 1 \rangle = 0$.

Hence, T is invertible. Following Section 5.3 of Chapter 4, we have $K = ST^{-1} = T^{-1}$ and the operator $K_1 = (T^{-1})^*T^{-1} : \mathcal{L}_2 \to \mathcal{L}_2$ has the eigenpairs $(|b_t|^{-2}, e_t)$ for $t = [t_1, t_2, \ldots, t_d]$ with integer $t_j, t \neq 0$.

Let us order the eigenvalues $\{|b_t|^{-2}\}$. That is, define the numbers $\{\lambda_n\}$ such that

$$\lambda_1 \geq \lambda_2 \geq \cdots > 0, \quad \{\lambda_n\} = \{|b_t|^{-2}\}.$$

Since the unique limit point of the set $\{|b_t|\}$ is infinity, the only limit point of the set $\{|b_t|^{-2}\}$ is zero. Therefore $\lim_n \lambda_n = 0$.

Kowalski and Sielski [87] studied this approximation problem and proved that

$$\sqrt{\lambda_n} = \frac{\alpha}{n^{1/\omega}} \left(1 + o(1)\right) \quad \text{as } n \to \infty, \text{ where } \omega = \sum_{j=1}^{d} \frac{1}{r_j},$$

and α is expressed in terms of the Γ (gamma) and B (beta) functions,

$$\alpha = \left(\frac{2^d}{\Gamma(1 + \omega)} \prod_{j=1}^{d} \frac{\Gamma(1/r_j)}{r_j |a_j|^{1/r_j}} \right)^{1/\omega}$$

if all r_j are even, and

$$\alpha = \left(\frac{2^{d-1} B\big(1/(2r_s), 1 + (\omega - 1/r_s)/2\big)}{\Gamma(1/r_s)\Gamma(1 + \omega - 1/r_s)} \prod_{j=1}^{d} \frac{\Gamma(1/r_j)}{r_j |a_j|^{1/r_j}} \right)^{1/\omega}$$

if r_s is odd.

This is proven by using Davenport's [51] theorem to find the number of integer coordinate points of the convex body B_m. Here B_m is of the form

$$B_m = \left\{ x \in \mathbb{R}^d : \sum_{j=1}^{d} |a_j| \, x_j^{r_j} \leq m \right\}$$

if r has no odd component, and

$$B_m = \left\{ x \in \mathbb{R}^d : \left(\sum_{j=1, j \neq s}^d |a_j| \, x_j^{r_j} \right)^2 + a_s^2 \, x_s^{2r_s} \leq m^2 \right\}$$

if r_s is odd.

From the form of λ_n, we conclude that the ε-cardinality number is given by

$$m(\varepsilon) = \left(\frac{\alpha}{\varepsilon} \right)^\omega \left(1 + o(1) \right) \quad \text{as } \varepsilon \to 0.$$

Applying Theorem 5.8.1 of Chapter 4 we conclude that the ε-complexity of the approximation problem for smooth periodic functions is given by

$$\text{comp}(\varepsilon) = (c + b) \left(\frac{\alpha}{\varepsilon} \right)^\omega \left(1 + o(1) \right) \quad \text{as } \varepsilon \to 0, \quad b \in [0, 2],$$

where c, as always, is the cost of one information evaluation. Furthermore, the information $N_{n^*}^*$ consisting of the inner products $\langle f, z_j \rangle$, where z_j is the eigenfunction of K_1 which corresponds to λ_j, $j = 1, 2, \ldots, m(\varepsilon)$, and the algorithm

$$\phi\left(N_{n^*}^*(f) \right) = \sum_{j=1}^{n^*} \langle f, z_j \rangle \, z_j, \quad n^* = m(\varepsilon),$$

are almost optimal. For $c \gg 1$ and small ε, we thus have

$$\text{comp}(\varepsilon) \simeq c \left(\frac{\alpha}{\varepsilon} \right)^{\sum_{j=1}^d r_j^{-1}}.$$

This exhibits how the complexity depends on dimension d and regularity parameters r_j.

EXAMPLE 3.1.1. We illustrate these results by setting $a_j = 1$, $r_j = 2$ for $j = 1, 2, \ldots, k$. Then $Tf = \sum_{j=1}^d \partial^2 f / \partial x_j^2$ is the d-dimensional Laplace operator. The vectors r and a satisfy (i) and (ii), and the ε-complexity is given by

$$\text{comp}(\varepsilon) = (c + b) \left(\frac{\alpha}{\varepsilon} \right)^{d/2} \left(1 + o(1) \right) \quad \text{as } \varepsilon \to 0,$$

where

$$b \in [0, 2] \quad \text{and} \quad \alpha = \frac{\pi}{\Gamma(1 + d/2)^{2/d}}.$$

Observe that the ε-complexity depends exponentially on d. For large d, the complexity is huge and the approximation problem of periodic functions is intractable.

We now consider the case when the vectors r and a do not satisfy (i) or (ii). Then $a_s = 0$ for some s, or

$$\left\{\left|\,|a_j|\,x^{r_j} - |a_k|\,y^{r_k}\,\right| : x, y \text{ integers}\right\} \subset \{|b_t|\}$$

for some j and k such that $0 < |a_k| \leq |a_j|$.

In the first case, when $a_s = 0$, we have $Te_{(0,\dots,0,t_s,0,\dots,0)} = 0$ for any integer t_s. Thus $\dim \ker T = +\infty$. From **NR 5.3:1** of Chapter 4 it follows that the radius of arbitrary information of finite cardinality is infinite. Hence

$$\text{comp}(\varepsilon) = +\infty, \quad \forall\,\varepsilon \geq 0.$$

Consider now the second case. It may then happen that the ε-complexity is infinite or finite depending on particular values of r_j and a_j. This is illustrated by the following two examples.

EXAMPLE 3.1.2. Let $d = 2$, $a = [1, -k]$, and $r = [2, 2]$, where k is an integer such that $k \neq m^2$ for all integers m. Then $A = \{x^2 - ky^2 : x, y \text{ integers}\} \subset \{|b_t|\}$. It is known that the equation $x^2 - ky^2 = 1$ has infinitely many integer solutions, see Sierpiński [68, Ch. 11, Sec. 17]. Thus, unity is a limit point of the spectrum of K_1, and consequently the radius of arbitrary information of a finite cardinality is at least 1. This implies that $\text{comp}(\varepsilon) = +\infty$, $\forall\,\varepsilon < 1$.

EXAMPLE 3.1.3. Let $d = 2$, $a = [a_1, -a_2]$, and $r = [m, m]$, where a_1, a_2 and m are positive integers, $m \geq 3$, such that the binary form $f(x, y) \equiv a_1 x^m - a_2 y^m$ is irreducible over the field of rational numbers. By the theorem of Thue [18], for any integer k, the inequality

$$|f(x, y)| \leq k$$

has at most finitely many integer solutions. The number of such solutions goes to infinity with k. Thus, the unique limit point of the set $\{|b_t|\}$ is infinity. Therefore the nth minimal radius of information goes to zero and the ε-complexity is finite for positive ε.

Kowalski and Sielski showed that if the conditions (i) and (ii) are not satisfied, then there exists an arbitrary small perturbation of the vector a for which the ε-complexity is infinite for all ε. More precisely, it is enough to consider the case when

$$\left\{\left|\,|a_j|\,x^{r_j} - |a_k|\,y^{r_k}\,\right| : x, y \text{ integers}\right\} \subset \{|b_t|\}$$

for some j and k with $0 < |a_k| \le |a_j|$. Let $\lambda = a_k/a_j$. Then $|\lambda|^{1/r_j} = \sum_{j=1}^{\infty} \beta_j 2^{-j}$ for some $\beta_j \in \{0, 1\}$. Define $a'_k = \text{sign}(a_k)\left(\sum_{p=1}^{m} \beta_p 2^{-p}\right)^{r_j} |a_j|$ for some integer m. Note that the equation

$$|a_j|x^{r_j} - |a'_k|y^{r_k} = 0$$

has infinitely many solutions. Indeed, $x = 2^{nr_k} \sum_{p=1}^{m} \beta_p 2^{-p}$ and $y = 2^{nr_j}$ are solutions for any integer n. Replacing the vector a by the vector $a' = [a_1, \ldots, a_{k-1}, a'_k, a_{k+1}, \ldots, a_d]$, we obtain the operator T', $T'f = Tf + (a'_k - a_k)\partial^{r_k}/\partial x_k^{r_k} f$, for which $\dim \ker T' = +\infty$. Therefore the ε-complexity for the class $\{f \in F_1 : \|T'f\| \le 1\}$ is infinite for all ε. Observe that $|a'_k - a_k|$ can be arbitrarily small if m is sufficiently large.

Notes and Remarks

NR 3.1:1 This section is based on Kowalski and Sielski [87].

NR 3.1:2 Consider the space $F_1 = F_1(r, \mathcal{L}_2)$ without assuming that $\langle f, 1 \rangle = 0$. Then T is many-to-one and $\dim \ker T = 1$. From **NR 5.3:1** of Chapter 4, we know that we have to compute $\langle f, e_0 \rangle$. The nth optimal information is now given by $N_n(f) = [\langle f, e_0 \rangle, \langle f, z_1 \rangle, \ldots, \langle f, z_{n-1} \rangle]$, where z_j are, as before, the eigenfunctions of T which corresponds to the largest eigenvalues. The optimal error algorithm ϕ takes now the form

$$\phi(N_n(f)) = \langle f, e_0 \rangle e_0 + \sum_{j=1}^{n-1} \langle f, z_j \rangle z_j.$$

The asymptotic expressions of the ε-cardinality and of the ε-complexity remain the same.

NR 3.1:3 The Gelfand n-widths and linear Kolmogorov n-widths of the set F are the same as the nth minimal radius of information, see Sections 5.4 and 5.6 of Chapter 4. Thus,

$$d^n(F, \mathcal{L}_2) = \lambda_n(F, \mathcal{L}_2) = \alpha \, n^{-1/\omega} (1 + o(1)) \quad \text{as } n \to +\infty$$

with α and ω defined as in Section 3.1. This coincides with the asymptotic values of the Gelfand and linear Kolmogorov n-width of some other classes of smooth multivariate functions, see Babenko [79].

Exercises

E 3.1:1 Assume that $d = 1$. Show that

$$N_n(f) = [\langle f, 1 \rangle, \langle f, \sin \cdot \rangle, \ldots, \langle f, \sin n_1 \cdot \rangle, \langle f, \cos \cdot \rangle, \ldots, \langle f, \cos n_1 \cdot \rangle]$$

with $n_1 = \lfloor (n-1)/2 \rfloor$ is nth optimal information in the class $\Lambda = F_1^*$, and $r(n) = \lceil n/2 \rceil^{-r}$.

E 3.1:2 Assume that $a_1 = \cdots = a_d = 1$ and $r_1 = \cdots = r_d = r$. Find out how many eigenvalues of T are smaller than $d \, k^r$ for an integer k. Based on that, derive an algorithm which computes n vectors $t = [t_1, t_2, \ldots, t_d]$ corresponding to the indices of the first n eigenfunctions e_t which correspond to the n largest eigenvalues.

3.2. Smooth Nonperiodic Functions: Hilbert Case

Consider the approximation problem for functions $f : D = [0,1]^d \to \mathbb{R}$ which are $r_j \geq 1$ times continuously differentiable in direction j, $j = 1, 2, \ldots, d$. Let $D^{i_1, \ldots, i_d}$ denote the partial derivative operator, $D^{i_1, \ldots, i_d} f = \partial^{i_1 + \cdots + i_d} f / (\partial x_1^{i_1} \cdot \ldots \cdot \partial x_d^{i_d})$. Define the linear space $F_1 = F_1(r)$, $r = [r_1, \ldots, r_d]$ by

$$F_1 = \{ f \in C^{r_1, \ldots, r_d}(D) : (D^{i_1, \ldots, i_d} f)(t) = 0, \ \forall i_j = 0, \ldots, r_j, \ j = 1, \ldots d,$$

$$\text{when one of the components of } t \text{ is zero} \}.$$

Define the linear restriction operator T by

$$T = D^{r_1, \ldots, r_d} : F_1 \to X = \mathcal{L}_2(D).$$

Observe that the boundary conditions in the definition of the space F_1 imply that the operator T is bijective.

We wish to approximate $S(f) = f$ for f from $F = \{ f \in F_1 : \|Tf\| \leq 1 \}$, with $G = \mathcal{L}_2(D)$ and $\Lambda = F_1^*$. Thus, we approximate smooth functions assuming that the range of S and T is the Hilbert space $\mathcal{L}_2(D)$.

As we know from Chapter 4, the ε-complexity depends on the eigenvalues of the operator $K_1 = (T^{-1})^* T^{-1} : \mathcal{L}_2(D) \to \mathcal{L}_2(D)$. To find the explicit form of K_1, define the operators $T_0^{r_1, \ldots, r_d}, T_1^{r_1, \ldots, r_d} : \mathcal{L}_2(D) \to \mathcal{L}(D)$ by

$$(T_0^{r_1, \ldots, r_d} f)(x_1, \ldots, x_d) = \int_D \prod_{j=1}^d \frac{(x_j - t_j)_+^{r_j - 1}}{(r_j - 1)!} f(t_1, \ldots, t_d) \, dt_1 \ldots dt_d,$$

$$(T_1^{r_1, \ldots, r_d} f)(x_1, \ldots, x_d) = \int_D \prod_{j=1}^d \frac{(t_j - x_j)_+^{r_j - 1}}{(r_j - 1)!} f(t_1, \ldots, t_d) \, dt_1 \ldots dt_d.$$

Then we have

$$D^{r_1, \ldots, r_d} T_0^{r_1, \ldots, r_d} = (-1)^{r_1 + \cdots + r_d} D^{r_1, \ldots, r_d} T_1^{r_1, \ldots, r_d} = I,$$
$$(T_0^{r_1, \ldots, r_d})^* = T_1^{r_1, r_2, \ldots, r_d}.$$

This yields that
$$K_1 = T_0^{r_1, \ldots, r_d} T_1^{r_1, \ldots, r_d}.$$

Let (λ, z) be an eigenpair of K_1, $K_1 z = \lambda z$. Then, by applying T^2 to the equation $K_1 z = \lambda z$, we obtain

$$\lambda D^{2r_1, \ldots, 2r_d} z - (-1)^{r_1 + \cdots + r_d} z = 0, \tag{i}$$

with boundary conditions

$$
\left.\frac{\partial^i z(x_1,\ldots,x_d)}{\partial x_j^i}\right|_{x_j=0} = 0, \quad i = 0,\ldots,r_j-1,
$$

$$
\left.\frac{\partial^i z(x_1,\ldots,x_d)}{\partial x_j^i}\right|_{x_j=1} = 0, \quad i = r_j,\ldots,2r_j-1,
$$

(ii)

for $j = 1,2,\ldots,d$. It is known, see e.g., Tikhomirov [76, p. 128], that the eigenvalues of (i) and (ii) are given by

$$
\lambda_{i_1,\ldots,i_d} = \prod_{j=1}^d \left(\frac{1}{\pi\, i_j}\right)^{2r_j}(1+o(1)) \quad \text{as } \min\{i_1,\ldots,i_d\} \to +\infty.
$$

Here $i_j = 1,2,\ldots$ and $j = 1,2,\ldots,d$. We order the eigenvalues $\{\lambda_{i_1,\ldots,i_d}\}$. That is, define the numbers $\{\lambda_n\}$ such that

$$
\lambda_1 \geq \lambda_2 \geq \cdots > 0 \quad \text{and} \quad \{\lambda_n\} = \{\lambda_{i_1,\ldots,i_d}\}.
$$

This approximation problem was analyzed by Micchelli and Wahba [81] for $r_1 = r_2 = \cdots = r_d$, and by Papageorgiou and Wasilkowski [86] for arbitrary r_j. They proved that

$$
\sqrt{\lambda_n} = \alpha\left(\frac{(\ln n)^{k-1}}{n}\right)^{r_{\min}}(1+o(1)) \quad \text{as } n \to +\infty,
$$

where $r_{\min} = \min\{r_j : 1 \leq j \leq d\}$, k is the number of r_j that are equal to $r_{\min}$, and the constant α is given by $\alpha = \alpha_{d,k}^{r_{\min}}/\pi^\beta$ with $\beta = \sum_{j=1}^d r_j$ and

$$
\alpha_{d,k} = \begin{cases} 1 & \text{if } d = 1, \\ 1/(d-1)! & \text{if } k = d, \\ \left((k-1)!\prod_{j=1,r_j\neq r_{\min}}^d \left(\frac{r_j}{r_{\min}}-1\right)\right)^{-1} & \text{otherwise.} \end{cases}
$$

From this we conclude that the ε-cardinality number is given by

$$
m(\varepsilon) = \frac{\alpha_{d,k}}{\pi^{\beta/r_{\min}}}\left(\frac{1}{\varepsilon}\right)^{1/r_{\min}}\left(\frac{1}{r_{\min}}\ln\frac{\alpha}{\varepsilon}\right)^{(k-1)}(1+o(1)) \quad \text{as } \varepsilon \to 0.
$$

Hence, the ε-complexity of the approximation problem for smooth nonperiodic functions is given by

$$
\text{comp}(\varepsilon) = (c+b)\frac{\alpha_{d,k}}{\pi^{\beta/r_{\min}}}\left(\frac{1}{\varepsilon}\right)^{1/r_{\min}}\left(\frac{1}{r_{\min}}\ln\frac{\alpha}{\varepsilon}\right)^{(k-1)}(1+o(1)) \quad \text{as } \varepsilon \to 0,
$$

with $b \in [0, 2]$. Furthermore, the information N_n^* consisting of the inner products $\langle f, z_j \rangle$, where z_j satisfies (i) and (ii) with $\lambda = \lambda_j$, $j = 1, 2, \ldots, n$, and the algorithm

$$\phi\big(N_n^*(f)\big) = \sum_{j=1}^{n} \langle f, z_j \rangle z_j, \quad n = m(\varepsilon),$$

are almost optimal. For $c \gg 1$ and small ε, we thus have

$$\text{comp}(\varepsilon) \simeq c \, \frac{\alpha_{d,k}}{r_{\min}^{k-1} \pi^{\beta/k}} \left(\frac{1}{\varepsilon} \right)^{1/r_{\min}} \left(\ln \frac{1}{\varepsilon} \right)^{k-1}.$$

Observe the mild dependence on the dimension d. The only dependence on d is through k, $k \leq d$. If all $r_j \equiv r_{\min}$ then $k = d$ and there is a $(\ln \varepsilon^{-1})^{d-1}$ factor in the ε-complexity. This factor is multiplied by $\varepsilon^{-1/r}$ which, obviously, goes to infinity faster as ε approaches zero. Therefore, for any d and r_j we can write

$$\text{comp}(\varepsilon) = O\!\left(c \left(\frac{1}{\varepsilon} \right)^{\eta + 1/r_{\min}} \right), \quad \forall \eta > 0.$$

We now indicate why the complexity is almost independent of the dimension d. This is because d plays a double role in the definition of the class F_1. It denotes the number of variables of f and also determines the smoothness of f. The increase of d implies more variables of f which makes the problem harder, but also the additional smoothness of functions in the class F_1 which makes the problem easier. These two effects of the change of d almost neutralize each other, and that's why the complexity depends so mildly on d.

Notes and Remarks

NR 3.2:1 This section is based on Papageorgiou and Wasilkowski [86].

NR 3.2:2 We have assumed that $r_j \geq 1$. It is easy to check that if one of the parameters r_j is zero then there exists a positive number $\varepsilon_0 = \varepsilon_0(r_1, r_2, \ldots, r_n)$ such that $r(N) \geq \varepsilon_0$ for any information of a finite cardinality. Therefore $\text{comp}(\varepsilon) = +\infty$ for $\varepsilon < \varepsilon_0$.

NR 3.2:3 Wahba [78] considered the bivariate, $d = 2$, approximation problem for the space $F = W_2^r \otimes W_2^r$ being the tensor product of Sobolev spaces W_2^r, and the class Λ consisting of only function values. She exhibited a sequence of information operators of cardinality n whose radii approach $O(n^{-(r-1/2)})$. This should be compared with the nth minimal radius in the class of *all* linear functionals which is proportional to $n^{-r} \ln(n)$. Thus, one can lose roughly at most $\sqrt{n}/\ln(n)$ by using function values instead of optimally chosen linear functionals. This is not too significant for large r.

Exercises

E 3.2:1 Show that for $r_1 = r_2 = \cdots = r_d = 0$, ε_0 defined in **NR 3.2:2** is equal to one.

3.3. Smooth Nonperiodic Functions: Banach Case

In this section we briefly consider a modification of the approximation problem studied in Section 3.2. This modification is needed for the average case and probabilistic settings.

We use the notation of Section 3.2. Consider the operator $T = D^{r_1,\ldots,r_d}$, this time with the range $C(D)$, the class of continuous functions equipped with the sup norm, $\|f\|_{\sup} = \sup_{t \in D} |f(t)|$. The set $F = F_q$ is now given by

$$F = \{f \in F_1 : \|D^{r_1,\ldots,r_d} f\|_{\sup} \le q\}, \quad q > 0.$$

We approximate $S(f) = f$ for $f \in F$ with $G = \mathcal{L}_2(D)$ and for the same class Λ as in Section 3.2. Let $\text{comp}(\varepsilon; q)$ denote the ε-complexity of this problem.

We show relations between $\text{comp}(\varepsilon; q)$ and the ε-complexity $\text{comp}(\varepsilon; \mathcal{L}_2)$ of the approximation problem studied in Section 3.2. Observe that $\|f\|_2 = \left(\int_D f^2(t)\, dt\right)^{1/2} \le \|f\|_{\sup}$, and therefore $\text{comp}(\varepsilon; q) \le \text{comp}(\varepsilon/q; \mathcal{L}_2)$. This yields

$$\text{comp}(\varepsilon; q) = O\left(c \left(\frac{q}{\varepsilon}\right)^{\eta + 1/r_{\min}}\right) \quad \text{as } \varepsilon \to 0, \quad \forall \eta > 0,$$

where $r_{\min} = \min\{r_j : 1 \le j \le d\}$.

We now find a lower bound on $\text{comp}(\varepsilon; q)$. Without loss of generality assume that $r_{\min} = r_1$. Consider the set

$$\widetilde{F} = \left\{ g(t_1) \prod_{j=2}^{d} \frac{t_j^{r_j + 1}}{(r_j + 1)!} : g \text{ is } r_{\min}\text{-times continuously differentiable}, \right.$$

$$\left. g(0) = g'(0) = \cdots = g^{(r_{\min})}(0) = 0, \text{ and } \max_{0 \le t \le 1} |g^{(r_{\min})}(t)| \le q \right\}.$$

Then $\widetilde{F} \subset F_q$ and $\text{comp}(\varepsilon; q)$ is no smaller than the ε-complexity of the approximation problem for the set $\widetilde{F}$. The latter problem corresponds to the approximation of smooth *scalar* functions whose complexity is proportional to $c\,(q/\varepsilon)^{1/r_{\min}}$, see e.g., GTOA p. 129-132. Thus,

$$\text{comp}(\varepsilon; q) = \Omega\left(c \left(\frac{q}{\varepsilon}\right)^{1/r_{\min}}\right) \quad \text{as } \varepsilon \to 0.$$

The last two equations show that modulo η, $\text{comp}(\varepsilon; q)$ is proportional to $c\,(q/\varepsilon)^{1/r_{\min}}$. The information $N^*_{m(\varepsilon)}$ and the algorithm ϕ^* which are almost optimal for the approximation problem of Section 3.2, are also almost optimal for the approximation problem of this section.

Exercises

E 3.3:1 Consider the approximation problem with the range of T given by $\mathcal{L}_p(D)$, $F = \{f : \|Tf\|_p \leq q\}$. Let $\text{comp}(\varepsilon; p, q)$ denote the ε-complexity of this problem. Show that

$$\text{comp}(\varepsilon; p, q) = \Omega\left(c \left(\frac{q}{\varepsilon} \right)^{1/r_{\min}} \right) \quad \text{as } \varepsilon \to 0, \quad \forall\, p \in [1, +\infty],$$

$$\text{comp}(\varepsilon; p, q) = O\left(c \left(\frac{q}{\varepsilon} \right)^{\eta + 1/r_{\min}} \right) \quad \text{as } \varepsilon \to 0, \quad \forall\, \eta > 0,\ p \in [2, +\infty].$$

4. Computer Vision

This section presents a problem which arises in human and computer vision, namely the problem of visual surface reconstruction. Our goal is to combine depth, surface normals, and curvature information about a surface into a single representation. Commonly used algorithms for acquiring the information to be combined include stereo, shape from shading, shape from texture, and shape from contours.

One of the most difficult parts of applying the theory of information-based complexity to practical problems is choosing the correct class F. While other elements of the model are generally fixed by the goals of the practitioner and the limits of the data acquisition schema, the choice of F is dictated only by the need for the formal mathematical definition of the problem to reflect the underlying physical problem. This section discusses not only the formulation and solution of a problem in vision but, more importantly, work in using the optimality properties of the resulting algorithms to better understand and refine the models underlying the problem and the human visual system.

The problem of visual surface reconstruction can be viewed as a function approximation problem with the solution operator $S: F_1 \to G$ being the embedding mapping, $S(f) = f$, where F_1 is our model of world surfaces and G is the solution space of functions. The space G is taken to be $\mathcal{L}_2(B)$ for some bounded set B of $\mathbb{R}^2$. (See also **NR 4:2**).

In the traditional formulation, Grimson [79, 81] and Terzopoulos [83] make no explicit assumptions on F_1. The formal definition below does not precisely specify F_1 because it is our attempt to use psychological experiments to determine the most appropriate class. A two parameter class $D^{-r}H^s$ will be considered for F_1, with $r > 1$. The precise definition of $D^{-r}H^s$ may be found in Duchon [76], see also Meinguet [79]. Here, we mention that $D^{-r}H^s$ is a semi-Hilbert space of functions f on $\mathbb{R}^2$ such that their rth derivative $D^r f$ (in the distributional sense) is a tempered distribution on $\mathbb{R}^2$ whose Fourier transform $\widehat{D^r f}$ satisfies

$$\|f\| = \left(\int_{\mathbb{R}^2} (x_1^2 + x_2^2)^s |\widehat{D^r f}(x)|^2 \, dx_1 \, dx_2 \right)^{1/2} < +\infty.$$

Note that $\|\cdot\|$ is a seminorm. The set F is taken as the unit ball in F_1.

The class Λ of permissible information operations consists of function values, first and sometimes second order derivatives, see **NR 4:3**.

Since F_1 is a semi-Hilbert space, Section 5.7 implies that the spline algorithm is strongly optimal, i.e., it is central and minimizes the local error for any information. Duchon [76], extending the work of Atteia [66] to the case of semi-Hilbert spaces, noted that a spline can be explicitly represented in terms of the reproducing kernel of the space. In particular, for $F_1 = D^{-r}H^s$ and for the information $N(f) = [f(x_1), f(x_2), \ldots, f(x_n)]$ consisting of n function evaluations, $x_i \in \mathbb{R}^2$, the spline σ takes the form

$$\sigma(x) = \sum_{i=1}^{n} \alpha_i g(x, x_i) + \sum_{i=1}^{d} \beta_i q_i(x).$$

(For the particular choice of $F_1 = D^{-2}H^0$, these are sometimes referred to as thin-plate splines.) Here, $\{q_i\}_{i=1}^{d}$ is a basis for the null space of the semi-norm and d is its dimension. We assume that $n \geq d$. The function $g(\cdot, \cdot)$ is closely related to the reproducing kernel of the space F_1 and takes the form

$$g(u, v) = \begin{cases} \|u - v\|^{2(m+s-1)} \ln \|u - v\| & \text{if } (m + s) \text{ is an even integer,} \\ \|u - v\|^{2(m+s-1)} & \text{otherwise,} \end{cases}$$

where $\|\cdot\|$ stands for the Euclidean norm in $\mathbb{R}^2$. The coefficients α_i and β_i of the spline σ can be found by solving the $(n + d) \times (n + d)$ dense linear system:

$$\sum_{i=1}^{n} \alpha_i g(x_j, x_i) + \sum_{i=1}^{d} \beta_i q_i(x_j) = f(x_j), \text{ for } j = 1, 2, \ldots, n,$$

$$\sum_{i=1}^{n} \alpha_i q_j(x_i) = 0, \qquad \text{for } j = 1, 2 \ldots, d.$$

Here, we assume that the points x_i include a subset $\{x_1, x_2, \ldots, x_d\}$ for which the matrix $\left(q_j(x_k)\right)_{j,k=1}^{d}$ is nonsingular. Then the spline is unique, see Duchon [76].

As indicated above, our main problem is to determine the best choice of r and s in $F_1 = D^{-r}H^s$. There are at least two basic approaches for doing this. The first approach is to derive (by some means unknown to the author) the classes and semi-norms from psychological/physiological models of human perception. The second approach, which we discuss here, is to take a collection of reasonable class/norm pairs and use psychological experimentation to subjectively order the pairs. In designing such an experiment, it is imperative that one compares only strongly optimal error algorithms. Otherwise, differences in the computed solutions might be caused by differences in the quality of the algorithms rather than by differences in the assumed models, see Boult [87].

The details of the experimental procedure appear elsewhere, see Boult [86]. Presented here is only enough context to allow the discussion of the results of the experiment. The experiments included the following nine classes as the choices for F_1:

$$\begin{aligned}
&\mathcal{A} = D^{-2}H^{-0.75} \quad &\mathcal{B} = D^{-3}H^{-1.75} \quad &\mathcal{C} = D^{-4}H^{-2.75} \\
&\mathcal{D} = D^{-2}H^{-0.50} \quad &\mathcal{E} = D^{-2}H^{-0.25} \quad &\mathcal{F} = D^{-2}H^{0} \\
&\mathcal{G} = D^{-2}H^{+0.50} \quad &\mathcal{H} = D^{-4}H^{0} \quad &\mathcal{I} = D^{-5}H^{0}.
\end{aligned}$$

In addition, nine different data-sets were considered, each generated by a different underlying surface. These underlying surfaces can be broken up into three classes:

(1) Jump discontinuities (data-sets 1, 2, 3, 6)
(2) Orientation discontinuities (data-sets 5, 8)
(3) No discontinuities (data-sets 4, 7, 9)

The number of points selected to form the data-sets ranged from 16 to 100 points. For the reconstructed surfaces, each sample presents two shaded perspective views of a surface generated by spline algorithm under different class/norm assumptions. The reconstructed surface was generated by computing the spline from the interpolation data and by evaluating that spline on a 70×70 grid of points which were plotted using a simple shading model.

The subjects were presented with nine packages each containing four views of the initial data and 36 sample reconstructions. The subjects rated each sample on "how well it fits their impression of the surface generating the initial data". They also compared each sample with five others, stating if it appeared to be a better, equal, or worst fit to the initial data. In total, each of the six subjects ranked 324 sample reconstructions and made 1485 pairwise comparisons. The rankings are given in Table 4.1.

Discontinuity	$\mathcal{A}$	$\mathcal{B}$	$\mathcal{C}$	$\mathcal{D}$	$\mathcal{E}$	$\mathcal{F}$	$\mathcal{G}$	$\mathcal{H}$	$\mathcal{I}$
Jump	3.97	3.94	3.99	3.97	3.49	3.22	2.67	2.39	1.73
Orientation	2.73	2.77	2.85	3.60	3.90	4.06	4.31	3.98	2.94
None	1.92	4.54	4.50	3.04	4.29	4.60	4.39	4.38	3.97
Overall	3.01	3.88	3.91	3.58	3.85	3.87	3.61	3.40	2.75

Table 4.1: Mean quality responses for the various data groupings

Examination of the ratings for data-sets from underlying functions with a jump discontinuity shows that classes $\mathcal{C}$, $\mathcal{A}$, $\mathcal{D}$, and $\mathcal{B}$ are superior; for those data-sets with underlying orientation discontinuities, class $\mathcal{G}$ is most suitable; for those data-sets sampled from infinitely differentiable surfaces classes $\mathcal{F}$, $\mathcal{B}$, and $\mathcal{C}$ are superior; and finally, when considering overall performance, classes $\mathcal{C}$, $\mathcal{B}$, $\mathcal{F}$, and $\mathcal{E}$ are the overall most appropriate, see **NR 4:4**.

From the data in Table 4.1, there appears to be a relationship between the number $s - r$ of apparent derivatives in the class $D^{-r}H^s$ and the quality of the associated reconstructions. The exact nature of the relationship seems dependent on the actual data-set, but it appeared to be a unimodal relationship with the location of the peak depending on the data-set (taking into account the fact that some classes produced exact answers because of their null-space).

Finally, for the case when the underlying surface had jump or orientation discontinuities, the change of the norm, while keeping the class of functions basically fixed, did not greatly affect the quality of reconstructions as can be seen by comparing the ratings for classes $\mathcal{A}$, $\mathcal{B}$, and $\mathcal{C}$. Conversely, for all data-sets considered, fixing the norm and varying the class of functions did produce significant changes in reported quality, as is apparent by comparing the ratings for classes $\mathcal{A}$, $\mathcal{D}$, $\mathcal{E}$, $\mathcal{F}$, and $\mathcal{G}$.

As an application of optimal algorithms, this section demonstrates models which yield reasonable and sometimes far better solutions to the visual surface reconstruction problem than those used in Terzopoulos [84] and Grimson [81]. While the computational aspects of these trade-offs have not been fully explored, it is already known that some of the non-traditional classes are computationally more efficient when employing the spline algorithm.

Note that the most appropriate model may be affected by the "smoothness" of the underlying data. Indeed, if the underlying data contains more than one surface (i.e., contains jump discontinuities), then some of the non-traditional classes were considerably better. If the underlying surfaces were smooth, most of the classes performed reasonably well.

We end this section with a final remark to those who question if humans would actually use an "optimal error algorithm". We are not claiming that spline algorithms are actually being used by the human visual system (nor are we saying that they should necessarily be used in computer vision). Instead, we are using these optimal algorithms to refine our models. Once we have developed an appropriate model for a problem, nothing is to prevent us from using that knowledge to develop approximate algorithms which are amenable to neural implementation or that are computationally more efficient than the optimal error algorithm.

Notes and Remarks

NR 4:1 This section was written by T. E. Boult.

NR 4:2 Based on some psychophysical evidence and the current understanding of the operation of the human visual system, Grimson [79] proposed a computational model of human visual surface reconstruction from stereo data. This model formulates the problem as one of finding the surface passing through the points that is of minimal norm. In that seminal work, Grimson presented *ad hoc* arguments as to which class of functions to assume. He also presented a discrete minimization algorithm which approximately solved the particular problem.

NR 4:3 One might question the use of surface derivatives since they are not direct observables using vision. However, first order derivatives can be obtained in many ways, including: texture and or occluding contours, e.g., see Aloimonos [86], Ikeuchi [80], Kender [86], and Stevens [79], shape-from-shading, e.g., Wolff [87a], Pentland [84], or other shape-from-X algorithms. Second order derivatives may be directly calculated using the algorithms presented in Wolff [87b].

NR 4:4 Note that the overall performance of any classes in the experiment is very dependent on the different individual data-sets chosen. This observation is supported by the large standard deviation in overall rating responses; the smallest standard deviation of overall responses for any class was 1.04 (for class $\mathcal{E}$ where the mean was 3.85), and the largest was 1.75 (for class $\mathcal{I}$ where the mean was 2.75).

NR 4:5 We comment on various restrictive assumptions which our problem definition implies about the workings of the visual system and the perceived visual world. They are:

(1) that the problem of visual surface reconstruction can be modeled as a semi-norm minimization in a semi-Hilbert space,
(2) that one should develop strongly optimal error algorithms using worst case error,
(3) and that data presented to the system is from one surface.

5. Linear Partial Differential Equations

In this section, we deal with the complexity of the approximate solution of $2m$th-order elliptic linear partial differential equations $Au = f$. First, we consider the case where any linear functional is permissible, i.e., $\Lambda = \Lambda^*$. We give necessary and sufficient conditions for the algorithm which is known as the finite element method (FEM) to be almost optimal. Unfortunately, the assumption that any linear functional is permissible is usually too strong. It is more common in practice to design algorithms whose sole information about a given problem element f is the "standard" information which consists of function values of f at some points. So, we next consider what happens when the class Λ of permissible information is restricted to be the class Λ^{std} of standard information. We find that the penalty involved in going from arbitrary linear information to standard information is unbounded when $m > 0$. Moreover, we show that a suitable variant of the FEM (which uses standard information) is an optimal algorithm in this case.

Let $r \geq -m$. Choose $F_1 = H^r(\Omega)$ as the usual Sobolev space consisting of all functions on a bounded, simply-connected, C^∞ region Ω of $\mathbb{R}^d$. We choose the unit ball of $H^r(\Omega)$ as our set F of problem elements. That is, we let

$$F = \{\, f \in H^r(\Omega) : \|f\|_r \leq 1 \,\},$$

where the norm $\|\cdot\|_r$ is defined by

$$\|f\|_r := \left(\sum_{|\alpha| \leq r} \int_\Omega \left((D^\alpha f)(x) \right)^2 dx \right)^{1/2},$$

see **NR 5:2** for further discussion of multi-index notation and Sobolev spaces. Recalling that $H_0^m(\Omega)$ denotes the space of $H^m(\Omega)$-functions whose normal derivatives of order at most $m - 1$ vanish on $\partial\Omega$, we choose $G = H_0^m(\Omega)$ as the range of the solution operator.

Let A be a $2m$th-order regularly-elliptic operator given by

$$(Av)(x) = \sum_{|\alpha|,|\beta| \leq m} (-1)^{|\alpha|} D^\alpha \left(a_{\alpha,\beta}(x) D^\beta v(x) \right), \qquad \forall\, x \in \Omega.$$

We assume that the (real) coefficients $a_{\alpha,\beta} \in C^\infty(\overline{\Omega})$ are chosen so that

$$a_{\alpha,\beta}(x) = a_{\beta,\alpha}(x), \qquad \forall\, x \in \Omega.$$

We define the *principal part* A_0 of A by

$$(A_0 v)(x) = \sum_{|\alpha|,|\beta| = m} (-1)^{|\alpha|} D^\alpha \left(a_{\alpha,\beta}(x) D^\beta v(x) \right), \qquad \forall\, x \in \Omega.$$

For any vector $\xi \in \mathbb{R}^d$ and for any point $x_0 \in \Omega$, we define the polynomial

$$A_0(x_0, \xi) = \sum_{|\alpha|,|\beta|=m} (-1)^{|\alpha|} \xi^\alpha \left(a_{\alpha,\beta}(x_0)\xi^\beta \right).$$

We assume that A is *uniformly strongly elliptic* on Ω, i.e., there exists a constant $C > 0$ such that the following conditions hold for all $x_0 \in \Omega$:

(1) If $\xi \in \mathbb{R}^d$ is nonzero, then $A_0(x_0, \xi) \neq 0$.
(2) For any pair of linearly independent vectors $\xi, \eta \in \mathbb{R}^d$, the polynomial equation
$$A_0(x_0, \lambda\xi + \eta) = 0$$

in the complex variable λ has exactly m roots with positive imaginary parts.
(3) Let $\|\cdot\|$ denote the Euclidean norm on $\mathbb{R}^d$. Then

$$|A_0(x_0, \xi)| \geq C\|\xi\|^{2m}, \qquad \forall\, \xi \in \mathbb{R}^d.$$

(Note that here, and in what follows, we will follow the well-established custom of letting C denote a generic positive constant whose value may change from place to place.)

We are interested in solving the *boundary value problem* of finding $u \in G$ such that

$$\begin{cases} (Au)(x) = f(x), & \forall\, x \in \Omega, \\ \partial_\nu^j u(x) = 0, & \forall\, x \in \partial\Omega \quad (0 \leq j \leq m-1), \end{cases}$$

where $f \in F$ and ∂_ν^j is the jth normal derivative operator.

We are interested in approximating the *variational solution* of our boundary-value problem. We define a symmetric, continuous bilinear form B on $H_0^m(\Omega)$ by

$$B(v, w) = \sum_{|\alpha|,|\beta|\leq m} \int_\Omega a_{\alpha\beta}(x) D^\alpha v(x) D^\beta w(x)\, dx, \qquad \forall\, v, w \in H_0^m(\Omega).$$

We additionally assume that B is $H_0^m(\Omega)$-*coercive*, i.e., there exists a constant $C > 0$ such that

$$B(v, v) \geq C\|v\|_m^2, \qquad \forall\, v \in H_0^m(\Omega).$$

The solution operator $S\colon F \to G$ is defined as $S(f) := u$, where $u \in G = H_0^m(\Omega)$ is chosen such that

$$B(u, v) = \langle f, v \rangle_0 = \int_\Omega f(x)v(x)\, dx, \qquad \forall\, v \in H_0^m(\Omega).$$

Since B is coercive and $r \geq -m$, the Lax-Milgram Theorem implies that the solution operator S is well-defined.

EXAMPLE 5.1. Let Δ, $(\Delta u)(x) = \sum_{j=1}^{d} (\partial^2/\partial x_j^2)u(x)$, be the Laplace operator. Then *Poisson's equation*

$$-\Delta u = f \quad \text{in } \Omega \qquad \text{and} \qquad u = 0 \quad \text{on } \partial\Omega$$

is a second-order elliptic problem with $m = 1$. The corresponding solution operator $S \colon H^r(\Omega) \to H_0^1(\Omega)$ is then defined as follows. Let $f \in F$. Then $u = S(f) \in H_0^1(\Omega)$ satisfies

$$\int_\Omega \langle \nabla u(x), \nabla v(x) \rangle \, dx = \int_\Omega f(x)v(x) \, dx, \qquad \forall\, v \in H_0^1(\Omega),$$

where $\langle \cdot, \cdot \rangle$ denotes the Euclidean inner product in $\mathbb{R}^n$.

EXAMPLE 5.2. The *biharmonic equation*

$$\Delta^2 u = f \quad \text{in } \Omega \qquad \text{and} \qquad u = \partial_\nu u = 0 \quad \text{on } \partial\Omega$$

is a fourth-order elliptic problem with $m = 2$. The corresponding solution operator $S \colon H^r(\Omega) \to H_0^2(\Omega)$ is then defined as follows. Let $f \in F$. Then $u = S(f) \in H_0^2(\Omega)$ satisfies

$$\int_\Omega \Delta u(x)\Delta v(x) \, dx = \int_\Omega f(x)v(x) \, dx, \qquad \forall\, v \in H_0^2(\Omega).$$

For future reference, we recall the important

SHIFT THEOREM. *If $f \in H^r(\Omega)$, then $S(f) \in H^{2m+r}(\Omega) \cap H_0^m(\Omega)$. Moreover, there exists a constant $C \geq 1$ such that*

$$C^{-1}\|S(f)\|_{2m+r} \leq \|f\|_r \leq C\|S(f)\|_{2m+r}, \qquad \forall\, f \in H^r(\Omega).$$

(The proof of the Shift Theorem may be found in Chapter 3 of Babuška and Aziz [72] or Chapter 8 of Oden and Reddy [76].) Using the shift theorem, the Sobolev embedding theorem and an m-fold integration by parts, we see that for sufficiently smooth f, the variational solution $S(f)$ is also the solution of the original boundary value problem.

We measure the quality of an approximation by the $G = H_0^m(\Omega)$-norm. Hence, the error of an algorithm ϕ using information N is given by

$$e(\phi, N) = \sup_{f \in F} \|S(f) - \phi(N(f))\|_m.$$

We first consider what happens when $\Lambda = \Lambda^*$ is the class of all linear functionals on $F_1 = H^r(\Omega)$. The nth minimal radius is given by the following theorem, which we prove in **NR 5:8**.

THEOREM 5.1.

$$r(n, \Lambda^*) = \Theta(n^{-(r+m)/d}) \quad as \quad n \to \infty.$$

We now describe the algorithm known as the finite element method. First, we define finite element spaces. Let $\{\mathcal{T}_n\}_{n=1}^{\infty}$ be a *quasi-uniform* family of triangulations of Ω. That is, there exists a constant $C > 0$, independent of n, such that

$$\max_{K \in \mathcal{T}_n} \operatorname{diam}(K) \leq C \min_{K \in \mathcal{T}_n} \sup\{\operatorname{diam}(S) : S \text{ a sphere contained in } K\}.$$

Next, we let $\mathcal{S}_{n,k}$ be the n-dimensional subspace of $H_0^m(\Omega)$ consisting of piecewise polynomials of degree k over the triangulation $\mathcal{T}_n$. That is, $s \in \mathcal{S}_{n,k}$ iff

  (1) for every element $K \in \mathcal{T}_n$, the restriction of s to K is a polynomial of degree at most k, and
  (2) $s \in C_0^{m-1}(\Omega)$.

We let $\{s_1, \ldots, s_n\}$ be a basis for $\mathcal{S}_{n,k}$ having a special form. Namely, we let $\{x_1^*, \ldots, x_n^*\}$ be a set of points in $\overline{\Omega}$, called the *nodes* of the finite element space $\mathcal{S}_{n,k}$. It is customary to choose basis functions $\{s_1, \ldots, s_n\}$ so that $s_i(x_j^*) = \delta_{i,j}$, $1 \leq i, j \leq n$, and therefore

$$v(x) = \sum_{j=1}^{n} v(x_j^*) s_j(x), \qquad \forall v \in \mathcal{S}_{n,k}.$$

Moreover, the nodes $\{x_1^*, \ldots, x_n^*\}$ are typically chosen so that the support of any given basis function is small; that is, the cardinality of the set of elements in $\mathcal{T}_n$ at which a given basis function is nonzero is independent of n.

We now define *finite element information* (FEI) $N_{n,k}$ of cardinality n and degree k by

$$N_{n,k}(f) = [\langle f, s_1 \rangle_0, \ldots, \langle f, s_n \rangle_0], \qquad \forall f \in F.$$

Since we have assumed that $\Lambda = \Lambda^*$, any linear functional is permissible. In particular, this means that $N_{n,k}$ is permissible information.

Now that we have defined finite element information, we can describe the finite element method using $N_{n,k}$; namely, for any $f \in F$, we let $u_{n,k} \in \mathcal{S}_{n,k}$ satisfy

$$B(u_{n,k}, s_i) = \langle f, s_i \rangle_0 \qquad (1 \leq i \leq n).$$

This may be easily reduced to the solution of an $n \times n$ linear system. Indeed, we define a matrix $M \in \mathbb{R}^{n \times n}$ and a vector $b \in \mathbb{R}^n$ by

$$M = \big(B(s_j, s_i)\big)_{1 \le i, j \le n} \qquad \text{and} \qquad b = N_{n,k}(f).$$

The matrix M is sparse since the support of basis functions is small. Let $a \in \mathbb{R}^n$ satisfy $Ma = b$. Since B is coercive, the matrix M is positive definite so that there is a unique $a = [a_1, \ldots, a_n]$ satisfying this set of equations for any $f \in F$. Then $u_{n,k}$ is well-defined and

$$u_{n,k}(x) = \sum_{j=1}^{n} a_j s_j(x).$$

Since $u_{n,k}$ depends on f only through the information $N_{n,k}(f)$, we may write

$$u_{n,k} = \phi_{n,k}(N_{n,k}(f)).$$

The algorithm $\phi_{n,k}$ is called the nth *finite element method* (FEM) of degree k using $N_{n,k}$. Clearly, the FEM is a linear algorithm that uses FEI and can be expressed as

$$\phi_{n,k}(N_{n,k}(f)) = \sum_{j=1}^{n} \langle f, s_j \rangle_0 \, g_j$$

for some functions $g_1, \ldots, g_n$.

We now comment on the implementation of the FEM. Since g_j are independent of f, they can be precomputed. Thus, the combinatory cost of the FEM is n multiplications and $n-1$ additions. On the other hand, if the functions g_j are hard to obtain then we can compute $\phi_{n,k}(N_{n,k}(f)) = \sum_{j=1}^{n} a_j s_j(x)$ by solving the sparse linear system $Ma = b$. There is a huge literature on the efficient solution of such systems, and in many cases the vector a can be computed in $\Theta(n)$ or $\Theta(n \log n)$ arithmetic operations using such techniques as FFT, matrix capacitance, or multigrid methods, see George and Liu [81], Swarztrauber [77], Dryja [84], Börgers and Widlund [86], and Hackbush [85].

Our next step is to determine the error of the FEM. Let

$$\gamma = \min\{k + 1 - m, r + m\}.$$

THEOREM 5.2. *The error of the FEM of degree k is*

$$e(\phi_{n,k}, N_{n,k}) = \Theta(n^{-\gamma/d}) \qquad \text{as } n \to \infty.$$

Hence, the FEM is an almost optimal error algorithm iff $k \geq 2m - 1 + r$.

There are two reasons why the error of the FEM of degree k, $k < 2m - 1 + r$, is not almost minimal. Either

(1) the FEM does not make good use of its information, and there is another algorithm using FEI whose error is almost minimal, regardless of whether $k \geq 2m - 1 + r$; or

(2) the FEM is an almost optimal error algorithm using FEI, and FEI is not strong enough information to have the radius close to $r(n, \Lambda^*)$.

It turns out that (1) is the reason the FEM (of too low a degree) does not have almost optimal error. Namely,

THEOREM 5.3. *The spline algorithm using FEI is an almost optimal error algorithm, i.e.,*

$$e(\phi_{n,k}^{s}, N_{n,k}) = \Theta\big(r(n, \Lambda^*)\big) = \Theta(n^{-(r+m)/d}) \qquad as \ \ n \to \infty.$$

Hence the information $N_{n,k}$ is always almost nth optimal information, whereas the FEM of degree k is an almost optimal error algorithm using FEI iff $k \geq 2m - 1 + r$.

We now determine the ε-complexity of our boundary value problem. In addition, we determine

$$\mathrm{cost}^{\mathrm{FEM}}(\varepsilon, k) = \inf\{\, \mathrm{cost}(\phi_{n,k}, N_{n,k}) : n \ \ \text{such that} \ \ e(\phi_{n,k}, N_{n,k}) \leq \varepsilon \,\},$$

which is the minimal cost of using the FEM of degree k to compute ε-approximations. Comparing these, we can determine whether the FEM is an almost optimal complexity algorithm. We are also interested in the minimal cost of the spline algorithm using FEI $N_{n,k}$ of degree k to compute ε-approximations, i.e.,

$$\mathrm{cost}^{\mathrm{SPLINE}}(\varepsilon, k) = \inf\{\mathrm{cost}(\phi_{n,k}^{s}, N_{n,k}) : n \ \ \text{such that} \ \ e(\phi_{n,k}^{s}, N_{n,k}) \leq \varepsilon \,\}.$$

From the results of Section 5.8 of Chapter 4, along with Theorems 5.1, 5.2, and 5.3, we immediately find

THEOREM 5.4.

(1) *The ε-complexity is given by*

$$\mathrm{comp}(\varepsilon, \Lambda^*) = \Theta(c\,\varepsilon^{-d/(r+m)}) \qquad as \ \ \varepsilon \to 0.$$

(2) *If $k \geq 2m - 1 + r$, the FEM is an almost optimal complexity algorithm, i.e.,*

$$\mathrm{cost}^{\mathrm{FEM}}(\varepsilon, k) = \Theta\big(\mathrm{comp}(\varepsilon, \Lambda^*)\big) = \Theta(c\,\varepsilon^{-d/(r+m)}) \qquad as \ \ \varepsilon \to 0.$$

(3) *If $k < 2m - 1 + r$, then*

$$\frac{\text{cost}^{\text{FEM}}(\varepsilon, k)}{\text{comp}(\varepsilon, \Lambda^*)} = \Theta(\varepsilon^{-\lambda d}) \qquad \text{as } \varepsilon \to 0,$$

where $\lambda = (k + 1 - m)^{-1} - (r + m)^{-1} > 0$, so that

$$\lim_{\varepsilon \to 0} \frac{\text{cost}^{\text{FEM}}(\varepsilon, k)}{\text{comp}(\varepsilon, \Lambda^*)} = \infty.$$

(4) *The spline algorithm using FEI of degree k is an almost optimal complexity algorithm, regardless of the value of k, i.e.,*

$$\text{cost}^{\text{SPLINE}}(\varepsilon, k) = \Theta(\text{comp}(\varepsilon, \Lambda^*)) = \Theta(\varepsilon^{-d/(r+m)}) \qquad \text{as } \varepsilon \to 0.$$

So the asymptotic penalty for using an FEM of too low a degree is unbounded as $\varepsilon \to 0$. This means that for sufficiently small $\varepsilon > 0$, it is cheaper to use the spline algorithm using FEI of degree k than to use the FEM of degree k. Obviously, one would use the FEM of degree at least $2m - 1 + r$ rather than the spline algorithm in practice if the latter is hard to implement.

As mentioned at the beginning of this section, the assumption that FEI is permissible information is often unrealistic. Instead, it is more often assumed that one can compute the value $f(x)$ of any function f from F at any point $x \in \overline{\Omega}$. So, we now analyze what happens when the permissible information operations are such evaluations. More precisely, let $\Lambda = \Lambda^{\text{std}}$, where the class Λ^{std} of *standard information* operations is defined by

$$L \in \Lambda^{\text{std}} \qquad \text{iff} \qquad \exists x \in \overline{\Omega} : L(f) = f(x), \quad \forall f \in F.$$

The analysis of standard information is new, and so proofs are given in some detail. In what follows, we assume that $r > d/2$. Hence, the Sobolev embedding theorem implies that standard information is well defined for any $f \in F$.

We first show a lower bound for the nth minimal radius of standard information.

THEOREM 5.5. *There exists a positive constant C, independent of n, such that*

$$r(n, \Lambda^{\text{std}}) \geq Cn^{-r/d} \qquad \text{as } n \to \infty.$$

PROOF: Given information $N(f) = [f(x_1), \ldots, f(x_n)]$, we must show that

$$r(N) \geq Cn^{-r/d} \qquad \text{as } n \to \infty.$$

Let Ω^0 be a C^∞ region whose closure is a subset of the interior of Ω. Let l denote the number of sample points $x_1, \ldots, x_n$ which lie in Ω^0. Without loss of generality, we may assume that $l \geq 1$ and $x_1, \ldots, x_l \in \Omega^0$. We claim that there exists a non-zero function $z \in F \cap \ker N$ such that

$$\int_{\Omega^0} z(x)\, dx \geq Cl^{-r/d}.$$

To see this, note that Poincare's inequality implies that there exists a positive constant κ such that

$$\kappa \|v\|_{r,\Omega^0} \leq |v|_{r,\Omega^0}, \qquad \forall\, v \in H_0^r(\Omega^0).$$

From Bakhvalov [77, pp. 301–304], there exists a positive constant C (independent of n and l) and a non-negative function $z \in H_0^r(\Omega^0)$ such that

$$|z|_{r,\Omega^0} \leq \kappa,$$
$$z(x_1) = \cdots = z(x_l) = 0, \text{ and}$$
$$\int_{\Omega^0} z(x)\, dx \geq Cl^{-r/d}.$$

Extending z from Ω^0 to Ω by letting z be zero outside Ω^0, we find that $z \in \ker N$. Moreover, $\|z\|_r = \|z\|_{r,\Omega^0} \leq \kappa^{-1}|z|_r \leq 1$, i.e., $z \in F \cap \ker N$ is the desired function.

Choose a function $v \in H_0^m(\Omega)$ such that $v = 1$ on Ω^0. Since $v = 1$ on the support Ω^0 of z, we find that the continuity of the bilinear form B implies that there exists a constant $C > 0$, independent of z and n, such that

$$C\|S(z)\|_m \|v\|_m \geq B\big(S(z), v\big) = \int_\Omega z(x)v(x)\, dx = \int_{\Omega^0} z(x)\, dx.$$

Since $l \leq n$, we may use this inequality and the properties of z to find that

$$\|S(z)\|_m \geq \frac{C}{\|v\|_m}\, n^{-r/d}$$

for a positive constant C. Finally, since $z \in F \cap \ker N$, Lemma 5.2.1 of Chapter 4 implies that

$$r(N) \geq \|S(z)\|_m \geq \frac{C}{\|v\|_m}\, n^{-r/d},$$

completing the proof of the theorem. ∎

We now show that the lower bound in Theorem 5.5 is sharp by presenting an algorithm using standard information whose error is $\Theta(n^{-r/d})$. Let $x_1^*, \ldots, x_n^*$ be the nodes of the finite element subspace $\mathcal{S}_{n,k}$. We define information N_n^* by

$$N_{n,k}^*(f) = [f(x_1^*), \ldots, f(x_n^*)], \qquad \forall f \in F.$$

The main idea is to replace each appearance of the problem element f in the finite element method by its $\mathcal{S}_{n,k}$-*interpolant* $\Pi_{n,k} f$, which is defined by

$$(\Pi_{n,k} f)(x) := \sum_{j=1}^{n} f(x_j^*) s_j(x), \qquad \forall x \in \overline{\Omega},$$

where, as before, $\{s_1, \ldots, s_n\}$ is a basis of $\mathcal{S}_{n,k}$ satisfying $s_j(x_i^*) = \delta_{i,j}$. Hence, for any $f \in F$, we let $u_{n,k}^* \in \mathcal{S}_{n,k}$ satisfy

$$B(u_{n,k}^*, s_i) = \langle \Pi_n f, s_i \rangle_0 \qquad (1 \leq i \leq n).$$

Once again, this may be reduced to the solution of an $n \times n$ linear system. Recall that the matrix $M \in \mathbb{R}^{n \times n}$ was given by

$$M = [B(s_j, s_i)]_{1 \leq i,j \leq n}.$$

For each problem element $f \in F$, define a vector $b^* = [b_1^*, \ldots, b_n^*] \in \mathbb{R}^n$ by

$$b_i^* = (\Pi_n f, s_i) = \sum_{k=1}^{n} f(x_k^*) \langle s_k, s_i \rangle_0 \qquad (1 \leq i \leq n).$$

(Note that this sum may be reduced to a sum over the indices k in the support of s_i. Hence, our conditions on the basis functions imply that the number of terms in the sum is independent of n.) We now let $a^* \in \mathbb{R}^n$ be the (necessarily unique) solution of $M a^* = b^*$. Then

$$u_{n,k}^*(x) = \sum_{j=1}^{n} a_j^* s_j(x).$$

Since $u_{n,k}^*$ depends on f only through the information $N_{n,k}^*(f)$, we may write

$$u_{n,k}^* = \phi_{n,k}^*(N_{n,k}^*(f)).$$

This algorithm is called the nth *modified finite element method* (MFEM) of degree k using $N_{n,k}^*$. We then have

THEOREM 5.6. *Let $k \geq m+r-1$. Then the error of the MFEM of degree k is*

$$e(\phi^*_{n,k}, N^*_{n,k}) = \Theta(n^{-r/d}) \qquad \text{as } n \to \infty.$$

PROOF: Since Theorem 5.5 yields

$$e(\phi^*_{n,k}, N^*_{n,k}) \geq r(n, \Lambda^{\text{std}}) = \Theta(n^{-r/d}) \qquad \text{as } n \to \infty,$$

it suffices to show the upper bound

$$e(\phi^*_{n,k}, N^*_{n,k}) = O(n^{-r/d}) \qquad \text{as } n \to \infty.$$

Let $f \in F$. Using the triangle inequality and Theorem 5.2, we have

$$\|S(f) - \phi^*_{n,k}(N^*_{n,k}(f))\|_m \leq \|S(f) - \phi_{n,k}(N_{n,k}(f))\|_m + \|u_{n,k} - u^*_{n,k}\|_m$$
$$\leq Cn^{-\gamma/d}\|f\|_r + \|u_{n,k} - u^*_{n,k}\|_m,$$

where (as before) $\gamma = \min\{k + 1 - m, m + r\}$. Here, $u_{n,k}$ and $u^*_{n,k}$, respectively, denote the FEM and MFEM approximations $\phi_{n,k}(N_{n,k}(f))$ and $\phi^*_{n,k}(N^*_{n,k}(f))$. From the coercivity of B, we find

$$C\|u_{n,k} - u^*_{n,k}\|^2_m \leq B(u_{n,k} - u^*_{n,k}, u_{n,k} - u^*_{n,k}) = \langle f - \Pi_n f, u_{n,k} - u^*_{n,k}\rangle_0$$
$$\leq \|f - \Pi_n f\|_0 \|u_{n,k} - u^*_{n,k}\|_m.$$

Hence, there exists a positive constant C, independent of n and f, such that

$$\|u_{n,k} - u^*_{n,k}\|_m \leq C\|f - \Pi_n f\|_0.$$

Since the results in Chapter 3 of Ciarlet [78] state that

$$\|f - \Pi_n f\|_0 \leq Cn^{-r/d}\|f\|_r$$

for a positive constant C, independent of n and f, we may combine the previous inequalities to find that

$$\|S(f) - \phi^*_{n,k}(N^*_{n,k}f)\|_m \leq C(n^{-r/d} + n^{-\gamma/d})\|f\|_r.$$

Now $k \geq m + r - 1$ implies that $\gamma \geq r$, while $f \in F$ implies that $\|f\|_r \leq 1$. So we have

$$\|S(f) - \phi^*_{n,k}(N^*_{n,k}f)\|_m \leq Cn^{-r/d}.$$

Take the supremum over all $f \in F$ to complete the proof of the theorem. ∎

From Theorems 5.5 and 5.6, we immediately have

THEOREM 5.7. *The nth minimal radius of standard information is given by*

$$r(n, \Lambda^{\text{std}}) = \Theta(n^{-r/d}) \qquad \text{as } n \to \infty.$$

Moreover, the MFEM of degree $k \geq m + r - 1$ is an almost optimal error algorithm.

We now determine the ε-complexity of our boundary-value problem when using only standard information. In addition, we determine

$$\text{cost}^{\text{MFEM}}(\varepsilon, k) = \inf\{\text{cost}(\phi_{n,k}, N_{n,k}) : n \text{ such that } e(\phi_{n,k}^*, N_{n,k}^*) \leq \varepsilon\},$$

which is the minimal cost of using the modified FEM of degree k to find an ε-approximation. From the results of Section 5.8 of Chapter 1, along with Theorems 5.6 and 5.7, we find

THEOREM 5.8.

(1) *The ε-complexity is given by*

$$\text{comp}(\varepsilon, \Lambda^{\text{std}}) = \Theta(\varepsilon^{-d/r}) \qquad \text{as } \varepsilon \to 0.$$

(2) *If $k \geq m + r - 1$, then the MFEM is an almost optimal complexity algorithm, i.e.,*

$$\text{cost}^{\text{MFEM}}(\varepsilon, \Lambda^{\text{std}}) = \Theta(\varepsilon^{-d/r}) \qquad \text{as } \varepsilon \to 0.$$

Finally, we compare the strengths of arbitrary information and standard information.

THEOREM 5.9.

(1) *If $m = 0$, then*

$$\text{comp}(\varepsilon, \Lambda^{\text{std}}) = \Theta\big(\text{comp}(\varepsilon, \Lambda^*)\big) \qquad \text{as } \varepsilon \to 0.$$

(2) *If $m > 0$, then*

$$\frac{\text{comp}(\varepsilon, \Lambda^{\text{std}})}{\text{comp}(\varepsilon, \Lambda^*)} = \Theta(\varepsilon^{-\lambda d}) \qquad \text{as } \varepsilon \to 0,$$

where $\lambda = d/r - d/(r + m) > 0$, so that

$$\lim_{\varepsilon \to 0} \frac{\text{comp}(\varepsilon, \Lambda^{\text{std}})}{\text{comp}(\varepsilon, \Lambda^*)} = \infty.$$

So the asymptotic penalty for using standard information instead of arbitrary information is unbounded as $\varepsilon \to 0$ whenever $m > 0$.

Notes and Remarks

NR 5:1 This section is written by A. G. Werschulz and much of the material in this section is taken from Werschulz [82, 86a, 87b]. The material on standard information is new.

NR 5:2 We briefly define Sobolev spaces $H^r(\Omega)$ and $H_0^r(\Omega)$. For more details, see Chapter 2 of Babuška and Aziz [72] and Chapter 4 of Oden and Reddy [76].

We first introduce the standard multi-index notation. Let $x = [x_1, \ldots, x_d] \in \Omega$. Then for a *multi-index* $\alpha = [\alpha_1, \ldots, \alpha_d]$ of non-negative integers, we write

$$D^\alpha v(x) := \left(\frac{\partial}{\partial x_1}\right)^{\alpha_1} \cdots \left(\frac{\partial}{\partial x_d}\right)^{\alpha_d} v(x)$$

and $|\alpha| := \alpha_1 + \ldots + \alpha_d$. It is also useful to write $\xi^\alpha := \xi_1^{\alpha_1} \ldots \xi_d^{\alpha_d}$ for a vector $\xi = [\xi_1, \ldots, \xi_n] \in \mathbb{R}^d$.

Next, we define Sobolev inner products, norms, and seminorms for the case where r is a non-negative integer. The inner product $\langle \cdot, \cdot \rangle_r$ is given on the space $C^\infty(\Omega)$ of infinitely-differentiable functions on Ω by

$$\langle v, w \rangle_r := \sum_{|\alpha| \le r} \int_\Omega D^\alpha v(x) D^\alpha w(x)\, dx, \qquad \forall\, v, w \in C^\infty(\Omega).$$

Then the *Sobolev r-norm* $\|\cdot\|_r$ denotes the norm induced by this inner product, i.e.,

$$\|v\|_r := \sqrt{\langle v, v \rangle_r}, \qquad \forall\, v, w \in C^\infty(\Omega).$$

We define the *Sobolev l-seminorm* $|\cdot|_l$ by

$$|v|_l = \sum_{|\alpha| = l} \int_\Omega \left((D^\alpha v)(x)\right)^2 dx, \qquad \forall\, v \in C^\infty(\Omega).$$

Of course, $\|v\|_r = \left(\sum_{l=0}^r |v|_l^2\right)^{1/2}$, $\forall\, v \in C^\infty(\Omega)$. If it is ever necessary to explicitly indicate the domain Ω, we write $\|\cdot\|_{r,\Omega}$ for $\|\cdot\|_r$ and $|\cdot|_{l,\Omega}$ for $|\cdot|_l$.

We are now ready to define Sobolev spaces. First, we suppose that r is an integer. Then the space $H^r(\Omega)$ is defined to be the closure of $C^\infty(\Omega)$ in $\mathcal{L}_2(\Omega)$ under the Sobolev r-norm. Similarly, the space $H_0^r(\Omega)$ is defined to be the closure of $C_0^\infty(\Omega)$ in $\mathcal{L}_2(\Omega)$ under the Sobolev r-norm, where $C_0^\infty(\Omega)$ denotes the infinitely-differentiable functions over Ω having compact support. It may be shown that $H_0^r(\Omega)$ is the space of $H^r(\Omega)$-functions whose normal derivatives of order at most $r-1$ vanish on $\partial\Omega$, i.e.,

$$H_0^r(\Omega) = \{\, v \in H^r(\Omega) : \partial_\nu^j v = 0 \text{ for } 0 \le j \le r-1 \,\},$$

(where $\partial_\nu^j u$ denotes the jth normal derivative of u).

For r a non-negative real number, the space $H^r(\Omega)$ and $H_0^r(\Omega)$ may be defined by "Hilbert space interpolation", which is *not* to be confused with "interpolation" as discussed in texts on numerical analysis. Finally, for negative values of r, we define $H^r(\Omega)$

to be the space of continuous linear functionals on $H_0^{-r}(\Omega)$, see Babuška and Aziz [72] for details.

NR 5:3 Note that all the analysis has been done modulo a constant C, whose value is unknown. This is typical of problems arising in partial differential equations. Although it is hopeless to determine a general value for C (as a function of, e.g., the coefficients of the operator A), it would be worthwhile to determine the value of C for specific model problems (such as the Laplace equation on a cube).

NR 5:4 The assumption that the coefficients of the operator A and the boundary of the region Ω are infinitely differentiable is made only for the sake of exposition. It can be greatly relaxed. More precise statements of the requirements can be found in Chapter 5 of Oden and Reddy [76].

NR 5:5 Not every elliptic problem generates a coercive bilinear form B. One of the most important examples of such a problem is the Helmholtz equation:

$$\Delta u + \lambda u = f \text{ in } \Omega \quad \text{and} \quad u = 0 \text{ on } \partial\Omega.$$

If λ is positive, and larger than the smallest eigenvalue of the Laplace operator Δ, then the bilinear form is no longer coercive. However, the finite element method still satisfies all the properties of Section 5.5. Hence, the FEM is almost optimal iff $k \geq 2m + r - 1$, even for such "indefinite" elliptic problems. For further details, see Werschulz [86a].

NR 5:6 We have assumed that the problem has been given with *Dirichlet boundary conditions*. That is, the first $m - 1$ normal derivatives of the solution of the problem were constrained to be zero on the boundary of the region Ω. This has been done solely for expository purposes. The results of this section remain the same if the boundary conditions form a "normal covering system" for the problem, see Chapter 5 of Oden and Reddy [76].

NR 5:7 One often wants to approximate the solution in one of other standard Sobolev norms $\|\cdot\|_l$ instead of the $\|\cdot\|_m$-norm. It is shown in Werschulz [86a] that under this norm, the FEM is (again) almost optimal iff $k \geq 2m + r - 1$.

NR 5:8 We present the proof of Theorem 5.1 in detail to show an example of the proof techniques often used. In what follows, we let

$$H_*^l(\Omega) = H^l(\Omega) \cap H_0^m(\Omega), \text{ normed under } \|\cdot\|_l, \qquad \forall l \geq 0.$$

Moreover, we let $\mathcal{B}X$ denote the unit ball of the Hilbert space X, i.e., $\mathcal{B}X = \{x \in X : \|x\| \leq 1\}$.

Since our problem is a linear problem in a Hilbert setting, the results in Section 5.4 of Chapter 4 imply

$$r(n, \Lambda^*) = d^n\big(S(F), H_0^m(\Omega)\big),$$

where d^n denotes the Gelfand n-width. For any $\theta > 0$, let

$$X(\theta) = \{\, u \in H_*^{2m+r}(\Omega) : \|u\|_{2m+r} \leq \theta\,\} = \theta\,\mathcal{B}H_*^{2m+r}(\Omega).$$

Letting C be the constant in the Shift Theorem, we find that $X(C^{-1}) \subseteq S(F) \subseteq X(C)$ and so

$$d^n\left(X(C^{-1}), H_0^m(\Omega)\right) \leq r(n, \Lambda^*) \leq d^n\left(X(C), H_0^m(\Omega)\right).$$

But $d^n\left(X(\theta),H_0^m(\Omega)\right) = \theta\,d^n\left(\mathcal{B}H_*^{2m+r}(\Omega),H_0^m(\Omega)\right)$, $\forall\,\theta > 0$, so that

$$C^{-1}d^n\left(\mathcal{B}H_*^{2m+r}(\Omega),H_0^m(\Omega)\right) \le r(n,\Lambda^*) \le Cd^n\left(\mathcal{B}H_*^{2m+r}(\Omega),H_0^m(\Omega)\right).$$

From Theorem IV.2.2 of Pinkus [85] and Theorem 2.5.1 of Babuška and Aziz [72], we find

$$d^n\left(\mathcal{B}H_*^{2m+r}(\Omega),H_0^m(\Omega)\right) = \Theta\left(d^n\left(\mathcal{B}H_0^1(\Omega),\mathcal{L}_2(\Omega)\right)^{r+m}\right).$$

Finally, Theorem VII.1.1 of Pinkus [85] states that

$$d^n\left(\mathcal{B}H_0^1(\Omega),\mathcal{L}_2(\Omega)\right) = \Theta(n^{-1/d}).$$

Combining these last three results, the proof is complete.

NR 5:9 Since Ω is C^∞, it is not generally true that $\mathcal{S}_{n,k} \subseteq H_0^m(\Omega)$. In this section, we ignored this source of error. If necessary, this error may be removed by using isoparametric elements as in Ciarlet and Raviart [78].

NR 5:10 The idea of using the $\mathcal{S}_{n,k}$-interpolant of f instead of f was originated by Fried [73].

Exercises

E 5:1 In this section, we assumed that the boundary conditions were *homogeneous*, i.e., the solution and some of its normal derivatives were constrained to be zero on the boundary. What happens with inhomogeneous problems? Consider the inhomogeneous Dirichlet problem for the Poisson equation

$$-\Delta u = f \text{ in } \Omega \quad \text{and} \quad u = g \text{ on } \partial\Omega$$

as a model problem.

E 5:2 (Werschulz [87a]) When does the FEM turn out to be the spline algorithm using FEI? Clearly, the results of this section imply that the FEM is not the spline algorithm when $k < 2m - 1 + r$. In Werschulz [87a], it is conjectured that the FEM is never a spline algorithm. Prove or disprove this conjecture.

E 5:3 (Werschulz [87a]) As mentioned in the notes and remarks for this section, all the results in this section are asymptotic, involving unknown (and often, unknowable) constants. The statement that the spline algorithm using FEI of degree k is cheaper than the FEM of degree k is true for "sufficiently small" values of $\varepsilon > 0$. This might lead one to believe that the threshold value ε_0 for which

$$\text{cost}^{\text{SPLINE}}(\varepsilon,k) < \text{cost}^{\text{FEM}}(\varepsilon,k), \qquad \forall\,\varepsilon \in (0,\varepsilon_0)$$

is too small to make the spline algorithm of practical use. To see that this is not true, consider the (variational form of the) following model problem:

$$-u''(x) = f(x) \quad \text{for } x \in (0,\pi) \quad \text{and} \quad u(0) = u(\pi) = 0.$$

Let $k = 1$, and take $\mathcal{S}_{n,k}$ to be the n-dimensional subspace of $H_0^1(0,\pi)$ consisting of piecewise linear polynomials with nodes at $x_j = j\pi/(n+1)$ for $0 \le j \le n+1$, so that $k = 1$. Show that we may choose

$$\varepsilon_0 = \varepsilon_0(c) = \left(\tfrac{1}{2}c + 1 - \sqrt{\left(\tfrac{1}{2}c+1\right)^2 - \tfrac{1}{\sqrt{12}}\pi(c+1)}\right)^2.$$

Note that $\varepsilon_0(c)$ increases with positive c and $\varepsilon_0(0) = (1 - (1 - \pi/\sqrt{12})^{1/2})^2 \doteq 0.4829$. Hence for this model problem, the spline algorithm using linear elements finds an ε-approximation more cheaply than the FEM using linear elements for all ε less than (roughly) one half.

E 5:4 Let $\gamma_1 = \min\{k+1-m, r\}$. Show that regardless of the value of k, $e(\phi_{n,k}^*, N_{n,k}^*) = \Theta(n^{-\gamma_1/d})$ as $n \to \infty$, and so the MFEM of too low a degree is not an almost optimal error algorithm using standard information. Compute $r(N_{n,k}^*)$, and determine whether the MFEM is always an almost optimal error algorithm.

E 5:5 One disadvantage of the MFEM is that it requires precomputation of $\langle s_j, s_i \rangle_0$ and $B(s_j, s_i)$ for all the basis functions. Define a *finite element method with quadrature* (FEMQ) which approximates the integrals appearing in the (original, unmodified) FEM by numerical quadrature rules of sufficiently high (piecewise) degree, i.e., a numerical quadrature rule which integrates exactly piecewise polynomials of sufficiently high degree. Determine the degree such that the FEMQ is an almost optimal error algorithm using standard information.

E 5:6 Investigate the complexity when the class Λ^{std} is extended to allow evaluation of the derivatives of functions f.

6. Integral Equations

We now discuss the complexity of Fredholm integral equations of the second kind. Let $I = [0,1]$ denote the unit interval. Let $r \geq 0$, and set $F_1 = H^r(I)$. We choose the unit ball of $H^r(I)$ as our set F of problem elements, i.e.,

$$F = \{ f \in H^r(I) : \|f\|_r \leq 1 \},$$

and we let $G = \mathcal{L}_2(I)$ be the range of the solution elements. Let $K: G \to G$ be a compact integral operator. We wish to solve the variational form of the Fredholm problem of finding $u \in G$ such that $(I - K)u = f$ for $f \in F$.

As in the previous section, we first suppose that the class Λ of permissible information operations is the class Λ^* of all linear functionals on $H^r(I)$. We define a finite element method (FEM) of degree k and show that the FEM is an optimal algorithm if and only if $k \geq r - 1$. When this inequality is violated, we show that the lack of optimality is because the FEM does not use its finite element information (FEI) optimally; the error of the spline algorithm using FEI is proportional to the minimal radius.

Next, we consider what happens when only function evaluations are permissible. We show that the class Λ^{std} of standard information is as strong as the class Λ^*. Moreover, we exhibit a modified FEM that is an almost optimal algorithm.

We now describe the operator K more precisely. Let $k: I \times I \to \mathbb{R}$ be a function such that $\partial_1^j k$ is continuous for $0 \leq j \leq r$, where ∂_1^j denotes the jth partial derivative with respect to the first variable. Define a linear operator $K: \mathcal{L}_2(I) \to \mathcal{L}_2(I)$ by

$$(Kv)(x) = \int_I k(x, y)v(y)\, dy.$$

Then K is a compact integral operator. In the rest of this section, we assume that K satisfies

$$\|K\| = \sup_{\substack{v \in \mathcal{L}_2(I) \\ v \neq 0}} \frac{\|Kv\|_0}{\|v\|_0} < 1,$$

where the norm $\|\cdot\|_0$ is the norm on $\mathcal{L}_2(I) = H^0(I)$. Then the operator $I - K: \mathcal{L}_2(I) \to \mathcal{L}_2(I)$ is invertible.

We wish to solve the variational (or weak) form of the Fredholm problem of the second kind of finding, for $f \in F$, a function $u \in G$ such that

$$(I - K)u = f.$$

We do this by defining a bilinear form $B: \mathcal{L}_2(I) \times \mathcal{L}_2(I) \to \mathbb{R}$ to be

$$B(v, w) = \langle (I - K)v, w \rangle_0, \quad \forall\, v, w \in \mathcal{L}_2(I).$$

Then our solution operator $S: F \to G$ is defined as $S(f) := u$, where $u \in G = \mathcal{L}_2(I)$ is chosen such that $B(u, v) = \langle f, v \rangle_0$, $\forall\, v \in \mathcal{L}_2(I)$, i.e.,

$$\int_I u(x)v(x)\, dx - \int_I \int_I k(x, y)u(y)v(x)\, dy\, dx = \int_I f(x)v(x)\, dx$$

for any $v \in \mathcal{L}_2(I)$. Since $\|K\| < 1$, we find that

$$B(v, v) \geq (1 - \|K\|)\|v\|_0^2,$$

i.e., B is $\mathcal{L}_2(I)$-coercive (in the sense of the previous section). Thus, the solution operator S is well-defined. As in Section 5, we find that a Shift Theorem holds and that variational solutions $S(f)$ coincide with solutions of the original Fredholm problem of the second kind, for sufficiently smooth f.

We measure the quality of an approximation by the $\mathcal{L}_2$-norm. Hence, the error of an algorithm ϕ using information N is given by

$$e(\phi, N) = \sup_{f \in F} \|S(f) - \phi(N(f))\|_0.$$

We first consider what happens when $\Lambda = \Lambda^*$ is the class of all linear functionals on $F_1 = H^r(I)$. The nth minimal radius is given by

THEOREM 6.1.
$$r(n, \Lambda^*) = \Theta(n^{-r}) \qquad \text{as } n \to \infty.$$

Next, we describe the algorithm known as the finite element method for this problem. As before, let $\{\mathcal{T}_n\}_{n=1}^{\infty}$ be a quasi-uniform family of meshes for I. Let $\mathcal{S}_{n,k}$ be the n-dimensional subspace of $\mathcal{L}_2(I)$ consisting of piecewise polynomials of degree k over the mesh $\mathcal{T}_n$. That is, $s \in \mathcal{S}_{n,k}$ if and only if for every subinterval of $\mathcal{T}_n$, the restriction of s that subinterval is a polynomial of degree at most k. In other words, no inter-element continuity is required. The basis functions $\{s_1, \ldots, s_n\}$ and nodes $\{x_1^*, \ldots, x_n^*\}$ of the finite element space $\mathcal{S}_{n,k}$ are chosen as in Section 5.

Finite element information (FEI) $N_{n,k}$ of cardinality n and degree k is defined as in Section 5,

$$N_{n,k}(f) = [\langle f, s_1 \rangle_0, \ldots, \langle f, s_n \rangle_0], \qquad \forall f \in F.$$

The *finite element method* $\phi_{n,k}$ of degree k using $N_{n,k}$ is then defined by

$$\phi_{n,k}(N_{n,k}(f)) = u_{n,k},$$

where $u_{n,k} \in \mathcal{S}_{n,k}$ satisfies

$$B(u_{n,k}, s_i) = \langle f, s_i \rangle_0 \qquad (1 \le i \le n).$$

As in Section 5, determining the approximation given by the FEM can be reduced to the solution of an $n \times n$ positive definite linear system $Ma = b$. Hence, the FEM is once again well-defined.

What is the error of the FEM? Let

$$\gamma = \min\{k+1, r\}.$$

THEOREM 6.2. *The error of the FEM of degree k is*

$$e(\phi_{n,k}, N_{n,k}) = \Theta(n^{-\gamma}) \qquad \text{as } n \to \infty.$$

Hence, the FEM is an almost optimal error algorithm iff $k \ge r - 1$.

As in the previous section, there might be two reasons why the error of the FEM of degree k, $k < r - 1$, is not almost minimal. Either

(1) the FEM does not make good use of its information, and there is another algorithm using FEI whose error is almost minimal, regardless of whether $k \ge r - 1$, or

(2) the FEM is an almost optimal error algorithm using FEI, and FEI is not strong enough information to have the radius close to $r(n, \Lambda^*)$.

From our experience in Section 5, it should come as no surprise that (1) is the reason the FEM (of too low a degree) does not have almost optimal error, and the spline algorithm $\phi_{n,k}^s$ using FEI $N_{n,k}$ has almost optimal error.

THEOREM 6.3. *The spline algorithm using FEI is an almost optimal error algorithm, i.e.,*

$$e(\phi^s_{n,k}, N_{n,k}) = \Theta\left(r(n, \Lambda^*)\right) = \Theta(n^{-r}) \qquad as \ n \to \infty.$$

Hence the information $N_{n,k}$ is always almost nth optimal information, whereas the FEM of degree k is an almost optimal error algorithm using FEI iff $k \geq r - 1$.

We now determine the ε-complexity of the Fredholm problem of the second kind. In addition, we determine

$$\text{cost}^{\text{FEM}}(\varepsilon, k) = \inf\{\, \text{cost}(\phi_{n,k}, N_{n,k}) : n \ \text{such that} \ e(\phi_{n,k}, N_{n,k}) \leq \varepsilon \,\},$$

which is the minimal cost of using the FEM of degree k to compute ε-approximations. Comparing these, we can determine whether the FEM is an almost optimal complexity algorithm. We are also interested in

$$\text{cost}^{\text{SPLINE}}(\varepsilon, k) = \inf\{\, \text{cost}(\phi^s_{n,k}, N_{n,k}) : n \ \text{such that} \ e(\phi^s_{n,k}, N_{n,k}) \leq \varepsilon \,\},$$

the minimal cost of the spline algorithm using FEI $N_{n,k}$ of degree k to compute ε-approximations. Since the FEM is a linear algorithm, the results of Section 5.8 of Chapter 4, along with Theorems 6.1, 6.2, and 6.3, yield

THEOREM 6.4.

(1) *The ε-complexity is given by*

$$\text{comp}(\varepsilon, \Lambda^*) = \Theta(c\,\varepsilon^{-1/r}) \qquad as \ \varepsilon \to 0.$$

(2) *If $k \geq r - 1$, the FEM is an almost optimal complexity algorithm, i.e.,*

$$\text{cost}^{\text{FEM}}(\varepsilon, k) = \Theta\left(\text{comp}(\varepsilon, \Lambda^*)\right) = \Theta(c\,\varepsilon^{-1/r}) \qquad as \ \varepsilon \to 0.$$

(3) *If $k < r - 1$, then*

$$\frac{\text{cost}^{\text{FEM}}(\varepsilon, k)}{\text{comp}(\varepsilon, \Lambda^*)} = \Theta(c\,\varepsilon^{-\lambda}) \qquad as \ \varepsilon \to 0,$$

where $\lambda = (k+1)^{-1} - r^{-1} > 0$, so that

$$\lim_{\varepsilon \to 0} \frac{\text{cost}^{\text{FEM}}(\varepsilon, k)}{\text{comp}(\varepsilon, \Lambda^*)} = \infty.$$

(4) *The spline algorithm using FEI of degree k is an almost optimal complexity algorithm, regardless of the value of k, i.e.,*

$$\text{cost}^{\text{SPLINE}}(\varepsilon, k) = \Theta\left(\text{comp}(\varepsilon, \Lambda^*)\right) = \Theta(\varepsilon^{-1/r}) \qquad as \ \varepsilon \to 0.$$

As in the previous section, we find that the asymptotic penalty for using an FEM of too low a degree is unbounded as $\varepsilon \to 0$. So, for sufficiently small $\varepsilon > 0$, it is cheaper to use the spline algorithm using FEI of degree k than to use the FEM of degree k. Again, one would use the FEM of degree at least $r - 1$ instead of the spline algorithm if the latter is hard to implement.

We now suppose that we can only compute standard information, i.e., that $\Lambda = \Lambda^{\mathrm{std}}$. Since we wish to compute the value of any $f \in F$ at any point in the interval I, we must assume that $r > 1/2$ by the Sobolev embedding theorem.

It is easy to show a lower bound for the nth minimal radius of standard information. Since $\Lambda^{\mathrm{std}} \subset \Lambda^*$, we have

$$r(n, \Lambda^{\mathrm{std}}) \geq r(n, \Lambda^*) = \Theta(n^{-r}) \qquad \text{as } n \to \infty.$$

We now show that this lower bound is sharp. Define the $S_{n,k}$-interpolant $\Pi_{n,k} f$ of the problem element $f \in F$ as in Section 5. Then for any $f \in F$, we let $u^*_{n,k} \in S_{n,k}$ satisfy

$$B(u^*_{n,k}, s_i) = \langle \Pi_n f, s_i \rangle_0 \qquad (1 \leq i \leq n).$$

As in the previous section, this may be reduced to the solution of an $n \times n$ linear system $M a^* = b^*$. Since $u^*_{n,k}$ depends on f only through the information

$$N^*_{n,k}(f) := [f(x^*_1), \ldots, f(x^*_n)],$$

we may write

$$u^*_{n,k} = \phi^*_{n,k}\big(N^*_{n,k}(f)\big).$$

This algorithm is called the nth *modified finite element method* (MFEM) of degree k using $N^*_{n,k}$. We then have

THEOREM 6.5.

(1) *The nth minimal radius of standard information is given by*

$$r(n, \Lambda^{\mathrm{std}}) = \Theta(n^{-r}) \qquad \text{as } n \to \infty.$$

(2) *Let $k \geq r - 1$. Then the error of the MFEM of degree k is*

$$e(\phi^*_{n,k}, N^*_{n,k}) = \Theta(n^{-r}) \qquad \text{as } n \to \infty.$$

Hence, the MFEM of degree $k \geq r-1$ is an almost optimal error algorithm.

We now determine the ε-complexity of the Fredholm problem of the second kind when using only standard information. In addition, we determine

$$\text{cost}^{\text{MFEM}}(\varepsilon, k) = \inf\{\text{cost}(\phi_{n,k}, N_{n,k}) : n \text{ such that } e(\phi_{n,k}^*, N_{n,k}^*) \leq \varepsilon\},$$

which is the minimal cost of using the MFEM of degree k to compute ε-approximations. From the results of Section 5.8 of Chapter 4, along with Theorem 6.5, we find

THEOREM 6.6.

(1) *The ε-complexity is given by*

$$\text{comp}(\varepsilon, \Lambda^{\text{std}}) = \Theta(\varepsilon^{-1/r}) \qquad as \ \varepsilon \to 0.$$

(2) *If $k \geq r - 1$, then the MFEM is an almost optimal complexity algorithm, i.e.,*

$$\text{cost}^{\text{MFEM}}(\varepsilon, \Lambda^{\text{std}}) = \Theta(\varepsilon^{-1/r}) \qquad as \ \varepsilon \to 0.$$

Finally, we compare the strengths of arbitrary information and standard information.

THEOREM 6.7.

$$\text{comp}(\varepsilon, \Lambda^{\text{std}}) = \Theta\big(\text{comp}(\varepsilon, \Lambda^*)\big) \qquad as \ \varepsilon \to 0.$$

So there is no penalty for using standard information instead of (say) finite element information. This should be contrasted with what happens for $2m$th-order elliptic problems when $m > 0$, see Theorem 5.9.

Notes and Remarks

NR 6:1 This section is written by A. G. Werschulz and the material is taken from Werschulz [85]. However, the approach used for standard information is new. The first work on complexity of Fredholm problems of the second kind appears to be in Emelyanov and Ilin [67], in which error is measured in the sup norm.

NR 6:2 The conditions on the function k that we have given for compactness of the operator K can be considerably weakened. See, e.g., Dunford and Schwartz [63, p. 518] for alternative conditions on k which yield compactness of K.

NR 6:3 In this section we have assumed that the operator K satisfies the condition $\|K\| < 1$ and that error is measured in the $\mathcal{L}_2(I)$-norm. This has been done solely for ease of exposition. In Werschulz [85], we show that the results of this section hold under weaker conditions:

(1) Error is measured in the $\mathcal{L}_p(I)$-norm (where $1 < p \leq \infty$).
(2) We only assume that 1 is not an eigenvalue of K.

Of course, condition (2) is necessary for the operator $I - K$ to be invertible. Note that condition (1) with $p = +\infty$ covers the results in Emelyanov and Ilin [67].

Exercises

E 6:1 Extend the results of this section so that the interval $I = [0, 1]$ is replaced by a region $\Omega \subset \mathbb{R}^d$. (The easy part of this problem is that all references to "n" are replaced by references to "$n^{1/d}$". The hard part is to figure a precise statement of the Shift Theorem.)

E 6:2 (Rokhlin [86]) Sometimes, the function k does not satisfy the continuity requirements of this section. Often, k is a function that is piecewise analytic on the unit square, and discontinuity of k or its derivatives occurs only on the diagonal. Extend the results of this section to this case.

E 6:3 Let $\gamma_1 = \min\{k + 1, r\}$. Show that regardless of the value of k, $e(\phi^*_{n,k}, N^*_{n,k}) = \Theta(n^{-\gamma_1})$ as $n \to \infty$, and so the MFEM of too low a degree is not an almost optimal error algorithm using standard information. Compute $r(N^*_{n,k})$, and determine whether the MFEM is always an almost optimal error algorithm using $N^*_{n,k}$.

E 6:4 One disadvantage of the MFEM is that it requires precomputation of $\langle s_j, s_i \rangle_0$ and $B(s_j, s_i)$ for all the basis functions. Define a *finite element method with quadrature* (FEMQ) which approximates the integrals appearing in the (original, unmodified) FEM by numerical quadrature rules of sufficiently-high (piecewise) degree. Determine the degree such that the FEMQ is an almost optimal error algorithm using standard information.

E 6:5 Investigate the complexity of the Fredholm problem of the second kind when the class Λ^{std} is extended to allow evaluation of the derivatives of functions f.

7. Ill-Posed Problems

In this section, we investigate the complexity of ill-posed problems for the absolute and relative error criteria in the worst-case setting. The average case setting is analyzed in Section 4 of Chapter 7. In our study of ill-posed problems, we assume that $\Lambda = F_1^*$, i.e., that any continuous linear functional is permissible.

We first define what is meant by an ill-posed problem. Let F_1 and G be normed linear spaces, and let D be an infinite-dimensional subspace of F_1. Let

$$S \colon D \subseteq F_1 \to G$$

be a linear solution operator with domain D. Then the problem consisting of solution operator S and problem elements

$$F = \{\, f \in D : \|f\| \le 1 \,\}$$

is said to be *ill-posed* if the solution operator S is *unbounded*, i.e., if there exist linearly independent elements $f_1, f_2, \cdots \in D$ of unit norm such that $\lim_{n \to +\infty} \|S(f_n)\| = +\infty$.

REMARK 7.1. Our primary example of such a problem is the solution of a *Fredholm problem of the first kind*, i.e., the inversion of a compact linear operator. Let $M \colon G \to F_1$ be a compact linear injection, where G is infinite-dimensional. Let $D = M(G)$ be the range of M. Define $S \colon D \subseteq F_1 \to G$ by

$$u = S(f) \quad \text{iff} \quad Mu = f.$$

Then S is an unbounded linear solution operator. Note that in many applications F_1 or G are Banach spaces. However, the closed graph theorem shows that D is *not* a closed subspace of F_1, i.e., D is not a Banach space. Moreover, there are situations in which an explicit description of D is difficult to determine, i.e., we cannot easily determine whether a given element of F_1 is in D. It is for these reasons that we prefer to use both the domain D of the solution operator *and* the "domain space" F_1 in our formulation of the problem.

As a particular example of a Fredholm problem, choose $F_1 = H^r(0,1)$, $G = L_2(0,1)$, and consider the compact operator $M \colon G \to F_1$ given by

$$(Mu)(s) = \int_0^1 \exp(-st) u(t)\, dt, \qquad \forall\, u \in G.$$

That is, Mu is the *finite Laplace transform* of u, already discussed in Section 5.5 of Chapter 4. The problem of inverting the finite Laplace transform arises in "measurement of the distribution of an absorbing gas (such as ozone in the earth's atmosphere) from the spectrum of scattered light", see Dunn [67] and Twomey [77] for details.

We first report results for the absolute error criterion; for proofs see Werschulz [87a].

THEOREM 7.1. *There exists no algorithm using arbitrary adaptive information of finite cardinality whose error is finite for the ill-posed problem.*

Things are even worse than suggested by this theorem. Although no algorithm can give finite (worst case) error for our problem, one might hope that there exists an algorithm whose worst case behavior does not happen often. The next result quashes that hope. For any information N, define the *zero algorithm* ϕ^0 *using* N by

$$\phi^0\big(N(f)\big) = 0, \qquad \forall\, f \in D.$$

Admittedly, the zero algorithm is about as naive an algorithm as one could possibly concoct. We now indicate that no algorithm can be much better than the zero algorithm.

Recall that for any subset $A \subseteq F$, we say that $w \in F$ belongs to the *relative interior of A in F* iff w is the center of an open F-ball that is contained in A.

THEOREM 7.2. *Let $q \in [0, 1)$. For any linear continuous adaptive information N of varying cardinality and for any algorithm ϕ using N, let*

$$A_q = \left\{ f \in F : \frac{\|S(f) - \phi(N(f))\|}{\|S(f) - \phi^0(N(f))\|} \leq q \right\}.$$

Then the relative interior of A_q in F is empty.

Note that in Theorem 7.2, q can be arbitrarily close to 1. So we find that not only is there no algorithm for an ill-posed problem whose worst case error is finite, but that there are many problem elements that are "bad cases."

From Theorem 7.1 and Theorem 4.1 of Chapter 4, we immediately have

THEOREM 7.3. *For any $\varepsilon > 0$,*

$$\text{comp}(\varepsilon, F_1^*) = +\infty.$$

Thus the ε-complexity of an ill-posed problem is infinite in the worst case setting using the absolute error criterion, no matter how large we choose ε to be. If we wish to solve ill-posed problems in the worst case setting, this means that we have to use another error criterion. We briefly report results for the residual error criterion for the Fredholm problem $Mu = f$ of the first kind, which is studied in Werschulz [87c]. Here, the error of an algorithm ϕ using information N is given by

$$e(\phi, N) = \sup_{f \in F} \|f - M(\phi(N(f)))\|_V,$$

where V is a normed linear space in which F_1 is embedded. For instance, we may take $V = \mathcal{L}_2(0, 1)$ for inversion of the finite Laplace transform so that smoothness of the problem elements is measured by the H^r-norm, but the residual error is measured by the $\mathcal{L}_2$-norm.

For the residual error criterion, we have the following

THEOREM 7.4.

(1) *For any nonadaptive continuous linear information N,*

$$r(N) = \sup\{\|f\|_V : f \in \ker N, \ \|f\|_{F_1} \leq 1\}.$$

Furthermore, there exists a linear optimal error algorithm using N.

(2) *Adaption is no more powerful than nonadaption, i.e., for any adaptive continuous linear information N^{a}, there exists nonadaptive continuous linear information N^{non} such that* $\mathrm{card}(N^{\mathrm{non}}) \leq \mathrm{card}(N^{\mathrm{a}})$ *and* $r(N^{\mathrm{non}}) \leq r(N^{\mathrm{a}})$.

(3) *Let $r(n)$ denote the nth minimal radius of information. Then $r(n)$ tends to 0 iff the embedding E of F_1 into V is compact. If E is compact, then $r(n)$ is the $(n+1)$st singular value of E.*

(4) *If E is not compact, then there exists $\varepsilon_0 > 0$ such that*

$$\mathrm{comp}(\varepsilon) = +\infty, \qquad \forall \varepsilon \leq \varepsilon_0.$$

If E is compact then $\mathrm{comp}(\varepsilon)$ is finite for every $\varepsilon > 0$, and

$$c\, m(\varepsilon) \leq \mathrm{comp}(\varepsilon) \leq (c+2)m(\varepsilon) - 1 \quad \text{with} \quad m(\varepsilon) = \min\{n : r(n) \leq \varepsilon\}.$$

If we apply this result to our problem of inverting the finite Laplace transform using problem elements of smoothness r, we find that $r(n) = \Theta(n^{-r})$ as $n \to \infty$, and $\mathrm{comp}(\varepsilon) = \Theta(\varepsilon^{-1/r})$ as $\varepsilon \to 0$.

Notes and Remarks

NR 7:1 This section is written by A. G. Werschulz and the material is taken from Werschulz [86b, 87a,c].

NR 7:2 The concept of a well-posed problem was introduced in Hadamard [52]. A problem is said to be well-posed if its solution exists, is unique, and depends continuously on its data; a problem that is not well-posed is said to be ill-posed. Hadamard [52] gives the impression that any correctly-formulated physical problem must be well-posed. However, in the years since the appearance of Hadamard's treatise, many important practical problems have been found to be ill-posed. Examples include Fujita's equation relating molecular weight distribution to the steady-state concentration or optical density in a centrifuged sample (Gehatia and Wiff [70]), problems in computational vision (Poggio, Torre, and Koch [85]), and problems in remote sensing (Twomey [77]).

NR 7:3 For further discussion of the approximate solution of ill-posed problems, see Carasso and Stone [75], Hämmerlin and Hoffmann [83], Lattes and Lions [69], Morozov [85], Tikhonov [63], and Tikhonov and Arsenin [77], as well as the references contained therein.

NR 7:4 Using classical computability theory, Pour-El and Richards [83] have shown that the only linear transformations of Banach spaces that map computable input data onto computable solutions are those that are bounded. That is, bounded operators preserve computability, whereas unbounded operators do not. Let us say that a problem is "strongly non-computable" if there exists no algorithm for its solution whose error is finite. The main results of this section then state that a problem is strongly non-computable iff the solution operator is unbounded.

NR 7:5 In this section, we have assumed that $\Lambda = F_1^*$. For the absolute error criterion, we have found that $r(n, F_1^*) = +\infty$ for all n and that $\text{comp}(\varepsilon, F_1^*) = +\infty$ for all $\varepsilon > 0$. Suppose now that $\Lambda = \Lambda^*$, i.e., that *any* linear functional (not necessarily continuous) is permissible. The proof of Theorem 7.1 relies heavily on the continuity of the linear functionals making up the information, and hence is not valid when $\Lambda = \Lambda^*$. If we consider Fredholm problems of the first kind in the Hilbert case (i.e., F_1 and G are Hilbert spaces) and we consider information of finite cardinality using arbitrary linear functionals, then we can show that the radius of information is always infinite and that $\text{comp}(\varepsilon, \Lambda^*) = +\infty$ for all $\varepsilon > 0$. The main point in the proof is to note that such information is an example of the mildly discontinuous nonlinear information discussed in **NR 5.3:3** of Chapter 4 and to use the Borsuk-Ulam theorem. See Werschulz [86b] for details.

8. Optimization

In this section we report two results from a seminal book by Nemirovsky and Yudin [83]. The book studies the following nonlinear constrained optimization problem. Let F be a class of functions $f = [f_0, f_1, \ldots, f_m]$, where $f_j : D \subseteq \mathbb{R}^d \to \mathbb{R}$ is a continuous scalar function, $j = 0, 1, \ldots m$. The solution operator is defined by

$$S(f) = \min \big\{ f_0(x) : x \in D, \ f_j(x) \leq 0, \ j = 0, 1, \ldots, m \big\}.$$

The class Λ of permissible information operations consists of the evaluations of f and f' at points from D.

Nemirovsky and Yudin give tight estimates on the ε-cardinality number for a number of classes F. These estimates are for deterministic as well as for random approximations. (See Chapter 11, where randomization is discussed.) We give two examples as a sample of their results.

Let F be the class of r-times continuously differentiable functions such that the rth derivative of f_j in any direction is uniformly bounded on a nonempty compact set D. Then the ε-cardinality number is given by

$$m(\varepsilon) = \Theta\big(\varepsilon^{-d/r}\big),$$

see also Ivanov [72], and Nemirovsky and Yudin [78]. The almost optimal information consists of the evaluation of f at the points on a regular grid of the set D and the optimal algorithm is provided by the minimal value of f at the grid points. Clearly, the combinatory cost of this algorithm is linear in the cardinality of the information, and therefore

$$\text{comp}(\varepsilon) = \Theta\big(c\,m(\varepsilon)\big).$$

As in Section 3.1, we see that the ε-complexity is exponential in the dimension d. Thus, even for moderate ε but large d, the problem is intractable.

Consider now F as the class of *convex* functions which satisfy a Lipschitz condition with a uniform constant on a bounded convex set D. Then

$$m(\varepsilon) = \Theta\left(\ln\frac{1}{\varepsilon}\right),$$

where the constant in the Θ notation depends polynomially on d and m.

Observe a drastic difference in the formulas for the ε-cardinality numbers. For the convex case, the ε-cardinality number goes to infinity quite slowly as ε approaches zero. This quantifies the relative value of convexity as opposed to smoothness.

Levin [73] suggested an algorithm using information of cardinality roughly $m(\varepsilon)$ whose error is at most ε, however, its combinatory cost is much greater than $m(\varepsilon)$. Nemirovsky and Yudin present an algorithm that uses information of cardinality proportional to $d\,m(\varepsilon)$ whose error is at most ε and whose combinatory cost is proportional to $d^4\ln(d/\varepsilon)$. For large d, the combinatory cost significantly exceeds $m(\varepsilon)$ and hence the information cost. Nevertheless, for fixed d, we have

$$\mathrm{comp}(\varepsilon) = \Theta\left(c\ln\frac{1}{\varepsilon}\right)\quad\text{as}\quad\varepsilon\to 0.$$

An interesting open problem is to find how the ε-complexity of this nonlinear optimization problem depends on the dimension d.

The reader interested in many different aspects of the optimization problem may consult Nemirovsky and Yudin as well as a long list of relevant papers in a forthcoming book of Sukharev [88].

9. Large Linear Systems

In this section we study the solution of large linear systems $Ax = b$, where A is an $n \times n$ nonsingular large sparse matrix and b is a given normalized vector, $\|b\|_2 = 1$. Assume that A belongs to a class F. The class F consists of matrices with some global properties such as symmetry, positive definiteness, or a uniform bound on the condition numbers. In what follows, we assume that the class F is *orthogonally invariant*, i.e.,

$$A \in F \;\Rightarrow\; Q^T A Q \in F$$

for any orthogonal matrix Q, $Q^T Q = I$.

For each A in F we want to compute a vector x_ε such that $\|Ax_\varepsilon - b\| \le \varepsilon$, where $\varepsilon \in [0,1)$. That is, the solution operator is now defined as in Remark 2.1.1 of Chapter 3, with

$$W(A,\varepsilon) = \{x \in \mathbb{R}^n : \|Ax - b\| \le \varepsilon\}.$$

If n is large, say, of the order 10^{+3} or 10^{+4}, then it is prohibitively expensive to store the matrix A in memory. Therefore, it is reasonable to assume that the information about the matrix A is supplied by a subroutine that computes Az for any vector z. That is, the class Λ is now of the form: $L \in \Lambda$ iff there exists a vector z such that $L(A) = Az$ for every A.

As always, c denotes the cost of one information operation. In this case, c is the cost of one matrix-vector multiplication. If A is sparse and has at most k nonzero elements in each row, then c is equal to the cost of $(2k-1)n$ arithmetic operations. Thus, c is a linear function of n.

An example of permissible information is provided by *Krylov* information of cardinality k,

$$N^{\mathrm{kr}}(A) = [Ab, A^2 b, \ldots, A^k b].$$

This information can be written as $[Az_1, Az_2, \ldots, Az_k]$ with $z_1 = b$ and $z_i = Az_{i-1}$. This shows that Krylov information is adaptive and can be computed in time $c\,k$.

An example of an algorithm that uses Krylov information is the *minimal residual* algorithm ϕ^{mr} which is a variant of the conjugate gradient algorithm, see Hestenes and Stiefel [52] or any advanced textbook on numerical analysis. The algorithm ϕ^{mr} computes the vector x_k for which the residual is minimized in the space $E_k = \mathrm{span}(b, Ab, \ldots, A^{k-1}b)$. That is,

$$\|Ax_k - b\| = \min\big\{\|Az - b\| : z \in E_k\big\}.$$

The vector x_k can be computed by the well known three-term recurrence formula with combinatory cost at most $10\,k\,n$.

Krylov information and the minimal residual algorithm are close to optimal in the following sense. Let $m(\varepsilon, \phi^{\mathrm{mr}}, N^{\mathrm{kr}})$ denote the minimal number k of matrix-vector multiplications needed to compute ε-approximations by the minimal residual algorithm using Krylov information of cardinality k. As always, $m(\varepsilon)$ denotes the ε-cardinality number, which is now the minimal number of matrix-vector multiplications needed to compute ε-approximations by *any* algorithm using *arbitrary* information. Obviously, both $m(\varepsilon, \phi^{\mathrm{mr}}, N^{\mathrm{kr}})$ and $m(\varepsilon)$ depend on the class F. For any orthogonally invariant class F, we have

$$m(\varepsilon) \;\leq\; m(\varepsilon, \phi^{\mathrm{mr}}, N^{\mathrm{kr}}) \;\leq\; 2\,m(\varepsilon) + 2, \tag{1}$$

see Chou [87], and Nemirovsky and Yudin [83, p. 262]. Usually $m(\varepsilon)$ is large for small ε and the additive term 2 in the upper bound is insignificant. The question as to whether the multiplicative factor 2 in the upper bound is necessary is open.

The estimates above state that it is impossible to compute ε-approxima-tions using less than one half of the matrix-vector multiplications of the minimal residual algorithm that uses Krylov information.

Let $\text{comp}(\varepsilon, F)$ denote the ε-complexity in the class F. From (1) it easily follows that

$$\text{comp}(\varepsilon, F) = c \, a \, m(\varepsilon, \phi^{\text{mr}}, N^{\text{kr}}), \tag{2}$$

where $a \in [0.5 - 1/m(\varepsilon, \phi^{\text{mr}}, N^{\text{kr}}), 1 + 10\,n/c]$. For small ε and $c \gg n$, we have roughly $a \in [0.5, 1]$.

Thus, the problem of obtaining the complexity reduces to the problem of finding the number $m(\varepsilon, \phi^{\text{mr}}, N^{\text{kr}})$. This number is known for some classes F, see Traub and Woźniakowski [84b]. We discuss two such classes:

$$F_1 = \left\{ A : A = A^T > 0, \text{ and } \|A\|_2 \, \|A^{-1}\|_2 \leq M \right\},$$
$$F_2 = \left\{ A : A = A^T, \quad \text{ and } \|A\|_2 \, \|A^{-1}\|_2 \leq M \right\}.$$

That is, F_1 is the class of symmetric positive definite matrices with condi-tion numbers bounded uniformly by M. Here M is a given number, $M \geq 1$. The class F_2 differs from F_1 by the lack of positive definiteness.

For the class F_1, we have

$$m(\varepsilon, \phi^{\text{mr}}, N^{\text{kr}}) = \min\left\{ n, \left\lceil \frac{\ln \frac{1+(1-\varepsilon^2)^{1/2}}{\varepsilon}}{\ln \frac{M^{1/2}+1}{M^{1/2}-1}} \right\rceil \right\}.$$

For small ε, large M, and $n > M^{1/2} \ln(2/\varepsilon)/2$,

$$m(\varepsilon, \phi^{\text{mr}}, N^{\text{kr}}) \simeq \frac{\sqrt{M}}{2} \, \ln \frac{2}{\varepsilon}.$$

For the class F_2, we have

$$m(\varepsilon, \phi^{\text{mr}}, N^{\text{kr}}) = \min\left\{ n, \left\lceil \frac{\ln \frac{1+(1-\varepsilon^2)^{1/2}}{\varepsilon}}{\ln \frac{M+1}{M-1}} \right\rceil \right\}.$$

For small ε, large M, and $n > M \ln(2/\varepsilon)$,

$$m(\varepsilon, \phi^{\text{mr}}, N^{\text{kr}}) \simeq M \ln \frac{2}{\varepsilon}.$$

These formulas enable us to compare the complexities for both classes F_1 and F_2. For small ε, large M, and $n > M \ln(2/\varepsilon)$, we have

$$\sqrt{M}\big(1 + o(1)\big) \leq \frac{\text{comp}(\varepsilon, F_2)}{\text{comp}(\varepsilon, F_1)} \leq 4\sqrt{M}\big(1 + o(1)\big).$$

This shows how the lack of positive definiteness increases the ε-complexity.

We state a few open problems for the approximate solution of large linear systems. The ratio between the lower and upper bounds on the complexity in (2) is roughly 2 for small ε and $c >> n$. It would be of interest to improve these estimates. We believe that the upper bound is sharp, or almost sharp, i.e., a in (2) is close to 1.

Another open problem is to determine the ε-complexity of large linear systems for more general information. So far we assumed matrix-vector multiplications. It is natural to assume that the inner products of some row (or column) of the matrix and a given vector can be computed, i.e., $\langle a_i, z \rangle$ can be computed, where a_i is the ith row of A and z is a vector. This type of information was studied by Rabin [72] for the exact solution of linear systems, $\varepsilon = 0$, with an arbitrary matrix. He proved that, roughly, $n^2/2$ inner products are enough to find the exact solution. Open problems are how many inner products are needed for an ε-approximation with a positive ε and to determine the ε-complexity. Another open problem is to permit even more general information given by the evaluation of arbitrary linear functionals L_i, and to find the optimal functionals L_i and the ε-complexity. We believe this problem is difficult.

Notes and Remarks

NR 9:1 We have discussed so far the complexity of linear systems assuming partial information on matrices and using the real number model. Linear systems have been also analyzed for different settings.

If the matrix A is assumed to be known, then one wants to find an algorithm that computes an ε-approximation using the minimal number of arithmetic operations and comparisons.

In the real number model, the complexity for $\varepsilon = 0$ satisfies the inequalities

$$c_1 n^2 \leq \text{comp}(0) \leq c_2 n^\beta, \quad \forall n,$$

where c_1, c_2 are positive and $\beta = 2.376....$The lower bound is trivial, since we have $n^2 + n$ inputs. The upper bound is due to Coppersmith and Winograd [87]. The exact value of the ε-complexity, $\varepsilon \geq 0$, is unknown.

Linear systems have been also analyzed in models of computation different from the real number model. A discussion may be found in IUC [83, pp. 97-100]. In particular, for floating point arithmetic with fixed precision, a relation between numerically stable algorithms and optimal error algorithms is exhibited. See also an interesting paper of Miller [75] about trade-offs between complexity and stability.

For floating point arithmetic with variable precision, Kiełbasiński [81] presents an algorithm based on iterative refinement and the algorithm of Schönhage and Strassen [71] for fast multiplication of t-digit numbers. His algorithm finds an ε-approximation with cost $O\big(n^2 \log(n) \log(1/\varepsilon) \log\big(\log(1/\varepsilon)\big) \log\big(\log(\log(1/\varepsilon)))\big)$. Note that the dependence is on $n^2 \log n$ instead of n^β with $\beta = 3$ for the classical algorithms or $\beta = 2.376...$ for Coppersmith and Winograd's algorithm.

Bojańczyk [84] analyzes linear systems in variable precision using the parallel model of computation. He presents an algorithm based on Newton iteration that uses $\Theta(n^3)$

processors and computes an ε-approximation for small ε, in time proportional to the time of one multiplication of two $t = \log(1/\varepsilon)$ digit numbers. We stress that the cost of Bojańczyk's algorithm is independent of n.

NR 9:2 Numerical stability of the minimal residual and conjugate gradients algorithms have been studied by Bollen [84] and Woźniakowski [80]. It is known that in floating point arithmetic, the computed residual vectors $\|Ax_k - b\|$ for large k are at worst of order $2^{-t} \kappa(A) \|A\| \|x_k\|$, where 2^{-t} is the relative computer precision and $\kappa(A) = \|A\|_2 \|A^{-1}\|_2$ is the condition number in the spectral norm. This should be compared to direct algorithms, such as Gaussian elimination with pivoting, Householder, and Gram-Schmidt, which compute a vector x whose residual $\|Ax - b\|$ is of order $2^{-t} \|A\| \|x\|$. Thus, for direct algorithms the residual does not depend on the condition number.

By the use of iterative refinement, it is possible to guarantee that the residuals in the minimal residual or conjugate gradient algorithms are independent of the condition number and are of order $2^{-t} \|A\| \|x_k\|$.

This can be achieved even if iterative refinement is performed in single precision provided $2^{-t} \kappa(A)^2$ is at most of order unity, see Jankowski and Woźniakowski [77], and Skeel [80].

NR 9:3 Consider the following orthogonally invariant classes

$$F_3 = \{A : A = I - B, \; B = B^T \text{ and } \|B\|_2 \leq \rho\},$$

$$F_4 = \{A : A = I - B, \qquad \text{and } \|B\|_2 \leq \rho\},$$

where $\rho < 1$. For the class F_3, we have

$$m(\varepsilon, \phi^{\mathrm{mr}}, N^{\mathrm{kr}}) = \min \left\{ n, \left\lceil \frac{\ln\left((1 + (1 - \varepsilon^2)^{1/2})/\varepsilon\right)}{\ln\left((1 + (1 - \rho^2)^{1/2})/\rho\right)} \right\rceil \right\}.$$

For the class F_4, we have

$$m(\varepsilon, \phi^{\mathrm{mr}}, N^{\mathrm{kr}}) = \min \left\{ n, \left\lceil \frac{\ln(1/\varepsilon)}{\ln(1/\rho)}(1 + o(1)) \right\rceil \right\} \quad \text{as } \varepsilon \to 0,$$

see Traub and Woźniakowski [84b]. For small ε, ρ close to unity, and n so large that the minima are attained for the second argument, we have from (2) the following bounds on the complexities

$$\frac{1}{2} \left(\frac{2}{1 - \rho} \right)^{1/2} (1 + o(1)) \leq \frac{\mathrm{comp}(\varepsilon, F_3)}{\mathrm{comp}(\varepsilon, F_4)} \leq 2 \left(\frac{2}{1 - \rho} \right)^{1/2} (1 + o(1)).$$

This shows how the lack of symmetry in B increases the complexity.

For classes F_3 and F_4, Krylov information is close to optimal. There are algorithms beside the minimal residual algorithm which make almost optimal use of Krylov information. Namely, the Chebyshev algorithm is optimal for the class F_3, and the simple iteration algorithm is almost optimal for the class F_4, see Traub and Woźniakowski [84b]. Rounding error analysis of the Chebyshev and simple iteration algorithms can be found in Woźniakowski [77, 78]. Results are similar to those described in **NR 9:2**.

NR 9:4 The solution of large linear systems may be also considered for different error criteria. For example, consider the relative error criterion, $\|x - \alpha\| \leq \varepsilon \|\alpha\|$, where

$\alpha = A^{-1}b$ is the exact solution. For the classes F_3 and F_4 of **NR 9:3**, Krylov information is still optimal modulo a multiplicative factor 2. For the class F_3, the problem is solved by using

$$m(\varepsilon, N^{\mathrm{kr}}) = \min \left\{ n, \left\lceil \frac{\ln \left(\varepsilon/(1 - (1 - \varepsilon^2)^{1/2})\right)}{\ln \left((1 + (1 - \rho^2)^{1/2})/\rho\right)} \right\rceil \right\}$$

matrix-multiplications. If n is so large that the minimum is achieved by the second argument, then the Chebyshev algorithm uses Krylov information optimally.

For the class F_4, the problem is solved by

$$m(\varepsilon, N^{\mathrm{kr}}) = \min \left\{ n, \left\lceil \frac{\ln(1/\varepsilon)}{\ln(1/\rho)} \right\rceil \right\}$$

matrix-vector multiplications. If n is so large that the last minimum is attained for the second argument then the simple iteration algorithm, i.e., $x_{i+1} = Bx_i + b$ with $x_0 = 0$, uses Krylov information optimally, see Chou [87] and Traub and Woźniakowski [84b]. For both classes, the complexity is of the form

$$\mathrm{comp}(\varepsilon, F_i) = c\, a\, m(\varepsilon, N^{\mathrm{kr}}),$$

where a is at least roughly 0.5 and at most roughly 1.

10. Eigenvalue Problem

In this section we study the eigenvalue problem for $n \times n$ large sparse symmetric matrices A. As in Section 9, we assume that information about the matrix A is given by a subroutine that computes Az for any vector z.

It would be desirable to compute an ε-approximation to the pth largest eigenvalue of A, for a preassigned p. We shall prove that this requires the computation of n matrix-vector multiplications. That is, there exists *no* algorithm that can compute an ε-approximation to the pth largest eigenvalue using less than n matrix-vector multiplications.

On the other hand, if we are willing to settle for an approximation to an eigenvalue for an unspecified p, then it can be computed using $\min\{n, \lceil \varepsilon^{-1} \rceil\}$ matrix-vector multiplications. The generalized minimal residual (gmr) algorithm that uses Krylov information is in this case almost optimal. We conclude this section by briefly comparing the gmr algorithm with the widely used Lanczos algorithm.

We first establish that n matrix-vector multiplications are necessary to compute an ε-approximation to the p largest eigenvalue $\lambda_p(A)$ of the symmetric matrix A. More precisely, let F be the class of $n \times n$ symmetric matrices. For all $A \in F$, we wish to compute $U(A)$ such that

$$|\lambda_p(A) - U(A)| \leq \varepsilon \|A\|_2, \tag{1}$$

where $\varepsilon < 1$. This means that the solution operator is given by $S(A) = \lambda_p(A)$ and we are now using the normalized error criterion.

Let $m(\varepsilon)$ be the ε-cardinality number, i.e., the minimal number of matrix-vector multiplications needed to compute $U(A)$ satisfying (1) for all matrices A from F.

Obviously, the problem can be solved by using n matrix-vector multiplications which can recover the matrix A exactly and provide enough information to produce ε-approximations for any ε, see **NR 10:1**. This shows that $m(\varepsilon) \le n$, $\forall \varepsilon \in [0, 1)$. One may hope that $m(\varepsilon)$ is significantly smaller than n, especially when ε is not too small. Unfortunately, this is *not* the case. Namely, we have

$$m(\varepsilon) = n, \qquad \forall \varepsilon \in [0, 1). \qquad (2)$$

To prove this, assume first that $p = 1$. Take any adaptive information N. As always in the worst case setting, we may assume that N has fixed cardinality. Thus, $N(A) = [Az_1, Az_2, \ldots, Az_k]$, where $z_i = z_i(Az_1, \ldots, Az_{i-1})$ and $k < n$.

No matter how the vectors z_i are chosen, define the information value $y = N(A) = -[z_1, z_2, \ldots, z_k]$, i.e., $Az_i = -z_i$ for $i = 1, 2, \ldots, k$. Knowing y, we conclude that the matrix A is equal to $-I$ in the linear subspace $X = \mathrm{span}(z_1, z_2, \ldots, z_k)$. In particular, we know that $\lambda = -1$ is a $\dim(X)$-multiple eigenvalue of A. Since $\dim(X)$ is at most equal to $n - 1$, we still know nothing about the location of the largest eigenvalue. Indeed, the matrix A can be equal to $-I$ in the whole space, or A can be equal to $-I + 2ww^T$, where w, $\|w\|_2 = 1$, is orthogonal to X. Note that in both cases the norm of A is 1, and $\lambda_1(-I) = -1$ and $\lambda_1(-I + 2ww^T) = +1$.

Let $U(A) = \phi(N(A))$, where ϕ is an algorithm that uses N. Since the information N about $-I$ and $-I + 2ww^T$ is the same, we have $x = \phi(N(-I)) = \phi(N(-I + 2ww^T))$. Suppose that x satisfies (1). Then

$$2 = |1 - x + 1 + x| \le |1 - x| + |-1 - x|$$
$$= |\lambda_1(-I + 2ww^T) - x| + |\lambda_1(-I) - x| \le 2\varepsilon.$$

This yields $\varepsilon \ge 1$, which is a contradiction.

For arbitrary p, we proceed as follows. For the first vectors z_i we set $Az_i = z_i$, $i \le p - 1$. If we perform more than $(p - 1)$ matrix-vector multiplications, then for $j = p, p + 1, \ldots, k$, the vector z_j is decomposed as $z_j = z_{j,1} + z_{j,2}$, where $z_{j,1} \in X = \mathrm{span}(z_1, z_2, \ldots, z_{p-1})$ and $z_{j,2}$ is orthogonal to X. We set $Az_j = z_{j,1} - z_{j,2}$. Knowing the information $y = N(A)$, we conclude that A restricted to X is equal to $+I$, and restricted to $V = \mathrm{span}(z_{p,2}, z_{p+1,2}, \ldots, z_{k,2})$ is equal to $-I$. Still the pth eigenvalue may be -1 or $+1$. Therefore (1) cannot be satisfied for ε less than 1.

Observe that the same argument shows that it is impossible to approximate eigenvalues from a given interval $[a, b]$ or to verify whether the interval $[a, b]$ contains some eigenvalues of A by performing less than n matrix-vector multiplications.

We stress that this negative result is in the worst case setting. It would be of interest to find the cardinality number $m(\varepsilon)$ in the average case and probabilistic settings and verify when $m(\varepsilon)$ is much smaller than n. An example of average case analysis may be found in Kostlan [86] who shows that the power method requires on the average an infinite number of matrix-vector multiplications to compute an ε-approximate eigenpair.

In the worst case setting, we have to relax the formulation of an ε-approximation to get a positive result. This can be achieved if we settle for approximating an unspecified eigenvalue and the eigenvector corresponding to it. That is, we wish to compute an approximate eigenpair (x, ρ), with the normalization $\|x\|_2 = 1$, such that

$$\|Ax - \rho x\|_2 \leq \varepsilon \|A\|_2, \tag{3}$$

where as before $\varepsilon < 1$. Thus, the solution operator is now defined in the generalized way by $W(A, \varepsilon) = \{(x, \rho) : \|x\|_2 = 1, \|Ax - \rho x\|_2 \leq \varepsilon\}$.

Consider now Krylov information, $N^{\mathrm{kr}}(A) = [Ab, A^2 b, \ldots, A^k b]$, where b is a normalized vector $\|b\|_2 = 1$, and the generalized minimal residual (gmr) algorithm ϕ^{gmr} which computes the pair (x_k, ρ_k) such that $\|x_k\|_2 = 1$, $x_k \in E_k = \mathrm{span}(b, Ab, \ldots, A^{k-1} b)$, and

$$\|Ax_k - \rho_k x_k\|_2 = \min \{\|Ax - \rho x\|_2 : \rho \in C \text{ and } x \in E_k, \|x\|_2 = 1\},$$

see Kuczyński [86].

In what follows, we assume that A belongs to an orthogonally invariant class F, see Section 9. Then Krylov information and the minimal residual algorithm enjoy optimality properties in the following sense. Let $m(\varepsilon, \phi^{\mathrm{gmr}}, N^{\mathrm{kr}})$ denote the minimal number of matrix-vector multiplications needed to compute ε-approximations (3) by the gmr algorithm using Krylov information. Let $m(\varepsilon)$ denote the ε-cardinality number. For an orthogonally invariant class F, we have

$$m(\varepsilon) \leq m(\varepsilon, \phi^{\mathrm{gmr}}, N^{\mathrm{kr}}) \leq 2 m(\varepsilon) + 1,$$

see Chou [87]. As in Section 9, the additive term 1 is usually insignificant, but it is not known whether the multiplicative factor 2 in the upper bound is necessary.

Thus, the number of matrix-vector multiplications used by the gmr algorithm with Krylov information is, at most, within a factor of 2 of being minimal.

The number $m(\varepsilon, \phi^{\mathrm{gmr}}, N^{\mathrm{kr}})$ is known for the class F of symmetric $n \times n$ matrices. Kuczyński [86] shows that

$$\min\left\{n, \lceil(2\varepsilon)^{-1}\rceil\right\} \leq m\left(\varepsilon, \phi^{\mathrm{gmr}}, N^{\mathrm{kr}}\right) \leq \min\left\{n, \lceil\varepsilon^{-1}\rceil\right\}.$$

Kuczyński [85, 86] presents an implementation and numerical tests of the gmr algorithm for symmetric matrices. Since the combinatory cost of this algorithm is proportional to $m(\varepsilon, \phi^{\mathrm{gmr}}, N^{\mathrm{kr}})^2$, we have the following bound on the complexity,

$$\mathrm{comp}(\varepsilon) = c\,a\,m(\varepsilon, \phi^{\mathrm{gmr}}, N^{\mathrm{kr}}),$$

where $a \in [0.5 - 1/(2m(\varepsilon, \phi^{\mathrm{gmr}}, N^{\mathrm{kr}})), 1 + O(1/(c\,m(\varepsilon, \phi^{\mathrm{gmr}}, N^{\mathrm{kr}})))]$. Thus, for $n > \varepsilon^{-1}$, we have

$$\mathrm{comp}(\varepsilon) = \frac{c\,a}{\varepsilon},$$

with $a \in [0.25 - \varepsilon/2, 1 + O(1/(\varepsilon n))]$. For large sparse matrices, c is linear in n and the gmr algorithm using Krylov information computes an ε-approximation in time proportional to n/ε. Observe that this is linear in n.

Kuczyński [86] also compares the gmr algorithm to the Lanczos algorithm. The latter is widely used in practice. The gmr algorithm never takes more time and sometimes takes substantially less time than the Lanczos algorithm to compute an approximate eigenpair. Furthermore, the gmr algorithm has the same numerical stability characteristics as the Lanczos algorithm.

Notes and Remarks

NR 10:1 Problem (1) can be solved by using n matrix-vector multiplications as follows. The matrix A can be exactly recovered by computing its columns Ae_i for the unit vectors e_i, $i = 1, 2 \ldots, n$, with cost $c\,n$. Then A can be transformed to a tridiagonal symmetric matrix using orthogonal similarity transformations by Householder's algorithm with cost proportional to n^3. Then the pth eigenvalue can be approximated by bisection from a Sturm sequence with cost proportional to $n \log_2(1/\varepsilon)$, see Wilkinson [65].

11. Ordinary Differential Equations

In this section we report work of Kacewicz [82, 83, 84, 87b] on the solution of systems of ordinary differential equations. See also Section 3.3 of Chapter 10, where this problem is discussed in the asymptotic setting. Let

$$F_1 = \left\{f : \mathbb{R}^{d+1} \rightarrow \mathbb{R}^d : f^{(r)} \text{ is continuous, } f(x) = 0 \text{ for } x \notin D\right\}$$

for a bounded open convex set $D \subset \mathbb{R}^{d+1}$. Then F_1 is a Banach space when equipped with the norm $\|f\| = \sum_{|\alpha| \le r} \|\partial^{|\alpha|}/(\partial^{\alpha_1} y_1 \dots \partial^{\alpha_{d+1}} y_{d+1}) f\|_{\sup}$, where $\alpha = [\alpha_1, \dots, \alpha_{d+1}]$ and $|\alpha| = \sum_{i=1}^{d+1} \alpha_i$. Let F be the unit ball in F_1 and let $G = C[0,1]$ be equipped with the sup norm. The operator S, $S : F \to G$, is defined by letting $S(f) = z$, where z is the solution of the initial value problem

$$
\begin{cases}
z'(x) = f(x, z(x)), & \forall x \in [0,1], \\
z(0) = \eta.
\end{cases}
$$

Kacewicz studies three classes Λ of permissible information operations:

(a) Λ consists of function and derivative evaluations,
(b) Λ consists of arbitrary linear functionals,
(c) Λ consists of arbitrary nonlinear functionals which are finitely continuous.

Finite continuity of a nonlinear functional L means that L is continuous on an arbitrary finite dimensional subspace.

For the first class Λ, we have

$$
\operatorname{comp}(\varepsilon) = \Theta(c\varepsilon^{-r}).
$$

The upper bound on the complexity is achieved, for instance, by the *Taylor* information and the *Taylor* series algorithm. Taylor information consists of a number of finite Taylor series at *adaptively* chosen points. The constant in the Θ notation depends polynomially on d.

For the second and third class Λ, the complexity is roughly the same and

$$
\operatorname{comp}(\varepsilon) = \Theta(c\varepsilon^{-(r+1)}).
$$

The upper bound on the complexity is now achieved by the *Taylor-integral* information and the *Taylor-integral* algorithm. Taylor-integral information consists of Taylor information plus a number of evaluations of integrals of f. As before, the constant in the Θ notation depends polynomially on d.

We now comment on these results. First of all, observe that the exponent of $1/\varepsilon$ in the complexity does not depend on the dimension d. This may seem surprising, especially when compared to the multivariate function approximation or topological degree problems. However, for the initial value problem we want to approximate a function $z : [0,1] \to \mathbb{R}^d$ which has only one scalar variable. Hence, we can view this problem as approximating d scalar functions $z_1, \dots, z_d$, where z_i is the ith component of z. Therefore, the parameter d plays here a different role than in the function approximation problem.

Secondly, observe that z, as a function of t, is $(r+1)$ times continuously differentiable. This suggests that the complexity should be proportional to $\varepsilon^{-(r+1)}$. This is only true if we can compute the values of z at some points in $[0,1]$, or equivalently some integrals of f, which is the case for the second and third class Λ. For the first class, we can only compute values of f, and there is no way to use the extra smoothness of z. Hence, for this class Λ, the complexity is proportional to ε^{-r} with r measuring the smoothness of f, not z.

We now comment on Kacewicz's result for the class Λ of nonlinear and finitely continuous functionals. He was the first to analyze such a general class of information, using the classic Borsuk-Ulam theorem. Observe that the restriction to finitely continuous functionals is quite natural. Without such a restriction, we might be led to consider the highly nonrealistic class of *all* nonlinear functionals. This class is too powerful since any problem for which the set $S(F)$ has power at most that of the continuum can be solved for an arbitrary positive ε using only one nonlinear functional, see GTOA p. 152 and **NR 5.3:4** of Chapter 4. The lack of power of finitely continuous nonlinear information for the nonlinear problem of solving ordinary differential equations agrees with a similar result for linear problems as proven by Kacewicz and Wasilkowski [86], see also **NR 5.3:3** of Chapter 4.

12. Nonlinear Equations

In this section we report some complexity results concerning the solution of nonlinear equations $f(\alpha) = 0$, where f is a scalar or multivariate function. We discuss some optimality results for computing ε-approximations. Both iterative and non-iterative algorithms are considered. A brief discussion of iterative algorithms which maximize the speed of convergence, as well as work in different models of computation other than the real number model, may be found in **NR 12:1** and **NR 12:2**.

We begin by discussing the approximate solution of scalar polynomial equations. This problem has been studied in many papers, a partial list being supplied in **NR 12:3**. Here we only report a recent result of Renegar [87b], see also Renegar [87c] where systems of polynomial equations are considered.

For given $R > 0$ and an integer $d \geq 2$, let F be the class of scalar complex polynomials of degree d whose all zeros are bounded by R, i.e., $f(\alpha) = 0$ implies that $|\alpha| \leq R$. The information about f is *complete* and is provided by the degree d of f and its coefficients a_j, where $f(x) = \sum_{j=0}^{d} a_j x^j$. The class of permissible combinatory operations is restricted to arithmetic operations, conjugation of complex numbers, and comparisons of real numbers. In particular, this means that calculating of roots is not now permitted.

Renegar exhibits an algorithm which approximates all zeros of f to within ε with the worst case cost $O\big(d^2(\log_2 d)\big(\log_2\log_2(R/\varepsilon)\big)+d^3\log_2 d\big)$. He also proves that the complexity of approximating only one zero of f is bounded from below by $\Omega\left(\log_2\log_2 R/\varepsilon - \log_2 d\right)$. This means that for an arbitrary but fixed degree d, the complexity of approximating all zeros of $f \in F$ is given by

$$\text{comp}(\varepsilon) = \Theta\left(\log_2\log_2\frac{R}{\varepsilon}\right) \quad \text{as } \varepsilon \to 0$$

and that Renegar's algorithm is almost optimal modulo a multiplicative constant. It would be interesting to extend this result to the class of permissible combinatory operations defined above augmented by calculations of roots.

We now report two negative results for polynomials of *arbitrary* degree. More specifically, let F consist of scalar complex polynomials f of arbitrary degree for which all zeros are simple, and one of the zeros being at most δ-apart from a given initial guess x_0, see Wasilkowski [83a]. That is, letting $Z(f)$ be the set of all zeros of f, we have

$$f(\alpha) = 0 \neq f'(\alpha), \quad \forall \alpha \in Z(f), \qquad \text{and} \qquad \text{dist}\big(Z(f), x_0\big) \leq \delta.$$

Consider the following problem. For given $\varepsilon < 1$, compute $U(f)$ such that

$$\text{dist}\big(Z(f), U(f)\big) \leq \varepsilon \, \text{dist}\big(Z(f), x_0\big).$$

We assume that Λ consists of all linear functionals and that there is no restriction on the class of permissible combinatory operations. Let $\text{comp}(\varepsilon, \delta, x_0)$ denote the worst case complexity of this problem. Then we have

$$\text{comp}(\varepsilon, \delta, x_0) = +\infty, \quad \forall \varepsilon < 1, \forall \delta > 0, \forall x_0 \in \mathcal{C}.$$

We stress that this result holds even if ε is very close to 1 and the error δ of the initial approximation is arbitrarily small. Thus, it is impossible to improve the quality of the initial approximation x_0 even slightly with finite cost in the worst case setting.

We now report one of Saari's [87] results on chaotic behavior of iterative algorithms for polynomial zero finding. Let F be as above. Let Λ consist of function and derivative evaluations, and let the approximation $U(f)$ have the following iterative form,

$$U(f) = x_k, \quad \text{with}$$
$$x_i = x_{i-1} + M\big(f(x_{i-1}), \ldots, f^{(p)}(x_{i-1}), \ldots, f(x_{i-s}), \ldots, f^{(p)}(x_{i-s})\big)$$

for some k, $p \geq 0$, $s \geq 1$, and for some continuous mapping M. Saari proves that if the mapping M is not constant then

$$\sup_{f \in F} \text{dist} \left(Z(f), U(f) \right) = +\infty.$$

Note that the class of algorithms considered by Saari includes the class of stationary iterative algorithms which are commonly used in practice. This result has therefore the following important implication. Consider a convergent stationary iteration which computes the sequence of successive approximations $\{x_i\}$ such that $\lim_i \text{dist} \left(Z(f), x_i \right) = 0$, $\forall f \in F$. Then for some polynomial f from the class F, the ith approximation is arbitrarily far away from any zero of f although we started with a very good initial approximation. Hence, the ith error might be arbitrarily bad even though the error goes to zero in the limit. We refer the reader to Saari [87] for more results on peculiarities in the behavior of iterative algorithms for polynomial zero finding.

We now turn to classes of smooth functions for which positive results are known. More material can be found in **NR 12:4**. For $r \geq 0$, consider the following class

$$F = \left\{ f : [a, b] \to \mathbb{R} : f(a) \leq 0, \ f(b) \geq 0, \ f^{(r)} \text{ is continuous} \right\}.$$

It is known that for the class Λ consisting of only function evaluations, optimal information and an optimal algorithm are provided by bisection, see Kung [76]. Bisection remains optimal even for Λ consisting of all linear functionals, see Sikorski [82a, 84b]. The ε-complexity is thus given by

$$\text{comp}(\varepsilon) = (c + a_1) \left\lceil \log_2 \frac{b - a}{\varepsilon} \right\rceil + a_2,$$

where $a_1 \in [0, 3]$ and $a_2 \in [0, 1]$. We stress that bisection information is adaptive. If one insists on using only nonadaptive information, then the minimal cost of any algorithm that uses nonadaptive information with the worst case error not exceeding ε is proportional to ε^{-1}, see GTOA p. 166. Hence, adaption is exponentially more efficient than nonadaption for this problem.

Finally, we report a recent result on approximating a fixed point of a function, see Sikorski and Woźniakowski [87]. Let F be the class of functions $f : D \to D$ which satisfies a Lipschitz condition with constant $\rho < 1$, i.e.,

$$F = \left\{ f : D \to D : \| f(x) - f(y) \| \leq \rho \| x - y \|, \ \forall x, y \in D \right\}.$$

That is, F is the class of ρ-contractive mappings on D. Here, D is a closed subset of a Banach space B such that $0 \in D$. As in Example 5.2.1 of Chapter 4, let $S(f) = \alpha$, where α is the unique solution of $x = f(x)$ for $x \in D$. Hence, we want to approximate the fixed point of f. Obviously, letting $\tilde{f}(x) = x - f(x)$ we have $\tilde{f}(\alpha) = 0$, and therefore the fixed point problem is an instance of nonlinear equation. Consider the relative error criterion, with the distance between $S(f)$ and $U(f)$ defined by $\|S(f) - U(f)\|/\|S(f)\|$. The class Λ consists of function values.

Suppose first that $D = \mathbb{R}^d$ is equipped with the spectral norm and

$$d \geq \left\lceil \frac{\log_2 \frac{1}{\varepsilon}}{\log_2 \frac{1}{\rho}} \right\rceil. \tag{1}$$

Observe that an affine mapping $f(x) = Ax + b$ with an $d \times d$ matrix whose spectral norm does not exceed ρ and an arbitrary $d \times 1$ vector b belongs to the class F. Thus the complexity of the fixed point problem is at least equal to the complexity of solving linear systems of the form $x = Ax + b$ with $\|A\| \leq \rho$. A lower bound on the complexity of the latter is known, see **NR 9:4**, and therefore

$$\text{comp}(\varepsilon) \geq \frac{c}{2} \left\lceil \frac{\log_2 \frac{1}{\varepsilon}}{\log_2 \frac{1}{\rho}} \right\rceil - c.$$

On the other hand, the first $k = k(\varepsilon, \rho) = \lceil \log_2(1/\varepsilon)/\log_2(1/\rho) \rceil$ steps of the simple iteration algorithm, i.e.,

$$U(f) = x_k, \quad \text{with } x_i = f(x_{i-1}), \ x_0 = 0,$$

solve the problem with cost equal to ck. Hence, the simple iteration algorithm is almost optimal (modulo a multiplicative constant $1/2$), and

$$\text{comp}(\varepsilon) = a\,c\, \frac{\log_2 \frac{1}{\varepsilon}}{\log_2 \frac{1}{\rho}},$$

where a is roughly at least 0.5 and at most 1. This means that for ρ close to 1 and large d, the fixed point problem has large complexity.

Consider now the same problem with $d = 1$, for which (1) obviously does not hold. Let $D = [0, 1]$. Then again, simple iteration requires $k(\varepsilon, \rho) = \lceil \log_2(1/\varepsilon)/\log_2(1/\rho) \rceil$ function evaluations to solve the problem. Let $m(\varepsilon, \rho)$ denote the number of function evaluations needed by an optimal algorithm. For $\varepsilon \leq 0.5$ and $\rho \in (1/3, 1)$, we have

$$\left\lfloor \log_2 \log_2 \frac{1}{1-\rho} \right\rfloor + \left\lceil \frac{\log_2(2\varepsilon)^{-1}}{\log_2 \frac{2+2\rho}{3\rho-1}} \right\rceil \leq m(\varepsilon, \rho) \leq \left\lceil \log_2 \log_2 \frac{1}{1-\rho} \right\rceil$$

$$+ \left\lceil \frac{\log_2(2\varepsilon)^{-1}}{0.9 + \log_2 \frac{2+2\rho}{3\rho-1}} \right\rceil + 1.$$

The optimal algorithm relies on constructing envelopes, which interpolate the data, and then solving a quadratic equation. This can be done in linear combinatory cost, and therefore, for large c, we have

$$\mathrm{comp}(\varepsilon) \simeq c\, m(\varepsilon, \rho).$$

Observe that for fixed ρ and small ε, the complexity is roughly $c \log_2(1/\varepsilon)$. On the other hand, if ε is fixed and ρ increases to 1, then the complexity is roughly $c \log_2 \log_2(1/(1-\rho))$, which goes extremely slowly to infinity.

Note that $m(\varepsilon, \rho)$ is significantly smaller than $k(\varepsilon, \rho)$ for ρ close to 1. Hence, for $d = 1$ the fixed point problem has small complexity which depends on ρ very mildly, whereas the simple iteration algorithm may be very expensive with cost very much dependent on ρ.

Notes and Remarks

NR 12:1 We briefly mention work on iterative algorithms which enjoy optimality properties in an asymptotic setting. More precisely, we seek an iterative algorithm which converges to a zero of a function with the best possible speed of convergence. This approach is related to the asymptotic setting discussed in Chapter 10.

The study of iterative complexity was initiated by Traub [61, 64]. The concept of order of information, which plays a role similar to the concept of radius of information in the worst case setting, was introduced by Woźniakowski [72]. Since the complexity depends inversely on the order of information, a tight upper bound on the order is needed to get a tight lower bound on the complexity, see Traub and Woźniakowski [76a]. Papers dealing with optimal iterative algorithms include Brent [73, 76a,b], Brent, Winograd, and Wolfe [73], Jankowska [79], Kacewicz [76a,b, 79], Kung [76], Kung and Traub [74, 76], Meersman [76a,b], Saari and Simon [78], Sikorski and Trojan [87], Traub [72], Traub and Woźniakowski [76a,b, 79, 80a,b,c], Trojan [80a,b], Wasilkowski [80, 81a], Werschulz [81b], and Woźniakowski [72, 74, 75a,b, 76].

NR 12:2 There is an interesting stream of work on polynomial equations in a bit operation model of computation. For an overview, the reader is referred to a survey of Schönhage [86].

NR 12:3 There is a number of significant results on finding efficient algorithms for polynomial equations in the real number model with the class of combinatory operations restricted to arithmetic operations, comparisons, conjugation of complex numbers, and/or radicals. A partial list of papers devoted to this study includes Hirsch and Smale [79], Kim [85], McMullen [85], Murota [82], Renegar [85a,b,c, 87a,b,c], Saari [87], Saari and Urenko [84], Shub and Smale [85, 86], Smale [81, 85, 86, 87], and Wongkew [85]. Some of the papers use average or probabilistic approaches to analyze the efficiency of algorithms.

NR 12:4 A recent survey on the optimal solution of nonlinear equations may be found in Sikorski [85]. A partial list of papers on optimal noniterative algorithms include Aird and Rice [77], Booth [67], Boult and Sikorski [84], Chernousko [68], Eichhorn [68], Gross and Johnson [59], Hyafil [77], Kiefer [53, 57], Kung [76], Majstrovskij [72], Micchelli and Miranker [75], Pevnyj [82], Plaskota [86], Sikorski [82a, 84a,b,], Sikorski and Trojan [87], Sikorski and Woźniakowski [86], Sukharev [71, 76, 88], Todd [78],

Traub and Woźniakowski [80a], Veroy [86], Wasilkowski [84], and Zaliznyak and Ligun [78]. Some of these papers deal with approximating extrema, a problem that is closely related to nonlinear equations. See also Wasilkowski [83b], where the inverse function problem and its relation to nonlinear equations is discussed.

We end this remark by a historical note. Probably the first paper written in the spirit of information-based complexity was by Kiefer [53] and contained the results of his master's thesis written in 1948. He studied the search for the maximum of scalar unimodal functions. Kiefer proved that if function evaluations are used, then the optimal information consists of function values at the Fibonnaci points and the optimal algorithm is the midpoint of the smallest interval containing the solution. The ε-complexity of this problem is equal to

$$\text{comp}(\varepsilon) = (c + O(1)) \frac{\log_2(1/\varepsilon)}{\log_2\left((1 + \sqrt{5})/2\right)} \simeq 1.44\, c\, \log_2(1/\varepsilon).$$

Fibonacci information is adaptive. If only nonadaptive information is used, then the cost of computing an ε-approximation is much higher, since it is proportional to c/ε, see GTOA pp. 176–197. Thus, adaptive information is exponentially more powerful than nonadaptive information for approximating the maximum of unimodal functions.

Note that for the class Λ consisting of all linear functionals, Fibonacci search is not optimal. From Sikorski [82a], it follows that the ε-complexity is roughly $c\, \log_2(1/\varepsilon)$.

13. Topological Degree

We now report some results of Boult [86], and Boult and Sikorski [85, 86] concerning the computation of topological degree. For a formal definition of topological degree the reader is refered to Ortega and Rheinboldt [70]. Here we only mention that the topological degree $\deg(f)$ of a function f, if it exists, is related to the number of zeros of f including their multiplicities. This makes it a useful tool for solving nonlinear equations, see, e.g., Eiger, Sikorski, and Stenger [84], Harvey and Stenger [76], Kearfott [77, 79], Prüfer and Siegberg [80], Sikorski [79, 84c], Stenger [75], and Stynes [79a,b, 81]. Let

$$F = \left\{ f : D \to \mathbb{R}^d : \|f(x) - f(y)\| \leq K\|x - y\|, \forall\, x, y \in D, \text{ and} \right.$$
$$\left. \|f(x)\| \geq \kappa, \forall\, x \in \partial D \right\},$$

where $D = [0,1]^d$ and ∂D is its boundary. Here we use the $\mathcal{L}_\infty$ norm, $\|\cdot\| = \|\cdot\|_\infty$, and K and κ are positive numbers.

The assumption that f does not vanish on the boundary ∂D guarantees that $\deg(f)$ is well defined for every $f \in F$. We set $S(f) = \deg(f)$. The class Λ consists of function evaluations.

It is easy to see that $\text{comp}(\varepsilon) = \text{comp}(0)$ for $\varepsilon < 1/2$. Indeed, if $|S(f) - U(f)| \leq \varepsilon < 1/2$ then the fact that $S(f)$ is an integer implies that $S(f)$

can be recovered exactly, $S(f) = \lfloor U(f) + 1/2 \rfloor$. Therefore we assume that $\varepsilon = 0$.

For $d = 1$, the topological degree is $\big(\text{sign}(f(1)) - \text{sign}(f(0))\big)/2$ and can be computed using two function evaluations.

For $d = 2$, Boult and Sikorski [85] find very tight bounds on the complexity,

$$\text{comp}(0) = 4\,(c + a)\,\left\lceil \frac{K}{4\kappa} \right\rceil - 1, \quad \text{with } a \in [2, 24].$$

For $d > 2$ and $K \geq 8\kappa$, Boult and Sikorski [86] prove that

$$a\,d\,(c + d)\,\left(\frac{K}{8\kappa} \right)^{d-1} \leq \text{comp}(0) \leq a\,d\,\left(c + \frac{d^2(d-1)!}{2} \right)\left(\frac{K}{2\kappa} \right)^{d-1},$$

where $a \simeq 2$.

Thus, the complexity is exponential in d. For large d or large $K/(8\kappa)$, the problem is intractable. The same negative result holds even if random information and random algorithms are permitted, see Section 4.1.4 of Chapter 11.

In either case, i.e., $d = 2$ or $d > 2$, the upper bound on complexity is achieved by an algorithm that uses nonadaptive information and is based on Kearfott's [79] algorithm. A Fortran subroutine for computing the topological degree for the class F can be found in a forthcoming paper of Boult and Sikorski [87].

Chapter 6

Average Case Setting: Theory

1. Introduction

In this chapter we analyze the average case setting. In this setting, the error and cost are defined by the average performance with respect to a probability measure μ on the set F.

The choice of a measure μ is a delicate problem. It depends on our belief of how often certain elements of F, or subsets of F, occur. For instance, consider a finite set F, $F = \{f_1, f_2, \ldots, f_k\}$. Let $p(f)$ denote the probability of occurrence of f, so that $p(f) \geq 0$, and $\sum_{f \in F} p(f) = 1$. Then for $A \subset F$, $\mu(A) = \sum_{f \in A} p(f)$. In many cases, it seems reasonable to assume that all elements f are equi-probable, i.e., $p(f) = 1/k, \forall f \in F$.

Consider now the case when F is a subset of the k dimensional Euclidean space, $F \subset \mathbb{R}^k$. Then a natural choice of μ might be a weighted Lebesgue measure, $\mu(A) = \int_A p(f) \, df$ for a Borel set A from $\mathbb{R}^k$. Here $p : \mathbb{R}^k \to \mathbb{R}_+$ is a weight (density) function.

However, if F lies in an infinite dimensional space, the choice of μ is less obvious. There exists no Lebesgue-like measure on an infinite dimensional space, and certain intuitions from the finite dimensional case do not carry over to the infinite dimensional case.

Many problems treated in information-based complexity are defined on subsets of infinite dimensional spaces. For such problems, measure theory on infinite dimensional spaces must be used. Elements of this theory are presented in Section 2 of the appendix. We believe that for many problems, a Gaussian measure may serve as a good candidate for the probability measure on the set F. A substantial portion of this chapter is devoted to linear problems on spaces equipped with Gaussian measures. The basic properties of Gaussian measures are briefly reviewed in Section 5.2.

The structure of this chapter is similar to that of Chapter 4. Our main goal is to find tight bounds on the average complexity. We present a number of theoretical results which allow us to obtain such bounds. In the next chapter we will apply these results to a number of specific problems such as integration, function approximation, or ill-posed problems.

We begin our analysis by introducing the concept of the average radius of information, which is a sharp lower bound on the average error of any algorithm using this information. Thus, to compute ε-approximations on the average, we must use information whose average radius does not exceed ε. Let $m^{\mathrm{avg}}(\varepsilon)$ be the minimal average cardinality of information whose average radius is at most ε.

The average cost of computing ε-approximations on the average must then be at least $c\, m^{\mathrm{avg}}(\varepsilon)$, where c is, as always, the cost of one information operation. Therefore, $c\, m^{\mathrm{avg}}(\varepsilon)$ is a lower bound on the average ε-complexity.

This bound is tight if there exists information of average cardinality $m^{\mathrm{avg}}(\varepsilon)$ and average radius at most ε such that an optimal error algorithm using this information has combinatory cost negligible compared to $c\, m^{\mathrm{avg}}(\varepsilon)$.

We show that this holds for *linear* problems. Recall that a linear problem was defined in Chapter 4. Here we specialize this definition by adding an assumption on the *a priori* probability measure μ. As mentioned before, we choose to work with Gaussian measures. The major part of this chapter is devoted to the study of linear problems.

We first study nonadaptive information for linear problems. Unlike the worst case setting, we show that there always exists a linear optimal error algorithm. This algorithm is the mean of the conditional measure and depends linearly on the data.

We then study adaptive information. We show that adaptive selection of information operations does not help in the average case setting. On the other hand, adaptive selection of the *number* of information operations may help. These issues are studied in detail in Section 5, and the introduction to this section explains how much can be gained by using adaptive information.

The analysis of the average case setting in Sections 2–5 is done for the absolute error criterion. In the final section we extend this analysis for other error criteria including relative, normalized, and general error criteria.

Notes and Remarks

NR 1:1 The average case and probabilistic approach to algorithmic analysis has gained considerable attention in theoretical computer science. Many important discrete and continuous problems defined on finite dimensional spaces have been analyzed on the average. These problems have been studied assuming complete information (i.e., N is the identity mapping) and atomic or weighted Lebesgue measure. A partial list of papers includes Karp [76, 79, 80] on the probabilistic behavior of algorithms for various combinatorial problems; Karp and Luby [83, 85] on reliability; Rabin [76], and Solovay and Strassen [77] on primality testing; Rabin [83] on the Byzantine general problem; Blum and Shub [86] on the evaluation of rational functions; Renegar [87a], Shub and Smale [85, 86], and Smale [81, 85, 86] on polynomial zero-finding; and Adler, Karp, and Shamir [87], Adler and Megiddo [85], Borgwardt [82], and Smale [82, 83, 85] on linear programming.

As far as we know, the first papers dealing with the average case setting with partial information are due to Suldin [59, 60]. He studied integration for continuous functions equipped with the classical Wiener measure. Larkin, in a series of papers commencing with Larkin [72], studied the approximation of linear problems utilizing a finitely additive Gauss measure. Both Suldin and Larkin assume linear algorithms that use nonadaptive information.

There is also an interesting stream of work in the statistical literature dealing with the approximation of linear functionals defined on function spaces. Information consists of function and derivative evaluations and is assumed to be nonadaptive. Usually linear algorithms are studied. For linear algorithms, the full knowledge of a measure is not needed. It is enough to know its mean and correlation operator. A partial list of such papers includes Kimeldorf and Wahba [70a,b], Sacks and Ylvisaker [66, 68, 70a,b], and Wahba [78]. Relations between Bayesian statistics and average case information-based complexity are discussed in Kadane and Wasilkowski [85].

NR 1:2 The problem of how a probability measure should be chosen is addressed in Novak [87a], see also Novak [86b,c]. He concludes that many natural properties of measures can only hold if the space F_1 is finite dimensional.

2. Radius of Information

In this section we define the average radius of information. This will be done similarly to the worst case setting. Recall that we wish to approximate $S(f)$ knowing $y = N(f)$, where $S: F \to G$ is a solution operator and N is an information operator defined as in Section 2.2 of Chapter 3.

In the average case setting, we assume that the set F is equipped with a probability measure μ defined on Borel sets from F. The measure μ represents our belief about the distribution of problem elements f. We assume that the solution operator S is a measurable mapping. Then the probability measure $\nu = \mu S^{-1}$ is an *a priori* measure of solution elements $S(f)$. Both μ and ν represent distributions which are known before any information about problem elements f have been computed.

Given the computed information $y = N(f)$, we concentrate, as in the worst case setting, on

$$SN^{-1}(y) = \{S(\tilde{f}) : \tilde{f} \in F, N(\tilde{f}) = y\},$$

the set of indistinguishable solution elements. In the worst case setting, the radius of information was defined via the (worst case) radius of a subset A of the normed space G,

$$\mathrm{rad}^{\mathrm{wor}}(A) = \inf_{x \in G} \sup_{a \in A} \|x - a\|.$$

In the average case setting, we would like to replace the maximal distance of $\|x - a\|$ by its average value. Assuming for a moment that an appropriate probability measure ν_A on A is available, the average radius of A is defined by

$$\mathrm{rad}^{\mathrm{avg}}(A) = \inf_{x \in G} \sqrt{\int_A \|x - a\|^2 \, \nu_A(da)}.$$

Clearly, $\mathrm{rad}^{\mathrm{avg}}(A) \le \mathrm{rad}^{\mathrm{wor}}(A)$.

With the set $SN^{-1}(y)$ playing the role of A, what measure should be chosen to represent the distribution of solution elements from $SN^{-1}(y)$? This measure must depend on the *a priori* measure μ, the solution operator S, the information operator N as well as on the value $y = N(f)$.

To get such a measure we proceed as follows. Assume that N is a measurable mapping. Then $\mu_1 = \mu N^{-1}$ is a probability measure defined on Borel sets of $N(F)$. For a measurable set A of $N(F)$, $\mu_1(A)$ is the probability that information N takes values from A.

We assume that there exists a unique (modulo sets of μ_1-measure zero) family of probability measures $\mu_2(\cdot|y)$ defined on Borel sets of F such that

(i) $\mu_2\big(N^{-1}(y)|y\big) = 1$ for almost all $y \in N(F)$,
(ii) $\mu_2(B|\cdot)$ is μ_1-measurable for any Borel set B of F,
(iii) $\mu(B) = \int_{N(F)} \mu_2(B|y) \, \mu_1(dy)$ for any Borel set B of F.

Such a family is called a *conditional measure*. It exists, for instance, if F is a measurable subset of a separable Banach space. See Sections 2.7 and 2.9.2 of the appendix for a more detailed discussion of conditional measures.

Property (i) requires $\mu_2(\cdot|y)$ to be concentrated on the set $N^{-1}(y)$ of problem elements which share the same information. Hence, it is a probability measure on $N^{-1}(y)$. Property (ii) ensures that the integral in (iii) is well-defined. Property (iii) relates the measures μ_1 and $\mu_2(\cdot|y)$ to the *a priori* measure μ. The essence of (iii) is that for any measurable function $Q : F \to \mathbb{R}_+$ we have

$$\int_F Q(f) \, \mu(df) = \int_{N(F)} \left\{ \int_{N^{-1}(y)} Q(f) \, \mu_2(df|y) \right\} \mu_1(dy). \qquad (1)$$

Thus, we can first integrate over elements that share the same information y and then over all information values y.

We are ready to define the measure $\nu(\cdot|y)$ on the set $SN^{-1}(y)$. For each measurable set B of G, let

$$\nu(B|y) = \mu_2(S^{-1}(B)|y).$$

As a result of (i), $\nu(B|y) = \mu_2(S^{-1}(B) \cap N^{-1}(y)|y)$ and $\nu(SN^{-1}(y)|y) = 1$. Thus, $\nu(\cdot|y)$ is a probability measure on $SN^{-1}(y)$. The measure $\nu(\cdot|y)$ is an *a posteriori* measure that represents our belief about the distribution of solution elements which are indistinguishable with respect to the computed information $y = N(f)$.

The *local average radius of information* is defined by

$$r^{\text{avg}}(N, y) = \inf_{x \in G} \sqrt{\int_{SN^{-1}(y)} \|x - g\|^2 \, \nu(dg|y)}.$$

We would like to define the global radius of information as the average value of $r^{\text{avg}}(N, \cdot)$ in the $\mathcal{L}_2$ sense with respect to the measure μ_1. To do this we must guarantee that $r^{\text{avg}}(N, \cdot)$ is a μ_1-measurable function.

LEMMA 2.1. *If G is a separable normed linear space then the local average radius is μ_1-measurable.*

PROOF: It is enough to show that $B(a) = \{y \in N(F) : r^{\text{avg}}(N, y) \geq a\}$ is μ_1-measurable for any real number a. For $y \in N(F)$, let $R(y, \cdot) : G \to \mathbb{R}_+$ be defined by

$$R(y, x) = \sqrt{\int_{SN^{-1}(y)} \|x - g\|^2 \, \nu(dg|y)}.$$

Then $R(y, \cdot)$ is continuous and $r^{\text{avg}}(N, y) = \inf_{x \in G} R(y, x)$. Furthermore,

$$B(a) = \{y \in N(F) : \forall x \in G, \ R(y, x) \geq a\} = \bigcap_{x \in G} B_x(a),$$

where $B_x(a) = \{y \in N(F) : R(y, x) \geq a\}$. Since G is separable, there exists a countable subset A which is dense in G. Of course,

$$B(a) \subset \bigcap_{x \in A} B_x(a). \tag{2}$$

We show that $B(a) = \bigcap_{x \in A} B_x(a)$. Indeed, take $y \in \bigcap_{x \in A} B_x(a)$ and $\bar{x} \in G$. Then $R(y, x) \geq a, \ \forall x \in A$. Since $R(y, \cdot)$ is continuous and

$\overline{x} = \lim_i x_i$ for some $x_i \in G$, we have $R(y, \overline{x}) = \lim_i R(y, x_i) \geq a$. Thus, $y \in B_{\overline{x}}(a)$, $\forall \overline{x} \in G$, and therefore $y \in B(a)$. Hence $\bigcap_{x \in A} B_x(a) \subset B(a)$ which with (2) yields the desired equality.

Every set $B_x(a)$ is μ_1-measurable since $R(\cdot, x)$ is μ_1-measurable for every x. Hence the set $B(a)$, as an intersection of countably many μ_1-measurable sets, is also μ_1-measurable. This completes the proof. ∎

Thus, assuming separability of G, the (*global*) *average radius of information* is defined by

$$r^{\mathrm{avg}}(N) = \sqrt{\int_{N(F)} r^{\mathrm{avg}}(N, y)^2 \, \mu_1(dy)}.$$

Obviously, $r^{\mathrm{avg}}(N, y) \leq r^{\mathrm{wor}}(N, y)$ for any $y \in N(F)$ and $r^{\mathrm{avg}}(N) \leq r^{\mathrm{wor}}(N)$.

As we shall see in the next section, the average radius of information measures on the average the intrinsic uncertainty caused by partial information. This implies that ε-approximations can be obtained on the average only if $r^{\mathrm{avg}}(N) \leq \varepsilon$.

In the worst case setting, the radius of information has been defined also for generalized solution operators. Also the diameter of information has been discussed and proved to be useful in the analysis of the worst case. These concepts can be defined in the average case setting as well. Since they are not needed in the main stream of this chapter, we defer their presentation to **NR 2:3** and **2:4**.

Notes and Remarks

NR 2:1 This section is based on Wasilkowski [83c], where the average radius of information was defined. The notion of the average radius of information is conceptually similar to the concept of the minimal risk in Bayesian statistics. A discussion of relations between the average case setting and Bayesian statistics may be found in Kadane and Wasilkowski [85].

NR 2:2 As already mentioned in Chapter 3, we define the average radius in the $\mathcal{L}_2$ sense to simplify the analysis. In Section 6 we indicate how some of these results extend to more general error criteria.

NR 2:3 The average radius of information is defined for generalized solution operators W as follows. As in IUC, Appendix B, define the distance between elements of the sets F and G by

$$\mathrm{dist}_G(f, g) = \inf\{\delta : g \in W(f, \delta)\},$$

$f \in F$ and $g \in G$, with the convention that $\inf \emptyset = +\infty$. Then the local worst case radius of information, see **NR 2:3** of Chapter 4, can be rewritten as

$$r^{\mathrm{wor}}(N, y) = \inf_{g \in G} \sup_{f \in N^{-1}(y)} \mathrm{dist}_G(f, g).$$

From this formula it easily follows that the local average radius of information should be defined by replacing the maximal distance $\text{dist}_G(f,g)$ by its average value with respect to the conditional measure $\mu_2(\cdot|y)$,

$$r^{\text{avg}}(N,y) = \inf_{g \in G} \left\{ \int_{N^{-1}(y)} (\text{dist}_G(f,g))^2 \, \mu_2(df|y) \right\}^{1/2}.$$

Assuming μ_1-measurability of $r^{\text{avg}}(N,\cdot)$, the (global) average radius is defined as in Section 2 by

$$r^{\text{avg}}(N) = \left\{ \int_{N(F)} r^{\text{avg}}(N,y)^2 \, \mu_1(dy) \right\}^{1/2}.$$

Observe that for $W(f,\varepsilon) = \{g \in G : \|S(f) - g\| \leq \varepsilon\}$, we have $\text{dist}_G(f,g) = \|S(f) - g\|$. Since

$$\int_{N^{-1}(y)} \|S(f) - x\|^2 \, \mu_2(df|y) = \int_{SN^{-1}(y)} \|x - g\|^2 \, \nu(dg|y),$$

the above definitions of local and global average radii coincide with those presented in Section 2.

NR 2:4 We show how the diameter of information can be defined in the average case setting. We first recall the worst case diameter of a subset A of the normed space G,

$$\text{diam}^{\text{wor}}(A) = \sup_{a_1,a_2 \in A} \|a_1 - a_2\|.$$

Assuming a probability measure ν_A on the set A, the average diameter of A is defined by the average distance in the $\mathcal{L}_2$ sense between elements of A,

$$\text{diam}^{\text{avg}}(A) = \left\{ \int_A \int_A \|g_1 - g_2\|^2 \, \nu_A(dg_1) \, \nu_A(dg_2) \right\}^{1/2}.$$

Clearly, $\text{diam}^{\text{avg}}(A) \leq \text{diam}^{\text{wor}}(A)$.

We now find relations between the average radius and diameter of A. Observe that $\text{rad}^{\text{avg}}(A)^2 \leq \int_A \|a_1 - a_2\|^2 \, \nu_A(da_1)$ for any a_2. Integrating with respect to a_2, we get

$$\text{rad}^{\text{avg}}(A) \leq \text{diam}^{\text{avg}}(A).$$

On the other hand, $\|a_1 - a_2\|^2 \leq 2(\|a_1 - x\|^2 + \|a_2 - x\|^2)$ for any x. This yields

$$\text{diam}^{\text{avg}}(A) \leq 2 \, \text{rad}^{\text{avg}}(A).$$

We define the local average diameter of information by

$$d^{\text{avg}}(N,y) = \left\{ \int_{SN^{-1}(y)} \int_{SN^{-1}(y)} \|g_1 - g_2\|^2 \, \nu(dg_1|y) \, \nu(dg_2|y) \right\}^{1/2},$$

and assuming μ_1-measurability of $d^{\text{avg}}(N,\cdot)$, the global one by

$$d^{\text{avg}}(N) = \left\{ \int_{N(F)} d^{\text{avg}}(N,y)^2 \, \mu_1(dy) \right\}^{1/2}.$$

Obviously,

$$r^{\mathrm{avg}}(N,y) \leq d^{\mathrm{avg}}(N,y) \leq 2\,r^{\mathrm{avg}}(N,y), \ \forall\, y \in N(F),$$
$$r^{\mathrm{avg}}(N) \leq d^{\mathrm{avg}}(N) \leq 2\,r^{\mathrm{avg}}(N).$$

We now indicate how the average diameter of information is defined for generalized solution operators. Recall that the local worst case diameter is defined in **NR 2:4** of Chapter 4,

$$d^{\mathrm{wor}}(N,y) = \sup_{f_1,f_2 \in N^{-1}(y)} \mathrm{dist}(f_1,f_2).$$

This suggests that the local average case diameter should be defined by

$$d^{\mathrm{avg}}(N,y) = \left\{ \int_{N^{-1}(y)} \int_{N^{-1}(y)} \mathrm{dist}^2(f_1,f_2)\, \mu_2(df_1|y)\, \mu_2(df_2|y) \right\}^{1/2}$$

and the global one by (once more assuming that $d^{\mathrm{avg}}(N,\cdot)$ is μ_1-measurable)

$$d^{\mathrm{avg}}(N) = \left\{ \int_{N(F)} (d^{\mathrm{avg}}(N,y))^2\, \mu_1(dy) \right\}^{1/2}.$$

Obviously, $d^{\mathrm{avg}}(N,y) \leq d^{\mathrm{wor}}(N,y)$ and $d^{\mathrm{avg}}(N) \leq d^{\mathrm{wor}}(N)$. As in the worst case setting, we have

$$d^{\mathrm{avg}}(N,y) \leq 2\,r^{\mathrm{avg}}(N,y), \ \ \forall\, y \in N(F), \quad \text{and} \quad d^{\mathrm{avg}}(N) \leq 2\,r^{\mathrm{avg}}(N).$$

Indeed, this follows from the fact that

$$\mathrm{dist}(f_1,f_2) \leq \mathrm{dist}_G(f_1,g) + \mathrm{dist}_G(f_2,g), \ \forall\, g \in G.$$

For a regular generalized solution operator, see **NR 2:4** of Chapter 4, we have

$$r^{\mathrm{avg}}(N,y) \leq d^{\mathrm{avg}}(N,y), \ \ \forall\, y \in N(F), \quad \text{and} \quad r^{\mathrm{avg}}(N) \leq d^{\mathrm{avg}}(N).$$

Indeed, regularity of W implies that for $g \in W(f_1,0)$ and any $f_2 \in F$ we have $\mathrm{dist}_G(f_2,g) \leq \mathrm{dist}_G(f_1,f_2)$. Integrating with respect to f_2 we get

$$r^{\mathrm{avg}}(N,y)^2 \leq \int_{N^{-1}(y)} \mathrm{dist}_G^2(f_1,f_2)\, \mu_2(df_2|y),$$

and integrating with respect to f_1, we conclude that $r^{\mathrm{avg}}(N,y) \leq d^{\mathrm{avg}}(N,y)$, as claimed.

For a nonregular generalized solution operator, it can happen that $r^{\mathrm{avg}}(N,y) = +\infty$ and $d^{\mathrm{avg}}(N,y) = 0$, $\forall\, y \in N(F)$, see **E 2:6**.

We now check if the definitions of average diameters coincide for $W(f,\varepsilon) = \{g \in G : \|S(f) - g\| \leq \varepsilon\}$. This is the case since $\mathrm{dist}(f_1,f_2) = \|S(f_1) - S(f_2)\|$ and

$$\int_{N^{-1}(y)} \int_{N^{-1}(y)} \|S(f_1) - S(f_2)\|^2\, \mu_2(df_1|y)\, \mu_2(df_2|y)$$

$$= \int_{SN^{-1}(y)} \int_{SN^{-1}(y)} \|a_1 - a_2\|^2\, \nu(da_1|y)\, \nu(da_2|y).$$

NR 2:5 We now indicate how the average case radius can be defined for a nonseparable space G. For such a space, we can set

$$r^{\mathrm{avg}}(N) = \inf \left\{ \left(\int_F z^2(y)\, \mu(dy) \right)^{1/2} : z(\cdot) \text{ is } \mu_1\text{-measurable}, \right.$$

$$\left. z(y) \geq r^{\mathrm{avg}}(N, y) \text{ for almost every } y \right\}.$$

Another way is to set

$$r^{\mathrm{avg}}(N) = \inf_\phi \left\{ \int_F \|S(f) - \phi(N(f))\|^2\, \mu(df) \right\}^{1/2},$$

with the infimum taken over all measurable algorithms ϕ. Both definitions are equivalent and coincide with the definition from Section 2 for a separable G. The same, of course, can be done for generalized solution operators.

Exercises

E 2:1 Consider the average case setting of continuous binary search from Chapter 2. Find the measures μ_1 and $\mu_2(\cdot|y)$ for information consisting of n bit questions. Then find the local average radius of that information.

E 2:2 Suppose that $F = \mathbf{R}^m$ and that μ is a weighted Lebesgue measure,

$$\mu(B) = \int_B \varsigma(f)\, d_m f$$

for some positive $\varsigma : \mathbf{R}^m \to \mathbf{R}_+$, $\int_{\mathbf{R}^m} \varsigma(f)\, d_m f = 1$. Here d_m stands for m dimensional Lebesgue measure. Let $N(f) = [f_1, f_2, \ldots, f_n]$, where $n < m$ and $f = [f_1, f_2, \ldots, f_m]$. Show that

$$\mu_1(A) = \int_A \varsigma_1(y)\, d_n y \quad \text{and} \quad \mu_2(B|y) = \int_{B_y} \frac{\varsigma([y|x])}{\varsigma_1(y)}\, d_{m-n} x,$$

where $[y|x] = [y_1, \ldots, y_n, x_1, \ldots, x_{m-n}]$ and $\varsigma_1(y) = \int_{\mathbf{R}^{m-n}} \varsigma([y|x]) d_{m-n} x$.

E 2:3 For a subset A of a normed space define the average radius and diameter in the $\mathcal{L}_p$ sense,

$$\mathrm{rad}^{\mathrm{avg}}(A) = \inf_{x \in G} \left\{ \int_A \|x - a\|^p\, \nu_A(da) \right\}^{1/p},$$

$$\mathrm{diam}^{\mathrm{avg}}(A) = \left\{ \int_A \int_A \|a_1 - a_2\|^p\, \nu_A(da_1)\, \nu_A(da_2) \right\}^{1/p},$$

where $p \in [1, +\infty)$ and ν_A is a probability measure on A. Show that

$$\mathrm{rad}^{\mathrm{avg}}(A) \leq \mathrm{diam}^{\mathrm{avg}}(A) \leq 2\, \mathrm{rad}^{\mathrm{avg}}(A).$$

From this conclude that in the $\mathcal{L}_p$ sense,

$$r^{\text{avg}}(N, y) \leq d^{\text{avg}}(N, y), \quad \forall y \in N(F).$$

E 2:4 Let $A = [a, b]$ and ν_A be a normalized Lebesgue measure. Show that in the $\mathcal{L}_p$ sense,

$$\text{rad}^{\text{avg}}(A) = \tfrac{1}{2} \, \text{diam}^{\text{avg}}(A) \left(\frac{p+2}{2} \right)^{1/p}$$

E 2:5 Let $\alpha \in [0.5, 1]$ be arbitrary. Find a set A and a probability measure ν_A such that in the $\mathcal{L}_p$ sense

$$0 < \text{rad}^{\text{avg}}(A) = \alpha \, \text{diam}^{\text{avg}}(A) < +\infty.$$

E 2:6 Consider **E 2:3** from Chapter 4. Let $\mu(\{i\}) = p_i$, $i = 1, 2, 3$ with $p_i > 0$ and $\sum_{i=1}^{3} p_i = 1$. Show that $r^{\text{avg}}(N) = r^{\text{avg}}(N, y) = +\infty$ and $d^{\text{avg}}(N) = 0$.

E 2:7 Let μ be a one dimensional Gaussian measure with mean m and variance $\sigma > 0$, $\mu(A) = (2\pi\sigma)^{-1/2} \int_A \exp\left(-(t - m)^2 / (2\sigma) \right) dt$ for any Borel set A of $\mathbb{R}$. Show that in the $\mathcal{L}_2$ sense

$$\text{rad}^{\text{avg}}(\mathbb{R}) = \frac{1}{\sqrt{2}} \, \text{diam}^{\text{avg}}(\mathbb{R}) = \sqrt{\sigma}.$$

E 2:8 As in **E 2:4** of Chapter 4, let N_1 be contained in N_2. Prove that $r^{\text{avg}}(N_1) \leq r^{\text{avg}}(N_2)$. Prove that $r^{\text{avg}}(N_1) = r^{\text{avg}}(N_2)$ if N_1 is equivalent to N_2.

3. Algorithms

In this section we discuss algorithms with minimal average error. As we shall see, this minimal error is equal to the average radius of information. We shall analyze central and optimal error algorithms. In the worst case setting, a central algorithm is an optimal error algorithm but an optimal error algorithm is not necessarily central. In the average case setting we show that the concepts of central and optimal error algorithms coincide unless the average radius is infinite. Thus, unlike in the worst case, an algorithm is central iff it is optimal error.

Notes and Remarks

NR 3:1 Section 3 is based on Wasilkowski [83c].

3.1. Local and Global Average Errors

For given information N, let $y = N(f)$ denote the computed information about f. Let $U(f) = \phi(y)$ be an approximation to $S(f)$, where ϕ, $\phi: N(F) \to G$, is an algorithm. As in the worst case, the element $\phi(y)$

is an approximation to all elements g from the set $SN^{-1}(y)$. The *local average error* of ϕ is defined by the average distance between $\phi(y)$ and elements g in the $\mathcal{L}_2$ sense,

$$e^{\mathrm{avg}}(\phi, N, y) = \left(\int_{SN^{-1}(y)} \|g - \phi(y)\|^2 \, \nu(dg|y) \right)^{1/2}.$$

Observe that the local average error is well defined for *every* algorithm (not necessarily measurable). Indeed, since $\phi(y)$ is a fixed element from G, the existence of the last integral follows from the measurability of the function $\| \cdot - \phi(y) \|$. However, $e^{\mathrm{avg}}(\phi, N, \cdot)$ need not be a μ_1-measurable function.

Clearly, no matter how $\phi(y)$ is selected, we have the following estimate,

$$e^{\mathrm{avg}}(\phi, N, y) \geq r^{\mathrm{avg}}(N, y), \quad \forall y \in N(F).$$

Thus, the local average radius of information is a lower bound on the local average error of algorithms.

The *global average error* of an algorithm ϕ is the average value of the local error $e^{\mathrm{avg}}(\phi, N, \cdot)$ in the $\mathcal{L}_2$ sense with respect to the measure μ_1. That is, if $e^{\mathrm{avg}}(\phi, N, \cdot)$ is μ_1-measurable then

$$e^{\mathrm{avg}}(\phi, N) = \left(\int_{N(F)} (e^{\mathrm{avg}}(\phi, N, y))^2 \, \mu_1(dy) \right)^{1/2}. \tag{1}$$

From the definition of the local error and from (1) of Section 2 we can rewrite this as

$$
\begin{aligned}
e^{\mathrm{avg}}(\phi, N) &= \left(\int_{N(F)} \int_{SN^{-1}(y)} \|x - \phi(y)\|^2 \, \nu(dx|y) \, \mu_1(dy) \right)^{1/2} \\
&= \left(\int_{N(F)} \int_{N^{-1}(y)} \|S(f) - \phi(y)\|^2 \, \mu_2(df|y) \, \mu_1(dy) \right)^{1/2} \\
&= \left(\int_F \|S(f) - \phi(N(f))\|^2 \, \mu(df) \right)^{1/2}.
\end{aligned}
$$

This agrees with the definition of the global average error from Chapter 3.

On the other hand, if $e^{\mathrm{avg}}(\phi, N, \cdot)$ is not μ_1-measurable, we proceed as follows. Let

$$Z(\phi) = \{ z : N(F) \to \mathbb{R}_+ : z(y) \geq e^{\mathrm{avg}}(\phi, N, y)^2, \forall y, \tag{2}$$
$$\text{and } z \text{ is } \mu_1\text{-measurable} \}.$$

Then by the global average error of ϕ we mean

$$e^{\text{avg}}(\phi, N) = \inf_{z \in Z(\phi)} \sqrt{\int_{N(F)} z(y)\, \mu_1(dy)} \qquad (3)$$

if $Z(\phi)$ is nonempty. Otherwise, $e^{\text{avg}}(\phi, N) = +\infty$. Thus, the global average error is well defined for every algorithm ϕ. Furthermore, if $e^{\text{avg}}(\phi, N, \cdot)$ is μ_1-measurable, then (1) and (3) coincide.

Local and global average errors for generalized solution operators are discussed in **NR 3.1:1**.

Notes and Remarks

NR 3.1:1 For a generalized solution operator W, the local and global average errors of an algorithm ϕ are defined as follows. As in **NR 2:3**, $\text{dist}_G(f, \phi(y)) = \inf\{\delta : \phi(y) \in W(f, \delta)\}$ denotes the distance between f and $\phi(y)$. Then

$$e^{\text{avg}}(\phi, N, y) = \left(\int_{SN^{-1}(y)} \big(\text{dist}_G(f, \phi(y)) \big)^2 \mu_2(df|y) \right)^{1/2}$$

is the local average error of ϕ. Clearly, we have

$$e^{\text{avg}}(\phi, N, y) \geq r^{\text{avg}}(N, y), \quad \forall\, y \in N(F).$$

The global average error is defined as in Section 3.1 by (2) and (3). For $W(f, \varepsilon) = \{g \in G : \|S(f) - g\| \leq \varepsilon\}$, we have $\text{dist}_G(f, \phi(y)) = \|S(f) - \phi(y)\|$, and the above definitions of local and global average radii coincide with those in Section 3.1.

NR 3.1:2 Novak [86b, 87a] studied the global error of an algorithm defined as follows. Let λ be a probability measure defined on the information values $N(F)$. Observe that such a measure might be known without assuming an *a priori* measure of problem elements. Then consider the worst case local error, $e^{\text{wor}}(\phi, y)$, of an algorithm ϕ that uses information N, where $y = N(f)$. The global error of ϕ is then defined as the expected value of the worst case local errors with respect to the measure λ,

$$e(\phi, N) = \int_{N(F)} e^{\text{wor}}(\phi, y)\, \lambda(dy).$$

Novak shows that for a number of problems such global error differs only by a constant factor from the worst case global error.

3.2. Central Algorithms

We want to find an algorithm ϕ such that its local average error is minimal. It is clear that we can define an algorithm ϕ whose local errors are arbitrarily close to local radii.

More precisely, consider an (*average*) *center* of a subset A of the separable normed space G, that is, an element m_A for which

$$\int_A \|m_A - a\|^2 \, \nu_A(da) = r^{\mathrm{avg}}(A)^2 = \inf_{x \in G} \int_A \|x - a\|^2 \, \nu_A(da).$$

Observe that the center need not exist, be unique, nor be an element of A. See **E 3.2:1** and **3.2:2**.

Assume for a moment that for all y from $N(F)$, the set $SN^{-1}(y)$ has a center $m = m(y)$. Then, similarly to the worst case setting, the algorithm ϕ^c defined by

$$\phi^c(y) = m(y)$$

is called *central*. Its local average error is

$$e^{\mathrm{avg}}(\phi^c, N, y) = r^{\mathrm{avg}}(N, y), \quad \forall y \in N(F).$$

Then $e^{\mathrm{avg}}(\phi^c, N, \cdot)$ is μ_1-measurable and its global average error is

$$e^{\mathrm{avg}}(\phi^c, N) = r^{\mathrm{avg}}(N, y).$$

Thus, the central algorithm minimizes the local and global average errors among all algorithms that use the information N.

If the set $SN^{-1}(y)$ has no center for some y, then the central algorithm does not exist. In this case, for an arbitrary positive δ, there exists an element $m = m(y, \delta)$ such that $\int_{SN^{-1}(y)} \|m - a\|^2 \nu(da|y) \le (r^{\mathrm{avg}}(N, y) + \delta)^2$. Then the algorithm $\phi_\delta(y) = m(y, \delta)$ has local average error not greater than $r^{\mathrm{avg}}(N, y) + \delta$. Its global average error, defined by (3), is at most $r^{\mathrm{avg}}(N) + \delta$, since the function $r^{\mathrm{avg}}(N, \cdot) + \delta$ is μ_1-measurable. Since δ is arbitrary, this shows that we can find algorithms whose local and global average errors are arbitrarily close to $r^{\mathrm{avg}}(N, y)$ and $r^{\mathrm{avg}}(N)$. We summarize this in

THEOREM 3.2.1. *The local and global average radii of information are sharp lower bounds on the local and global average errors of any algorithm using the information N,*

$$r^{\mathrm{avg}}(N, y) = \inf_\phi e^{\mathrm{avg}}(\phi, N, y), \; \forall y \in N(F), \; \text{and} \; r^{\mathrm{avg}}(N) = \inf_\phi e^{\mathrm{avg}}(\phi, N).$$

A central algorithm ϕ^c, if it exists, minimizes the local and global average errors.

In the worst case setting, an algorithm which minimizes the global error does not necessarily minimize the local errors for all data y. In the average case setting, this cannot happen unless $r^{\mathrm{avg}}(N) = +\infty$.

More precisely, we say that an algorithm ϕ is an *optimal error algorithm* if $e^{\mathrm{avg}}(\phi, N) = r^{\mathrm{avg}}(N)$. We say that two algorithms ϕ_1 and ϕ_2 are *equal* if the set of elements for which $\phi_1(y) \neq \phi_2(y)$ has μ_1-measure zero.

In what follows, we assume that the measure μ is *complete*. That is, every subset of a set of μ-measure zero is a Borel set, see also Section 2.2 of the appendix.

THEOREM 3.2.2. *Let μ be complete and let the average radius $r^{\mathrm{avg}}(N)$ of information be finite. Then an algorithm ϕ is an optimal error algorithm iff it is central.*

PROOF: We need only prove that an optimal error algorithm ϕ is central. Let

$$P = \{y \in N(F) : e^{\mathrm{avg}}(\phi, N, y) > r^{\mathrm{avg}}(N, y)\}.$$

We prove that the set P is μ_1-measurable and that its measure is zero. Indeed, let $Q_i = \{y \in N(F) : e^{\mathrm{avg}}(\phi, N, y)^2 \geq r^{\mathrm{avg}}(N, y)^2 + i^{-1}\}$ for $i = 1, 2, \ldots$. Then $Q_i \subset Q_{i+1}$ and $\bigcup_{i=1}^{\infty} Q_i = P$. From (2) of Section 3.1, there exists a sequence $\{z_k\}$ of μ_1-measurable functions such that $z_k(y) \geq e^{\mathrm{avg}}(\phi, N, y)^2$ and $\lim_k \int_{N(F)} z_k(y) \, \mu_1(dy) = e^{\mathrm{avg}}(\phi, N)^2$. Define

$$Q_{i,k} = \{y \in N(F) : z_k(y) \geq r^{\mathrm{avg}}(N, y)^2 + i^{-1}\} \quad \text{and} \quad P_i = \bigcap_{k=1}^{\infty} Q_{k,i}.$$

Since $Q_i \subset Q_{k,i}$, $Q_i \subset P_i$. Observe now that

$$r^{\mathrm{avg}}(N)^2 = e^{\mathrm{avg}}(\phi, N)^2 = \lim_k \int_{N(F)} z_k(y) \, \mu_1(dy)$$

$$= r^{\mathrm{avg}}(N)^2 + \lim_k \int_{N(F)} (z_k(y) - r^{\mathrm{avg}}(N, y)^2) \, \mu_1(dy)$$

$$\geq r^{\mathrm{avg}}(N)^2 + \lim_k \int_{P_i} i^{-1} \, \mu_1(dy)$$

$$= r^{\mathrm{avg}}(N)^2 + i^{-1} \, \mu_1(P_i).$$

This means that $\mu_1(P_i) = 0$. Since $Q_i \subset P_i$ and μ_1 is complete (the completeness of μ_1 follows from the completeness of μ), then Q_i is μ_1-measurable and $\mu_1(Q_i) = 0$. This implies that $P = \bigcup_{i=1}^{\infty} Q_i$ is measurable and $\mu_1(P) = 0$, as claimed. Thus, $e^{\mathrm{avg}}(\phi, N, y) = r^{\mathrm{avg}}(N, y)$ for almost all $y \in N(F)$. This means that ϕ is central. ∎

We now comment on the assumptions of Theorem 3.2.2. The completeness of a measure μ is not crucial. Indeed, for incomplete μ, any optimal error algorithm may differ from a central algorithm on a set P which is a subset of a set of measure zero. Although P need not now be measurable, the difference between these algorithms is insignificant.

The assumption that $r^{\text{avg}}(N) < +\infty$ is essential. In **NR 3.2:1** we present an example with $r^{\text{avg}}(N) = +\infty$ and an optimal error algorithm which is not central.

We now discuss relations between central algorithms and mean elements of conditional measures $\nu(\cdot|y)$. Recall that the *mean* $m = m(y)$ of the measure $\nu(\cdot|y)$ is defined as an element of G for which

$$L(m) = \int_G L(g)\, \nu(dg|y),$$

for every continuous linear functional L, $L \in G^*$. Such an element needs not exist in general, see **E 3.2:3**. In Section 2.5 of the appendix the reader may find conditions on the space G and the measure $\nu(\cdot|y)$ under which the mean element exists. In particular, the mean element exists if G is a separable Banach space and the first moment $\int_G \|g\|\, \nu(dg|y)$ of $\nu(\cdot|y)$ is finite.

We now show two cases for which central algorithms coincide with mean elements of the conditional measures. They are presented in Lemmas 3.2.1 and 3.2.2. In Lemma 3.2.1, we assume that the space G is a separable Hilbert space with an arbitrary measure $\nu(\cdot|y)$ for which the mean $m(y)$ exists. In Lemma 3.2.2, the space G is arbitrary but the set $SN^{-1}(y)$ and the measure $\nu(\cdot|y)$ satisfy certain "symmetry" conditions.

LEMMA 3.2.1. *Let G be a separable Hilbert space and let $m(y)$ be the mean of the conditional measure $\nu(\cdot|y)$. Then the algorithm $\phi^c(y) = m(y)$ is central and*

$$r^{\text{avg}}(N, y)^2 = \int_G \|g\|^2\, \nu(dg|y) - \|m(y)\|^2, \quad \forall\, y \in N(F),$$

$$r^{\text{avg}}(N)^2 = \int_G \|g\|^2\, \nu(dg) - \int_{N(F)} \|m(y)\|^2\, \mu_1(dy).$$

As always, $\nu = \mu S^{-1}$ and $\nu(\cdot|y) = \mu_2(S^{-1}\cdot|y)$ are the a priori and conditional measures of solution elements, respectively.

PROOF: Without loss of generality assume that $\int_G \|g\|^2\, \nu(dg|y)$ is finite, since otherwise every element of G is a center of $SN^{-1}(y)$. For $m = m(y)$, $A = SN^{-1}(y)$, and $\langle \cdot, \cdot \rangle$ being the inner product of G, we have

$$\int_A \|x - g\|^2\, \nu(dg|y) = \|x\|^2 - 2\, \langle m, x \rangle - \int_A \|g\|^2\, \nu(dg|y)$$

$$= \|x - m\|^2 + \int_G \|g\|^2\, \nu(dg|y) - \|m\|^2.$$

This is minimized if $x = m$, and therefore $\phi^c(y) = m(y)$ is central. From this, the formulas for the radii easily follow. ∎

We now present the second case in which we assume that the set $A = SN^{-1}(y)$ is symmetric with respect to some element $p(y)$, i.e., $g + p(y) \in A$ implies $-g + p(y) \in A$. Define the mapping $D_y: G \to G$ by

$$D_y g = 2p(y) - g.$$

Then $D_y^2 g = g$ and $D_y A = A$.

LEMMA 3.2.2. *Let $SN^{-1}(y)$ be symmetric with respect to $p(y)$ and let*

$$\nu(D_y B | y) = \nu(B|y), \; \forall \; \text{Borel sets } B, \; \text{for almost all } y \in N(F).$$

Then $p(y)$ is the mean of $\nu(\cdot|y)$ for almost all $y \in N(F)$, the algorithm $\phi^c(y) = p(y)$ is central, and the average case radii are given as in Lemma 3.2.1.

PROOF: For an arbitrary continuous linear functional L, the invariance of the measure $\nu(\cdot|y)$ yields

$$\int_G L(g) \, \nu(dg|y) = \int_G L\big(2p(y) - g\big) \, \nu(dg|y).$$

Thus, $\int_G L(g) \, \nu(dg|y) = L(p(y))$ proving that $p(y)$ is the mean of $\nu(\cdot|y)$. Furthermore, we have

$$\int_A \|x - g\|^2 \, \nu(dg|y) = \tfrac{1}{2} \int_A \big(\|x - g\|^2 + \|2p(y) - x - g\|^2 \big) \, \nu(dg|y).$$

Since $p(y) - g = (x - g)/2 + \big(2p(y) - g - x\big)/2$, we get $\|p(y) - g\|^2 \le \big(\|x - g\|^2 + \|2p(y) - g - x\|^2 \big)/2$. Thus,

$$\int_A \|x - g\|^2 \, \nu(dg|y) \ge \int_A \|p(y) - g\|^2 \, \nu(dg|y).$$

This means that $p(y)$ is a center of $A = SN^{-1}(y)$. ∎

Lemmas 3.2.1 and 3.2.2 state conditions under which a central algorithm becomes the mean of the conditional measure $\nu(\cdot|y)$. If these conditions are violated then the central algorithm may be different than the mean. This is because the central algorithm depends also on the error criterion, whereas the mean does not. In **NR 3.2:3** we present such an example. See also Remark 6.1.3 in Section 6, where we present an error criterion for which the algorithm based on the mean of the conditional measure has infinite error, whereas the error of the central algorithm may be arbitrarily small.

Central algorithms for generalized solution operators as well as interpolatory algorithms are discussed in **NR 3.2:4** and **3.2:5**.

Notes and Remarks

NR 3.2:1 (Wasilkowski [83c]) Let $F = G$ be a separable Hilbert space with an orthonormal system $\eta_1, \eta_2, \ldots$. Let μ be defined by $\mu(\{2^{2k}\eta_k\}) = 2^{-k}$ for $k = 1, 2, \ldots$. Then μ is concentrated on the set $\{2^2\eta_1, 2^4\eta_2, \ldots\}$. Let $S(f) = f$ and $N(f) = \langle f, \eta_1 \rangle$. For every algorithm ϕ we have

$$e^{\mathrm{avg}}(\phi, N)^2 = 2^{-1}\|2^2\eta_1 - \phi(1)\|^2 + \sum_{k=2}^{\infty} 2^{-k}\|2^{2k}\eta_k - \phi(0)\|^2 = +\infty.$$

This means that $r^{\mathrm{avg}}(N) = +\infty$, and every algorithm is optimal.

Consider now the zero algorithm $\phi^*(y) = 0$, $\forall y \in \mathbb{R}$. Then its local average error is

$$e^{\mathrm{avg}}(\phi^*, N, 1)^2 = \|2^2\eta_1\|^2 = 16 > 0 = r^{\mathrm{avg}}(N, 1)^2.$$

Since $\mu_1(\{1\}) = 1/2 > 0$, then the algorithm ϕ^* is not central, although it is an optimal error algorithm.

NR 3.2:2 The use of the mean of the conditional measure (=the mean of the *a posteriori* measure) is also advocated in Bayesian statistics.

NR 3.2:3 Consider $F = G = \mathbb{R}$ and $S(f) = f$, $N(f) = 0$. Let

$$\mu(A) = (k+1)\int_{A \cap [0,1]} t^k\, dt, \quad k > -1,$$

be the probability measure on F. Then μ_1 is the atomic measure, $\mu_1(\{0\}) = 1$, and $\nu(\cdot|0) = \mu$ with the mean element

$$m(0) = \frac{k+1}{k+2}.$$

Suppose the average error is defined in the $\mathcal{L}_1$ sense. Then the assumptions of Lemma 3.2.1 do not hold. The assumptions of Lemma 3.2.2 do not hold either, unless $k = 0$. The central algorithm $\phi^c(y) \equiv a^*$, where a^* minimizes the function

$$(k+1)\int_0^1 t^k|t-a|\, dt = \frac{2\,a^{k+2}}{k+2} + \frac{k+1}{k+2} - a, \quad 0 \le a \le 1.$$

Thus, $\phi^c(y) = 2^{-1/(k+1)}$ and $\phi^c(y) \ne m(y)$ for $k \ne 0$.

NR 3.2:4 For a generalized solution operator W, a central algorithm $\phi^c(y)$ is given as an element $m = m(y)$, if it exists, for which, see **NR 2:3**,

$$r^{\mathrm{avg}}(N, y)^2 = \int_{N^{-1}(y)} \mathrm{dist}_G(f, m)^2\, \mu_2(df|g).$$

NR 3.2:5 An interpolatory algorithm ϕ^I is defined in Section 3.3 of Chapter 4 by $\phi^I(y) = S(\tilde{f})$, where $\tilde{f} \in N^{-1}(y)$. In the worst case setting, the interpolatory algorithms enjoy strong optimal error properties since their local errors do not exceed the local diameter of information.

In the average case setting, the local average error of an interpolatory algorithm can be arbitrarily larger than the local average diameter. Indeed, its local average error is given by

$$e^{\text{avg}}(\phi^I, N, y)^2 = \int_{SN^{-1}(y)} \|g - \phi^I(y)\|^2 \, \nu(dg|y)$$

and, in general, is not related to the local average diameter

$$d^{\text{avg}}(N, y)^2 = \int_{SN^{-1}(y)} \int_{SN^{-1}(y)} \|g_1 - g_2\|^2 \, \nu(dg_1|y) \, \nu(dg_2|y).$$

As we shall see in Section 5, for some problems $SN^{-1}(y) = \mathbb{R}$ and $\nu(\cdot|y)$ is a one dimensional Gaussian measure with mean $m = m(y)$ and variance $\sigma = \sigma(y) > 0$,

$$\nu(A|y) = \frac{1}{\sqrt{2\pi\sigma}} \int_A \exp\left(-(t-m)^2/(2\sigma)\right) dt.$$

Then

$$e^{\text{avg}}(\phi^I, N, y)^2 = \sigma + (m - \phi^I(y))^2 \quad \text{and} \quad d^{\text{avg}}(N, y)^2 = 2\sigma.$$

Observe that $\phi^I(y)$ can be any real number. Hence, $e^{\text{avg}}(\phi^I, N, y)$ may be arbitrarily larger than $d^{\text{avg}}(N, y)$, see also **E 3.2:5**.

Exercises

E 3.2:1 Let G be a linear space of sequences $g = (g_1, g_2, \dots)$ with only finitely many nonzero elements, i.e., for each g there exists $n = n(g)$ such that $g_i = 0$ for $i \geq n$. The space G is equipped with the norm $\|g\| = \left(\sum_{i=1}^{\infty} g_i^2\right)^{1/2}$. Let $e_i = (0, \dots, \underset{i}{1}, 0 \dots)$ be the ith unit vector. Define the measure ν by $\nu(\{e_i\}) = p_i \geq 0$, where $\sum_{i=1}^{\infty} p_i = 1$.

(i) Let $A = G$ and $\nu_A = \nu$. Show that $\text{rad}^{\text{avg}}(A) = \left(1 - \sum_{i=1}^{\infty} p_i^2\right)^{1/2}$ and that there exists no center of A if $p_i > 0$ for infinitely many i's.

(ii) Let $A = \{e_1, \dots, e_n\}$ and $\nu_A = \nu$ with $p_i > 0$ for $i = 1, 2, \dots, n$, and $p_i = 0$ for $i \geq n + 1$. Find a unique center of A and show that it is not an element of A.

E 3.2:2 Let $G = \mathbb{R}^2$ with the sup norm and let the average error be defined in the $\mathcal{L}_1$ sense. Define the set $A = [0, 1] \times \{-1, +1\}$. For $B \subset A$, we have $B = (B_1 \times \{-1\}) \cup (B_2 \times \{+1\})$, where $B_i \subset [0, 1]$. Define the measure ν_A by $\nu_A(B) = 1/2 \int_{B_1} dx_1 + 1/2 \int_{B_2} dx_2$. Show that the set A has infinitely many centers.

E 3.2:3 Consider the space G and the measure $\nu(\cdot|y) = \nu$ as in **E 3.2:1** with infinitely many positive p_i. Show that the mean element of ν does not exist.

E 3.2:4 Let $F = G = \mathbb{R}$ and let μ be the Cauchy measure, $\mu(A) = 2\pi^{-1} \int_A (1+t^2)^{-1} dt$. Let $S(f) = f$, $N(f) = 0$ and let the error be defined in the $\mathcal{L}_2$ sense. Show that $r^{\text{avg}}(N) = r^{\text{avg}}(N, y) = +\infty$ and therefore every algorithm is central.

E 3.2:5 Let $F_1 = G = \mathbb{R}^2$ with the Euclidean norm.

Consider $S(f) = f$, $N(f) = f_1$, and the error in the $\mathcal{L}_2$ sense. For $p \in (0,1)$, let $\mu([0,1] \times \{0\}) = p$ and $\mu([0,1] \times \{1\}) = 1 - p$. Show that

(i) a central algorithm is given by $[y, 1-p]$ and $d^{\mathrm{avg}}(N) = \sqrt{2}\, r^{\mathrm{avg}}(N) = \sqrt{2p(1-p)}$.

(ii) there exist two interpolatory ϕ_i^I algorithms with the average error $\sqrt{1-p}$ and $\sqrt{p}$.

Thus,

$$\frac{e^{\mathrm{avg}}(\phi_1^I, N)}{d^{\mathrm{avg}}(N)} = \frac{1}{\sqrt{2p}} \to +\infty \quad \text{as} \quad p \to 0$$

and

$$\frac{e^{\mathrm{avg}}(\phi_2^I, N)}{d^{\mathrm{avg}}(N)} = \frac{1}{\sqrt{2(1-p)}} \to +\infty \quad \text{as} \quad p \to 1.$$

E 3.2:6 Assume that G is a prehilbert space, i.e., G is equipped with an inner product but need not be complete. Prove that a measurable algorithm ϕ^* is central iff

$$\int_F \langle S(f) - \phi^*(N(f)), \phi(N(f)) \rangle\, \mu(df) = 0$$

for any measurable mapping ϕ. Here $\langle \cdot, \cdot \rangle$ stands for the inner product of G. Hint: Consider $\phi_1(N(f)) = \phi^*(N(f)) + \alpha\, \phi(N(f))$ for small α, and show that

$$e^{\mathrm{avg}}(\phi_1, N)^2 = e^{\mathrm{avg}}(\phi^*, N)^2$$
$$- 2\alpha \int_F \langle S(f) - \phi^*(N(f)), \phi(N(f)) \rangle\, \mu(df) + \alpha^2 \int_F \|\phi(N(f))\|^2\, \mu(df).$$

E 3.2:7 As in **E 3.2:6** let G be a prehilbert space. Consider the class $\Phi(N)$ of algorithms that use the information N such that $\phi_1, \phi_2 \in \Phi(N)$ implies that $\alpha_1 \phi_1 + \alpha_2 \phi_2 \in \Phi(N)$ for any real α_1 and α_2. Prove that an algorithm ϕ^* has minimal average error among the algorithms from $\Phi(N)$ iff

$$\int_F \langle S(f) - \phi^*(N(f)), \phi(N(f)) \rangle\, \mu(df) = 0, \quad \forall \phi \in \Phi(N).$$

4. Average Cardinality Number and Complexity

In this section we present bounds on the average complexity in terms of the average radius of information. The average radius $r^{\mathrm{avg}}(N)$ measures the intrinsic uncertainty caused by the information N as explained in Theorem 3.2.1. Thus, to compute ε-approximations on the average we must use information N such that $r^{\mathrm{avg}}(N) \leq \varepsilon$.

Information N is of the form presented in Section 2.2 of Chapter 3,

$$N(f) = [L_1(f), L_2(f; y_1), \ldots, L_{n(f)}(f; y_1, \ldots, y_{n(f)-1})],$$

where $y_1 = L_1(f)$ and $y_i = L_i(f; y_1, \ldots, y_{i-1})$, $L_i(\cdot; y_1, \ldots, y_{i-1}) \in \Lambda$, with $n(f) = \min\{i : \mathrm{ter}_i(y_1, y_2, \ldots, y_i) = 1\}$. The computation of $N(f)$ costs at least $c\,n(f)$, where c is the cost of one information operation. Therefore, the average cost of computing $N(f)$ is bounded from below by c times the average value of $n(f)$. The latter is called the *average cardinality of information N*,

$$\mathrm{card}^{\mathrm{avg}}(N) = \int_F n(f)\,\mu(df).$$

Obviously, $\mathrm{card}^{\mathrm{avg}}(N) \leq \mathrm{card}^{\mathrm{wor}}(N) = \sup_{f \in F} n(f)$. Note that for non-adaptive information, $n(f) \equiv n$ and $\mathrm{card}^{\mathrm{avg}}(N) = \mathrm{card}^{\mathrm{wor}}(N) = n$.

By the *average ε-cardinality number $m^{\mathrm{avg}}(\varepsilon)$* we mean the minimal average cardinality of information whose average radius does not exceed ε,

$$m^{\mathrm{avg}}(\varepsilon) = \inf\{\mathrm{card}^{\mathrm{avg}}(N) : N \text{ such that } r^{\mathrm{avg}}(N) \leq \varepsilon\}.$$

Obviously, $m^{\mathrm{avg}}(\varepsilon) \leq m^{\mathrm{wor}}(\varepsilon)$, where the (worst case) ε-cardinality number $m^{\mathrm{wor}}(\varepsilon)$ is defined in Section 4 of Chapter 4. Observe that $m^{\mathrm{avg}}(\varepsilon)$ can be a real number whereas $m^{\mathrm{wor}}(\varepsilon)$ is always an integer.

To compute ε-approximations on the average we have to use information N whose average cardinality is at least $m^{\mathrm{avg}}(\varepsilon)$, and its average cost is at least $c\,m^{\mathrm{avg}}(\varepsilon)$. Thus, similarly to the worst case setting, we found a lower bound on the average ε-complexity.

THEOREM 4.1.
$$\mathrm{comp}^{\mathrm{avg}}(\varepsilon) \geq c\,m^{\mathrm{avg}}(\varepsilon).$$

As in Section 4 of Chapter 4, the bound in Theorem 4.1 is tight if the following assumptions hold. Suppose that there exists information N of average cardinality $m^{\mathrm{avg}}(\varepsilon)$ such that

  (i) its average radius is at most ε, and
  (ii) its average information cost is $c\,m^{\mathrm{avg}}(\varepsilon)$.

Let ϕ be an algorithm that uses N and whose average error is equal to $r^{\mathrm{avg}}(N)$. Then $U(f) = \phi(N(f))$ provides ε-approximations on the average. Assume that the average combinatory cost of ϕ is dominated by the average information cost,

$$\int_F \mathrm{cost}(\phi, N(f))\,\mu(df) << c\,m^{\mathrm{avg}}(\varepsilon).$$

Then we have

$$\mathrm{cost}^{\mathrm{avg}}(U) = \mathrm{cost}^{\mathrm{avg}}(\phi, N) \simeq c\,m^{\mathrm{avg}}(\varepsilon).$$

From Theorem 4.1 we conclude that N and ϕ are almost *optimal informa-tion* and *optimal algorithm* in the average case setting, and $\text{comp}^{\text{avg}}(\varepsilon) \simeq c\, m^{\text{avg}}(\varepsilon)$. Thus, we have found the average ε-complexity almost exactly, and it is exhibited in terms of the average ε-cardinality number. We sum-marize this in

THEOREM 4.2. *If there exists information N of average cardinality $m^{\text{avg}}(\varepsilon)$ which satisfies assumptions (i) and (ii), and if there exists a central algo-rithm that uses N such that its average combinatory cost is dominated by the average information cost, then*

$$\text{comp}^{\text{avg}}(\varepsilon) \simeq c\, m^{\text{avg}}(\varepsilon)$$

and (ϕ, N) are almost optimal.

In Section 5, we show that the assumptions of Theorem 4.2 hold for linear problems whose spaces are equipped with Gaussian measures.

From this and Chapter 4 we thus conclude that the ε-complexities of linear problems are strongly related to the ε-cardinality numbers in both the worst case and average case settings.

5. Linear Problems

In this section we study linear problems in the average case setting. The definition of a linear problem is presented in Section 5.1 of Chapter 4. We specialize this definition by assuming that the set F is the ball of center zero and radius q in a separable Banach space F_1. We assume that F is equipped with a truncated Gaussian measure. We shall show that the average complexity depends only mildly on q and, for all q satisfying a weak assumption, the dependence is essentially the same as for $q = +\infty$. Therefore, in the first seven subsections we consider $F = F_1$ and then, in Section 5.8, we extend the analysis to finite q.

The analysis of this section heavily relies on properties of Gaussian mea-sures. For the reader's convenience, we list major properties of Gaussian measures in Section 5.2. More detailed discussion may be found in Section 2.9 of the appendix.

From Section 4 we know that under appropriate assumptions the central algorithm coincides with the mean of the conditional measure. This is the case for linear problems. Furthermore, for nonadaptive information the central algorithm is *linear* and therefore its combinatory cost is dominated by the information cost. This is studied in Section 5.3.

In the worst case setting, Chapter 4, we study spline algorithms which interpolate the data and have the minimal T-norm, where T is a linear operator which describes the set F. In Section 5.4, we show that the central algorithm is also a spline algorithm for an appropriately chosen operator T depending on the *a priori* measure μ. To stress the dependence on the measure μ, we call the central algorithm as the μ-*spline algorithm*. Properties of μ-spline algorithms for arbitrary measures are presented in **NR 5.4:1** and **5.4:2**.

Then, in Section 5.5, we turn our attention to *optimal nonadaptive* information. This is equivalent to selecting permissible functionals from a given class Λ so that the radius of information is minimal. In the class $\Lambda = F_1^*$ consisting of all continuous linear functionals, optimal nonadaptive information is given by the inner products of solution elements with eigenelements of the correlation operator C_ν of the *a priori* measure $\nu = \mu S^{-1}$. We take eigenelements which correspond to the largest eigenvalues of C_ν. In this case, the central algorithm (which is the μ-spline algorithm) that uses this optimal information is just the truncated Fourier series of the solution element in the orthonormal basis of eigenelements of C_ν. The average error is then the square root of the truncated trace of the correlation operator C_ν.

Section 5.6 deals with adaptive information. We ask how much can be gained by using adaptive information as compared to nonadaptive information. In general, adaptive information could be more powerful than nonadaptive information in either of two ways:

  (i) by adaptive selection of linear functionals, or
  (ii) by varying cardinality $n(f)$.

For linear problems (with Gaussian measures) we prove that adaptive selection of linear functionals does *not* help. That is, for adaptive information N^{a} with fixed cardinality $n(f) \equiv n$, one can find nonadaptive information N^{non} of cardinality n whose average radius $r^{\mathrm{avg}}(N^{\mathrm{non}})$ is no greater than $r^{\mathrm{avg}}(N^{\mathrm{a}})$. Furthermore, N^{non} consists of linear functionals which are used by N^{a}.

Then we analyze the effect of varying cardinality. In general, varying cardinality helps. On the other hand, we show that it is enough to restrict information operators to those whose cardinalities $n(\cdot)$ attain at most two values, $n(f) \in \{n_1, n_2\}, \forall f \in F$. More precisely, for adaptive information N^{a} we exhibit information N^* such that the average cardinality of N^* is the same as N^{a}, the average radius of N^* does not exceed the average radius of N^{a}, and N^* consists of *two* nonadaptive information operators. Information N^* has structure almost as simple as nonadaptive information. In particular, the μ-spline algorithm that uses N^* can be implemented with combinatory cost at most $(c + 2)\,\mathrm{card}^{\mathrm{avg}}(N^*)$.

How much can be lost by using nonadaptive information? We show that arbitrary adaptive information N^a is no more powerful than correspond-ingly chosen nonadaptive information N^{non} if either the average cardinality or the average radius of the latter does not exceed $x = (1 + \sqrt{5})/2 \simeq 1.618$ times the average cardinality or average radius of N^a, i.e., either

$$\text{card}^{avg}(N^{non}) \leq \text{card}^{avg}(N^a) \quad \text{and} \quad r^{avg}(N^{non}) \leq x\, r^{avg}(N^a)$$

or

$$\text{card}^{avg}(N^{non}) \leq x\, \text{card}^{avg}(N^a) \quad \text{and} \quad r^{avg}(N^{non}) \leq r^{avg}(N^a).$$

We do not know if $x = 1.618\ldots$ in the above inequalities is sharp. We do exhibit, however, an example for which $x = (1 + \sqrt{3})/2 \simeq 1.366$.

For some linear problems adaptive information is *no* more powerful than nonadaptive information. This holds if the sequence of the squares of nth minimal average radii is *convex*, see Section 5.6.2. This is the case for the class $\Lambda = F_1^*$.

The analysis of Sections 5.2–5.6 enables us to estimate the average ε-complexity of a linear problem. This is done in Section 5.7 by applying Theorem 4.2.

We then analyze which functions can be the average ε-complexity for a linear problem. Unlike the worst case setting, where an arbitrary increasing function is the ε-worst case complexity for some linear problem, we show that an increasing function g is the average ε-complexity of a linear problem if $(1/g^{-1}(\cdot))^2$ is convex. Although the average ε-complexity cannot be an arbitrary increasing function, it may go to infinity arbitrarily fast. Thus, there exist linear problems with arbitrary high average complexity.

In Section 5.8, we extend the analysis of the average case setting for linear problems to the case when the set $F = B_q$ is the ball with a finite radius q. The results of Section 5.8 state that, even for a modest q, the average ε-complexity is roughly the same as for $q = +\infty$. This enables us to compare the worst case and average case complexity of linear problems, which is the content of Chapter 9.

Finally, in Section 6 we study the average case setting with error criteria already analyzed in Chapter 4 for the worst case setting.

5.1. Linear Problems in the Average Case Setting

The definition of a linear problem is given in Section 5.1 of Chapter 4. Here we specialize this definition by assuming that:

(i) The space F_1 is a separable Banach space over the real field and the domain F is either the whole space F_1 or a ball of radius q, i.e., $F = \{f \in F_1 : \|f\| \leq q\}, \ q \in (0, +\infty]$.

(ii) The solution operator S, $S : F \to G$, is continuous and linear, and its range G is a separable Hilbert space over the real field.

(iii) The class Λ of permissible information operations is a subset of F_1^*, the class of all continuous linear functionals.

(iv) The ball F is equipped with a truncated Gaussian measure μ_q. That is, for any Borel set A of F_1 we have

$$\mu_q(A) = \frac{\mu(A \cap F)}{\mu(F)},$$

where μ is a Gaussian measure with mean zero and a correlation operator C_μ, $C_\mu : F_1^* \to F_1$.

We now comment on the assumptions (i)–(iv). Continuity of S as well as of functionals forming the information is needed to preserve some essential properties of the Gaussian measure. For technical reasons, we assume that F_1 and G are separable Banach and Hilbert spaces, respectively. Some of the results of this section hold for more general spaces as will be indicated in Notes and Remarks.

In the average case setting, we choose a special form of F as a ball of radius q, although in the worst case setting we analyze general balanced and convex sets F. The assumption that F is a ball is not so restrictive, since by the proper choice of a norm we can model sets of the form $\{f \in F_1 : \|Tf\| \leq 1\}$ with a one-to-one linear T. That is, the norm in F_1 can be given as $\|f\|_{F_1} = \|Tf\|$. Of course, depending on T, the space F_1 with such a norm may or may not be complete.

In the worst case setting, it is essential to restrict the domain F to a proper subset of F_1. Indeed, if $F = F_1$ then the (worst case) complexity is infinite, unless S is of a special form. For F being a ball of radius q, the complexity is a nondecreasing function of q and for nontrivial problems, it is infinite for $q = +\infty$.

In the average case setting, as we shall see, the (average) complexity depends very mildly on q. Since the tail of a Gaussian measure goes to zero exponentially fast, the complexity even for moderate q is roughly the same as the complexity for $q = +\infty$. The case $q = +\infty$ corresponds to $F = F_1$ and $\mu_q = \mu$, and is technically much simpler than the case with finite q. Therefore, in the first seven subsections of this chapter we deal with $q = +\infty$. In Section 5.8, we show how to translate the results for $q = +\infty$ to the case with finite q.

5.2. Gaussian Measures

In this section we list major properties of Gaussian measures which will be needed later. The detailed study of Gaussian measures can be found, for instance, in Kuo [75], Skorohod [74], and Vakhania [81]. A substantial portion of the appendix is also devoted to Gaussian measures.

Let us first assume that $F_1 = \mathbb{R}^k$ is the k dimensional Euclidean space. Then μ is Gaussian if

$$\mu(A) = \frac{1}{(2\pi \det(M))^{k/2}} \int_A \exp\left(-\tfrac{1}{2}\langle M^{-1}(x-m), x-m\rangle\right) dx,$$

for any Borel set A of $\mathbb{R}^k$. Here $m \in \mathbb{R}^k$ and M is a $k \times k$ symmetric and positive definite matrix. The vector m is called the *mean element* of μ and is uniquely characterized by the condition

$$\langle m, x\rangle = \int_{\mathbb{R}^k} \langle f, x\rangle \, \mu(df), \quad \forall\, x \in \mathbb{R}^k.$$

Here $\langle m, x\rangle = \sum_{i=1}^{k} m_i x_i$, where m_i and x_i are components of m and x, respectively. The matrix M is called the *correlation operator (matrix)* of μ and is uniquely characterized by the condition

$$\langle Mx, y\rangle = \int_{\mathbb{R}^k} \langle f-m, x\rangle \langle f-m, y\rangle \, \mu(df), \quad \forall\, x, y \in \mathbb{R}^k.$$

Assume now that F_1 is a separable Banach space and μ is a σ-additive probability measure defined on Borel sets of F_1. Then μ is *Gaussian* iff μL^{-1} is a one dimensional Gaussian measure for any continuous linear functional L, $L \in F_1^*$.

Gaussian measures, as well as arbitrary probability measures, can be uniquely defined through their characteristic functionals. The *characteristic functional* ψ_μ of a probability measure μ defined on Borel sets of F_1 is given by

$$\psi_\mu(L) = \int_{F_1} \exp\left(i\, L(f)\right) \mu(df), \quad \forall\, L \in F_1^*, \quad i = \sqrt{-1}.$$

The σ-additive measure μ is Gaussian iff its characteristic functional is of the form

$$\psi_\mu(L) = \exp\left(i\, L(m_\mu) - \tfrac{1}{2}\, L(C_\mu L)\right), \quad \forall\, L \in F_1^*,$$

for some element m_μ from F_1 and some linear operator $C_\mu : F_1^* \to F_1$. The element m_μ is called the *mean element* of μ and is uniquely defined by the condition

$$L(m_\mu) = \int_{F_1} L(f)\, \mu(df), \quad \forall\, L \in F_1^*.$$

The linear operator C_μ is called the *correlation operator* of μ and is uniquely defined by the condition

$$L_1(C_\mu L_2) = \int_{F_1} L_1(f - m_\mu) L_2(f - m_\mu) \, \mu(df), \quad \forall L_1, L_2 \in F_1^*.$$

The correlation operator is symmetric, $L_1(C_\mu L_2) = L_2(C_\mu L_1)$, and non-negative definite, $L(C_\mu L) \geq 0$, $\forall L_1, L_2, L \in F_1^*$. It generates a semi-inner product $\langle \cdot, \cdot \rangle_\mu$ on F_1^*,

$$\langle L_1, L_2 \rangle_\mu = L_1(C_\mu L_2), \quad \forall L_1, L_2 \in F_1^*,$$

and the corresponding semi-norm $\|\cdot\|_\mu$ on F_1^*,

$$\|L\|_\mu = \sqrt{\langle L, L \rangle_\mu}, \quad \forall L \in F_1^*.$$

If C_μ is positive definite, i.e., $L(C_\mu L) > 0$ (or equivalently $C_\mu L \neq 0$) for all $L \neq 0$ from F_1^*, then $\langle \cdot, \cdot \rangle_\mu$ and $\|\cdot\|_\mu$ become an inner product and a norm, respectively.

For separable Banach spaces, the complete characterization of the correlation operators of Gaussian measures is not known. If F_1 is a separable Hilbert space then they are fully characterized by being symmetric, non-negative definite, and having a finite trace. That is, C_μ is a correlation operator of a Gaussian measure μ on F_1 iff $C_\mu = C_\mu^* \geq 0$ and

$$\text{trace}(C_\mu) = \int_{F_1} \|f\|^2 \, \mu(df) = \sum_{i=1}^{\infty} \langle C_\mu \eta_i, \eta_i \rangle < +\infty,$$

where $\{\eta_i\}$ is an orthonormal system. In particular, one can choose $\{\eta_i\}$ as eigenelements of C_μ. Thus, the trace of C_μ is the sum of eigenvalues of C_μ.

For a Gaussian measure μ with mean zero and correlation operator C_μ, consider the continuous linear solution operator S, $S : F_1 \to G$, where F_1 and G are separable Banach and Hilbert spaces, respectively. Then the *a priori* measure of solution elements

$$\nu = \mu S^{-1}$$

is also Gaussian. Its mean is zero and its correlation operator $C_\nu \colon G^* = G \to G$, is given by

$$C_\nu g = S\big(C_\mu(L_g S)\big), \quad \forall g \in G,$$

where $L_g(h) = \langle g, h \rangle$ and $\langle \cdot, \cdot \rangle$ stands for the inner product of G. Note that $L_g S \in F_1^*$ and $(L_g S)(f) = \langle g, S(f) \rangle$. We have

$$\text{trace}(C_\nu) = \int_{F_1} \|S(f)\|^2 \mu(df).$$

Consider now the nonadaptive information $N(f) = [L_1(f), L_2(f), \ldots, L_n(f)]$, where $L_j \in F_1^*$. Without loss of generality we can assume that L_j are μ-orthonormal, i.e., $\langle L_i, L_j \rangle_\mu = L_i(C_\mu L_j) = \delta_{i,j}$. Indeed, take $K_i = \sum_{j=1}^{i} a_{i,j} L_j$ with numbers $a_{i,j}$ chosen in such a way that $K_i(C_\mu K_j) = \delta_{i,j}$, $i, j = 1, \ldots, p$. This can be done by, for instance, the Gram-Schmidt orthogonalization process with p denoting the maximal number of linearly independent linear functionals among $L_1, L_2, \ldots, L_n$. Then $K_1, K_2, \ldots, K_p$ play the role of $L_1, L_2, \ldots, L_n$.

As in Section 2, let $\mu_1 = \mu N^{-1}$ be a probability measure on $N(F_1) = \mathbb{R}^n$. Then μ_1 is Gaussian with mean zero. The correlation operator (matrix) of μ_1 is the identity due to μ-orthonormality of L_i, see Section 2.9.2 of the appendix. That is,

$$\mu_1(A) = \frac{1}{(2\pi)^{n/2}} \int_A \exp \left(\sum_{j=1}^{n} \frac{-t_j^2}{2} \right) dt_1 \ldots dt_n.$$

Let $y = N(f) = [y_1, y_2, \ldots, y_n]$. As shown in Section 2.9.2 of the Appendix, the conditional measure $\mu_2(\cdot | y)$ defined on Borel sets of F_1 and concentrated on $N^{-1}(y)$ is also Gaussian. Its mean is

$$m_{\mu,y} = \sum_{j=1}^{n} y_j\, C_\mu L_j.$$

Its correlation operator is given by $C_{\mu,N} : F_1^* \to F_1$,

$$C_{\mu,N}(L) = C_\mu L - \sum_{j=1}^{n} \langle L, L_j \rangle_\mu C_\mu L_j, \quad \forall L \in F_1^*.$$

Observe that $C_{\mu,N}$ does not depend on y. Furthermore, $C_{\mu,N}(L_i) = 0$, $i = 1, 2, \ldots, n$, and $C_{\mu,N}(L) = C_\mu L$ for all functionals L from F_1^* which are μ-orthogonal to L_i's, i.e., $\langle L, L_i \rangle_\mu = L(C_\mu L_i) = 0$, $i = 1, 2, \ldots, n$.

The information $y = N(f)$ changes the *a priori* measure μ by shifting the mean element from zero to $m_{\mu,y}$ and by annihilating the correlation operator C_μ in the linear subspace $\text{span}(L_1, L_2, \ldots, L_n)$.

The *a posteriori* measure $\nu(\cdot|y) = \mu_2(S^{-1}\cdot|y)$ is defined on Borel sets of the space G. It is also Gaussian with mean

$$m(y) = Sm_{\mu,y} = \sum_{j=1}^{n} y_j S(C_\mu L_j).$$

Its correlation operator does not depend on y and is given by $C_{\nu,N} \colon G \to G$,

$$C_{\nu,N}(g) = S(C_{\mu,N}(L_g S)) = C_\nu g - \sum_{j=1}^{n} \langle g, SC_\mu L_j \rangle \, SC_\mu L_j, \quad \forall\, g \in G.$$

Exercises

E 5.2:1 Let F_1 and G be Hilbert spaces. Let μ be a probability measure on F_1 with a finite second moment, $\int_{F_1} \|f\|^2 \, \mu(df) < +\infty$. For a continuous linear solution operator $S : F_1 \to G$, show that the correlation operator C_ν of $\nu = \mu S^{-1}$ is given by $C_\nu = SC_\mu S^*$.

E 5.2:2 Show that for an arbitrary probability measure μ with a finite second moment we have

$$\int_{F_1} \langle S(f), g \rangle \, L(f)\mu(df) = \langle SC_\mu L, g \rangle,$$

where $L \in F_1^*$, $g \in G$ and G is a Hilbert space, and S is a continuous linear operator from F_1 into G.

E 5.2:3 Prove that the correlation operator C_ν of the measure $\nu = \mu S^{-1}$ is also given by

$$C_\nu g = \int_{F_1} \langle S(f), g \rangle \, S(f)\, \mu(df), \quad \forall\, g \in G.$$

Here S is a continuous linear operator and $S(f) = \sum_{i=1}^{\infty} \langle S(f), \eta_i \rangle \, \eta_i$, where $\{\eta_i\}$ is an orthonormal system of the Hilbert space G. The integral above is understood as $\sum_{i=1}^{\infty} \left[\int_{F_1} \langle S(f), g \rangle \langle S(f), \eta_i \rangle \, \mu(df) \right] \eta_i$.

E 5.2:4 Let $F_1 = \mathbb{R}^k$. Consider the measure

$$\mu(B) = \int_B w(\|Mf\|)\, df, \quad \forall\ \text{Borel set } B \text{ of } F_1,$$

where M is a nonsingular matrix, $\|\cdot\|$ stands for the $\mathcal{L}_2$ norm, and $w : \mathbb{R}_+ \to \mathbb{R}_+$ is chosen so that $\mu(F_1) = 1$. Prove that the mean is zero and the correlation operator is given by $C_\mu = \alpha \, (M^*M)^{-1}$, where $\alpha = k^{-1} \int_{\mathbb{R}^k} \|Mf\|^2 w(\|Mf\|)\, df$ is assumed to be finite.

5.3. Central Algorithms

In this section we present central algorithms for linear problems with $F = F_1$. This will be done by directly using the results presented in Sections 3.2 and 5.2.

Let $N(f) = [L_1(f), L_2(f), \ldots, L_n(f)]$ be nonadaptive information with $L_i \in F_1^*$. Assume that $\langle L_i, L_j \rangle_\mu = L_i(C_\mu L_j) = \delta_{i,j}$. Lemma 3.2.1 states that the central algorithm is the mean of the conditional measure $\nu(\cdot|y)$, for $y = N(f) = [y_1, y_2, \ldots, y_n]$. From Section 5.2, we thus conclude that the algorithm

$$\phi^c(y) = \sum_{j=1}^{n} y_j \, S(C_\mu L_j)$$

is central.

The algorithm ϕ^c remains central for far more general spaces and error criteria, as discussed in **NR 5.4:1** and Section 6.3.

We now show that the local average error of ϕ^c, which is equal to the local average radius $r^{\mathrm{avg}}(N, y)$, does not depend on y and is equal to

$$r^{\mathrm{avg}}(N, y)^2 = \int_G \|g\|^2 \, \nu(dg|0) = \mathrm{trace}(C_{\nu, N})$$

$$= \mathrm{trace}(C_\nu) - \sum_{j=1}^{n} \|S(C_\mu L_j)\|^2.$$

Indeed, $r^{\mathrm{avg}}(N, y)$ is equal to the average radius of $SN^{-1}(y)$ and is given by

$$r^{\mathrm{avg}}(N, y)^2 = \int_G \|g - m(y)\|^2 \, \nu(dg|y),$$

see Section 2. Changing variables by $g := g - m(y)$, we get

$$r^{\mathrm{avg}}(N, y)^2 = \int_G \|g\|^2 \, \nu(dg|0) = \mathrm{trace}(C_{\nu, N}).$$

We now relate the trace of $C_{\nu, N}$ to the trace of the correlation operator C_ν of the *a priori* measure ν, the information N, and the solution operator S. Let $\{g_i\}$ be an orthonormal system of G. From the formula of $C_{\nu, N}$ in Section 5.2, we have

$$\mathrm{trace}(C_{\nu, N})$$
$$= \sum_{i=1}^{\infty} \langle C_{\nu, N} g_i, g_i \rangle = \sum_{i=1}^{\infty} \left[\langle C_\nu g_i, g_i \rangle - \sum_{j=1}^{n} \langle g_i, SC_\nu L_j \rangle^2 \right]$$
$$= \mathrm{trace}(C_\nu) - \sum_{j=1}^{n} \sum_{i=1}^{\infty} \langle g_i, SC_\mu L_j \rangle^2 = \mathrm{trace}(C_\nu) - \sum_{j=1}^{n} \|SC_\mu L_j\|^2,$$

as claimed. Thus, we have proven

THEOREM 5.3.1. *The algorithm* $\phi^c(y) = \sum_{j=1}^n y_j\, S(C_\mu L_j)$ *is central and*

$$r^{\mathrm{avg}}(N) = r^{\mathrm{avg}}(N, y) = \sqrt{\mathrm{trace}(C_{\nu,N})} = \sqrt{\mathrm{trace}(C_\nu) - \sum_{j=1}^n \|S(C_\mu L_j)\|^2}.$$

Theorem 5.3.1 can be interpreted as follows. Before any computation has been done, we only know the *a priori* measure ν. The best approximation to elements $g = S(f)$ is zero as the mean of the *a priori measure* ν. The average radius of information is then $\sqrt{\mathrm{trace}(C_\nu)}$. Formally, this corresponds to the zero information whose average radius is given by

$$r^{\mathrm{avg}}(0) = \sqrt{\mathrm{trace}(C_\nu)}.$$

Thus, $\sqrt{\mathrm{trace}(C_\nu)}$ measures the *a priori* uncertainty when only the formulation of the problem is known.

After computing $y = N(f)$, the best approximation is the mean of the *a posteriori* measure $\nu(\cdot|y)$ and the trace of its correlation operator $C_{\nu,N}$ measures the *a posteriori* uncertainty. The trace of $C_{\nu,N}$ is smaller than the trace of C_ν by $a = \sum_{j=1}^n \|S(C_\mu L_j)\|^2$. The number a depends on the solution operator S, the *a priori* measure μ through its correlation operator, and on the information N through functionals $L_1, L_2, \ldots, L_n$. The larger a, the better the information N.

Observe that if S is a continuous linear functional then ν and $\nu(\cdot|y)$ are one dimensional Gaussian measures. Then $\mathrm{trace}(C_{\nu,N})$ is the variance, and the radius of information $r^{\mathrm{avg}}(N) = \sqrt{\mathrm{trace}(C_{\nu,N})}$ is the standard deviation of the conditional measure $\nu(\cdot|y)$.

We now relate the average radius of information to the error of the least squares approximation, see **NR 5.5:7** of Chapter 4 where this was done in the worst case setting. Assume first that S is a continuous linear functional, $S \in F_1^*$ and $G = \mathbb{R}$. Observe that

$$\mathrm{trace}(C_\nu) = \int_{F_1} |S(f)|^2 \mu(df) = S(C_\mu S) = \|S\|_\mu^2.$$

Since $\langle L_i, L_j \rangle_\mu = \delta_{i,j}$, we can rewrite the average radius of information as

$$r^{\mathrm{avg}}(N) = \sqrt{\|S\|_\mu^2 - \sum_{i=1}^n \langle S, L_i \rangle_\mu^2} = \left\| S - \sum_{i=1}^n \langle S, L_i \rangle\, L_i \right\|_\mu$$

$$= \inf_{g_i \in G} \left\| S - \sum_{i=1}^n g_i L_i \right\|_\mu.$$

The same is true if S is a continuous linear operator. In this case, G is a Hilbert space, $\|S\|_\mu = \int_{F_1} \|S(f)\|^2 \mu(df)$, and $g_i L_i$ stands for the operator $g_i L_i : F_1 \to G$ such that $(g_i L_i)(f) = L_i(f)g_i$. Details can be found in **NR 5.3:2**. Thus, we have

COROLLARY 5.3.1. *The average radius of nonadaptive information is equal to the error of the least squares approximation of S by* $\mathrm{span}(L_1, L_2, \ldots, L_n)$ *with respect to the norm* $\|\cdot\|_\mu$,

$$r^{\mathrm{avg}}(N) = \inf_{g_i \in G} \left\| S - \sum_{i=1}^{n} g_i L_i \right\|_\mu.$$

We end this section by a remark on the nonadaptive information $N = [L_1, \ldots, L_n]$, $L_i \in \Lambda$, where Λ is the class of permissible information operations. In general, L_i's are not orthonormalized, i.e., $L_i(C_\mu L_j) = \delta_{i,j}$ does not necessarily hold. As in Section 5.2, let $K_i = \sum_{j=1}^{n} a_{i,j} L_j$, where the numbers $a_{i,j}$ are chosen so that $K_i(C_\mu K_j) = \delta_{i,j}$, $i, j = 1, 2, \ldots, p$, with the maximal $p \leq n$. (This can be done by the Gram-Schmidt orthogonalization process.) We stress that K_i's need not belong to the class Λ. However, the information $[K_1(f), \ldots, K_p(f)]$ can be recovered from $N(f)$, since $K_i(f) = \sum_{j=1}^{n} a_{i,j} L_j(f)$. Applying Theorem 5.3.1 to the information N, we conclude that the algorithm

$$\phi^c(N(f)) = \sum_{i=1}^{p} K_i(f) S C_\mu K_i = \sum_{j=1}^{n} L_j(f) g_j,$$

$$g_j = \sum_{i=1}^{p} a_{i,j} S C_\mu K_i$$

is central. Furthermore, Theorem 5.3.1 and Corollary 5.3.1 yield ,

$$r^{\mathrm{avg}}(N) = \left(\mathrm{trace}(C_\nu) - \sum_{j=1}^{p} \|S(C_\mu K_j)\|^2 \right)^{1/2} = \inf_{g_i \in G} \left\| S - \sum_{i=1}^{n} g_i L_i \right\|_\mu.$$

Notes and Remarks

NR 5.3:1 The average radius $r^{\mathrm{avg}}(N)$ of information can be also obtained from Lemma 3.1 by integrating

$$\int_{\mathbb{R}^n} \|m(y)\|^2 \mu_1(dy) = \sum_{i,j=1}^{n} \langle S C_\mu L_i, S C_\mu L_j \rangle \int_{\mathbb{R}^n} y_i \, y_j \, \mu_1(dy).$$

The last integral is equal to the Kronecker delta which yields the needed formula.

NR 5.3:2 In Section 5.2, we defined a semi-inner product and a semi-norm for continuous linear functionals. We now extend their definitions for the class $\mathcal{B}(F_1, G)$ of continuous linear operators from F_1 into G, (F_1 is a separable Banach space and G is a separable Hilbert space). Let $\{\eta_i\}$ be an orthonormal system of G. Then for $A \in \mathcal{B}(F_1, G)$ we have

$$Af = \sum_{i=1}^{\infty} A_i(f)\,\eta_i, \quad A_i(f) = \langle Af, \eta_i \rangle.$$

For A, B from $\mathcal{B}(F_1, G)$ define

$$\langle A, B \rangle_\mu = \sum_{i=1}^{\infty} \langle A_i, B_i \rangle_\mu = \sum_{i=1}^{\infty} \int_{F_1} \langle Af, \eta_i \rangle \langle Bf, \eta_i \rangle\, \mu(df),$$

$$\|A\|_\mu = \sqrt{\langle A, A \rangle_\mu} = \sqrt{\int_{F_1} \|Af\|^2\, \mu(df)}.$$

Obviously, $\langle \cdot, \cdot \rangle_\mu$ and $\|\cdot\|_\mu$ are a semi-inner product and a semi-norm on the space $\mathcal{B}(F_1, G)$, and they do not depend on a particular choice of $\{\eta_i\}$. For $G = \mathbb{R}$, they coincide with the semi-inner product and semi-norm defined in Section 5.2. We show that

$$r^{\mathrm{avg}}(N) = \inf_{g_i \in G} \left\| S - \sum_{i=1}^{n} g_i L_i \right\|_\mu.$$

Here $g_i L_i$ is an operator such that $(g_i L_i)(f) = L_i(f) g_i$. Indeed,

$$\left\| S - \sum_{i=1}^{n} g_i L_i \right\|_\mu^2 = \|S\|_\mu^2 - 2 \sum_{i=1}^{n} \langle S, g_i L_i \rangle_\mu + \sum_{i,j=1}^{n} \left\langle g_i L_i, g_j L_j \right\rangle_\mu.$$

It is easy to check, see **E 5.2:2**, that

$$\langle S, g_i L_i \rangle_\mu = \langle S C_\mu L_i, g_i \rangle \quad \text{and} \quad \left\langle g_i L_i, g_j L_j \right\rangle_\mu = \delta_{i,j} \|g_i\|^2.$$

Thus,

$$\left\| S - \sum_{i=1}^{n} g_i L_i \right\|_\mu^2 = \|S\|_\mu^2 + \sum_{i=1}^{n} \|g_i - S C_\mu L_i\|^2 - \sum_{i=1}^{n} \|S C_\mu L_i\|^2.$$

This is minimized for $g_i = S C_\mu L_i$ which corresponds to the central algorithm ϕ^c. Therefore, the average radius of information is the error of the least squares approximation of S by $\mathrm{span}(L_1, L_2, \ldots, L_n)$ in the space G with respect to the norm $\|\cdot\|_\mu$.

5.4. Spline Algorithms

Spline algorithms play the essential role in the worst case setting, as exhibited in Section 5.7 of Chapter 4. They are also important in the average case setting.

Splines are defined in the literature by two linear operators N and T, see among others Anselone and Laurent [68], Atteia [65], and Holmes [72]. Recall that a spline $\sigma = \sigma(y)$ interpolates the data y generated by the operator N and has the minimal T-norm among all interpolants,

$$N(\sigma) = y \quad \text{and} \quad \|T\sigma\| = \min\{\|Th\| : N(h) = y\}.$$

Here $\|\cdot\|$ is a norm in the range space of T.

In the worst case setting, N is an information operator and T is a restriction operator defining the set F of problem elements $F = \{f \in F_1 : \|Tf\| \leq 1\}$.

In the average case setting, N is also an information operator. The set F is equal to a separable Banach space F_1. It is then unclear how we should define an operator T to guarantee optimality properties of the spline algorithm $\phi^s(y) = S\sigma(y)$. Obviously, the operator T should depend on the *a priori* measure μ on F_1, since optimality properties of an algorithm depend on μ.

We use the results of Section 5.3 as a clue how to select a proper operator T. For $N(f) = [L_1(f), L_2(f), \ldots, L_n(f)]$ with $\langle L_i, L_j \rangle_\mu = \delta_{i,j}$ we know that the algorithm

$$\phi(y) = Sm_{\mu, y}$$

is central, where $\sigma = m_{\mu, y} = \sum_{j=1}^n y_j C_\mu L_j$ is the mean of the *a posteriori* measure $\mu_2(\cdot | y)$. The element σ has two properties:

(i) σ interpolates y, $N(\sigma) = y$,
(ii) for every functional $\overline{L} \in F_1^*$ such that $C_\mu \overline{L} = \sigma$, $\overline{L}$ has the minimal semi-norm

$$\|\overline{L}\|_\mu = \min\{\|L\|_\mu : L \in F_1^*, \ N(C_\mu L) = y\}.$$

Indeed, $L_i(\sigma) = \sum_{j=1}^n y_j \langle L_i, L_j \rangle_\mu = y_i$, which proves (i). To prove (ii), take $L \in F_1^*$ such that $N(C_\mu L) = y$. Let $f = C_\mu L$. Then $f = \sigma + h$, where $N(h) = 0$. Define $R = L - \overline{L}$. Then $R \in F_1^*$ and $C_\mu R = f - \sigma = h$. Thus, $N(C_\mu R) = 0$, i.e., $L_j(C_\mu R) = R(C_\mu L_j) = 0$, $j = 1, 2, \ldots, n$. Observe that $\|L\|_\mu^2 = \|\overline{L}\|_\mu^2 + \|R\|_\mu^2 + 2\langle \overline{L}, R \rangle_\mu$. Since

$$\langle \overline{L}, R \rangle_\mu = R(C_\mu \overline{L}) = R\sigma = \sum_{j=1}^n y_j R(C_\mu L_j) = 0,$$

we get $\|L\|_\mu \geq \|\overline{L}\|_\mu$, as claimed in (ii).

Assume now that C_μ is bijective. Then $\overline{L} = C_\mu^{-1}(\sigma)$ and (ii) can be rewritten as

$$\|C_\mu^{-1}(\sigma)\|_\mu = \min\left\{\|C_\mu^{-1}h\|_\mu : h \in C_\mu(F_1^*), N(h) = y\right\}.$$

From this we conclude that for $T = C_\mu^{-1} : C_\mu(F_1^*) \to F_1^*$ and for the norm $\|\cdot\|_\mu$, the element σ is a spline with respect to the linear operators N and T. We stress that the domain of the operator T is a linear subspace $C_\mu(F_1^*)$ which, in general, is a proper subset of F_1. In fact, for an infinite dimensional space F_1 with $\dim\left(C_\mu(F_1^*)\right) = +\infty$, the set $C_\mu(F_1^*)$ has μ-measure zero, see Vakhania [81, p. 59].

The central algorithm $\phi(y) = Sm(y)$ is thus a spline algorithm. To stress the dependence on the measure μ, the algorithm $\phi = \phi^s$ is sometimes called the μ-*spline algorithm*. Observe that the μ-spline algorithm is also well-defined for other than Gaussian measures. It is well defined for every probability measure μ with a finite second moment, $\int_{F_1}\|f\|^2\mu(df) < +\infty$, and still enjoys certain optimal error properties as explained in **NR 5.4:1** and **5.4:2**.

Notes and Remarks

NR 5.4:1 (Wasilkowski and Woźniakowski [86]) We exhibit optimal error properties of the μ-spline algorithm $\phi^s(N(f)) = \sum_{j=1}^n L_j(f)S(C_\mu L_j)$, $\left\langle L_i, L_j\right\rangle_\mu = \delta_{i,j}$, for a linear problem with an arbitrary probability measure μ with mean m_μ, correlation operator C_μ, and a finite second moment, $\int_{F_1}\|f\|^2\mu(df) < +\infty$. We first show that for any μ, the μ-spline algorithm is a unique linear algorithm with minimal average error among linear algorithms, i.e.,

$$e^{\mathrm{avg}}(\phi^s, N)^2 = \inf_{g_i \in G}\int_{F_1}\left\|S(f) - \sum_{j=1}^n L_j(f)g_i\right\|^2 \mu(df)$$

$$= \int_{F_1}\|S(f)\|^2\,\mu(df) - \sum_{j=1}^n\|S(C_\mu L_j)\|^2.$$

Indeed, for any linear algorithm $\phi(Nf) = \sum_{j=1}^n L_j(f)g_i$, we have

$$\int_{F_1}\langle S(f), \phi(Nf)\rangle_\mu^2\,\mu(df) = \sum_{j=1}^n\int_{F_1}\left\langle S(f), g_j\right\rangle L_j(f)\,\mu(df)$$

$$= \sum_{j=1}^n L_{g_j}S(C_\mu L_j) = \sum_{j=1}^n\left\langle S(C_\mu L_j), g_j\right\rangle,$$

where $L_{g_j} \in G^*$, and $L_{g_j}(g) = \left\langle g_j, g\right\rangle$. Furthermore,

$$\int_{F_1}\|\phi(Nf)\|^2\,\mu(df) = \sum_{i,j=1}^n\left\langle g_i, g_j\right\rangle\int_{F_1}L_j(f)\,L_i(f)\,\mu(df) = \sum_{j=1}^n\|g_j\|^2.$$

This yields

$$e^{\mathrm{avg}}(\phi, N)^2 = \int_{F_1} \|S(f)\|^2 \, \mu(df) + \sum_{j=1}^{n} \|g_j - S(C_\mu L_j)\|^2 - \sum_{j=1}^{n} \|S(C_\mu L_j)\|^2.$$

Thus, the average error is minimized iff $g_j = S(C_\mu L_j)$, which corresponds to the μ-spline algorithm.

We now provide a condition on the measure μ which guarantees that the μ-spline algorithm has minimal average error among *all* algorithms using N. Similarly to Section 3.2, define the mapping $D: F_1 \to F_1$ by

$$Df = 2 \sum_{j=1}^{n} L_j(f) \, C_\mu L_j - f.$$

The mapping D has two properties: $N(f) = N(Df)$ and $D^2 f = f, \forall f \in F_1$. If

$$\mu(DB) = \mu(B), \quad \forall \text{ Borel set } B \text{ of } F_1, \tag{i}$$

then the μ-spline algorithm is the unique algorithm which has minimal average error among all algorithms using N. Indeed, take an arbitrary algorithm ϕ. Then (i) and $N(f) = N(Df)$ imply

$$\int_{F_1} \|S(f) - \phi(Nf)\|^2 \, \mu(df) = \int_{F_1} \|S(Df) - \phi(Nf)\|^2 \, \mu(df).$$

Observe that

$$S(f) - \phi^s(Nf) = \tfrac{1}{2}(S(f) - S(Df)) = \tfrac{1}{2}(S(f) - \phi(Nf)) + \tfrac{1}{2}(\phi(Nf) - S(Df)). \tag{ii}$$

Thus,

$$\|S(f) - \phi^s(Nf)\|^2 \le \tfrac{1}{4}(\|S(f) - \phi(Nf)\| + \|\phi(Nf) - S(Df)\|)^2$$
$$\le \tfrac{1}{2}\left(\|S(f) - \phi(Nf)\|^2 + \|S(Df) - \phi(Nf)\|^2\right).$$

From this we conclude

$$e^{\mathrm{avg}}(\phi^s, N)^2 \le \tfrac{1}{2}\int_{F_1}\left(\|S(f) - \phi(Nf)\|^2 + \|S(Df) - \phi(Nf)\|^2\right)\mu(df) = e^{\mathrm{avg}}(\phi, N)^2.$$

Thus, ϕ^s has minimal average error. Uniqueness, up to a set of measure zero, follows from the fact that optimality of ϕ implies that (ii) holds with equality (almost everywhere) which, in turn, yields $\phi = \phi^s$.

If (i) holds, then the μ-spline algorithm remains optimal even for a more general error criterion. Indeed, let $\mathrm{ER}: G \to \mathbb{R}_+$ be convex and symmetric. Here it is enough to assume that G is a linear space. Redefine the average error as

$$e^{\mathrm{avg}}(\phi, N) = \left(\int_{F_1} \mathrm{ER}(S(f) - \phi(Nf))\mu(df)\right)^{1/2}.$$

Then (ii) yields

$$\mathrm{ER}\left(S(f) - \phi^s(Nf)\right) \le \tfrac{1}{2}\,\mathrm{ER}\left(S(f) - \phi(Nf)\right) + \tfrac{1}{2}\,\mathrm{ER}\left(S(Df) - \phi(Nf)\right).$$

This and (i) implies $e^{\mathrm{avg}}(\phi^s, N) \le e^{\mathrm{avg}}(\phi, N)$, as claimed.

For which measures does (i) hold? This is the case if

(iii) F_1 is finite dimensional and μ is a weighted Lebesgue measure of the form

$$\mu(B) = \int_B w(\|Mf\|)\, df, \quad \forall \ \text{Borel set } B \text{ of } F_1,$$

where $M: F_1 \to X$ is a symmetric positive definite matrix, X is a Hilbert space, and $w: \mathbb{R}_+ \to \mathbb{R}_+$ is chosen so that $\mu(F_1) = 1$, see Traub, Wasilkowski, and Woźniakowski [84a] or, more generally, if

(iv) F_1 is a separable Banach space and μ is elliptically contoured, see Crawford [77]. That is

$$\mu(B) = \int_0^\infty \mu_G\left(\frac{1}{\sqrt{t}}B\right)\alpha(dt), \quad \forall \ \text{Borel set } B \text{ of } F_1,$$

where α is a measure defined on Borel sets of $(0, +\infty)$ such that $\int_0^\infty \alpha(dt) = \int_0^\infty t\,\alpha(dt) = 1$, and μ_G is Gaussian with mean zero and correlation operator C_μ. Note that $\mu_t(B) = \mu_G\left(t^{-1/2}B\right)$ is also Gaussian with mean zero and correlation operator $t\,C_\mu$. Recently, Kwapień [85] proved that if $\dim(F_1) = +\infty$ and C_μ is bijective, then μ satisfies (i) for all information N iff μ is elliptically contoured.

It is interesting to notice that the last characteristic is not true if $\dim(F_1) < \infty$. That is, there exists an *orthogonally invariant* measure μ, i.e., a measure which is invariant under mappings D for all information, and which is not elliptically contoured, see **E 5.4:3**.

Elliptically contoured measures are proper combinations of Gaussian measures. Their projections on finite dimensional subspaces are weighted Lebesgue measures

$$\lambda(B) = \int_B w(\|Mf\|)\, df$$

for some symmetric positive definite matrix M. Thus, the weight function w is constant on the ellipsoids $\|Mf\| = \text{constant}$, and thus the name.

We emphasize that if (i) does not hold, then the μ-spline algorithm may be far from being optimal, see **E 5.4:4**.

NR 5.4:2 (Wasilkowski [86b]) We exhibit another optimality property of the μ-spline algorithm ϕ^s showing that it minimizes the *variance* of an algorithm that uses non-adaptive information. More precisely, consider a linear problem with $F = F_1$. Let $N = [L_1, L_2, \ldots, L_n]$, $\left\langle L_i, L_j \right\rangle_\mu = \delta_{i,j}$. The *variance* of an algorithm ϕ that uses N is defined to be

$$\mathrm{var}(\phi) = \int_{F_1} \left(\|S(f) - \phi(N(f))\|^2 - e^{\mathrm{avg}}(\phi, N)^2\right)^2 \mu(df).$$

Here $e^{\mathrm{avg}}(\phi, N)^2 = \int_{F_1} \|S(f) - \phi(N(f))\|^2 \mu(df)$. We now prove that

$$\mathrm{var}(\phi^s) = \inf_\phi \mathrm{var}(\phi).$$

Indeed, for an arbitrary algorithm ϕ, let $h = \phi - \phi^s$. Then

$$\text{var}(\phi) = \int_{\mathbb{R}^n} \int_{F_1} \left(\|S(f) - h(y)\|^2 - e^{\text{avg}}(\phi, N)^2 \right)^2 \mu_2(df|0) \, \mu_1(dy)$$

$$= \int_{\mathbb{R}^n} \int_G \left(\|g - h(y)\|^2 - e^{\text{avg}}(\phi, N)^2 \right)^2 \nu(dg|0) \, \mu_1(dy).$$

We have $\|g - h(y)\|^2 = \|g\|^2 - 2\langle g, h(y) \rangle + \|h(y)\|^2$. Since the mean of $\nu(\cdot|0)$ is zero, $\int_G \langle g, h(y) \rangle \, \nu(dg|0) = 0$ and

$$e^{\text{avg}}(\phi, N)^2 = \int_{\mathbb{R}^n} \int_G \|g - h(y)\|^2 \nu(dg|0)\mu_1(dy) = e^{\text{avg}}(\phi^s, N)^2 + \int_{\mathbb{R}^n} \|h(y)\|^2 \mu_1(dy).$$

Hence,

$$\text{var}(\phi) = \int_{\mathbb{R}^n} \int_G \left[\|g\|^2 - e^{\text{avg}}(\phi^s, N)^2 - 2\langle g, h(y) \rangle \right.$$

$$\left. + \|h(y)\|^2 - \int_{\mathbb{R}^n} \|h(z)\|^2 \mu_1(dz) \right]^2 \nu(dg|0) \, \mu_1(dy).$$

Change the variables by letting $g := -g$. Then

$$\text{var}(\phi) = \int_{\mathbb{R}^n} \int_G \left[\|g\|^2 - e^{\text{avg}}(\phi^s, N)^2 + 2\langle g, h(y) \rangle \right.$$

$$\left. + \|h(y)\|^2 - \int_{\mathbb{R}^n} \|h(z)\|^2 \mu_1(dz) \right]^2 \nu(dg|0) \, \mu_1(y).$$

Since $((a + b)^2 + (a - b)^2)/2 \geq a^2$,

$$\text{var}(\phi)$$

$$\geq \int_{\mathbb{R}^n} \int_G \left[\|g\|^2 - e^{\text{avg}}(\phi^s, N)^2 + \|h(y)\|^2 - \int_{\mathbb{R}^n} \|h(z)\|^2 \mu_1(dz) \right]^2 \nu(dg|0) \, \mu_1(dy).$$

Hence

$$\text{var}(\phi) \geq \text{var}(\phi^s) + 2H_1 + H_2,$$

where

$$H_1 = \int_{\mathbb{R}^n} \int_G \left[\|g\|^2 - e^{\text{avg}}(\phi^s, N)^2 \right] \left[\|h(y)\|^2 - \int_{\mathbb{R}^n} \|h(z)\|^2 \mu_1(dz) \right] \nu(dg|0) \, \mu_1(dy)$$

$$= \left[\int_{\mathbb{R}^n} \|h(y)\|^2 \mu_1(dy) - \int_{\mathbb{R}^n} \|h(z)\|^2 \mu_1(dz) \right] \left[\int_G \|g\|^2 \nu(dg|0) - e^{\text{avg}}(\phi^s, N)^2 \right]$$

$$= 0,$$

and

$$H_2 = \int_{\mathbb{R}^n} \left[\|h(y)\|^2 - \int_{\mathbb{R}^n} \|h(z)\|^2 \mu_1(dz) \right]^2 \mu_1(dy) \geq 0.$$

Therefore, $\text{var}(\phi) \geq \text{var}(\phi^s)$, as claimed. We stress that the minimal variance of the μ-spline algorithm depends strongly on the error criterion. For arbitrary ER, even convex and symmetric, see **NR 5.4:1**, the μ-spline algorithm needs not minimize the variance.

Exercises

E 5.4:1 Consider a linear problem with a Gaussian measure μ with mean m_μ and correlation operator C_μ. Prove that the affine spline algorithm

$$\phi^{as}(Nf) = \sum_{j=1}^{n} L_j(f - m_\mu)SC_\mu L_j + Sm_\mu$$

is a central algorithm and

$$r^{avg}(N,y)^2 = \int_{F_1} \|S(f)\|^2 \mu(df) - \sum_{j=1}^{n} \|SC_\mu L_j\|^2$$

$$= \text{trace}(C_\nu) + \|Sm_\mu\|^2 - \sum_{j=1}^{n} \|SC_\mu L_j\|^2.$$

Here $N = [L_1, L_2, \ldots, L_n]$ with $\left\langle L_i, L_j \right\rangle_\mu = \delta_{i,j}$.

E 5.4:2 Consider **E 5.4:1** with an arbitrary probability measure μ whose second moment, $\int_{F_1} \|f\|^2 \mu(df)$, is finite.
  (i) Prove that ϕ^{as} is a unique affine algorithm with minimal average error among affine algorithms that use N.
  (ii) Prove that the μ-spline algorithm has minimal average error among affine algorithms that use N if $m_\mu = 0$.

E 5.4:3 Let $F = \mathbb{R}$ and let μ be an atomic measure such that $\mu(\{-1\}) = \mu(\{+1\}) = 1/2$. Show that μ is *not* elliptically contoured, but μ satisfies (i) of **NR 5.4:1**.

E 5.4:4 Let $F = G = \overline{\text{span}(\xi_1, \xi_2, \ldots)}$, where $\left\langle z_i, z_j \right\rangle = \delta_{i,j}$. Define the measure μ by

$$\mu(\{\xi_i\}) = \mu(\{-\xi_i\}) = p_i,$$

where $\sum_{i=1}^{\infty} p_i = 1/2$ for distinct and positive p_i. Let $S(f) = f$ and $N(f) = \langle f, g_1 \rangle$ with $g_1 = \sum_{i=1}^{\infty} p_i \xi_i$. Show that
  (i) $m_\mu = 0$ and $C_\mu f = \sum_{i=1}^{\infty} 2p_i \langle f, \xi_i \rangle \xi_i$.
  (ii) The μ-spline algorithm has positive average error and takes the form

$$\phi^s(N(f)) = \left(\sum_{i=1}^{\infty} 2p_i^3 \right)^{-1} \langle f, g_1 \rangle \sum_{i=1}^{\infty} 2p_i^2 \xi_i.$$

  (iii) The algorithm

$$\phi(y) = \begin{cases} \xi_i & \text{if } y = p_i, \\ -\xi_i & \text{if } y = -p_i, \\ g & \text{otherwise,} \end{cases}$$

has average error zero, where g is an arbitrary element of G. Thus ϕ is central and ϕ^s is *not*.

(iv) The mapping D, see **NR 5.4:1**, now has the form

$$Df = \frac{2\langle f, g_1 \rangle}{\langle C_\mu g_1, g_1 \rangle} \sum_{i=1}^{\infty} 2p_i^2 \xi_i - f,$$

and μ is not invariant under the mapping D. Hint: Take $B = \{\xi_i\}$ and show that $\mu(B) = p_1$ and $\mu(DB) = 0$.

5.5. Optimal Nonadaptive Information

In this section we study how to select continuous linear functionals to minimize the average radius of nonadaptive information. Recall that Λ is the class of permissible information operations, $\Lambda \subset F_1^*$. Let

$$r^{\mathrm{avg}}(n, \Lambda) = \inf\left\{ r^{\mathrm{avg}}(N) : N = [L_1, L_2, \dots, L_n] \text{ and } L_i \in \Lambda \right\}$$

denote the *nth minimal average radius of (nonadaptive) information* in the class Λ. Information $N_n^* = [L_1^*, L_2^*, \dots, L_n^*]$ is called the *nth optimal (nonadaptive) information* in the class Λ iff $L_i^* \in \Lambda$ and

$$r^{\mathrm{avg}}(N_n^*) = r^{\mathrm{avg}}(n, \Lambda).$$

For brevity, we sometimes write $r^{\mathrm{avg}}(n)$ instead of $r^{\mathrm{avg}}(n, \Lambda)$ if $\Lambda = F_1^*$, i.e., when all continuous linear functionals are permissible.

We now present the nth minimal average radius and nth optimal information for the class $\Lambda = F_1^*$. Let $N = [L_1, L_2, \dots, L_n]$ with $L_i \in \Lambda$. As before we can assume without loss of generality that the functionals L_i are orthonormalized, $L_i(C_\mu L_j) = \delta_{i,j}$. Then Theorem 5.3.1 implies that the best choice of L_i is provided by functionals which maximize $\sum_{j=1}^n \|S(C_\mu L_j)\|^2$. That is,

$$r^{\mathrm{avg}}(n, \Lambda)^2 = \mathrm{trace}\ (C_\nu)$$
$$- \sup\left\{ \sum_{j=1}^n \|S(C_\mu L_j)\|^2 : L_i \in \Lambda \text{ and } L_i(C_\mu L_j) = \delta_{i,j} \right\}.$$

Let $\{\eta_i^*\}$ be the orthonormal eigenelements of the correlation operator C_ν, $C_\nu : G \to G$, where $\nu = \mu S^{-1}$ is the *a priori* measure of solution elements, G is a separable Hilbert space,

$$C_\nu \eta_i^* = \lambda_i^* \eta_i^*.$$

and $\lambda_1^* \geq \lambda_2^* \geq \cdots \geq 0$. If $\dim(G) < +\infty$, we formally set $\lambda_i^* = 0$ for $i > \dim(G)$. Let $k = \min\{n, \sup\{i \colon \lambda_i^* > 0\}\}$ with $\sup \emptyset = 0$. Thus $k = n$ if $\lambda_n^* > 0$, and otherwise k is the largest index of positive eigenvalues of C_μ. Define the nonadaptive information N_n^* as follows.

If $k = 0$ then $N_n^* = 0$, otherwise

$$N_n^*(f) = [L_1^*(f), L_2^*(f), \ldots, L_k^*(f)],$$

where $L_i^*(f) = (\lambda_i^*)^{-1/2} \langle S(f), \eta_i^* \rangle$. Obviously, the cardinality of N_n^* is at most n.

THEOREM 5.5.1. *Information N_n^* is nth optimal nonadaptive information in the class $\Lambda = F_1^*$ and*

$$r^{\mathrm{avg}}(n) = r^{\mathrm{avg}}(N_n^*) = \sqrt{\sum_{j=n+1}^{\infty} \lambda_i^*}.$$

PROOF: Observe that

$$L_i^*(C_\mu L_j^*) = \frac{1}{\sqrt{\lambda_i^* \lambda_j^*}} \int_{F_1} \langle S(f), \eta_i^* \rangle \langle S(f), \eta_j^* \rangle \, \mu(df)$$

$$= \frac{1}{\sqrt{\lambda_i^* \lambda_j^*}} \int_G \langle g, \eta_i^* \rangle \langle g, \eta_j^* \rangle \, \nu(dg) = \frac{1}{\sqrt{\lambda_i^* \lambda_j^*}} \langle C_\nu \eta_i^*, \eta_j^* \rangle = \delta_{i,j}.$$

From this it follows that

$$SC_\mu L_j^* = \sum_{i=1}^{\infty} \langle SC_\mu L_j^*, \eta_i^* \rangle \eta_i^* = \sum_{i=1}^{\infty} \sqrt{\lambda_i^*} L_i^* (C_\mu L_j^*) \eta_i^* = \sqrt{\lambda_j^*} \eta_j^*.$$

Applying Theorem 5.3.1 for the information N_n^*, we conclude that

$$r^{\mathrm{avg}}(N_n^*) = \sqrt{\sum_{i=1}^{\infty} \lambda_i^* - \sum_{i=1}^{n} \lambda_i^*} = \sqrt{\sum_{i=n+1}^{\infty} \lambda_i^*}.$$

We now show that $r^{\mathrm{avg}}(N) \geq r^{\mathrm{avg}}(N_n^*)$ for arbitrary information $N = [L_1, L_2, \ldots, L_n]$ with $\langle L_i, L_j \rangle_\mu = \delta_{i,j}$. Let $\{z_i\}$ be an orthonormal system of G such that

$$\mathrm{span}\left(S(C_\mu L_1), \ldots, S(C_\mu L_n)\right) \subset \mathrm{span}(z_1, z_2, \ldots, z_n).$$

From Theorem 5.3.1 we have

$$r^{\mathrm{avg}}(N)^2 = \int_{F_1} \left\| S(f) - \sum_{j=1}^{n} L_j(f) S C_\mu L_j \right\|^2 \mu(df)$$

$$= \int_{F_1} \left(\sum_{i=1}^{n} \left\langle S(f) - \sum_{j=1}^{n} L_j(f) S C_\mu L_j , z_i \right\rangle^2 + \sum_{i=n+1}^{\infty} \left\langle S(f), z_i \right\rangle^2 \right) \mu(df)$$

$$\geq \sum_{i=n+1}^{\infty} \int_{F_1} \left\langle S(f), z_i \right\rangle^2 \mu(df) = \sum_{i=n+1}^{\infty} \left\langle C_\nu z_i, z_i \right\rangle$$

$$= \mathrm{trace}\,(C_\nu) - \sum_{i=1}^{n} \left\langle C_\nu z_i, z_i \right\rangle.$$

Thus,

$$r^{\mathrm{avg}}(N)^2 \geq \mathrm{trace}\,(C_\nu) - \sup \left\{ \sum_{i=1}^{n} \left\langle C_\nu z_i, z_i \right\rangle : \left\langle z_i, z_j \right\rangle = \delta_{i,j} \right\}.$$

It is known that the last supremum is equal to $\sum_{i=1}^{n} \lambda_i^*$, see, e.g., Marcus and Minc [64, Theorem 4.1.4]. For completeness we provide a short proof. We have $z_i = \sum_{j=1}^{\infty} \left\langle z_i, \eta_j^* \right\rangle \eta_j^*$ and $\sum_{k=1}^{\infty} \left\langle z_i, \eta_k^* \right\rangle^2 = \sum_{k=1}^{\infty} \left\langle z_k, \eta_j^* \right\rangle^2 = 1$ for every i, j. Then

$$\sum_{i=1}^{n} \left\langle C_\nu z_i, z_i \right\rangle = \sum_{i=1}^{n} \left[\sum_{j=1}^{n} \lambda_j^* \left\langle z_i, \eta_j^* \right\rangle^2 + \sum_{j=n+1}^{\infty} \lambda_j^* \left\langle z_i, \eta_j^* \right\rangle^2 \right]$$

$$\leq \sum_{i=1}^{n} \left[\sum_{j=1}^{n} \lambda_j^* \left\langle z_i, \eta_j^* \right\rangle^2 + \lambda_{n+1}^* \left(1 - \sum_{j=1}^{n} \left\langle z_i, \eta_j^* \right\rangle^2 \right) \right]$$

$$= n \lambda_{n+1}^* + \sum_{j=1}^{n} (\lambda_j^* - \lambda_{n+1}^*) \sum_{i=1}^{n} \left\langle z_i, \eta_j^* \right\rangle^2$$

$$\leq n \lambda_{n+1}^* + \sum_{j=1}^{n} (\lambda_j^* - \lambda_{n+1}^*) = \sum_{j=1}^{n} \lambda_j^*,$$

as claimed. Thus, $r^{\mathrm{avg}}(N) \geq r^{\mathrm{avg}}(N_n^*)$, which completes the proof. ∎

Theorem 5.5.1 states that N_n^* is the nth optimal information. The μ-spline algorithm that uses N_n^* (and which is central) now takes the form

$$\phi^s(N_n^*(f)) = \sum_{j=1}^{n} L_j^*(f) S C_\mu L_j^* = \sum_{j=1}^{n} \left\langle S(f), \eta_j^* \right\rangle \eta_j^*$$

since $SC_\mu L_j^* = \sqrt{\lambda_j}\eta_j^*$. This is the truncated Fourier series of the solution element $S(f)$ in the orthonormal system which consists of eigenelements of the correlation operator of the *a priori* measure ν.

For the classes Λ of permissible information operations which are proper subsets of F_1^*, the problem of finding nth optimal information is hard. The nth optimal information depends very much on the structure of the class Λ, as well as on the solution operator S and specific Gaussian measure μ. In Chapter 7 we report nth optimal information assuming that Λ consists of only function and derivatives values, S is a continuous linear functional, and μ is the Wiener measure placed on derivatives of functions.

In any case, the optimal choice of functionals L_i from the class Λ minimizes the trace of the correlation operator of the conditional measure. Corollary 5.3.1 yields that this is equivalent to minimizing the least squares approximation error. More precisely, we have

COROLLARY 5.5.1. *Information* $N_n^* = [L_1^*, L_2^*, \ldots, L_n^*]$ *is* nth *optimal in the class* Λ *iff* $L_i^* \in \Lambda$ *and*

$$\inf_{g_i \in G} \left\| S - \sum_{i=1}^n g_i L_i^* \right\|_\mu = \inf_{L_i \in \Lambda} \inf_{g_i \in G} \left\| S - \sum_{i=1}^n g_i L_i \right\|_\mu.$$

The reader may find a brief discussion on optimal nonlinear information in **NR 5.5:2**.

Notes and Remarks

NR 5.5:1 This section is based on Papageorgiou and Wasilkowski [86].

NR 5.5:2 As already mentioned in **NR 5.3:3** of Chapter 4, Kacewicz and Wasilkowski [86] studied finitely continuous nonlinear information also in the average case setting. They consider the class Λ consisting of finitely continuous functionals, i.e., functionals which are continuous on any finite dimensional space. They proved that for linear problems, $r^{\mathrm{avg}}(1, \Lambda) = 0$. That is, the knowledge of one value $L(f)$ with appropriately chosen L from the class Λ enables us to approximate $S(f)$ on the average with an arbitrarily small error. This is contrary to the worst case setting, where the class Λ is as powerful as the class F_1^*. Thus, the class of finitely continuous nonlinear functionals is of the same power as the class of continuous linear functionals in the worst case setting and is much more powerful in the average case one.

For the class Λ of nonlinear (and not necessarily finitely continuous) functionals, we mentioned in **NR 5.3:4** of Chapter 4 that $r^{\mathrm{wor}}(1, \Lambda) = 0$ whenever the set $S(F)$ has power at most of the continuum. This holds for nonlinear S and arbitrary F. Obviously, we also have $r^{\mathrm{avg}}(1, \Lambda) = 0$.

5.6. Adaptive Information

In this section we study the power of adaptive information for linear problems with F being the whole space, $F = F_1$. This question was studied for the worst case setting in Section 5.2 of Chapter 4, where we showed that adaptive information is not significantly more powerful than nonadaptive information. As we shall see, the answer to this question in the average case setting depends on whether adaptive information is of fixed or varying cardinality. For fixed cardinality, we prove that adaptive information is *not* more powerful than the correspondingly chosen nonadaptive information.

For varying cardinality, it may happen that adaptive information *is* more powerful than nonadaptive information. In this case, however, we show that there exists information N^* whose cardinality $n(f)$ attains one of at most two values and which is as powerful as adaptive information N^a. Information N^* has a structure which is almost as simple as nonadaptive information. We also provide a condition under which varying cardinality does not help. These results will be used in Section 5.7 for deriving tight bounds on the average complexity of a linear problem.

5.6.1. Adaptive Information with Fixed Cardinality

In this subsection we consider adaptive information N^a with fixed cardinality, $n(f) \equiv n$. That is,

$$N^a(f) = [L_1(f), L_2(f; y_1), \ldots, L_n(f; y_1, \ldots, y_{n-1})],$$

where $y_1 = L_1(f)$, $y_i = L_i(f; y_1, \ldots, y_{i-1})$ and $L_{i,y} = L_i(\cdot; y_1, \ldots, y_{i-1})$ belongs to the class Λ of permissible information operations.

As mentioned several times before, we can assume without loss of generality that the functionals $L_{i,y}$ are orthonormal with respect to $\langle \cdot, \cdot \rangle_\mu$, i.e., $\langle L_{i,y}, L_{j,y} \rangle_\mu = \delta_{i,j}$ for all $i, j = 1, 2, \ldots, n$ and $y \in N^a(F_1)$. In Section 2.9.2 of the appendix we show that

(i) $\mu_1 = \mu(N^a)^{-1}$ is the Gaussian measure on $\mathbb{R}^n$ with mean zero and correlation operator (matrix) identity,

$$\mu_1(A) = \frac{1}{(2\pi)^{n/2}} \int_A \exp\left(\sum_{j=1}^n \frac{-y_j^2}{2} \right) dy, \quad \forall \text{ Borel set } A \text{ of } \mathbb{R}^n.$$

(ii) The measure $\mu_2(\cdot|y)$ is the Gaussian measure on F_1 with mean element $\sigma_n(y) = \sum_{j=1}^n y_j C_\mu L_{j,y}$, which is a spline element, and correlation operator

$$C_{n,y}(L) = C_\mu L - \sum_{j=1}^n \langle L, L_{j,y} \rangle_\mu C_\mu L_{j,y}.$$

Hence, the measure $\nu(\cdot|y) = \mu_2(S^{-1}\cdot|y)$ is Gaussian on the Hilbert space G with mean $m(y) = S\sigma_n(y)$ and correlation operator

$$C_{\nu,y}(g) = C_\nu(g) - \sum_{j=1}^{n} \langle g, SC_\mu L_{j,y} \rangle SC_\mu L_{j,y}.$$

LEMMA 5.6.1. *For arbitrary adaptive N^{a} with fixed cardinality, the μ-spline algorithm ϕ^s, $\phi^s(y) = \sum_{j=1}^{n} y_j SC_\mu L_{j,y}$, is central and*

$$e^{\mathrm{avg}}(\phi^s, N^{\mathrm{a}}, y) = r^{\mathrm{avg}}(N^{\mathrm{a}}, y) = \left(\mathrm{trace}(C_\nu) - \sum_{j=1}^{n} \|SC_\mu L_{j,y}\|^2 \right)^{1/2},$$

$$e^{\mathrm{avg}}(\phi^s, N^{\mathrm{a}}) = r^{\mathrm{avg}}(N^{\mathrm{a}}) = \left(\mathrm{trace}\ (C_\nu) - \int_{\mathbb{R}^n} \sum_{j=1}^{n} \|SC_\mu L_{j,y}\|^2 \mu_1(dy) \right)^{1/2}.$$

PROOF: The first part of Lemma 5.6.1 follows from Lemma 3.2.1 and Section 5.4. To prove the formula for $r^{\mathrm{avg}}(N^{\mathrm{a}}, y)$ observe that

$$r^{\mathrm{avg}}(N^{\mathrm{a}}, y)^2 = \int_F \|g - m(y)\|^2 \nu(dg|y) = \int_F \|g\|^2 \lambda(dg|y) = \mathrm{trace}(C_{\nu,y}),$$

where the measure $\lambda(\cdot|y)$ is equal to $\nu(\cdot|y)$ shifted by the element $m(y)$. Clearly, $\lambda(\cdot|y)$ is Gaussian with mean zero and correlation operator $C_{\nu,y}$. As in Section 5.3 we conclude that

$$\mathrm{trace}(C_{\nu,y}) = \mathrm{trace}(C_\nu) - \sum_{j=1}^{n} \|SC_\mu L_{j,y}\|^2,$$

which completes the proof. ∎

Note that the μ-spline algorithm ϕ^s is a nonlinear algorithm whenever $L_{j,y}$ varies with y. The computation of $\phi^s(y)$ can be easy if the elements $SC_\mu L_{j,y}$ are not hard to obtain.

Lemma 5.6.1 states that the global average radius of N^{a} is given by

$$r^{\mathrm{avg}}(N^{\mathrm{a}})^2 = \int_F \|S(f)\|^2 \mu(df) - \int_{\mathbb{R}^n} \sum_{j=1}^{n} \|SC_\mu L_{j,y}\|^2 \mu_1(dy),$$

whereas for nonadaptive information $N^{\mathrm{non}} = [L_1, \ldots, L_n]$ with $\langle L_i, L_j \rangle_\mu = \delta_{i,j}$, we have

$$r^{\mathrm{avg}}(N^{\mathrm{non}})^2 = \int_F \|S(f)\|^2 \mu(df) - \sum_{j=1}^{n} \|SC_\mu L_j\|^2.$$

Can adaption be more powerful than nonadaption? This could happen only if the integral $\int_{\mathbf{R}^n} \sum_{j=1}^{n} \|SC_\mu L_{j,y}\|^2 \mu_1(dy)$ were smaller than $\sum_{j=1}^{n} \|SC_\mu L_j\|^2$ for any choice of functionals L_j. But this is impossible. To see this, apply the mean value theorem to $\int_{\mathbf{R}^n} \sum_{j=1}^{n} \|SC_\mu L_{j,y}\|^2 \mu_1(dy)$ to conclude that there exists a vector $y^* = [y_1^*, y_2^*, \dots, y_n^*]$ such that

$$\sum_{j=1}^{n} \|SC_\mu L_{j,y^*}\|^2 \geq \int_{\mathbf{R}^n} \sum_{j=1}^{n} \|SC_\mu L_{j,y}\|^2 \mu_1(dy).$$

Then, letting

$$N_{y^*}^{\text{non}}(f) - [L_{1,y^*}(f), L_{2,y^*}(f), \dots, L_{n,y^*}(f)],$$

we get $r^{\text{avg}}(N_{y^*}^{\text{non}}) \leq r^{\text{avg}}(N^{\text{a}})$. The information $N_{y^*}^{\text{non}}$ is derived from N^{a} by setting all the values y_i in N^{a} to $y_i = y_i^*$. Clearly, $N_{y^*}^{\text{non}}$ has the same cardinality as N^{a}, and it consists of functionals from the class Λ, i.e., $L_{i,y^*} \in \Lambda$. We summarize this in the following

THEOREM 5.6.1. *For an arbitrary linear problem with $F = F_1$ and arbitrary adaptive information N^{a} with fixed cardinality $n(f) \equiv n$, there exists a vector y^* such that the nonadaptive information $N_{y^*}^{\text{non}}$ of the same cardinality n is as powerful as N^{a}, i.e.,*

$$r^{\text{avg}}(N_{y^*}^{\text{non}}) \leq r^{\text{avg}}(N^{\text{a}}).$$

We remark that in the worst case setting, the corresponding theorem, Theorem 5.2.1 of Chapter 4, holds with the vector $y^* = 0$ for any adaptive information N^{a}. In the average case setting the vector y^* is, in general, nonzero.

From Theorem 5.6.1 it follows that the only gain in the average case setting may be obtained by varying cardinality. This will be studied in the next section.

Notes and Remarks

NR 5.6.1:1 This section is based on Wasilkowski [86a].

NR 5.6.1:2 Theorem 5.6.1 was proven by Traub, Wasilkowski, and Woźniakowski [84a] for a finite dimensional Hilbert space F_1 equipped with a weighted Lebesgue measure discussed in (iii) of **NR 5.4:1**.

Theorem 5.6.1 was proven by Wasilkowski and Woźniakowski [84] for a separable Hilbert space F_1 equipped with an orthogonally invariant measure μ, i.e., $\mu(QB) = \mu(B)$ for any Borel set B and any linear mapping $Q : F_1 \to F_1$ of the form $Qf = 2\langle f, h \rangle C_\mu h - f$, where $\langle C_\mu h, h \rangle = 1$ or $h = 0$. In the two papers listed above, the proof technique is different from that of Theorem 5.6.1 since conditional measures were not used there. Theorem 5.6.1 was proven by Wasilkowski [86b] for a separable Hilbert space F_1 and by Lee and Wasilkowski [86] for a separable Banach space F_1. In both cases F_1 was equipped with a Gaussian measure and a general error criterion was used. That is, the average error of (ϕ, N) was defined by $e^{\mathrm{avg}}(\phi, N) = \int_{F_1} \mathrm{ER}\left(S(f) - \phi(N(f))\right) \mu(df)$, with an arbitrary functional $\mathrm{ER} : G \to \mathbb{R}_+$ such that $\mathrm{ER}(S(\cdot) - g)$ is measurable for any element $g \in G$. The proof was based on using conditional measures.

5.6.2. Adaptive Information with Varying Cardinality

In this subsection we allow the cardinality $n(\cdot)$ to vary. That is,

$$N^{\mathrm{a}}(f) = [L_1(f), L_2(f; y_1), \ldots, L_{n(f)}(f; y_1, \ldots, y_{n(f)-1})],$$

where $n(f) = \min\{i : \mathrm{ter}_i(y_1, \ldots, y_i) = 1\}$ as in Section 2.2 of Chapter 3. Recall that the average cardinality of N^{a} is given by

$$\mathrm{card}^{\mathrm{avg}}(N^{\mathrm{a}}) = \int_F n(f)\, \mu(df).$$

Let $B_k = B_k(N^{\mathrm{a}})$ be the set of all information values for which exactly k evaluations are performed, i.e.,

$$B_k = \{N^{\mathrm{a}}(f) : f \in F \text{ and } n(f) = k\}.$$

Obviously, B_k is a Borel set of $\mathbb{R}^k$ and

$$B_k = \big\{y = [y_1, \ldots, y_k] \in \mathbb{R}^k : \mathrm{ter}_k(y_1, y_2, \ldots, y_k) = 1 \text{ and }$$
$$\mathrm{ter}_i(y_1, \ldots, y_i) = 0, i = 1, \ldots, k - 1\big\}.$$

Let N_k consist of the first k evaluations of N^{a}. That is, for $f \in N_k^{-1}(B_k)$ we have $N_k(f) = N^{\mathrm{a}}(f)$. The measure $\lambda_k = \mu N_k^{-1}$ can be extended to be the Gaussian measure on $\mathbb{R}^k$ with mean zero and correlation matrix the identity. From Section 5.6.1, we conclude that for every $y \in B_k$, $\mu_2(\cdot|y)$ is the Gaussian measure on F with mean $\sigma_k(y) = \sum_{j=1}^{k} y_j C_\mu L_{j,y}$ and correlation operator $C_{k,y} L = C_\mu L - \sum_{j=1}^{k} \langle L, L_{j,y} \rangle_\mu C_\mu L_{j,y}$. We are ready to present a central algorithm that uses the information N^{a}.

LEMMA 5.6.2. For $y = [y_1, \ldots, y_k] \in N^{\mathrm{a}}(F)$, the μ-spline algorithm ϕ^s that uses adaptive information N^{a}, $\phi^s(y) = \sum_{j=1}^{k} y_j SC_\mu L_{j,y}$, is central and

$$e^{\mathrm{avg}}(\phi^s, N^{\mathrm{a}}, y) = r^{\mathrm{avg}}(N^{\mathrm{a}}, y) = \left(\mathrm{trace}(C_\nu) - \sum_{j=1}^{k} \| SC_\mu L_{j,y} \|^2 \right)^{1/2},$$

$$e^{\mathrm{avg}}(\phi^s, N^{\mathrm{a}}) = r^{\mathrm{avg}}(N^{\mathrm{a}})$$

$$= \left(\mathrm{trace}(C_\nu) - \sum_{k=1}^{\infty} \int_{B_k} \sum_{j=1}^{k} \| SC_\mu L_{j,y} \|^2 \, \lambda_k(dy) \right)^{1/2}.$$

PROOF: Centrality of the μ-spline algorithm and the formula for the local average radius follow directly from Lemma 3.2.1. The global average radius is obtained by noting that

$$\int_{N^a(F)} r^{\text{avg}}(N^a, y)^2\, \mu_1(dy) = \sum_{k=1}^{\infty} \int_{B_k} r^{\text{avg}}(N^a, y)^2\, \lambda_k(dy). \quad \blacksquare$$

As in Section 5.6.1, we conclude that for every k there exists a vector $y^k \in B_k$ such that

$$\lambda_k(B_k) \sum_{j=1}^{k} \|SC_\mu L_{j,y^k}\|^2 \geq \int_{B_k} \sum_{j=1}^{k} \|SC_\mu L_{j,y}\|^2 \lambda_k(dy).$$

For brevity, denote $M_k = N_{k,y^k}^{\text{non}}$. That is, M_k is nonadaptive information of cardinality k consisting of $L_1, L_{2,y^k}, \dots, L_{k,y^k}$. The average radius of M_k is given by

$$r^{\text{avg}}(M_k)^2 = \text{trace}(C_\nu) - \sum_{j=1}^{k} \|SC_\mu L_{j,y^k}\|^2.$$

From Lemma 5.6.2, we thus conclude

COROLLARY 5.6.1.

$$r^{\text{avg}}(N^a)^2 \geq \sum_{k=1}^{\infty} r^{\text{avg}}(M_k)^2\, \lambda_k(B_k).$$

We need the following

LEMMA 5.6.3. Let $z = \text{card}^{\text{avg}}(N^a)$ be finite and let

$$r = \inf\left\{ \sum_{k=1}^{\infty} r^{\text{avg}}(M_k)^2 a_k \; : \; a_k \geq 0, \sum_{k=1}^{\infty} a_k = 1, \sum_{k=1}^{\infty} k a_k \leq z \right\}.$$

Then there exist two indices k_1 and k_2 and a number $a^* \in [0,1]$ such that

$$r = r^{\text{avg}}(M_{k_1})^2 a^* + r^{\text{avg}}(M_{k_2})^2 (1 - a^*),$$
$$z = k_1 a^* + k_2 (1 - a^*).$$

PROOF: The constant r is a solution of a linear programming problem with an infinite number of parameters a_k. We show that r is also a solution of the same minimization problem with a finite number of parameters a_k,

$$r = \min\left\{ \sum_{k=1}^{m} r_k a_k \; : \; a_k \geq 0, \sum_{k=1}^{m} a_k = 1, \sum_{k=1}^{m} k a_k \leq z \right\}$$

for sufficiently large m, where $r_k = r^{\text{avg}}(M_k)^2$. Let $n = \lceil z \rceil$. Without loss of generality assume that $r_k \le r_n < r_{n-1}$ for $k \ge n$. Thus, there exists a positive constant d such that

$$r_k(1+d) < r_{n-1}, \quad \forall k \ge n.$$

Let $m = \lceil (n(1+d)-1)/d \rceil$. Take a feasible solution $\{a_k\}_{k=1}^\infty$ with $a_{m^*} > 0$ for some $m^* > m$. Since $\sum_{k=1}^m ka_k \le n$, there exists $j \le n-1$ such that $a_j > 0$. Let $t = \min\{a_j, a_{m^*}/(1+d)\}$. Consider now $\{a_k^*\}_{k=1}^\infty$ with $a_k^* = a_k$ for $k \notin \{j, n, m^*\}$, $a_j^* = a_j - t$, $a_n^* = a_n + t(1+d)$, and $a_{m^*}^* = a_{m^*} - td$. This is a feasible solution. Indeed,

$$a_k^* \ge 0, \text{ for every } k, \quad \text{and} \quad \sum_{k=1}^\infty a_k^* = 1,$$

as easily seen from the definition of t. Furthermore,

$$\sum_{k=1}^\infty ka_k^* - \sum_{k=1}^\infty ka_k = t\big((1+d)n - j - dm^*\big)$$

$$\le td\left(\frac{(1+d)n-1}{d} - m^*\right) \le td(m - m^*) \le 0.$$

Hence, $\{a_k^*\}_{k=1}^\infty$ is feasible. Note that

$$\sum_{k=1}^\infty r_k a_k^* - \sum_{k=1}^\infty r_k a_k = t(1+d)r_n - tr_j - tdr_{m^*} \le t\big((1+d)r_n - r_{n-1}\big) < 0.$$

This shows that $\{a_k\}_{k=1}^\infty$ with positive a_{m^*}, for some $m^* > m$, is not a solution of the minimization problem defining r. Thus, the formula for r with finitely many a_k is proven. Since there are two active constraints, the solution is obtained as

$$r = r_{k_1}a^* + r_{k_2}(1-a^*)$$

for some indices $k_1 \le z \le k_2$ and $a^* = (k_2 - z)/(k_2 - k_1)$ if $k_1 < k_2$, and $a^* = 1$ if $k_1 = k_2$. This completes the proof. ∎

We are ready to relate the power of adaptive information N^{a} to information N^* consisting of two nonadaptive information M_{k_1} and M_{k_2}, where k_1 and k_2 are from Lemma 5.6.3. More precisely, let A be any Borel set from

$\mathbb{R}$ whose λ_1-measure equals a^*, i.e., $(2\pi)^{-1/2} \int_A \exp(-t^2/2)\, dt = a^*$, where a^* is from Lemma 5.6.3. Define the information

$$N^*(f) = \begin{cases} M_{k_1}(f) & \text{if } L_1(f) \in A, \\ M_{k_2}(f) & \text{otherwise,} \end{cases}$$

where L_1 is the first functional of the information N^{a} (it is also the first functional of M_{k_1} and M_{k_2}).

THEOREM 5.6.2. *For arbitrary linear problem with $F = F_1$, and arbitrary adaptive information N^{a} with finite cardinality, $\mathrm{card}^{\mathrm{avg}}(N^{\mathrm{a}}) < +\infty$, the information N^* is as powerful as N^{a},*

$$\mathrm{card}^{\mathrm{avg}}(N^*) - \mathrm{card}^{\mathrm{avg}}(N^{\mathrm{a}}) \quad \text{and} \quad r^{\mathrm{avg}}(N^*) \le r^{\mathrm{avg}}(N^{\mathrm{a}}).$$

PROOF: From Corollary 5.6.1 and Lemma 5.6.3 we get $r^{\mathrm{avg}}(N^{\mathrm{a}})^2 \ge r$ since $\lambda_k(B_k) \ge 0$, $\sum_{k=1}^{\infty} \lambda_k(B_k) = 1$ and $\mathrm{card}^{\mathrm{avg}}(N^{\mathrm{a}}) = \sum_{k=1}^{\infty} k\lambda_k(B_k)$. On the other hand,

$$r^{\mathrm{avg}}(N^*)^2 = a^* r^{\mathrm{avg}}(M_{k_1})^2 + (1 - a^*) r^{\mathrm{avg}}(M_{k_2})^2 = r \le r^{\mathrm{avg}}(N^{\mathrm{a}})^2,$$

and

$$\mathrm{card}^{\mathrm{avg}}(N^*) = a^* k_1 + (1 - a^*) k_2 = \mathrm{card}^{\mathrm{avg}}(N^{\mathrm{a}}),$$

as claimed. ∎

Information N^* consists of two nonadaptive information M_{k_1} and M_{k_2}. The structure of N^* is almost as simple as the structure of nonadaptive information. It is enough to evaluate the first functional $y_1 = L_1(f)$, to check if y_1 belongs to the set A and then to proceed with nonadaptive information. Note that checking whether $y \in A$ need not be hard since the set A can be chosen as $(-\infty, \alpha]$, with α so that $\int_{-\infty}^{\alpha} \exp(-t^2/2)\, dt = \sqrt{2\pi}\, a^*$. Since a^* is given *a priori* by Lemma 5.6.3, the number α can be precomputed. Thus, the cost of computing $N^*(f)$ is equal to the cost of one comparison plus either the cost of k_1 information operations with probability a^* or the cost of k_2 information operations with probability $1 - a^*$. The implementation of the μ-spline algorithm ϕ^s which uses N^* is also easy. Indeed, Lemma 5.6.2 yields that

$$\phi^s(y) = \begin{cases} \sum_{j=1}^{k_1} y_j SC_{\mu} L_{j,k_1} & \text{if } y_1 \le \alpha, \\ \\ \sum_{j=1}^{k_2} y_j SC_{\mu} L_{j,k_2} & \text{if } y_1 > \alpha, \end{cases}$$

where $M_{k_1} = [L_{1,k_1}, L_{2,k_1}, \ldots, L_{k_1,k_1}]$ and $M_{k_2} = [L_{1,k_2}, L_{2,k_2}, \ldots, L_{k_2k_2}]$ with $L_{1,k_1} = L_{1,k_2} = L_1$. Thus, $\phi^s(y)$ can be computed at cost equal to the cost of k_1 multiplications and $(k_1 - 1)$ additions in the space G with probability a^* and k_2 multiplications and $(k_2 - 1)$ additions in the space G with probability $1 - a^*$. Information N^* and the algorithm ϕ^s can be also efficiently computed in parallel. Details are left to **E 5.6.2:1**. From this discussion we conclude

COROLLARY 5.6.2.

$$\mathrm{cost}^{\mathrm{avg}}(\phi^s, N^*) \leq (c + 2)\, \mathrm{card}^{\mathrm{avg}}(N^*). \quad \blacksquare$$

We showed that adaptive information N^{a} is not more powerful than information N^* consisting of two appropriately chosen nonadaptive information M_{k_1} and M_{k_2}. We now relate the power of N^{a} to nonadaptive information M_{k_1} or M_{k_2}.

Let $p > 0$. Suppose that $a^* \geq p$. For the nonadaptive information M_{k_1} we then have

$$r^{\mathrm{avg}}(M_{k_1}) \leq \frac{1}{\sqrt{p}}\, r^{\mathrm{avg}}(N^{\mathrm{a}}) \quad \text{and} \quad \mathrm{card}^{\mathrm{avg}}(M_{k_1}) \leq \mathrm{card}^{\mathrm{avg}}(N^{\mathrm{a}}).$$

On the other hand, if $a^* < p$ then for the nonadaptive information M_{k_2} we have

$$r^{\mathrm{avg}}(M_{k_2}) \leq r^{\mathrm{avg}}(N^{\mathrm{a}}) \quad \text{and} \quad \mathrm{card}^{\mathrm{avg}}(M_{k_2}) \leq \frac{1}{1 - p}\, \mathrm{card}^{\mathrm{avg}}(N^{\mathrm{a}}).$$

Choose now p such that $\sqrt{p} = 1 - p$. Then $p = 2/(3 + \sqrt{5}) = 0.3819651\ldots$ and $(1 - p)^{-1} = (1 + \sqrt{5})/2 = 1.618034\ldots$.

This means that increasing the average radius or the average cardinality by at most $1.618\ldots$ times we can find nonadaptive information which is as powerful as adaptive information. We summarize this in

COROLLARY 5.6.3. *For any adaptive information N^{a} with finite average cardinality, there exists nonadaptive information N^{non} such that*

$$\mathrm{card}^{\mathrm{avg}}(N^{\mathrm{non}}) \leq \mathrm{card}^{\mathrm{avg}}(N^{\mathrm{a}}) \quad \text{and} \quad r^{\mathrm{avg}}(N^{\mathrm{non}}) \leq x\, \mathrm{card}^{\mathrm{avg}}(N^{\mathrm{a}})$$

or

$$\mathrm{card}^{\mathrm{avg}}(N^{\mathrm{non}}) \leq x\, \mathrm{card}^{\mathrm{avg}}(N^{\mathrm{a}}) \quad \text{and} \quad r^{\mathrm{avg}}(N^{\mathrm{non}}) \leq r^{\mathrm{avg}}(N^{\mathrm{a}}),$$

where $x = (1 + \sqrt{5})/2 = 1.618\ldots$.

We now illustrate Theorem 5.6.2 by an example showing that adaptive information may indeed be more powerful than nonadaptive information.

EXAMPLE 5.6.1. Let $F = F_1 = \mathbb{R}^2$ be equipped with the Gaussian (normal) measure with mean zero and correlation operator (matrix) identity. Let S be the identity and $\Lambda = F_1^*$. Obviously, the nth minimal average radii are equal to $r^{\mathrm{avg}}(1) = 1$ and $r^{\mathrm{avg}}(n) = 0$ for $n \geq 2$. Consider adaptive information N^{a} of the form

$$N^{\mathrm{a}}(f) = \begin{cases} M_1(f) & \text{if } \langle f, e_1 \rangle \in A, \\ M_2(f) & \text{otherwise.} \end{cases}$$

Here $M_1(f) = \langle f, e_1 \rangle$, $M_2(f) = [\langle f, e_1 \rangle, \langle f, e_2 \rangle]$ for the unit vectors e_i, and A is a Borel set of $\mathbb{R}$ such that $\int_A \exp(-t^2/2) \, dt = \sqrt{2\pi}\, \alpha$, with $\alpha = 2(2 - \sqrt{3}) = 0.535\ldots$. This means that $N^{\mathrm{a}} = M_1$ with probability α, and $N^{\mathrm{a}} = M_2$ with probability $1 - \alpha$. Hence,

$$\mathrm{card}^{\mathrm{avg}}(N^{\mathrm{a}}) = 2 - \alpha \quad \text{and} \quad r^{\mathrm{avg}}(N^{\mathrm{a}}) = \sqrt{\alpha}.$$

Let N^{non} be nonadaptive information. Obviously, if $\mathrm{card}^{\mathrm{avg}}(N^{\mathrm{non}}) = 1 \leq \mathrm{card}^{\mathrm{avg}}(N^{\mathrm{a}})$ then $r^{\mathrm{avg}}(N^{\mathrm{non}}) \geq 1 \geq \alpha^{-1/2} r^{\mathrm{avg}}(N^{\mathrm{a}})$. On the other hand, if N^{non} has cardinality 2 then $r^{\mathrm{avg}}(N^{\mathrm{non}}) = 0 \leq r^{\mathrm{avg}}(N^{\mathrm{a}})$, but $\mathrm{card}^{\mathrm{avg}}(N^{\mathrm{non}}) = x_1 \, \mathrm{card}^{\mathrm{avg}}(N^{\mathrm{a}})$ with $x_1 = 2/(2 - \alpha) = \alpha^{-1/2} = (\sqrt{3} + 1)/2 = 1.366\ldots$. This shows that adaptive information can be more powerful than nonadaptive information.

Example 5.6.1 also shows that Corollary 5.6.3 can hold with the constant x no less than $x_1 = (\sqrt{3} + 1)/2$. We do not know the best constant x^* for which the estimates of Corollary 5.6.3 hold. What we do know is that the number x^* belongs to the interval $[1.366\ldots, 1.618\ldots]$.

We now compare adaptive information N^{a} of cardinality $\mathrm{card}(N^{\mathrm{a}})$ to nonadaptive information N^{non} of cardinality $\lceil \mathrm{card}(N^{\mathrm{a}}) \rceil$. That is, we now permit the cardinality of N^{non} to be at most one greater than the cardinality of N^{a}. We present a condition under which adaptive information is not more powerful than nonadaptive information. This condition is expressed by the convexity of the sequence $\{r^{\mathrm{avg}}(n, \Lambda)^2\}$, where $r^{\mathrm{avg}}(n, \Lambda)$ is nth minimal average radius of nonadaptive information in the class Λ, see Section 5.5. By the *convexity* of a sequence of real numbers $\{\alpha_n\}$ we mean that

$$\alpha_n \leq (\alpha_{n-1} + \alpha_{n+1})/2, \quad \forall n \geq 2.$$

As can be proven by induction, this is equivalent to the inequality

$$\alpha_n \leq t\alpha_i + (1 - t)\alpha_j$$

for any i, j and $t \in [0, 1]$ such that $n = ti + (1 - t)j$ is an integer.

Observe that for the class $\Lambda = F_1^*$, the sequence $r^{\mathrm{avg}}(n)^2 = r^{\mathrm{avg}}(n, F_1^*)^2$ is convex. Indeed, from Theorem 5.2 we have $r^{\mathrm{avg}}(n)^2 = \sum_{j=n+1}^{\infty} \lambda_j$, where λ_j are eigenvalues of the correlation operator C_ν, $\lambda_1 \geq \lambda_2 \geq \cdots \geq 0$. Then

$$\tfrac{1}{2}\left(r^{\mathrm{avg}}(n-1)^2 + r^{\mathrm{avg}}(n+1)^2\right) = r^{\mathrm{avg}}(n)^2 + \tfrac{1}{2}(\lambda_n - \lambda_{n+1}) \geq r^{\mathrm{avg}}(n)^2,$$

as claimed.

Without loss of generality we assume that there exists nth optimal non-adaptive information N_n^* in the class Λ, $r^{\mathrm{avg}}(N_n^*) = r^{\mathrm{avg}}(n, \Lambda)$.

THEOREM 5.6.3. *Consider arbitrary adaptive information N^{a} with finite* $\mathrm{card}^{\mathrm{avg}}(N^{\mathrm{a}})$.

(i) *Let the sequence $\{r^{\mathrm{avg}}(n, \Lambda)^2\}$ be convex. Then the nth optimal nonadaptive information N_n^* with $n = \lceil \mathrm{card}^{\mathrm{avg}}(N^{\mathrm{a}}) \rceil$ is as powerful as N^{a},*

$$r^{\mathrm{avg}}(N_n^*) \leq r^{\mathrm{avg}}(N^{\mathrm{a}}).$$

(ii) *Let the sequence $\{r^{\mathrm{avg}}(n, \Lambda)^2\}$ be semiconvex, i.e., there exist positive numbers a and b, and a convex sequence $\{\alpha_k\}$ such that $a\,\alpha_k \leq r^{\mathrm{avg}}(n, \Lambda)^2 \leq b\,\alpha_k$. Then for n and N_n^* as in (i), we have*

$$r^{\mathrm{avg}}(N_n^*) \leq \sqrt{\frac{b}{a}}\; r^{\mathrm{avg}}(N^{\mathrm{a}}).$$

PROOF: From the proof of Theorem 5.6.2 and from Lemma 5.6.3, we know that

$$r^{\mathrm{avg}}(N^{\mathrm{a}}) \geq \min\left\{r^{\mathrm{avg}}(M_i)^2 d + r^{\mathrm{avg}}(M_j)^2(1-d) : i \leq j,\; d \in [0,1]\right.$$
$$\left. \text{and } id + j(1-d) = x\right\},$$

where $x = \mathrm{card}^{\mathrm{avg}}(N^{\mathrm{a}})$. Observe that $r^{\mathrm{avg}}(M_i)^2 \geq r_i = r^{\mathrm{avg}}(N_k^*)^2$. Thus,

$$r^{\mathrm{avg}}(N^{\mathrm{a}})^2$$
$$\geq r := \min\left\{r_i d + r_j(1-d) : \; i \leq j,\, d \in [0,1] \text{ and } id + j(1-d) = x\right\}.$$

Assume that $\{r_i\}$ is convex. We prove that the last minimum is attained for $i = n - 1$ and $j = n = \lceil x \rceil$. For $i \leq n - 1$ and $j \geq n$, let

$$r(i, j) = r_i d + r_j(1-d) \quad \text{with} \quad d = \frac{j - x}{j - i}.$$

Then $r = \min\{r(i,j) : \; i \leq n - 1 \text{ and } j \geq n\}$. Note that

$$r(i,j) - r(i,n) = \left(\frac{r_i(j-n)}{j-i} + \frac{r_j(n-i)}{j-i} - r_n\right) \frac{x-i}{n-i}.$$

Set $t = (j - n)/(j - i)$. Then $t \in [0,1], 1 - t = (n - i)/(j - i)$, and $n = it + j(1 - t)$. Thus, convexity of $\{r_i\}$ yields that $r(i, j) - r(i, n) \geq 0$, and therefore $r = \min_{1 \leq i \leq n-1} r(i, n)$. Using a similar proof technique, it is easy to show that $r(i, n) - r(n - 1, n) \geq 0$. Thus, $r = r(n - 1, n)$, as claimed.

Since the minimum is attained for $i = n - 1$ and $j = n$, it is not smaller than r_n. Consequently, $r^{\mathrm{avg}}(N_n^*) \leq r^{\mathrm{avg}}(N^{\mathrm{a}})$ which completes the proof of part (i).

Assume now that $\{r_i\}$ is semiconvex. Then $r_i \geq a\,\alpha_i$ with convex $\{\alpha_i\}$. We have

$$r^{\mathrm{avg}}(N^{\mathrm{a}})^2$$
$$\geq a \min \left\{\alpha_i d + \alpha_j (1 - d) : i \leq j, d \in [0, 1] \text{ and } id + j(1 - d) = x\right\} \geq a\,\alpha_n.$$

Since $\alpha_n \geq r^{\mathrm{avg}}(N_n^*)^2/b$, we conclude that $r^{\mathrm{avg}}(N_n^*) \leq \sqrt{b/a}\, r^{\mathrm{avg}}(N^{\mathrm{a}})$, as claimed. ∎

From Theorem 5.6.3 and convexity of the sequence $r^{\mathrm{avg}}(n, F_1^*)$ we conclude

COROLLARY 5.6.4. *For the class* $\Lambda = F_1^*$, *adaptive information is not more powerful than nonadaptive information.*

Notes and Remarks

NR 5.6.2:1 Most results of this section are from Wasilkowski [86a]. Varying cardinality for *nonadaptive* selection of linear functionals is also studied in the statistical literature, see, e.g., Blackwell and Girshick [59], Ferguson [67], DeGroot [70], and Darling [72]. The problem is to find information, called *optimal design*, which is defined in relation to minimizing the expected loss. The loss incorporates the uncertainty and cardinality in one expression; most commonly, loss is a weighted sum of the uncertainty and the cardinality. A typical result is that under suitable assumptions, e.g., μ is Gaussian and the uncertainty is measured by the distance, varying cardinality does not help.

Our approach is different from the statistical one since we consider varying cardinality for *adaptive* selection of linear functionals, and we want to find information of minimal cardinality which guarantees a desired uncertainty. This explains why the result that varying cardinality may help differs from the statistical one mentioned above.

NR 5.6.2:2 Theorem 5.6.2 can be easily generalized for adaptive information with infinite average cardinality, $\mathrm{card}^{\mathrm{avg}}(N^{\mathrm{a}}) = +\infty$. Let $r^* = \lim_k r^{\mathrm{avg}}(N_k^*)^2$. Then $r^* \leq r^{\mathrm{avg}}(N_k^*)^2$ for all k, and $r^* \leq \sum_{k=1}^{\infty} r^{\mathrm{avg}}(N_k^*)^2 \lambda_k(B_k) \leq r^{\mathrm{avg}}(N^{\mathrm{a}})^2$. For any positive δ, there exists an index $k = k(\delta)$ such that $r^{\mathrm{avg}}(N_k^*) \leq \sqrt{r^*} + \delta$. Therefore

$$r^{\mathrm{avg}}(N_k^*) \leq r^{\mathrm{avg}}(N^{\mathrm{a}}) + \delta,$$

and, obviously, $k = \mathrm{card}^{\mathrm{avg}}(N_k^*) < \mathrm{card}^{\mathrm{avg}}(N^{\mathrm{a}}) = \infty$. Thus, the nonadaptive information N_k^* is as powerful as the adaptive information N^{a} modulo an arbitrary small δ.

Exercise

E 5.6.2:1 Consider the parallel evaluation of information N^* and the algorithm ϕ^s from Theorem 5.4.

(i) Assuming p processors, $p > k_1 + k_2$, show that $\phi^*(N^*(f))$ can be computed in time

$$c + 2 + \lceil \log_2 k_1 \rceil a^* + \lceil \log_2 k_2 \rceil (1 - a^*).$$

(ii) What is the cost of computing $\phi^*(N^*(y))$ if the number of processors p is less than $k_1 + k_2$?

E 5.6.2:2 Let $F = F_1 = G = \mathbb{R}^m$ be equipped with the Gaussian (normal) measure with mean zero and covariance operator (matrix) C_μ whose eigenvectors are $e_1, \ldots, e_m$, and eigenvalues are $\beta_1 = \beta_2 = 1$ and $\beta_3 = \cdots = \beta_m = x$, for $x \geq 1$. Let $Se_i = e_i$, $i = 1, 2$ and $Se_i = 0$, otherwise. Let the class Λ be defined by functionals which are inner products with $e_1, e_2 + e_3, \ldots, e_{m-1} + e_m$ and e_m. That is, $\Lambda = \{ \langle \cdot, e_1 \rangle, \langle \cdot, e_m \rangle, \langle \cdot, e_i + e_{i+1} \rangle : i = 2, \ldots, m - 1 \}$. Consider adaptive information N^a of the form

$$N^a(f) = \begin{cases} M_1(f) & \text{if } \langle f, e_1 \rangle \in A, \\ M_2(f) & \text{otherwise.} \end{cases}$$

Here $M_1(f) = \langle f, e_1 \rangle$, $M_2(f) = [\langle f, e_1 \rangle, \langle f, e_m \rangle, \langle f, e_2 + e_3 \rangle, \ldots, \langle f, e_{m-1} + e_m \rangle]$ and A is a Borel set of $\mathbb{R}$ such that $\int_A e^{-t^2/2} \, dt = \sqrt{2\pi} \, x/(x + m)$. Find x and m which minimize the number $p = p(x, m)$ for which

$$\text{card}^{\text{avg}}(N^{\text{non}}) \leq p \, \text{card}^{\text{avg}}(N^a) \quad \text{and} \quad r^{\text{avg}}(N^{\text{non}}) \leq p \, r^{\text{avg}}(N^a)$$

for some nonadaptive information N^{non}.

5.7. Complexity

In this section we analyze the average case complexity of linear problems with $F = F_1$. This will be done using already established results of Section 5 as well as general estimates of complexity presented in Section 4.

The average ε-complexity, $\text{comp}^{\text{avg}}(\varepsilon)$, is estimated from below in terms of the average ε-cardinality number $m^{\text{avg}}(\varepsilon)$. Recall that $m^{\text{avg}}(\varepsilon)$ is the smallest average cardinality of information with average radius at most ε, see Section 4. We now show that the upper bound on $\text{comp}^{\text{avg}}(\varepsilon)$ depends also on $m^{\text{avg}}(\varepsilon)$.

THEOREM 5.7.1. *The average ε-complexity of a linear problem satisfies*

$$c \, m^{\text{avg}}(\varepsilon) \leq \text{comp}^{\text{avg}}(\varepsilon) \leq (c + 2) \, m^{\text{avg}}(\varepsilon),$$

where c is the cost of one information operation. For $c \gg 1$, we have

$$\text{comp}^{\text{avg}}(\varepsilon) \simeq c \, m^{\text{avg}}(\varepsilon).$$

PROOF: It is enough to prove the upper bound, since the lower bound is provided by Theorem 4.1 of Section 4. Without loss of generality assume that $m^{\mathrm{avg}}(\varepsilon)$ is finite and there exists information N such that $r^{\mathrm{avg}}(N) \leq \varepsilon$ and $\mathrm{card}^{\mathrm{avg}}(N) = m^{\mathrm{avg}}(\varepsilon)$. Applying Theorem 5.6.2 to information N, we conclude the existence of information N^* for which $r^{\mathrm{avg}}(N^*) \leq r^{\mathrm{avg}}(N) \leq \varepsilon$ and $\mathrm{card}^{\mathrm{avg}}(N^*) = \mathrm{card}^{\mathrm{avg}}(N) = m^{\mathrm{avg}}(\varepsilon)$. Corollary 5.6.2 states that for the μ-spline algorithm ϕ^s that uses the information N^*, we have $e^{\mathrm{avg}}(\phi^s, N^*) \leq \varepsilon$ and $\mathrm{cost}^{\mathrm{avg}}(\phi^s, N^*) \leq (c+2)\,\mathrm{card}^{\mathrm{avg}}(N^*) = (c+2)m^{\mathrm{avg}}(\varepsilon)$. Thus, $\mathrm{comp}^{\mathrm{avg}}(\varepsilon) \leq \mathrm{cost}(\phi^s, N^*) \leq (c+2)\,m^{\mathrm{avg}}(\varepsilon)$, as claimed. ∎

Theorem 5.7.1 expresses the average ε-complexity in terms of the average ε-cardinality number $m^{\mathrm{avg}}(\varepsilon)$. We now show how $m^{\mathrm{avg}}(\varepsilon)$ is related to the nth minimal radii $r^{\mathrm{avg}}(n, \Lambda)$. Recall that $r^{\mathrm{avg}}(n, \Lambda)$ is the minimal average radius of nonadaptive information of cardinality at most n in the class Λ, see Section 5.5. Let

$$n^{\mathrm{avg}}(\varepsilon) = \min\{n : r^{\mathrm{avg}}(n, \Lambda) \leq \varepsilon\}$$

denote the minimal number of *nonadaptive* evaluations which are needed to find an ε-approximation.

THEOREM 5.7.2.

(i) *Denote* $r_i = r^{\mathrm{avg}}(i, \Lambda)$. *Then*

$$0 \leq m^{\mathrm{avg}}(\varepsilon) - \min\left\{\frac{\varepsilon^2 - r_j^2}{r_i^2 - r_j^2}i + \frac{r_i^2 - \varepsilon^2}{r_i^2 - r_j^2}j : i \leq j \text{ and } r_j \leq \varepsilon \leq r_i\right\} \leq \frac{1}{2},$$

with the convention $+\infty - (+\infty) = 0$, *and*

$$\sup_{x>1} \min\left\{n^{\mathrm{avg}}(x\varepsilon), \frac{x^2 - 1}{x^2}n^{\mathrm{avg}}(\varepsilon)\right\} \leq m^{\mathrm{avg}}(\varepsilon) \leq n^{\mathrm{avg}}(\varepsilon).$$

(ii) *Let* $\{r_i^2\}$ *be convex. Then*

$$\lceil m^{\mathrm{avg}}(\varepsilon)\rceil = n^{\mathrm{avg}}(\varepsilon).$$

PROOF: Recall that the average ε-cardinality number is defined by

$$m^{\mathrm{avg}}(\varepsilon) = \inf\left\{\mathrm{card}^{\mathrm{avg}}(N) : N \text{ such that } r^{\mathrm{avg}}(N) \leq \varepsilon\right\}.$$

From Corollary 5.6.1 we have

$$r^{\text{avg}}(N)^2 \geq \sum_{k=1}^{\infty} r^{\text{avg}}(M_k)^2 a_k,$$

for some nonadaptive information M_k of cardinality k and some numbers a_k, $a_k \geq 0$ and $\sum_{k=1}^{\infty} a_k = 1$. Clearly $r^{\text{avg}}(M_k) \geq r_k$, and

$$\text{card}^{\text{avg}}(N) = \sum_{k=1}^{\infty} k a_k.$$

Therefore

$$m^{\text{avg}}(\varepsilon) \geq \inf \left\{ \sum_{k=1}^{\infty} k a_k \; : \; a_k \geq 0, \; \sum_{k=1}^{\infty} a_k = 1, \; \sum_{k=1}^{\infty} r_k^2 a_k \leq \varepsilon^2 \right\}.$$

Lemma 5.6.3 yields that

$$m^{\text{avg}}(\varepsilon) \geq \min \left\{ ai + (1-a)j : a \in [0,1], \; i \leq j, \; r_i^2 a + r_j^2 (1-a) \leq \varepsilon^2 \right\}$$

$$= m^* := \min \left\{ \frac{\varepsilon^2 - r_j^2}{r_i^2 - r_j^2} i + \frac{r_i^2 - \varepsilon^2}{r_i^2 - r_j^2} j : i \leq j, \; r_j \leq \varepsilon \leq r_i \right\}.$$

Thus, $m^{\text{avg}}(\varepsilon) - m^* \geq 0$. If $m^* = +\infty$ then we are done. If $m^* < +\infty$, then there exists i^* and j^*, $i^* \leq j^*$ such that

$$m^* = a^* i^* + (1 - a^*) j^*,$$

where $a^* = (\varepsilon^2 - r_{j^*}^2)/(r_{i^*}^2 - r_{j^*}^2)$. Let N_{i^*} and N_{j^*} be the i^*th and j^*th optimal nonadaptive information in the class Λ. Let L_{1,i^*} and L_{1,j^*} be their first functionals. Observe that, in general, they are different. Let α be a number such that

$$\frac{1}{\sqrt{2\pi}} \int_{-\infty}^{\alpha} \exp\left(-t^2/2\right) dt = a^*.$$

Define the information N^* as follows. If $a^* \geq 1/2$ then

$$N^*(f) = \begin{cases} N_{i^*}(f) & \text{if } L_{1,i^*}(f) \leq \alpha, \\ N_{j^*}(f) & \text{otherwise.} \end{cases}$$

If $a^* < 1/2$ then

$$N^*(f) = \begin{cases} N_{j^*}(f) & \text{if } L_{1,j^*}(f) \geq \alpha, \\ N_{i^*}(f) & \text{otherwise.} \end{cases}$$

Then

$$r^{\mathrm{avg}}(N^*)^2 = r_{i^*}^2 a^* + r_{j^*}^2 (1 - a^*) = \varepsilon^2.$$

If $a^* \geq 1/2$ then the average cardinality of N^* is given by

$$\mathrm{card}^{\mathrm{avg}}(N^*) \leq 1 + (i^* - 1)a^* + j^*(1 - a^*) = 1 - a^* + m^* \leq \tfrac{1}{2} + m^*.$$

If $a^* < 1/2$, then

$$\mathrm{card}^{\mathrm{avg}}(N^*) \leq 1 + (j^* - 1)(1 - a^*) + i^* a^* = a^* + m^* \leq \tfrac{1}{2} + m^*.$$

In both cases, $m^* \geq \mathrm{card}^{\mathrm{avg}}(N^*) - 1/2$. Since $\mathrm{card}^{\mathrm{avg}}(N^*) \geq m^{\mathrm{avg}}(\varepsilon)$, we conclude that $m^{\mathrm{avg}}(\varepsilon) - m^* \leq 1/2$, as claimed.

We now prove the second part of (i). The inequality $m^{\mathrm{avg}}(\varepsilon) \leq n^{\mathrm{avg}}(\varepsilon)$ is obvious. To prove the lower bound on $m^{\mathrm{avg}}(\varepsilon)$ observe that

$$m^{\mathrm{avg}}(\varepsilon) \geq m^* = a^* i^* + (1 - a^*) j^*$$

for some $a^* \in [0, 1]$ and i^*, j^* such that $i^* \leq m^* \leq j^*$ and $a^* r_{i^*}^2 + (1 - a^*) r_{j^*}^2 \leq \varepsilon^2$.

Take $x > 1$. If $r_{i^*} = r^{\mathrm{avg}}(i^*, \Lambda) \leq x\varepsilon$ then $i^* \geq n^{\mathrm{avg}}(x\varepsilon)$, and therefore $m^{\mathrm{avg}}(\varepsilon) \geq n^{\mathrm{avg}}(x\varepsilon)$. If $r_{i^*} > x\varepsilon$, then $a^* x^2 \varepsilon^2 < a^* r_{i^*}^2 + (1 - a^*) r_{j^*}^2 \leq \varepsilon^2$. Thus, $a^* x^2 < 1$ and $1 - a^* \geq 1 - x^{-2} = (x^2 - 1)/x^2$. Consequently,

$$m^{\mathrm{avg}}(\varepsilon) \geq \frac{x^2 - 1}{x^2} j^* \geq \frac{x^2 - 1}{x^2} n^{\mathrm{avg}}(\varepsilon).$$

Since this holds for any $x > 1$, the proof of (i) is complete.

Assume now that $\{r_i^2\}$ is convex. Then $i^* = n - 1$ and $j^* = n$ with $n = n^{\mathrm{avg}}(\varepsilon)$. If $a^* = 0$ then $m^{\mathrm{avg}}(\varepsilon) = n$. If $a^* > 0$ then

$$n^{\mathrm{avg}}(\varepsilon) - 1 < m^{\mathrm{avg}}(\varepsilon) \leq n^{\mathrm{avg}}(\varepsilon).$$

In both cases, $\lceil m^{\mathrm{avg}}(\varepsilon) \rceil = n^{\mathrm{avg}}(\varepsilon)$, as claimed. ∎

We illustrate Theorem 5.7.2 by two sequences $\{r^{\mathrm{avg}}(i, \Lambda)\}$.

EXAMPLE 5.7.1.

(i) Suppose that $r^{\mathrm{avg}}(i, \Lambda) = i^{-\alpha}$ for some $\alpha > 1$. Since this sequence is convex, Theorem 5.7.2 yields that

$$\lceil m^{\mathrm{avg}}(\varepsilon) \rceil = n^{\mathrm{avg}}(\varepsilon) = \lceil \varepsilon^{-1/\alpha} \rceil.$$

We have chosen such a sequence to see how tight the estimates of the second part of Theorem 5.7.2 (i) are. Taking $x = \alpha$ we get for small ε,

$$\min\left\{1 - \alpha^{-2}, \alpha^{-1/\alpha}\right\} n^{\mathrm{avg}}(\varepsilon)\left(1 + o(1)\right) \le m^{\mathrm{avg}}(\varepsilon) \le n^{\mathrm{avg}}(\varepsilon).$$

Thus, for large α, we have rather tight estimates.

(ii) Suppose that $r^{\mathrm{avg}}(i, \Lambda) = \exp(-\lambda i^p)$ for $\lambda > 0$ and $p < 1$. This sequence needs not be convex. We have

$$n^{\mathrm{avg}}(\varepsilon) = \left\lceil \left(\frac{\ln(1/\varepsilon)}{\lambda}\right)^{1/p} \right\rceil.$$

Taking $x = \ln(1/\varepsilon)$ we get for small ε

$$\min\left\{1 - \ln^{-2}\frac{1}{\varepsilon}, \left(1 - \frac{\ln\ln\varepsilon^{-1}}{\ln\varepsilon^{-1}}\right)^{1/p}\right\} n^{\mathrm{avg}}(\varepsilon)\left(1 + o(1)\right) \le m^{\mathrm{avg}}(\varepsilon) \le n^{\mathrm{avg}}(\varepsilon).$$

Thus, $m^{\mathrm{avg}}(\varepsilon) = n^{\mathrm{avg}}(\varepsilon)(1 + o(1))$.

The proof of Theorem 5.7.2 presents the information N^* whose average cardinality is close to $m^{\mathrm{avg}}(\varepsilon)$. Observe that if the first functionals L_{1,i^*} and L_{1,j^*} are equal then $\mathrm{card}^{\mathrm{avg}}(N^*) = m^*$. Indeed, assume for instance that $a^* \ge 1/2$. Then

$$\mathrm{card}^{\mathrm{avg}}(N^*) = 1 + (i^* - 1)a^* + (j^* - 1)(1 - a^*) = i^*a^* + j^*(1 - a^*) = m^*.$$

Thus we have

COROLLARY 5.7.1. *If the first functionals L_{1,i^*} and L_{1,j^*} in the nth optimal information for the class Λ are the same for every $n \ge 1$, then*

$$m^{\mathrm{avg}}(\varepsilon) = \min\left\{\frac{\varepsilon^2 - r_j^2}{r_i^2 - r_j^2}\, i + \frac{r_i^2 - \varepsilon^2}{r_i^2 - r_j^2}\, j : \ i \le j \text{ and } r_j \le \varepsilon \le r_i\right\}.$$

Let ϕ^s be the μ-spline algorithm that uses N^*. For $a^* \ge 1/2$, we have

$$\phi^s(y) = \begin{cases} \sum_{i=1}^{i^*} y_i S(C_\mu L_{i,i^*}) & \text{if } y_1 \le \alpha, \\[2ex] \sum_{i=1}^{j^*} y_i S(C_\mu L_{i,j^*}) & \text{otherwise.} \end{cases}$$

For $a^* < 1/2$, we have

$$
\phi^s(y) = \begin{cases} \sum_{i=1}^{j^*} y_i S(C_\mu L_{i,j^*}) & \text{if } y_1 \geq \alpha, \\[2mm] \sum_{i=1}^{i^*} y_i S(C_\mu L_{i,i^*}) & \text{otherwise,} \end{cases}
$$

where the functionals L_{i,i^*} and L_{i,j^*} form the information N_{i^*} and N_{j^*}, respectively. Then $e^{\mathrm{avg}}(\phi^s, N^*) = \varepsilon$ and $\mathrm{cost}^{\mathrm{avg}}(\phi^s, N^*) \leq (c+2)\left(m^{\mathrm{avg}}(\varepsilon) + 1/2\right)$. From this and Theorems 5.7.1 and 5.7.2 we conclude

COROLLARY 5.7.2. *The information N^* and the algorithm ϕ^s are almost optimal,*

$$
c\, m^{\mathrm{avg}}(\varepsilon) \leq \mathrm{comp}^{\mathrm{avg}}(\varepsilon) \leq \mathrm{cost}^{\mathrm{avg}}(\phi^s, N^*) \leq (c+2)\left(m^{\mathrm{avg}}(\varepsilon) + \tfrac{1}{2}\right).
$$

For large c and $m^{\mathrm{avg}}(\varepsilon)$, we have

$$
\mathrm{comp}^{\mathrm{avg}}(\varepsilon) \simeq \mathrm{cost}^{\mathrm{avg}}(\phi^s, N^*) \simeq c\, m^{\mathrm{avg}}(\varepsilon).
$$

We now discuss the complexity for the class $\Lambda = F_1^*$. Recall that C_ν is the correlation operator of the Gaussian measure $\nu = \mu S^{-1}$ defined on the separable Hilbert space G of solution elements. For $\lambda_n^* > 0$, the nth optimal nonadaptive information is given by

$$
N_n^*(f) = \left[\frac{1}{\sqrt{\lambda_1}}\langle S(f), \eta_1^* \rangle, \ldots, \frac{1}{\sqrt{\lambda_n^*}}\langle S(f), \eta_n^* \rangle \right],
$$

where (λ_i^*, η_i^*) are eigenpairs of C_ν, $\lambda_1^* \geq \lambda_2^* \geq \cdots \geq 0$. In this case, the assumption of Corollary 5.7.1 holds. Furthermore, the sequence $\{r_i^2\}$ is convex. Therefore, we have

COROLLARY 5.7.3. *For the class $\Lambda = F_1^*$,*

$$
m^{\mathrm{avg}}(\varepsilon) = a^*(n^* - 1) + (1 - a^*)n^*,
$$

where $a^* = (\varepsilon^2 - r_{n^*}^2)/(r_{n^*-1}^2 - r_{n^*}^2)$, $r_n = \sqrt{\sum_{i=n+1}^{\infty} \lambda_i^*}$, and

$$
n^* = \lceil m^{\mathrm{avg}}(\varepsilon) \rceil = n^{\mathrm{avg}}(\varepsilon) = \min\left\{ n : \sum_{i=n+1}^{\infty} \lambda_i^* \leq \varepsilon^2 \right\}
$$

We illustrate Corollary 5.7.3 by two sequences of the eigenvalues $\{\lambda_i^*\}$.

EXAMPLE 5.7.2.

(i) Let $\lambda_i^* = i^{-p}$ for some $p > 1$. Then for the class $\Lambda = F_1^*$ we have

$$m^{\mathrm{avg}}(\varepsilon) = (p-1)^{-1/(p-1)}\,\varepsilon^{-2/(p-1)}\,(1+o(1)) \quad \text{as } \varepsilon \to 0.$$

For large c, Theorem 5.7.1 yields

$$\mathrm{comp}^{\mathrm{avg}}(\varepsilon) \simeq c\,(p-1)^{-1/(p-1)}\,\varepsilon^{-2/(p-1)}.$$

(ii) Let $\lambda_i^* = \rho^i$ for some $\rho \in (0,1)$. Then for the class $\Lambda = F_1^*$ we have

$$m^{\mathrm{avg}}(\varepsilon) = \frac{\ln\left((1-\rho)\varepsilon^2\right)}{\ln \rho}\,(1+o(1)) \quad \text{as } \varepsilon \to 0,$$

and for large c, Theorem 5.7.1 yields

$$\mathrm{comp}^{\mathrm{avg}}(\varepsilon) \simeq c\,\frac{\ln\left((1-\rho)\varepsilon^2\right)}{\ln \rho}.$$

It may happen that the value a^* in Corollary 5.7.3 is an arbitrary number in the interval $[0,1]$, see **E 5.7:1**. In any case, $m^{\mathrm{avg}}(\varepsilon) \in (n^*-1, n^*]$ and at most one extra information operation is needed when the nonadaptive information $N_{n^*}^*$ is used. The μ-spline algorithm ϕ^s that uses $N_{n^*}^*$ is of the form

$$\phi^s\left(N_{n^*}^*(f)\right) = \sum_{j=1}^{n^*} \langle S(f), \eta_j^* \rangle\, \eta_j^*.$$

Combining the results of this section we have

COROLLARY 5.7.4. *Let $\Lambda = F_1^*$. The nonadaptive information $N_{n^*}^*$ and the algorithm ϕ^s are almost optimal,*

$$c\,(n^*-1) \le \mathrm{comp}^{\mathrm{avg}}(\varepsilon) \le \mathrm{cost}^{\mathrm{avg}}(\phi^s, N_{n^*}^*) \le (c+2)\,n^*.$$

For large c and n^*,

$$\mathrm{comp}^{\mathrm{avg}}(\varepsilon) \simeq \mathrm{cost}^{\mathrm{avg}}(\phi^s, N_{n^*}^*) \simeq c\,n^* = c \min\left\{ n : \sum_{i=n+1}^{\infty} \lambda_i^* \le \varepsilon^2 \right\}.$$

In the worst case setting, we showed that an arbitrary increasing continuous function g with $\lim_{x\to\infty} g(x) = +\infty$ can be the complexity of an appropriately chosen linear problem with $\Lambda = F_1^*$, see Theorem 5.8.2 of Chapter 4. What is the situation in the average case setting? Is it still true that any increasing function g can be the average complexity of a linear problem?

Unlike the worst case, the answer is no. Since the average ε-complexity depends on the *convex* sequence $r^{\text{avg}}(n)^2$, we need to assume convexity of a function which is the square of the reciprocal of g^{-1}.

THEOREM 5.7.3. *Let $h(x) = (g^{-1}(x))^{-2}$ for $x > g(0)$. If h is convex then there exists a linear problem such that the ε-average complexity in the class $\Lambda = F_1^*$ is given by*

$$c \left\lceil g\left(\varepsilon^{-1}\right)\right\rceil \leq \text{comp}^{\text{avg}}(\varepsilon) \leq (c+2)\left\lceil g\left(\varepsilon^{-1}\right)\right\rceil, \ \forall \varepsilon \leq \varepsilon_0 = 1/g^{-1}(\lfloor g(0)\rfloor + 1).$$

PROOF: Let $F_1 = G$ be a separable Hilbert space and let $S(f) = f$ be the identity operator. Define $\lambda_i^* = h(i-1) - h(i)$ for $i - 1 \geq n^* := \lfloor g(0)\rfloor + 1$, and $\lambda_i^* = 2\lambda_{i+1}^* - \lambda_{i+2}^*$ for $i = n^*, n^* - 1, \ldots, 1$. Since g is increasing, h is decreasing. Then $\lambda_i^* > 0$. Since h is convex, $\lambda_i^* \geq \lambda_{i+1}^*, \forall i$, and $\sum_{i=1}^{\infty} \lambda_i^*$ is finite. Thus, there exists a Gaussian measure μ with mean zero whose correlation operator C_μ has the eigenvalues λ_i^*. Observe that for $n \geq n^*$,

$$\sum_{i=n+1}^{\infty} \lambda_i^* = h(n) \leq \varepsilon^2 \ \text{ iff } \ g^{-1}(n) \geq \varepsilon^{-1}.$$

Thus, for $\varepsilon \leq \varepsilon_0$ we have $m^{\text{avg}}(\varepsilon) = \min\{n : h(n) \leq \varepsilon\} = \lceil g(\varepsilon^{-1})\rceil$. Due to Theorem 5.7.1, this completes the proof. ∎

We now show that convexity of the function h is, in general, necessary to conclude that $c\lceil g(\varepsilon^{-1})\rceil$ is roughly the average ε-complexity.

EXAMPLE 5.7.3. Consider the function

$$g(x) = \begin{cases} x^d & \text{for } x \in [0, 3^{1/d}], \\ 3 + (x - 3^{1/d})/(4 - 3^{1/d}) & \text{otherwise}, \end{cases}$$

where $d > d^* = 2\ln 3/\ln(16/11) = 5.864058\ldots$. Observe that the function h is now given by

$$h(x) = \begin{cases} x^{-2/d} & \text{for } x \in [0, 3], \\ \left(3^{1/d} + (4 - 3^{1/d})(x - 3)\right)^{-2} & \text{otherwise}. \end{cases}$$

The function h is *not* convex. Indeed, it is not true that

$$3^{-2/d} = h(3) = h(\tfrac{1}{3} + \tfrac{2}{3}4) \leq \tfrac{1}{3}h(1) + \tfrac{2}{3}h(4) = \tfrac{3}{8} \text{ for } d > d^*.$$

Suppose there exists a linear problem whose average ε-cardinality number satisfies

$$\lceil m^{\text{avg}}(\varepsilon) \rceil = \lceil g(\varepsilon^{-1}) \rceil = \min\left\{ n : \sum_{i=n+1}^{\infty} \lambda_i^* \le \varepsilon^2 \right\}, \ \forall \varepsilon \le \varepsilon_0$$

with $\varepsilon_0 = 1/g^{-1}(\lfloor g(0) \rfloor + 1) = 1$ and λ_i^* being the eigenvalues of the correlation operator C_ν, $\lambda_1^* \ge \lambda_2^* \ge \cdots \ge 0$.

Let $\varepsilon = 1/4$. Then $g(4) = 4$ and $\sum_{i=5}^{\infty} \lambda_i^* \le 1/16$. Setting $\varepsilon = 3^{-1/d}$ and $\varepsilon = 1$, we conclude that

$$3^{-2/d} < \sum_{i=3}^{\infty} \lambda_i^* \le \sum_{i=2}^{\infty} \lambda_i^* \le 1.$$

From this we estimate λ_2^* by

$$\lambda_2^* \le 1 - \sum_{i=3}^{\infty} \lambda_i^* \le 1 - 3^{-2/d},$$

and

$$\lambda_2^* \ge (\lambda_3^* + \lambda_4^*)/2 \ge \left(3^{-2/d} - \sum_{i=5}^{\infty} \lambda_i^* \right)/2 \ge \left(3^{-2/d} - 2^{-4} \right)/2.$$

This implies that $3^{-2/d} - 2^{-4} \le 2(1 - 3^{-2/d})$, which is equivalent to $3^{-2/d} \le 11/16$. This is not true for $d > d^* = 2 \ln 3 / \ln(16/11) = 5.864058\ldots$. Thus, there exists no linear problem for which $m^{\text{avg}}(\varepsilon) = \lceil g(\varepsilon^{-1}) \rceil$.

Although the average complexity cannot be an arbitrary increasing function, it may go to infinity arbitrarily fast as ε goes to zero. Indeed, take

$$g(x) = \underbrace{\exp(\exp(\cdots((\exp(x^2)\cdots)\cdots))}_{k \text{ times}}.$$

It is easy to check that $h(x) = (g^{-1}(x))^{-2}$ is convex. Therefore, Theorem 5.7.3 implies that there exists a linear problem such that for small ε,

$$\text{comp}^{\text{avg}}(\varepsilon) \simeq c \lceil g(\varepsilon^{-1}) \rceil.$$

Thus, the average ε-complexity is k-fold exponential and k can be arbitrarily large. See also **E 5.7:2**, where such a linear problem is presented in more detail.

Notes and Remarks

NR 5.7:1 A major part of this section is based on Wasilkowski [86a].

Exercises

E 5.7:1 Let $a \in [0,1]$ and let λ_i^* be arbitrary eigenvalues. Find ε such that a^* in Corollary 5.7.3 is equal to a.

E 5.7:2 Consider the linear problem $S(f) = f$ with $F_1 = G$, and the Gaussian measure μ with mean zero and the correlation operator C_μ with eigenvalues $\lambda_i^* = \beta_i - \beta_{i+1}$. Here $\beta_i = 1/\ln(k, i-1)$, with $\ln(k, x) = \underbrace{\ln \ln \ldots \ln}_{k \text{ times}}(x + d_k)$ and $d_k = \underbrace{\exp(\cdots \exp}_{k \text{ times}}(1) \cdots)$. Show that for small ε

$$\text{comp}^{\text{avg}}(\varepsilon) = c \underbrace{\exp(\cdots \exp}_{k \text{ times}} (\varepsilon^{-2}) \cdots)(1 + o(1))(1 + 0(c^{-1})),$$

$$\lambda_i^* = \left\{ i \ln(1, i) \cdots \ln(k-1, i) \ln^2(k, i) \right\}^{-1} (1 + o(1)).$$

5.8. Linear Problems for Bounded Domains

So far, we have analyzed linear problems in the average case setting assuming that F is the whole space, $F = F_1$. In this section we extend this analysis to the case when

$$F = B_q = \{f \in F_1 : \|f\| \le q\}$$

is the ball of a finite radius q. As mentioned earlier, such a set is needed to guarantee that the complexity in the worst case setting is finite. Recall that the ball $F = B_q$ is equipped with the probability measure μ_q,

$$\mu_q(A) = \frac{\mu(A \cap F)}{\mu(F)}, \quad \text{for any Borel set } A,$$

where μ is the Gaussian measure with mean zero and a correlation operator C_μ. Observe that for finite q the measure μ_q is not Gaussian. However for large q, μ_q "resembles" μ. To preserve essential properties of a Gaussian measure, it is necessary to assume that q is not too small. However, since the tail of a Gaussian measure goes to zero exponentially fast, we need only a mild assumption on q.

Let $\text{comp}^{\text{avg}}(\varepsilon, q)$ be the average complexity of a linear problem with $F = B_q$. As before, $\text{comp}^{\text{avg}}(\varepsilon) = \text{comp}^{\text{avg}}(\varepsilon, +\infty)$ denotes the average complexity for the whole space, $F = F_1$.

It is intuitively obvious that for large q, the average complexity should be close to the average complexity for the whole space. We prove this in quantitative terms even for moderate q. We find lower and upper bounds on the average complexity for the ball B_q in terms of the average complexity for the whole space. These bounds are quite tight. Under mild assumptions, the average complexities for finite q and $q = +\infty$ differ by a factor $1 + O\left(\exp(-q^2b)\right)$, where b depends only on the given Gaussian measure μ.

Relations between $\mathrm{comp}^{\mathrm{avg}}(\varepsilon, q)$ and $\mathrm{comp}^{\mathrm{avg}}(\varepsilon)$ depend on the measure $\mu(B_q)$ of the ball B_q. More precisely, they depend on how fast $\mu(B_q)$ goes to one as q tends to infinity. For Gaussian measures, $\mu(B_q)$ goes to one exponentially fast. Indeed, from Borell [75, 76] we have

$$\mu(B_q) = 1 - \exp\left(-q^2 a^*\left(1 + o(1)\right)\right) \quad \text{as} \quad q \to +\infty, \tag{1}$$

where

$$a^* = \left(2 \sup\{\|L\|_\mu \, : \, L \in F_1^*, \, \|L\| = 1\}\right)^{-1}. \tag{2}$$

The difference $1 - \mu(B_q)$ can be also estimated using Fernique's theorem, see for instance Araujo and Giné [80,p.141], which states together with (1) that $\int_{F_1} \exp\left(a\|f\|^2\right) \mu(df) < +\infty$ for any number a such that $a < a^*$. Then

$$\begin{aligned} 1 - \mu(B_q) &= \int_{\|f\|>q} \mu(df) \le \exp\left(-q^2 a\right) \int_{\|f\|>q} \exp\left(a\|f\|^2\right) \mu(df) \\ &< \exp\left(-q^2 a\right) \int_{F_1} \exp\left(a\|f\|^2\right) \mu(df). \end{aligned} \tag{3}$$

Let $x = 1 - \mu(B_q)$. In what follows we assume that q is chosen so that

$$1 - x - \sqrt{3x} > 0. \tag{4}$$

That is, $\mu(B_q) \ge \left(\sqrt{21} - 3\right)/2 \simeq 0.8$. Due to (1) and (3), we have for any $a < a^*$,

$$x \le \frac{5 - \sqrt{21}}{2} \simeq 0.2, \quad x \le \exp\left(-q^2 a\right) \int_{F_1} \exp\left(a\|f\|^2\right) \mu(df), \tag{5}$$

$$\text{and} \quad x = \exp\left(-q^2 a^*\left(1 + o(1)\right)\right) \quad \text{as} \quad q \to +\infty.$$

REMARK 5.8.1. We illustrate (5) for a separable Hilbert space F_1. Let β_i be the eigenvalues of the correlation operator C_μ of μ. Then $a^* = (2 \max \beta_i)^{-1}$, and for $a < a^*$

$$\int_{F_1} \exp\left(a\|f\|^2\right) \mu(df) = \prod_{i=1}^{\infty} \frac{1}{\sqrt{1 - 2a\beta_i}}.$$

Since trace$(C_\mu) = \sum_{i=1}^{\infty} \beta_i$, the above integral is no greater than $\left(1 - 2a\ \text{trace}(C_\mu)\right)^{-1/2}$ for $a < \left(2\ \text{trace}(C_\mu)\right)^{-1}$. Thus,

$$0 \leq x \leq \frac{\exp\left(-q^2 a\right)}{\sqrt{1 - 2a\ \text{trace}(C_\mu)}}.$$

Assume that $\beta_i = i^{-p}$ for some $p > 1$. Then trace$(C_\mu) = \zeta(p)$ is Riemann's zeta function at p and $\zeta(p) \leq 1 + 1/(p-1)$. For $a = (p-1)/(4p)$, we get

$$0 \leq x \leq \sqrt{2}\ \exp\left(\frac{-q^2(p-1)}{4p}\right).$$

We are ready to state relations between the two average complexities for the ball B_q and for the whole space.

THEOREM 5.8.1.

(i) Let q be so that $x = 1 - \mu(B_q)$ satisfies (4). Then

$$\frac{c}{c+2}\ \frac{1 - x - \sqrt{3x}}{1 - x}\ \text{comp}^{\text{avg}}\left(\varepsilon\sqrt{\frac{1-x}{1 - x - \sqrt{3x}}}\right)$$

$$\leq \text{comp}^{\text{avg}}(\varepsilon, q) \leq \frac{1}{1-x}\ \text{comp}^{\text{avg}}\left(\varepsilon\sqrt{1-x}\right). \tag{6}$$

(ii) If

$$\text{comp}^{\text{avg}}\left(\varepsilon(1+\delta)\right) = \text{comp}^{\text{avg}}(\varepsilon)\left(1 + O(\delta)\right) \quad \text{as} \quad \delta \to 0 \tag{7}$$

then for any $a < a^*$ we have

$$\text{comp}^{\text{avg}}(\varepsilon, q) = \text{comp}^{\text{avg}}(\varepsilon)\left(1 + o\left(\exp\left(-q^2 a/2\right)\right)\right)\left(1 + O\left(c^{-1}\right)\right)$$

as q and c go to infinity.

The proof of this theorem is given in Section 5.8.2 and is based on the analysis of Section 5.8.1.

Notes and Remarks

NR 5.8:1 This section is based on Woźniakowski [87].

5.8.1. Average Radius of Information

To get complexity bounds, we study the average radius $r^{\text{avg}}(N, q)$ for adaptive information N. Recall that $r^{\text{avg}}(N, q)$ is the minimal average error of algorithms using N for problem elements from the ball B_q.

We find relations between $r^{\mathrm{avg}}(N,q)$ and $r^{\mathrm{avg}}(N) = r^{\mathrm{avg}}(N,+\infty)$. One may hope that both radii are essentially the same for large q. More precisely, one may hope that there exists a function $\delta : \mathbb{R}_+ \to \mathbb{R}_+$, $\lim_{q\to\infty} \delta(q) = 0$ such that for any adaptive information N we have

$$r^{\mathrm{avg}}(N,q) = \big(1 + \delta(N,q)\big)\, r^{\mathrm{avg}}(N) \qquad \text{with} \qquad |\delta(N,q)| \le \delta(q). \qquad (8)$$

We show this for *nonadaptive* information N, i.e., for $N = [L_1, L_2, \ldots, L_k]$, $L_i \in \Lambda$, with $\delta(q) = \sqrt{3(1 - \mu(B_q))} = o\big(\exp\big(-q^2 a/2\big)\big)$, see (1)–(3).

For adaptive information, (8) is in general false. For any finite q, there exists adaptive information N such that $r^{\mathrm{avg}}(N,q) = 0$ and $r^{\mathrm{avg}}(N) > 0$, as illustrated by the following example.

EXAMPLE 5.8.1. Let $F_1 = G$ be a separable Hilbert space with an orthonormal system $\{\zeta_i\}$. Define $y_1 = L_1(f) = \langle f, \zeta_1 \rangle$ and

$$y_i = L_{i,y}(f) = \begin{cases} \langle f, \zeta_i \rangle & \text{if } \sum_{j=1}^{i-1} y_j^2 \le q^2, \\ 0 & \text{otherwise.} \end{cases}$$

Then $N(f) = [L_1(f), L_{2,y}(f), \ldots]$ is adaptive. Observe that for $\|f\| \le q$, we can recover f exactly from $N(f)$. Therefore the algorithm $\phi(N(f)) = S(f)$ is well defined and its average error is zero. Thus, $r^{\mathrm{avg}}(N,q) = 0$.

On the other hand, $N(f) = \langle f, \zeta_1 \rangle$ for $|\langle f, \zeta_1 \rangle| > q$. Therefore,

$$r^{\mathrm{avg}}(N)^2 \ge \int_{|\langle f,\zeta_1\rangle|>q} \|S(f) - \langle f,\zeta_1\rangle\, S\zeta_1\|^2\, \mu(df),$$

which is positive for injective S and C_μ. Thus, (8) is false in this case.

For adaptive information N, we relax (8) by showing that

$$r^{\mathrm{avg}}(N,q) \ge \big(1 - \delta(q)\big) r^{\mathrm{avg}}(N^*) \qquad (9)$$

for some information N^* whose cardinality is roughly the same as the cardinality of N and whose structure is simpler than the structure of N. This will be done by applying the results of Section 5.6.

Recall that the average cardinality of adaptive information N is given by $\mathrm{card}^{\mathrm{avg}}(N,q) = \int_{B_q} n(f)\, \mu_q(df)$. As before, we denote $\mathrm{card}^{\mathrm{avg}}(N,+\infty)$ by $\mathrm{card}^{\mathrm{avg}}(N)$.

The function $\delta(q)$ in (9) will be given in terms of $x = 1 - \mu(B_q)$, and we shall have $\delta(q) = o\big(\exp\big(-q^2 a/2\big)\big)$ as $q \to +\infty$.

To define the information N^* in (9), we proceed as in Section 5.6. For a vector $y \in N(B_q) \cap \mathbb{R}^k$, define

$$N_y(f) = [L_{1,y}(f), L_{2,y}(f), \ldots, L_{k,y}(f)]. \qquad (10)$$

Let $r^{\mathrm{avg}}(N_y)$ denote its average radius. Let

$$r_k = \inf_{y \in N(B_q) \cap \mathbb{R}^k} r^{\mathrm{avg}}(N_y), \qquad (11)$$

with the convention that $r_k = 0$ if $N(B_q) \cap \mathbb{R}^k = \emptyset$. Without loss of generality we assume that the infimum in (11) is attained, and so there exists M_k such that $r_k = r^{\mathrm{avg}}(M_k)$.

We state relations between $r^{\mathrm{avg}}(N, q)$, $r^{\mathrm{avg}}(N)$, and $r^{\mathrm{avg}}(N^*)$.

THEOREM 5.8.2. *Let q be such that $x = 1 - \mu(B_q)$ satisfies (4).*

(i) *Let N be nonadaptive information. Then*

$$r^{\mathrm{avg}}(N, q) \geq r^{\mathrm{avg}}(N)\sqrt{1 - \sqrt{3x}},$$
$$r^{\mathrm{avg}}(N, q) = \left(1 + \delta(N, q)\right) r^{\mathrm{avg}}(N), \quad \text{where } |\delta(N, q)| \leq \sqrt{3x}.$$

(ii) *Let N be adaptive information with $n(f) \equiv k$. Then*

$$r^{\mathrm{avg}}(N, q) \geq r^{\mathrm{avg}}(M_k)\sqrt{1 - \sqrt{3x}}.$$

(iii) *Let N be arbitrary adaptive information with finite $\mathrm{card}^{\mathrm{avg}}(N)$. Then there exists information N^* such that*

$$r^{\mathrm{avg}}(N, q) \geq r^{\mathrm{avg}}(N^*)\sqrt{\frac{1 - x - \sqrt{3x}}{1 - x}},$$

$$\mathrm{card}^{\mathrm{avg}}(N, q) \geq \mathrm{card}^{\mathrm{avg}}(N^*)\frac{1 - x - \sqrt{3x}}{1 - x},$$

and N^* consists of two nonadaptive information

$$N^*(f) = \begin{cases} M_{k_1}(f) & \text{if } L_1(f) \in A, \\ M_{k_2}(f) & \text{otherwise,} \end{cases}$$

for some indices k_1 and k_2, and a Borel set A of $\mathbb{R}$.

PROOF: Let N be adaptive information with normalized $L_{i,y}$, $\langle L_{i,y}, L_{j,y} \rangle_\mu = \delta_{i,j}$. Let $\nu(\cdot|y) = \mu_2(S^{-1}(\cdot)|y)$ be the conditional measure on the space G of solution elements. Then $\nu(\cdot|y)$ is Gaussian on the separable Hilbert space G with mean $S\sigma(y)$ and correlation operator $C_{\nu,y}$, as shown in Section 5.6. The operator $C_{\nu,y}$ is self-adjoint, nonnegative definite, and has a finite trace. Let $\lambda_i = \lambda_i(y)$ and $\zeta_i = \zeta_i(y)$ be its orthonormal eigenpairs, $C_{\nu,y}\zeta_i = \lambda_i\zeta_i$, $\lambda_1 \geq \lambda_2 \geq \cdots \geq 0$ and $\sum_{i=1}^{\infty} \lambda_i < +\infty$.

Let ϕ be an arbitrary algorithm using N with a finite average error. Since $\|S(f) - \phi(N(f))\|^2 = \sum_{i=1}^{\infty} \langle S(f) - \phi(N(f)), \zeta_i(N(f)) \rangle^2$, its average error can be expressed by

$$u := \mu(B_q)\, e(\phi, N, q)^2 = \int_{N(F)} \int_{F_1} \sum_{i=1}^{\infty} \langle S(f) - \phi(y), \zeta_i(y) \rangle^2 \tag{12}$$
$$\times\, (1 - b(f, q))\, \mu_2(df|y)\, \mu_1(df),$$

where $b(\cdot, q)$ is the characteristic function of the complement of the ball B_q, i.e., $b(f, q) = 1$ for $\|f\| > q$, and $b(f, q) = 0$ otherwise. For $\lambda_i = \lambda_i(y) > 0$, define $\eta_i = \eta_i(y) = \lambda_i^{-1/2} \zeta_i$ and

$$g_i(y) = \int_{F_1} \langle S(f) - \phi(y), \eta_i \rangle^2\, b(f, q)\, \mu_2(df|y).$$

Note that

$$0 \le g_i(y) \le \int_{F_1} \langle S(f) - \phi(y), \eta_i \rangle^2\, \mu_2(df|y)$$
$$= \int_G \langle g - \phi(y), \eta_i \rangle^2\, \nu(dg|y)$$
$$= \frac{1}{\sqrt{2\pi}} \int_{\mathbb{R}} (t - \langle \phi(y), \eta_i \rangle)^2\, \exp\left(\frac{-(t - \langle S\sigma(y), \eta_i \rangle)^2}{2} \right) dt \tag{13}$$
$$= 1 + \langle S\sigma(y) - \phi(y), \eta_i \rangle^2 = 1 + e_i^2,$$

where $e_i = e_i(y) = \langle S\sigma(y) - \phi(y), \eta_i \rangle$. Furthermore,

$$g_i^2(y) \le \int_{F_1} \langle S(f) - \phi(y), \eta_i \rangle^4\, \mu_2(df|y) \int_{F_1} b(f, q)\, \mu_2(df|y)$$
$$= \frac{1}{\sqrt{2\pi}} \int_{\mathbb{R}} (t - e_i)^4\, \exp\left(-t^2/2 \right) dt\, (1 - \mu_2(B_q|y)) \tag{14}$$
$$= (3 + 6e_i^2 + e_i^4)(1 - \mu_2(B_q|y)).$$

We now rewrite (12) as

$$u = \int_{N(F)} \sum_{i=1}^{\infty} \lambda_i(y)\, \left(1 + e_i^2(y) - g_i(y) \right) \mu_1(dy). \tag{15}$$

The last series is convergent since it is no greater than $\sum_{i=1}^{\infty} \lambda_i(y) + \|S\sigma(y) - \phi(y)\|^2$. Let

$$h(y) = \frac{\sum_{i=1}^{\infty} \lambda_i(y) g_i(y)}{\sum_{i=1}^{\infty} \lambda_i(y) \left(1 + e_i^2(y) \right)}.$$

Then (13) yields that $h(y) \in [0, 1]$, and (14) yields that

$$h(y) \leq \sup_i \frac{g_i(y)}{1 + e_i^2(y)} \leq \sqrt{1 - \mu_2(B_q|y)} \sup_{t \geq 0} \frac{\sqrt{3 + 6t + t^2}}{1 + t}$$

$$= \sqrt{3(1 - \mu_2(B_q|y))}. \tag{16}$$

From this we conclude that

$$\int_{N(F)} h(y)\, \mu_1(dy) \leq \left(\int_{N(F_1)} h^2(y)\, \mu_1(dy) \right)^{1/2}$$

$$= \sqrt{3} \left(1 - \int_{N(F_1)} \mu_2(B_q|y)\, \mu_1(dy) \right)^{1/2} = \sqrt{3 (1 - \mu(B_q))} = \sqrt{3x}. \tag{17}$$

Finally we rewrite (15) as

$$u = \int_{N(F)} \sum_{i=1}^{\infty} \lambda_i(y) \left(1 + e_i^2(y)\right) \left(1 - h(y)\right) \mu_1(dy)$$

$$\geq \int_{N(F)} \sum_{i=1}^{\infty} \lambda_i(y) \left(1 - h(y)\right) \mu_1(dy). \tag{18}$$

We consider three cases as indicated in Theorem 5.8.2.

(i) Nonadaptive information.

For nonadaptive information, the correlation operator $C_{\nu,y}$ does not depend on y. Therefore $\lambda_i(y) \equiv \lambda_i, \forall y$. As we know

$$r^{\text{avg}}(N)^2 = \sum_{i=1}^{\infty} \lambda_i.$$

(This also follows from (18) with $q = +\infty$. Then $g_i \equiv h \equiv 0$ and (18) is minimized for $e_i = 0$, i.e., for $\phi(y) = S\sigma(y)$.) From (18) and (17) we have

$$e^{\text{avg}}(\phi, N, q) \geq \sqrt{u} \geq r^{\text{avg}}(N) \left(1 - \int_{N(F)} h(y)\, \mu_1(dy) \right)^{1/2}$$

$$\geq r^{\text{avg}}(N) \sqrt{1 - \sqrt{3x}}.$$

This holds for any ϕ, and therefore $r^{\text{avg}}(N, q) \geq r^{\text{avg}}(N)\sqrt{1 - \sqrt{3x}}$.

On the other hand, $r^{\mathrm{avg}}(N,q) \leq r^{\mathrm{avg}}(N)/\sqrt{\mu(B_q)}$ which, with the previous estimate, leads to the equation

$$r^{\mathrm{avg}}(N,q) = \left(1 + \delta(N,q)\right) r^{\mathrm{avg}}(N), \qquad |\delta(N,q)| \leq \sqrt{3x},$$

as claimed.

(ii) Adaptive information with $n(f) \equiv k$.

For nonadaptive information N_y given by (10) we have $r^{\mathrm{avg}}(N_y) = \sqrt{\sum_{i=1}^{\infty} \lambda_i(y)}$. Then (11) yields $\sqrt{\sum_{i=1}^{\infty} \lambda_i(y)} \geq r_k = r^{\mathrm{avg}}(M_k)$. Applying this to (18) we have

$$e(\phi, N, q) \geq \sqrt{u} \geq r^{\mathrm{avg}}(M_k)\sqrt{1 - \sqrt{3x}}.$$

This implies (ii) of Theorem 5.8.2.

(iii) Adaptive information with varying $n(f)$.

Let $A_k = N(B_q) \cap \mathbb{R}^k$. Then

$$\mathrm{card}^{\mathrm{avg}}(N,q) = \frac{1}{\mu(B_q)} \int_{B_q} n(f)\,\mu(df) = \frac{1}{1-x} \sum_{k=1}^{\infty} k\,\mu_1(A_k)$$

and $\sum_{k=1}^{\infty} \mu_1(A_k) = \mu(B_q)$. We rewrite (18) using (11) as

$$u \geq \sum_{k=1}^{\infty} \int_{A_k} \sum_{i=1}^{\infty} \lambda_i(y)\left(1 - h(y)\right)\mu_1(dy)$$

$$\geq \sum_{k=1}^{\infty} r_k^2 \int_{A_k} \left(1 - h(y)\right)\mu_1(dy) = \sum_{k=1}^{\infty} r_k^2\,\beta_k,$$

where $\beta_k = \mu_1(A_k) - \int_{A_k} h(y)\,\mu_1(dy)$. Obviously, $\beta_k \geq 0$ and for $\beta = \sum_{k=1}^{\infty} \beta_k$ we have $\beta = \mu(B_q) - \int_{N(B_q)} h(y)\,\mu_1(dy) \geq 1 - x - \sqrt{3x} > 0$, due to (4). Let $a_k = \beta_k/\beta$. Then $\sum_{k=1}^{\infty} a_k = 1$ and

$$\sum_{k=1}^{\infty} k\,a_k \leq \frac{1}{\beta} \sum_{k=1}^{\infty} k\,\mu_1(A_k) \leq \frac{1-x}{1-x-\sqrt{3x}}\,\mathrm{card}^{\mathrm{avg}}(N,q) =: b.$$

From this we conclude that

$$(1-x)\,r^{\mathrm{avg}}(N,q)^2 \geq \beta \inf\left\{\sum_{k=1}^{\infty} r_k^2\,a_k \ : \ a_k \geq 0, \sum_{k=1}^{\infty} a_k = 1, \sum_{k=1}^{\infty} k\,a_k \leq b\right\}.$$

The above minimization problem has been studied in Section 5.6.2. Lemma 5.6.3 states that there exists a Borel set A of $\mathbb{R}$ and two indices k_1 and k_2 such that the infimum is attained by the square of the average radius of information N^* with $\mathrm{card}^{\mathrm{avg}}(N^*) \leq (1-x)/(1-x-\sqrt{3x})\,\mathrm{card}^{\mathrm{avg}}(N,q)$. Furthermore, $N^*(f) = M_{k_1}(f)$ if $L_1(f) \in A$, and $N^*(f) = M_{k_2}(f)$ otherwise. Thus,

$$r^{\mathrm{avg}}(N,q) \geq \sqrt{\frac{\beta}{1-x}}\; r^{\mathrm{avg}}(N^*) \geq \sqrt{1 - \frac{\sqrt{3x}}{1-x}}\; r^{\mathrm{avg}}(N^*),$$

as claimed. ∎

5.8.2. Proof of Theorem 5.8.1

Without loss of generality we can assume that the complexity is finite,

$$\mathrm{comp}^{\mathrm{avg}}(\varepsilon, q) \leq +\infty,$$

and is attained by a pair (ϕ, N). Thus, $\mathrm{cost}^{\mathrm{avg}}(\phi, N, q) = \mathrm{comp}^{\mathrm{avg}}(\varepsilon, q)$ and $e^{\mathrm{avg}}(\phi, N, q) \leq \varepsilon$. We have

$$\mathrm{comp}^{\mathrm{avg}}(\varepsilon, q) \geq \int_{B_q} \mathrm{cost}(N, f)\, \mu_q(df)$$

$$\geq c \int_{B_q} n(f)\, \mu_q(df) = c\, \mathrm{card}^{\mathrm{avg}}(N, q).$$

Obviously, $r^{\mathrm{avg}}(N,q) \leq \varepsilon$. Theorem 5.8.2 (iii) yields that

$$r^{\mathrm{avg}}(N^*) \leq \varepsilon \sqrt{\frac{1-x}{1-x-\sqrt{3x}}},$$

$$\mathrm{card}^{\mathrm{avg}}(N^*) \leq \frac{1-x}{1-x-\sqrt{3x}}\, \mathrm{card}^{\mathrm{avg}}(N,q)$$

$$\leq \frac{1-x}{c\,(1-x-\sqrt{3x})}\, \mathrm{comp}^{\mathrm{avg}}(\varepsilon, q).$$

Information N^* is of the form given in Theorem 5.8.2 (iii). From Section 5.6 we know that the algorithm $\phi^*(N^*(f)) = S\sigma(N^*(f))$ has average error equal to $r^{\mathrm{avg}}(N^*)$, consists of two linear algorithms, and can be computed with average cost equal to

$$(c+2)\,\mathrm{card}^{\mathrm{avg}}(N^*) \leq \frac{c+2}{c}\, \frac{1-x}{1-x-\sqrt{3x}}\, \mathrm{comp}^{\mathrm{avg}}(\varepsilon, q).$$

Since (ϕ^*, N^*) solves the problem for $\varepsilon_1 = \varepsilon\sqrt{(1-x)/\left(1 - x - \sqrt{3x}\,\right)}$, we have

$$\text{comp}(\varepsilon_1) \leq \frac{c+2}{c} \frac{1-x}{1-x-\sqrt{3x}} \text{comp}^{\text{avg}}(\varepsilon, q),$$

as claimed in the left-hand side of (6).

To prove the right-hand side of (6), take a pair (ϕ, N) for which $e^{\text{avg}}(\phi, N)$ $\leq \varepsilon\sqrt{1-x}$ and $\text{cost}^{\text{avg}}(\phi, N) = \text{comp}^{\text{avg}}(\varepsilon\sqrt{1-x})$. Then

$$e^{\text{avg}}(\phi, N, q) \leq \frac{1}{\sqrt{1-x}} e^{\text{avg}}(\phi, N) \leq \varepsilon.$$

Thus,

$$\text{comp}^{\text{avg}}(\varepsilon, q) \leq \frac{1}{1-x} \text{cost}^{\text{avg}}(\phi, N) = \frac{1}{1-x} \text{comp}^{\text{avg}}\left(\varepsilon\sqrt{1-x}\right),$$

as claimed. This proves (i) of Theorem 5.8.1.

The estimate (ii) of Theorem 5.8.1 easily follows from (6) and the fact that $x = o\left(\exp\left(-q^2 a\right)\right)$ as $q \to +\infty$. This completes the proof. ∎

Notes and Remarks

NR 5.8.2:1 The results of Section 5.8 can be generalized if the absolute error is defined in the $\mathcal{L}_p$ sense, $p \in [1, +\infty)$, provided that S is a continuous linear functional, $S \in F_1^*$. That is, the average error is now defined by

$$e^{\text{avg}}(\phi, N) = \left(\int_{B_q} |S(f) - \phi(N(f))|^p \mu_q(df)\right)^{1/p}.$$

Define

$$d_p = \max_{x \in \mathbb{R}} \frac{\sqrt{(2\pi)^{-1/2} \int_{\mathbb{R}} |t + x|^{2p} \exp\left(-t^2/2\right) dt}}{(2\pi)^{-1/2} \int_{\mathbb{R}} |t + x|^p \exp\left(-t^2/2\right) dt}.$$

Observe that d_p is finite since the function whose maximum is sought tends to 1 as $|x| \to +\infty$. For $p = 2$, we have $d_2 = \sqrt{3}$, for $p = 1$ we have $\sqrt{\pi/2} \leq d_1 \leq \sqrt{(\pi + 8)/2}$. It is possible to check that d_p goes to infinity exponentially with p. (Take $x = 0$ and use the formulas for the pth moments of the Gaussian measure, see Gradshteyn and Ryzhik [80, 3.46-3.48].)

Theorem 5.8.1 can be generalized as follows. Let $x = 1 - \mu(B_q)$. Assume that $q = q(p)$ is chosen such that $1 - x - d_p\sqrt{x} > 0$. Since $d_p \to +\infty$, $q(p) \to +\infty$ as $p \to +\infty$. Let $\text{comp}^{\text{avg}}(\varepsilon, q, p)$ denote the ε-average complexity for the ball B_q with the absolute error criterion defined in the $\mathcal{L}_p$ sense. By $\text{comp}^{\text{avg}}(\varepsilon, p)$ we mean $\text{comp}^{\text{avg}}(\varepsilon, +\infty, p)$. Then

$$\frac{c}{c+2} \frac{1 - x - d_p\sqrt{x}}{1-x} \text{comp}^{\text{avg}}\left(\varepsilon\left(\frac{1-x}{1-x-d_p\sqrt{x}}\right)^{1/p}, p\right)$$

$$\leq \text{comp}^{\text{avg}}(\varepsilon, q, p) \leq \frac{1}{1-x} \text{comp}^{\text{avg}}\left(\varepsilon(1-x)^{1/p}, p\right).$$

The proof of these inequalities is based on an analog of Theorem 5.8.2, which in this case is as follows.

Let $r^{\mathrm{avg}}(N,q,p)$ and $r^{\mathrm{avg}}(N,p)$ denote the average radii of information for the ball B_q and for the whole space, respectively, with the absolute error in the $\mathcal{L}_p$ sense. As before, let $1 - x - d_p\sqrt{x} > 0$ with $x = 1 - \mu(B_q)$. Then

(i) For nonadaptive information N,

$$r^{\mathrm{avg}}(N,q,p) \geq r^{\mathrm{avg}}(N,q)\left(1 - d_p\sqrt{x}\right)^{1/p}.$$

(ii) For adaptive information N with $n(f) \equiv k$,

$$r^{\mathrm{avg}}(N,q,p) \geq r^{\mathrm{avg}}(M_k,q)\left(1 - d_p\sqrt{x}\right)^{1/p},$$

where M_k is nonadaptive information of cardinality k such that $M_k = N_{y_k}$ with minimal $\sigma(y_k)$, i.e., $\sigma(y_k) = \min_y \sigma(y)$. Here $\sigma(y)$ denotes the variance of the conditional Gaussian measure $\nu(\cdot|y)$ defined on $\mathbb{R}$.

(iii) For arbitrary adaptive information N,

$$r^{\mathrm{avg}}(N,q,p) \geq r^{\mathrm{avg}}(N^*,q)\left(1 - \frac{d_p\sqrt{x}}{1-x}\right)^{1/p}$$

and

$$\mathrm{card}^{\mathrm{avg}}(N,q) \geq \mathrm{card}(N^*)\left(1 - \frac{d_p\sqrt{x}}{1-x}\right),$$

where N^* consists of two nonadaptive information

$$N^*(f) = \begin{cases} M_{k_1}(f) & \text{if } L_1(f) \in A, \\ M_{k_2}(f) & \text{otherwise,} \end{cases}$$

for some indices k_1 and k_2, and a Borel set A of $\mathbb{R}$. Here L_1 is the first functional of N.

The proof of (i)-(iii) is exactly the same as the proof of Theorem 5.8.2. Since $S \in F_1^*$, the sum with respect to i reduces to the one term. The corresponding definitions of the functions g_1 and h are as follows:

$$g_1(y) := \frac{1}{\sigma(y)^{p/2}} \int_{F_1} |S(f) - \phi(y)|^p\, b(f,q)\, \mu_2(df|y)$$

$$\leq \bar{g}(y) := \frac{1}{\sqrt{2\pi}} \int_{\mathbb{R}} \left| t + \frac{m(y) - \phi(y)}{\sigma(y)} \right|^p \exp\left(-t^2/2\right) dt,$$

$$h(y) := g(y)/\bar{g}(y) \leq \sqrt{1 - \mu_2(B_q|y)}\, \frac{\sqrt{(2\pi)^{-1/2}\int_{\mathbb{R}} |t + x(y)|^{2p} \exp\left(-t^2/2\right) dt}}{(2\pi)^{-1/2}\int_{\mathbb{R}} |t + x(y)|^p \exp\left(-t^2/2\right) dt}$$

$$\leq \sqrt{1 - \mu_2(B_q|y)}\, d_p,$$

where $x(y) = (m(y) - \phi(y))/\sigma(y)$, and $m(y)$ is the mean of the conditional measure $\nu(\cdot|y)$.

As in Section 5.8, we thus conclude that the ε-average complexities $\text{comp}^{\text{avg}}(\varepsilon, q, p)$ and $\text{comp}^{\text{avg}}(\varepsilon, p)$ are closely related if q is chosen in such a way that $1 - x - d_p\sqrt{x}$ is close to one. The ε-average complexity $\text{comp}^{\text{avg}}(\varepsilon, p)$ is studied in Section 6.3.

Exercises

E 5.8.2:1 Consider a linear problem with $F = B_q$. Let $N = [L_1, L_2, \ldots, L_n]$ be nonadaptive information and let ϕ^* be an algorithm which uses N and has minimal average error. Show that

(i) $\phi^*(0) = 0$ minimizes the local average radius for $y = 0$,

(ii) ϕ^* is, in general, nonlinear.

E 5.8.2:2 Consider a linear problem with an arbitrary measurable F, $F \subset F_1$. Let $N = [L_1, L_2, \ldots, L_n]$ with $\left\langle L_i, L_j \right\rangle_\mu = \delta_{i,j}$. As in **NR 5.4:1**, let

$$Df = 2 \sum_{j=1}^{n} L_j(f) C_\mu L_j - f.$$

Prove that $\mu D = \mu$ and $D(F) = F$ imply that the μ-spline algorithm has minimal average error.

6. Different Error Criteria

So far our analysis of the average case setting has been for the absolute error criterion. We now discuss the average case setting for relative, normalized, and convex and symmetric error criteria. Recall that these error criteria were analyzed in the worst case setting in Section 6 of Chapter 4.

6.1. Relative Error

Let N be adaptive information and let ϕ be an algorithm that uses N. For the relative error criterion, the distance between $S(f)$ and $\phi(N(f))$ is defined by $\|S(f) - \phi(N(f))\|/\|S(f)\|$. The *average relative error* is then defined by

$$e^{\text{rel}}(\phi, N) = \left(\int_{F_1} \frac{\|S(f) - \phi(N(f))\|^2}{\|S(f)\|^2} \, \mu(df) \right)^{1/2},$$

with the convention that $0/0 = 0$.

Let $\text{comp}^{\text{rel}}(\varepsilon)$ denote the average complexity under the relative error criterion defined as in Chapter 3 with $e^{\text{avg}}(\phi, N)$ replaced by $e^{\text{rel}}(\phi, N)$. To avoid the trivial case, we assume that $\varepsilon < 1$.

We analyze the relative error criterion for linear problems with $F = F_1$, see Section 5.1. That is, we assume that F_1 is a separable Banach space equipped with a Gaussian measure μ with mean zero and an injective correlation operator C_μ, G is a separable Hilbert space, and $S : F_1 \to G$ is a continuous linear operator. The class Λ of permissible information operations is a subset of F_1^*. To avoid the trivial case, we assume that the solution operator S *cannot* be expressed as a finite sum of functionals from Λ, i.e., there is no finite collection of $L_1, L_2, \ldots, L_n$ and $g_1, g_2, \ldots, g_n$ such that $S = \sum_{i=1}^n g_i L_i$.

We show that the dimension of the range $S(F_1)$ plays a crucial role. Namely, if $\dim S(F_1) \le 2$ then $\mathrm{comp}^{\mathrm{rel}}(\varepsilon) = +\infty$, $\forall \varepsilon < 1$. That is, a continuous linear functional or a two dimensional operator cannot be approximated at finite cost with the relative error criterion. This is contrary to the result obtained for the absolute error criterion, where the average complexity is finite for *all* positive ε if $r^{\mathrm{avg}}(n, \Lambda) \to 0$ as $n \to +\infty$.

On the other hand, if $\dim S(F_1) \ge 3$ and $r^{\mathrm{avg}}(n, \Lambda) \to 0$ as $n \to +\infty$, then $\mathrm{comp}^{\mathrm{rel}}(\varepsilon)$ is finite and related to the average complexity $\mathrm{comp}^{\mathrm{avg}}(\varepsilon)$ for the absolute error criterion. For instance,

$$\mathrm{comp}^{\mathrm{rel}}(\varepsilon) = \Theta\big(\mathrm{comp}^{\mathrm{avg}}(\varepsilon)\big) \quad \text{as} \quad \varepsilon \to 0$$

if $\mathrm{comp}^{\mathrm{avg}}(a\varepsilon) = \Theta(\mathrm{comp}^{\mathrm{avg}}(\varepsilon))$ for all positive a. Thus, operators of dimension greater than two can be approximated at a finite cost with the relative error criterion. From this point of view, the higher dimension of the space $S(F)$ helps.

We now prove the results mentioned above.

THEOREM 6.1.1. *Let* $\dim S(F_1) \le 2$. *Then*

$$\mathrm{comp}^{\mathrm{rel}}(\varepsilon) = +\infty.$$

PROOF: We use the notation and properties of Gaussian measures from Section 5. Let N be adaptive information with orthonormalized $L_{i,y}$, $\langle L_{i,y}, L_{j,y} \rangle_\mu = \delta_{i,j}$, and with finite $\mathrm{card}^{\mathrm{avg}}(N)$. Then $n(f) < +\infty$ for almost all f. The average relative error of an algorithm ϕ that uses N is given by

$$e^{\mathrm{rel}}(\phi, N)^2 = \int_{N(F_1)} \int_{F_1} \frac{\|S(f) - \phi(y)\|^2}{\|S(f)\|^2} \, \mu_2(df|y) \, \mu_1(dy)$$

$$= \int_{N(F_1)} \int_{S(F_1)} \frac{\|g - \phi(y)\|^2}{\|g\|^2} \, \nu(dg|y) \, \mu_1(dy).$$

Here $\nu(\cdot|y) = \mu_2(S^{-1}\cdot|y)$ is Gaussian on the linear space $S(F)$ with mean $m(y)$ and correlation matrix $C_{\nu,y}$, both given in Section 5.6. From Section

5.3 we have for $y = N(f)$ with $n(f) = k$,

$$\text{trace}(C_{\nu,y}) = \inf_{g_i \in G} \left\| S - \sum_{i=1}^{k} g_i L_{i,y} \right\|_{\mu}^2 .$$

Since $S \neq \sum_{i=1}^{k} g_i L_{i,y}$ and C_μ is injective, $\text{trace}(C_{\nu,y}) > 0$. Thus, the Gaussian measure $\nu(\cdot|y)$ is not atomic.

Let $p = \dim S(F_1) \in \{1, 2\}$. Let (λ_i, η_i), $i \leq p$, be the eigenpairs of $C_{\nu,y}$. Then $\lambda_1 > 0$ and $\lambda_p \geq 0$. Let $\phi(y) = z_1\eta_1 + z_2\eta_2$, and $m(y) = m_1\eta_1 + m_2\eta_2$. Then for $a = \int_{S(F_1)} \|g - \phi(y)\|^2/\|g\|^2 \, \nu(dg|y)$ we have

$$a = \frac{1}{\sqrt{\prod_{i=1}^{p} 2\pi\lambda_i}} \int_{\mathbb{R}^p} \frac{\sum_{i=1}^{p}(x_i - z_i)^2}{\sum_{i=1}^{p} x_i^2} \exp\left(-\sum_{i=1}^{p} \frac{(x_i - m_i)^2}{2\lambda_i} \right) dx_1 \ldots dx_p.$$

Note that for $\phi(y) = 0$, i.e., $z_1 = z_2 = 0$, the last integral is equal to one. If $\phi(y) \neq 0$, i.e., $z_1^2 + z_2^2 \neq 0$, then the last integral is equal to infinity.

Indeed, replacing $\mathbb{R}^p$ by a ball B_q with center 0 and small positive radius q, we estimate the numerator from below by a positive number b, say, to find out that

$$a \geq b \int_{B_q} \frac{1}{\sum_{i=1}^{p} x_i^2} \, dx_1 \ldots dx_p = +\infty.$$

Thus,

$$e^{\text{rel}}(\phi, N) = \begin{cases} 1 & \text{if } \phi(N(f)) = 0 \text{ for almost all } f, \\ +\infty & \text{otherwise.} \end{cases}$$

Therefore, we cannot solve the problem with finite average cardinality if $\varepsilon < 1$. This implies that $\text{comp}^{\text{rel}}(\varepsilon) = +\infty$, as claimed. ∎

REMARK 6.1.1. The proof of Theorem 6.1.1 yields that the radius of information

$$r^{\text{rel}}(N) = \inf_{\phi} e^{\text{rel}}(\phi, N) = 1$$

for any information N of a finite average cardinality. Furthermore, the only algorithm with a finite average relative error is the zero algorithm, whose error is equal to one.

REMARK 6.1.2. It is interesting to notice that if one interchanges the role of $S(f)$ and $\phi(N(f))$ in the definition of relative error, then the complexity is finite no matter what the dimension of $S(F_1)$. This is discussed in **NR 6.1:4**, see also the next remark.

REMARK 6.1.3. Throughout this chapter we discussed the μ-spline algorithm ϕ^s which is the mean of the conditional measure. For the absolute error criterion, this algorithm minimizes the average error. For the relative error criterion, the situation is quite different.

Assume that S is a continuous linear functional which cannot be expressed by finite linear combinations of functionals from the class Λ. Then the average error of the μ-spline algorithm ϕ^s is infinite no matter whether the relative error is defined by $|S(f)-U(f)|/|S(f)|$ or $|S(f)-U(f)|/|U(f)|$. For the second case, the algorithm with minimal average error is given by

$$\phi^*(y) = m(y) + \sigma(y)/m(y),$$

where $m(y)$ and $\sigma(y)$ are the mean and the variance of the conditional measure $\nu(\cdot|y), y = N(f)$ for adaptive information N, see **NR 6.1:4**. Observe that

$$\phi^*(y) - \phi^s(y) = \sigma(y)/m(y).$$

For small $m(y)$ relative to $\sigma(y)$, the optimal algorithm ϕ^* is far away from the μ-spline algorithm. Note that ϕ^* is not well defined for $m(y) = 0$ but it can only happen for a set of measure zero.

Thus, under this error criterion, the mean of the conditional measure does not lead to a good algorithm.

We now turn to the case $\dim S(F_1) \geq 3$. As mentioned before, we show that $\mathrm{comp}^{\mathrm{rel}}(\varepsilon)$ is finite and related to the average complexity for the absolute error criterion. To prove this, we need the following lemmas.

LEMMA 6.1.1. Let $p > 0$. If $2p < \dim F_1$ then $\int_{F_1} \|f\|^{-2p} \mu(df)$ is finite.

PROOF: Take a finite integer k such that $2p < k \leq \dim F_1$. Then there exist $L_1, L_2, \ldots, L_k$ from F_1^* such that $L_i(C_\mu L_j) = \delta_{i,j}$ for $i, j = 1, 2, \ldots, k$. Define $Qf = \sum_{i=1}^k L_i(f) C_\mu L_i$. Then $\|f\| \geq \|Qf\|/\|Q\|$ and

$$u := \int_{F_1} \|f\|^{-2p} \mu(df) \leq \int_{F_1} \left(\frac{\|Qf\|}{\|Q\|}\right)^{-2p} \mu(df) = \|Q\|^{2p} \int_X \|x\|^{-2p} \lambda(dx),$$

where $X = \mathrm{span}(C_\mu L_1, \ldots, C_\mu L_k)$ and $\lambda = \mu Q^{-1}$ is Gaussian with mean zero and the identity correlation operator. Since X is finite dimensional, $\|\cdot\|$ restricted to X is equivalent to the Euclidean norm, i.e., there exists a positive constant b such that

$$\left\| \sum_{i=1}^k x_i C_\mu L_i \right\| \geq b \left(\sum_{i=1}^k x_i^2\right)^{1/2} = b\|x\|_2, \quad \forall\, x \in X.$$

Thus,

$$\int_X \|x\|^{-2p}\, \lambda(dx) \le (2\pi)^{-k/2} b^{-2p} \int_{\mathbf{R}} \|t\|_2^{-2p} \exp\big(-\|t\|_2^2/2\big)\, dt$$

$$\le (2\pi)^{-k/2} b^{-2p} \int_{\|t\|_2 \le 1} \|t\|^{-2p}\, dt + b^{-2p}.$$

The last integral $v = \int_{\|t\|_2 \le 1} \|t\|_2^{-2p} dt$ is finite iff $k > 2p$, see Gradshteyn and Ryzhik [80, 4.642], and then $v = 2\sqrt{\pi^k}/\big(\Gamma(k/2)(k-2p)\big)$. ∎

LEMMA 6.1.2. Let $\dim S(F_1) \ge 3$ and let $p \in \big(1, 0.5 \dim S(F_1)\big)$. For nonadaptive information N and the μ-spline algorithm ϕ^s that uses N, we have

$$e^{\mathrm{rel}}(\phi^s, N) \le d_p\, r^{\mathrm{avg}}(N)$$

with finite

$$d_p = \left(\int_G \|g\|^{-2p}\, \nu(dg)\right)^{1/(2p)} \left(\frac{1}{\sqrt{2\pi}} \int_{\mathbf{R}} |t|^{\frac{2p}{p-1}} \exp\big(-t^2/2\big)\, dt\right)^{(p-1)/(2p)}.$$

PROOF: We use the notation of Section 5.8. Let (λ_i, ζ_i) be the eigenpairs of the correlation operator $C_{\nu,N}$. For $\rho = (p-1)/p$ we have

$$e^{\mathrm{rel}}(\phi^s, N)^2 = \sum_i \int_{F_1} \frac{\langle Sf - \phi^s(Nf), \zeta_i\rangle^2}{\|Sf\|^2}\, \mu(df) \le$$

$$\left(\int_{S(F_1)} \|Sf\|^{-2p}\, \mu(df)\right)^{1/p} \sum_i \left(\int_{F_1} |\langle Sf - \phi^s(Nf), \zeta_i\rangle|^{2/\rho}\, \mu(df)\right)^{\rho}.$$

The last expression is equal to

$$\left(\int_G \|g\|^{-2p}\, \nu(dg)\right)^{1/p}$$

$$\times \sum_i \left(\int_{N(F_1)} \int_{F_1} |\langle S(f) - S\sigma(y), \zeta_i\rangle|^{2/\rho}\, \mu_2(df|y)\, \mu_1(dy)\right)^{\rho}$$

$$= \left(\int_G \|g\|^{-2p}\, \nu(dg)\right)^{1/p} \sum_i \left(\frac{1}{\sqrt{2\pi\lambda_i}} \int_{\mathbf{R}} |t|^{2/\rho} \exp\left(\frac{-t^2}{2\lambda_i}\right) dt\right)^{\rho}$$

$$= d_p^2 \sum_i \lambda_i = d_p^2\, r^{\mathrm{avg}}(N)^2,$$

proving that $e^{\text{rel}}(\phi^s, N) \leq d_p \, r^{\text{avg}}(N)$. To see that d_p is finite, apply Lemma 6.1.1 with $F_1 = G$. Then $C_\nu(G) = C_\nu(S(F_1))$ and $\dim C_\nu(G) = \dim S(F_1) > 2p$. ∎

We are ready to present relations between $\text{comp}^{\text{rel}}(\varepsilon)$ and $\text{comp}^{\text{avg}}(\varepsilon)$. As in Section 5.8, let $x = 1 - \mu(B_q)$ satisfy (4).

THEOREM 6.1.2. Let $\dim S(F_1) \geq 3$ and $p \in \big(1, 0.5 \dim S(F_1)\big)$.

  (i) Then

$$\text{comp}^{\text{rel}}(\varepsilon) \leq \frac{c+2}{c} \inf_{0 \leq t \leq 1} \max \left\{ \frac{1}{1-t} \, \text{comp}^{\text{avg}} \left(\frac{\varepsilon}{d_p} \right), \text{comp}^{\text{avg}} \left(\frac{\varepsilon}{d_p} \sqrt{t} \right) \right\},$$

$$\text{comp}^{\text{rel}}(\varepsilon) \geq \frac{c}{c+2} \left(1 - x - \sqrt{3x} \right) \text{comp}^{\text{avg}} \left(\frac{\varepsilon \, \|S\| \, q}{\sqrt{1 - x - \sqrt{3x}}} \right)$$

  with d_p defined in Lemma 6.1.2.
  (ii) If, for all positive b, $\text{comp}^{\text{avg}}(b\,\varepsilon) = \Theta\big(\text{comp}^{\text{avg}}(\varepsilon)\big)$ as ε goes to zero
       then
$$\text{comp}^{\text{rel}}(\varepsilon) = \Theta\big(\text{comp}^{\text{avg}}(\varepsilon)\big).$$

PROOF: Take information N for which $r^{\text{avg}}(N) \leq \varepsilon$ and $\text{card}^{\text{avg}}(N) = m^{\text{avg}}(\varepsilon) \leq c^{-1} \text{comp}^{\text{avg}}(\varepsilon)$. From Theorem 5.6.2 there exists information N^* such that $\text{card}^{\text{avg}}(N^*) \leq \text{card}^{\text{avg}}(N)$, $r^{\text{avg}}(N^*) \leq r^{\text{avg}}(N)$, and N^* has the form

$$N^*(f) = \begin{cases} M_1(f) & \text{if } L_1(f) \in A, \\ M_2(f) & \text{otherwise,} \end{cases}$$

where M_1 and M_2 are both nonadaptive, L_1 is the first functional of M_1 and M_2, and the set A from $\mathbb{R}$ has measure t. Let k_i be the cardinality of M_i. Then $k_1 \leq \text{card}^{\text{avg}}(N^*) \leq k_2$ and $k_1 t + k_2(1 - t) = \text{card}^{\text{avg}}(N^*)$. Let r_i be the average radius of N_i. Then $r_2 \leq r^{\text{avg}}(N^*) \leq r_1$ and $\sqrt{t \, r_1^2 + (1-t) r_2^2} = r^{\text{avg}}(N^*)$.

Assume for a moment that $t > 0$. Consider the nonadaptive information M_1. Its average radius is no greater than $r^{\text{avg}}(N^*)/\sqrt{t}$. Apply Lemma 6.1.2 for the information M_1. Let ϕ_1 be the μ-spline algorithm using M_1. Then

$$e^{\text{rel}}(\phi_1, M_1) \leq \frac{d_p \, \varepsilon}{\sqrt{t}}.$$

Thus, the pair (ϕ_1, M_1) solves the problem for $\varepsilon_1 = \varepsilon \, d_p / \sqrt{t}$ with the average cost

$$(c+2) k_1 - 1 \leq (c+2) \, \text{card}^{\text{avg}}(N^*) \leq \frac{c+2}{c} \, \text{comp}^{\text{avg}}(\varepsilon).$$

Therefore

$$\text{comp}^{\text{rel}}(\varepsilon_1) \leq \frac{c+2}{c} \, \text{comp}^{\text{avg}} \left(\frac{\varepsilon_1}{d_p} \sqrt{t} \right). \tag{1}$$

Observe that (1) trivially holds for $t = 0$.

Assume now that $t < 1$. Consider the nonadaptive information M_2. Since $r_2 \leq r^{\text{avg}}(N^*)$, Lemma 6.1.2 yields for the μ-spline algorithm ϕ_2 that uses M_2,

$$e^{\text{rel}}(\phi_2, M_2) \leq d_p \, \varepsilon.$$

The pair (ϕ_2, M_2) solves the problem for $\varepsilon_2 = d_p \, \varepsilon$ with the average cost

$$(c+2)k_2 - 1 \leq \frac{(c+2) \, \text{card}^{\text{avg}}(N^*)}{1-t} \leq \frac{c+2}{c} \frac{1}{1-t} \, \text{comp}^{\text{avg}}(\varepsilon).$$

Therefore

$$\text{comp}^{\text{rel}}(\varepsilon_2) \leq \frac{c+2}{c} \frac{1}{1-t} \, \text{comp}^{\text{avg}} \left(\frac{\varepsilon_2}{d_p} \right). \tag{2}$$

Note that (2) holds trivially for $t = 1$.

We established (1) and (2) for arbitrary ε. Therefore (1) holds for any ε_1 and (2) for any ε_2. From this we conclude that

$$\text{comp}^{\text{rel}}(\varepsilon) \leq \frac{c+2}{c} \sup_{0 \leq t \leq 1} \min \left\{ \frac{1}{1-t} \, \text{comp}^{\text{avg}} \left(\frac{\varepsilon}{d_p} \right), \text{comp}^{\text{avg}} \left(\frac{\varepsilon}{d_p} \sqrt{t} \right) \right\}$$

$$= \frac{c+2}{c} \inf_{0 \leq t \leq 1} \max \left\{ \frac{1}{1-t} \, \text{comp}^{\text{avg}} \left(\frac{\varepsilon}{d_p} \right), \text{comp}^{\text{avg}} \left(\frac{\varepsilon}{d_p} \sqrt{t} \right) \right\},$$

as claimed.

We now prove a lower bound on $\text{comp}^{\text{rel}}(\varepsilon)$. Take a pair (ϕ, N) such that $e^{\text{rel}}(\phi, N) \leq \varepsilon$ and $\text{cost}^{\text{avg}}(\phi, N) = \text{comp}^{\text{rel}}(\varepsilon)$. Observe that for any positive q,

$$\varepsilon^2 \geq \int_{F_1} \frac{\|S(f) - \phi(N(f))\|^2}{\|S(f)\|^2} \, \mu(df) \geq \int_{B_q} \frac{\|S(f) - \phi(N(f))\|^2}{\|S(f)\|^2} \, \mu(df)$$

$$\geq (q\|S\|)^{-2} \mu(B_q) \int_{B_q} \|S(f) - \phi(N(f))\|^2 \, \mu_q(df)$$

$$= (q\|S\|)^{-2} (1 - x) \, e^{\text{avg}}(\phi, N, q)^2.$$

This proves that $r^{\text{avg}}(N, q) \leq \varepsilon q \|S\| / \sqrt{1-x}$. Furthermore, $\text{cost}^{\text{avg}}(\phi, N, q)$ $\leq (1-x)^{-1} \text{cost}^{\text{avg}}(\phi, N) = (1-x)^{-1} \text{comp}^{\text{rel}}(\varepsilon)$. Thus, the pair (ϕ, N) solves the problem for the ball B_q with $\varepsilon_1 = q \varepsilon \|S\| / \sqrt{1-x}$. Therefore,

$$\text{comp}^{\text{avg}}(\varepsilon_1, q) \leq \frac{1}{1-x} \, \text{comp}^{\text{rel}}(\varepsilon).$$

Now applying Theorem 5.8.1, we get

$$\text{comp}^{\text{rel}}(\varepsilon) \geq \frac{c}{c+2} \left(1 - x - \sqrt{3x}\right) \text{comp}^{\text{avg}} \left(\frac{\varepsilon \|S\| q}{\sqrt{1 - x - \sqrt{3x}}}\right),$$

as claimed. The proof of (ii) follows easily from (i). ∎

Theorem 6.1.2 relates the average complexity for the relative error to the average complexity for the absolute error. The bounds only permit us to find lower and upper estimates on $\text{comp}^{\text{rel}}(\varepsilon)$. These estimates, in general, are not tight. Better bounds on $\text{comp}^{\text{rel}}(\varepsilon)$ will require a more refined analysis than has been carried out here.

We end this section by a brief remark on the modified relative error criterion, see Section 6.1 of Chapter 4. That is, the error of an algorithm ϕ that uses information N is now defined by

$$e^{\text{rel}}(\phi, N; \eta) = \left(\int_{F_1} \frac{\|S(f) - \phi(N(f))\|^2}{(\|S(f)\| + \eta)^2} \mu(df)\right)^{1/2},$$

where η is a given, presumably small, number. Clearly,

$$e^{\text{rel}}(\phi, N; \eta) \leq \eta^{-1} e^{\text{avg}}(\phi, N).$$

Thus, no matter what the dimension of $S(F)$ is, the average complexity for the modified relative error is finite and

$$\text{comp}^{\text{rel}}(\varepsilon; \eta) \leq \text{comp}^{\text{avg}}(\varepsilon \eta).$$

On the other hand,

$$e^{\text{rel}}(\phi, N; \eta) \geq \frac{\sqrt{\mu(B_q)}}{q\|S\| + \eta} e^{\text{avg}}(\phi, N, q),$$

and

$$\text{comp}^{\text{rel}}(\varepsilon; \eta) \geq \text{comp}^{\text{avg}} \left(\frac{\varepsilon(\|S\| q + \eta)}{\sqrt{\mu(B_q)}}, q\right).$$

If, for all positive b, $\text{comp}^{\text{avg}}(b\varepsilon) = \Theta\left(\text{comp}^{\text{avg}}(\varepsilon)\right)$ as $\varepsilon \to 0$ then Theorem 5.8.1(ii) yields

$$\text{comp}^{\text{rel}}(\varepsilon; \eta) = \Theta\left(\text{comp}^{\text{avg}}(\varepsilon)\right).$$

This establishes a Θ-relation between the average complexities for the absolute and modified relative error no matter what the dimension of $S(F_1)$.

Tight bounds on $\text{comp}^{\text{rel}}(\varepsilon;\eta)$ are not known. It seems especially interesting to obtain them for small η and $\dim S(F_1) \leq 2$, and to see how fast $\text{comp}^{\text{rel}}(\varepsilon;\eta)$ approaches $\text{comp}^{\text{rel}}(\varepsilon;0) = +\infty$, see **NR 6.1:5**.

Notes and Remarks

NR 6.1:1 This section is based on Jackowski and Woźniakowski [87], and Woźniakowski [87].

NR 6.1:2 Theorem 6.1.1 remains valid if G is a normed linear space. Indeed, since $\dim S(F_1) \leq 2$, the norm $\|g\|$ for $g \in S$ is equivalent to the $\mathcal{L}_2$ norm, $d_1 \|g\|_2 \leq \|g\| \leq d_2 \|g\|_2$ for some $d_i > 0$. Therefore,

$$\int_{S(F_1)} \frac{\|g - \phi(y)\|^2}{\|g\|^2}\, \nu(dg|y) \geq \left(\frac{d_1}{d_2}\right)^2 \int_{\mathbb{R}^p} \frac{\|g - \phi(y)\|_2^2}{\|g\|_2^2}\, \nu(dg|y),$$

and the rest of the proof is unchanged.

NR 6.1:3 Lemma 6.1.1 remains valid if C_μ is not necessarily one-to-one. We only need to assume that $2p < \dim C_\mu(F_1^*)$.

NR 6.1:4 We now discuss a linear problem with a relative error criterion in which the roles of $S(f)$ and $U(f) = \phi(N(f))$ are interchanged. That is,

$$e^{\text{rel}}(U) = \left(\int_{F_1} \frac{\|S(f) - U(f)\|^2}{\|U(f)\|^2}\, \mu(df)\right)^{1/2}.$$

Contrary to the worst case setting, see Remark 6.1.1 of Chapter 4, we show that the complexity with this definition of relative error becomes finite independently of the dimension of $S(F_1)$. For simplicity, we consider here the case when S is a continuous linear functional. Compare with **E 6.1:2** and **6.1:3**, where S is an operator.

Let N be adaptive information with fixed cardinality $n(f) = n$ and with μ-orthonormal functionals $L_{i,y}$, $\langle L_{i,y}, L_{j,y}\rangle_\mu = \delta_{i,j}$. Let ϕ be an algorithm that uses N. Let $\phi(y) = m(y) + z(y)$, where $m(y)$ is the mean of the conditional measure $\nu(\cdot|y)$, and let $\sigma(y)$ be its variance. It is easy to show that the square of the local average error of ϕ is given by

$$\frac{\sigma + z^2}{(m + z)^2},$$

where $\sigma = \sigma(y)$, $z = z(y)$, and $m = m(y)$. To minimize the local average error, it is enough to find z which minimizes the last expression. Such a number z is equal to σ/m. Thus, the algorithm

$$\phi^*(y) = m(y) + \sigma(y)/m(y)$$

minimizes the local and global average errors. Observe that ϕ^* is not well defined if $m(y) = 0$. This can happen, however, only on a set of measure zero. The local average error is equal to

$$\sqrt{\frac{\sigma(y)}{m^2(y) + \sigma(y)}}.$$

Since it is a decreasing function of $\sigma(y)$, this proves that adaptive selection of linear functionals does not help and

$$e^{\text{rel}}(\phi^*, N)^2 \geq \frac{2\sigma_n}{\sqrt{2\pi} \|w\|^2} \int_0^\infty \left(x^2 + \frac{\sigma_n}{\|w\|^2} \right)^{-1} \exp\left(-x^2/2 \right) dx,$$

where σ_n is the smallest variance obtained after n evaluations. That is,

$$\sigma_n = \|S\|_\mu^2 - \sum_{i=1}^n [S(C_\mu L_i^*)]^2 = \min_{L_i \in \Lambda} \min_{a_i \in \mathbb{R}} \|S - \sum_{i=1}^n a_i L_i\|_\mu^2,$$

and

$$\|w\|^2 = \sum_{i=1}^n [S(C_\mu L_i^*)]^2.$$

Note that the last inequality becomes an equality if $N = N_n^* = [L_1^*, L_2^*, \ldots, L_n^*]$.
It is easy to check that

$$\int_0^\infty \frac{\exp\left(-x^2/2 \right)}{x^2 + a} dx = \frac{\pi}{2\sqrt{a}} (1 + o(1)) \quad \text{as } a \to 0^+.$$

Therefore, the error of $U_n^*(f) = \phi^*(N_n^*(f))$ is given by

$$e^{\text{rel}}(U_n^*) = \left(\frac{\pi}{2} \frac{\sigma_n}{S(C_\mu S) - \sigma_n} \right)^{1/4} (1 + o(1)).$$

Let

$$n^* = n^*(\varepsilon) = \min \left\{ n : \sigma_n \leq \left(\varepsilon^2 \|S\|_\mu \sqrt{2/\pi} \right)^2 \right\}.$$

Then the error of $U_{n^*}^*$ is $\varepsilon(1 + o(1))$. This proves that the complexity is finite and at most roughly equal to $c\, n^*(\varepsilon)$. It is not known if this bound is sharp. Observe that $c\, n^*(\varepsilon)$ is roughly equal to the average complexity with the absolute error criterion for $\varepsilon^2 \|S\|_\mu \sqrt{2/\pi}$.

Observe that the local average error of the μ-spline algorithm, $\phi^s(y) = m(y)$, is given by $\sqrt{\sigma(y)}/|m(y)|$. Then the global error can be estimated by

$$e^{\text{rel}}(\phi^s, N)^2 \geq \sigma_n \int_{\mathbb{R}^n} \frac{1}{|m(y)|} \mu_1(dy) = \frac{\sigma_n}{\|w\|} \sqrt{\frac{2}{\pi}} \int_0^\infty x^{-1} \exp\left(-x^2/2 \right) dx = +\infty.$$

This shows that the mean of the conditional measure leads to a poor algorithm for this relative error criterion.

NR 6.1:5 We discuss the modified relative error assuming that S is a continuous linear functional. We sketch the proof that

$$\text{comp}^{\text{rel}}(\varepsilon; \eta) \leq \text{comp}^{\text{avg}} \left(\varepsilon \sqrt{\eta \|S\|_\mu} \sqrt{\pi/2} (1 + o(1)) \right) \quad \text{as } \varepsilon \to 0.$$

That is, the average complexity with the modified relative error is roughly at most equal to the average complexity with the absolute error criterion for $\varepsilon \left(\eta \, \|S\|_\mu \, \sqrt{\pi/2} \, \right)^{1/2}$.

Let $N = [L_1, L_2, \ldots, L_n]$ be nonadaptive information with $\left\langle L_i, L_j \right\rangle_\mu = \delta_{i,j}$. The error of the μ-spline algorithm ϕ^s is now given by

$$e^{\mathrm{rel}}(\phi^s, N; \eta)^2 = \frac{\sigma}{2\pi} \int_{\mathbb{R}^2} \frac{t^2 \, \exp\left(-(t^2 + x^2)/2 \right)}{\left(|t \sqrt{\sigma} + b\, x| + \eta \right)^2} \, dt \, dx,$$

where $\sigma = S(C_\mu S) - \sum_{j=1}^{n} [S(C_\mu L_j)]^2$ and $b = \sqrt{S(C_\mu S) - \sigma}$. It is easy to show that for small positive a,

$$\int_0^\infty (x + a)^{-2} \, \exp\left(-x^2/2 \right) dx = a^{-1} \left(1 + o(1) \right).$$

From this we conclude that for small σ and η

$$e^{\mathrm{rel}}(\phi^s, N; \eta) = \sqrt{\frac{\sigma}{\eta\, b}} \, \sqrt{2/\pi} \, (1 + o(1)).$$

Thus, the error is roughly ε if $N = N_{n^*}^*$ is the n^*th optimal nonadaptive information in the class Λ with

$$n^* = \min \left\{ n : \, r^{\mathrm{avg}}(n, \Lambda) \le \varepsilon \sqrt{\eta} \, \left(\pi (\|S\|_\mu^2 - r^{\mathrm{avg}}(n, \Lambda)^2)/2 \right)^{1/4} \right\}.$$

This proves the upper bound on the complexity. The actual value of $\mathrm{comp}^{\mathrm{rel}}(\varepsilon; \eta)$ is not known. In any case, the dependence on η is at most through $\sqrt{\eta}$.

Exercises

E 6.1:1 Consider the relative error in the $\mathcal{L}_p$ sense, $p \ge 1$. That is,

$$e^{\mathrm{rel}}(\phi, N) = \left(\int_{F_1} \frac{\|S(f) - \phi(N(f))\|^p}{\|S(f)\|^p} \, \mu(df) \right)^{1/p}.$$

Show that for linear problems with $\dim S(F_1) \le p$ we have $\mathrm{comp}^{\mathrm{rel}}(\varepsilon) = +\infty, \, \forall \varepsilon < 1$.

E 6.1:2 Consider a linear problem with the relative error criterion as in **NR 6.1:4**. Let N be adaptive information and let ϕ^s be the μ-spline algorithm. Prove that the average error of ϕ^s is infinite iff $\dim S(F) \le 2$.

E 6.1:3 Consider the problem as in **E 6.1:2**. Prove that the algorithm

$$\phi^*(y) = \left(1 + \mathrm{trace}(C_{\nu,y})/\|m(y)\|^2 \right) m(y)$$

minimizes the local average radii. Here $m(y)$ is the mean of the conditional measure $\nu(\cdot|y)$ and $C_{\nu,y}$ is its correlation operator.

E 6.1:4 For linear problems, analyze the average case setting with the following error criteria
(i) $\|S(f) - U(f)\|/(\|U(f)\| + \eta)$,

(ii) $\|S(f) - U(f)\|/\max\{\|S(f)\|, \|U(f)\|\}$,

(iii) $\|S(f) - U(f)\|/(\max\{\|S(f)\|, \|U(f)\|\} + \eta)$, where $\eta > 0$.

E 6.1:5 Consider a linear problem with a continuous linear functional S and with the relative error criterion as in **NR 6.1:4** in the $\mathcal{L}_1$ sense. That is,

$$e^{\mathrm{rel}}(U) = \int_{F_1} \frac{|S(f) - U(f)|}{|U(f)|} \mu(df).$$

Let N be nonadaptive information. Prove that the μ-spline algorithm ϕ^s has infinite error. Prove that the algorithm

$$\phi^*(y) = m(y) + \sqrt{\sigma} \, \mathrm{sign}\,(m(y))$$

almost minimizes the error. Here $m(y)$ is the mean of the conditional measure and $\sigma = \sigma(N)$ is its variance. Hence, the "small" difference between the algorithms ϕ^s and ϕ^*, $|\phi^s(y) - \phi^s(y)| = \sqrt{\sigma}$, is essential and makes the error of ϕ^* finite.

E 6.1:6 Consider the problem of **E 6.1:5**. Prove that for large c and small ε the complexity is at most proportional to $c\,n^*$, where n^* is the smallest n for which

$$\sqrt{\frac{\sigma_n}{\|S\|_\mu^2 - \sigma_n}} \, \ln \frac{\|S\|_\mu^2 - \sigma_n}{\sigma_n} \le 2\varepsilon,$$

with $\sigma_n = \inf_{L_i \in \Lambda} \inf_{a_i \in \mathbb{R}} \|S - \sum_{i=1}^n a_i L_i\|_\mu^2$ being the smallest variance of the conditional measure after n evaluations.

E 6.1:7 Consider a linear problem with a continuous linear functional S and with the modified relative error criterion in the $\mathcal{L}_1$ sense. That is, $e^{\mathrm{rel}}(U) = \int_{F_1} |S(f) - U(f)|/(|S(f)| + \eta)\,\mu(df)$. Prove that for large c, and small ε and η the complexity $\mathrm{comp}^{\mathrm{rel}}(\varepsilon; \eta)$ is no greater than $\mathrm{comp}^{\mathrm{avg}}\left(\varepsilon\,(1 + o(1))/\ln \eta^{-1}\right)(1 + o(1))$, i.e., no greater than the average complexity with the absolute error criterion for $\varepsilon\,(1 + o(1))/\ln \eta^{-1}$.

6.2. Normalized Error

We now discuss the average case setting for linear problems with the normalized error criterion. That is, the distance between $S(f)$ and $\phi(N(f))$ is defined by $\|S(f) - \phi(N(f))\|/\|f\|$. Observe that the first norm is the norm of the Hilbert space G, whereas the second is the norm of the Banach space F_1. The average normalized error is defined by

$$e^{\mathrm{nor}}(\phi, N) = \left(\int_{F_1} \frac{\|S(f) - \phi(N(f))\|^2}{\|f\|^2} \mu(df) \right)^{1/2}.$$

Let $\mathrm{comp}^{\mathrm{nor}}(\varepsilon)$ denote the average complexity with the normalized error criterion. It is defined as in Chapter 3 with $e^{\mathrm{avg}}(\phi, N)$ replaced by $e^{\mathrm{nor}}(\phi, N)$.

We now show that the complexity $\text{comp}^{\text{nor}}(\varepsilon)$ is related to the average complexity with the absolute error criterion. Let q be so that $x = 1 - \mu(B_q)$ satisfies (4) of Section 5.8.

THEOREM 6.2.1.

(i) *Lower Bound:*

$$\text{comp}^{\text{nor}}(\varepsilon) \geq \frac{c\left(1 - x - \sqrt{3x}\right)}{c+2}\, \text{comp}^{\text{avg}}\left(\frac{q\,\varepsilon}{\sqrt{1 - x - \sqrt{3x}}}\right).$$

(ii) *Upper Bound: Assume that* $\dim F_1 \geq 3$. *Let* $p \in \left(1, 1/2 \dim F_1\right)$. *Then*

$$\text{comp}^{\text{nor}}(\varepsilon)$$
$$\leq \frac{c+2}{c}\, \inf_{0 \leq t \leq 1}\, \max\left\{\frac{1}{1-t}\, \text{comp}^{\text{avg}}\left(\frac{\varepsilon}{c_p}\right), \text{comp}^{\text{avg}}\left(\frac{\varepsilon}{c_p}\sqrt{t}\right)\right\}$$

with finite

$$c_p = \left(\int_{F_1} \|f\|^{-2p}\, \mu(df)\right)^{1/(2p)} \left(\frac{1}{\sqrt{2\pi}} \int_{\mathbb{R}} |t|^{2p/(p-1)}\, dt\right)^{(p-1)/(2p)}.$$

(iii) *If, for all positive* b, $\text{comp}^{\text{avg}}(b\,\varepsilon) = \Theta\left(\text{comp}^{\text{avg}}(\varepsilon)\right)$ *as* ε *goes to zero then*

$$\text{comp}^{\text{nor}}(\varepsilon) = \Theta\left(\text{comp}^{\text{avg}}(\varepsilon)\right).$$

PROOF: The proof is essentially the same as the proof of Theorem 6.1.2. To get (i), we switch to the ball B_q, estimate $(\|S(f) - \phi(N(f))\|/\|f\|)^2 \geq q^{-2}\|S(f) - \phi(N(f))\|^2$, and apply Theorem 5.8.1. To get (ii), it is enough to notice that a modification of Lemma 6.1.2 yields that the average normalized error of the μ-spline algorithm ϕ^s using nonadaptive information N is estimated by

$$e^{\text{nor}}(\phi^s, N) \leq c_p\, r^{\text{avg}}(N).$$

The number c_p is finite due to Lemma 6.1.1. Of course, (iii) follows easily from (ii). ∎

Observe that the assumption $\dim F_1 \geq 3$, which is needed for the upper bound on $\text{comp}^{\text{nor}}(\varepsilon)$, is not restrictive. If $\dim F_1 \leq 2$ then the problem is trivial since at most two evaluations of linear functionals are enough to compute $S(f)$ exactly.

Theorem 6.2.1 provides bounds on $\text{comp}^{\text{nor}}(\varepsilon)$ in terms of the average complexity with the absolute error criterion. As for the relative error criterion, these bounds need not be sharp. Tight bounds on $\text{comp}^{\text{nor}}(\varepsilon)$ will require a more refined analysis than has been done here.

Notes and Remarks

NR 6.2:1 This section is based on Woźniakowski [87].

NR 6.2:2 The upper bound on $\text{comp}^{\text{nor}}(\varepsilon)$ in Theorem 6.2.1 remains valid if the assumption $\dim F_1 \geq 3$ is replaced by the assumption $\dim C_\mu(F_1^*) \geq 3$, where C_μ is a correlation operator of the Gaussian measure which needs not be one-to-one. Thus, $\dim C_\mu(F_1^*) \geq 3$ means that the Gaussian measure μ is concentrated on a subspace of dimension at least three. If F_1 is a Hilbert space, this means that C_μ has at least three nonzero eigenvalues.

Exercises

E 6.2:1 For linear problems, analyze the average case setting with the error criterion $\|S(f) - U(f)\|/(\|f\| + \eta)$ for $\eta > 0$.

6.3. General Error Functional

In this section, we study the average case setting under the error criterion defined by an *error functional*

$$\text{ER} : G \to \mathbb{R}_+.$$

Here we assume only that G is a linear space. In Section 6.3 of Chapter 4 we discussed the worst case setting under this error criterion assuming that ER is convex and symmetric. In the average case setting these assumptions on ER are not always needed. Furthermore, a number of important error criteria correspond to nonconvex ER. The major example is provided by the probabilistic setting studied in Chapter 8 which corresponds to $\text{ER}(g) = 0$ if $\|g\| \leq \varepsilon$, and $\text{ER}(g) = 1$ otherwise.

The distance between $S(f)$ and $\phi(N(f))$ is now given by $\text{ER}(S(f) - \phi(N(f)))$. The average error is then defined by

$$e^{\text{avg}}(\phi, N) = \int_{F_1} \text{ER}(S(f) - \phi(N(f)))\, \mu(df).$$

To guarantee the existence of $e^{\text{avg}}(\phi, N)$, we assume that the mapping $\text{ER}(S(\cdot) - \phi(N(\cdot)))$ is measurable. This assumption can be weakened by defining first the local average error of the algorithm ϕ and by proceeding as in Section 3.1. Then we need only to assume that $\text{ER}(S(\cdot) - g)$ is measurable for every $g \in G$. To make the radius of information finite, we also assume that $\int_{F_1} \mathrm{ER}(Sf)\,\mu(df)$ is finite. We show how the results of Section 5 generalize for the error functional ER.

We first analyze adaptive information N^{a} with fixed cardinality $n(f) \equiv k$,

$$N^{\mathrm{a}}(f) = [L_1(f), L_2(f;y_1), \ldots, L_k(f;y_1, \ldots, y_{k-1})],$$

where $y_1 = L_1(f)$, $y_i = L_i(f;y_1, \ldots, y_{i-1})$, and $L_{i,y} = L_i(\cdot;y_1, \ldots, y_{i-1}) \in F_1^*$. The functionals $L_{i,y}$ are μ-orthonormal, $\langle L_{i,y}, L_{j,y} \rangle_\mu = \delta_{i,j}$. Recall that the conditional measure $\mu_2(\cdot|y)$ is Gaussian with mean element $m_{\mu,y} = \sum_{i=1}^k y_i C_\mu L_{i,y}$ and correlation operator $C_{k,y} = C_\mu - \sum_{i=1}^k L_{i,y}(\cdot) C_\mu L_{i,y}$. Let $\gamma_k(\cdot|y)$ denote the Gaussian measure with mean zero and correlation operator $C_{k,y}$. It is a translation of $\mu_2(\cdot|y)$, i.e., $\gamma_k(B|y) = \mu_2(B - m_{\mu,y}|y)$. Furthermore, for nonadaptive information $L_{i,y} \equiv L_i$ and $\gamma_k(\cdot|y)$ does not depend on y. Without loss of generality we assume that for every $y \in \mathbb{R}^k$ there exists an element $g^*(y)$ of G such that

$$\int_{F_1} \mathrm{ER}\left(S(f) - g^*(y)\right)\gamma_k(df|y) = \inf_{g \in G} \int_{F_1} \mathrm{ER}(S(f) - g)\gamma_k(df|y). \quad (1)$$

Note that if ER is convex and symmetric then $g^*(y) \equiv 0$. Indeed, convexity of ER yields

$$\mathrm{ER}(S(f)) \leq \tfrac{1}{2}\mathrm{ER}(S(f) - g) + \tfrac{1}{2}\mathrm{ER}(S(f) + g), \quad \forall g \in G.$$

Integrating the last inequality, we have

$$\int_{F_1} \mathrm{ER}(Sf)\,\gamma_k(df|y)$$

$$\leq \tfrac{1}{2}\int_{F_1} \mathrm{ER}(S(f) - g)\,\gamma_k(df|y) + \tfrac{1}{2}\int_{F_1} \mathrm{ER}(S(f) + g)\,\gamma_k(df|y).$$

Since ER is symmetric and $\gamma_k(A|y) = \gamma_k(-A|y)$ for any Borel set A, where $-A = \{f \in F_1, -f \in A\}$, we change the variable f to $-f$ to conclude that the second integral on the right-hand side is equal to the first one. Thus,

$$\int_{F_1} \mathrm{ER}(Sf)\,\gamma_k(df|y) \leq \int_{F_1} \mathrm{ER}(S(f) - g)\,\gamma_k(df|y), \quad \forall g \in G.$$

Hence $g^*(y) \equiv 0$, as claimed.

Define the translated μ-spline algorithm ϕ^* by

$$\phi^*(y) = \phi^s(y) + g^*(y) = Sm_{\mu,y} + g^*(y). \quad (2)$$

The mapping ϕ^* is, in general, nonlinear. If, however, the information is nonadaptive then $m_{\mu,y}$ depends linearly on y and $g^*(y) \equiv g^*$ for some element g^* from G. Thus, ϕ^* is an *affine* mapping. Since g^* can be precomputed, the computation of $\phi^*(y)$ requires at most n multiplications and additions in the space G and thus $\text{cost}(\phi^*, y) \leq 2n$.

We now prove an optimal error property of the algorithm ϕ^*.

THEOREM 6.3.1. *The translated μ-spline algorithm ϕ^* that uses adaptive information N^{a} with fixed cardinality $n(f) \equiv k$ minimizes the average error,*

$$e^{\text{avg}}(\phi^*, N^{\text{a}}) = r^{\text{avg}}(N^{\text{a}}) = \inf_{\phi} \int_{F_1} \text{ER}\left(S(f) - \phi(N(f))\right) \mu(df)$$

$$= (2\pi)^{-k/2} \int_{\mathbb{R}^k} \int_{F_1} \text{ER}\left(S(f) - g^*(y)\right) \gamma_k(df|y) \exp(-\langle y, y \rangle /2) \, dy.$$

PROOF: Take an arbitrary algorithm ϕ that uses N^{a}. Decomposing the measure μ as in Section 5.6, we get

$$e^{\text{avg}}(\phi, N^{\text{a}}) = \int_{\mathbb{R}^k} \int_{F_1} \text{ER}\left(S(f) - \phi(y)\right) \mu_2(df|y) \mu_1(dy)$$

$$= \int_{\mathbb{R}^k} \int_{F_1} \text{ER}\left(S(f) - (\phi(y) - Sm_{\mu,y})\right) \gamma_k(df|y) \mu_1(dy)$$

$$\geq \int_{\mathbb{R}^k} \inf_{g \in G} \int_{F_1} \text{ER}(S(f) - g) \gamma_k(df|y) \mu_1(dy)$$

$$= (2\pi)^{-k/2} \int_{\mathbb{R}^k} \text{ER}\left(S(f) - g^*(y)\right) \exp(-\langle y, y \rangle /2) \, dy.$$

For $\phi = \phi^*$, we get equality which shows that ϕ^* minimizes the average error. ∎

From Theorem 6.3.1 it easily follows that adaptive information N^{a} with fixed cardinality is no more powerful than nonadaptive information $N^{\text{non}}_{y^*}$ for an appropriately chosen y^*. Indeed, there exists a vector y^* for which

$$\int_{\mathbb{R}^k} \int_{F_1} \text{ER}\left(S(f) - g^*(y)\right) \gamma_k(df|y) \mu_1(dy)$$

$$\geq \int_{F_1} \text{ER}\left(S(f) - g^*(y^*)\right) \gamma_k(df|y^*), \tag{3}$$

where μ_1 stands, as before, for the Gaussian measure with mean zero and correlation matrix identity. For such a vector y^*, define the nonadaptive information,

$$N^{\text{non}}_{y^*} = [L_{1,y^*}, L_{2,y^*}, \ldots, L_{k,y^*}].$$

Then the translated μ-spline algorithm ϕ^* that uses $N_{y^*}^{\text{non}}$ takes the form

$$\phi^*(y) = \sum_{i=1}^{k} y_i \, SC_\mu L_{i,y^*} + g^*,$$

where $g^* = g^*(y^*)$. The average radius of $N_{y^*}^{\text{non}}$ is given by

$$r^{\text{avg}}(N_{y^*}^{\text{non}}) = e^{\text{avg}}(\phi^*, N_{y^*}^{\text{non}}) = \int_{\mathbb{R}^k} \int_{F_1} \text{ER}(S(f) - g^*) \, \gamma_k(df|y^*) \, \mu_1(dy)$$

$$= \int_{F_1} \text{ER}(S(f) - g^*) \, \gamma_k(df|y^*).$$

Hence, (3) implies that $r^{\text{avg}}(N^{\text{a}}) \geq r^{\text{avg}}(N_{y^*}^{\text{non}})$. We summarize this in

THEOREM 6.3.2. *For any error functional ER, adaptive information N^{a} with fixed cardinality $n(f) \equiv k$ is no more powerful than nonadaptive information $N_{y^*}^{\text{non}}$ of cardinality k,*

$$r^{\text{avg}}(N_{y^*}^{\text{non}}) \leq r^{\text{avg}}(N^{\text{a}}).$$

We now analyze adaptive information N^{a} with varying cardinality,

$$N^{\text{a}}(f) = [L_1(f), L_2(f; y_1), \ldots, L_{n(f)}(f; y_1, \ldots, y_{n(f)-1})],$$

where $y_1 = L_1(f)$, $y_i = L_i(f; y_1, \ldots, y_{i-1})$, and

$$n(f) = \min \{i : \text{ter}_i(y_1, \ldots, y_i) = 1\}.$$

Let $B_k = \{N^{\text{a}}(f) : f \in F_1 \text{ and } n(f) = k\}$. We assume that the average cardinality of N^{a} is finite,

$$\text{card}^{\text{avg}}(N^{\text{a}}) = \sum_{k=1}^{\infty} k \lambda_k(B_k) < +\infty,$$

where λ_k is the Gaussian measure on $\mathbb{R}^k$ with mean zero and correlation matrix identity.

Assume that the solution of (1) exists for $k = 1, 2, \ldots$. That is, for every integer k and $y \in \mathbb{R}^k$, let $g_k^*(y)$ be an element of G such that (1) holds.

Let $y \in N^{\text{a}}(F)$. Then $y = [y_1, \ldots, y_k]$ for some k. Repeating the proof of Theorem 6.3.1, it is easy to see that the translated μ-spline algorithm that uses N^{a},

$$\phi^*(y) = \sum_{i=1}^{k} y_i \, SC_\mu L_{i,y} + g_k^*(y),$$

minimizes the average error and that the radius of information of N^{a} is given by

$$e(\phi^*, N^{\mathrm{a}}) = r^{\mathrm{avg}}(N^{\mathrm{a}}) = \sum_{k=1}^{\infty} \int_{B_k} \int_{F_1} \mathrm{ER}\left(S(f) - g_k^*(y)\right) \gamma_k(df|y) \lambda_k(dy).$$

Similarly to (3) we conclude that for any integer k, there exists a vector y_k^* such that

$$\int_{B_k} \int_{F_1} \mathrm{ER}\left(S(f) - g_k^*(y)\right) \gamma_k(df|y) \lambda_k(dy)$$
$$\geq \int_{F_1} \mathrm{ER}\left(S(f) - g_k^*(y_k^*)\right) \gamma_k(df|y_k^*) \lambda_k(B_k) = r^{\mathrm{avg}}(M_k) \lambda_k(B_k).$$

Here, $M_k = N_{y_k^*}^{\mathrm{non}} = [L_1, L_{2,y_k^*}, \dots, L_{k,y_k^*}]$ is nonadaptive information of cardinality k. From this we conclude that

$$r^{\mathrm{avg}}(N^{\mathrm{a}}) \geq \sum_{k=1}^{\infty} r^{\mathrm{avg}}(M_k) \lambda_k(B_k).$$

Consider the following minimization problem

$$r = \inf\left\{ \sum_{k=1}^{\infty} r^{\mathrm{avg}}(M_k) a_k : a_k \geq 0, \ \sum_{k=1}^{\infty} a_k = 1, \ \sum_{k=1}^{\infty} k a_k \leq \mathrm{card}^{\mathrm{avg}}(N^{\mathrm{a}}) \right\}.$$

From Lemma 5.6.3 it follows that there exist two indices k_1 and k_2 and a number $a^* \in [0, 1]$ such that

$$r = r^{\mathrm{avg}}(M_{k_1}) a^* + r^{\mathrm{avg}}(M_{k_2})(1 - a^*),$$
$$\mathrm{card}^{\mathrm{avg}}(N^{\mathrm{a}}) = k_1 a^* + k_2(1 - a^*).$$

Let A be any Borel set of $\mathbb{R}$ whose λ_1-measure is equal to a^*. Define the information

$$N^*(f) = \begin{cases} M_{k_1}(f) & \text{if } L_1(f) \in A, \\ M_{k_2}(f) & \text{otherwise,} \end{cases}$$

where L_1 is the first functional of M_{k_1} (and of M_{k_2}). Then $r^{\mathrm{avg}}(N^*) = r \leq r^{\mathrm{avg}}(N^{\mathrm{a}})$ and $\mathrm{card}^{\mathrm{avg}}(N^*) = \mathrm{card}^{\mathrm{avg}}(N^{\mathrm{a}})$. We thus obtain the generalization of Theorem 5.6.2.

THEOREM 6.3.3. *For any error functional* ER, *adaptive information* N^{a} *with finite cardinality* $\mathrm{card}^{\mathrm{avg}}(N^{\mathrm{a}})$ *is no more powerful than the information* N^*,

$$\mathrm{card}^{\mathrm{avg}}(N^*) = \mathrm{card}^{\mathrm{avg}}(N^{\mathrm{a}}) \quad \text{and} \quad r^{\mathrm{avg}}(N^*) \leq r^{\mathrm{avg}}(N^{\mathrm{a}}).$$

As in Section 5.6, one can compare the power of adaptive information N^{a} to the power of the optimal nonadaptive information in the class Λ. Namely, let

$$r^{\mathrm{avg}}(n, \Lambda) = \inf \left\{ r^{\mathrm{avg}}(N) : N = [L_1, L_2, \ldots, L_n] \text{ with } L_i \in \Lambda \right\}$$

be the nth minimal radius of nonadaptive information in the class Λ. Let N_n^* be the nth optimal nonadaptive information in this class, $r^{\mathrm{avg}}(N_n^*) = r^{\mathrm{avg}}(n, \Lambda)$. We stress that $r^{\mathrm{avg}}(n, \Lambda)$ and N_n^* depend on the error functional ER. Then proceeding exactly as in the proof of Theorem 5.6.3, we obtain the following

THEOREM 6.3.4. *Consider arbitrary adaptive information N^{a} with finite* $\mathrm{card}^{\mathrm{avg}}(N^{\mathrm{a}})$ *which consists of functionals from the class Λ. For any error functional* ER *we have*

(i) *If the sequence $\{r^{\mathrm{avg}}(n, \Lambda)\}$ is convex, then the nth optimal non-adaptive information N_n^* with $n = \lceil \mathrm{card}^{\mathrm{avg}}(N^{\mathrm{a}}) \rceil$ is as powerful as N^{a},*

$$r^{\mathrm{avg}}(N_n^*) \leq r^{\mathrm{avg}}(N^{\mathrm{a}}).$$

(ii) *If the sequence $\{r^{\mathrm{avg}}(n, \Lambda)\}$ is semiconvex, i.e., $a\, \alpha_n \leq r^{\mathrm{avg}}(n, \Lambda) \leq b\, \alpha_n$ for a convex sequence $\{\alpha_k\}$ and positive constants a and b, then for n and N_n^* as in (i) we have*

$$r^{\mathrm{avg}}(N_n^*) \leq \frac{b}{a}\, r^{\mathrm{avg}}(N^{\mathrm{a}}).$$

We now discuss optimal nonadaptive information for the error functional of the form

$$\mathrm{ER}(g) = \mathrm{H}(\|g\|), \quad g \in G, \tag{4}$$

where $\mathrm{H} : R_+ \to \mathbb{R}_+$ is convex and nondecreasing. From now on, we assume that G is a separable Hilbert space. The error functional ER is convex and symmetric and therefore $g^*(y) \equiv 0$ in (1). This means that for every information the μ-spline algorithm is optimal.

We discuss two cases of linear problems. In the first one, we assume that S is a continuous linear functional and the class Λ is an arbitrary subset of F_1^*. In the second one, we assume that S is a continuous linear operator and $\Lambda = F_1^*$ consists of all continuous linear functionals.

Case 1: $S \in F_1^*$ and $\Lambda \subset F_1^*$.

The average radius of nonadaptive information $N = [L_1, L_2, \ldots, L_n]$ with $\langle L_i, L_j \rangle_\mu = \delta_{i,j}$ is given by Theorem 6.3.1,

$$r^{\text{avg}}(N) = \int_{F_1} H(\|S(f)\|)\, \gamma_n(df|0)$$

$$= \sqrt{\frac{2}{\pi}} \int_0^\infty H\left(\sqrt{\sigma(N)}\, t\right) \exp\left(-t^2/2\right) dt,$$

where the variance $\sigma(N)$ is given by

$$\sigma(N) = S(C_{n,0}S) = \|S\|_\mu^2 - \sum_{i=1}^n \langle S, L_i \rangle_\mu^2 = \inf_{a_i \in \mathbb{R}} \left\| S - \sum_{i=1}^n a_i L_i \right\|_\mu^2.$$

Observe that the average radius $r^{\text{avg}}(N)$ is a nonincreasing function of $\sigma(N)$. Therefore, the optimal nonadaptive information does *not* depend on the function H. Let

$$\sigma_n = \inf_{L_i \in \Lambda} \inf_{a_i \in \mathbb{R}} \left\| S - \sum_{i=1}^n a_i L_i \right\|_\mu^2$$

be the minimal variance obtained after n evaluations. Let the first minimum be obtained by $L_1^*, \ldots, L_n^*$, and let $N_n^* = [L_1^*, L_2^*, \ldots, L_n^*]$. We thus have

COROLLARY 6.3.1. *Information N_n^* is nth optimal nonadaptive information in the class Λ for any error functional ER of the form* (4).

Case 2: Continuous linear operator S and $\Lambda = F_1^*$.

The average radius of information $N = [L_1, L_2, \ldots, L_n]$ with $\langle L_i, L_j \rangle_\mu = \delta_{i,j}$ is now equal to

$$r^{\text{avg}}(N) = \int_{F_1} H(\|S(f)\|)\, \gamma_n(df|0) = \int_G H(\|g\|)\, \nu(dg|N), \qquad (5)$$

where $\nu(\cdot|N)$ is Gaussian with mean zero and correlation operator

$$C_{\nu,N} = C_\nu - \sum_{i=1}^n \langle \cdot, SC_\mu L_i \rangle\, SC_\mu L_i. \qquad (6)$$

Here C_ν stands for the correlation operator of the *a priori* Gaussian measure $\nu = \mu S^{-1}$.

As in Section 5.5, let (λ_i^*, η_i^*) be the eigenpairs of the operator C_ν,

$$C_\nu \eta_i^* = \lambda_i^* \eta_i^*, \quad \lambda_1^* \geq \lambda_2^* \geq \cdots \geq 0,$$

with the convention that for $\dim(G) < +\infty$ we formally set $\lambda_i^* = 0$ for $i > \dim(G)$. Let $k = \min\{n, \sup\{i : \lambda_i^* > 0\}\}$ with $\sup \emptyset = 0$. Define the nonadaptive information N_n^* of cardinality at most n as follows. If $k = 0$ then $N_n^* = 0$, otherwise

$$N_n^*(f) = [L_1^*(f), L_2^*(f), \ldots, L_k^*(f)],$$

where $L_i^*(f) = (\lambda_i^*)^{-1/2} \langle S(f), \eta_i^* \rangle$. Theorem 5.5.1 states that N_n^* is nth optimal for the error functional given in the $\mathcal{L}_2$ sense. We extend this result by showing that N_n^* remains nth optimal for arbitrary convex and nondecreasing H in (4).

THEOREM 6.3.5. *Information N_n^* is nth optimal nonadaptive information in the class $\Lambda = F_1^*$ for any error functional ER of the form (4).*

PROOF: Assume first that the space G has a finite dimension, $\dim(G) = m$. Consider the correlation operator $A = C_{\nu, N_n^*}$ of the Gaussian measure $\nu(\cdot | N_n^*)$.

If $m \leq n$ then $A = 0$ and $\nu(\cdot | N_n^*)$ is atomic. Then $r^{\text{avg}}(N_n^*) = \text{H}(0)$. Note that $\text{H}(0) \leq \text{H}(\|g\|)$, $\forall g \in G$. Integrating this with respect to $\nu(dg|N)$, where N is arbitrary information, we get from (5),

$$r^{\text{avg}}(N_n^*) = \text{H}(0) \leq \int_G \text{H}(\|g\|) \, \nu(dg|N) = r^{\text{avg}}(N).$$

Thus, N_n^* is kth optimal for all k.

Suppose then that $m > n$. Let α_i be eigenvalues of A, $\alpha_1 \geq \alpha_2 \geq \cdots \geq \alpha_m \geq 0$. Then $\alpha_i = \lambda_{i+n}^*$ for $i = 1, 2, \ldots, m - n$, and $\alpha_i = 0$ for $i = m - n + 1, \ldots, m$. As before, λ_i^* are eigenvalues of C_ν. Take an arbitrary nonadaptive information N of cardinality at most n. The correlation operator $B = C_{\nu, N}$ of the Gaussian measure $\nu(\cdot | N)$ is given by (6). Of course, $B = B^* \geq 0$. Let $\{\beta_i\}$ be its eigenvalues, $\beta_1 \geq \beta_2 \geq \cdots \geq \beta_m \geq 0$. From (6) we have

$$B = C_\nu - C,$$

where $C = C^* \geq 0$ and whose rank is at most n. From Weyl's monotonicity theorem, see e.g., Parlett [80, pp. 191-194], it follows that

$$\beta_i \geq \lambda_{i+n}^*, \quad i = 1, 2, \ldots, m - n.$$

This yields that $\alpha_i \leq \beta_i$ for $i = 2, \ldots, m$.

The measures $\nu(\cdot|N_n^*)$ and $\nu(\cdot|N)$ are Gaussian and therefore (5) can be rewritten as

$$r^{\mathrm{avg}}(N_n^*) = (2\pi)^{-m/2} \int_{\mathbb{R}^m} \mathrm{H}\left(\left(\sum_{i=1}^{m} \alpha_i \, t_i^2\right)^{1/2}\right) \exp\left(-\sum_{i=1}^{m} t_i^2/2\right) dt,$$

$$r^{\mathrm{avg}}(N_n^*) = (2\pi)^{-m/2} \int_{\mathbb{R}^m} \mathrm{H}\left(\left(\sum_{i=1}^{m} \beta_i \, t_i^2\right)^{1/2}\right) \exp\left(-\sum_{i=1}^{m} t_i^2/2\right) dt.$$

Clearly, $r^{\mathrm{avg}}(N_n^*) \leq r^{\mathrm{avg}}(N)$ since $\alpha_i \leq \beta_i$ and H is nondecreasing. Thus, N_n^* is nth optimal information.

Suppose now that $\dim(G) = +\infty$. Then

$$r^{\mathrm{avg}}(N) = \lim_{m \to \infty} \int_G \mathrm{H}\left(\|P_m g\|\right) \nu(dg|N),$$

where P_m is the orthogonal projection onto the space spanned by the first m eigenelements $\eta_1^*, \eta_2^*, \ldots, \eta_m^*$ of C_ν. As above one can show that

$$\int_G \mathrm{H}(\|P_m g\|) \, \nu(dg|N) \geq \int_G \mathrm{H}(\|P_m g\|) \, \nu(dg|N_n^*)$$

and therefore $r^{\mathrm{avg}}(N) \geq r^{\mathrm{avg}}(N_n^*)$. Thus, N_n^* is nth optimal information which completes the proof. ∎

The essence of Theorem 6.3.5 and Corollary 6.3.1 is that the same information and the same algorithm remain optimal for a variety of different error criteria. This shows the robustness of optimality properties of information N_n^* and the μ-spline algorithm ϕ^s with respect to the error functional ER of the form (4).

We now briefly discuss the average complexity, $\mathrm{comp}^{\mathrm{avg}}(\varepsilon)$, under the general error functional ER. As in Section 5.7, the complexity bounds depend on $m^{\mathrm{avg}}(\varepsilon)$ and $n^{\mathrm{avg}}(\varepsilon)$. Recall that

$$m^{\mathrm{avg}}(\varepsilon) = \min\left\{\mathrm{card}^{\mathrm{avg}}(N) : r^{\mathrm{avg}}(N) \leq \varepsilon\right\}$$

is the average ε-cardinality number and

$$n^{\mathrm{avg}}(\varepsilon) = \min\left\{n : r^{\mathrm{avg}}(n, \Lambda) \leq \varepsilon\right\}$$

is the minimal number of nonadaptive evaluations needed to find an ε-approximation. Then we have

THEOREM 6.3.6.

(i) *The ε-complexity $\mathrm{comp}^{\mathrm{avg}}(\varepsilon)$ is bounded by*

$$c\, m^{\mathrm{avg}}(\varepsilon) \le \mathrm{comp}^{\mathrm{avg}}(\varepsilon) \le (c+2)\, m^{\mathrm{avg}}(\varepsilon) + 1,$$

where c is the cost of one information operation. For $c \gg 1$, we have

$$\mathrm{comp}^{\mathrm{avg}}(\varepsilon) \simeq c\, m^{\mathrm{avg}}(\varepsilon).$$

(ii) *Let $r_i = r^{\mathrm{avg}}(i, \Lambda)$. The ε-cardinality number $m^{\mathrm{avg}}(\varepsilon)$ is bounded by*

$$0 \le m^{\mathrm{avg}}(\varepsilon) - \min\left\{ \frac{\varepsilon - r_j}{r_i - r_j} i + \frac{r_i - \varepsilon}{r_i - r_j} j \ : i \ \le j \text{ and } r_j \le \varepsilon \le r_i \right\} \le \tfrac{1}{2},$$

$$\sup_{x>1} \min\left\{ n^{\mathrm{avg}}(x\varepsilon), \frac{x-1}{x} n^{\mathrm{avg}}(\varepsilon) \right\} \le m^{\mathrm{avg}}(\varepsilon) \le n^{\mathrm{avg}}(\varepsilon).$$

(iii) *If $\{r^{\mathrm{avg}}(n, \Lambda)\}$ is convex then*

$$\left\lceil m^{\mathrm{avg}}(n) \right\rceil = n^{\mathrm{avg}}(\varepsilon).$$

PROOF: The proof is essentially the same as the proofs of Theorems 5.7.1 and 5.7.2. Note that the upper bound on $\mathrm{comp}^{\mathrm{avg}}(\varepsilon)$ in Theorem 5.7.1 is $(c+2)\, m^{\mathrm{avg}}(\varepsilon)$, whereas in Theorem 6.3.6 we have $(c+2)\, m^{\mathrm{avg}}(\varepsilon) + 1$ since we use the translated μ-spline algorithm which requires one more addition than the (untranslated) μ-spline algorithm. Of course, if the error functional ER is convex and symmetric, the μ-spline algorithm is optimal and this extra addition is not needed.

Note that the lower bounds on $m^{\mathrm{avg}}(\varepsilon)$ in Theorem 6.3.6 differ from the lower bounds in Theorem 5.7.2. This is because in the earlier analysis we worked with the square root of the local average radii of information in the $\mathcal{L}_2$ sense. ∎

The upper bounds on $\mathrm{comp}^{\mathrm{avg}}(\varepsilon)$ in Theorem 6.3.6 can be achieved by information N^* constructed as in Corollary 5.7.2 and by the translated μ-spline algorithm ϕ^s that uses N^*.

Notes and Remarks

NR 6.3:1 This section is based on Wasilkowski [86a,b] and Lee and Wasilkowski [86].

NR 6.3:2 Probably the most natural example of the error criterion ER which satisfies (4) is $ER(g) = \|g\|^p$ for $p \ge 1$. This is a convex and symmetric error criterion, with the function $\mathrm{H}(t) = t^p$ which is convex and nondecreasing. Therefore, the same information

N_n^* and the μ-spline algorithm ϕ^s that uses N_n^* are optimal no matter what the value of p is. However, the ε-complexity depends on the error criterion since the value of $r^{\mathrm{avg}}(n, \Lambda)$ depends on p. For example, consider a continuous linear functional S. Then

$$r^{\mathrm{avg}}(N) = \sqrt{\frac{2}{\pi}}\, \sigma(N)^{p/2} \int_0^\infty t^p \exp\left(-t^2/2\right) dt.$$

For even integers p, we have

$$r^{\mathrm{avg}}(N) = (p-1)!!\, \sigma(N)^{p/2},$$

for odd integers p, we have

$$r^{\mathrm{avg}}(N) = \sqrt{2^p/\pi}\, ((p-1)/2)!\, \sigma(N)^{p/2},$$

see Gradshteyn and Ryzhik [80, 3.46-3.48].

NR 6.3:3 To establish the ε-complexity under the error criterion given by ER, it is necessary to know the behavior of the sequence $r^{\mathrm{avg}}(n, \Lambda)$. For a general error criterion, the computation of $r^{\mathrm{avg}}(n, \Lambda)$ can be hard. For instance, let $\Lambda = F_1^*$, $\mathrm{ER}(g) = \|g\|^p$ with $p \geq 1$, and let $G = \mathbb{R}^m$ with $k = m - n \geq 0$. Then the computation of n for which

$$r^{\mathrm{avg}}(n, \Lambda) = (2\pi)^{-k/2} \int_{\mathbb{R}^k} \left(\sum_{i=1}^k \gamma_i t_i^2\right)^{p/2} \exp\left(-\sum_{i=1}^k t_i^2/2\right) dt \leq \varepsilon^p$$

for some positive γ_i, is not obvious for $p \neq 2$.

NR 6.3:4 Consider $S \in F_1^*$, $\Lambda \subset F_1^*$, and the error criterion in the $\mathcal{L}_p$ sense, $p \in [1, +\infty)$, i.e.,

$$e^{\mathrm{avg}}(\phi, N) = \left(\int_{F_1} |S(f) - \phi(N(f))|^p \, \mu(df)\right)^{1/p}.$$

For nonadaptive $N = [L_1, \ldots, L_n]$, **NR 6.3:2** and the form of $\sigma(N)$ yield

$$r^{\mathrm{avg}}(N) = \alpha_p \inf_{g_i \in \mathbb{R}} \left\| S - \sum_{i=1}^n g_i L_i \right\|_\mu,$$

where $\alpha_p = \left(\sqrt{2/\pi} \int_0^\infty t^p \exp\left(-t^2/2\right) dt\right)^{1/p}$. In particular, $\alpha_1 = \sqrt{2/\pi}$ and $\alpha_2 = 1$.

This generalizes Corollary 5.3.1 for the $\mathcal{L}_p$ error criterion and states that modulo a multiplicative factor α_p the average radius of nonadaptive information is equal to the error of the least squares approximation of S by $\mathrm{span}(L_1, \ldots, L_n)$ with respect to the norm $\|\cdot\|_\mu$.

NR 6.3:5 Consider Cases 1 and 2 for the function H given by (4) which is nondecreasing but not necessarily convex. Then the translated μ-spline algorithm that uses nonadaptive information N is optimal and

$$r^{\mathrm{avg}}(N) = \int_{F_1} \mathrm{H}(\|S(f) + g^*\|)\, \gamma_n(df|0)$$

for some element $g^* = g^*(N)$. If, however, one can show that $g^*(N) = 0$ for arbitrary nonadaptive information N, then the analysis of Cases 1 and 2 carries over. This shows that the same information remains optimal if the μ-spline algorithms are optimal and H is nondecreasing. As we shall see in Chapter 8, this is the case in the probabilistic setting.

Exercises

E 6.3:1 Consider a linear problem with a continuous linear functional S and with the error functional $\mathrm{ER}(g) = |g|^p$ for $p \geq 1$. Let $r^{\mathrm{avg}}(N,p)$ denote the average radius of nonadaptive information. Prove that

$$\lim_{p \to \infty} r^{\mathrm{avg}}(N,p)^{1/p} = +\infty$$

whenever $\sigma(N) > 0$, see Case 1 and **NR 6.3:2**.

E 6.3:2 Consider a convex and symmetric error functional ER for a linear problem with an arbitrary measurable set F of problem elements. That is, the average error is defined by

$$e^{\mathrm{avg}}(\phi, N) = \frac{1}{\mu(F)} \int_F \mathrm{ER}\left(S(f) - \phi(N(f))\right) \mu(df).$$

Let $N = [L_1, L_2, \ldots, L_n]$ with $\left\langle L_i, L_j \right\rangle = \delta_{i,j}$, and let $Df = 2 \sum_{j=1}^n L_j(f) C_\mu L_j - f$. Prove that $D(F) = F$ implies that the μ-spline algorithm has minimal average error, see **E 5.8.2:2**.

E 6.3:3 Consider the case when the error of an algorithm ϕ that uses information N is defined in the $\mathcal{L}_\infty$ sense,

$$e(\phi, N) = \inf_{A:\mu(A)=0} \sup_{f \in F - A} \|S(f) - \phi(N(f))\|$$

$$= \lim_{p \to \infty} \left(\int_F \|S(f) - \phi(N(f))\|^p \mu(df) \right)^{1/p}.$$

Show that for a linear problem with $F = F_1$ and $S \notin \mathrm{span}\,(L_1, L_2, \ldots, L_n)$, $\forall n$, $\forall L_i \in \Lambda$, we have $e(\phi, N) = +\infty$ for any pair (ϕ, N) such that $\mathrm{card}^{\mathrm{avg}}(N) < +\infty$.

6.4. Precision Error

We now briefly discuss the precision error functional ER in the average case setting, see Remark 6.3.1 of Chapter 4. That is,

$$\mathrm{ER}(g) = \log_2 \frac{1}{\|g\|}, \quad g \in G.$$

For an algorithm ϕ that uses information N, define

$$e^{\mathrm{pre}}(\phi, N) = \int_F \mathrm{ER}\left(S(f) - \phi(N(f))\right) \mu(df).$$

Then $e^{\mathrm{pre}}(\phi, N)$ is equal to the average number of significant bits of $S(f)$ recovered by ϕ and N. Let $\mathrm{comp}^{\mathrm{pre}}(k)$ be the average complexity of computing k bits of the solution elements on the average,

$$\mathrm{comp}^{\mathrm{pre}}(k) = \inf \{ \, \mathrm{cost}^{\mathrm{avg}}(\phi, N) : e^{\mathrm{pre}}(\phi, N) \ge k \, \}.$$

We find bounds on $\mathrm{comp}^{\mathrm{pre}}(k)$ for a linear problem with $F = F_1$. Consider nonadaptive information $N = [L_1, L_2, \ldots, L_n]$, $\langle L_i, L_j \rangle_\mu = \delta_{i,j}$. We first want to find an algorithm ϕ^* that uses N and whose average number of significant bits is maximal, i.e.,

$$e^{\mathrm{pre}}(\phi^*, N) = \sup_{\phi} e^{\mathrm{pre}}(\phi, N).$$

Observe that

$$e^{\mathrm{pre}}(\phi^*, N) = -\inf_{\phi} \int_{F_1} \overline{\mathrm{ER}}\big(S(f) - \phi(N(f))\big) \, \mu(df),$$

where $\overline{\mathrm{ER}}(g) = -\mathrm{ER}(g) = \log_2 \|g\|$. Although $\overline{\mathrm{ER}}$ changes sign, the results of Section 6.3 carry over. This means that the translated μ-spline $\phi^*(y) = \sum_{i=1}^{n} y_i C_\mu L_i + g^*$ maximizes $e^{\mathrm{avg}}(\cdot, N)$. Here the element g^* is chosen to minimize the function

$$z(t) = \int_G \log_2 \|g - t\| \, \nu(dg|0), \quad \forall t \in G.$$

It is not hard to observe that $g^* = 0$. Indeed, it is enough to check it for finite dimensional spaces $G = \mathbb{R}^m$. Then

$$z(t) = \tfrac{1}{2} \prod_{i=1}^{m} \frac{1}{\sqrt{2\pi\sigma_i}} \int_{\mathbb{R}^m} \log_2 \left(\sum_{i=1}^{m} x_i^2 \right) \exp\left(-\sum_{i=1}^{m} \frac{(x_i - t_i)^2}{2\sigma_i} \right) dx_1 \ldots dx_m$$

for some nonnegative σ_i. The function z is even. It can be checked that its gradient is zero only for $t = 0$. Since $z(t) \to +\infty$ as $\|t\| \to +\infty$, this proves that the minimum of z is at 0. Thus $g^* = 0$, as claimed.

We now turn to the problem of optimal nonadaptive information for a given class Λ. Suppose first that $S \in F_1^*$, i.e., S is a continuous linear functional. From the form of the function z, it is obvious that the information N_n^* which minimizes the variance of the conditional measure is optimal.

Assume now that S is an arbitrary continuous linear operator and $\Lambda = F_1^*$. Once more, the form of the function z yields that the information N_n^* presented in Theorem 6.3.5 remains optimal under the precision error functional.

Chapter 7

Average Case Setting: Applications

1. Introduction

In this chapter we apply the results of Chapter 6 to three linear problems: integration, function approximation, and ill-posed problems. The integration problem is studied for two classes of scalar functions assuming that only values of the function and/or its derivatives can be computed. The function approximation problem is studied for two classes of multivariate functions assuming that all continuous linear functionals can be computed. The ill-posed problem requires the extension of the theory of Chapter 6 to unbounded linear solution operators S. We show that if S is "bounded on the average", then most of the results of Chapter 6 hold.

We exhibit tight complexity bounds, (almost) optimal information, and optimal algorithms. In particular, we show how a Gaussian measure increases the "effective" smoothness of functions and how much the average case complexity is decreased compared to the worst case complexity.

As in Chapter 5, the complexity analysis of linear problems is usually based on specific results obtained in a number of papers as cited in corresponding sections and in Notes and Remarks. We report many such results without proofs; they can be found in the cited references. Contrary to the worst case setting, we restrict ourselves to only linear problems. No average case complexity analysis of nonlinear problems presented in Chapter 5 has been performed.

2. Integration

In this section we analyze the integration problem for two classes of scalar functions. The first one consists of smooth functions equipped with the sup norm and the Wiener measure placed on rth derivatives. The second class consists of functions from a reproducing kernel Hilbert space. In particular, the class of periodic and smooth functions is an example of such a class. The worst case setting for these classes was analyzed in Section 2 of Chapter 5. Here we study the average case.

Notes and Remarks

NR 2:1 Novak [87a] studied the following variant of the average case setting for the integration problem. Let $r^{\mathrm{avg}}(n, \mu)$ denote the minimal average case error with respect to a probability measure μ among all algorithms that use n adaptive function values. Let $r^{\mathrm{avg}}(n, \mathrm{worst}) = \sup_{\mu} r^{\mathrm{avg}}(n, \mu)$ denote the maximal such radius with respect to all probability measures μ. As in **NR 2:1** of Chapter 5, consider two classes

$$C_d^{r,\alpha} = \{f : [0,1]^d \to \mathbb{R} : |D^{(i)}f(x) - D^{(i)}f(y)| \le \|x - y\|_\infty^\alpha$$
$$\text{for all partial derivatives } D^{(i)}, |i| \le r\},$$

where $r \ge 1$ and $\alpha \in (0,1]$, and

$$W_p^{r,d} = \{f : [0,1]^d \to \mathbb{R} : \sum_{|i|=r} \|f^{(i)}\|_p \le 1\}$$

with $p \in [1, +\infty]$, $r \ge 1$, $i = [i_1, \ldots, i_d]$ is a multiindex with $|i| = \sum_{j=1}^d i_j$, and $f^{(i)}$ denotes the distributional derivative in $\mathcal{L}_p$. Novak proved that for the class $C_d^{r,\alpha}$,

$$r^{\mathrm{avg}}(n, \mathrm{worst}) = \Theta\left(n^{-(r+\alpha)/d-1/2}\right).$$

This should be contrasted with the nth minimal worst case radius $r^{\mathrm{wor}}(n)$ which is equal to $\Theta(n^{-(r+\alpha)/d})$, see **NR 2:1** of Chapter 5. For the class $W_p^{r,d}$ with $rp > d$, Novak proved

$$r^{\mathrm{avg}}(n, \mathrm{worst}) = \Theta\left(n^{-r/d-\max\{1/2, 1-1/p\}}\right).$$

This should be compared with the nth minimal worst case radius $r^{\mathrm{wor}}(n) = \Theta(n^{-r/d})$.

For both classes, this means that no matter how the probability measure is selected, the nth minimal average radius is much smaller than the corresponding radius for the worst case setting. This is especially evident if d is large relative to r. This also implies that the average ε-complexity is at most proportional to $\varepsilon^{-1/2}$ for all d, whereas the worst case ε-complexity is exponential in d.

2.1. Smooth Functions

In this section we analyze the integration problem for the space

$$F_1 = \{f : [0,1] \to \mathbb{R} : f^{(r)} \text{ is continuous}, f(0) = f'(0) = \cdots = f^{(r)}(0)\}.$$

The space F_1 is equipped with the norm $\|f\| = \max_{0 \le t \le 1} |f^{(r)}(t)|$. Thus, F_1 is a separable Banach space. We equip the space F_1 with a Wiener measure placed on rth derivatives,

$$\mu(B) = w\big(D^r(B)\big), \quad \forall \text{ Borel set } B,$$

where w is the classical Wiener measure defined on Borel sets of the space of continuous functions which vanish at zero, see Section 2.9 of the appendix.

The measure μ is Gaussian with mean zero and correlation operator C_μ given as follows. For every $L \in F_1^*$ there exists a function $s_L : [0,1] \to \mathbb{R}$, which is of bounded variation, continuous from the left, and satisfying $s_L(1) = 0$, such that

$$L(f) = \int_0^1 f^{(r)}(t)\, d\big(s_L(t)\big), \quad \forall f \in F_1.$$

Then $C_\mu L = -T^{r+1} s_L$, where

$$\left(T^{r+1} f\right)(x) = \int_0^1 f(t)\, \frac{(x - t)_+^r}{r!}\, dt.$$

We first consider the integration problem $S(f) = \int_0^1 f(t)\, dt$ for the whole space F_1. Let Λ consist of linear functionals of the form $L(f) = f^{(j)}(x)$, $\forall f \in F_1$, where $x \in [0,1]$ and $j \le r$.

Let $N(f) = [L_1(f), \ldots, L_n(f)]$ be nonadaptive information with the functionals L_i of the form $L_i(f) = f^{(j_i)}(t_i)$. Then $L_i(f) = \int_0^1 f^{(r)}(t)\, ds_i(t)$, where $s_i(t) = (t_i - t)_+^{r-j_i} / (r - j_i)!$. From Corollary 5.3.1 of Chapter 6, we know that the average radius $r^{\text{avg}}(N)$ is given by

$$r^{\text{avg}}(N) = \inf_{g_i \in \mathbb{R}} \left\| S - \sum_{i=1}^n g_i L_i \right\|_\mu.$$

Note that $\langle L_i, L_j \rangle_\mu = \int_0^1 s_i(t) s_j(t)\, dt = \langle s_i, s_j \rangle_{\mathcal{L}_2}$, and

$$S(f) = -\int_0^1 f^{(r)}(t)\, d\big(s(t)\big)$$

with $s(t) = (1 - t)^{r+1} / (r + 1)!$. Therefore,

$$r^{\text{avg}}(N) = \inf_{g_i \in \mathbb{R}} \left(\int_0^1 \left(\frac{(1 - t)^{r+1}}{(r + 1)!} - \sum_{i=1}^n g_i \frac{(t_i - t)_+^{r - j_i}}{(r - j_i)!} \right)^2 dt \right)^{1/2}.$$

Thus, the average radius of information corresponds to the worst case radius of information in the space $W_2^{r+1}(0,1)$ with $q = 1$, see Section 2.2 of Chapter 5. Hence we can use the results for the worst case setting. In particular,

$$r^{\text{avg}}(n, \Lambda) = \inf \left\{ \left(\int_0^1 \left(\frac{(1-t)^{r+1}}{(r+1)!} - \sum_{i=1}^{n} g_i \frac{(t_i - t)_+^{r-j_i}}{(r-j_i)!} \right)^2 dt \right)^{1/2} : \right.$$

$$\left. g_i \in \mathbb{R}, 0 \le t_i \le 1, j_i \le r \right\}.$$

From Žensykbaev [82] we know that the nth optimal information consists of n function values, $j_i = 0$. The optimal points t_i^* and weights g_i^* satisfy the system of nonlinear equations presented in Section 2.2 of Chapter 5 with r replaced by $r + 1$ and with $p = p' = 2$. The exact form of t_i^* and g_i^* is not known for $r \ge 3$. We have, however, for $n > 2\lfloor (r + 1)/2 \rfloor + 1$, the following bounds from (5) of Section 2.2 of Chapter 5,

$$\frac{1}{n^{r+1}} \le r^{\text{avg}}(n, \Lambda) \sqrt{\frac{(2r+2)!}{|B_{2r+2}|}} \le \frac{1}{(n - 2\lfloor (r+1)/2 \rfloor - 1)^{r+1}}, \quad (1)$$

where B_{2r+2} is the Bernoulli number. Asymptotically we thus have

$$r^{\text{avg}}(n, \Lambda) = \sqrt{\frac{|B_{2r+2}|}{(2r+2)!}} \frac{1}{n^{r+1}} (1 + o(1)) \quad \text{as } n \to \infty. \quad (2)$$

Recall that $B_2 = 1/6$, $B_4 = -1/30$, $B_6 = 1/42$, $B_8 = -1/30$, $B_{10} = 5/66$, $B_{12} = -691/2730$, see Gradshteyn and Ryzhik [80, pp. 1079-1080].

The upper bound in (1) can be slightly improved. Indeed, consider the information

$$N_n(f) =$$

$$\left[f(1), f'(1), f^{(3)}(1), \ldots, f^{(s)}(1), f\left(\frac{1}{m}\right), f\left(\frac{2}{m}\right), \ldots, f\left(\frac{m-1}{m}\right) \right], \quad (3)$$

where $s = 0$ if $r = 1$, and $s = 2\lfloor (r+1)/2 \rfloor - 1$ otherwise, and $n = m + \lfloor (r+1)/2 \rfloor$. Since $f(0) = \cdots = f^{(r)}(0) = 0$, Sections 2.1 and 2.2 of Chapter 5 yield

$$r^{\text{avg}}(n, \Lambda) \le r^{\text{avg}}(N_n) \le r^{\text{avg}}(n - \lfloor (r+1)/2 \rfloor, \Lambda),$$

$$r^{\text{avg}}(N_n) = \sqrt{\frac{|B_{2r+2}|}{(2r+2)!}} \frac{1}{m^{r+1}}.$$

This shows that $n-2\lfloor(r+1)/2\rfloor-1$ in (1) can be replaced by $n-\lfloor(r+1)/2\rfloor$. This also shows that for large n, $r^{\mathrm{avg}}(N_n) \simeq r^{\mathrm{avg}}(n, \Lambda)$ which means that the information N_n is almost nth optimal.

We now discuss the μ-spline algorithm that uses the information N_n and, more generally, *Hermitian* information

$$N(f) = [f(t_1), \ldots f^{(j_1)}(t_1), \ldots, f(t_k), \ldots, f^{(j_k)}(t_k)]$$

for distinct $t_i \in [0,1]$, $j_i \in [0,r]$, and $n = (j_1 + 1) + \cdots + (j_k + 1)$. Let $\sigma = \sigma(N(f))$ be the μ-spline element interpolating $N(f)$. That is, $\sigma^{(j)}(0) = 0$, $j = 0, 1, 2, \ldots, r$, and

$$\sigma^{(j)}(t_i) = f^{(j)}(t_i), \quad i = 1, 2, \ldots, k, \quad j = 0, 1, \ldots, j_i.$$

Furthermore, $\|C_\mu^{-1}\sigma\|_\mu$ is minimal among all elements interpolating the data. Since

$$\|C_\mu^{-1}\sigma\|_\mu = \sqrt{(C_\mu^{-1}\sigma)\sigma} = \|\sigma^{(r+1)}\|_{\mathcal{L}_2},$$

σ is the *natural spline of degree* $2r + 1$. This shows that the μ-spline algorithm ϕ^s is the integral of the natural spline of degree $2r + 1$ which interpolates the data. The value of $\phi^s(N(f))$ can be computed by a well known technique of spline theory in cost proportional to solving a system of linear equations with a band matrix of size proportional to n whose band width is proportional to r. This can be done in $O(nr^2)$ arithmetic operations.

For almost nth optimal information N_n given by (3), the μ-spline algorithm ϕ_n takes an especially simple form. Namely as in Section 2.2 of Chapter 5, we have

$$\phi_n(N_n(f)) = \frac{f(1)}{2m} + \frac{1}{m}\sum_{i=1}^{m-1} f\left(\frac{i}{m}\right) + \sum_{i=1}^{\lfloor(r+1)/2\rfloor} a_{2i-1}f^{(2i-1)}(1), \quad (4)$$

where $a_{2i-1} = -m^{-2i}B_{2i}/(2i)!$. Since a_{2i-1} can be precomputed, the cost of evaluating $\phi_n(N_n(f))$ is no greater than $c(n+1) + \lfloor(r+1)/2\rfloor + 1$.

We briefly discuss the average ε-complexity. Due to (1), we see that the sequence $\{r^{\mathrm{avg}}(n, \Lambda)^2\}$ is bounded by two convex sequences. Therefore, Theorem 5.7.2 of Chapter 6 yields that the average ε-cardinality number $m^{\mathrm{avg}}(\varepsilon)$ is given by

$$n^{\mathrm{avg}}(\varepsilon) \le \lceil m^{\mathrm{avg}}(\varepsilon)\rceil \le n^{\mathrm{avg}}(\varepsilon) + \lfloor(r+1)/2\rfloor,$$

where

$$n^{\mathrm{avg}}(\varepsilon) = \min\left\{n : r^{\mathrm{avg}}(n, \Lambda) \le \varepsilon\right\} = \left\lceil\left(\sqrt{\frac{|B_{2r+2}|}{(2r+2)!}}\frac{1}{\varepsilon}\right)^{1/(r+1)}\right\rceil.$$

Due to Theorem 5.7.1 of Chapter 6, the average ε-complexity is given by

$$c\, m^{\mathrm{avg}}(\varepsilon) \le \mathrm{comp}^{\mathrm{avg}}(\varepsilon) \le (c+2)\, m^{\mathrm{avg}}(\varepsilon).$$

For small ε, the nonadaptive information N_n given by (3) and the algorithm ϕ_n given by (4) with $n = n^{\mathrm{avg}}(\varepsilon) + \lfloor (r+1)/2 \rfloor$ are *almost optimal* and for large c,

$$\mathrm{comp}^{\mathrm{avg}}(\varepsilon) \simeq \mathrm{cost}^{\mathrm{avg}}(\phi_n, N_n) \simeq c \left(\sqrt{\frac{|B_{2r+2}|}{(2r+2)!}} \frac{1}{\varepsilon} \right)^{1/(r+1)}.$$

We now briefly discuss the integration problem defined on the ball $F = B_q = \{ f \in F_1 : \|f\| \le q \}$. The set F is equipped with the truncated Gaussian measure $\mu_q(\cdot) = \mu(\cdot \cap B_q)/\mu(B_q)$. To apply the results of Section 5.8 of Chapter 6, we calculate

$$a^* = \left(2 \sup\{ \|L\|_\mu : L \in F_1^*, \|L\| = 1 \} \right)^{-1}.$$

For $L(f) = \int_0^1 f^{(r)}(t)\, d(s_L(t))$ we obtain $\|L\|_\mu = \left(\int_0^1 s_L^2(t)\, dt \right)^{1/2}$ and $\|L\| = \sup\{ |L(f)| : f \in F_1, \|f\| \le 1 \} = \max_{0 \le t \le 1} |s_L(t)|$. This yields $a^* = 1/2$.

For $x = 1 - \mu(B_q)$ we thus have $x = \exp\left(-q^2/2 \right) (1 + o(1))$ as $q \to +\infty$. Since (7) of Theorem 5.8.1 of Chapter 6 is satisfied, we conclude that the ε-complexity $\mathrm{comp}^{\mathrm{avg}}(\varepsilon, q)$ for the ball B_q is given by

$$\mathrm{comp}^{\mathrm{avg}}(\varepsilon, q) = \mathrm{comp}^{\mathrm{avg}}(\varepsilon) \left(1 + o\left(\exp(-q^2 a/2) \right) \right) \left(1 + O(c^{-1}) \right)$$

for any $a < 1/2$. For small ε, and large q and c, we have

$$\mathrm{comp}^{\mathrm{avg}}(\varepsilon, q) \simeq c \left(\sqrt{\frac{|B_{2r+2}|}{(2r+2)!}} \frac{1}{\varepsilon} \right)^{1/(r+1)}.$$

Notes and Remarks

NR 2.1:1 A part of this section is based on Lee and Wasilkowski [86].

NR 2.1:2 (Lee and Wasilkowski [86]) The μ-spline is the mean of the conditional measure. Thus, for the space F_1 and Hermitian information, it turns out that the natural spline of degree $2r+1$ is the mean of the conditional (*a posteriori*) measure. This fact is mentioned in the statistical literature. For instance, Diaconis and Freedman [83, p.110] write that this result is a well known part of the folklore. There is a number of interesting papers (see, e.g., Kimeldorf and Wahba [70a,b] and Wahba [78]) where similar problems are analyzed and relations between Bayesian statistics and spline functions are exhibited. In particular, Kimeldorf and Wahba [70a] show that for a number of stochastic processes (excluding the Wiener case) spline functions (different from natural splines) are the means of conditional measures.

NR 2.1:3 The integration problem for $r = 0$ was studied by Lee [86]. He found the explicit form of the unique nth optimal nonadaptive information which consists of function evaluations at $t_i^* = 2i/(2n + 1)$ and $r^{\mathrm{avg}}(n, \Lambda) = 1/(\sqrt{3}\,(2n + 1))$.

Exercises

E 2.1:1 Consider Hermitian information

$$N(f) = [f(t_1), \ldots, f^{(j_1)}(t_1), \ldots, f(t_k), \ldots, f^{(j_k)}(t_k)]$$

for the integration problem of Section 2.1. Prove that $r^{\mathrm{avg}}(m, \Lambda) \le r^{\mathrm{avg}}(N)$, where $m = \lceil \sum_{i=1}^{k} (j_i + 2)/2 \rceil$. Hint: see Bojanov [80] and **NR 2.2:3** of Chapter 5.

2.2. Weighted Integration in a Reproducing Kernel Hilbert Space

We discuss the weighted integration problem for functions $f : [a, b] \to \mathbb{R}$ from a separable Hilbert space F_1 with a reproducing kernel $k : [a, b] \times [a, b] \to \mathbb{R}$. We assume that F_1 is a subspace of $\mathcal{L}_2(a, b)$, and $\langle \cdot, \cdot \rangle$ denotes the inner product of F_1. We have $f(x) = \langle f, k(\cdot, x) \rangle$, $\forall f \in F_1$ and $\forall x \in [a, b]$. We equip the space F_1 with a Gaussian measure μ with mean zero and injective correlation operator C_μ. Let (λ_i, z_i) be the eigenpairs of C_μ, $C_\mu z_i = \lambda_i z_i$, where $\langle z_i, z_j \rangle = \delta_{i,j}$ and $\lambda_1 \ge \lambda_2 \ge \cdots \ge 0$. Then

$$k(x, t) = \sum_{i=1}^{\infty} z_i(x)\, z_i(t).$$

Let $R_\mu : [a, b] \times [a, b] \to \mathbb{R}$ be a covariance kernel function of the measure μ, i.e.,

$$R_\mu(x, t) = \int_{F_1} f(x) f(t)\, \mu(df).$$

Since $f(t) = \langle f, k(\cdot, t) \rangle = \sum_{i=1}^{\infty} \langle f, z_i \rangle z_i(t)$, the function R_μ is related to the kernel k and the correlation operator C_μ as follows

$$R_\mu(x, t) = \int_{F_1} \langle f, k(\cdot, x) \rangle \langle f, k(\cdot, t) \rangle \, \mu(dt) = \sum_{i=1}^{\infty} \lambda_i\, z_i(x)\, z_i(t),$$

$$R_\mu(\cdot, t) = C_\mu k(\cdot, t), \quad \forall t \in [a, b].$$

Define the solution operator by

$$S(f) = \int_a^b f(x)\, \rho(x)\, dx, \quad \forall f \in F_1,$$

where ρ is a known (weight) function from $\mathcal{L}_2(a,b)$. Suppose that only function evaluations are permitted, i.e., Λ consists of $L(f) = f(x), \forall f \in F_1$, and $x \in [a,b]$.

We first analyze the average case setting for the whole space, $F = F_1$. Consider the nonadaptive information

$$N_n(f) = [L_1(f), L_2(f), \ldots, L_n(f)],$$

where $L_j(f) = f(t_j)$ for distinct t_j from $[a,b]$. Since

$$C_\mu L_j = C_\mu k(\cdot, t_j) = R_\mu(\cdot, t_j),$$

the spline element σ is given by

$$\sigma(x) = \sum_{j=1}^{n} g_j\, R_\mu(x, t_j).$$

The numbers g_j are chosen so that $\sigma(t_i) = f(t_i)$. This can be done since $R_\mu(\cdot, t_1), \ldots, R_\mu(\cdot, t_n)$ are linearly independent, and the Gram matrix $M = \left(R_\mu(t_i, t_j)\right)$ is nonsingular. Thus, $g_j = \sum_{i=1}^{n} a_{i,j}\, f(t_i)$, where $a_{i,j}$ corresponds to the entries of the inverse of M. The μ-spline algorithm ϕ^s is of the form

$$\phi^s\left(N_n(f)\right) = \sum_{i=1}^{n} g_i^*\, f(t_i) \quad \text{with} \quad g_i^* = \sum_{j=1}^{n} a_{i,j} \int_a^b R_\mu(x, t_j)\, \rho(x)\, dx.$$

From Corollary 5.3.1 of Chapter 6, we have

$$e^{\text{avg}}(\phi^s, N_n) = r^{\text{avg}}(N) = \inf_{a_i \in \mathbb{R}} \left\| S - \sum_{i=1}^{n} a_i\, L_i \right\|_\mu.$$

Define the function

$$f_\mu^*(t) = \int_a^b \rho(x)\, R_\mu(x, t)\, dx. \tag{1}$$

Then

$$r^{\text{avg}}(N) = \inf_{a_i \in \mathbb{R}} \left\| f_\mu^* - \sum_{i=1}^{n} a_i\, R_\mu(\cdot, t_i) \right\|_*. \tag{2}$$

Here $\|\cdot\|_* = \langle\cdot,\cdot\rangle_*^{1/2}$, where $\langle\cdot,\cdot\rangle_*$ is the inner product of the Hilbert space

$$H = C_\mu^{1/2}(F_1) = \left\{ f \in F_1 : \sum_{i=1}^{\infty} \langle f, z_i\rangle^2 / \lambda_i < +\infty \right\}$$

given by $\langle f, y \rangle_* = \langle C_\mu^{-1/2} f, C_\mu^{-1/2} g \rangle = \sum_{i=1}^\infty \langle f, z_i \rangle \langle g, z_i \rangle / \lambda_i$. Observe that the function R_μ is the reproducing kernel of H. Indeed, $R_\mu(\cdot, x) \in H$ and

$$\langle f, R_\mu(\cdot, x) \rangle_* = \sum_{i=1}^\infty \lambda_i \langle f, z_i \rangle_* z_i(x) = \sum_{i=1}^\infty \langle f, z_i \rangle z_i(x) = f(x).$$

Thus, the average radius of information is the least squares error of approximation of the function f_μ^* by span $\left(R_\mu(\cdot, t_1), \ldots, R_\mu(\cdot, t_n) \right)$ in the space H, compare with (2) of Section 2.3 of Chapter 5.

We now turn to the nth optimal nonadaptive information. Due to (2), we need to choose t_i, or equivalently basis functions $R_\mu(\cdot, t_1), \ldots, R_\mu(\cdot, t_n)$, for which the error of approximation of the function f_μ^* is minimized,

$$r^{\mathrm{avg}}(n, \Lambda) = \inf_{a \le t_i \le b} \; \inf_{a_i \in \mathbb{R}} \left\| f_\mu^* - \sum_{i=1}^n a_i \, R_\mu(\cdot, t_i) \right\|_*. \qquad (3)$$

The average ε-complexity can be estimated in terms of $r^{\mathrm{avg}}(n, \Lambda)$ as shown in Section 5.7 of Chapter 6. Let $n^{\mathrm{avg}}(\varepsilon) = \min\{n : r^{\mathrm{avg}}(n, \Lambda) \le \varepsilon\}$ denote the smallest number of points t_i for which the average error is at most ε. Then Theorems 5.7.1 and 5.7.2 of Chapter 6 yield

$$c \sup_{x > 1} \min \left\{ n^{\mathrm{avg}}(x\varepsilon), \frac{x^2 - 1}{x^2} \, n^{\mathrm{avg}}(x) \right\} \le \mathrm{comp}^{\mathrm{avg}}(\varepsilon) \le (c + 2) \, n^{\mathrm{avg}}(\varepsilon).$$

Furthermore, if the sequence $\{r^{\mathrm{avg}}(n, \Lambda)^2\}$ is convex then

$$c \left(n^{\mathrm{avg}}(\varepsilon) - 1 \right) < \mathrm{comp}^{\mathrm{avg}}(\varepsilon) \le (c + 2) \, n^{\mathrm{avg}}(\varepsilon).$$

For large c and small ε, we then have

$$\mathrm{comp}^{\mathrm{avg}}(\varepsilon) \simeq c \, n^{\mathrm{avg}}(\varepsilon).$$

REMARK 2.2.1. The analysis presented above shows that the average case setting of the weighted integration problem for the reproducing kernel Hilbert space F_1 reduces to the approximation of the function f_μ^* by functions of the form $R_\mu(\cdot, t_i)$. The latter problem is equivalent to the worst case setting of the weighted integration problem for the unit ball in the reproducing kernel Hilbert space H, as explained in Section 2.3 of Chapter 5.

More precisely, the average radius $r^{\mathrm{avg}}(N)$ and the nth minimal average radius $r^{\mathrm{avg}}(n, \Lambda)$ for the space F_1 are equal to the worst case radius $r^{\mathrm{wor}}(N)$

and to the nth minimal worst case radius $r^{\text{wor}}(n, \Lambda)$ for the unit ball of the space H, respectively. Furthermore, if the sequence $\{r^{\text{avg}}(n, \Lambda)\}$ is convex, then the average ε-complexity for the space F_1 is roughly equal to the worst case ε-complexity for the unit ball in the space H.

We summarize this by saying that the weighted integration problem for the reproducing kernel Hilbert space F_1 in the average case setting is equivalent to the weighted integration problem for the unit ball of the reproducing kernel Hilbert space H in the worst case setting. We stress that the space H as well as the functions f_μ^* and $R_\mu(\cdot, t_i)$ *do* depend on the Gaussian measure of the space F_1. The space H is a subset of F_1. Furthermore, $\mu(H) = 0$, as explained in **NR 2.2:2**.

We now briefly discuss the weighted integration problem in the average case setting for the ball B_q, $F = B_q = \{f \in F_1 : \|f\| \leq q\}$. The set F is equipped with the truncated Gaussian measure $\mu_q(\cdot) = \mu(\cdot \cap B_q)/\mu(B_q)$. From Section 5.8 of Chapter 6 we conclude that for large c and q, the ε-complexity $\text{comp}^{\text{avg}}(\varepsilon, q)$ for the ball q is given by

$$\text{comp}^{\text{avg}}(\varepsilon, q) = \text{comp}^{\text{avg}}\left(\varepsilon(1 + o(1))\right)(1 + o(1)).$$

If $n^{\text{avg}}(x\varepsilon) = \Theta(n^{\text{avg}}(\varepsilon))$ then

$$\text{comp}^{\text{avg}}(\varepsilon, q) = \Theta(c\, n^{\text{avg}}(\varepsilon)) \quad \text{and} \quad \text{comp}^{\text{avg}}(\varepsilon) = \Theta(c\, n^{\text{avg}}(\varepsilon)).$$

We illustrate the analysis of this section by two examples.

EXAMPLE 2.2.1. Consider $F_1 = \{f \in W_2^r(0, 1) : f(0) = \cdots = f^{(r-1)}(0) = 0\}$ as in Example 2.3.1 of Chapter 5. Define the Gaussian measure μ by

$$\mu(A) = \mu_0(D^r A),$$

where $D^r f = f^{(r)}$. The measure μ_0 is defined on Borel sets of $\mathcal{L}_2(0, 1)$ through the Wiener measure w. More precisely, for the space C_0^0 of continuous functions vanishing at zero, we have

$$\mu_0(B) = w(B \cap C_0^0).$$

It is easy to check that

$$R_\mu(x, t) = \int_0^1 \int_0^1 \frac{(x - u_1)_+^{r-1}}{(r-1)!} \frac{(t - u_2)_+^{r-1}}{(r-1)!} \int_{C_0^0} f(u_1)\, f(u_2)\, w(df)\, du_1\, du_2.$$

Since $\int_{C_0^0} f(u_1)\, f(u_2)\, w(df) = \min\{u_1, u_2\}$, we have

$$R_\mu(x, t) = \int_0^1 \frac{(x - u)_+^r (t - u)_+^r}{(r!)^2}\, du.$$

Recall that the reproducing kernel $k(x, t)$ of the space F_1 is of the same form but with r replaced by $r - 1$. This means that the Gaussian measure μ increases the parameter r by one and this corresponds to the increased smoothness of functions in the space H. Indeed, we now have $H = \{f \in W_2^{r+1}(0, 1) : f^{(i)}(0) = 0, i \le r\}$, and $\langle f, g \rangle_* = \int_0^1 f^{(r+1)}(t) g^{(r+1)}(t) \, dt$. Proceeding exactly as in Example 2.3.1 of Chapter 5 with r replaced by $r + 1$, we conclude that the function f_μ^* is of the form

$$f_\mu^*(t) = \int_0^1 \int_0^1 \rho(x) \frac{(x - u)_+^r (t - u)_+^r}{(r!)^2} \, du \, dx.$$

Assume now that $\rho(x) \equiv 1$. Then the nth minimal average radius of information is given by

$$r^{\mathrm{avg}}(n, \Lambda) = \sqrt{\frac{|B_{2r+2}|}{(2r + 2)!}} \frac{1}{n^{r+1}} (1 + o(1)) \quad \text{as } n \to +\infty,$$

where B_{2r+2} is the $(2r + 2)$nd Bernoulli number. Since $\{r^{\mathrm{avg}}(n, \Lambda)^2\}$ is, at least, asymptotically convex, we have for large c and small ε,

$$\mathrm{comp}^{\mathrm{avg}}(\varepsilon) \simeq c\, n^{\mathrm{avg}}(\varepsilon) \simeq c \left(\sqrt{\frac{|B_{2r+2}|}{(2r + 2)!}} \frac{1}{\varepsilon} \right)^{1/(r+1)}.$$

For large q, the average complexity $\mathrm{comp}^{\mathrm{avg}}(\varepsilon, q)$ is roughly the same as $\mathrm{comp}^{\mathrm{avg}}(\varepsilon)$.

We comment on optimal information and an optimal algorithm. Consider

$$N_n(f)$$
$$= \left[f(1), f'(1), f^{(3)}(1), \ldots, f^{(s)}(1), f\left(\frac{1}{m}\right), f\left(\frac{2}{m}\right), \ldots f\left(\frac{m-1}{m}\right) \right]$$

with $s = 2\lfloor (r + 1)/2 \rfloor - 1$, $n = m + \lfloor (r + 1)/2 \rfloor$, and

$$\phi_n^*(N_n(t)) = \frac{f(1)}{2m} + \frac{1}{m} \sum_{i=1}^{m-1} f\left(\frac{i}{m}\right) + \sum_{i=1}^{\lfloor (r+1)/2 \rfloor} a_{2i-1} f^{(2i-1)}(1)$$

with $a_{2i-1} = -m^{-2i} B_{2i}/(2i)!$, see **NR 2.2:6** of Chapter 5. Then we have

$$e^{\mathrm{avg}}(\phi_n^*, N_n) = r^{\mathrm{avg}}(N_n) = \sqrt{\frac{|B_{2r+2}|}{(2r + 2)!}} \frac{1}{n^{(r+1)}} (1 + o(1)) \quad \text{as } n \to +\infty.$$

The information N_n is, however, not permissible because the evaluations of derivatives are not now permissible. Nevertheless, we can approximate $f^{(2i-1)}(1)$ by a few additional function evaluations as explained in **NR 2.2:5** of Chapter 5. After such a modification the pair (ϕ_n^*, N_n) with $n = n^{\mathrm{avg}}(\varepsilon)$ is almost optimal.

EXAMPLE 2.2.2. Consider the space $F_1 = \{f \in \widetilde{W}_2^r(0, 2\pi) : f(0) = 0\}$ with the inner product $\langle f, g \rangle = \int_0^{2\pi} f^{(r)}(t) g^{(r)}(t) \, dt$, $r \geq 1$, as in Example 2.3.2 of Chapter 5. It is easy to check that the functions $z_{2k-1}(x) = (-1 + \cos kx)/(k^r \sqrt{\pi})$, $z_{2k}(x) = (\sin kx)/(k^r \sqrt{\pi})$ form an orthonormal system of the space F_1.

We equip F_1 with a Gaussian measure μ whose mean is zero and whose correlation operator C_μ has eigenfunctions z_k, $C_\mu z_k = \lambda_k z_k$ with $\sum_{k=1}^\infty \lambda_k < +\infty$. Then the covariance kernel function R_μ takes the form

$$R_\mu(x, t) = \pi^{-1} \sum_{k=1}^\infty \lambda_{2k} \, k^{-2r} \sin kx \sin kt$$

$$+ \, \pi^{-1} \sum_{k=1}^\infty \lambda_{2k-1} \, k^{-2r} (-1 + \cos kx)(-1 + \cos kt).$$

Assume now that $\lambda_{2k-1} = \lambda_{2k}$. Then

$$R_\mu(x, t) = \pi^{-1} \sum_{k=1}^\infty \lambda_{2k} \, k^{-2r} \left(\cos k(x - t) - \cos kt - \cos kx + 1 \right).$$

Recall that the reproducing kernel $k(x, t)$ of the space F_1 is of the form

$$k(x, t) = \pi^{-1} \sum_{k=1}^\infty k^{-2r} \left(\cos k(x - t) - \cos kt - \cos kx + 1 \right).$$

Thus, for $\lambda_{2k} = k^{-2s}$ with a positive integer s, the covariance kernel function R_μ is of the same form as the reproducing kernel k with r replaced by $r + s$. This means that the Gaussian measure μ (with $\lambda_{2k-1} = \lambda_{2k} = k^{-2s}$) increases the smoothness of functions, and $H = \{f \in \widetilde{W}_2^{r+s}(0, 2\pi) : f(0) = 0\}$ with $\langle f, g \rangle_* = \int_0^{2\pi} f^{(r+s)}(t) \, g^{(r+s)}(t) \, dt$.

From Example 2.3.2 of Chapter 5 with r replaced by $r + s$, we conclude that

$$(f_\mu^*)^{(r)}(t) = \frac{1}{\pi} \int_0^{2\pi} \rho(x) \left(D_{r+s}(x - t) - D_{r+s}(-t) \right) dx.$$

Assume now that $\rho(x) \equiv 1$. Then $(f_\mu^*)^{(r)}(t) = -2D_{r+s}(-t)$ and the nth minimal average radius of information is given by

$$r^{\text{avg}}(n, \Lambda) = (2\pi)^{r+s+1/2} \sqrt{\frac{|B_{2(r+s)}|}{(2(r+s))!}} \frac{1}{(n+1)^{r+s}}.$$

The information $N_n^*(f) = \left[f(2\pi/(n+1)), \ldots, f(2\pi n/(n+1)) \right]$ and the rectangle (or trapezoid) formula $\phi_n^* \left(N_n^*(f) \right) = 2\pi/(n+1) \sum_{i=1}^n f(2\pi i/(n+1))$ is nth optimal information and a linear optimal error algorithm. For

$$n = n^{\text{avg}}(\varepsilon) = \left\lceil 2\pi \left(\frac{1}{\varepsilon} \sqrt{\frac{2\pi |B_{2(r+s)}|}{[2(r+s)]!}} \right)^{1/(r+s)} \right\rceil - 1,$$

the average error $e^{\text{avg}}(\phi_n^*, N_n^*) \leq \varepsilon$. Furthermore, the average ε-complexity is bounded by

$$(c+1) \left(n^{\text{avg}}(\varepsilon) - 1 \right) - 1 < \text{comp}^{\text{avg}}(\varepsilon) \leq (c+1) \, n^{\text{avg}}(\varepsilon).$$

For large c and q, and small ε, we have

$$\text{comp}^{\text{avg}}(\varepsilon) \simeq \text{comp}^{\text{avg}}(\varepsilon, q) \simeq c \, n^{\text{avg}}(\varepsilon).$$

Notes and Remarks

NR 2.2:1 The approach of this section follows Sacks and Ylvisaker [70b], see **NR 2.3:1** of Chapter 5.

NR 2.2:2 It is interesting to notice that $\mu(H) = 0$ for $H = C_\mu^{1/2}(F_1)$, see, e.g., Vakhania [81, p. 59]. This means that the average case setting for the whole space $F = F_1$ is equivalent to the worst case setting for the unit ball in H whose average measure is zero. There is an elegant characterization of a Gaussian measure of linear subspaces $A, A \subset F_1$, which is known as the Kolmogorov (or zero-one) principle, see Shilov and Fan Dyk Tin [67]. Namely, for a separable Hilbert space F_1, we have $\mu(A) = 0$ or $\mu(A) = 1$. If $A = \{f \in F_1 : \sum_{i=1}^\infty \langle f, z_i \rangle^2 \, a_i < +\infty\}$ for an orthonormal system $\{z_i\}$ of eigenelements of C_μ, $C_\mu z_i = \lambda_i z_i$, and for a positive sequence $\{a_i\}$, then

$$\mu(A) = \begin{cases} 0 & \text{if } \sum_{i=1}^\infty a_i \lambda_i = +\infty, \\ 1 & \text{if } \sum_{i=1}^\infty a_i \lambda_i < +\infty. \end{cases}$$

Since $H = C_\mu^{1/2}(F_1)$ corresponds to $a_i = 1/\lambda_i$, we have $\sum_{i=1}^\infty a_i \lambda_i = +\infty$, and therefore $\mu(H) = 0$.

3. Function Approximation

In this section we analyze the approximation problems for smooth periodic and nonperiodic functions. These problems have been studied in the worst case setting in Sections 3.1 and 3.3 of Chapter 5. Here we study them in the average case setting.

Notes and Remarks

3:1 Novak [87a] also studied the problem defined in **NR 2:1** for function approximation with $G = \mathcal{L}_\infty$. He showed that there exists a probability measure on the classes $C_d^{r,\alpha}$ and $W_d^{r,d}$ such that the average case nth minimal radius of information with fixed cardinality $n(f) \equiv n$ is proportional to the worst case radius. Since the worst case radii are (modulo a multiplicative constant) convex, see **NR 3:1** of Chapter 5, this means that for such a measure the average ε-complexity is proportional to the worst case complexity and is exponential in d. Contrary to the integration problem, which is always significantly easier in the average case setting, see **NR 2:1**, this shows that the average and worst case complexities can be essentially the same for the approximation problem.

3.1. Smooth Periodic Functions

Consider the approximation problem defined in Section 3.1 of Chapter 5. Recall that $Tf = \sum_{j=1}^{d} a_j \, \partial^{r_j} f / \partial x_j^{r_j}$. Assume that $r = [r_1, \ldots, r_d]$ and $a = [a_1, \ldots, a_n]$ satisfy (i) and (ii) of Section 3.1 of Chapter 5. That is,

$$r \text{ contains at most one odd component,} \tag{i}$$

$$\text{sign } a_j \begin{cases} \neq 0 & \text{if } r_j \text{ is odd,} \\ = u & \text{if } r_j \text{ is multiple of 4,} \\ = -u & \text{otherwise,} \end{cases} \quad \forall j, \tag{ii}$$

where $u = \pm 1$.

Then T is bijective and $K_1 = (T^{-1})^* T^{-1}$ is well defined. Recall that (λ_j, ζ_j) are eigenpairs of the operator K_1, $\lambda_1 \geq \lambda_2 \geq \cdots > 0$, $\{\lambda_n\} = \{|b_t|^{-2}\}$, $\{\zeta_j\} = \{e_t\}$ with b_t and e_t being eigenpairs of T. For $f, g \in F_1$ let $\langle f, g \rangle = \int_{t \in D} f(t) \overline{g(t)} \, dt$, $D = [0, 2\pi]^d$ and

$$\langle f, g \rangle_1 = \langle Tf, Tg \rangle = \langle K_1^{-1} f, g \rangle = \sum_{j=1}^{\infty} \lambda_j^{-1} \langle f, z_j \rangle \langle g, z_j \rangle.$$

The space F_1 can then be written as

$$F_1 = \{f : \|f\|_1^2 = \langle f, f \rangle_1 < +\infty\}.$$

Clearly, F_1 is a separable Hilbert space. We equip the space F_1 with a Gaussian measure μ with mean zero and correlation operator C_μ. We assume that ζ_j are eigenfunctions of $C_\mu, C_\mu \zeta_j = \beta_j \zeta_j$, with $\beta_j = a^* j^{-v}$, where $a^* > 0$ and $v > 1$. Then $\text{trace}(C_\mu) = a^* \sum_{j=1}^{\infty} j^{-v} = a^* \zeta(v)$, ζ is Riemann's zeta function, and $\text{trace}(C_\mu) \le a^* \left(1 + 1/(v-1)\right)$.

Recall that the solution operator S is an embedding operator from F_1 to $G = L_2(D)$. It is easy to check that the *a priori* measure $\nu = \mu S^{-1}$ is Gaussian with mean zero and correlation operator C_ν whose eigenpairs (λ_j^*, η_j^*) are given by

$$\lambda_j^* = \lambda_j \, \beta_j \quad \text{and} \quad \eta_j^* = \zeta_j.$$

Indeed, from Section 5.2 of Chapter 6, we have $C_\nu g = S(C_\mu L_g S)$ for $g \in G$. Here $(L_g S)(f) = \langle g, S(f) \rangle = \langle g, f \rangle = \langle K_1 g, K_1^{-1} f \rangle = \langle f, K_1 g \rangle_1$. Hence $C_\nu = C_\mu K_1$ and therefore $C_\nu \zeta_j = \lambda_j \, \beta_j \, \zeta_j$, as claimed.

We first consider the approximation problem for the whole space F_1. Since $\Lambda = F_1^*$, Corollary 5.7.3 of Chapter 6 states that the average ε-cardinality number is given by

$$\lceil m^{\text{avg}}(\varepsilon) \rceil = \min \left\{ n : \sum_{j=n+1}^{\infty} \lambda_j \, \beta_j \le \varepsilon^2 \right\}.$$

Since $\lambda_j = \alpha^2 j^{-2/\omega}\left(1 + o(1)\right)$, $\beta_j = a^* j^{-v}$ with $\omega = \sum_{j=1}^{d} r_j^{-1}$, and α is given in Section 3.1 of Chapter 5, we have

$$m^{\text{avg}}(\varepsilon) = \left(\sqrt{\frac{a^* \, \omega}{2 + (v-1)\,\omega}} \, \frac{\alpha}{\varepsilon} \right)^{\omega/(1+(v-1)\,\omega/2)} \left(1 + o(1)\right) \quad \text{as } \varepsilon \to 0.$$

Theorem 5.7.1 of Chapter 6 states that the average ε-complexity is given by

$$\text{comp}^{\text{avg}}(\varepsilon, F_1) = (c + b)\, m^{\text{avg}}(\varepsilon), \quad b \in [0, 2].$$

Furthermore, the information $N_{n^*}^*(f) = [\langle f, \zeta_1 \rangle, \ldots, \langle f, \zeta_{n^*} \rangle]$ and the algorithm

$$\phi^*(N_{n^*}^*(f)) = \sum_{j=1}^{n^*} \langle f, \zeta_j \rangle \, \zeta_j, \quad n^* = m^{\text{avg}}(\varepsilon),$$

are almost optimal. For $c \gg 1$ and small ε, we thus have

$$\text{comp}^{\text{avg}}(\varepsilon, F_1) \simeq c \left(\sqrt{\frac{a^* \, \omega}{2 + (v-1)\,\omega}} \, \frac{\alpha}{\varepsilon} \right)^{\omega/(1+(v-1)\,\omega/2)}.$$

Observe that for v close to one, the exponent of the last formula is close to ω, which corresponds to the exponent of the worst case ε-complexity.

We now discuss the function approximation problem defined on the set $F = \{f \in F_1 : \|Tf\| \leq 1\} = \{f \in F_1 : \|f\|_1 \leq 1\}$. Thus, F is a ball of radius 1 equipped with the truncated Gaussian measure as explained in Section 5.8 of Chapter 6. Let $x = 1 - \mu(F)$. From Remark 5.8.1 of Chapter 6 we conclude that

$$0 \leq x \leq \sqrt{2} \exp\left(\frac{1-v}{4a^*v}\right).$$

Thus, for small a^*, $\mu(F)$ is close to one. Note also that $\text{comp}^{\text{avg}}(\varepsilon, F_1)$ satisfies assumption (7) of Theorem 5.8.1 of Chapter 6. Therefore, Theorem 5.8.1 yields that for the set F,

$$\text{comp}^{\text{avg}}(\varepsilon, F)$$
$$= \text{comp}^{\text{avg}}(\varepsilon, F_1) \left(1 + o\left(\exp((1-v)/(4a^*v))\right)\right) \left(1 + O(c^{-1})\right).$$

Thus, for a^* and ε small and large c we have

$$\text{comp}^{\text{avg}}(\varepsilon, F) \simeq c \left(\sqrt{\frac{a^* \, \omega}{2 + (v-1)\omega}} \, \frac{\alpha}{\varepsilon}\right)^{\omega/(1+(v-1)\,\omega/2)}.$$

The information N_n^* and the algorithm ϕ^* presented above remain almost optimal for the set F.

Notes and Remarks

NR 3.1:1 Suppose that the condition (i) or (ii) does not hold. It is easy to see that the average ε-complexity is finite for all positive ε. If, however, the worst case ε-complexity is infinite, then one can define a Gaussian measure on the set F (or on the space F_1) such that the average ε-complexity goes to infinity arbitrarily fast, see **E 3.1:1**.

NR 3.1:2 It is possible to extend the analysis of this section to the space F_1 without assuming that $\langle f, 1 \rangle = 0$. The results remain essentially the same.

Exercises

E 3.1:1 Assume that $\dim \ker T = +\infty$. Take a Gaussian measure μ with mean zero and the eigenvalues of C_μ given by $\beta_j = j^{-v}$, $v > 1$, such that $\mu(\ker T) > 0$. Prove that the average ε-complexity goes to infinity as $v \to 1^+$.

3.2. Smooth Nonperiodic Functions

Consider the approximation problem defined in Section 3.3 of Chapter 5. Recall that the space

$$F_1 = \{f \in C^{r_1, \ldots, r_d}(D) : (D^{i_1, \ldots, i_d} f)(t) = 0, \; \forall \, i_j = 0, \ldots, r_j, \; j = 1, \ldots d,$$
$$\text{when one of the components of } t \text{ is zero}\}.$$

is equipped with the sup norm $\|f\| = \sup_{t \in D} |D^{r_1,\dots,r_d} f(t)|$, $D = [0,1]^d$. Thus, F_1 is a separable Banach space. We equip the space F_1 with a Wiener measure placed on partial derivatives,

$$\mu(B) = w(D^{r_1,\dots,r_d}(B)), \quad \forall \text{ Borel sets } B,$$

where w is the classical Wiener measure defined on Borel sets of the space $C^{0,\dots,0}(D)$, see, e.g., Adler [81] and Kuo [75]. The measure w is Gaussian with mean zero and covariance kernel function

$$R_w(s,t) = \int_{C^{0,\dots,0}(D)} f(s) \, f(t) \, w(dt) = \prod_{j=1}^{d} \min\{s_j, t_j\},$$

where s_j and t_j are components of s and t, respectively.

Recall that $S : F_1 \to \mathcal{L}_2(D)$ is the embedding operator. Let $\nu = \mu S^{-1}$ be the *a priori* measure on solution elements. Papageorgiou and Wasilkowski [86] studied this problem and proved that ν is Gaussian with mean zero and covariance operator

$$C_\nu = T_0^{r_1+1,\dots,r_d+1} \, T_1^{r_1+1,\dots,r_d+1}.$$

Observe that C_ν differs from the operator K_1 in Section 3.2 of Chapter 5 only by the increased values of r_j. This corresponds to the increased smoothness of functions due to the Gaussian measure μ. From Section 3.2 of Chapter 5 we thus have that the eigenvalues λ_i^* of C_ν are given by

$$\lambda_i^* = \overline{\alpha} \left(i^{-1} (\ln i)^{k-1} \right)^{2 r_{\min}+2} (1 + o(1)) \quad \text{as } i \to +\infty.$$

Here $r_{\min} = \min\{r_j : 1 \le j \le d\}$, k is the number of r_j equal to $r_{\min}$, and the constant $\overline{\alpha}$ is given by the formula $\overline{\alpha} = \overline{\alpha}_{d,k}^{2r_{\min}+2}/\pi^{2\overline{\beta}}$ with $\overline{\beta} = d + \sum_{j=1}^{d} r_j$ and

$$\overline{\alpha}_{d,k} = \begin{cases} 1 & \text{if } d = 1, \\ 1/(d-1)! & \text{if } k = d, \\ \left((k-1)! \prod_{j=1, j \neq r_{\min}}^{d} \left(\dfrac{r_j+1}{r_{\min}+1} - 1 \right) \right)^{-1} & \text{otherwise.} \end{cases}$$

The eigenfunctions η_i^* and eigenvalues λ_i^* of C_ν, $C_\nu \eta_i^* = \lambda_i^* \eta_i^*$, are the solutions z and λ of the differential equation

$$\lambda_i^* \, D^{2r_1+2,\dots,2r_d+2} \, z - (-1)^{d+r_1+\dots+r_d} \, z = 0,$$

with boundary conditions

$$\left.\frac{\partial^i z(x_1,\ldots,x_d)}{\partial x_j^i}\right|_{x_j=0} = 0, \quad i = 0,\ldots,r_j,$$

$$\left.\frac{\partial^i z(x_1,\ldots,x_d)}{\partial x_j^i}\right|_{x_j=1} = 0, \quad i = r_j+1,\ldots,2r_j+1$$

for $j = 1, 2, \ldots, d$.

We first consider the approximation problem for the whole space F_1. Since $\Lambda = F_1^*$, Corollary 5.7.3 of Chapter 6 states that the average ε-cardinality number is given by

$$\lceil m^{\text{avg}}(\varepsilon) \rceil = \min \left\{ n : \sum_{j=n+1}^{\infty} \lambda_j^* \le \varepsilon^2 \right\}.$$

From the form of λ_j^* we thus have

$$m^{\text{avg}}(\varepsilon) = \left(\sqrt{\frac{\overline{\alpha}}{2r_{\min}+1}} \frac{1}{\varepsilon} \right)^{1/(r_{\min}+1/2)}$$

$$\times \left(\frac{1}{2r_{\min}+1} \ln \frac{\overline{\alpha}}{\varepsilon^2 (2r_{\min}+1)} \right)^{\rho} (1 + o(1)),$$

where $\rho = (k-1)(r_{\min}+1)/(r_{\min}+1/2)$. Theorem 5.7.1 of Chapter 6 states that the average ε-complexity is given by

$$\text{comp}^{\text{avg}}(\varepsilon) = (c + b) \, m^{\text{avg}}(\varepsilon), \quad b \in [0, 2].$$

Furthermore, the information $N_{n^*}^*(f) = [\langle f, \eta_1^* \rangle, \ldots, \langle f, \eta_{n^*}^* \rangle]$ and the algorithm

$$\phi^*(N_{n^*}^*(f)) = \sum_{j=1}^{n^*} \langle f, \eta_j^* \rangle \, \eta_j^*, \quad n^* = m^{\text{avg}}(\varepsilon),$$

are almost optimal. For $c \gg 1$ and small ε, we thus have

$$\text{comp}^{\text{avg}}(\varepsilon) \simeq c \left(\frac{\overline{\alpha}}{\sqrt{2r_{\min}+1}} \frac{1}{\varepsilon} \right)^{1/(r_{\min}+1/2)}$$

$$\times \left(\frac{1}{r_{\min}+1/2} \ln \frac{1}{\varepsilon} \right)^{(k-1)(r_{\min}+1)/(r_{\min}+1/2)}.$$

Observe that even for $r_{\min} = 0$ and $k = d$, we have

$$\text{comp}^{\text{avg}}(\varepsilon) = \Theta\left(c\left(\frac{1}{\varepsilon}\right)^2\left(\ln\frac{1}{\varepsilon}\right)^{2(d-1)}\right).$$

Thus, for arbitrary values of r_j and d, the average ε-complexity goes to infinity slower than $\varepsilon^{-(2+\eta)}$, $\forall\,\eta > 0$. We stress that the dependence on the dimension d is only through at most $(-\ln\varepsilon)^{2(d-1)}$.

We now discuss the function approximation problem defined on the set $F = F_q = \{f : \|f\|_1 \le q\}$. The ball F_q is equipped with the truncated Gaussian measure μ_q, $\mu_q(\cdot) = \mu(\cdot \cap F_q)/\mu(B_q)$. Let $\text{comp}^{\text{avg}}(\varepsilon, q)$ denote the complexity of this problem. Due to the form of the average ε-complexity $\text{comp}^{\text{avg}}(\varepsilon) = \text{comp}^{\text{avg}}(\varepsilon, +\infty)$, assumption (7) of Theorem 5.8.1 is satisfied and

$$\text{comp}^{\text{avg}}(\varepsilon, q) = \text{comp}^{\text{avg}}(\varepsilon)\left(1 + o\left(\exp(-q^2 a/2)\right)\right)\left(1 + O(c^{-1})\right),$$

where $a < \left(2\sup\{\|L\|_\mu : L \in F_1^*, \|L\| = 1\}\right)^{-1}$. Thus, for small ε and large q,

$$\text{comp}^{\text{avg}}(\varepsilon, q) \simeq \text{comp}(\varepsilon)$$

and the information $N_{n^*}^*$ and the algorithm ϕ^* presented above remain almost optimal for the set F_q.

Notes and Remarks

NR 3.2:1 This section is based on Papageorgiou and Wasilkowski [86].

NR 3.2:2 (Papageorgiou and Wasilkowski [86]). We have discussed so far the class $\Lambda = F_1^*$ consisting of *all* continuous linear functionals. Sometimes, some restrictions on permissible functionals may be imposed. Assume that only function and/or partial derivative evaluations are allowed. Then the class Λ of such functionals is a proper subset of F_1^*. What is then the average ε-complexity of the approximation problem? For $d = 1$, Speckman [79a] proved that the information $N_n(f) = [f(1/(n+1)), f(2/(n+1)), \ldots, f(n/(n+1))]$ is nth optimal in the class Λ and $r^{\text{avg}}(N) = \Theta\left(n^{-(r_1+1/2)}\right)$.

Since the nth minimal radii in the class $\Lambda = F_1^*$ are also of order $n^{-(r_1+1/2)}$, this shows that function evaluations at n equally spaced points provide nearly as good information as any n continuous linear functionals.

For the multivariate case, $d \ge 2$, optimal information in the class Λ is unknown. However, one can easily prove that partial derivative evaluations do not help, i.e., function evaluations form optimal information. Furthermore, among information consisting of function values taken at grid points,

$$N(f) = [f(h_1, \ldots, h_d), \ldots, f(i_1 h_1, \ldots, i_d h_d), \ldots, f(1 - h_1, \ldots, 1 - h_d)]$$

for some $h_1, \ldots, h_d$, the information with function evaluations on a regular grid, $h_1 = \cdots = h_d$, is nearly optimal. The average radius of such information is proportional to $\left(n^{-(r_{\min}+1/2)/d}\right)$, which depends heavily on the dimension d. Nevertheless, it is plausible to conjecture that there exist points $t_1, \ldots, t_n$ such that the information consisting of n function evaluations at these points has average radius proportional to the nth minimal radius $r(n) = \Theta\left((\ln\ n)^{(k-1)(r_{\min}+1)/(r_{\min}+1/2)} n^{-r_{\min}-1/2}\right)$ in the class $\Lambda = F_1^*$. The location of points $t_1, \ldots, t_n$ which form nth optimal information in the class Λ seems to be very irregular and hard to find.

NR 3.2:3 Assume now that $d = 1$ and $r = 0$. Then the eigenpairs of the correlation operator C_ν are given by

$$\lambda_j^* = (j\pi - \pi/2)^{-2} \quad \text{and} \quad \eta_j^*(x) = \sqrt{2}\,\sin\left((j\pi - \pi/2)x\right).$$

If arbitrary continuous linear functionals are allowed, $\Lambda = F_1^*$, then the average ε-complexity in the class F_1^* is given by

$$\text{comp}^{\text{avg}}(\varepsilon, F_1^*) = (c + a_1)\,\frac{1}{(\pi\,\varepsilon)^2}\,(1 + o(1)) \quad \text{as } \varepsilon \to 0, \quad a_1 \in [0, 2].$$

Assume now that Λ consists of only function evaluations. This problem was analyzed by Lee [86]. He showed that the best points of function evaluations are $t_i^* = 3i/(3n+1)$, $i = 1, 2, \ldots, n$, with the average radius of information $1/\sqrt{2(3n+1)}$. The average ε-complexity in the class Λ is given by

$$\text{comp}^{\text{avg}}(\varepsilon, \Lambda) = (c + a_2)\,\frac{1}{6\,\varepsilon^2}\,(1 + o(1)) \quad \text{as } \varepsilon \to 0,$$

where $a_2 \in [0, 2]$. For large c and small ε we thus have

$$\frac{\text{comp}^{\text{avg}}(\varepsilon, \Lambda)}{\text{comp}^{\text{avg}}(\varepsilon, F_1^*)} \simeq \frac{\pi^2}{6} \simeq 1.645.$$

This proves that one loses about 64.5% by using function evaluations instead, if possible, of optimally chosen linear functionals.

Exercises

E 3.2:1 Consider the approximation problem of smooth nonperiodic functions defined in Section 3.2 of Chapter 5. Using a technique of this section, find the average ε-complexity for the Gaussian measure μ of mean zero and correlation C_μ such that $C_\mu z_j = \beta_j z_j$, where z_j is an eigenfunction of the operator K_1 and $\beta_j = a\,j^{-v}$, $a > 0$, $v > 1$. Show that the average ε-complexity tends to the worst case complexity if $v \to 1^+$.

4. Ill-Posed Problems

In this section, we investigate the complexity of ill-posed problems in the average case setting. Our analysis is done only for the Hilbert case. That is, as in Section 7 of Chapter 5, we assume that F_1 and G are separable Hilbert spaces, and the solution operator, $S: D \subseteq F_1 \to G$, is an unbounded linear operator with domain D. Here, D is a linear subspace of F_1. Analogously to Section 5 of Chapter 6, we will assume that the set F of problem elements is the domain D of the solution operator. (The case in which F is a ball of radius q in D is left as an exercise.) We allow any continuous linear functional as a permissible information operation so that $\Lambda = F_1^*$. We assume that the Gaussian measure μ is concentrated on D, i.e., $\mu(D) = 1$, has mean zero and correlation operator C_μ. Furthermore, we assume that S is measurable, although $\int_D \|S(f)\|^2 \, \mu(df)$ need not be finite.

We begin with the study of the absolute error criterion. The residual error criterion is discussed in the second part of this section.

We say that S is *bounded on the average* iff $\int_D \|S(f)\|^2 \, \mu(df) < +\infty$. It is easy to show that for any information N,

$$r^{\mathrm{avg}}(N) < +\infty \qquad \text{iff} \qquad \int_D \|Sf\|^2 \, \mu(df) < +\infty.$$

Indeed, if S is bounded on the average then for arbitrary information N, $r^{\mathrm{avg}}(N)$ is no greater than the error of the zero algorithm whose square is equal to $\int_D \|S(f)\|^2 \, \mu(df)$. Hence, $r^{\mathrm{avg}}(N)$ is finite. On the other hand, if S is not bounded on the average, then from Section 6.3 of Chapter 6, we know that for arbitrary information N,

$$r^{\mathrm{avg}}(N) \geq \sum_{k=1}^{\infty} r^{\mathrm{avg}}(M_k)\, b_k$$

for some nonadaptive information M_k of cardinality k and some non-negative numbers b_k, $\sum_{k=1}^{\infty} b_k = 1$. However, for any nonadaptive M_k, $M_k = [L_1, \dots, L_k]$ with μ-orthonormal L_i, Section 6.3 of Chapter 6 yields that

$$r^{\mathrm{avg}}(M_k) = \left(\int_D \|S(f)\|^2 \, \mu(df) - \sum_{j=1}^{k} \|S(C_\mu L_j)\|^2 \right)^{1/2}.$$

Since $C_\mu(F_1) \subset D$, which follows from general properties of Gaussian measures and the assumptions on D, the sum above is well defined and finite, and so $r^{\mathrm{avg}}(M_k) = +\infty$. Hence, $r^{\mathrm{avg}}(N) = +\infty$.

We now assume that S is bounded on the average. In Section 6.3 of Chapter 6 we do not assume continuity of S. Hence, the results of this section hold, and therefore the μ-spline algorithm is optimal, and nonadaptive information is as powerful as adaptive information.

We now discuss the selection of nth optimal information. Since $C_\mu(F_1) \subset D$, SC_μ is a well defined bounded linear operator from F_1 into G, the results in Section 2.2 of Gelfand and Vilenkin [64] imply that $SC_\mu^{1/2}$ is a *Hilbert-Schmidt* operator. That is, the operator $SC_\mu^{1/2}$ is compact, and the sum of the squares of its singular values is finite.

Note that the adjoint $\left(SC_\mu^{1/2}\right)^*$ of the bounded linear operator $SC_\mu^{1/2}$ is well defined. However, since S is unbounded, the domain of S^* will be a proper subspace of G. Hence, $\left(SC_\mu^{1/2}\right)^* \neq C_\mu^{1/2} S^*$ since the domain of $\left(SC_\mu^{1/2}\right)^*$ is the whole space G, while the domain of $C_\mu^{1/2} S^*$ is only a proper subspace of G.

Since $SC_\mu^{1/2}$ is a Hilbert-Schmidt operator, the *a priori* measure $\nu = \mu S^{-1}$ on the space of solution elements is Gaussian with zero mean and correlation operator

$$C_\nu = (SC_\mu^{1/2})(SC_\mu^{1/2})^*,$$

which has finite trace (as is required of the correlation operator of a Gaussian measure). More precisely, let $\lambda_1^* \geq \lambda_2^* \geq \cdots \geq 0$ be the eigenvalues of the correlation operator C_ν, $C_\nu \eta_i^* = \lambda_i^* \eta_i^*$ for orthonormal η_i^*. Then $\text{trace}(C_\nu) = \sum_{i=1}^\infty \lambda_i^* = \int_D \|Sf\|^2 \, \mu(df) < +\infty$. Recall that $r^{\text{avg}}(n)$ denotes the nth minimal average radius. From Section 5.5 of Chapter 6, we immediately have

THEOREM 4.1.

(i) *If S is bounded on the average then*

$$r^{\text{avg}}(n)^2 \geq \int_D \|Sf\|^2 \, \mu(df) - \sum_{i=1}^n \lambda_i^*.$$

(ii) *In addition, suppose that η_i^* is in the domain of S^* for $1 \leq i \leq n$, and set*

$$f_i^* = \begin{cases} \lambda_i^{*-1/2} S^* \eta_i^* & \text{if } \lambda_i^* > 0, \\ 0 & \text{if } \lambda_i^* = 0. \end{cases}$$

Then the information N_n^* given by

$$N_n^* f = [\langle f, f_1^* \rangle, \ldots, \langle f, f_n^* \rangle]$$

is nth optimal information, the μ-spline algorithm ϕ_n^* using N_n^* is optimal error algorithm, and

$$e^{\text{avg}}(\phi_n^*, N_n^*) = r^{\text{avg}}(N_n^*) = r^{\text{avg}}(n) = \left(\int_D \|Sf\|^2 \, \mu(df) - \sum_{i=1}^n \lambda_i^* \right)^{1/2}.$$

Hence, we have optimal information and optimal error algorithms in the case when η_i^* are in the domain of S^*. However, since S is an unbounded operator, this is not the case in general. See **E 4:2** for further discussion.

We now extend part (ii) of Theorem 4.2 to the general case. The proof is given in some detail since it shows how to find almost nth optimal information.

THEOREM 4.2. *If S is bounded on the average then*

$$r^{\text{avg}}(n) = \left(\int_D \|Sf\|^2 \, \mu(df) - \sum_{i=1}^{n} \lambda_i^* \right)^{1/2} = \left(\sum_{i=n+1}^{\infty} \lambda_i^* \right)^{1/2}.$$

PROOF: It suffices to prove the first expression for $r^{\text{avg}}(n)$. Define an orthonormal set $\{\zeta_1^*, \ldots, \zeta_n^*\}$ by

$$\zeta_i^* = \frac{1}{\sqrt{\lambda_i^*}} (SC_\mu^{1/2})^* \eta_i^*, \quad 1 \le i \le n.$$

Next, let $\delta > 0$. Choose positive θ,

$$\theta \le \min \left\{ \lambda_n^{*\,1/2}, \delta \sum_{i=n+1}^{\infty} \lambda_i^* / \left(2 \sum_{i=1}^{n} \lambda_i^{*\,1/2} \right) \right\}.$$

Choose $f_1, \ldots, f_n$ such that $\langle C_\mu f_i, f_j \rangle = \delta_{i,j}$ for $1 \le i, j \le n$, and $\|\zeta_i^* - C_\mu^{1/2} f_i\| < \theta / \|SC_\mu^{1/2}\|$ for $1 \le i \le n$. Since $\zeta_1^*, \ldots, \zeta_n^*$ are orthonormal eigenelements of $(SC_\mu^{1/2})^*(SC_\mu^{1/2})$ corresponding to the eigenvalues $\lambda_1^*, \ldots, \lambda_n^*$, this inequality and the triangle inequality imply that $\|SC_\mu f_i\| \ge \lambda_i^{*\,1/2} - \theta \ge 0$, $\forall\, 1 \le i \le n$, and so

$$\sum_{i=1}^{n} \|SC_\mu f_i\|^2 \ge \sum_{i=1}^{n} \lambda_i^* - 2\theta \sum_{i=1}^{n} \lambda_i^{*\,1/2} + n\theta^2 \ge \sum_{i=1}^{n} \lambda_i^* - \delta.$$

Define information $N_{n,\delta}$ by

$$N_{n,\delta} f = [\langle f, f_1 \rangle, \ldots, \langle f, f_n \rangle], \quad \forall\, f \in F_1.$$

Then the previous inequality yields that

$$r^{\text{avg}}(n)^2 \le r^{\text{avg}}(N_{n,\delta})^2 \le \int_D \|Sf\|^2 \, \mu(df) - \sum_{i=1}^{n} \lambda_i^* + \delta.$$

Since $\delta > 0$ is arbitrary, this implies that $r^{\text{avg}}(n)^2 \le \int_D \|Sf\|^2 \, \mu(df) - \sum_{i=1}^{n} \lambda_i^*$. By part (i) of Theorem 4.1, the opposite of this inequality also holds. This establishes the first expression for $r^{\text{avg}}(n)$, completing the proof of the theorem. ∎

As a result, we see that if S is bounded on the average, then for any $\delta > 0$, the information $N_{n,\delta}$ is within δ of being nth optimal information. In the remainder of this section, we assume without essential loss of generality that for any n, there exists N_n^* which is nth optimal information, and we let ϕ_n^* denote the spline algorithm using N_n^*.

We now give sharp bounds on the ε-complexity $\mathrm{comp}^{\mathrm{avg}}(\varepsilon)$ of ill-posed problems. Recall that $m^{\mathrm{avg}}(\varepsilon)$ and $n^{\mathrm{avg}}(\varepsilon)$, respectively, denote the average ε-cardinality numbers for adaptive information of varying cardinality and for nonadaptive information. Since $\Lambda = F_1^*$, the results of this section and of Chapter 6 immediately yield

THEOREM 4.3.

(i) *If S is not bounded on the average then*

$$\mathrm{comp}^{\mathrm{avg}}(\varepsilon) = +\infty, \qquad \forall\, \varepsilon > 0.$$

(ii) *Suppose that S is bounded on the average. Let $\varepsilon > 0$. Then the average ε-cardinality numbers satisfy*

$$\lceil m^{\mathrm{avg}}(\varepsilon)\rceil = n^{\mathrm{avg}}(\varepsilon) = \inf\left\{ n : \sum_{i=n+1}^{\infty} \lambda_i^* \le \varepsilon^2 \right\}.$$

Let $n = n^{\mathrm{avg}}(\varepsilon)$. Then the information N_n^* and the algorithm ϕ_n^* are almost optimal, with

$$c\, m^{\mathrm{avg}}(\varepsilon) \le \mathrm{comp}^{\mathrm{avg}}(\varepsilon) \le \mathrm{cost}^{\mathrm{avg}}(\phi_n^*, N_n^*) \le (c+2)n^{\mathrm{avg}}(\varepsilon) - 1$$
$$\le (c+2)\big(m^{\mathrm{avg}}(\varepsilon) + 1\big) - 1.$$

For large c and small ε, we have

$$\mathrm{comp}^{\mathrm{avg}}(\varepsilon) \simeq \mathrm{cost}^{\mathrm{avg}}(\varepsilon) \simeq c\, m^{\mathrm{avg}}(\varepsilon).$$

We conclude this part of the section by pointing out an important difference between the worst and average case settings for the absolute error criterion. Suppose that we are solving a linear problem in the Hilbert case for the unit ball in the domain of the solution operator. We say that the problem is *convergent* if there exists a sequence of algorithms whose error converges to zero, i.e., if for any $\varepsilon > 0$, there exists an algorithm giving an ε-approximation. In the worst case setting, we have three different possibilities:

(1) The solution operator is unbounded. Then every algorithm has infinite error.
(2) The solution operator is bounded, but not compact. Then there exist algorithms with finite error, but the problem is not convergent.
(3) The solution operator is compact. Then the problem is convergent.

However, in the average case setting, there are only two possibilities:

(1) The solution operator is not bounded on the average. Then every algorithm has infinite error.
(2) The solution operator is bounded on the average. Then the problem is convergent.

We now consider the residual error criterion for the Fredholm problem $Ku = f$ of the first kind. Here, the error of an algorithm ϕ using information N is given by

$$e^{\text{res}}(\phi, N) = \left(\int_D \|f - K(\phi(Nf))\|_V^2 \, \mu(df) \right)^{1/2},$$

where V is a normed linear space in which F_1 is embedded. The measure μ is to satisfy the properties mentioned at the beginning of this section. Letting $\text{ER}(\cdot) = \|\cdot\|_V$, we get from Section 6.3 of Chapter 6 that our problem is now equivalent to the approximation problem, $S = I$ for the spaces F_1 and $G = V$.

THEOREM 4.4.

(i) For any nonadaptive information N, the μ-spline algorithm using N is an optimal error algorithm and

$$r^{\text{res}}(N) = \left(\int_{F_1} \|f\|_V^2 \, \mu_2(df|0) \right)^{1/2} < +\infty,$$

where $\mu_2(\cdot|0)$ is the conditional measure for $y = 0$.

(ii) Adaption is no more powerful than nonadaption, i.e., for any adaptive information N^{a}, there exists nonadaptive information N^{non} such that $\text{card}(N^{\text{non}}) \le \lceil \text{card}(N^{\text{a}}) \rceil$ and $r^{\text{res}}(N^{\text{non}}) \le r^{\text{res}}(N^{\text{a}})$.

(iii) Let $r^{\text{res}}(n)$ denote the nth minimal radius of information. Then

$$r^{\text{res}}(n) = \left(\sum_{i=n+1}^{\infty} \lambda_i \right)^{1/2},$$

where $\lambda_1 \ge \lambda_2 \ge \ldots \ge 0$ are the eigenvalues of the correlation operator C_μ. In particular, $\lim_{n \to \infty} r^{\text{res}}(n) = 0$.

(iv) Let $n(\varepsilon) = \inf\{n : r^{\text{res}}(n) \le \varepsilon\}$. Then

$$c\left(n(\varepsilon) - 1\right) \le \text{comp}(\varepsilon) \le (c + 2)n(\varepsilon) - 1, \qquad \forall \varepsilon > 0,$$

and so $\text{comp}(\varepsilon)$ is finite for all $\varepsilon > 0$.

Notes and Remarks

NR 4:1 This section is written by A. G. Werschulz, and the material is taken from Werschulz [86b, 87a].

NR 4:2 We show that for the Fredholm problem of the first kind in a Hilbert space, there always exists a Gaussian measure μ concentrated on the subspace domain D. Recall that the Fredholm problem is defined to be the inversion of a compact injection $K: G \to F_1$ of Hilbert spaces. Without loss of generality, we may assume that the range D of K is dense in F_1. Let u_i denote the eigenelement of K^*K corresponding to the eigenvalue κ_i^2, where $\kappa_1 \geq \kappa_2 \geq \ldots > 0$. Then $\{u_i\}_{i=1}^{\infty}$ is an orthonormal system for G. For each index i, let $e_i = \kappa_i^{-1}Ku_i$, so that $\{e_i\}_{i=1}^{\infty}$ is an orthonormal system for F_1. The range D of K is, of course, the domain of the solution operator $S = K^{-1}$, and it is straightforward to check that $D = \{f \in F_1 : \sum_{i=1}^{\infty} \langle f, e_i \rangle / \kappa_i^2 < +\infty\}$.

Suppose now that the Gaussian measure μ has covariance operator C_μ defined by $C_\mu e_i = \sigma_i e_i$ for $i = 1, 2, \ldots$, where $\sigma_1 \geq \sigma_2 \geq \ldots > 0$ with $\lim_{i \to \infty} \sigma_i = 0$ satisfies $\sum_{i=1}^{\infty} \sigma_i / \kappa_i^2 < +\infty$. Using Kolmogorov's principle (sometimes called the zero-one law), see Shilov and Fan Dyk Tin [67] and **NR 2.2:2**, it is easy to show that $\mu(D) = 1$. Since $Sf = \lim_{n \to \infty} \sum_{i=1}^{n} \kappa_i^{-1} \langle f, e_i \rangle e_i$ for every $f \in D$, we see that S is the pointwise limit of measurable linear operators. Hence, S is a measurable linear operator.

NR 4:3 Note that for any Fredholm problem of the first kind in a Hilbert space, there exists a measure such that the solution operator is bounded on the average. To see this, let S be the inverse of a compact injection K of Hilbert spaces. Let μ be the Gaussian measure whose covariance operator is described in **NR 4:2**. A simple calculation shows that $\int_D \|Sf\|^2 \mu(df) = \sum_{i=1}^{\infty} \sigma_i / \kappa_i^2 < +\infty$.

NR 4:4 Note that our presentation of nth optimal information differs from that of Theorem 5.5.1 of Chapter 6. That is, we did not choose to represent the nth optimal information as

$$N_n^* f = [L_1^*(f), \ldots, L_n^*(f)]$$

for the functionals $L_i^*(f) = (\lambda_i^*)^{-1/2} \langle Sf, \eta_i^* \rangle$. There are two reasons. The first is that since we are in a Hilbert space, we wish to use the Riesz representation of bounded linear functionals as inner products to get an explicit formula for the nth optimal information. The second is more subtle: The linear functional L_i^* is not bounded unless η_i^* is in the domain of S^*. Hence, the information consisting of $L_1^*, \ldots, L_n^*$ is, generally, not permissible.

Exercises

E 4:1 Extend the results of this section to the case where the problem elements form a ball of radius q in D, i.e., $F = \{f \in D : \|f\| \leq q\}$.

E 4:2 Let S be the inverse of a compact operator. Show that for any n, there always exists a correlation operator C_μ such that S is bounded on the average, yet η_i^* is not in the domain of S^* for $i = 1, \ldots, n$.

E 4:3 In Chapter 6, we study the average case setting under the assumption that any permissible information operation must be a continuous linear functional. This led to the conclusion that the optimal information for an ill-posed problem need not be permissible. Suppose that we allow a linear functional L to be a permissible linear functional iff $\int_F |L(f)|^2 \mu(df)$ is finite. Show that the main results of this section still hold. That is, algorithms with finite error exist iff S is bounded on the average, the standard formula for nth optimal average radius remains true, and adaption does not help. Moreover, the nth optimal information of **NR 4:4** is now permissible. (Hint: A measurable linear functional may be approximated by a bounded linear functional, see Skorohod [74].)

E 4:4 Determine the nth optimal information N_n^* and the μ-spline algorithm ϕ_n^* using N_n^* for the problem described in **NR 4:2**. Specializing to the case where $\sigma_i/\kappa_i^2 = i^{-\alpha}$ for some $\alpha > 1$, determine $\text{comp}^{\text{avg}}(\varepsilon)$.

E 4:5 Extend the results of this section to include ill-posed problems in which F_1 is a separable Banach space and G is a separable Hilbert space.

Chapter 8

Probabilistic Setting

1. Introduction

In this chapter we analyze the probabilistic setting. This is the setting in which the error of an algorithm is defined in a worst case sense, disregarding a set of preassigned measure δ. The cost of an algorithm is defined by its worst performance.

We begin with an overview of this chapter. In Section 2 we show that the probabilistic setting is closely related to the average case setting with a special error criterion. This relation enables us to apply many results from Chapter 6, and it makes the analysis of the probabilistic setting quite straightforward.

In Section 3 we define the probabilistic radius of information. It is a sharp lower bound on the errors of algorithms that use this information. Roughly speaking, the probabilistic radius of information is the smallest radius of a ball whose conditional measure is at least $1-\delta$. We can compute ε-approximations using the information N only if its probabilistic radius is at most ε.

In Section 4 we define the probabilistic cardinality number $m^{\text{prob}}(\varepsilon, \delta)$ to be the smallest cardinality of information whose probabilistic radius is at most ε. The cardinality of information is defined in a worst case sense. Clearly, the probabilistic cardinality number multiplied by the cost c of one information operation is a lower bound on the probabilistic complexity. As in the worst and average case settings, this bound is sharp if there exists information of cardinality $m^{\mathrm{prob}}(\varepsilon, \delta)$ with probabilistic radius at most ε such that an optimal error algorithm that uses this information has combinatory cost negligible compared to $c\, m^{\mathrm{prob}}(\varepsilon, \delta)$.

Linear problems are studied in Section 5. We begin with $F = F_1$ and show that the assumption on negligible combinatory cost holds in this case. We do this in two steps. We first consider nonadaptive information. Then the μ-spline algorithm, which is optimal in the average case setting, is also optimal in the probabilistic setting. Thus, for nonadaptive information, the combinatory cost of an optimal algorithm is negligible. We then show that adaption does not help. The proof is much easier than in the average case setting since, without loss of generality, we can restrict ourselves to information of fixed cardinality and apply the corresponding result from Chapter 6.

To get complexity bounds, we must estimate the probabilistic radius of nonadaptive information. The upper bound on the probabilistic radius depends on the trace of the correlation operator of the conditional measure, and this estimate is essentially sharp if δ is small but fixed and the trace goes to zero. In this case, the probabilistic radius behaves like the average radius of information. We also exhibit a lower bound on the probabilistic radius in terms of the largest eigenvalue of the correlation operator. This estimate is sharp if the trace is fixed and δ goes to zero.

These estimates show that the probabilistic radius of information changes its behavior depending on the relation between δ and the trace of the correlation operator.

When the solution operator is a continuous linear functional, there is, of course, no difference between the trace and the largest eigenvalue of the correlation operator of the conditional measure. In this case, we have a pleasing relation between the average and probabilistic radii. Namely, the probabilistic radius is equal to $\psi^{-1}(1 - \delta)$ times the average radius, where $\psi(x) = \sqrt{2/\pi} \int_0^x \exp(-t^2/2)\, dt$ is the probability integral and ψ^{-1} is its inverse. For small δ, we have $\psi^{-1}(1 - \delta) \simeq \sqrt{2\ln(1/\delta)}$.

We next study optimal nonadaptive information. We consider two classes Λ of permissible information operations. Namely, for $S \in F_1^*$ we study arbitrary $\Lambda \subseteq F_1^*$, and for arbitrary S we study $\Lambda = F_1^*$. In both cases, we show that the same information is optimal in the probabilistic and average case settings.

These results yield tight complexity bounds in terms of the probabilistic cardinality number. Depending on the relation between ε and δ, the probabilistic (ε, δ)-cardinality number is fully determined by the trace of the correlation operator of the conditional measure (δ fixed, ε tending to zero) or by the largest eigenvalue of the same operator (ε fixed, δ tending to zero). For $S \in F_1^*$, we have a straightforward relation between the average case and probabilistic complexities.

We show that bounds on the probabilistic (ε, δ)-complexity depend on $\psi^{-1}(1 - \delta)/\varepsilon = \sqrt{2\ln(1/\delta)}(1 + o(1))/\varepsilon$ as $\delta \to 0$. Thus, the dependence on ε is much more crucial than the dependence on δ. The dependence on δ is in fact quite weak since it is only through $\sqrt{2\ln(1/\delta)}$ and, even for very small δ, the factor $\sqrt{2\ln(1/\delta)}$ is not too large.

In Section 5.5 we analyze linear problems over the ball B_q with a finite radius q. One might hope that the probabilistic complexity over B_q is essentially the same as the probabilistic complexity over the whole space. Indeed, this is the case if δ is at least equal to $x = 1 - \mu(B_q) = \exp\left(-q^2 a^*\left(1 + o(1)\right)\right)$ as $q \to +\infty$ with a^* depending on the *a priori* Gaussian measure μ. On the other hand, if $\delta << x$ then the two probabilistic complexities are not related. This is because the probabilistic complexity over the whole space usually goes to infinity as δ goes to zero, whereas the probabilistic complexity over the ball B_q is bounded for all δ by the worst case complexity, which is usually finite for positive ε and independent of δ. Thus, even for $\delta = 0$, the probabilistic complexity over the ball B_q is usually finite.

Different error criteria in the probabilistic setting are discussed in Section 6. As in the previous settings, we begin with relative error. The analysis of relative error is only done for continuous linear functionals S and an arbitrary class Λ. To make the problem meaningful, we assume that S cannot be expressed by finite linear combinations of permissible functionals from Λ. With this assumption, the worst and average case complexities are infinite. We prove that the probabilistic complexity is in general finite and related to the average case complexity under the absolute error criterion with ε replaced by roughly $\varepsilon\delta$. Observe that the dependence on δ is now much more crucial than the dependence for the absolute error criterion. It is interesting to notice that despite the relation to the average case setting, the μ-spline algorithm is only an *almost* optimal error algorithm. An optimal error algorithm is nonlinear, and its implementation requires the solution of a quadratic equation.

The relative error criterion for arbitrary linear operators is currently under investigation. We present only crude preliminary bounds on the probabilistic complexity.

We next turn to the normalized error criterion. We present some rather crude estimates that relate the probabilistic complexities under the normalized and absolute error criteria. As in Section 5.5, we remark that these two complexities are related only if δ is relatively large compared to ε. For all δ, the probabilistic complexity under the normalized error criterion is bounded by the worst case complexity, which is usually finite; whereas the probabilistic complexity under the absolute error criterion usually goes to criterion ER_x. Due to (3) from Section 2, we define the *probabilistic radius of information* N by

$$r^{\text{prob}}(N, \delta) = M^{-1}(N, \delta) = \inf \{ x : M(N, x) \leq \delta \}. \qquad (2)$$

Roughly speaking, $r^{\text{prob}}(N, \delta)$ is the smallest radius of balls with varying centers whose expected value of the conditional measures is at least $1 - \delta$. Clearly, if the infimum in (2) is attained then

$$r^{\text{prob}}(N, \delta) \leq \varepsilon \quad \text{iff} \quad M(N, \varepsilon) \leq \delta. \qquad (3)$$

The radius $r^{\text{prob}}(N, \delta)$ is a sharp lower bound on the probabilistic error of any algorithm that uses N,

$$r^{\text{prob}}(N, \delta) = \inf_{\phi} e^{\text{prob}}(\phi, N, \delta). \qquad (4)$$

As always, ϕ^* is an *optimal error algorithm* iff

$$e^{\text{prob}}(\phi^*, N, \delta) = r^{\text{prob}}(N, \delta).$$

In general, the optimal error algorithm ϕ^* is hard to implement. For linear problems with $F = F_1$, we show in Section 5 that ϕ^* is just the μ-spline algorithm. Hence the same algorithm is optimal in both the average case and probabilistic settings.

Notes and Remarks

NR 3:1 As in Lemma 2.1 of Chapter 6, one may show that the integrand of (1) is μ_1-measurable if G is a separable normed linear space.

4. Probabilistic Cardinality Number and Complexity

As in the worst and average case settings, the concept of the radius of information is crucial for determining the complexity. From (4) of Section 3, it follows that to compute ε-approximations in the probabilistic setting we must use information with $r^{\text{prob}}(N, \delta) \leq \varepsilon$.

Let N be adaptive information defined as in Section 2.2 of Chapter 3. Let $\text{card}^{\text{wor}}(N)$ denote its worst case cardinality, $\text{card}^{\text{wor}}(N) = \sup_{f \in F} n(f)$. Since in the probabilistic setting the cost is defined in a worst case sense, we conclude that varying cardinality does not help. Hence, we can restrict ourselves to information with fixed cardinality, $n(f) \equiv$ constant.

By the *probabilistic (ε, δ)-cardinality number* $m^{\mathrm{prob}}(\varepsilon, \delta)$ we mean the minimal cardinality of information whose probabilistic radius does not exceed ε,

$$m^{\mathrm{prob}}(\varepsilon, \delta) = \min \left\{ \mathrm{card}^{\mathrm{wor}}(N) : N \text{ such that } r^{\mathrm{prob}}(N, \delta) \leq \varepsilon \right\}.$$

Due to (3) of Section 3, we have

$$m^{\mathrm{prob}}(\varepsilon, \delta) = \min \left\{ \mathrm{card}^{\mathrm{wor}}(N) : N \text{ such that } M(N, \varepsilon) \leq \delta \right\}.$$

Clearly, the definition of the cost in a worst case sense implies that

$$\mathrm{comp}^{\mathrm{prob}}(\varepsilon, \delta) \geq c\, m^{\mathrm{prob}}(\varepsilon, \delta), \tag{1}$$

where c is the cost of one information operation. As in the worst and average case settings, this bound is sharp if there exists information N of cardinality $m^{\mathrm{prob}}(\varepsilon, \delta)$ with probabilistic radius at most ε whose cost dominates the combinatory cost of an optimal error algorithm that uses N. Under these assumptions,

$$\mathrm{comp}^{\mathrm{prob}}(\varepsilon, \delta) \simeq c\, m^{\mathrm{prob}}(\varepsilon, \delta). \tag{2}$$

Notes and Remarks

NR 4:1 As indicated in Chapter 3, one can analyze the probabilistic setting with the average case definition of cost. Then the probabilistic (ε, δ)-cardinality number is redefined by

$$m^{\mathrm{prob}}(\varepsilon, \delta) = \min \left\{ \mathrm{card}^{\mathrm{avg}}(N) : N \text{ such that } r^{\mathrm{prob}}(N, \delta) \leq \varepsilon \right\},$$

where $\mathrm{card}^{\mathrm{avg}}(N) = \int_F n(f)\, \mu(df)$ is the average cardinality of information N. Obviously, estimates (1) and (2) remain true. The analysis of the probabilistic setting with the cost defined in an average case sense will be presented in Notes and Remarks after successive sections of this chapter.

5. Linear Problems

In this section we analyze the probabilistic setting for linear problems. The formal definition of a linear problem is given in Section 5.1 of Chapter 6. As in that chapter, we first discuss linear problems when F is the whole space, $F = F_1$. This is done in Sections 5.1–5.4. In Section 5.5, we extend the analysis to the case when F is a ball with finite radius q.

5.1. Optimal Error Algorithms

Let N be nonadaptive information, $N = [L_1, L_2, \ldots, L_n]$ with μ-orthonormal functionals L_j. From Section 6.3 of Chapter 6, we conclude that the affine μ-spline algorithm $\phi(\cdot) = \phi^s(\cdot) + g^*$ is an optimal error algorithm. We now prove that despite the lack of convexity of ER_x, the μ-spline algorithm is optimal, i.e., $g^* = 0$. Indeed, $\nu(\cdot|y)$ is Gaussian with mean $m(y) = \sum_{j=1}^n y_j S(C_\mu L_j)$ and correlation operator

$$C_{\nu,N} = C_\nu - \sum_{j=1}^n \langle \cdot, S(C_\mu L_j) \rangle S(C_\mu L_j),$$

where C_ν is the correlation operator of $\nu = \mu S^{-1}$ and $\langle \cdot, \cdot \rangle$ stands for the inner product of G. From Section 3, we have that for an arbitrary algorithm ϕ, $M(\phi, N, x) = 1 - \int_{\mathbb{R}^n} \nu(B(\phi(y), x)|y) \, \mu_1(dy)$. Hence

$$M(\phi, N, x) = 1 - \int_{\mathbb{R}^n} \nu_N (B(\phi(y) - m(y), x)) \, \mu_1(dy),$$

where ν_N is Gaussian with mean zero and correlation operator $C_{\nu,N}$. Lemma 2.9.3 from the appendix yields that for every $x \in \mathbb{R}_+$, $M(\phi, N, x)$ is minimized by the μ-spline algorithm $\phi^s(y) = m(y)$. Since this holds for arbitrary x, the μ-spline algorithm is an optimal error algorithm in the probabilistic setting, as claimed.

We now discuss the probabilistic error of ϕ^s. We have

$$M(\phi^s, N, x) = M(N, x) = 1 - \int_{\mathbb{R}^n} \nu_N (B(0, x)) \, \mu_1(dy) = 1 - \nu_N (B(0, x)).$$

Hence

$$e^{\mathrm{prob}}(\phi^s, N, \delta) = r^{\mathrm{prob}}(N, \delta) = M^{-1}(N, \delta) = \inf \{ x : \nu_N(B(0, x)) \geq 1 - \delta \}.$$

This means that for nonadaptive information, the probabilistic radius is the smallest radius of a ball whose conditional measure is at least $1 - \delta$. We summarize this in

COROLLARY 5.1.1. *For arbitrary nonadaptive information N and arbitrary δ, the μ-spline algorithm $\phi^s(y) = \sum_{j=1}^n y_j S(C_\mu L_j)$ is optimal in the probabilistic setting and*

$$r^{\mathrm{prob}}(N, \delta) = \inf \{ x : \nu_N(B(0, x)) \geq 1 - \delta \}.$$

We now interpret Corollary 5.1.1. Before any computation is performed, the best approximation to solution elements $g = S(f)$ is zero as the mean of the *a priori* measure $\nu = \mu S^{-1}$. Then the probabilistic radius $r^{\mathrm{prob}}(0, \delta) = \inf \{ x : \nu(B(0, x)) \geq 1 - \delta \}$ is the smallest radius of a ball whose ν-measure is at least $1-\delta$. After computing $y = N(f)$, the measure ν is changed to the conditional measure $\nu(\cdot|y)$ whose mean, the value of the μ-spline algorithm at y, is the best approximation to the solution elements. Its probabilistic radius is the smallest radius of a ball whose ν_N-measure is at least $1-\delta$. The correlation operator $C_{\nu,N}$ of ν_N depends on the information N. As we know from Chapter 6, the trace of this operator goes to zero when the cardinality n of N increases. Thus, for large n, the conditional measure resembles an atomic measure concentrated over the exact solution, and the ν_N-measure of the ball with radius ε tends to one.

5.2. Estimates of the Radius of Information

We now estimate the probabilistic radius $r^{\mathrm{prob}}(N,\delta)$ for nonadaptive information. We begin with the case when the solution operator is a continuous linear functional.

For $S \in F_1^*$, the measure ν_N is one dimensional Gaussian with mean zero and variance $\sigma(N)$, where

$$\sigma(N) = \inf_{g_j \in \mathbb{R}} \left\| S - \sum_{j=1}^{n} g_j\, L_j \right\|_{\mu}^2.$$

As we know from Chapter 6, $\sqrt{\sigma(N)}$ is equal to the average radius of N with the absolute error criterion, $\sqrt{\sigma(N)} = r^{\mathrm{avg}}(N)$. Note that

$$\nu_N\big(B(0,x)\big) = \sqrt{\frac{2}{\pi\sigma(N)}} \int_0^x \exp\left(\frac{-t^2}{2\sigma(N)}\right) dt = \psi\left(\frac{x}{r^{\mathrm{avg}}(N)}\right),$$

where

$$\psi(z) = \sqrt{\frac{2}{\pi}} \int_0^z \exp\left(-t^2/2\right) dt$$

is the probability integral. This yields

COROLLARY 5.2.1. *Let S be a continuous linear functional. Then for nonadaptive N,*

$$r^{\mathrm{prob}}(N,\delta) = \psi^{-1}(1-\delta)\, r^{\mathrm{avg}}(N).$$

Observe that for large z, $\psi(z) = 1 - \sqrt{2/\pi}\, z^{-1}\exp(-z^2/2)\,(1+o(1))$ as $z \to +\infty$ and therefore $\psi^{-1}(1-\delta) = \sqrt{2\ln(1/\delta)}\,(1+o(1))$ as $\delta \to 0$. Hence for small δ, the probabilistic radius of N is equal, roughly, to $\sqrt{2\ln(1/\delta)}$ times the average radius of N with the absolute error criterion.

We now estimate $r^{\mathrm{prob}}(N,\delta)$ for an arbitrary continuous linear solution operator. We start with an upper bound. From Lemma 2.9.2 of the appendix, we conclude that

$$r^{\mathrm{prob}}(N,\delta) \le \sqrt{2\,\mathrm{trace}(C_{\nu,N})\,\ln\frac{5}{\delta}}. \tag{1}$$

We show that this estimate is essentially sharp if δ is small but fixed, and if $\mathrm{trace}(C_{\nu,N})$ goes to zero. Namely, we have

$$r^{\mathrm{prob}}(N,\delta) = \left(\sqrt{2\,\mathrm{trace}(C_{\nu,N})\,\ln\frac{5}{\delta}}\right)^{(1+o(1))} \qquad \text{as } \mathrm{trace}(C_{\nu,N}) \to 0. \tag{2}$$

Indeed, apply Lemma 2.9.1 from the Appendix with $a = \left(\mathrm{trace}(C_{\nu,N})\right)^{-p/2}$ for a positive p. Note that for small $\mathrm{trace}(C_{\nu,N})$, $a > 1$. For $x = r^{\mathrm{prob}}(N,\delta)$ we have

$$1 - \delta = \nu_N\left(B(0,x)\right) \le \left(1 - a^{-2}\right)^{-1}\psi(z),$$

where $z = ax/\sqrt{\mathrm{trace}(C_{\nu,N})}$. Since δ and a^{-2} are small, z is large and therefore,

$$(1-\delta)\left(1-a^{-2}\right) \le 1 - \sqrt{\frac{2}{\pi}}\,z^{-1}\exp\left(\frac{-z^2}{2}\right)\left(1 + o(1)\right).$$

This yields for small $\mathrm{trace}(C_{\nu,N})$,

$$x \ge \sqrt{2\left(\mathrm{trace}(C_{\nu,N})\right)^{1+p}\ln\frac{1}{\delta}}\left(1 + o(1)\right).$$

Let $u = \sqrt{2\,\mathrm{trace}(C_{\nu,N})\ln(5/\delta)}$. Then the last estimate and (1) yield

$$1 + p\left(1 + o(1)\right) \le \frac{\ln x}{\ln u} \le 1 \quad \text{as } \mathrm{trace}(C_{\nu,N}) \to 0.$$

Since p can be arbitrarily small, this implies that $\lim_{\mathrm{trace}(C_{\nu,N})\to 0} \ln x/\ln u$ $= 1$ and $x = u^{1+o(1)}$, as claimed in (2).

We now present a lower bound on the probabilistic radius for arbitrary $\mathrm{trace}(C_{\nu,N})$ and δ. Let λ_N be the largest eigenvalue of $C_{\nu,N}$, and let η_N be its normalized eigenelement, $\|\eta_N\| = 1$. Observe that $B(0,x) \subset \{g \in G : |\langle g, \eta_N\rangle| \le x\}$ and

$$\nu_N\left(B(0,x)\right) \le \nu_N\left(\{g \in G : |\langle g,\eta_N\rangle| \le x\}\right) = \psi\left(\frac{x}{\sqrt{\lambda_N}}\right).$$

Therefore,

$$r^{\text{prob}}(N,\delta) \geq \sqrt{\lambda_N}\,\psi^{-1}(1-\delta) = \sqrt{2\,\lambda_N \ln \frac{1}{\delta}}\,(1+o(1)) \quad \text{as } \delta \to 0. \quad (3)$$

This bound is sharp if the information N is fixed and δ goes to zero. Indeed, from Borell's [75, 76] estimate, see Section 5.8 of Chapter 6, we know that

$$\nu_N\big(B(0,x)\big) = 1 - \exp\left(\frac{-x^2(1+o(1))}{2\,\lambda_N}\right) \quad \text{as } x \to +\infty.$$

Then $1 - \delta = \nu_N\big(B(0,x)\big)$ for $x = r^{\text{prob}}(N,\delta)$ and small δ imply

$$r^{\text{prob}}(N,\delta) = \sqrt{2\,\lambda_N \ln \frac{1}{\delta}}\,(1+o(1)) \quad \text{as } \delta \to 0. \quad (4)$$

Thus, (3) is sharp for small δ. We summarize this in

COROLLARY 5.2.2. *Let S be a continuous linear operator. Then*

$$\sqrt{\lambda_N}\,\psi^{-1}(1-\delta) \leq r^{\text{prob}}(N,\delta) \leq \sqrt{2\,\text{trace}(C_{\nu,N}) \ln \frac{5}{\delta}}.$$

These two bounds are essentially sharp. Namely, the probabilistic radius is roughly equal to the lower bound if the information N is fixed and δ goes to zero, and it is roughly equal to the upper bound if δ is fixed and $\text{trace}(C_{\nu,N})$ goes to zero.

We now compare the probabilistic and average case radii of information. From Section 5.3 of Chapter 6, we know that in the average case setting with the absolute error criterion,

$$r^{\text{avg}}(N) = \sqrt{\text{trace}(C_{\nu,N})}.$$

Therefore, (1) can be rewritten as

$$r^{\text{prob}}(N,\delta) \leq \sqrt{2 \ln \frac{5}{\delta}}\, r^{\text{avg}}(N).$$

For fixed δ and small $\text{trace}(C_{\nu,N})$, this estimate is essentially sharp. Then the intrinsic uncertainty in the probabilistic setting is roughly $\sqrt{2\ln(5/\delta)}$ times larger than in the average case setting.

On the other hand, for the fixed information N and small δ, we have from (4),

$$r^{\text{prob}}(N,\delta) \simeq \sqrt{2\ln\frac{1}{\delta}}\ \sqrt{\frac{\lambda_N}{\text{trace}(C_{\nu,N})}}\ r^{\text{avg}}(N).$$

Observe that $a_N = \sqrt{\lambda_N/\text{trace}(C_{\nu,N})}$ depends on the eigenvalues $\lambda_{i,N}$ of $C_{\nu,N}$. For some values of $\lambda_{i,N}$, a_N can be arbitrarily small. Indeed, assume that $\lambda_{i,N} = (n+i)^{-p}$, $i = 1, 2, \ldots$, for $p > 1$. Then $a_N = \sqrt{(p-1)n^{-1}}(1+o(1))$. In this case, the intrinsic uncertainty in the probabilistic setting is much less than $\sqrt{2\ln(1/\delta)}$ times the intrinsic uncertainty in the average case setting.

For some other values of $\lambda_{i,N}$, it can happen that a_N is of order one. Indeed, take now $\lambda_{i,N} = \rho^{i+n}$, $i = 1, 2, \ldots$, for $\rho < 1$. Then $a_N = \sqrt{1-\rho}$ is of order one for small ρ. In this case, the intrinsic uncertainty in the probabilistic setting is roughly equal to $\sqrt{2\ln(1/\delta)}$ times the intrinsic uncertainty in the average case setting.

5.3. Optimal Information

We want to find nonadaptive information N of cardinality n with the smallest probabilistic radius. Recall that Λ is the class of permissible information operations, $\Lambda \subset F_1^*$. Let

$$r^{\text{prob}}(n,\delta,\Lambda) = \inf\left\{r^{\text{prob}}(N,\delta) : N = [L_1,\ldots,L_n] \text{ and } L_i \in \Lambda\right\}$$

denote the *nth minimal probabilistic radius of* (*nonadaptive*) *information* in the class Λ. Information $N^* = [L_1^*, L_2^*, \ldots, L_n^*]$ is called *nth optimal* (*nonadaptive*) *information* in the class Λ iff $L_i^* \in \Lambda$ and

$$r^{\text{prob}}(N^*,\delta) = r^{\text{prob}}(n,\delta,\Lambda).$$

As in the previous settings, $r^{\text{prob}}(n,\delta)$ stands for $r^{\text{prob}}(n,\delta,F_1^*)$.

We stress that $r^{\text{prob}}(n,\delta,\Lambda)$ is defined as the minimal probabilistic radius among *nonadaptive* information only. This restriction is without loss of generality since we have

COROLLARY 5.3.1. *Adaption does not help for linear problems in the probabilistic setting, i.e., for every adaptive information N^{a} from the class Λ of cardinality n,*

$$r^{\text{prob}}(N^{\text{a}},\delta) \geq r^{\text{prob}}(n,\delta,\Lambda).$$

PROOF: Let $x > r^{\text{prob}}(N^{\text{a}},\delta)$. Then (3) of Section 3 yields $M(N^{\text{a}},x) \leq \delta$. Since adaption does not help in the average case setting with an arbitrary error functional, see Theorem 6.3.3 of Chapter 6, then there exists a vector $y = y(N^{\mathrm{a}}, x)$ such that for the nonadaptive information N_y^{non} we have $M(N_y^{\mathrm{non}}, x) \leq M(N^{\mathrm{a}}, x) \leq \delta$. Thus, $r^{\mathrm{prob}}(n, \delta, \Lambda) \leq r^{\mathrm{prob}}(N_y^{\mathrm{non}}, \delta) \leq x$. Since x can be arbitrary close to $r^{\mathrm{prob}}(N^{\mathrm{a}}, \delta)$, the proof is complete. ∎

For general S and Λ, nth optimal information is difficult to find. However, for $S \in F_1^*$ and arbitrary Λ, or for arbitrary S and $\Lambda = F_1^*$, the nth optimal information can be obtained easily by applying the results of Section 6.3 from Chapter 6. In our case, the μ-spline algorithms are optimal and $M(N, x)$ corresponds to $\mathrm{ER}_x(g) = H_x(\|g\|)$, where $H_x(t) = 0$ for $t \leq x$ and $H_x(t) = 1$ otherwise. Observe that H_x is nondecreasing. Hence the assumptions of **NR 6.3.5** of Chapter 6 hold for any x. Therefore, we have

COROLLARY 5.3.2.

(i) Let S be a continuous linear functional. Then for arbitrary δ and Λ, the nth optimal information in the probabilistic setting coincides with the nth optimal information in the average case setting under the absolute error criterion. Furthermore,

$$r^{\mathrm{prob}}(n, \delta, \Lambda) = \psi^{-1}(1 - \delta) \, r^{\mathrm{avg}}(n, \Lambda)$$

and $r^{\mathrm{avg}}(n, \Lambda) = \inf_{L_i \in \Lambda} \inf_{g_i \in \mathbb{R}} \left\| S - \sum_{i=1}^{n} g_i \, L_i \right\|_\mu$.

(ii) Let S be a continuous linear operator and $\Lambda = F_1^*$. Then for arbitrary δ, the nth optimal information in the probabilistic setting coincides with the nth optimal information in the average case setting under the absolute error criterion. Hence,

$$N^* = [L_1^*, L_2^* \ldots, L_n^*] \quad \text{with} \quad L_i^*(f) = (\lambda_i^*)^{-1/2} \langle S(f), \eta_i^* \rangle,$$

where η_i^* are the eigenelements of C_ν corresponding to the eigenvalues λ_i^*, $\lambda_1^* \geq \lambda_2^* \geq \cdots \geq 0$.

Based on (1)–(4) from Section 5.2, we present a few estimates of the nth minimal radius $r^{\mathrm{prob}}(n, \delta)$ for the class $\Lambda = F_1^*$. Recall that $r^{\mathrm{avg}}(n) = \sqrt{\sum_{i=n+1}^{\infty} \lambda_i^*}$. We have

$$r^{\mathrm{prob}}(n, \delta) \leq r^{\mathrm{avg}}(n) \sqrt{2 \ln \frac{5}{\delta}} \tag{1}$$

$$r^{\mathrm{prob}}(n, \delta) \geq \sqrt{\lambda_{n+1}^*} \, \psi^{-1}(1 - \delta) = \sqrt{2 \lambda_{n+1}^* \ln \frac{1}{\delta}} \, (1 + o(1)). \tag{2}$$

Estimate (1) is essentially sharp if δ is fixed and the cardinality n goes to infinity,

$$r^{\text{prob}}(n, \delta) = \left(r^{\text{avg}}(n) \sqrt{2 \ln(5/\delta)}\right)^{1+o(1)} \quad \text{as } n \to +\infty. \tag{3}$$

Estimate (2) is sharp if the cardinality n is fixed and δ goes to zero,

$$r^{\text{prob}}(n, \delta) = \sqrt{2 \lambda_{n+1}^{*} \ln(1/\delta)} \left(1 + o(1)\right) \quad \text{as } \delta \to 0. \tag{4}$$

5.4. Complexity

In this section we provide bounds on the probabilistic complexity of linear problems defined over $F = F_1$.

THEOREM 5.4.1. *The probabilistic (ε, δ)-complexity of a linear problem satisfies*

$$c\, m^{\text{prob}}(\varepsilon, \delta) \leq \text{comp}^{\text{prob}}(\varepsilon, \delta) \leq (c + 2)\, m^{\text{prob}}(\varepsilon, \delta) - 1,$$

where c is the cost of one information operation, and the probabilistic (ε, δ)-cardinality number is given by

$$m^{\text{prob}}(\varepsilon, \delta) = \min\left\{n : r^{\text{prob}}(n, \delta, \Lambda) \leq \varepsilon\right\}$$
$$= \min\left\{n : \nu_N\left(B(0, \varepsilon)\right) \geq 1 - \delta \text{ with } N = [L_1, \ldots, L_n], \ L_i \in \Lambda\right\}.$$

Here ν_N is the conditional measure for $y = N(f) = 0$, $\nu_N = \nu(\cdot|0)$. Furthermore, for $n = m^{\text{prob}}(\varepsilon, \delta)$, the nth optimal information N_n^* in the class Λ and the μ-spline algorithm ϕ^s that uses N_n^* are almost optimal.

PROOF: The lower bound on the complexity is from Section 4. The upper bound as well as optimality of N_n^* and ϕ^s follow from the fact that adaption does not help and the μ-spline algorithm is a linear optimal error algorithm. The form of $m^{\text{prob}}(\varepsilon, \delta)$ follows from the relation which states that $r^{\text{prob}}(N, \delta) \leq \varepsilon$ iff $\nu_N(B(0, \varepsilon)) \geq 1 - \delta$. ∎

We now present a few estimates on $m^{\text{prob}}(\varepsilon, \delta)$. Recall that for given information N, $C_{\nu, N}$ denotes the correlation operator of the measure ν_N, λ_N is its largest eigenvalue, and $\psi(x) = \sqrt{2/\pi} \int_0^x \exp(-t^2/2)\, dt$ is the probability integral.

From (1) and (3) of Section 5.2 we have

$$m_L^{\text{prob}}(\varepsilon, \delta) \leq m^{\text{prob}}(\varepsilon, \delta) \leq m_U^{\text{prob}}(\varepsilon, \delta), \tag{1}$$

where the lower bound is given by

$$m_L^{\text{prob}}(\varepsilon, \delta)$$
$$= \min\left\{ n : \psi\left(\frac{\varepsilon}{\sqrt{\lambda_N}}\right) \geq 1 - \delta \ \text{ with } N = [L_1, \ldots, L_n], \ L_i \in \Lambda \right\},$$

and the upper bound is given by

$$m_U^{\text{prob}}(\varepsilon, \delta)$$
$$= \min\left\{ n : \text{trace}(C_{\nu,N}) \leq \frac{\varepsilon^2}{2 \ln \frac{5}{\delta}} \ \text{ with } N = [L_1, \ldots, L_n], \ L_i \in \Lambda \right\}.$$

We now show that, in a certain sense, both estimates in (1) are sharp depending on the relation between ε and δ.

THEOREM 5.4.2.

(i) For any function $h : \mathbb{R}_+ \to (0, 1)$ with $\lim_{\varepsilon \to 0+} h(\varepsilon) = 0$ and for any positive ε, there exists a positive δ_0 such that

$$m_L^{\text{prob}}(\varepsilon, \delta) \leq m^{\text{prob}}(\varepsilon, \delta) \leq m_L^{\text{prob}}\big(\varepsilon(1 - h(\varepsilon)), \delta\big), \quad \forall \delta \leq \delta_0.$$

(ii) For any function $h : \mathbb{R}_+ \to \mathbb{R}_+$ with $\lim_{\varepsilon \to 0+} h(\varepsilon) = +\infty$ and for any small positive δ, there exists a positive ε_0 such that

$$m_U^{\text{prob}}\big(\varepsilon h(\varepsilon), \delta\big) \leq m^{\text{prob}}(\varepsilon, \delta) \leq m_U^{\text{prob}}(\varepsilon, \delta), \quad \forall \varepsilon \leq \varepsilon_0.$$

PROOF: Due to (1), we need only show the upper bound of (i) and the lower bound of (ii). To prove (i), we use estimate (5) from Section 5.8 of Chapter 6,

$$1 - \nu_N(B(0, \varepsilon)) \leq \exp(-\varepsilon^2 a) \prod_{i=1}^{\infty} (1 - 2a\lambda_{i,N})^{-1/2},$$

where $\lambda_{i,N}$ are the eigenvalues of $C_{\nu,N}$ in decreasing order, $\lambda_{1,N} = \lambda_N$, and $a < (2\lambda_N)^{-1}$. Take a positive η and set $a = (2\lambda_N(1 + \eta))^{-1}$. Then

$$\exp\left(\frac{-\varepsilon^2}{2\lambda_N(1 + \eta)}\right) \prod_{i=1}^{\infty} \left[1 - \frac{\lambda_{i,N}}{\lambda_N(1 + \eta)}\right] \leq \delta$$

implies $\nu_N(B(0, \varepsilon)) \geq 1 - \delta$. The last inequality can be rewritten as

$$\frac{\varepsilon^2}{2\lambda_N(1 + \eta)} \left[1 + \frac{2\lambda_N(1 + \eta)}{\varepsilon^2} \sum_{i=1}^{\infty} \ln\left(1 - \frac{\lambda_{i,N}}{\lambda_N(1 + \eta)}\right)\right] \geq \ln \frac{1}{\delta}.$$

For $x \in [0, (1+\eta)^{-1}]$, there exists a positive $b(\eta)$ such that $-xb(\eta) \le \ln(1-x) \le -x$. This yields

$$\frac{-\operatorname{trace}(C_{\nu,N})\, b(\eta)}{1+\eta} \le \lambda_N \sum_{i=1}^{\infty} \ln\left(1 - \frac{\lambda_{i,N}}{\lambda_N(1+\eta)}\right) \le \frac{-\operatorname{trace}(C_{\nu,N})}{1+\eta}.$$

For $\delta \to 0$, the trace of $C_{\nu,N}$ goes to zero. Therefore

$$\lambda_N \ge \frac{\varepsilon^2}{2\ln\frac{1}{\delta}} \frac{1}{1+\eta}\left(1 + o(1)\right) \quad \text{as } \delta \to 0.$$

Take now positive η such that for small δ,

$$\frac{1+o(1)}{2\ln\frac{1}{\delta}} \frac{1}{1+\eta} \ge \left[\frac{1-h(\varepsilon)}{\psi^{-1}(1-\delta)}\right]^2.$$

Such a number η exists since $\psi^{-1}(1-\delta) = \sqrt{2\ln(1/\delta)}\left(1 + o(1)\right)$. Then

$$\psi\left(\frac{\varepsilon\left(1 - h(\varepsilon)\right)}{\sqrt{\lambda_N}}\right) \le 1 - \delta.$$

Thus, the cardinality of N is no greater than $m_L^{\mathrm{prob}}\left(\varepsilon(1-h(\varepsilon)), \delta\right)$ which proves (i).

To prove (ii), take information N for which $\nu_N\left(B(0,\varepsilon)\right) \ge 1 - \delta$. From Lemma 2.9.1 of the appendix with $a = h(\varepsilon)/2 > 1$, we have

$$(1-\delta)\left(1 - 4\,h(\varepsilon)^{-2}\right) \le \psi\left(\frac{\varepsilon\,h(\varepsilon)}{2\sqrt{\operatorname{trace}(C_{\nu,N})}}\right).$$

This yields

$$\operatorname{trace}(C_{\nu,N}) \le \frac{\left(\varepsilon\,h(\varepsilon)\right)^2}{8\ln\frac{1}{\delta}}\left(1 + o(1)\right) \le \frac{\left(\varepsilon\,h(\varepsilon)\right)^2}{2\ln\frac{5}{\delta}} \quad \text{as } \varepsilon \to 0.$$

Therefore the cardinality of N has to be at least $m_U^{\mathrm{prob}}\left(\varepsilon h(\varepsilon), \delta\right)$ which proves (ii). $\blacksquare$

This theorem states that for fixed ε and small δ, the probabilistic cardinality depends on the largest eigenvalue of the correlation operator of the conditional measure. On the other hand, if δ is fixed and ε is small, then cardinality depends on the trace of the same operator.

We now specialize Theorems 5.4.1 and 5.4.2 for the class $\Lambda = F_1^*$. In this case, the nth optimal information is given by

$$N_n^*(f) = [\langle S(f), \eta_1^* \rangle, \ldots, \langle S(f), \eta_n^* \rangle],$$

where (λ_i^*, η_i^*) with $\lambda_1^* \geq \lambda_2^* \geq \ldots \lambda_n^* \geq \lambda_{n+1}^* \geq \cdots \geq 0$ are eigenpairs of the correlation operator C_ν of the *a priori* measure $\nu = \mu S^{-1}$. The μ-spline algorithm ϕ^s takes the form

$$\phi^s(N_n^*(f)) = \sum_{j=1}^n \langle S(f), \eta_j^* \rangle \, \eta_j^*.$$

The correlation operator of the conditional measure $\nu_n = \nu_{N_n^*}$ has eigenvalues λ_{n+i}^*, $i = 1, 2, \ldots$. Thus, we have

COROLLARY 5.4.1. *For the class* $\Lambda = F_1^*$, *the probabilistic* (ε, δ)-*cardinality,* $m^{\mathrm{prob}} = \min\{n : \nu_n(B(0, \varepsilon)) \geq 1 - \delta\}$, *is bounded by*

$$\min\left\{n : \psi\left(\frac{\varepsilon}{\sqrt{\lambda_{n+1}^*}}\right) \geq 1 - \delta\right\}$$

$$\leq m^{\mathrm{prob}}(\varepsilon, \delta) \leq \min\left\{n : \sum_{i=n+1}^\infty \lambda_i^* \leq \frac{\varepsilon^2}{2 \ln \frac{5}{\delta}}\right\}.$$

We now exhibit tight estimates for $m^{\mathrm{prob}}(\varepsilon, \delta)$ assuming that $\{\lambda_i^*\}$ satisfies some special conditions. We show that $m^{\mathrm{prob}}(\varepsilon, \delta)$ is asymptotically in ε independent of δ, and essentially the same as the average cardinality number $m^{\mathrm{avg}}(\varepsilon)$, $\lceil m^{\mathrm{avg}}(\varepsilon)\rceil = \min\{n : \sum_{k=n+1}^\infty \lambda_k^* \leq \varepsilon^2\}$.

THEOREM 5.4.3. *Let* $\Lambda = F_1^*$ *and let* $\{\lambda_i^*\}$, $\lambda_i^* > 0$, *satisfy*

$$\lim_n \frac{\sum_{k=n+1}^\infty (\lambda_k^*)^3}{\left(\sum_{k=n+1}^\infty (\lambda_k^*)^2\right)^{3/2}} = 0 \tag{2}$$

and

$$\lim_n \frac{\sum_{k=\lceil tn\rceil+1}^n \lambda_k^*}{\left(\sum_{k=n+1}^\infty (\lambda_k^*)^2\right)^{1/2}} = +\infty, \quad \forall t \in (0, 1). \tag{3}$$

Then

$$\lim_{\varepsilon \to 0} \frac{m^{\mathrm{prob}}(\varepsilon, \delta)}{m^{\mathrm{avg}}(\varepsilon)} = 1, \quad \forall \delta \in (0, 1/2).$$

PROOF: Fix $\delta \in (0, 1/2)$. Consider $\xi_k(g) = \langle g, \eta_k^* \rangle / \sqrt{\lambda_k^*}$ for $g \in G$. Then $\{\xi_k\}$ is a sequence of independent random variables, each having Gaussian distribution with mean zero and variance one. Obviously,

$$\nu_n\big(B_n(0, \varepsilon)\big) = \text{Prob}\left(\sum_{k=n+1}^{\infty} \lambda_k^*(\xi_k^2 - 1) \leq \varepsilon^2 - \sum_{k=n+1}^{\infty} \lambda_k^* \right).$$

Take $X_k = \lambda_k^*(\xi_k^2 - 1)$. Then $\{X_k\}$ is a sequence of independent random variables, each having mean zero and variance $2(\lambda_k^*)^2$. Furthermore, the expected value of $|X_k|^3$ is equal to $\alpha (\lambda_k^*)^3$ for a positive constant α independent of k. Then from Esseen's inequality, see, e.g., Petrov [75] page 111, we get

$$\left| \text{Prob}\left(\sum_{k=n+1}^{\infty} X_k < x \sqrt{\sum_{k=n+1}^{\infty} 2(\lambda_k^*)^2} \right) - \Psi(x) \right| \leq \beta_n, \quad \forall x,$$

where

$$\Psi(x) = \frac{1}{\sqrt{2\pi}} \int_{-\infty}^{x} e^{-t^2/2} \, dt$$

and

$$\beta_n = A \frac{\sum_{k=n+1}^{\infty} \alpha(\lambda_k^*)^3}{\left(\sum_{k=n+1}^{\infty} 2(\lambda_k^*)^2\right)^{3/2}}$$

with A being an absolute positive constant. Due to (2),

$$\lim_n \beta_n = 0.$$

Take $x = \left(\varepsilon^2 - \sum_{k=n+1}^{\infty} \lambda_k^*\right)/\sqrt{2\sum_{k=n+1}^{\infty}(\lambda_k^*)^2}$. Then

$$\left| \nu_n\big(B_n(0, \varepsilon)\big) - \Psi\left(\frac{\varepsilon^2 - \sum_{k=n+1}^{\infty} \lambda_k^*}{\sqrt{2\sum_{k=n+1}^{\infty}(\lambda_k^*)^2}} \right) \right| \leq \beta_n, \quad \forall \varepsilon > 0.$$

Hence for $n = m^{\text{prob}}(\varepsilon, \delta)$, we have

$$\Psi\left(\frac{\varepsilon^2 - \sum_{k=n+1}^{\infty} \lambda_k^*}{\sqrt{2\sum_{k=n+1}^{\infty}(\lambda_k^*)^2}} \right) = 1 - \delta + o(1) \quad \text{as } \varepsilon \to 0,$$

and consequently,

$$\varepsilon^2 = \sum_{k=n+1}^{\infty} \lambda_k^* + \Psi^{-1}\big(1 - \delta + o(1)\big) \sqrt{2\sum_{k=n+1}^{\infty}(\lambda_k^*)^2}.$$

For $\delta < 1/2$ and small ε, we have $\Psi^{-1}(1 - \delta + o(1)) > 0$. Thus, $\varepsilon^2 > \sum_{k=n+1}^{\infty} \lambda_k^*$ which implies that $m^{\mathrm{avg}}(\varepsilon) \leq m^{\mathrm{prob}}(\varepsilon, \delta)$.

For any $t \in (0, 1)$, (3) yields

$$\sum_{k=\lceil tn \rceil + 1}^{n} \lambda_k^* > \Psi^{-1}(1 - \delta + o(1)) \sqrt{2 \sum_{k=n+1}^{\infty} (\lambda_k^*)^2}$$

for small ε. Thus, $\varepsilon^2 < \sum_{k=\lceil tn \rceil + 1}^{\infty} \lambda_k^*$, which implies that $t\, m^{\mathrm{prob}}(\varepsilon, \delta) \leq \lceil m^{\mathrm{avg}}(\varepsilon) \rceil$. Hence the proof is complete. ∎

Theorem 5.4.3 gives assumptions under which the average ε-cardinality and the probabilistic (ε, δ)-cardinality are essentially the same independently of δ, $\delta \in (0, 1/2)$. As can be easily checked, these assumptions are satisfied for sequences of eigenvalues λ_k^* such as $\lambda_k^* = \Theta(k^{-p}(\ln k)^q)$ with $p > 1$ and q arbitrary.

Theorems 5.4.1, 5.4.2, and Corollary 5.4.1 enable us to compare the probabilistic and average case complexities. Recall that

$$c\, m^{\mathrm{avg}}(\varepsilon) \leq \mathrm{comp}^{\mathrm{avg}}(\varepsilon) \leq (c + 2)\, m^{\mathrm{avg}}(\varepsilon).$$

Then

$$\mathrm{comp}^{\mathrm{prob}}(\varepsilon, \delta) \leq \frac{c + 2}{c}\, \mathrm{comp}^{\mathrm{avg}}\left(\frac{\varepsilon}{\sqrt{2 \ln \frac{5}{\delta}}}\right) + c + 2.$$

From (ii) of Theorem 5.4.2 we have for fixed δ and small ε,

$$\mathrm{comp}^{\mathrm{prob}}(\varepsilon, \delta) \geq \frac{c}{c + 2}\, \mathrm{comp}^{\mathrm{avg}}\left(\frac{\varepsilon\, h(\varepsilon)}{\sqrt{2 \ln \frac{5}{\delta}}}\right),$$

where h is a function whose value $h(\varepsilon)$ goes to infinity as ε goes to zero. Since it can go to infinity arbitrarily slowly, we get

COROLLARY 5.4.2. *For the class $\Lambda = F_1^*$ and large c, we have*

$$\mathrm{comp}^{\mathrm{prob}}(\varepsilon, \delta) \simeq \mathrm{comp}^{\mathrm{avg}}\left(\frac{\varepsilon^{1 + o(1)}}{\sqrt{2 \ln \frac{5}{\delta}}}\right)$$

for small fixed δ and ε going to zero. If, additionally, the eigenvalues of C_ν satisfy the assumptions of Theorem 5.4.3 then

$$\mathrm{comp}^{\mathrm{prob}}(\varepsilon, \delta) \simeq \mathrm{comp}^{\mathrm{avg}}(\varepsilon)$$

for any $\delta \in (0, 1/2)$ and ε going to zero.

We end this section with a remark on an arbitrary class Λ of permissible information operations, $\Lambda \subset F_1^*$, assuming that S is a continuous linear functional. From Corollary 5.3.2 (i) we know that

$$r^{\mathrm{prob}}(n, \delta, \Lambda) = \psi^{-1}(1 - \delta)\, r^{\mathrm{avg}}(n, \Lambda).$$

This yields that the probabilistic (ε, δ)-cardinality number is given by

$$m^{\mathrm{prob}}(\varepsilon, \delta) = \min \left\{ n : \sqrt{\sigma_n} \leq \frac{\varepsilon}{\psi^{-1}(1 - \delta)} \right\},$$

where $\sigma_n = \left(r^{\mathrm{avg}}(n, \Lambda)\right)^2$ is the minimal variance of the conditional measure after n permissible information operations. This and Theorem 5.7.2 of Chapter 6 enable us to relate the probabilistic and average case complexities. We have

COROLLARY 5.4.3. *If S is a continuous linear functional then*

$$\frac{c}{c + 2}\, \mathrm{comp}^{\mathrm{avg}} \left(\frac{\varepsilon}{\psi^{-1}(1 - \delta)} \right) \leq \mathrm{comp}^{\mathrm{prob}}(\varepsilon, \delta),$$

and

$$\mathrm{comp}^{\mathrm{avg}}(\varepsilon) \geq$$
$$\frac{c}{c + 2}\, \sup_{x > 1} \min \left\{ \mathrm{comp}^{\mathrm{prob}}\left(x\varepsilon_1, \delta\right), \frac{x^2 - 1}{x^2}\, \mathrm{comp}^{\mathrm{prob}}\left(\varepsilon_1, \delta\right) \right\},$$

where $\varepsilon_1 = \varepsilon\, \psi^{-1}(1 - \delta)$. If, additionally, the sequence $\{r^{\mathrm{avg}}(n, \Lambda)^2\}$ is convex then

$$\mathrm{comp}^{\mathrm{prob}}(\varepsilon, \delta) \leq \frac{c + 2}{c}\, \mathrm{comp}^{\mathrm{avg}} \left(\frac{\varepsilon}{\psi^{-1}(1 - \delta)} \right) + c + 2$$

and for large c,

$$\mathrm{comp}^{\mathrm{prob}}(\varepsilon, \delta) \simeq \mathrm{comp}^{\mathrm{avg}} \left(\frac{\varepsilon}{\psi^{-1}(1 - \delta)} \right).$$

Notes and Remarks

NR 5.4:1 Theorem 5.4.3 is due to Kwapień [87] .

NR 5.4:2 In Section 5.7 of Chapter 6, we show that the average ε-complexity for the class $\Lambda = F_1^*$ may go to infinity arbitrarily fast as ε goes to zero. The same is true for the probabilistic complexity. In fact, Theorem 5.7.3 of Chapter 6 can be easily generalized for the probabilistic setting.

NR 5.4:3 Consider the probabilistic case setting with the cost defined as in the average case setting. Let $\text{comp}_1^{\text{prob}}(\varepsilon, \delta)$ denote the (ε, δ)-complexity in this setting. This setting can be treated as the average case setting with the error functional $\text{ER} = \text{ER}_\varepsilon$ and δ playing the role of error tolerance. From Chapter 6 we conclude that

$$c \sup_{1 \leq x \leq 1/\delta} \min \left\{ m^{\text{prob}}(\varepsilon, x\delta), \frac{x-1}{x} m^{\text{prob}}(\varepsilon, \delta) \right\}$$
$$\leq \text{comp}_1^{\text{prob}}(\varepsilon, \delta) \leq (c+2) m^{\text{prob}}(\varepsilon, \delta) - 1.$$

In particular, if

$$m^{\text{prob}}\left(\varepsilon, \delta \ln \frac{1}{\delta}\right) = m^{\text{prob}}(\varepsilon, \delta)(1 + o(1)) \quad \text{as } \delta \to 0$$

then setting $x = \ln(1/\delta)$ we get

$$\text{comp}_1^{\text{prob}}(\varepsilon, \delta) = (c+a) m^{\text{prob}}(\varepsilon, \delta)(1 + o(1)) \quad \text{as } \delta \to 0,$$

where $a \in [0, 2]$. For $c \gg 1$, we have tight bounds on $\text{comp}_1^{\text{prob}}(\varepsilon, \delta)$,

$$\text{comp}_1^{\text{prob}}(\varepsilon, \delta) \simeq c\, m^{\text{prob}}(\varepsilon, \delta).$$

In this case, the complexity is essentially the same, whether the cost is defined in a worst or average case sense.

NR 5.4:4 One can modify the definition of cost by disregarding a set of measure at most δ for which the error may exceed ε. That is, the cost of U is given by

$$\text{cost}(U) = \frac{1}{1-\delta} \inf \left\{ \int_A \text{cost}(U, f) : A \text{ such that } \mu(A) \geq 1 - \delta, \right.$$

$$\left. \text{and } \|S(f) - U(f)\| \leq \varepsilon, \forall f \in A \right\}.$$

Let $\text{comp}_2^{\text{prob}}(\varepsilon, \delta)$ denote the probabilistic (ε, δ)-complexity with this definition of cost. For $\delta < 1/2$, it is easy to show that

$$\text{comp}_1^{\text{prob}}(\varepsilon, \delta) \leq \text{comp}_2^{\text{prob}}(\varepsilon, \delta) \leq \frac{1}{1 - \delta_1} \text{comp}_1^{\text{prob}}(\varepsilon, \delta),$$

where $1 - \delta_1 = (1 - 2\delta)/(1 - \delta)$. For small δ, $\delta_1 = \delta(1 + o(1))$ and therefore $\text{comp}_2^{\text{prob}}(\varepsilon, \delta)$ is practically equal to $\text{comp}_1^{\text{prob}}(\varepsilon, \delta)$.

One may also disregard a set of measure at most δ in the worst case definition of cost. Then it is easy to see that the corresponding (ε, δ)-complexity will be the same as $\text{comp}^{\text{prob}}(\varepsilon, \delta)$.

NR 5.4:5 We indicate in this section that for linear problems, the probabilistic (ε, δ)-complexity is related to the average ε_1-complexity with $\varepsilon_1 = \varepsilon / \sqrt{2 \ln(1/\delta)}$ for small ε. This holds for Gaussian measures. For arbitrary measures, this is not true in general. In fact, it may happen that the average ε-complexity is infinite, whereas the probabilistic (ε, δ)-complexity is finite for positive ε and δ. If, however, the average ε-complexity is finite then Chebyshev's inequality yields $\mathrm{comp}^{\mathrm{prob}}(\varepsilon, \delta) \le \mathrm{comp}^{\mathrm{avg}}\left(\sqrt{\delta}\,\varepsilon\right)$.

5.5. Linear Problems for Bounded Domains

We now analyze linear problems for $F = B_q$ being the ball in the space F_1 with radius q and center zero. Recall that $B(0, q)$ denotes the ball with radius q and center zero but in the space G. As in Chapter 6, F is equipped with the truncated Gaussian measure μ_q,

$$\mu_q(A) = \frac{\mu(A \cap F)}{\mu(F)}, \quad \text{for any Borel set } A.$$

Let $\mathrm{comp}^{\mathrm{prob}}(\varepsilon, \delta, q)$ be the probabilistic complexity of a linear problem with $F = B_q$. As in Section 5.4, $\mathrm{comp}^{\mathrm{prob}}(\varepsilon, \delta) = \mathrm{comp}^{\mathrm{prob}}(\varepsilon, \delta, +\infty)$ denotes the probabilistic complexity for the whole space, $F = B_\infty = F_1$.

We wish to find relations between $\mathrm{comp}^{\mathrm{prob}}(\varepsilon, \delta, q)$ and $\mathrm{comp}^{\mathrm{prob}}(\varepsilon, \delta)$. One may hope that these two complexities are almost the same for large q, as it was the case in the average case setting, see Section 5.8 of Chapter 6. Can this be true for small δ?

Observe that the probabilistic complexity $\mathrm{comp}^{\mathrm{prob}}(\varepsilon, \delta, q)$ is bounded from above by the worst case complexity $\mathrm{comp}^{\mathrm{wor}}(\varepsilon, q)$. The latter is finite for a reasonable choice of the class Λ since the radius q is finite. In this case,

$$\mathrm{comp}^{\mathrm{prob}}(\varepsilon, \delta, q) \le \mathrm{comp}^{\mathrm{prob}}(\varepsilon, 0, q) \le \mathrm{comp}^{\mathrm{wor}}(\varepsilon, q) < +\infty.$$

On the other hand, we conclude from Section 5.4 that, in general, the probabilistic complexity $\mathrm{comp}^{\mathrm{prob}}(\varepsilon, \delta)$ goes to infinity as δ goes to zero. This shows that $\mathrm{comp}^{\mathrm{prob}}(\varepsilon, \delta, q)$ and $\mathrm{comp}^{\mathrm{prob}}(\varepsilon, \delta)$, unlike in the average case setting, are not related for small δ. We show that this is the only case in which this can happen.

As in Section 5.8 of Chapter 6, let $x = 1 - \mu(B_q)$. Then

$$x \le \exp\left(-q^2 a\right) \int_F \exp\left(a\|f\|^2\right) \mu(df) \quad \text{and} \quad x = \exp\left(-q^2 a^*(1 + o(1))\right)$$

for any $a < a^* = \left(2 \sup\left\{\|L\|_\mu : L \in F_1^*, \|L\| = 1\right\}\right)^{-1}$ as $q \to 0$. Thus, x is very close to zero even for a modest q. We are ready to state relations between the probabilistic complexities.

THEOREM 5.5.1.

$$\frac{c}{c+2}\,\mathrm{comp}^{\mathrm{prob}}(\varepsilon,\delta(1-x)+x)\leq\mathrm{comp}^{\mathrm{prob}}(\varepsilon,\delta,q)\leq\mathrm{comp}^{\mathrm{prob}}(\varepsilon,\delta(1-x)).$$

PROOF: Let $\delta_1 = \delta(1-x)+x$. Take information N and an algorithm ϕ that uses N such that $U(f) = \phi(N(f))$ solves the problem over the ball B_q with minimal cost. That is,

$$1-\delta \leq \mu_q\big(\{f \in F : \|S(f)-U(f)\| \leq \varepsilon\}\big),$$

and $\mathrm{comp}^{\mathrm{prob}}(\varepsilon,\delta,q) \geq c\,\mathrm{card}^{\mathrm{wor}}(N)$. As explained before, we can assume that N has fixed cardinality, $n(f) \equiv \mathrm{card}^{\mathrm{wor}}(N)$. We have

$$1-\delta \leq \frac{1}{1-x}\,\mu\big(\{f \in F_1 : \|S(f)-U(f)\| \leq \varepsilon\}\big).$$

Hence U solves the problem over the whole space for ε and δ_1. This implies that

$$m^{\mathrm{prob}}(\varepsilon,\delta_1) \leq \mathrm{card}^{\mathrm{wor}}(N) \leq \frac{1}{c}\,\mathrm{comp}^{\mathrm{prob}}(\varepsilon,\delta,q),$$

and together with Theorem 5.4.1 proves the lower bound.

To prove the upper bound, take U which solves the problem over the whole space for ε and $\delta(1-x)$ with minimal cost. Then

$$\begin{aligned}
1-\delta(1-x) &\leq \mu\big(\{f \in F_1 : \|S(f)-U(f)\| \leq \varepsilon\}\big)\\
&\leq \mu\big(\{f \in F_1 : \|S(f)-U(f)\| \leq \varepsilon \text{ and } \|f\| \leq q\}\big) + x\\
&= (1-x)\mu_q\big(\{f \in F : \|S(f)-U(f)\| \leq \varepsilon\}\big) + x.
\end{aligned}$$

Hence $1-\delta \leq \mu_q\big(\{f \in F : \|S(f)-U(f)\| \leq \varepsilon\}\big)$, i.e., U solves the problem over the ball B_q for ε and δ. Therefore $\mathrm{comp}^{\mathrm{prob}}(\varepsilon,\delta,q) \leq \mathrm{cost}^{\mathrm{wor}}(U) = \mathrm{comp}^{\mathrm{prob}}\big(\varepsilon,\delta(1-x)\big)$. This completes the proof. $\blacksquare$

Theorem 5.5.1 states that as long as δ is no less than x, the two probabilistic complexities $\mathrm{comp}^{\mathrm{prob}}(\varepsilon,\delta,q)$ and $\mathrm{comp}^{\mathrm{prob}}(\varepsilon,\delta)$ are practically the same. The situation changes if δ is smaller than x. For $\delta \ll x$, the lower bound in Theorem 5.5.1 becomes roughly $\mathrm{comp}^{\mathrm{prob}}(\varepsilon,x)$, which enables the probabilistic complexity $\mathrm{comp}^{\mathrm{prob}}(\varepsilon,\delta,q)$ to stay finite even for $\delta = 0$.

We want to stress that for properly chosen q, all practically important values of δ are much larger than $x = \exp\big(-q^2 a^*(1+o(1))\big)$. Indeed, take $q = 10$ for a separable Hilbert space F_1 with the jth eigenvalue of the correlation operator equal to j^{-2}. (This corresponds to the classical Wiener measure on a Hilbert space.) Then Remark 5.8.1 of Chapter 6 yields that $0 \leq x \leq \sqrt{2} \exp(-100/8) < 10^{-5}$. Thus, as long as $\delta > 10^{-5}$, both probabilistic complexities are essentially the same.

On the other hand, if one, rather theoretically, considers δ much smaller than x then the probabilistic complexity $\text{comp}^{\text{prob}}(\varepsilon, \delta, q)$ is not known. It is then interesting to find a relation between $\text{comp}^{\text{prob}}(\varepsilon, \delta, q)$ and the worst case complexity $\text{comp}^{\text{wor}}(\varepsilon, q)$.

Notes and Remarks

NR 5.5:1 Consider the probabilistic setting with cost defined as in the average case setting. Proceeding as in Section 5.8 of Chapter 6, one can show that the corresponding complexity is essentially the same as the probabilistic complexity $\text{comp}^{\text{prob}}(\varepsilon, \delta)$ as long as $x = 1 - \mu(B_q)$ is small and $\delta >> x$.

6. Different Error Criteria

In the previous sections we analyze the probabilistic setting with the absolute error criterion. We now discuss the probabilistic setting with different error criteria including relative, normalized, and defined by general error functionals. Recall that these error criteria have been analyzed in the worst case setting in Section 6 of Chapter 4, and in the average case setting in Section 6 of Chapter 6.

6.1. Relative Error

The probabilistic relative error of $U = (\phi, N)$ is defined by

$$e^{\text{rel}}(U, \delta) = \inf_{A:\mu(A) \leq \delta} \sup_{f \in F - A} \frac{\|S(f) - U(f)\|}{\|S(f)\|},$$

with the convention that $0/0 = 0$. As in Section 2,

$$e^{\text{rel}}(U) \leq \varepsilon \quad \text{iff} \quad M(U) \leq \delta,$$

where

$$M(U) = M(U, \varepsilon) = \mu(\{f \in F : \|S(f) - U(f)\|/\|S(f)\| > \varepsilon\}).$$

Let $\text{comp}^{\text{rel}}(\varepsilon, \delta)$ denote the probabilistic complexity under the relative error criterion,

$$\text{comp}^{\text{rel}}(\varepsilon, \delta) = \min \{\text{cost}^{\text{wor}}(U) : e^{\text{rel}}(U, \delta) \leq \varepsilon\}.$$

To avoid the trivial case, we assume that $\varepsilon < 1$.

We restrict our analysis to linear problems with a continuous linear functional S and $F = F_1$. A more general case is briefly discussed in **NR 6.2:1** after analyzing the normalized error criterion.

To make the problem nontrivial, we assume that S does not belong to span(Λ). That is, S cannot be represented as a finite linear combination of permissible functionals from Λ.

Let N be adaptive information. As explained before, we can assume without loss of generality that $n(f) \equiv n$ and that

$$N(f) = [L_1(f), L_2(f; y_1), \ldots, L_n(f; y_1, \ldots, y_{n-1})],$$

where $y_i = L_{i,y}(f) = L_i(f; y_1, \ldots, y_{i-1})$ and $\langle L_{i,y}, L_{j,y} \rangle = \delta_{i,j}$. Recall that the conditional measure $\nu(\cdot | y)$ is a one-dimensional Gaussian measure with mean $m = m(y)$ and variance $\sigma = \sigma(y)$. We have

$$m(y) = \langle y, w(y) \rangle, \tag{1}$$

$$\sigma(y) = S(C_\mu S) - \langle w(y), w(y) \rangle = \inf_{g_i \in \mathbb{R}} \left\| S - \sum_{i=1}^{n} g_i L_{i,y} \right\|_\mu^2, \tag{2}$$

for the vector

$$w(y) = [S(C_\mu L_1), S(C_\mu L_{2,y}), \ldots, S(C_\mu L_{n,y})]. \tag{3}$$

Let

$$\sigma' = \sigma'(y) = \frac{\sigma(y)}{2\varepsilon} \ln \frac{1+\varepsilon}{1-\varepsilon}. \tag{4}$$

For small ε, we have $\sigma' \simeq \sigma$. Define the algorithm

$$\phi^*(y) = \left(m + \operatorname{sign}(m) \sqrt{m^2 + 4\sigma'} \right) \frac{1 - \varepsilon^2}{2}. \tag{5}$$

Observe that the algorithm ϕ^* is nonlinear even for nonadaptive information. However, its combinatory cost is roughly the same as that of a linear algorithm. For small ε, ϕ^* is close to the mean of conditional measure, $\phi^*(y) \simeq m(y)$, which depends linearly on y for nonadaptive information. We prove optimality properties of this algorithm. To do this, observe that for any $U(f) = \phi(N(f))$ we have

$$M(U) = M(\phi, N) = \int_{\mathbb{R}^n} M(\phi, N, y) \, \mu_1(dy), \tag{6}$$

where μ_1 is Gaussian with mean zero and correlation operator equal to the identity matrix, and

$$M(\phi, N, y) = \nu\big(\{x \in \mathbb{R} : |x - \phi(y)|/|x| > \varepsilon\}|y\big). \tag{7}$$

LEMMA 6.1.1. *The algorithm* ϕ^* *minimizes* $M(\cdot, N, y)$ *for all* $y \in \mathbb{R}^n$.

PROOF: The equation (7) implies that it is enough to find $u = \phi(y)$ which minimizes $\nu\big(\{x \in \mathbb{R} : |x - u|/|x| > \varepsilon\}|y\big)$. Observe that

$$\frac{|x - u|}{|x|} > \varepsilon \quad \Longleftrightarrow \quad x < u_1 = \frac{u - |u|\varepsilon}{1 - \varepsilon^2} \quad \text{or} \quad x > u_2 = \frac{u + |u|\varepsilon}{1 - \varepsilon^2}. \tag{8}$$

Hence

$$M(\phi, N, y) = 1 - \frac{1}{\sqrt{2\pi\sigma}} \int_{u_1}^{u_2} \exp\left(\frac{-(x - u)^2}{2\sigma}\right) dx =: 1 - \frac{1}{\sqrt{2\pi\sigma}} H(u).$$

We seek $u = u^*$ which maximizes $H(u)$. Since H is differentiable for $u \neq 0$ and $u = 0$ does not maximize H, we consider the equation $H'(u) = 0$ and find that

$$u^* = \phi^*(y) = \big(m + \text{sign}(m)\sqrt{m^2 + 4\sigma'}\big)\frac{1 - \varepsilon^2}{2},$$

which completes the proof. ∎

We now estimate $M(\phi^*, N)$ for nonadaptive information.

LEMMA 6.1.2. *For nonadaptive information* $N = [L_1, \ldots, L_n]$ *in which* $\langle L_i, L_j \rangle = \delta_{i,j}$, *we have*

$$\left(1 - \sqrt{\frac{\pi}{4}\varepsilon \ln \frac{1 + \varepsilon}{1 - \varepsilon}}\right)\frac{2}{\pi} \text{arc cot}\left(\frac{\varepsilon}{\sqrt{\sigma}}\|w\|\right)$$
$$\leq M(\phi^*, N) \leq \frac{2}{\pi} \text{arc cot}\left(\frac{\varepsilon}{\sqrt{\sigma}}\|w\|\right),$$

where $w = [S(C_\mu L_1), \ldots, S(C_\mu L_n)]$. *For small* ε, *we have*

$$M(\phi^*, N) \simeq \frac{2}{\pi} \text{arc cot}\left(\frac{\varepsilon}{\sqrt{\sigma}}\|w\|\right).$$

PROOF: Let $\gamma_m = u^*/(1 - \varepsilon^2) - m$ with $m = \langle y, w \rangle$, and let $\rho = \sigma^{-1/2}$. For the algorithm ϕ^* we have

$$
M(\phi^*, N, y) = 1 - \frac{\text{sign}(m)}{\sqrt{2\pi}} \left[\int_{-m\varepsilon\rho}^{m\varepsilon\rho} e^{-t^2/2} \, dt - \int_{-m\varepsilon\rho}^{-m\varepsilon\rho+\gamma_m(1-\varepsilon)\rho} e^{-t^2/2} \, dt \right.
$$
$$
\left. + \int_{m\varepsilon\rho}^{m\varepsilon\rho+\gamma_m(1+\varepsilon)\rho} e^{-t^2/2} \, dt \right]
$$
$$
= 1 - \frac{\text{sign}(m)}{\sqrt{2\pi}} \left[\int_{-m\varepsilon\rho}^{m\varepsilon\rho} e^{-t^2/2} \, dt - \int_{m\varepsilon\rho-\gamma_m(1-\varepsilon)\rho}^{m\varepsilon\rho} e^{-t^2/2} \, dt \right.
$$
$$
\left. + \int_{m\varepsilon\rho}^{m\varepsilon\rho+\gamma_m(1-\varepsilon)\rho} e^{-t^2/2} \, dt + \int_{m\varepsilon\rho+\gamma_m(1-\varepsilon)\rho}^{m\varepsilon\rho+\gamma_m(1+\varepsilon)\rho} e^{-t^2/2} \, dt \right].
$$

Note that the absolute value of the second integral is no less than the absolute value of the third one. The absolute value of the fourth integral can be estimated from above by shifting the interval by $\gamma_m(1 - \varepsilon)/\sqrt{\sigma}$. This yields

$$
M(\phi^*, N, y) \geq 1 - \frac{\text{sign}(m)}{\sqrt{2\pi}} \left[\int_{-m\varepsilon\rho}^{m\varepsilon\rho} e^{-t^2/2} \, dt + \int_{m\varepsilon\rho}^{m\varepsilon\rho+2\varepsilon\gamma_m\rho} e^{-t^2/2} \, dt \right]. \quad (9)
$$

Because $|\gamma_m| \leq \sqrt{\sigma'}$, we have

$$
\left| \int_{m\varepsilon\rho}^{m\varepsilon\rho+2\varepsilon\gamma_m\rho} e^{-t^2/2} \, dt \right| \leq 2\varepsilon \sqrt{\frac{\sigma'}{\sigma}} e^{-(m\varepsilon)^2/(2\sigma)}. \quad (10)
$$

We now integrate $M(\phi^*, N, y)$ with respect to y. To do this, we use the formula

$$
\int_{\mathbf{R}^n} h(\langle y, w \rangle) \, \mu_1(dy) = \frac{1}{\sqrt{2\pi}} \int_{\mathbf{R}} h(x\|w\|) e^{-x^2/2} \, dx,
$$

which holds for any measurable function $h : \mathbf{R} \to \mathbf{R}$ and vector $w \in \mathbf{R}^n$. Using this formula and (6), and combining (9) with (10) we obtain

$$
M(\phi^*, N)
$$
$$
\geq \frac{2}{\pi} \int_0^\infty \int_{x\varepsilon\|w\|\rho}^\infty e^{-(t^2+x^2)/2} \, dt \, dx - \frac{2\varepsilon}{\pi} \sqrt{\frac{\sigma'}{\sigma}} \int_0^\infty e^{-(x\varepsilon\|w\|)^2/(2\sigma)} e^{-x^2/2} \, dx
$$
$$
= \frac{2}{\pi} \int_0^\infty \int_{x\varepsilon\|w\|\rho}^\infty e^{-(t^2+x^2)/2} \, dt \, dx - \varepsilon\pi \sqrt{\frac{2\sigma'}{\pi\sigma}} \left(\frac{(\varepsilon\|w\|)^2}{\sigma} + 1 \right)^{-1/2}.
$$

Let $\tau = \varepsilon \|w\|/\sqrt{\sigma}$. Define

$$g(\tau) = \frac{2}{\pi} \int_0^\infty \int_{x\tau}^\infty e^{-(t^2+x^2)/2} \, dt \, dx.$$

Obviously, $g(0) = 1$ and $g'(\tau) = -2/(\pi(1+\tau^2))$. Hence $g(\tau) = 1 - 2\pi^{-1} \arctan(\tau) = 2\pi^{-1} \operatorname{arc cot}(\tau)$. Thus,

$$\frac{2}{\pi} \int_0^\infty \int_{x\varepsilon\|w\|\rho}^\infty e^{-(t^2+x^2)/2} \, dt \, dx = \frac{2}{\pi} \operatorname{arc cot}\left(\frac{\varepsilon}{\sqrt{\sigma}}\|w\|\right).$$

Since $\operatorname{arc cot}(\tau) = \arcsin\left(1/\sqrt{1+\tau^2}\right) \geq 1/\sqrt{1+\tau^2}$, (10) yields

$$M(\phi^*, N) \geq \frac{2}{\pi} \operatorname{arc cot}(\tau) - \varepsilon \sqrt{\frac{2\sigma'}{\pi\sigma}} \frac{1}{\sqrt{\tau^2+1}}$$

$$\geq \left(1 - \varepsilon\sqrt{\frac{\pi\sigma'}{2\sigma}}\right) \frac{2}{\pi} \operatorname{arc cot}\left(\frac{\varepsilon}{\sqrt{\sigma}}\|w\|\right).$$

This proves the lower bound.

We now prove the upper bound on $M(\phi^*, N)$. Define the algorithm $\phi(y) = m(y)(1-\varepsilon^2)$. Obviously, $M(\phi^*, N) \leq M(\phi, N)$. We have

$$M(\phi, N, y) = 1 - \frac{\operatorname{sign}(m)}{\sqrt{2\pi}} \int_{-m\varepsilon\rho}^{m\varepsilon\rho} e^{-t^2/2} \, dt.$$

As before, we find out that $M(\phi, N) = 2\pi^{-1} \operatorname{arc cot}(\varepsilon\|w\|/\sqrt{\sigma})$. Thus, the upper bound is proved. The rest of the theorem easily follows. ∎

We now show that adaptive information is not more powerful than non-adaptive information.

THEOREM 6.1.1. *For every adaptive information* N^{a} *with fixed cardinality* $n(f) \equiv n$, *there exists nonadaptive information* N^* *of cardinality* n *such that*

$$M(\phi^*, N^*) \leq M(\phi^{\mathrm{a}}, N^{\mathrm{a}}),$$

where ϕ^* *and* ϕ^{a} *are defined by* (5) *for* N^* *and* N^{a}, *respectively, i.e., they minimize* $M(\cdot, N^*)$ *and* $M(\cdot, N^{\mathrm{a}})$, *respectively.*

To prove this theorem, we need two lemmas. In both lemmas, $\|\cdot\|$ denotes the $\mathcal{L}_2$ norm in $\mathbb{R}^n$.

LEMMA 6.1.3. *Let* $w : \mathbb{R}^n \to \mathbb{R}^n$ *be a measurable mapping such that* $\|w(y)\| \equiv 1$ *and*

$$w(y) = [w_1, w_2(y_1), \ldots, w_n(y_1, \ldots, y_{n-1})]. \tag{11}$$

Let $h, g : \mathbb{R} \to \mathbb{R}$ *be measurable functions. Then for every* $z \in \mathbb{R}^n$ *with* $\|z\| = 1$, *we have*

$$\int_{\mathbb{R}^n} g(\langle y, w(y)\rangle)\, h(\langle y, y\rangle)\, dy = \int_{\mathbb{R}^n} g(\langle y, z\rangle)\, h(\langle y, y\rangle)\, dy.$$

PROOF: For every $y = [y_1, \ldots, y_n] \in \mathbb{R}^n$, define $n \times n$ orthogonal matrices $D_1, D_2, \ldots, D_n$ such that $D_n \circ D_{n-1} \cdots \circ D_1\, z = w(y)$. We choose the matrix D_i to have the form

$$D_i = \begin{pmatrix} I_i & 0 \\ 0 & \overline{D_i} \end{pmatrix},$$

where I_i is the $(i-1) \times (i-1)$ identity matrix and $\overline{D_i}$ is an $(n - i + 1) \times (n - i + 1)$ orthogonal matrix depending only on $y_1, \ldots, y_{i-1}$. To construct D_i, we first take $\overline{D_1} = D_1$ to be an orthogonal matrix for which the first component of $D_1 z$ is w_1. Assume inductively that $D_{i-1} \circ \cdots \circ D_1 z$ agrees with the first $(i-1)$ components of $w(y)$. Thus, $D_{i-1} \circ \cdots \circ D_1 z = [w_1, w_2(y), \ldots, w_{i-1}(y_1, \ldots, y_{i-2}), v]^T$. Define $\overline{D_i}$ such that the first component of $\overline{D_i} v$ is $w_i(y_1, \ldots, y_{i-1})$. Clearly, $\overline{D_i}$ depends only on $y_1, \ldots, y_{i-1}$ and $D_i \circ \cdots \circ D_1 z$ agrees with $w(y)$ on the first i components. For $i \in [1, n]$, we have

$$\int_{\mathbb{R}^{n-i+1}} g(\langle y, D_i \circ \cdots \circ D_1 z\rangle)\, dy_n\, dy_{n-1} \ldots dy_i$$

$$= \int_{\mathbb{R}^{n-i+1}} g(\langle D_i^T y, D_{i-1} \circ \cdots \circ D_1 z\rangle)\, dy_n\, dy_{n-1} \ldots dy_i$$

$$= \int_{\mathbb{R}^{n-i+1}} g(\langle y, D_{i-1} \circ \cdots \circ D_1 z\rangle)\, dy_n\, dy_{n-1} \ldots dy_i.$$

The last equality follows from the change of variables $y' = D_i^T y$ and the facts that y' agrees with y on the first $(i-1)$ components and D_i^T depends only on $y_1, \ldots, y_{i-1}$.

Using the last equality for $i = n, n-1, \ldots, 1$, we get

$$\int_{\mathbb{R}^n} g(\langle y, w(y)\rangle)\, h(\langle y, y\rangle)\, dy = \int_{\mathbb{R}^n} g(\langle y, D_n \circ \cdots \circ D_1 z\rangle)\, h(\langle y, y\rangle)\, dy$$

$$= \int_{\mathbb{R}^{n-1}} \left[\int_{\mathbb{R}} g(\langle y, D_{n-1} \circ \cdots \circ D_1 z\rangle)\, h(\langle y, y\rangle)\, dy_n \right] dy_{n-1} \ldots dy_1$$

$$= \cdots = \int_{\mathbb{R}^n} g(\langle y, z\rangle)\, h(\langle y, y\rangle)\, dy.$$

This completes the proof. ∎

LEMMA 6.1.4. *Let* $w : \mathbb{R}^n \to \mathbb{R}^n$ *be a measurable mapping of the form (11) such that*

$$\sup_{y \in \mathbb{R}^n} \|w(y)\| < +\infty.$$

Let $h : \mathbb{R} \to \mathbb{R}$ *be a nonnegative measurable function. Let* $g : \mathbb{R} \to \mathbb{R}$ *be a measurable function such that*

$$|x_1| \le |x_2| \implies g(x_1) \ge g(x_2) \qquad \forall\, x_1, x_2 \in \mathbb{R}. \qquad (12)$$

Then for every $z \in \mathbb{R}^n$ *with* $\|z\| \ge \sup_{y \in \mathbb{R}^n} \|w(y)\|$, *we have*

$$\int_{\mathbb{R}^n} g(\langle y, w(y)\rangle)\, h(\langle y, y\rangle)\, dy \ge \int_{\mathbb{R}^n} g(\langle y, z\rangle)\, h(\langle y, y\rangle)\, dy.$$

PROOF: Without loss of generality we can assume that for all $y \in \mathbb{R}$, $w(y) \ne 0$. Let $r = \sup_{y \in \mathbb{R}^n} \|w(y)\|$. Then using (12) and Lemma 6.1.3 we obtain

$$\int_{\mathbb{R}^n} g(\langle y, w(y)\rangle)\, h(\langle y, y\rangle)\, dy$$

$$= \int_{\mathbb{R}^n} g(\|w(y)\| \langle y, w(y)/\|w(y)\|\rangle)\, h(\langle y, y\rangle)\, dy$$

$$\ge \int_{\mathbb{R}^n} g(r\langle y, w(y)/\|w(y)\|\rangle)\, h(\langle y, y\rangle)\, dy$$

$$= \int_{\mathbb{R}^n} g(r\langle y, z/\|z\|\rangle)\, h(\langle y, y\rangle)\, dy$$

$$\ge \int_{\mathbb{R}^n} g(\|z\| \langle y, z/\|z\|\rangle)\, h(\langle y, y\rangle)\, dy = \int_{\mathbb{R}^n} g(\langle y, z\rangle)\, h(\langle y, y\rangle)\, dy,$$

which completes the proof. ∎

PROOF OF THEOREM 6.1.1: For information N^{a}, consider $w(y)$, $m(y)$, and $\sigma(y)$ defined by (1)–(4). Let the algorithm ϕ^{a} be defined by (5). Without loss of generality we can assume that there exists y^* such that for $w^* = w(y^*)$,

$$\sup_{y \in \mathbb{R}^n} \|w(y)\| = \|w^*\|.$$

This is equivalent to $\inf_{y \in \mathbb{R}^n} \sigma(y) = \sigma(y^*) = \sigma^*$. Consider $M(\phi^{\mathrm{a}}, N^{\mathrm{a}}, y)$. It is easy, although tedious, to show that $M(\phi^{\mathrm{a}}, N^{\mathrm{a}}, y)$ is decreasing as a function of $\sigma(y)$. Thus,

$$M(\phi^{\mathrm{a}}, N^{\mathrm{a}}, y) \ge g(m) := 1 - \frac{1}{\sqrt{2\pi}\sigma^*} \int_{u_1^*}^{u_2^*} e^{-(x-m)^2/(2\sigma^*)}\, dx, \qquad (13)$$

where u_1^* and u_2^* are defined by (8) with $u = \left(m + \text{sign}(m)\sqrt{m^2 + 4\sigma'}\right)(1 - \varepsilon^2)/2$, and σ' is defined by (4) with $\sigma(y) = \sigma^*$. It is easy to show that g satisfies (12) of Lemma 6.1.4.

Define nonadaptive information $N^* = [L_1, L_{2,y^*}, \ldots, L_{n,y^*}]$, and let ϕ^* be defined by (5) for information N^*. Then using (13) and Lemma 6.1.4 we get

$$M(\phi^a, N^a) \geq (2\pi)^{-n/2} \int_{\mathbb{R}^n} g(\langle y, w(y)\rangle) e^{-\|y\|^2/2}\, dy$$

$$\geq (2\pi)^{-n/2} \int_{\mathbb{R}^n} g(\langle y, w^*\rangle) e^{-\|y\|^2/2}\, dy = M(\phi^*, N^*),$$

which completes the proof of Theorem 6.1.1. ∎

We are ready to estimate the probabilistic complexity $\text{comp}^{\text{rel}}(\varepsilon, \delta)$ under the relative error criterion. As in Chapter 6, let

$$\sigma_n = \inf_{L_i \in \Lambda} \inf_{g_i \in \mathbb{R}} \left\| S - \sum_{i=1}^n g_i L_i \right\|_\mu^2 \tag{14}$$

denote the minimal variance of the conditional measure after n information evaluations. Observe that $\sigma_n \leq \sigma_0 = \|S\|_\mu^2 = S(C_\mu S)$, and σ_n is positive for all n since $S \notin \text{span}(\Lambda)$.

For given ε and δ, define

$$m^{\text{rel}}(\varepsilon, \delta) = \min\left\{ n : \sqrt{\frac{\sigma_n}{\sigma_0 - \sigma_n}} \leq \varepsilon \tan\left(\frac{\pi}{2}\delta\right)\right\}.$$

Note that $m^{\text{rel}}(\varepsilon, \delta)$ is finite for all positive ε and δ iff $\sigma_n \to 0$.

We prove that $m^{\text{rel}}(\varepsilon, \delta)$ is roughly equal to the probabilistic cardinality number, i.e., we need to compute roughly $m^{\text{rel}}(\varepsilon, \delta)$ information operations. More precisely we have

THEOREM 6.1.2.

$$c\, m^{\text{rel}}(\varepsilon, \delta_1) \leq \text{comp}^{\text{rel}}(\varepsilon, \delta) \leq (c+2)\, m^{\text{rel}}(\varepsilon, \delta) - 1, \tag{15}$$

where c is the cost of one information operation and

$$\delta_1 = \min\left\{1, \delta\left[1 - \sqrt{\frac{\pi\varepsilon}{4}\ln\frac{1+\varepsilon}{1-\varepsilon}}\right]_+^{-1}\right\}.$$

For small ε and δ, and large c we have

$$\text{comp}^{\text{rel}}(\varepsilon, \delta) \simeq c\, m^{\text{rel}}(\varepsilon, \delta(1 + o(1))) \quad \text{as } \varepsilon \to 0.$$

PROOF: We first prove the upper bound of (15). Let $n = m^{\text{rel}}(\varepsilon, \delta)$. For simplicity, assume that the first infimum in (14) is attained for $L_1^*, \ldots, L_n^*$. Let $N = [L_1, \ldots, L_n]$ with $L_i \in \text{span}(L_1^*, \ldots, L_i^*)$ such that $\langle L_i, L_j \rangle = \delta_{i,j}$. Consider the linear algorithm $\phi(y) = m(y)(1 - \varepsilon^2)$. Its cost is equal to $(c + 2)n - 1$. To check that $e^{\text{rel}}(\phi, N) \leq \varepsilon$, it is enough to show that $M(\phi, N) \leq \delta$. From the proof of Lemma 6.1.2, we know that

$$M(\phi, N) = \frac{2}{\pi} \operatorname{arc\,cot}\left(\frac{\varepsilon \|w\|}{\sqrt{\sigma}}\right),$$

where $\|w\|^2 = \sum_{i=1}^{n} \left[S(C_\mu L_i)\right]^2$. From (14) we have

$$\sigma_n = \inf_{g_i \in \mathbb{R}} \left\| S - \sum_{i=1}^{n} g_i L_i \right\|_\mu^2 = \sigma_0 - \|w\|^2.$$

This and the definition of n yield

$$\frac{\varepsilon \|w\|}{\sqrt{\sigma_n}} = \varepsilon \sqrt{\frac{\sigma_0 - \sigma_n}{\sigma_n}} \geq \cot\left(\frac{\pi}{2} \delta\right).$$

Therefore $2\pi^{-1} \operatorname{arc\,cot}(\varepsilon \|w\| / \sqrt{\sigma_n}) \leq \delta$, which completes the proof of the upper bound of (15).

To prove the lower bound, assume first that

$$\delta \geq \left(1 - \sqrt{\varepsilon \pi / 4 \ln\left((1 + \varepsilon)/(1 - \varepsilon)\right)}\,\right)_+.$$

Then $\delta_1 = 1$ and $m^{\text{rel}}(\varepsilon, 1) = 0$. Thus, (15) trivially holds. Assume then that

$$1 - \sqrt{\varepsilon \pi / 4 \ln\left((1 + \varepsilon)/(1 - \varepsilon)\right)} > 0$$

and

$$\delta_1 = \delta / \left(1 - \sqrt{\varepsilon \pi / 4 \ln\left((1 + \varepsilon)/(1 - \varepsilon)\right)}\,\right) < 1.$$

Take an arbitrary U, $U(f) = \phi(N(f))$, such that $e^{\text{rel}}(U) \leq \varepsilon$. Thus, $M(\phi, N) \leq \delta$. We can assume that information N is of fixed and finite cardinality, i.e., $n(f) \equiv k$. Due to Theorem 6.1.1, we can assume that N is nonadaptive. From Lemmas 6.1.1 and 6.1.2 we conclude that

$$\delta \geq M(\phi, N) \geq \left[1 - \sqrt{\frac{\pi}{4} \varepsilon \ln \frac{1 + \varepsilon}{1 - \varepsilon}}\,\right] \frac{2}{\pi} \operatorname{arc\,cot}\left(\varepsilon \sqrt{\frac{\sigma_0 - \sigma}{\sigma}}\right),$$

where $\sigma \in [\sigma_k, \sigma_0]$. From this we get

$$\sqrt{\frac{\sigma_k}{\sigma_0 - \sigma_k}} \le \varepsilon \tan\left(\frac{\pi}{2}\delta_1\right).$$

Hence, $k \ge m^{\mathrm{rel}}(\varepsilon, \delta_1)$ and $\mathrm{cost}(U) \ge c\,m^{\mathrm{rel}}(\varepsilon, \delta_1)$. This completes the proof. ∎

From the proof of Theorem 6.1.2 it follows that N and ϕ are almost optimal. Observe that the linear algorithm ϕ is *not* an optimal error algorithm since it differs slightly from the nonlinear optimal error algorithm ϕ^* defined by (5). Obviously, for small ε, the difference between the algorithms ϕ and ϕ^* is insignificant.

Notes and Remarks

NR 6.1:1 One may consider the relative error criterion in which the roles of $S(f)$ and $U(f)$ are interchanged. Unlike the average case setting, this change does not really affect the probabilistic complexity. Indeed, for $\varepsilon < 1$ we have

$$\frac{|S(f) - U(f)|}{|U(f)|} \le \varepsilon \implies \frac{|S(f) - U(f)|}{|S(f)|} \le \frac{\varepsilon}{1 - \varepsilon},$$

and vice versa,

$$\frac{|S(f) - U(f)|}{|S(f)|} \le \varepsilon \implies \frac{|S(f) - U(f)|}{|U(f)|} \le \frac{\varepsilon}{1 - \varepsilon}.$$

Therefore, the probabilistic (ε, δ)-complexity with the new definition of the relative error is no smaller than $\mathrm{comp}^{\mathrm{rel}}(\varepsilon/(1 - \varepsilon), \delta)$ and is no greater than $\mathrm{comp}^{\mathrm{rel}}(\varepsilon/(1 + \varepsilon), \delta)$. Hence, for small ε they are practically the same.

NR 6.1:2 Consider the modified error criterion, see Section 6 of Chapter 4, when the distance between $S(f)$ and $U(f)$ is given by $|S(f) - U(f)|/(|S(f)| + \eta)$ for a positive η. Clearly, the probabilistic complexity $\mathrm{comp}^{\mathrm{rel}}(\varepsilon, \delta; \eta)$ is no greater than the probabilistic complexity under the absolute error criterion with ε replaced by $\varepsilon\eta$. This means that for small ε, δ, and η, $\mathrm{comp}^{\mathrm{rel}}(\varepsilon, \delta; \eta)$ is roughly at most equal to cn, where n is the minimal integer such that $\sqrt{\sigma_n} \le \varepsilon\eta/\sqrt{2\ln(1/\delta)}$. Observe the change in the dependence on δ. For the relative error criterion, the probabilistic complexity $\mathrm{comp}^{\mathrm{rel}}(\varepsilon, \delta)$ depends fully on δ since

$$\mathrm{comp}^{\mathrm{rel}}(\varepsilon, \delta) \simeq c \min\left\{ n : \sqrt{\sigma_n} \le \varepsilon\delta\sqrt{\sigma_0}\,\frac{\pi}{2}\,(1 + o(1)) \right\} \quad \text{as } \varepsilon, \delta \to 0.$$

The upper bound on $\mathrm{comp}^{\mathrm{rel}}(\varepsilon, \delta; \eta)$ depends merely on $1/\sqrt{2\ln(1/\delta)}$. The actual value of $\mathrm{comp}^{\mathrm{rel}}(\varepsilon, \delta; \eta)$ is not known.

6.2. Normalized Error

We briefly discuss the normalized error for linear problems with $F = F_1$ in the probabilistic setting. The probabilistic normalized error of $U =$

(ϕ, N) is defined by

$$e^{\mathrm{nor}}(U, \delta) = \inf_{A:\mu(A) \leq \delta} \sup_{f \in F-A} \frac{\|S(f) - U(f)\|}{\|f\|}.$$

Let $\mathrm{comp}^{\mathrm{nor}}(\varepsilon, \delta)$ denote the probabilistic complexity under the normalized error criterion,

$$\mathrm{comp}^{\mathrm{nor}}(\varepsilon, \delta) = \inf \left\{ \mathrm{cost}^{\mathrm{wor}}(U) : e^{\mathrm{nor}}(U, \delta) \leq \varepsilon \right\}.$$

We present bounds on $\mathrm{comp}^{\mathrm{nor}}(\varepsilon, \delta)$ in terms of $\mathrm{comp}^{\mathrm{prob}}(\varepsilon, \delta)$. These bounds are not always tight, and a more refined analysis is needed to fully understand relations between these two complexities.

As in Section 5.5, we first notice that $\mathrm{comp}^{\mathrm{nor}}(\varepsilon, \delta)$ is bounded for all δ by the worst case complexity. The latter is independent of δ and is, in general, finite. Thus, $\mathrm{comp}^{\mathrm{nor}}(\varepsilon, \delta)$ is finite even for $\delta = 0$, whereas $\mathrm{comp}^{\mathrm{prob}}(\varepsilon, \delta)$ usually goes to infinity as δ goes to zero. Therefore, a relation between $\mathrm{comp}^{\mathrm{nor}}(\varepsilon, \delta)$ and $\mathrm{comp}^{\mathrm{prob}}(\varepsilon, \delta)$ can be established only if δ is not too small.

LEMMA 6.2.1. Let $b(x) = \mu(B_x)$ denote the μ-measure of the ball in F_1 with radius x and center zero. Then for every $x \in \mathbb{R}_+$,

$$\mathrm{comp}^{\mathrm{nor}}(\varepsilon, \delta) \geq \mathrm{comp}^{\mathrm{prob}} \left(\varepsilon\, x, \delta + 1 - b(x) \right),$$

and for every x with $b(x) \leq \delta$,

$$\mathrm{comp}^{\mathrm{nor}}(\varepsilon, \delta) \leq \mathrm{comp}^{\mathrm{prob}} \left(\varepsilon\, x, \delta - b(x) \right).$$

PROOF: Take any U that solves the problem for the normalized error criterion. Then for any $x \in \mathbb{R}_+$,

$$\begin{aligned}
1 - \delta &\leq \mu\big(\{f : \|S(f) - U(f)\|/\|f\| \leq \varepsilon\}\big) \\
&\leq \mu\big(\{f : \|S(f) - U(f)\|/\|f\| \leq \varepsilon \text{ and } \|f\| \leq x\}\big) + 1 - b(x) \\
&\leq \mu\big(\{f : \|S(f) - U(f)\| \leq \varepsilon x\}\big) + 1 - b(x).
\end{aligned}$$

Thus, U solves the problem for the absolute error criterion with $\varepsilon_1 = \varepsilon\, x$ and $\delta_1 = \delta + 1 - b(x)$. This proves the first inequality.

Take now U which solves the problem for the absolute error criterion with $\varepsilon_1 = \varepsilon\, x$ and $\delta_1 = \delta - b(x)$. Then

$$\begin{aligned}
\mu\big(\{f : \|S(f) - U(f)\|/\|f\| \leq \varepsilon\}\big) \\
\geq \mu\big(\{f : \|S(f) - U(f)\|/\|f\| \leq \varepsilon \text{ and } \|f\| \geq x\}\big) \\
\geq \mu\big(\{f : \|S(f) - U(f)\| \leq \varepsilon x \text{ and } \|f\| \geq x\}\big) \\
\geq \mu\big(\{f : \|S(f) - U(f)\| \leq \varepsilon x\}\big) - b(x) \geq 1 - \delta.
\end{aligned}$$

Thus, U solves the problem for the normalized error criterion and this completes the proof. ∎

For a positive δ, the first estimate of Lemma 6.2.1 can be used for large x such that $\delta + 1 - b(x) \simeq \delta$, and the second estimate for small x such that $\delta - b(x) \simeq \delta$. We can rewrite Lemma 6.2.1 in a somewhat more convenient form.

COROLLARY 6.2.1. *For any function* $h : \mathbb{R}_+ \to \mathbb{R}_+$ *with* $\lim_{\varepsilon \to 0^+} h(\varepsilon) = 0$ *and any* δ, *we have*

$$\text{comp}^{\text{prob}}\left(\frac{\varepsilon}{h(\varepsilon)}, \delta + o_1(\varepsilon)\right) \leq \text{comp}^{\text{nor}}(\varepsilon, \delta) \leq \text{comp}^{\text{prob}}(\varepsilon\, h(\varepsilon), \delta - o_2(\varepsilon))$$

for every ε, $o_2(\varepsilon) \leq \delta$, *where* $o_1(\varepsilon) = 1 - b(1/h(\varepsilon))$ *and* $o_2(\varepsilon) = b(h(\varepsilon))$, *and both* $o_i(\varepsilon) \to 0$ *as* $\varepsilon \to 0$.

PROOF: Apply the first estimate of Lemma 6.2.1 with $x = 1/h(\varepsilon)$ and the second estimate with $x = h(\varepsilon)$. ∎

Choosing a function h which goes to zero very slowly, we obtain for fixed δ and small ε that the complexity for the normalized error is tightly related to the probabilistic complexity for the absolute error. For example, choose $h(\varepsilon) = 1/\ln(1/\varepsilon)$. Then

$$\text{comp}^{\text{prob}}\left(\varepsilon \ln(1/\varepsilon), \delta + o(1)\right)$$
$$\leq \text{comp}^{\text{nor}}(\varepsilon, \delta) \leq \text{comp}^{\text{prob}}\left(\frac{\varepsilon}{\ln(1/\varepsilon)}, \delta + o(1)\right)$$

as $\varepsilon \to 0$, which can be rewritten as

$$\text{comp}^{\text{nor}}(\varepsilon, \delta) = \text{comp}^{\text{prob}}\left(\varepsilon^{1 + o(1)}, \delta + o(1)\right) \quad \text{as } \varepsilon \to 0, \tag{1}$$

with the understanding that $o(1)$ takes positive values for the lower bound and negative values for the upper bound, respectively.

Notes and Remarks

NR 6.2:1 Lemma 6.2.1 can be readily generalized for the relative error. In this case, the only difference is that $b(x) = \nu(B(0, x))$ stands for the ν-measure, $\nu = \mu S^{-1}$, of the ball in the space G. Thus,

$$\text{comp}^{\text{rel}}(\varepsilon, \delta) \geq \text{comp}^{\text{prob}}\left(\varepsilon\, x, \delta + 1 - b(x)\right), \quad \forall\, x \in \mathbb{R}_+,$$
$$\text{comp}^{\text{rel}}(\varepsilon, \delta) \leq \text{comp}^{\text{prob}}\left(\varepsilon\, x, \delta - b(x)\right), \quad \forall\, x, b(x) \leq \delta.$$

Observe, however, that for the relative error, the estimates above are even weaker than for the normalized error. Indeed, set $\delta = 0$. Then, unlike for the normalized error, $\mathrm{comp}^{\mathrm{rel}}(\varepsilon, 0)$ is, in general, infinite, whereas the lower bound is $\mathrm{comp}^{\mathrm{prob}}(\varepsilon x, 1 - b(x))$ which may be finite for every x. Nevertheless, for a fixed positive δ, one may get the same estimate as in (1),

$$\mathrm{comp}^{\mathrm{rel}}(\varepsilon, \delta) = \mathrm{comp}^{\mathrm{prob}}\left(\varepsilon^{1+o(1)}, \delta + o(1)\right) \quad \text{as } \varepsilon \to 0.$$

6.3. General Error Functional

We briefly discuss the probabilistic setting with the error criterion defined by an error functional $\mathrm{ER} : G \to \mathbb{R}_+$, see Sections 6.3 of Chapters 4 and 6, where this error criterion is analyzed for the worst and average case settings, respectively. The probabilistic error of $U = (\phi, N)$ is now defined by

$$e^{\mathrm{prob}}(U, \delta) = \inf_{A : \mu(A) \leq \delta} \sup_{f \in F - A} \mathrm{ER}\left(S(f) - U(f)\right).$$

Obviously, $e^{\mathrm{prob}}(U, \delta) \leq \varepsilon$ iff $M(U, \varepsilon) \leq \delta$, where

$$M(U, \varepsilon) = \mu\left(\{f \in F : \mathrm{ER}\left(S(f) - U(f)\right) > \varepsilon\}\right).$$

The probabilistic complexity is defined in the usual way by

$$\mathrm{comp}^{\mathrm{prob}}(\varepsilon, \delta)$$
$$= \inf\left\{\, \mathrm{cost}^{\mathrm{wor}}(U) : e^{\mathrm{prob}}(U, \delta) \leq \varepsilon \right\} = \inf\left\{\, \mathrm{cost}^{\mathrm{wor}}(U) : M(U, \varepsilon) \leq \delta \right\}.$$

Consider now a linear problem with $F = F_1$. As in Section 5.3, it is easy to show that adaption does not help for arbitrary ER. For nonadaptive information N and for $U = (\phi, N)$, we have

$$M(\phi, N, x) = 1 - \nu_N\left(B + \phi(y) - \phi^s(y)\right),$$

where, as always, $\nu_N = \nu(\cdot|0)$ is the conditional measure with mean $\phi^s(y)$, and B is now a "generalized" ball, $B = \{g \in G : \mathrm{ER}(g) \leq x\}$.

Observe that for a convex and symmetric error functional ER, the set B is convex and balanced, and therefore Lemma 2.9.3 of the appendix yields that $M(\phi, N, x)$ is minimized by $\phi(y) = \phi^s(y)$ independently of x. Thus, the μ-spline algorithm is optimal for any convex and balanced ER.

Assume now that $\mathrm{ER}(g) = \mathrm{H}(\|g\|)$ for a nondecreasing H. Obviously,

$$M(U, \varepsilon) = \mu\left(\{f \in F_1 : \|S(f) - U(f)\| > \mathrm{H}^{-1}(\varepsilon)\}\right),$$

which corresponds to the absolute error with the error demand $\mathrm{H}^{-1}(\varepsilon)$. Therefore, all results of Section 5 hold for any nondecreasing H with ε replaced by $\mathrm{H}^{-1}(\varepsilon)$.

Similarly, the precision error functional $ER(g) = -\log_2 \|g\|$, see Section 6.4 of Chapter 6, is equivalent to the absolute error with $\varepsilon = \exp(-k)$, where k is the required number of correct bits.

7. Applications

We indicate how the results of this chapter can be applied to linear problems discussed in Chapters 5 and 7 for the worst and average case settings, respectively.

The first of these linear problems is integration for the three classes of scalar functions with Λ consisting of function and derivative evaluations, see Section 2 of Chapter 7. Since the solution operator is now a continuous linear functional and the nth minimal average radii are semi-convex, Corollary 5.4.3 states that the probabilistic setting is essentially equivalent to the average case setting with ε replaced by $\varepsilon/\psi^{-1}(1-\delta) = \varepsilon/\sqrt{2\ln(1/\delta)}\,(1+o(1))$. Therefore, one can readily translate the results of Section 2 of Chapter 7 to the integration problem in the probabilistic setting.

In particular, consider the integration problem for

$$F = F_1 = \{f : [0,1] \to \mathbb{R} : f^{(r)} \text{ is continuous, } f^{(i)}(0) = 0, \ i = 0,1,\ldots,r\},$$

with μ being the Wiener measure placed on rth derivatives. From Section 2.1 of Chapter 7, we conclude that for small ε and δ, and large c,

$$\text{comp}^{\text{prob}}(\varepsilon,\delta) \simeq c\,m^{\text{prob}}(\varepsilon,\delta) = c\left[\sqrt{\frac{|B_{2r+2}|}{(2r+2)!}}\,\frac{\sqrt{2\ln\frac{1}{\delta}}}{\varepsilon}\right]^{1/(r+1)}(1+o(1)),$$

where B_{2r+2} is the Bernoulli number.

Function values at $n = m^{\text{prob}}(\varepsilon,\delta)$ equally spaced points plus a few odd derivatives at the endpoint 1 form almost optimal information, and the integral of the natural spline of degree $2r+1$ that interpolates this information is an almost optimal algorithm. The exact form of the information and the algorithm is given in (4) of Section 2.1 of Chapter 7.

Consider now the same problem with F being the ball B_q. From Theorem 5.5.1, we get

$$\text{comp}^{\text{prob}}(\varepsilon,\delta,q) \simeq \text{comp}^{\text{prob}}(\varepsilon,\delta)$$

for q satisfying $1 - \mu(B_q) << \delta$. This can be rewritten as $q >> \sqrt{2\ln(1/\delta)}$.

For the integration problem with F_1 and μ given as in Example 2.2.1 of Chapter 7, the formulas for the probabilistic complexity and for almost optimal information and algorithm are essentially the same.

For the integration problem for periodic functions with F_1 and μ given as in Example 2.2.2 of Chapter 7, we have for small ε and δ, and large c,

$$\text{comp}^{\text{prob}}(\varepsilon, \delta)$$

$$\simeq c\, m^{\text{prob}}(\varepsilon, \delta) = 2\pi\, c \left(\sqrt{\frac{2\pi |B_{2(r+s)}|}{(2(r+s))!}}\, \frac{\sqrt{2 \ln \frac{1}{\delta}}}{\varepsilon} \right)^{1/(r+s)} \left(1 + o(1)\right).$$

Function values at $n = m^{\text{prob}}(\varepsilon, \delta)$ equally spaced points and the rectangle formula are almost optimal. For $q \gg \sqrt{2 \ln(1/\delta)}$ we have

$$\text{comp}^{\text{prob}}(\varepsilon, \delta, q) \simeq \text{comp}^{\text{prob}}(\varepsilon, \delta).$$

We now turn to the function approximation problem for two classes of multivariate functions with Λ consisting of all continuous linear functionals, see Section 3 of Chapter 7. For small ε and δ, and large c, we have from Sections 5.1 and 5.4,

$$\text{comp}^{\text{prob}}(\varepsilon, \delta) \simeq c\, m^{\text{prob}}(\varepsilon, \delta)$$

and

$$m_L^{\text{prob}}(\varepsilon, \delta) = \min\left\{ n : \lambda_{n+1}^* \le \frac{\varepsilon^2}{2 \ln \frac{1}{\delta}} \left(1 + o(1)\right) \right\} \le m^{\text{prob}}(\varepsilon, \delta)$$

$$\le m_U^{\text{prob}}(\varepsilon, \delta) = \min\left\{ n : \sum_{i=n+1}^{\infty} \lambda_i^* \le \frac{\varepsilon^2}{2 \ln \frac{1}{\delta}} \left(1 + o(1)\right) \right\}$$

as $\delta \to 0$, where λ_i^* are the eigenvalues of the correlation operator C_ν in decreasing order. Furthermore, Theorem 5.4.2 states that for fixed ε and δ tending to zero, we have

$$m^{\text{prob}}(\varepsilon, \delta) \simeq m_L^{\text{prob}}(\varepsilon, \delta),$$

whereas for fixed δ and ε tending to zero, we have

$$m^{\text{prob}}(\varepsilon, \delta) \simeq m_U^{\text{prob}}(\varepsilon^{1+o(1)}, \delta).$$

Information consisting of $n = m^{\text{prob}}(\varepsilon, \delta)$ inner products $\langle f, \eta_1^* \rangle, \ldots, \langle f, \eta_n^* \rangle$ and the μ-spline algorithm, $\phi^s(N(f)) = \sum_{i=1}^{n} \langle f, \eta_i^* \rangle \eta_i^*$, are almost optimal. Here, η_i^* is the eigenelement of C_ν which corresponds to the ith eigenvalue λ_i^*.

Consider the function approximation problem for specific classes of functions. We first consider smooth periodic functions with $F = F_1$ and μ given as in Section 3.1 of Chapter 7. Then $\lambda_j^* = a^* \alpha^2 j^{-(v+2/\omega)} (1 + o(1))$ for large j, where $a^* > 0$, $v > 1$, $\omega = \sum_{j=1}^{d} r_j^{-1}$, and α are given in Section 3.1 of Chapter 5. For small ε and δ we thus have

$$m_L^{\mathrm{prob}}(\varepsilon, \delta) = \left[\alpha \frac{\sqrt{2 a^* \ln \frac{1}{\delta}}}{\varepsilon} \right]^{\omega/(1+v\omega/2)} (1 + o(1)),$$

$$m_U^{\mathrm{prob}}(\varepsilon, \delta) = \left[\alpha \sqrt{\frac{a^* \omega}{2 + (v-1)\omega}} \frac{\sqrt{2 \ln \frac{1}{\delta}}}{\varepsilon} \right]^{\omega/(1+(v-1)\omega/2)} (1 + o(1)).$$

Since λ_j^* satisfy the assumptions of Theorem 5.4.3, we also have

$$m^{\mathrm{prob}}(\varepsilon, \delta) = \left[\frac{\alpha}{\varepsilon} \sqrt{\frac{a^* \omega}{2 + (v-1)\omega}} \right]^{\omega/(1+(v-1)\omega/2)} (1 + o(1))$$

for any $\delta \in (0, 1/2)$ and ε going to zero.

When F is the unit ball in F_1, the complexity, optimal information, and optimal algorithm are essentially the same if a^* is small.

Consider now the function approximation problem for nonperiodic functions with $F = F_1$ and μ given as in Section 3.2 of Chapter 7. Then $\lambda_j^* = \overline{\alpha} \left((\ln j)^{k-1}/j \right)^{2r_{\min}+2} (1 + o(1))$ for large j, where $\overline{\alpha}$, k, and $r_{\min}$ are defined in Section 3.2 of Chapter 7. For small ε and δ we thus have

$$m_L^{\mathrm{prob}}(\varepsilon, \delta) = \left[\frac{\sqrt{2 \overline{\alpha} \ln \frac{1}{\delta}}}{\varepsilon} \right]^{1/(r_{\min}+1)} \left[\frac{1}{2r_{\min}+2} \ln \frac{2\overline{\alpha} \ln \frac{1}{\delta}}{\varepsilon^2} \right]^{k-1} (1 + o(1))$$

and

$$m_U^{\mathrm{prob}}(\varepsilon, \delta) = \left[\frac{1}{\sqrt{2r_{\min}+1}} \frac{\sqrt{2 \overline{\alpha} \ln \frac{1}{\delta}}}{\varepsilon} \right]^{1/(r_{\min}+1/2)}$$

$$\times \left[\frac{1}{r_{\min}+\frac{1}{2}} \ln \frac{\sqrt{2 \ln \frac{1}{\delta}}}{\varepsilon} \right]^{(k-1)(r_{\min}+1)/(r_{\min}+1/2)} (1 + o(1)).$$

As before, λ_j^* satisfy the assumptions of Theorem 5.4.3. Hence,

$$m^{\mathrm{prob}}(\varepsilon, \delta) = \left[\sqrt{\frac{\overline{\alpha}}{2r_{\min}+1}} \frac{1}{\varepsilon} \right]^{1/(r_{\min}+1/2)}$$

$$\times \left[\frac{1}{r_{\min}+\frac{1}{2}} \ln \frac{1}{\varepsilon} \right]^{(k-1)(r_{\min}+1)/(r_{\min}+1/2)} (1 + o(1))$$

for any $\delta \in (0, 1/2)$ and ε going to zero.

For $F = B_q$ with $q \gg \sqrt{2 \ln(1/\delta)}$, we get essentially the same results,

$$\mathrm{comp}^{\mathrm{prob}}(\varepsilon, \delta, q) \simeq \mathrm{comp}^{\mathrm{prob}}(\varepsilon, \delta).$$

We now discuss the probabilistic setting for ill-posed problems, see Section 7 of Chapter 5 and Section 4 of Chapter 7. Recall that we are given separable Hilbert spaces F_1 and G, and an unbounded linear operator $S : D \subseteq F_1 \to G$ defined on a dense subspace D of F_1 having full measure. We consider only the case where the class F of problem elements is the domain D of S, leaving the case in which F is a ball in D of finite radius as an exercise.

Suppose first that S is bounded on the average. Then $\nu = \mu S^{-1}$ is a Gaussian measure with correlation operator C_ν. It is then easy to see that the results in Section 5 hold as before. In particular:

(1) The μ-spline algorithm is optimal.
(2) The estimates for the probabilistic radius given in Section 5.2 hold.
(3) nth optimal information is the same as in the average case.
(4) The estimates of the nth minimal probabilistic radius given in Section 5.3 hold.
(5) The complexity estimates of Section 5.4 hold.

Note especially that $r^{\mathrm{prob}}(N, \delta)$ is finite for any $\delta \in (0, 1]$ and for any information N.

Suppose now that S is not bounded on the average. We claim that $r^{\mathrm{prob}}(N, \delta) = +\infty$ for any information N from the class $\Lambda = F_1^*$ and for any $\delta \in [0, 1)$. It is enough to show this for nonadaptive information. Recalling that $\mu_2(\cdot | y)$ is conditional measure, we first note that

$$\mu_2(\{f \in D : \|S(f) - g\| \leq \varepsilon\}|0) \leq \mu_2(\{f \in D : \|S(f)\| \leq \varepsilon\}|0),$$

due to Lemma 2.9.3 in the appendix. Let $\{\zeta_j\}$ be an orthonormal system for G and let P_k denote the orthonormal projection onto $\mathrm{span}\{\zeta_1, \ldots, \zeta_k\}$. Since G is a Hilbert space,

$$\mu_2(\{f \in D : \|S(f)\| \leq \varepsilon\}|0) \leq \mu_2(\{f \in D : \|P_k S(f)\| \leq \varepsilon\}|0).$$

Since $P_k S$ is continuous, the measure $\nu_k = \mu_2(P_k S)^{-1}$ is Gaussian on $\mathbb{R}^k$. Let C_{ν_k} denote the correlation operator of ν_k. Hence

$$\mu_2(\{f \in D : \|P_k S(f)\| \leq \varepsilon\}|0)$$
$$= \nu_k(\{g \in \mathbb{R}^k : \|g\| \leq \varepsilon\}|0) \leq \tfrac{4}{3} \int_0^{x_k} e^{-t^2/2} \, dt,$$

where $x_k = 2\varepsilon/\sqrt{\text{trace}(C_{\nu_k})}$ due to Lemma 2.9.1 of the appendix. Now

$$\text{trace}(C_{\nu_k}) = \int_D \|P_k S(f)\|^2 \, \mu(df).$$

Since $\{\|P_k S(f)\|\}$ is an increasing sequence, the Lebesgue theorem yields that

$$\lim_{k\to\infty} \int_D \|P_k S(f)\|^2 \, \mu(df) = \int_D \|S(f)\|^2 \, \mu(df).$$

Since S is not bounded on the average, $\lim_{k\to\infty} \text{trace}(C_{\nu_k}) = +\infty$, and so $\lim_{k\to\infty} x_k = 0$. It then follows that $\mu_2(\{f \in D : \|S(f) - g\| \le \varepsilon\}|0) = 0$, which (when integrated) implies that $r^{\text{prob}}(N, \delta) = +\infty$, as claimed.

Notes and Remarks

NR 7:1 The material on ill-posed problems was written by A. G. Werschulz.

Exercises

E 7:1 Extend the results on ill-posed problems to include the case where F is a ball of finite radius q in D.

Chapter 9

Comparison between Different Settings

1. Introduction

In previous chapters we studied the complexity of various problems in a fixed setting. In this chapter we will fix the problem and compare its complexity in the worst case, average case, and probabilistic settings. We will consider five error criteria. Thus, we determine the effect of setting and error criterion on complexity. The integration problem will be discussed for two classes of scalar functions with the class Λ consisting of function and derivative evaluations. The approximation problem will be studied for two classes of multivariate functions with the class Λ consisting of all continuous linear functionals.

The error criteria are:

- absolute error, denoted by Abs, with the distance between $S(f)$ and $U(f)$ defined by $\|S(f) - U(f)\|$,
- normalized error, denoted by Nor, with the distance defined by $\|S(f) - U(f)\|/\|f\|$,
- relative error, denoted by Rel_1, with the distance defined by $\|S(f) - U(f)\|/\|S(f)\|$,
- relative error, denoted by Rel_2, with the roles of $S(f)$ and $U(f)$ interchanged, i.e., with the distance defined by $\|S(f) - U(f)\|/\|U(f)\|$,
- modified relative error, denoted by Rel_3, with the distance defined by $\|S(f) - U(f)\|/ (\|S(f)\| + \eta)$ for a positive η.

The absolute and modified relative error criteria are studied for the ball $F = B_q \subseteq F_1$ of radius q. The normalized and relative errors Rel_1 and Rel_2 are studied for the whole space $F = F_1$. In the average case and probabilistic settings, $F = B_q$ is equipped with a truncated Gaussian measure μ_q, whereas $F = F_1$ is equipped with a Gaussian measure μ. The specific form of μ is the same as in Chapter 7.

In Chapters 5, 7, and 8, we presented lower and upper bounds on the complexity. To simplify comparison between the three settings, we recall these estimates only for small ε, for fixed but small δ in the probabilistic setting, for large c, and for q such that $1 - \mu(B_q) << 1$ and $1 - \mu(B_q) << \delta$ in the probabilistic setting. That is, the ε-complexity is of the form

$$\text{comp}(\varepsilon) = c\,Z(\varepsilon)\,\big(1 + o(1)\big) \quad \text{as } \varepsilon \to 0.$$

The function Z will be given in the corresponding tables and will have the form $Z(\varepsilon) = \alpha\,z(\varepsilon)$, where α is an asymptotic constant.

For each problem, we will present a 5×3 table with formulas for the complexity under five error criteria in three settings. Since we have two integration and two approximation problems, we will present altogether 60 such formulas. For some cases, we know only upper bounds on the complexity. This will be indicated by the sign $\leq$ in the corresponding place of a table. For some cases, we know the complexity modulo an arbitrary increasing or decreasing function of ε. In this case, the function Z will be expressed in terms of a function γ whose bounds will be given above or below the corresponding table. For some other cases, we do not know α. In such a case, we use the symbol β. Thus, each appearance of $\leq$, γ, or β indicates an open problem.

2. Integration of Smooth Functions

We summarize the complexity results for the integration problem for the Banach space

$$F_1 = \big\{f : [0,1] \to \mathbb{R} : f^{(r)} \text{ is continuous, } f^{(i)}(0) = 0,\ i = 0,1,\ldots,r\big\},$$

with the norm $\|f\| = \max_{0 \leq t \leq 1} |f^{(r)}(t)|$.

The probability measure μ in the average case and probabilistic settings is the Wiener measure placed on the rth derivative. This problem has been studied in **NR 2.2:6** of Section 2.2 in Chapter 5, Section 2.1 of Chapter 7, and Section 7 of Chapter 8. We have

$$\text{comp}(\varepsilon) = c\,Z(\varepsilon)\,\big(1 + o(1)\big) \quad \text{as } \varepsilon \to 0$$

with $Z(\varepsilon)$ given in Table 2.1.

	Worst	Average	Probabilistic
Abs	$\alpha_1 \left(\dfrac{q}{\varepsilon}\right)^{1/r}$	$\alpha_2 \left(\dfrac{1}{\varepsilon}\right)^{1/(r+1)}$	$\alpha_2 \left(\dfrac{\sqrt{2\ln\delta^{-1}}}{\varepsilon}\right)^{1/(r+1)}$
Nor	$\alpha_1 \left(\dfrac{1}{\varepsilon}\right)^{1/r}$	$\beta \left(\dfrac{1}{\varepsilon}\right)^{1/(r+1)}$	$\alpha_2 \left(\dfrac{\sqrt{2\ln\delta^{-1}}}{\varepsilon\,\gamma(\varepsilon)}\right)^{1/(r+1)}$
Rel_1	$+\infty$	$+\infty$	$\alpha_3 \left(\dfrac{1}{\varepsilon\tan(\frac{1}{2}\delta\pi)}\right)^{1/(r+1)}$
Rel_2	$+\infty$	$\leq \alpha_4 \left(\dfrac{1}{\varepsilon}\right)^{2/(r+1)}$	$\alpha_3 \left(\dfrac{1}{\varepsilon\tan(\frac{1}{2}\delta\pi)}\right)^{1/(r+1)}$
Rel_3	$\alpha_1 \left(\dfrac{q}{\varepsilon\eta}\right)^{1/r}$	$\leq \alpha_5 \left(\dfrac{1}{\varepsilon\sqrt{\eta}}\right)^{1/(r+1)}$	$\leq \alpha_2 \left(\dfrac{\sqrt{2\ln\delta^{-1}}}{\varepsilon\eta}\right)^{1/(r+1)}$

Table 2.1

The asymptotic constants α_i are:

$$\alpha_1 = \frac{K_r^{1/r}}{2\pi}, \quad \alpha_2 = \left(\frac{|B_{2r+2}|}{(2r+2)!}\right)^{1/(2(r+1))},$$

$$\alpha_3 = \alpha_2\big((r+1)!\sqrt{2r+3}\,\big)^{1/(r+1)},$$

$$\alpha_4 = \alpha_2\big((r+1)!\sqrt{\pi(2r+3)/2}\,\big)^{1/(r+1)},$$

$$\alpha_5 = \alpha_2\big((r+1)!\sqrt{2(2r+3)/\pi}\,\big)^{1/(2(r+1))}.$$

The function γ is bounded in terms of a function h. Here, h is any function such that $h : \mathbb{R}_+ \to \mathbb{R}_+$ with $\lim_{\varepsilon\to 0} h(\varepsilon) = 0$. Then we have

$$h(\varepsilon) \leq \gamma(\varepsilon) \leq h(\varepsilon)^{-1} \quad \text{as } \varepsilon \to 0.$$

Here, K_i and B_i are the ith Favard and Bernoulli numbers, respectively.

We now comment on the successive rows of Table 2.1. We begin with the absolute error criterion. The worst case is studied in **NR 2.2:6** of Chapter 5. Observe that the worst case complexity is finite iff $r \geq 1$, and it goes to infinity with q. The smoothness parameter r determines how fast the ε-complexity goes to infinity as ε approaches zero. The average case is studied in Section 2.1 of Chapter 7. As we know, the average case is equivalent (modulo the finite q) to the worst case setting for the unit ball in the space $W_2^{r+1}(0,1)$. The probabilistic setting is studied in Chapter 8. We know that the probabilistic complexity is the same as the average case complexity with ε replaced roughly by $\varepsilon/\sqrt{2\ln \delta^{-1}}$.

We now turn to the normalized error criterion. For the worst case setting, the normalized error is equivalent to the absolute error on the unit ball, see Section 6.2 of Chapter 4. For the average case, the complexity under the normalized error is the same, modulo the asymptotic constant, as the complexity under the absolute error, see Theorem 6.2.1 (iii) of Chapter 6. In this case, we do not know the asymptotic constant, which is indicated by the presence of β. For the probabilistic setting, Corollary 6.2.1 of Chapter 8 relates the complexity under the normalized error to the complexity under the absolute error with ε replaced by $\varepsilon h(\varepsilon)$ for the upper bound and $\varepsilon h(\varepsilon)^{-1}$ for the lower bound, where h is an arbitrary function which takes positive values and goes to zero with ε. This yields bounds on the function γ. Since h can go to zero extremely slowly, $\varepsilon\gamma(\varepsilon)$ behaves essentially as ε, and therefore we have a fairly good estimate on the probabilistic complexity under the normalized error criterion.

For the relative error Rel_1, the worst and average case complexities are infinite. That is, it is impossible to compute ε-approximations for $\varepsilon < 1$ with finite cost. This follows from Section 6.1 of Chapter 4, where it is shown that the worst case radius of any information of finite cardinality is equal to 1, and from Theorem 6.1.1 of Chapter 6 since $\dim(S(F_1)) = 1$. For the probabilistic setting, the complexity is finite. Its form follows from Theorem 6.1.2 of Chapter 8, which states that the probabilistic complexity is essentially the same as the average case complexity for the absolute error criterion with ε replaced by $\varepsilon \tan(\delta\,\pi/2)\,\|S\|_\mu$. In our case, $\|S\|_\mu = \left((r+1)!\sqrt{2r+3}\right)^{-1}$.

For the relative error Rel_2, where the roles of $S(f)$ and $U(f)$ are interchanged, we still have the infinite worst case complexity, as explained in Remark 6.1.1 of Chapter 4. On the other hand, the average case complexity becomes finite and is at most equal to the average case complexity under the absolute error criterion for $\varepsilon^2\sqrt{2/\pi}\,\|S\|_\mu$, as explained in **NR 6.1:4** of Chapter 6. Note that we now know only an upper bound which is indicated by the sign $\leq$. For the probabilistic setting, the relative errors Rel_1 and Rel_2 are practically the same, see **NR 6.1:1** of Chapter 8.

Finally, we discuss the modified relative error criterion, Rel_3. From Section 6.1 of Chapter 4, we know that the worst case is equivalent to the absolute error with ε replaced by $\varepsilon\,\eta$. For the average case, we know from **NR 6.1:5** of Chapter 6 that the complexity is at most equal to the average case complexity under the absolute error with ε replaced by $\varepsilon \sqrt{\eta \|S\|_\mu} (\pi/2)^{1/4}$. We also know that for fixed η, the complexity is $\Theta\big(\varepsilon^{-1/(r+1)}\big)$. For the probabilistic setting, the complexity is bounded by the average case complexity with ε replaced by $\varepsilon\, \eta/\sqrt{2\ln\delta^{-1}}$, see **NR 6.1:2** of Chapter 8.

We now comment on the columns of Table 2.1. Observe that the exponent of the worst case complexity is $1/r$, whereas the exponent of the average case and probabilistic complexities is $1/(r+1)$. For small r, the difference between these exponents is crucial. For the worst case setting, r has to be at least 1 to make the complexity finite. For the average case and probabilistic settings, r can be equal to zero and the complexities are still finite. The change in the exponent is caused by the Gaussian measure which supplies the extra smoothness on the class of functions.

Observe how the probabilistic complexity depends on δ. The dependence on δ is quite weak for the absolute, normalized, and modified error criteria. For the relative error criteria Rel_1 and Rel_2, the dependence on δ is much stronger and is the same as the dependence on ε.

Information and algorithms for which upper bounds on the complexity are achieved may be found in the corresponding sections of the book. Roughly speaking, in most cases, optimal information consists of function values at equally spaced points plus a few odd derivatives at the endpoint 1. The integral of a natural spline which interpolates this information is close to an optimal algorithm. The degree of the natural spline as well as the cardinality of the information depend on the setting and the error criterion.

3. Integration of Smooth Periodic Functions

We now consider the integration problem for the Hilbert space $\widetilde{W_2^r}(0, 2\pi)$ of periodic r times differentiable functions which vanish at zero. The probability measure in the average case and probabilistic settings is given in Example 2.2.2 of Chapter 7. It is a Gaussian measure with mean zero and correlation operator with eigenvalues $\lambda_{2k-1} = \lambda_{2k} = k^{-2s}$ for some positive integer s. This problem has been studied in Section 2.3 of Chapter 5, Section 2.2 of Chapter 7, and Section 7 of Chapter 8. We have

$$\mathrm{comp}(\varepsilon) = c\, Z(\varepsilon)\, \big(1 + o(1)\big) \quad \text{as } \varepsilon \to 0$$

with $Z(\varepsilon)$ given in Table 3.1, whose asymptotic constants α_i and the function γ are given by

$$\alpha_1 = 2\pi \left(\frac{2\pi |B_{2r}|}{(2r)!}\right)^{1/(2r)}, \qquad \alpha_2 = 2\pi \left(\frac{2\pi |B_{2(r+s)}|}{(2(r+s))!}\right)^{1/(2(r+s))},$$

$$\alpha_3 = 1 \qquad \alpha_4 = \left(\frac{\pi}{2}\right)^{1/(2(r+s))}, \qquad \alpha_5 = \left(\frac{2}{\pi}\right)^{1/(4(r+s))} \sqrt{\alpha_2},$$

and for any function $h : \mathbb{R}_+ \to \mathbb{R}_+$ with $\lim_{\varepsilon \to 0} h(\varepsilon) = 0$, we have

$$h(\varepsilon) \le \gamma(\varepsilon) \le h(\varepsilon)^{-1} \quad \text{as } \varepsilon \to 0.$$

As before, B_i is the ith Bernoulli number.

	Worst	Average	Probabilistic
Abs	$\alpha_1 \left(\dfrac{q}{\varepsilon}\right)^{1/r}$	$\alpha_2 \left(\dfrac{1}{\varepsilon}\right)^{1/(r+s)}$	$\alpha_2 \left(\dfrac{\sqrt{2\ln \delta^{-1}}}{\varepsilon}\right)^{1/(r+s)}$
Nor	$\alpha_1 \left(\dfrac{1}{\varepsilon}\right)^{1/r}$	$\beta \left(\dfrac{1}{\varepsilon}\right)^{1/(r+s)}$	$\alpha_2 \left(\dfrac{\sqrt{2\ln \delta^{-1}}}{\varepsilon \gamma(\varepsilon)}\right)^{1/(r+s)}$
Rel_1	$+\infty$	$+\infty$	$\alpha_3 \left(\dfrac{1}{\varepsilon \tan(\frac{1}{2}\delta\pi)}\right)^{1/(r+s)}$
Rel_2	$+\infty$	$\le \alpha_4 \left(\dfrac{1}{\varepsilon}\right)^{2/(r+s)}$	$\alpha_3 \left(\dfrac{1}{\varepsilon \tan(\frac{1}{2}\delta\pi)}\right)^{1/(r+s)}$
Rel_3	$\alpha_1 \left(\dfrac{q}{\varepsilon\eta}\right)^{1/r}$	$\le \alpha_5 \left(\dfrac{1}{\varepsilon\sqrt{\eta}}\right)^{1/(r+s)}$	$\le \alpha_2 \left(\dfrac{\sqrt{2\ln \delta^{-1}}}{\varepsilon\eta}\right)^{1/(r+s)}$

Table 3.1

We now comment on Table 3.1. The derivation of formulas in Table 3.1 is analogous to Section 2. In this case,

$$\|S\|_\mu = (2\pi)^{r+s+0.5} \sqrt{|B_{2(r+s)}|/(2(r+s))!}.$$

Observe that the exponent of the worst case complexity is $1/r$, as in Section 2, whereas the exponent of the average case and probabilistic complexities is now $1/(r+s)$. The latter depends on s, and for large s, the average case or probabilistic complexity goes to infinity much more slowly than the worst case complexity as ε approaches zero. The value of s determines the eigenvalues of the correlation operator of the Gaussian measure. It corresponds to the extra smoothness imposed on the class of functions by the Gaussian measure. For $s = 1$, the average case and probabilistic complexities are, modulo the asymptotic constants, the same as in Section 2.

In all cases for which the complexity is at least asymptotically known, information consisting of function values at equally spaced points is almost optimal information, and the rectangle formula is an almost optimal algorithm. Observe, however, that under the relative error criterion Rel_2, the average error of the rectangle formula is infinite, as shown in **NR 6.1:4** of Chapter 6. The algorithm whose average error achieves the upper bound presented in Table 3.1 is of the form $\phi^*(y) = m(y) + \sigma/m(y)$, where $m(y)$ is the mean of the conditional measure, which is also the value of the rectangle algorithm, and σ is the variance of the conditional measure, see again **NR 6.1:4** of Chapter 6.

4. Approximation of Smooth Periodic Functions

We now turn to the approximation problem for the Hilbert space F_1 of multivariate functions studied in Sections 3.1 of Chapters 5 and 7, and Section 7 of Chapter 8. The space F_1 consists of functions of d variables that are r_j differentiable with respect to the jth variable and for which $\|\sum_{j=1}^{d} a_j \partial^{r_j} f/\partial x_j^{r_j}\| \leq 1$. Here, $\|\cdot\|$ denotes the $\mathcal{L}_2$ norm. As in the previous sections, let $\omega = \sum_{j=1}^{d} r_j^{-1}$. We assume that coefficients r_j and a_j satisfy (i) and (ii) of Section 3.1 of Chapter 5. These assumptions are needed to make the worst case complexity finite.

The Gaussian measure μ is as in Section 3.1 of Chapter 7. The eigenvalues of its correlation operator are given by $\beta_j = a^* j^{-v}$, where a^* is positive and $v > 1$. In this section, we set $q = 1$. To guarantee that the measure of the unit ball is almost one, we assume that a^* is small.

We recall that the class Λ consists now of all continuous linear functionals. The complexity is then given by

$$\text{comp}(\varepsilon) = c\, Z(\varepsilon)\, \big(1 + o(1)\big) \quad \text{as } \varepsilon \to 0$$

with $Z(\varepsilon)$ presented in Table 4.1. The exponent ω^* and the asymptotic constants α_i are given by

$$\omega^* = \frac{2\omega}{2 + (v-1)\omega}, \quad \alpha_1 = \alpha^\omega, \quad \alpha_2 = \left(\alpha\sqrt{\frac{a^*\,\omega}{2 + (v-1)\omega}}\right)^{\omega^*},$$

where the constant α is defined in Section 3.1 of Chapter 5. The function γ is bounded as follows. For any function $h : \mathbb{R}_+ \to \mathbb{R}_+$ with $\lim_{\varepsilon \to 0} h(\varepsilon) = 0$, we have

$$h(\varepsilon) \le \gamma(\varepsilon) \le h(\varepsilon)^{-1} \quad \text{as } \varepsilon \to 0.$$

We now comment on Table 4.1. The formulas of this table follow from the results presented in Section 3.1 of Chapter 5 for the worst case setting, in Section 3.1 of Chapter 7 for the average case setting, and in Section 7 of Chapter 8 for the probabilistic setting. Unlike the integration problems of Sections 2 and 3, the average case complexity under the relative error Rel_1 is now finite and, modulo the asymptotic constant, is the same as the average case complexity under the absolute or normalized error criteria. This follows from Theorem 6.1.2 of Chapter 6 since $\dim(S(F_1)) = +\infty$.

	Worst	Average	Probabilistic
Abs	$\alpha_1 \left(\dfrac{1}{\varepsilon} \right)^{\omega}$	$\alpha_2 \left(\dfrac{1}{\varepsilon} \right)^{\omega^*}$	$\alpha_2 \left(\dfrac{1}{\varepsilon} \right)^{\omega^*}$
Nor	$\alpha_1 \left(\dfrac{1}{\varepsilon} \right)^{\omega}$	$\beta \left(\dfrac{1}{\varepsilon} \right)^{\omega^*}$	$\alpha_2 \left(\dfrac{1}{\varepsilon \gamma(\varepsilon)} \right)^{\omega^*}$
Rel_1	$+\infty$	$\beta \left(\dfrac{1}{\varepsilon} \right)^{\omega^*}$	$\alpha_2 \left(\dfrac{1}{\varepsilon \gamma(\varepsilon)} \right)^{\omega^*}$
Rel_2	$+\infty$	$\beta \left(\dfrac{1}{\varepsilon} \right)^{\omega^*}$	$\alpha_2 \left(\dfrac{1}{\varepsilon \gamma(\varepsilon)} \right)^{\omega^*}$
Rel_3	$\alpha_1 \left(\dfrac{1}{\varepsilon \eta} \right)^{\omega}$	$\le \alpha_2 \left(\dfrac{1}{\varepsilon \eta} \right)^{\omega^*}$	$\le \alpha_2 \left(\dfrac{1}{\varepsilon \eta} \right)^{\omega^*}$

Table 4.1

For the relative error Rel_2, bounds on the average case complexity can be established similarly as for the relative error Rel_1. For the relative error Rel_3, we also know that for fixed η the complexity is $\Theta(\varepsilon^{-\omega^*})$. For the probabilistic setting, bounds for the absolute error criterion follow from Theorem 5.4.3 of Chapter 8. Similarly, bounds for the normalized and relative error Rel_1 follow from the relation to the probabilistic complexity under the absolute error criterion, as shown in Corollary 6.2.1 and **NR 6.2:1** of Chapter 8. As always, the relative error Rel_2 in the probabilistic setting is essentially the same as Rel_1. Finally, the probabilistic complexity under the relative error Rel_3 is at most equal to the probabilistic complexity under the absolute error with ε replaced by $\varepsilon \eta$.

We stress once more that the function h can go to zero extremely slowly. Therefore, $\varepsilon\gamma(\varepsilon)$ behaves roughly as ε and, without much loss of precision, one can ignore the influence of γ on the complexities.

We now comment on the exponents of the complexities. For the worst case setting, the exponent is $\omega = \sum_{j=1}^{d} r_j^{-1}$. Observe that for the same regularity in each direction, $r_j \equiv r$, we have $\omega = d/r$. In this case, the worst case complexity is exponential in dimension d. Thus, even for a modest ε but large d, the worst case complexity is so huge that the problem of multivariate function approximation is intractable.

For the average case and probabilistic complexities, the exponent is $\omega^* = \omega/(1 + (v-1)\omega/2)$. Obviously, $\omega^* < \omega$. This means, not surprisingly, that the average case and probabilistic complexities go to infinity more slowly than the worst case complexity as ε approaches zero. The behavior of the average case and probabilistic complexities depends, in particular, on v. The parameter v characterizes the eigenvalues of the correlation operator of the Gaussian measure μ. It corresponds to the extra smoothness imposed on the class of functions by the Gaussian measure. Observe that v can be chosen arbitrarily closely to 1. For v close to 1, this extra smoothness becomes less significant since ω^* is close to ω, and the behavior of all the complexities is more or less the same. In this case, for $r_j \equiv r$ and large d, the problem of multivariate function approximation becomes intractable also in the average case and probabilistic settings.

In all cases for which the complexity is at least asymptotically known, information consisting of inner products $\langle f, \zeta_j \rangle$, where ζ_j are eigenfunctions of the correlation operator of the *a priori* measure $\nu = \mu S^{-1}$ which correspond to the largest eigenvalues, is almost optimal information, and the truncated Fourier series is an almost optimal algorithm. The cardinality of the information depends on the particular setting and error criterion.

5. Approximation of Smooth Nonperiodic Functions

In this section we consider the approximation problem for the Banach space F_1 of multivariate functions studied in Section 3.3 of Chapter 5, Section 3.2 of Chapter 7, and Section 7 of Chapter 8. This is the space of functions of d variables which are r_j times continuously differentiable in the jth direction and for which the supremum norm of $D^{r_1,\ldots,r_d} f$ is finite, where $D^{r_1,\ldots,r_d}$ stands for the partial derivative operator. As in the previous sections, let

$$r_{\min} = \min\{r_j : 1 \le j \le d\},$$

and let k denote the number of r_j that are equal to $r_{\min}$.

The Gaussian measure μ is the classical Wiener measure placed on the partial derivatives, see Section 3.2 of Chapter 7. As in Section 4, the class Λ consists of all continuous linear functionals. The complexity is given by

$$\text{comp}(\varepsilon) = c\, Z(\varepsilon) \left(1 + o(1)\right) \quad \text{as } \varepsilon \to 0$$

with $Z(\varepsilon)$ presented in Table 5.1. The exponents p_i and the asymptotic constant α are given by

$$p_1 = \frac{1}{r_{\min}}, \quad p_2 = \frac{1}{r_{\min} + \frac{1}{2}}, \quad p_3 = \frac{(k-1)(r_{\min}+1)}{r_{\min} + \frac{1}{2}},$$

$$\alpha_1 = \left(\sqrt{\frac{\overline{\alpha}}{2r_{\min}+1}}\right)^{p_2} \left(\frac{1}{r_{\min}+\frac{1}{2}}\right)^{p_3},$$

where $\overline{\alpha}$ is defined in Section 3.2 of Chapter 7. The functions γ_i are bounded as follows,

$$1 \leq \gamma_1(\varepsilon) \leq \left(\ln\frac{1}{\varepsilon}\right)^{k-1},$$

and for any function $h : \mathbb{R}_+ \to \mathbb{R}_+$ with $\lim_{\varepsilon \to 0} h(\varepsilon) = 0$,

$$h(\varepsilon) \leq \gamma_2(\varepsilon) \leq h(\varepsilon)^{-1} \quad \text{as } \varepsilon \to 0.$$

	Worst	Average	Probabilistic
Abs	$\beta\gamma_1 \left(\dfrac{q}{\varepsilon}\right)^{p_1}$	$\alpha_1 \left(\dfrac{1}{\varepsilon}\right)^{p_2} \left(\ln\dfrac{1}{\varepsilon}\right)^{p_3}$	$\alpha_1 \left(\dfrac{1}{\varepsilon}\right)^{p_2} \left(\ln\dfrac{1}{\varepsilon}\right)^{p_3}$
Nor	$\beta\gamma_1 \left(\dfrac{1}{\varepsilon}\right)^{p_1}$	$\beta \left(\dfrac{1}{\varepsilon}\right)^{p_2} \left(\ln\dfrac{1}{\varepsilon}\right)^{p_3}$	$\alpha_1\gamma_2 \left(\dfrac{1}{\varepsilon}\right)^{p_2} \left(\ln\dfrac{1}{\varepsilon}\right)^{p_3}$
Rel$_1$	$+\infty$	$\beta \left(\dfrac{1}{\varepsilon}\right)^{p_2} \left(\ln\dfrac{1}{\varepsilon}\right)^{p_3}$	$\alpha_1\gamma_2 \left(\dfrac{1}{\varepsilon}\right)^{p_2} \left(\ln\dfrac{1}{\varepsilon}\right)^{p_3}$
Rel$_2$	$+\infty$	$\beta \left(\dfrac{1}{\varepsilon}\right)^{p_2} \left(\ln\dfrac{1}{\varepsilon}\right)^{p_3}$	$\alpha_1\gamma_2 \left(\dfrac{1}{\varepsilon}\right)^{p_2} \left(\ln\dfrac{1}{\varepsilon}\right)^{p_3}$
Rel$_3$	$\beta\gamma_1 \left(\dfrac{q}{\varepsilon\eta}\right)^{p_1}$	$\leq \alpha_1 \left(\dfrac{1}{\varepsilon\eta}\right)^{p_2} \left(\ln\dfrac{1}{\varepsilon\eta}\right)^{p_3}$	$\alpha_1 \left(\dfrac{1}{\varepsilon\eta}\right)^{p_2} \left(\ln\dfrac{1}{\varepsilon\eta}\right)^{p_3}$

Table 5.1

We comment on Table 5.1. Observe that the worst case complexity is now not known exactly. As explained in Section 3.3 of Chapter 5, the worst case complexity for the absolute error criterion is bounded from above by the corresponding complexity for the $\mathcal{L}_2$ norm and from below by the corresponding complexity for the one dimensional case. This yields bounds on the function γ_1. Since γ_1 can go to infinity rather slowly, we have fairly good estimates on the worst case complexity under the absolute error criterion as well as for the other error criteria. The rest of the formulas follow more or less directly from Section 3.2 of Chapter 7 and Section 7 of Chapter 8, as explained in Section 4.

We now comment on the exponents of the complexities. For the worst case setting, the exponent is $p_1 = 1/r_{\min}$. To make the worst case complexity finite, we have to assume that $r_{\min} \geq 1$, which means that the regularity of functions in each direction must be at least one. Nevertheless, it is important that the exponent is independent of the dimension d. The reason for that was explained in Section 3.2 of Chapter 5 and is based on the double role of the parameter d which not only denotes the number of variables but also determines the smoothness of functions.

For the average case and probabilistic settings, the exponent is determined by p_2 and p_3. Obviously, the parameter p_2 plays a much more important role since it is the exponent of $1/\varepsilon$. Note that the maximal value of p_2 is 2 and is achieved for $r_{\min} = 0$. Thus, even if functions are only continuous, the average case and probabilistic complexities are finite although the worst case complexity is infinite. Furthermore, the average case and probabilistic complexities go to infinity as ε approaches zero no faster than $(1/\varepsilon)^{2+a}$ for any positive a. On the other hand, if we assume that $r_{\min} \geq 1$, which makes the worst case complexity finite, then the average case and probabilistic complexities go to infinity no faster than $(1/\varepsilon)^{2/3+a}$ for any positive a.

The average case and probabilistic complexities also depend on the parameter p_3, which is an exponent of $\ln(1/\varepsilon)$. Its value is at most $2(d-1)$. Once more, this shows that the average case and probabilistic complexities depend weakly on the dimension d.

As in Section 4, information consisting of inner products with eigenfunctions of the correlation operator of the *a priori* measure ν and the truncated Fourier series are almost optimal information and algorithm. As always, the cardinality of information depends on the specific setting and error criterion.

Chapter 10

Asymptotic Setting

1. Introduction

In this chapter we analyze the asymptotic setting in which one considers a particular problem element and then uses a sequence of approximations for which the error goes to zero as fast as possible.

Asymptotically convergent algorithms are widely used in practice. Examples include algorithms such as Romberg and Bulirsch-Gregg-Stoer for integration as well as algorithms for the solution of ordinary or partial differential equations with meshsize tending to zero. This commonly used approach in numerical analysis motivates our study.

One might expect that the asymptotic setting would have some advantages over the worst case or average case settings. To illustrate this point, consider a simple integration example.

EXAMPLE 1.1. Suppose one approximates $S(f) = \int_0^1 f(t)\,dt$, where $f : [0,1] \to \mathbb{R}$ belongs to the set F of functions whose second derivative is continuous and bounded by a constant q on the interval $[0,1]$.

In the worst case setting, we know that for any information $N_n(f) = [f(t_1), \ldots, f(t_n)]$, $t_i \in [0,1]$, and any algorithm ϕ_n that uses N_n, the worst case error of (ϕ_n, N_n) satisfies

$$e^{\mathrm{wor}}(\phi_n, N_n) \geq \alpha_1 \frac{q}{n^2}$$

for some positive constant α_1 independent of n. Furthermore, there exist points t_i^* forming information N_n^* and an algorithm ϕ_n^* that uses N_n^* such that

$$e^{\mathrm{wor}}(\phi_n^*, N_n^*) = \Theta\left(\frac{q}{n^2}\right) \quad \text{as } n \to +\infty.$$

Note that the set F consists of smooth functions f such that $\|f''\| \le q$, with $\|\cdot\|$ denoting the sup norm. The existence of such a bound for a given f might be a reasonable assumption. However, finding the bound q might be very hard in practice. Note that if q is large (or even $q = +\infty$) then the worst case error of any algorithm is large (or even infinite). Thus, for the worst case setting the bound q is essential.

For the asymptotic setting we do not have to know the value of q, but merely that $\|f''\|$ is finite. Indeed, for a reasonable choice of points t_i and algorithm ϕ_n we have

$$S(f) - \phi_n(N_n(f)) = O\left(\frac{\|f''\|}{n^2}\right).$$

Since now f is fixed and n tends to infinity, we get convergence regardless of the magnitude of $\|f''\|$. Note, however, that although $\|f''\|$ does not affect the speed of convergence, it *does* affect the absolute error. If one wants to have an algorithm which enjoys a good speed of convergence and a small absolute error then a bound on $\|f''\|$ is once again necessary. Also the problem of termination, which is not addressed in this chapter, becomes much harder if the bound on $\|f''\|$ is not known.

In our example, the worst case error of any sequence of algorithms cannot go to zero faster than n^{-2}. One might hope that in the asymptotic setting it is possible to beat this bound. That is, one seeks a sequence of information $\overline{N} = \{N_n\}$ and a sequence of algorithms $\overline{\phi} = \{\phi_n\}$ such that $S(f) - \phi_n(N_n(f))$ goes to zero faster than does n^{-2} for each f from F. The reason for hoping this is as follows. The worst case error being of order n^{-2} means that for each n there exists a function f which depends on n, $f = f_n$, such that $f_n \in F$ and

$$|S(f)_n - \phi_n(N_n(f_n))| \simeq \frac{q}{n^2}. \tag{1}$$

If n is changed, the function f_n may also change. One may hope that there exists *no* function f from F for which (1) holds for all n (or for some subsequence of n). Since in the asymptotic setting f is fixed and n varies, it would explain why a better speed of convergence than n^{-2} might be possible. However, we prove that this is *not* the case. More precisely, from general results applied to this particular example, it follows that the set of functions f for which the speed of convergence is better than n^{-2} has empty interior (for any norm on F under which F becomes a Banach space). This holds for any sequence of information and any sequence of algorithms.

Consider now the same integration problem in the average case setting. Let F be equipped with the Wiener measure placed on the second derivatives of the functions, see Section 2 of Chapter 7. Then one can find points t_i, $i = 1, 2, \ldots, n$, forming the information N_n such that the average error of the μ-spline algorithm ϕ_n^s that uses N_n is of the form

$$e^{\text{avg}}(\phi_n^s, N_n) = \Theta(n^{-3}) \quad \text{as } n \to +\infty.$$

In the asymptotic setting it is natural to ask: Do there exist information $\{N_n\}$ and algorithms $\{\phi_n\}$ such that $S(f) - \phi_n(N_n(f))$ goes to zero faster than n^{-3} for all functions f from a set with a positive measure? One might hope that the measure of such a set is close to one.

However, this is impossible. From general results applied to this example, it follows that the set $\left\{ f \in F : \lim_{n\to\infty} |S(f) - \phi_n(N_n(f))| \, n^3 = 0 \right\}$ is of measure zero. This holds for any sequences $\{N_n\}$ and $\{\phi_n\}$.

Example 1.1 suggests that for the integration example not much can be gained in the asymptotic setting. We show in this chapter that this is the case for *linear* problems. For nonlinear problems the situation may be different, as explained in Section 3.

Our main interest in this chapter is to find an asymptotically optimal algorithm. We first motivate our definitions of asymptotically optimal algorithms by the following discussion.

Suppose we want to approximate $S(f)$ for f from F. Let $\overline{\phi} = \{\phi_n\}$ and $\overline{\phi^*} = \{\phi_n^*\}$ be two algorithms that use information $\overline{N} = \{N_n\}$ for approximating $S(f)$. Let $A(\overline{\phi}, \overline{\phi^*})$ denote the set of functions f for which the algorithm $\overline{\phi}$ converges to $S(f)$ with a better rate of convergence than the algorithm $\overline{\phi^*}$. That is,

$$A(\overline{\phi}, \overline{\phi^*}) = \left\{ f \in F : \lim_{n\to\infty} \frac{\|S(f) - \phi_n(N_n(f))\|}{\|S(f) - \phi_n^*(N_n(f))\|} = 0 \right\}. \tag{2}$$

One might attempt to define $\overline{\phi^*}$ as optimal if $\overline{\phi^*}$ *never* "loses" to $\overline{\phi}$. That is, $\overline{\phi^*}$ is optimal if $A(\overline{\phi}, \overline{\phi^*}) = \emptyset$, $\forall \overline{\phi}$. We show that such an algorithm $\overline{\phi^*}$ does not exist. Another attempt is to define $\overline{\phi^*}$ as optimal by requiring that $A(\overline{\phi}, \overline{\phi^*})$ is finite or perhaps countable for all $\overline{\phi}$. Unfortunately, this also does not work, as proven in **NR 1:1**. Thus, optimality of $\overline{\phi^*}$ must be defined differently.

In this chapter we analyze two definitions of optimality in the asymptotic setting. The first one is due to Trojan [83] and does not use a measure on the set F. The second definition, due to Wasilkowski and Woźniakowski [87], uses the fact that the set F is equipped with a probability measure. We stress that neither definition leads to unique optimal algorithms. However, the difference between optimal algorithms is insignificant as far as the rate of convergence is concerned. Indeed, let $h_n = \phi_{1,n} - \phi_{2,n}$ be the difference between two optimal algorithms $\{\phi_{1,n}\}$ and $\{\phi_{2,n}\}$. Then $\|h_n(N_n(f))\| \leq \|S(f) - \phi_{1,n}(N_n(f))\| + \|S(f) - \phi_{2,n}(N_n(f))\|$ goes to zero at least as fast as the errors of optimal algorithms.

We now discuss the two definitions of optimality and the results obtained. The first definition of optimality is as follows. An algorithm $\overline{\phi}^*$ is *optimal* if the set

$$\left\{ f \in F : \lim_{n \to \infty} \frac{\|S(f) - \phi_n(N_n(f))\|}{\delta_n \|S(f) - \phi_n^*(N_n(f))\|} = 0 \right\}$$

has empty interior for any $\overline{\phi}$ and any positive sequence $\{\delta_n\}$ converging to zero. We report Trojan's results for *linear* problems in Section 2 . We show that for a given sequence of information $\overline{N} = \{N_n\}$, the sequence $\{\phi_n^s\}$ of spline algorithms (and more generally "ρ-spline" algorithms) that uses $\{N_n\}$ is optimal. The speed of convergence of the sequence of spline algorithms is characterized by the sequence of radii $\{r(N_n, f)\}$ of information. Here $r(N_n, f)$ stands for the radius of the set of elements $S\tilde{f}$ which are indistinguishable from $S(f)$, $N_n(\tilde{f}) = N_n(f)$, and for which $\|\tilde{f} - f\| \leq 1$. More precisely, we show that for any sequence of algorithms $\{\phi_n\}$, the set of elements f for which $S(f) - \phi_n(N_n(f))$ goes to zero faster than $\delta_n \, r(N_n, f)$ has empty interior. This holds for any sequence $\{\delta_n\}$ of positive numbers converging to zero. The presence of the sequence $\{\delta_n\}$ is necessary. We also show that the sequence $\{r(N_n, f)\}$ is a sharp bound on the speed of convergence. That is, the errors $\{\|S(f) - \phi_n^*(N_n(f))\|\}$ of the spline algorithm go to zero at least as fast as $\{r(N_n, f)\}$.

EXAMPLE 1.2.   As an application of this result, consider the example where S is the identity operator and $F_1 = G$ is an infinite dimensional Hilbert space with an orthonormal system ζ_i, $\langle \zeta_i, \zeta_j \rangle = \delta_{i,j}$. That is, we approximate f knowing n continuous linear (possibly adaptive) functionals evaluated at f. From Chapter 4 it easily follows that $r(N_n, f) = 1$, $\forall n$, $\forall f \in F_1$. This means that it is impossible to approximate f in the worst case setting with error less than 1 no matter how many evaluations are performed and what algorithm is used. However, in the asymptotic setting we *can* approximate f. Indeed, it is enough to compute $N_n(f) = [\langle f, \zeta_1 \rangle, \langle f, \zeta_2 \rangle, \dots, \langle f, \zeta_n \rangle]$ and take the algorithm $\phi_n(N_n(f)) = \sum_{i=1}^n \langle f, \zeta_i \rangle \, \zeta_i$. Then $\phi_n(N_n(f))$ converges to f as n goes to $+\infty$, and this holds for all f from F_1^*. The result mentioned above implies that although we can approximate f, the speed of convergence is arbitrarily slow. More precisely, for *any* sequence $\{\delta_n\}$ converging to zero, the set of f's for which $\lim_{n\to\infty} \|f - \phi_n(N_n(f))\|/\delta_n = 0$ has empty interior. That is, for a dense subset of F_1, $\phi_n(N_n(f))$ goes to f no faster than δ_n goes to zero. This holds for any choice of $\{N_n\}$ and $\{\phi_n\}$.

We then turn to the problem of finding information $\overline{N} = \{N_n\}$ for which the speed of convergence is maximal. The solution is obtained in terms of the worst case optimal information. Namely, as in Chapter 4, let $r(n, \Lambda)$ denote the minimal radius of nonadaptive information of cardinality n with linear functionals from the class Λ and for F being the unit ball of F_1. We prove, roughly speaking, that the best possible convergence cannot be faster than the convergence of the sequence $\{r(n, \Lambda)\}$. We also present two general situations for which it is possible to find a sequence of information $\{N_n^*\}$ with convergence given by $\{r(n, \Lambda)\}$. We show that the sequence of information operators which enjoy the best convergence are *nonadaptive*. Thus, although we permit adaptive information, adaption does *not* help for linear problems in the asymptotic setting. This agrees with the same result obtained in Chapter 4 for the worst case setting.

These results exhibit a close relation between the asymptotic and the worst case settings. Neglecting some details (such as the sequence δ_n) the best speed of convergence is achieved by information operators and algorithms which are optimal in the worst case setting. The equivalence between the asymptotic and worst case settings has some good effects. Since the theory of the worst case setting is quite well established, the equivalence enables one to use worst case results to analyze the asymptotic setting.

Note that we may decide to vary n by a subsequence $\{n_k\}$ rather than using every possible value of n, $n = 1, 2, \ldots$. Although the results of this chapter are stated in terms of the behavior of the sequence $\{\|S(f) - \phi_n(N_n(f))\|\}_{n=1}^{\infty}$, completely analogous results hold for the subsequence $\{\|S(f) - \phi_{n_k}(N_{n_k}(f))\|\}_{k=1}^{\infty}$. In this case $r(N_n, f)$ and $r(n, \Lambda)$ should be replaced by $r(N_{n_k}, f)$ and $r(n_k, \Lambda)$, respectively. We choose $n_k = k$ only for convenience and sake of exposition.

Section 2 deals with linear problems. In Section 3 we report the results of Kacewicz [87a] who generalizes Trojan's analysis to nonlinear solution operators and nonlinear information. For some nonlinear problems, such as the solution of ordinary differential equations, the asymptotic setting is still related to the worst case setting. On the other hand, for the problem of solving scalar nonlinear equations the asymptotic setting leads to different results than those in the worst case setting, as shown by Sikorski and

Trojan [87].

In Section 4 we turn to the second definition of optimality in the asymptotic setting. We assume that the set F is equipped with a probability measure μ. Optimality of the algorithm $\overline{\phi^*}$ is then defined by zero measure of the set $A(\overline{\phi}, \overline{\phi^*})$ for any algorithm $\overline{\phi}$, see (2). Thus, $\overline{\phi^*}$ is optimal if it "loses" to any algorithm $\overline{\phi}$ only on a set of measure zero.

We show that for linear problems the asymptotic setting under this definition of optimality is related to the average case setting. More precisely, let F_1 be a separable Banach space over the real field equipped with a Gaussian measure μ with mean zero and correlation operator C_μ. Let G be a separable Hilbert space over the real field. The solution operator $S : F_1 \to G$ is a continuous linear operator, and the class Λ of permissible information operations is a subset of F_1^*. The optimality of the algorithm $\overline{\phi^*} = \{\phi_n^*\}$ that uses information $\overline{N} = \{N_n\}$ means that

$$\mu\left(\left\{f \in F_1 : \lim_{n \to \infty} \frac{\|S(f) - \phi_n(N_n(f))\|}{\|S(f) - \phi_n^*(N_n(f))\|} = 0\right\}\right) = 0$$

for any algorithm $\overline{\phi} = \{\phi_n\}$. The first problem studied in Section 4 is to find an optimal algorithm for given information $\overline{N} = \{N_n\}$. Let $\overline{\phi^*} = \{\phi_n^s\}$ be the sequence of μ-spline algorithms, where ϕ_n^s uses the information N_n and is defined as in Section 5.4 of Chapter 6. We prove that $\overline{\phi^*}$ is optimal. This is very desirable from a practical point of view. The algorithm $\overline{\phi^*}$ which has the best possible rate of convergence also has the minimal average case error at each step.

REMARK 1.1. The concept of optimality in the asymptotic setting can be weakened. Instead of collecting elements f for which $\overline{\phi}$ converges with a better rate than $\overline{\phi^*}$, let us collect elements f for which $\overline{\phi}$ converges "faster" than $\overline{\phi^*}$. That is, for $q \in [0, 1)$ let

$$B_q(\overline{\phi}, \overline{\phi^*}) = \left\{f \in F_1 : \overline{\lim_{n \to \infty}} \frac{\|S(f) - \phi_n(N_n(f))\|}{\|S(f) - \phi_n^*(N_n(f))\|} \leq q\right\}. \tag{3}$$

Note that for $q = 0$, (3) coincides with the set in (2). Then, one might define $\overline{\phi^*}$ as optimal if $\mu(B_q(\overline{\phi}, \overline{\phi^*}))$ is close to zero for any $\overline{\phi}$. For small q, we prove that the algorithm which is optimal in the sense of (2) is also optimal in the sense of (3). For q close to one we do not know which algorithm is optimal.

The second problem studied in Section 4 is to characterize the rate of convergence of the μ-spline algorithms. Once more, we solve this by showing a relation to the average case setting. This relation is exhibited in terms of local average radii. We show that the sequence of local average radii fully characterizes the rate of convergence of the μ-spline algorithms.

The final problem studied in Section 4 is to find information $\overline{N}^* = \{N_n^*\}$ for which the rate of convergence of local radii is best possible, or equivalently, for which the rate of convergence of the optimal algorithm is best possible. It turns out that $\overline{N}^*$ is given by that sequence of *nonadaptive* information which is optimal in the average case setting.

Thus, although adaptive information and nonlinear algorithms are permitted, the optimal information is *nonadaptive* and the optimal algorithm is *linear*.

These results exhibit a close relation between the average case setting and the asymptotic setting for linear problems. As before, this is desirable from a practical point of view. Algorithms and information which minimize the average case error also yield the best rate of convergence.

Notes and Remarks

NR 1:1 (Wasilkowski and Woźniakowski [87]) We now show that optimality in the asymptotic setting cannot be defined by requiring that the set $A(\overline{\phi}, \overline{\phi}^*)$ is countable. Assume that F_1 is an infinite dimensional Banach space, G is a normed linear space, and S is a one-to-one operator (not necessarily linear). Let $\overline{\phi} = \{\phi_n\}$ be an algorithm that uses information $\overline{N} = \{N_n\}$. Here we assume that

$$N_n(f) = [L_1(f), L_2(f; y_1), \ldots, L_n(f; y_1, \ldots, y_{n-1})],$$

where $y_1 = L_1(f)$, $y_i = L_i(f; y_1, y_2, \ldots, y_{i-1})$ and $L_i(\cdot; y_1, \ldots, y_{i-1})$ is a continuous linear functional. We also assume that $L_1 \not\equiv 0$. Define

$$A(\overline{\phi}) = \{f \in F_1 : \phi_n(N_n(f)) = S(f), \ \forall n \geq k(f)\}$$

as the set of elements for which the algorithm $\overline{\phi}$ solves the problem exactly for sufficiently large n.

LEMMA. *The set $A(\overline{\phi})$ has empty interior for every algorithm $\overline{\phi}$.*

PROOF: Assume, on the contrary, that $A(\overline{\phi})$ contains a ball $B(f_1, r) = \{f \in F_1 : \|f - f_1\| \leq r\}$ for $r > 0$. We construct a Cauchy sequence $\{f_j\}$ from the ball $B(f_1, r)$. Suppose inductively that f_j is defined. Since $f_j \in B(f_1, r) \subset A(\overline{\phi})$, then there exists $k_j = k(f_j)$ such that $\phi_n(N_n(f_j)) = S(f)$ for $n \geq k_j$. Take $h_j \in F_1$ such that $L_1(h_j) = L_2(h_j; y_1) = \cdots = L_{k_j}(h_j; y_1, \ldots, y_{k_j-1}) = 0$ and $\|h_j\| = r/3^j$. Here $y_i = L_i(f_j; y_1, \ldots, y_{i-1})$. Observe that such an element h_j exists since $\dim F_1 = +\infty$. Define $f_{j+1} = f_j + h_j$. Then $f_{j+1} = f_1 + \sum_{i=1}^{j} h_j$ and $\|f_{j+1} - f_1\| \leq r \sum_{i=1}^{j} 3^{-i} < r/2$. Thus, $f_{j+1} \in B(f_1, r)$ and $N_{k_j}(f_{j+1}) = N_{k_j}(f_j)$. Hence, $\phi_{k_j}(N_{k_j}(f_{j+1})) = \phi_{k_j}(N_{k_j}(f_j)) = S(f_j) \neq S(f_{j+1})$ since $f_{j+1} \neq f_j$ and S is one-to-one. Thus, $k_{j+1} = k(f_{j+1}) \geq k_j + 1$.

Define $f = \lim_{j \to \infty} f_j = f_1 + \sum_{j=1}^{\infty} h_j$. The element f exists since $\{f_j\}$ is a Cauchy sequence and F_1 is a Banach space. Note that $f \in B(f_1, r)$ and

$$\|f - f_j\| = \left\| \sum_{i=j}^{\infty} h_i \right\| \geq \|h_j\| - \sum_{i=j+1}^{\infty} \|h_i\| = \frac{r}{3^j 2} > 0.$$

Thus, $f \neq f_j$, $\forall j$. Continuity of functionals which form $\overline{N}$ yields that

$$N_{k_j}(f) = N_{k_j}\left(f_1 + \sum_{i=1}^{j-1} h_i\right) = N_{k_j}(f_j), \quad \forall j.$$

Thus, we have

$$\phi_{k_j}(N_{k_j}(f)) = \phi_{k_j}(N_{k_j}(f_j)) = S(f_j) \neq S(f).$$

Since k_j goes to infinity with j, this proves that $f \notin A(\overline{\phi})$. This is a contradiction which completes the proof. ∎

REMARK. In fact, the proof of the Lemma supplies a slightly stronger result. Namely, it yields that for every $f \in A(\overline{\phi})$ and for every $r > 0$, there exists an element h such that $\|h\| \leq r$, $f + h \notin A(\overline{\phi})$, and additionally $L_1(h) = 0$.

Based on the Lemma and Remark, we prove the result mentioned in the introduction. Let $\overline{\phi} = \{\phi_n\}$ and $\overline{\phi^*} = \{\phi^*\}$ be two algorithms that use information $\overline{N} = \{N_n\}$. Let $a_n(f) = \|S(f) - \phi_n(N_n(f))\|$ and $b_n(f) = \|S(f) - \phi_n^*(N_n(f))\|$. Then

$$A(\overline{\phi}, \overline{\phi^*}) = \{f \in F_1 : \lim_{n \to \infty} a_n(f)/b_n(f) = 0\}.$$

We need to consider the case $a_n(f) = 0$ for all $n \geq n_0$ for some n_0. Then, if $b_n(f) = 0$ for all $n \geq n_1$ for some n_1, the two algorithms $\overline{\phi}$ and $\overline{\phi^*}$ solve the problem exactly and none of them is superior. It is therefore reasonable to set in this case $\lim_{n \to \infty} a_n(f)/b_n(f) = 1$. On the other hand, if $\{b_n(f)\}$ contains a nonzero subsequence then the algorithm $\overline{\phi}$ is superior to the algorithm $\overline{\phi^*}$ and it is reasonable to set in this case $\lim_{n \to \infty} a_n(f)/b_n(f) = 0$. Having this convention in mind, we are ready to prove

THEOREM. *For every algorithm $\overline{\phi^*}$ there exists an algorithm $\overline{\phi}$ such that $A(\overline{\phi}, \overline{\phi^*})$ is uncountable.*

PROOF: Choose an element $f_1 \in F_1$ such that $L_1(f_1) = 1$. For $y \in \mathbb{R}$, define

$$g_y = \begin{cases} y f_1 & \text{if } y f_1 \notin A(\overline{\phi^*}), \\ y f_1 + h & \text{if } y f_1 \in A(\overline{\phi^*}). \end{cases}$$

Here h is chosen such that $L_1(h) = 0$ and $y f_1 + h \notin A(\overline{\phi^*})$. Such an element h exists due to the Remark.

We now define the algorithm $\overline{\phi} = \{\phi_n\}$ by

$$\phi_n(N_n(f)) = S g_{N_1(f)}.$$

Note that $\phi_n(N_n(g_y)) = S g_y$, $\forall n \geq 1$ $\forall y \in \mathbb{R}$. Since $g_y \notin A(\overline{\phi^*})$, there exists a subsequence $\{n_i\}$ such that

$$\phi_{n_i}^*(N_{n_i}(g_y)) \neq S g_y.$$

This means that $g_y \in A(\overline{\phi}, \overline{\phi^*})$, $\forall y \in \mathbb{R}$. Note that g_y varies with y, which means that $A(\overline{\phi}, \overline{\phi^*})$ contains at least as many elements as $\mathbb{R}$. This completes the proof. ∎

Consider now the set $B(\overline{\phi}, \overline{\phi^*}) = \{f \in F_1 : \lim_{n \to \infty} a_n(f)/(\delta_n b_n(f)) = 0\}$ for any positive sequence $\{\delta_n\}$. Then the same proof as above yields that for every algorithm

$\overline{\phi^*}$ there exists an algorithm $\overline{\phi}$ such that the set $B(\overline{\phi}, \overline{\phi^*})$ is uncountable. As we shall see in the next section, it is possible to find an algorithm $\overline{\phi^*}$ such that the set $B(\overline{\phi}, \overline{\phi^*})$ has empty interior for any algorithm $\overline{\phi}$ and any positive sequence $\{\delta_n\}$ converging to zero.

2. Asymptotic and Worst Case Settings: Linear Problems

In this section we exhibit relations between the asymptotic and worst case settings for linear problems. The same issue is studied for nonlinear problems in Section 3.

Let F_1 be a Banach space and let G be a normed linear space. Consider a continuous linear operator S, $S : F_1 \to G$. Our problem is to approximate $S(f)$ for all $f \in F_1$. The information about f is provided by adaptive information $\overline{N}$ of the form,

$$\overline{N}(f) = [L_1(f), L_2(f; y_1), \dots, L_n(f; y_1, \dots, y_{n-1}), \dots],$$

where $y_1 = L_1(f)$, $y_n = L_n(f; y_1, \dots, y_{n-1})$, and $L_n(\cdot; y_1, \dots, y_{n-1}) \in F_1^*$. Thus, the information operator $\overline{N}$ in the asymptotic setting consists of a sequence of continuous linear functionals chosen adaptively or nonadaptively. Let

$$N_n(f) = [L_1(f), L_2(f; y_1), \dots, L_n(f; y_1, \dots, y_{n-1})]$$

denote the first n functionals of $\overline{N}$. By the *algorithm* $\overline{\phi} = \{\phi_n\}$ that uses information $\overline{N} = \{N_n\}$ we mean a sequence of mappings such that

$$\phi_n : N_n(F_1) \subset \mathbf{R}^n \to G.$$

Observe that $\|S(f) - \phi_n(N_n(f))\|$ is the nth error of the algorithm $\overline{\phi}$ that uses the information $\overline{N}$ for the element f.

Notes and Remarks

NR 2:1 Section 2 is based on unpublished results of Trojan [83].

2.1. Optimal Algorithms

In the asymptotic setting we wish to find $\overline{\phi}$ and $\overline{N}$ such that for any f from F_1, the error $\|S(f) - \phi_n(N_n(f))\|$ goes to zero as fast as possible when n goes to infinity. We show that, roughly speaking, the errors cannot go to zero faster than the radii $r(N_n, f)$ of information which are defined as follows. Let

$$U_n(f) = \{S(\tilde{f}) : N_n(\tilde{f}) = N_n(f), \|\tilde{f} - f\| \leq 1\}$$

be the set of $S(\tilde{f})$ for all elements $\tilde{f}$ which are indistinguishable from f under the information N_n and which are "close" to f. This can be rewritten as

$$U_n(f)$$
$$= \left\{ S(\tilde{f}) : L_1(\tilde{f} - f) = \cdots = L_n(\tilde{f} - f; y_1, \ldots, y_{n-1}) = 0, \|\tilde{f} - f\| \le 1 \right\}.$$

Let $r(N_n, f)$ be the radius of the set $U_n(f)$. From Section 5 of Chapter 4, we know that $r(N_n, f) \in [d(N_n, f)/2, d(N_n, f)]$, where $d(N_n, f)$ is the diameter of the set $U_n(f)$,

$$d(N_n, f) = \sup \left\{ \|S(\tilde{f}_1) - S(\tilde{f}_2)\| : S(\tilde{f}_1), S(\tilde{f}_2) \in U_n(f) \right\}$$
$$= \sup \left\{ \|S(h)\| : L_1(h) = \cdots = L_n(h; y_1, \ldots, y_{n-1}) = 0, \|h\| \le 2 \right\}. \tag{1}$$

As a matter of fact, we have $r(N_n, f) = d(N_n, f)/2$ since $U_n(f)$ is symmetric with respect to $S(f)$.

We are ready to prove the main theorem of this section.

THEOREM 2.1.1. *For any algorithm $\overline{\phi}$ that uses $\overline{N}$ and any positive sequence $\{\delta_n\}$ converging to zero, the set*

$$A_1 = \left\{ f \in F_1 : \lim_{n \to \infty} \frac{\|S(f) - \phi_n(N_n(f))\|}{\delta_n \, r(N_n, f)} = 0 \right\}$$

has empty interior, i.e., $\overline{F_1 - A_1} = F_1$. (We use the convention $0/0 = 1$.)

PROOF: Suppose, on the contrary, that for some $\overline{N}$, $\overline{\phi}$, and $\{\delta_n\}$, there exists a closed ball B with center w and radius r, $r > 0$, such that

$$\|S(f) - \phi_n(N_n(f))\| = o(\delta_n \, r(N_n, f)), \quad \forall f \in B. \tag{2}$$

We inductively construct a sequence $\{f_k\}$, $f_k \in B$, such that $f^* = \lim_k f_k$ belongs to B and (2) does not hold for f^*.

Let $f_1 = w$ be the center of B. Choose $a \in (0.9, 1)$. Suppose that $f_1, f_2, \ldots, f_k$ are constructed, $f_i \in B$. To construct f_{k+1} we proceed as follows. From (2), there exists an index n_k such that

$$\|S(f_k) - \phi_{n_k}(N_{n_k}(f_k))\| \le \tfrac{1}{3} \delta_{n_k} r(N_{n_k}, f_k), \tag{3}$$

where $\delta_{n_1} \le ar/3$ for $k = 1$, and $\delta_{n_k} \le \delta_{n_{k-1}}/3$ for $k \ge 2$. Using (1), we can find h_k, $\|h_k\| \le 2$, such that

$$L_1(h_k) = L_2(h_k; y_{1,k}) = \cdots = L_{n_k}(h_k; y_{1,k}, \ldots, y_{n_k-1,k}) = 0,$$

where $y_{i,k} = L_i(f_k; y_{1,k}, \ldots, y_{i-1,k})$, and

$$a\, d(N_{n_k}, f_k) \leq \|Sh_k\| \leq d(N_{n_k}, f_k). \tag{4}$$

Define

$$f_{k+1} = f_k + a^{-1} \delta_{n_k} h_k = w + a^{-1} \sum_{i=1}^{k} \delta_{n_i} h_i. \tag{5}$$

Note that $\delta_{n_i} \leq 3^{-(i-1)} \delta_{n_1} \leq a\, r\, 3^{-i}$. From this we have $\|f_{k+1} - w\| \leq 2\, r \sum_{i=1}^{k} 3^{-i} \leq r$. Thus, $f_{k+1} \in B$ and the construction of $\{f_k\}$ is completed.

Observe that (5) yields

$$N_{n_k}(f_k) = N_{n_k}(f_{k+j}), \quad \forall j \geq 1, \tag{6}$$

i.e., the n_kth information on f_{k+j} is the same as on f_k. This implies

$$d(N_{n_k}, f_k) = d(N_{n_k}, f_{k+j}) \geq d(N_{n_{k+j}}, f_{k+j}), \quad \forall j \geq 1. \tag{7}$$

Let

$$f^* = \lim_{k \to \infty} f_k = w + a^{-1} \sum_{i=1}^{\infty} \delta_{n_i} h_i.$$

Observe that f^* exists. This follows from the fact that F_1 is complete and the series $a^{-1} \sum_{i=1}^{\infty} \delta_{n_i} h_i$ is convergent since $\|a^{-1} \sum_{i=1}^{\infty} \delta_{n_i} h_i\| \leq 2a^{-1} \sum_{i=1}^{\infty} \delta_{n_i} \leq r$. This also proves that $f^* \in B$. Since S is continuous, $S(f^*) = \lim_{k \to \infty} S(f_k)$. Note that

$$\|S(f^*) - S(f_k)\| = a^{-1} \left\| \sum_{i=k}^{\infty} \delta_{n_i} S(h_i) \right\|$$

$$\geq a^{-1} \left(\delta_{n_k} \|S(h_k)\| - \sum_{i=k+1}^{\infty} \delta_{n_i} \|S(h_i)\| \right).$$

From (4) and (7) we get

$$\|S(f^*) - S(f_k)\| \geq \delta_{n_k} d(N_{n_k}, f_k) - a^{-1} \sum_{i=k+1}^{\infty} \delta_{n_i} d(N_{n_i}, f_i)$$

$$\geq \left(\delta_{n_k} - a^{-1} \sum_{i=k+1}^{\infty} \delta_{n_i} \right) d(N_{n_k}, f_k).$$

Since $\delta_{n_i} \leq 3^{k-i} \delta_{n_k}$ and $a \geq 0.9$, we get

$$\|S(f^*) - S(f_k)\| \geq \left(1 - (2a)^{-1}\right) \delta_{n_k} d(N_{n_k}, f_k) \geq \tfrac{4}{9} \delta_{n_k} d(N_{n_k}, f_k). \quad (8)$$

From (6) and continuity of the functionals forming N_{n_k}, we have

$$N_{n_k}(f_k) = N_{n_k}(f^*),$$

and consequently

$$d(N_{n_k}, f_k) = d(N_{n_k}, f^*) \quad \text{and} \quad \phi_{n_k}\big(N_{n_k}(f_k)\big) = \phi_{n_k}\big(N_{n_k}(f^*)\big).$$

From this, (8), and (3) we get

$$\|S(f^*) - \phi_{n_k}(N_{n_k}(f^*))\| \geq \|S(f^*) - S(f_k)\| - \|S(f_k) - \phi_{n_k}(N_{n_k}(f_k))\|$$
$$\geq \tfrac{4}{9} \delta_{n_k} d(N_{n_k}, f_k) - \tfrac{1}{3} \delta_{n_k} r(N_{n_k}, f_k) \geq \tfrac{5}{9} \delta_{n_k} r(N_{n_k}, f^*).$$

Hence,

$$\varlimsup_{n \to \infty} \frac{\|S(f^*) - \phi_n(N_n(f^*))\|}{\delta_n r(N_n, f^*)} \geq \tfrac{5}{9},$$

which contradicts (2) for $f = f^*$. This completes the proof. ∎

Theorem 2.1.1 gives a lower bound on the error of an arbitrary algorithm $\overline{\phi}$. Roughly speaking, the sequence $\{\|S(f) - \phi_n(N_n(f))\|\}$ cannot converge faster than $\{\delta_n r(N_n, f)\}$ for a dense subset of F_1. We stress that this holds for any positive sequence $\{\delta_n\}$ converging to zero. Thus, one can choose an arbitrarily slowly convergent sequence as $\{\delta_n\}$. We show later that the sequence $\{\delta_n\}$ in Theorem 2.1.1 cannot be omitted.

We now present an algorithm $\overline{\phi}$ that uses $\overline{N}$ for which $\{r(N_n, f)\}$ is an upper bound on the error. Choose a number $\rho > 1$. For every $f \in F_1$, choose an element $\sigma_n = \sigma(N_n(f))$ such that

$$N_n(\sigma_n) = N_n(f), \text{ and}$$
$$\|\sigma_n\| \leq \rho \inf \big\{\|g\| : g \in F_1, N_n(g) = N_n(f)\big\}. \quad (9)$$

Define the ρ-spline algorithm $\overline{\phi}^* = \{\phi_n^*\}$ by

$$\phi_n^*(N_n(f)) = S\sigma_n\big(N_n(f)\big). \quad (10)$$

The element σ_n interpolates $N_n(f)$ and has small norm. Observe that such an element exists since $\rho > 1$. (If $\rho = 1$ in (9), the element σ_n might not exist.) Recall from Chapter 4 that if σ_n exists for $\rho = 1$ then σ_n is the spline interpolating $N_n(f)$ and $\overline{\phi^*}$ is a *spline* algorithm. The analysis of existence and properties of spline algorithms may be found in Section 5.7 of Chapter 4.

THEOREM 2.1.2. *The error of a ρ-spline algorithm $\overline{\phi^*}$ that uses $\overline{N}$ satisfies the estimate*

$$\|S(f) - \phi_n^* (N_n(f))\| \leq (\rho + 1) \|f\| \, r(N_n, f) \tag{11}$$

for any $f \in F_1$ and any $n \geq 1$.

PROOF: Take $f \in F_1$ and $n = 1, 2, \ldots$. Without loss of generality we can assume that $f \neq \sigma_n = \sigma(N_n(f))$ since otherwise $S(f) = \phi_n^*(N_n(f))$. Then

$$\|S(f) - \phi_n^* (N_n(f))\| = \|S(f - \sigma_n)\| = \|f - \sigma_n\| \, \|S(h)\|,$$

where $h = (f - \sigma_n)/\|f - \sigma_n\|$. Then $\|h\| \leq 1$ and due to (9) we have

$$L_1(h) = L_2(h; y_1) = \cdots = L_n(h; y_1, \ldots, y_{n-1}) = 0$$

with $y_i = L_i(f; y_1, \ldots, y_{i-1})$. From (1) and the relation between radius and diameter, we get $\|Sh\| \leq r(N_n, f)$. Next, observe that (9) implies

$$\|f - \sigma_n\| \leq \|f\| + \|\sigma_n\| \leq (1 + \rho) \|f\|.$$

Thus, $\|S(f) - \phi_n^* (N_n(f))\| \leq (\rho + 1) \|f\| \, r(N_n, f)$, as claimed. ∎

Theorems 2.1.1 and 2.1.2 yield

COROLLARY 2.1.1. *The ρ-spline algorithm $\overline{\phi^*}$ that uses $\overline{N}$ is optimal in the asymptotic setting, i.e., for any algorithm $\overline{\phi}$ that uses $\overline{N}$ and any positive sequence $\{\delta_n\}$ converging to zero, the set*

$$A_2 = \left\{ f \in F_1 : \lim_{n \to \infty} \frac{\|S(f) - \phi_n(N_n(f))\|}{\delta_n \|S(f) - \phi_n^* (N_n(f))\|} = 0 \right\}$$

has empty interior.

PROOF: Note that for $f = 0$ we have $S(f) - \phi_n^*(N_n(f)) = 0$, due to (11). Thus, $0 \notin A_2$. For $f \neq 0$ we have from (11),

$$\frac{\|S(f) - \phi_n(N_n(f))\|}{\delta_n \|S(f) - \phi_n^* (N_n(f))\|} \geq \frac{1}{(\rho + 1)\|f\|} \frac{\|S(f) - \phi_n(N_n(f))\|}{\delta_n \, r(N_n, f)}.$$

Hence, $f \in A_2$ implies that $f \in A_1$, where A_1 is the set defined in Theorem 2.1.1. Thus, $A_2 \subseteq A_1$ and Corollary 2.1.1 follows from Theorem 2.1.1. ∎

We now present two examples showing that the estimates of Theorem 2.1.1 and 2.1.2 are best possible.

EXAMPLE 2.1.1. We show that the sequence $\{\delta_n\}$ in Theorem 2.1.1 is needed. (Observe that Example 1.2 also indicates the need for the sequence of $\{\delta_n\}$.) Let $F_1 = F_2$ be an infinite dimensional Hilbert space with an orthonormal system ζ_i, $\langle \zeta_i, \zeta_j \rangle = \delta_{i,j}$. Let $S(f) = \sum_{i=1}^{\infty} i^{-p} \langle f, \zeta_i \rangle \zeta_i$ for some nonnegative p. Let $\overline{N}(f) = [\langle f, \zeta_1 \rangle, \langle f, \zeta_2 \rangle, \ldots, \langle f, \zeta_n \rangle, \ldots]$ be nonadaptive information. Then

$$r(N_n, f) = \sup \left\{ \left(\sum_{i=n+1}^{\infty} i^{-2p} \langle h, \zeta_i \rangle^2 \right)^{1/2} : \sum_{i=1}^{\infty} \langle h, \zeta_i \rangle^2 \leq 1 \right\} = (n+1)^{-p}.$$

It is easy to check that $\overline{\phi^*} = \{\phi_n\}$ with $\phi_n^*(N_n(f)) = \sum_{i=1}^{n} i^{-p} \langle f, \zeta_i \rangle$ is the unique spline algorithm. The error of $\overline{\phi^*}$ is estimated by

$$\|S(f) - \phi_n^*(N_n(f))\| = \left\| \sum_{i=n+1}^{\infty} i^{-p} \langle f, \zeta_i \rangle \zeta_i \right\| \leq (n+1)^{-p} \sum_{i=n+1}^{\infty} \langle f, \zeta_i \rangle^2.$$

Since $\sum_{i=n+1}^{\infty} \langle f, \zeta_i \rangle^2$ goes to zero as n tends to infinity, we have

$$\lim_{n \to \infty} \frac{\|S(f) - \phi_n^*(N_n(f))\|}{r(N_n, f)} = 0, \quad \forall f \in F_1.$$

This proves that the sequence $\{\delta_n\}$ in Theorem 2.1.1 cannot be omitted. Indeed, if one sets $\delta_n \equiv 1$ in Theorem 2.1.1 then the set A_1 can be equal to the whole space.

EXAMPLE 2.1.2. We show that the dependence on $(\rho+1)\|f\|$ in Theorem 2.1.2 is essential. Let $F_1 = G = \ell_{\infty}$ be the space of $f = [f_1, f_2, \ldots]$ such that $\|f\| = \sup_i |f_i| < +\infty$. Let $p \geq 0$. We then set $S(f) = [1^{-p} f_1, 2^{-p} f_2, \ldots, n^{-p} f_n, \ldots]$, and $\overline{N}(f) = [f_1, f_2, \ldots, f_n, \ldots]$. Then we have $r(N_n, f) = (n+1)^{-p}$. For any $\rho \geq 1$, the algorithm $\overline{\phi^*} = \{\phi_n\}$ given by

$$\phi_n^*(N_n(f)) = [1^{-p} f_1, 2^{-p} f_2, \ldots, n^{-p} f_n, (n+1)^{-p} \rho a, 0, \ldots],$$

with $a = \max_{1 \leq i \leq n} |f_i|$, is a ρ-spline algorithm. For any $f \in F_1$, we have

$$\|S(f) - \phi_n^*(N_n(f))\|$$
$$= \left\| [0, \ldots, 0, (n+1)^{-p}(f_{n+1} - \rho a), (n+2)^{-p} f_{n+2}, \ldots] \right\|$$
$$\leq (\rho+1)\|f\| r(N_n, f),$$

while for $f = [-1, -1, \ldots]$, we have

$$\|S(f) - \phi_n^* \left(N_n(f)\right)\| = (\rho + 1) \|f\| \, r(N_n, f).$$

This proves that (11) of Theorem 2.1.2 is sharp.

2.2. Optimal Information

In this section we study the optimal choice of linear functionals which form information $\overline{N}$. An optimal choice of functionals means that the speed of convergence of the ρ-spline algorithms is maximized.

Let Λ be a permissible class of linear continuous functionals L, $L : F_1 \to \mathbb{R}$. Let $\overline{N}$ be *adaptive* information

$$\overline{N}(f) = [L_1(f), L_2(f; y_1), \ldots, L_n(f; y_1, \ldots, y_{n-1}), \ldots],$$

where $y_i = y_i(f) = L_i(f; y_1, \ldots, y_{i-1})$. We say that $\overline{N}$ *is from* Λ iff $L_i(\cdot; y_1, \ldots, y_{i-1}) \in \Lambda$ for every $y_i \in \mathbb{R}$ and $i = 1, 2, \ldots$.

As in Section 5.3 of Chapter 4, let Λ_n denote the class of permissible *nonadaptive* information N of cardinality n, $N(f) = [L_1(f), \ldots, L_n(f)]$ with $L_i \in \Lambda$ for $i = 1, 2, \ldots, n$. Let $r(N)$ be the worst case radius of N for the class F being the unit ball of F_1. As we know from Chapter 4, the radius of information $r(N) \in [d(N)/2, d(N)]$, where the diameter of information N is given by $d(N) = \sup \{\|Sh\| : L_i(h) = 0, \|h\| \le 2, i \le n\}$. Recall that the *nth minimal radius* of nonadaptive information in the class Λ is given by

$$r(n, \Lambda) = \inf_{N \in \Lambda} r(N).$$

From Theorem 2.1.1 we easily obtain

THEOREM 2.2.1. *Let $\overline{N}$ be arbitrary adaptive information from Λ. For any algorithm $\overline{\phi}$ that uses $\overline{N}$ and any positive sequence $\{\delta_n\}$ converging to zero, the set*

$$A_3 = \left\{ f \in F_1 : \lim_{n \to \infty} \frac{\|S(f) - \phi_n(N_n(f))\|}{\delta_n \, r(n, \Lambda)} = 0 \right\}$$

has empty interior.

PROOF: Since $L_i(\cdot; y_1, \ldots, y_{i-1}) \in \Lambda$, we have that $r(N_n, f) \ge r(n, \Lambda)/2$ for every $f \in F_1$. Thus,

$$\frac{\|S(f) - \phi_n(N_n(f))\|}{\delta_n \, r(n, \Lambda)} \ge \frac{\|S(f) - \phi_n(N_n(f))\|}{2\delta_n \, r(N_n, f)}.$$

Hence, $f \in A_3$ implies that $f \in A_1$, and therefore $A_3 \subset A_1$. Theorem 2.2.1 then follows from Theorem 2.1.1. ∎

Theorem 2.2.1 states, roughly speaking, that the best possible convergence cannot be faster than the sequence of nth minimal radii $\{r(n, \Lambda)\}$. We now give a condition under which the convergence $\{r(n, \Lambda)\}$ is achieved. Let

$$N_n^{\mathrm{non}}(f) = [L_{1,n}(f), L_{2,n}(f), \ldots, L_{n,n}(f)], \quad L_{i,n} \in \Lambda, \tag{1}$$

be a sequence of nearly optimal nonadaptive information, i.e., there exists a constant α_1, $\alpha_1 \geq 1$, independent of n such that

$$r(N_n^{\mathrm{non}}) \leq \alpha_1 \, r(n, \Lambda), \quad \forall n.$$

Define the nonadaptive information

$$\overline{N^*}(f) = [N_1^{\mathrm{non}}(f), N_2^{\mathrm{non}}(f), N_4^{\mathrm{non}}(f), \ldots, N_{2^k}^{\mathrm{non}}(f), \ldots].$$

This means that $\overline{N^*}$ consists of the following functionals from the class Λ,

$$\overline{N^*}(f) = [L_{1,1}(f), L_{1,2}(f), L_{2,2}(f), \ldots, L_{1,2^k}(f), \ldots, L_{2^k,2^k}(f), \ldots].$$

From Theorem 2.1.2 we easily obtain

LEMMA 2.2.1. *The error of a ρ-spline algorithm $\overline{\phi^*}$ that uses $\overline{N^*}$ satisfies the estimate*

$$\|S(f) - \phi_n^*(N_n^*(f))\| \leq \alpha_1 \, (\rho + 1) \, \|f\| \, r(\lceil (n+1)/4 \rceil, \Lambda),$$

for any $f \in F_1$ and any $n \geq 1$.

PROOF: From Theorem 2.1.2 we have

$$\|S(f) - \phi_n^*(N_n^*(f))\| \leq (\rho + 1) \, \|f\| \, r(N_n^*, f).$$

Note that $r(N_n^*, f) \leq r(N_n^*)$, where N_n^* consists of the first n functionals of $\overline{N^*}$. For $k = \lfloor \log_2(n+1) \rfloor - 1$, we have $\sum_{i=0}^{k} 2^i \leq n$, which means that $N_{2^k}^{\mathrm{non}}$ is a part of N_n^*. Thus, $r(N_n^*, f) \leq r(N_{2^k}^{\mathrm{non}})$. Since $2^k \geq \lceil (n+1)/4 \rceil$, we get

$$r(N_n^*, f) \leq \alpha_1 \, r(2^k, \Lambda) \leq \alpha_1 \, r(\lceil (n+1)/4 \rceil, \Lambda).$$

This completes the proof. ∎

We are ready to prove optimality of information $\overline{N^*}$ under the assumption that $r(n, \Lambda)$ does not go to zero too quickly.

THEOREM 2.2.2. *Assume that*

$$r\big(\lceil (n+1)/4\rceil, \Lambda\big) = \Theta\big(r(n, \Lambda)\big) \quad \text{as } n \to +\infty. \tag{2}$$

Then the nonadaptive information $\overline{N}^*$ and a ρ-spline algorithm $\overline{\phi}^*$ that uses $\overline{N}^*$ are optimal, i.e., for arbitrary adaptive information $\overline{N}$ from Λ, an arbitrary algorithm $\overline{\phi}$ that uses $\overline{N}$, and an arbitrary positive sequence $\{\delta_n\}$ converging to zero, the set

$$A_4 = \left\{ f \in F_1 : \lim_{n \to \infty} \frac{\|S(f) - \phi_n(N_n(f))\|}{\delta_n \|S(f) - \phi_n^*(N_n^*(f))\|} = 0 \right\} \tag{3}$$

has empty interior.

PROOF: From (2), $r\big(\lfloor (n+1)/4\rfloor, \Lambda\big) \le \alpha_2\, r(n, \Lambda)$ for some $\alpha_2 \ge 1$. Then for $f \ne 0$, Lemma 2.2.1 yields

$$\frac{\|S(f) - \phi_n(N_n(f))\|}{\delta_n \|S(f) - \phi_n^*(N_n^*(f))\|} \ge \frac{1}{(\rho+1)\,\alpha_1\,\alpha_2\,\|f\|} \frac{\|S(f) - \phi_n(N_n(f))\|}{\delta_n\, r(n, \Lambda)}.$$

Then $f \in A_4$ implies that $f \in A_3$, and so $A_4 \subset A_3$. Hence, Theorem 2.2.2 follows from Theorem 2.2.1. ∎

We comment on the assumption (2). It holds, for instance, if $r(n, \Lambda) = \Theta(n^{-r})$ for some $r \ge 0$. As we know from Chapter 5, $r(n, \Lambda) = \Theta(n^{-r})$ for many problems of practical interest. On the other hand, (2) is not satisfied if $r(n, \Lambda)$ goes to zero exponentially fast, i.e., $r(n, \Lambda) = \Theta(q^{n^p})$ with $q < 1$ and $p > 0$.

We now exhibit information which is optimal under a a different assumption than (2). In (1), we indicate that the functionals $L_{i,n}$ forming N_n^{non} may depend on n. For some problems, $L_{i,n}$ does *not* depend on n, i.e., the $(n+1)$st information N_{n+1}^{non} consists of the nth information N_n^{non} and one additional functional L_{n+1},

$$N_{n+1}^{\mathrm{non}}(f) = [N_n^{\mathrm{non}}(f), L_{n+1}(f)], \quad n = 1, 2, \dots. \tag{4}$$

We stress that (4) holds if F_1 and G are separable Hilbert spaces and Λ is the class of all linear continuous functionals. Then $L_n(f) = \langle f, \zeta_n \rangle$, where ζ_n is an orthonormalized eigenelement corresponding to the nth largest eigenvalue of S^*S, see Section 5.3 of Chapter 4.

Define the *nonadaptive* information

$$\overline{N}^{**}(f) = [L_1(f), L_2(f), \dots, L_n(f), \dots].$$

Since $r(N_n^{**}, f) \le r(N_n^{\mathrm{non}}) \le \alpha_1\, r(n, \Lambda)$, we have

COROLLARY 2.2.1. *The error of the ρ-spline algorithm $\overline{\phi^{**}}$ that uses $\overline{N^{**}}$ satisfies the estimate*

$$\|S(f) - \phi^{**}(N_n^{**}(f))\| \leq \alpha_1 (\rho + 1) \|f\| r(n, \Lambda).$$

From this we have the following theorem corresponding to Theorem 2.2.2.

THEOREM 2.2.3. *Assume that (4) holds. Then the nonadaptive information $\overline{N^{**}}$ and a ρ-spline algorithm $\overline{\phi^{**}}$ that uses $\overline{N^{**}}$ are optimal, i.e., (3) holds with $\overline{N^*}$ and $\overline{\phi^*}$ replaced by $\overline{N^{**}}$ and $\overline{\phi^{**}}$, respectively.*

We stress that the optimal information $\overline{N^*}$ and $\overline{N^{**}}$ are *nonadaptive* even though we permit the use of *adaptive* information. Thus, if (2) or (4) holds, then in the asymptotic setting *adaption* does not help for linear problems. We recall that the same result holds for worst and average case settings. We stress that for some *nonlinear* problems S, adaption does help significantly in the worst or asymptotic setting, see Chapter 5 and Section 3 of this chapter.

Notes and Remarks

NR 2.2:1 (Trojan [83]) So far, we have shown relations between the asymptotic and the worst case settings for linear problems defined with the identity restriction operator $T = I$. In Chapter 4, we study the worst case setting also for arbitrary linear restriction operators T, i.e., for subsets F of the form

$$F = \{f \in F_1 : \|Tf\| \leq 1\},$$

where $T : F_1 \rightarrow G$ is a linear surjection and G is a linear normed space.

Let $N_n(f) = [L_1(f), L_2(f; y_1), \ldots, L_n(f; y_1, \ldots, y_{n-1})]$ be adaptive information. As always, $y_i = L_i(f; y_1, \ldots, y_{i-1})$. Let $r(N_n, T, f)$ (and $d(N_n, T, f)$) denote the radius (and the diameter) of the set $\{S(\tilde{f}) : N_n(\tilde{f}) = N_n(f), \|T(\tilde{f} - f)\| \leq 1\}$. It is natural to ask about the relations between the sequence $\{r(N_n, T, f)\}$ and the sequence $\{r(N_n, f)\}$ studied in Section 2. We have

THEOREM. *Let F_1 and G be Banach spaces and let $T : F_1 \rightarrow G$ be a continuous linear bijection. Then there exist positive numbers a_1, a_2 such that*

$$a_1 r(N_n, f) \leq r(N_n, T, f) \leq a_2 r(N_n, f)$$

for any $f \in F$ and for any adaptive information operator N_n.

PROOF: From the open mapping theorem, the operator T^{-1} is continuous and therefore

$$\|T^{-1}\|^{-1} \|f\| \leq \|Tf\| \leq \|T\| \|f\|, \quad \forall f \in F_1.$$

Let $\alpha_2 = \|T^{-1}\|$. Take an arbitrary h from F_1 such that $\|Th\| \leq 2$. Then $\|h\| \leq 2\alpha_2$. From the formulas for the radii and diameters, we have

$$
\begin{aligned}
2 r(N_n, T, f) &= d(N_n, T, f) \\
&\leq \sup \{\alpha_2 \|S(h/\alpha_2)\| : \\
&\quad L_1(h/\alpha_2) = \cdots = L_n(h/\alpha_2; y_1, \ldots, y_{n-1}) = 0, \|h/\alpha_2\| \leq 2\} \\
&= \alpha_2 d(N_n, I, f) = 2\alpha_2 r(N_n, f).
\end{aligned}
$$

This proves the upper bound with $a_2 = 2\|T^{-1}\|$.

To prove the lower bound, let $a_1 = 1/(\|T\|)$. Take h from F_1 such that $\|h\| \leq 1$. Then $\|Th\| \leq 1/a_1$. We have

$$
\begin{aligned}
2a_1\, r(N_n, f) &= a_1\, d(N_n, I, f) \\
&= \sup\left\{ \|S(a_1 h)\| : L_1(h) = \cdots = L_n(h; y_1, \ldots, y_{n-1}) = 0,\ \|h\| \leq 2 \right\} \\
&\leq \sup\big\{ \|(Sa_1 h)\| : \\
&\qquad L_1(a_1 h) = \cdots = L_n(a_1 h; y_1, \ldots, y_{n-1}) = 0,\ \|T(a_1 h)\| \leq 2 \big\} \\
&= 2\, r(N_n, T, f),
\end{aligned}
$$

which completes the proof. ∎

We comment on the assumptions of the theorem. We assume that T is one-to-one. This is done only for simplicity. One can formulate an analogous theorem assuming that $\ker N_n \cap \ker T \subset \ker S$ (which is necessary for the radius of information to be finite) instead of assuming that T is one-to-one. The assumptions on continuity of T and completeness of F_1 and G are essential.

The essence of the theorem is that the operator T does not change the behavior of the sequence $\{r(N_n, T, f)\}$. This is why $T = I$ is chosen in the asymptotic setting of Section 2.

Let ϕ_n be an arbitrary algorithm that uses the information N_n. Let $e(\phi_n, N_n, T, f) = \sup\{\|S(\tilde{f}) - \phi_n(N_n(f))\| : N_n(\tilde{f}) = N_n(f) \text{ and } \|T\tilde{f}\| \leq 1\}$ be the worst case local error. Then we have from the theorem,

$$
e(\phi_n, N_n, T, f) \geq a_1\, r(N_n, f), \quad \forall f \in F.
$$

This means that $a_1 r(N_n, f)$ is a lower bound on the local error of any algorithm in the worst case setting. This should be compared to Theorem 2.1.1, which states that $\delta_n\, r(N_n, f)$ is a lower bound on the error of any algorithm in the asymptotic setting.

Let ϕ_n^* be a ρ-spline algorithm that uses N_n, see Section 2.1. Then

$$
e(\phi_n^*, N_n, T, f) \leq (\rho + 1)\, r(N_n, T, f) \leq (\rho + 1)\, a_2\, r(N_n, f), \quad \forall f \in F.
$$

This means that a multiple of $r(N_n, f)$ is an upper bound on the local error of any ρ-spline algorithm in the worst case setting. This should be compared to Theorem 2.1.2, which states that a multiple of $r(N_n, f)$ is also an upper bound on the error of any ρ-spline algorithm in the asymptotic setting. The same correspondence between the worst case and asymptotic settings may be obtained for optimal information.

This shows that (neglecting some unimportant details, such as the sequence $\{\delta_n\}$) the worst case and asymptotic settings do not differ for linear problems with an arbitrary restriction operator T.

2.3. Continuous Algorithms

Theorem 2.2.1 states that the sequence of errors $\{\|S(f) - \phi_n(N_n(f))\|\}$ can tend to zero faster than the sequence $\{\delta_n\, r(n, \Lambda)\}$ only on a set A_3 of empty interior. This result can be strengthened for the class of continuous algorithms. An algorithm $\overline{\phi}$ that uses $\overline{N}$ is called *continuous* if all the mappings $\phi_n(N_n(\cdot))$ are continuous. This holds, for instance, if $\overline{N}$ is nonadaptive and ϕ_n are linear mappings.

We recall some concepts of topological character, see for instance Rudin [74]. A subset A of F_1 is said to be *nowhere dense* if its closure $\overline{A}$ has empty interior. The set A is of the *first category* in F_1 if it is a countable union of nowhere dense sets. Since F_1 is complete, Baire's category theorem says that a set of the first category has empty interior.

We are ready to state a stronger version of Theorem 2.2.1.

THEOREM 2.3.1. *Let $\overline{N}$ be arbitrary information from Λ. For any continuous algorithm $\overline{\phi}$ that uses $\overline{N}$ and any positive sequence $\{\delta_n\}$ converging to zero, the set*

$$A_3 = \left\{ f \in F_1 : \lim_{n \to \infty} \frac{\|S(f) - \phi_n(N_n(f))\|}{\delta_n \, r(n, \Lambda)} = 0 \right\}$$

is of the first category.

PROOF: Note that if $r(n_0, \Lambda) = 0$ for some n_0, then $r(n, \Lambda) = 0$ for $n \geq n_0$, and the set A_3 is empty. Thus, without loss of generality, we can assume that $r(n, \Lambda) > 0$, $\forall n \geq 1$.

Define $B_j = \{ f \in F_1 : \|S(f) - \phi_m(N_m(f))\| \leq \delta_m \, r(m, \Lambda), \; \forall m \geq j \}$. Let $B = \bigcup_{j=1}^{\infty} B_j$. Obviously, $A_3 \subset B$. Therefore, it suffices to show that B_j is nowhere dense, i.e., $\operatorname{int} \overline{B}_j = \emptyset$. Since $\|S(\cdot) - \phi_m(N_m(\cdot))\|$ is continuous for any m, B_j is closed, i.e., $B_j = \overline{B}_j$. We now show that $\operatorname{int} B_j = \emptyset$. Take an arbitrary $f \in B_j$. We shall construct a sequence $\{f_k\}$ such that $f_k \notin B_j$ and $\lim_{k \to \infty} f_k = f$. This will imply that $\operatorname{int} B_j = \emptyset$.
Define

$$V_n = \{ h \in F_1 : L_1(h) = \cdots = L_n(h, y_1, \ldots, y_{n-1}) = 0, \|h\| \leq 4\delta_n \},$$

where $y_i = L_i(f; y_1, \ldots, y_{i-1})$. Note that

$$\sup_{h \in V_n} \|S(h)\| = 2\delta_n \, d(N_n, f). \tag{1}$$

Take $k \geq 1$. Let $n = n(k) \geq j$ be such that $\delta_n \leq 1/k$. Since $f \in B_j$, we have

$$\|S(f) - \phi_n(N_n(f))\| \leq \delta_n \, r(n, \Lambda). \tag{2}$$

Due to (1), it is possible to find h_k from V_n such that

$$\|S(h_k)\| > \delta_n \, d(N_n, f) = 2\delta_n \, r(n, \Lambda). \tag{3}$$

Define $f_k = f + h_k$. Since $h_k \in V_n$, we have $N_n(f_k) = N_n(f)$ and $\phi_n(N_n(f_k)) = \phi_n(N_n(f))$. This, (2), and (3) yield

$$\|S(f_k) - \phi_n(N_n(f_k))\| \geq \|Sh_k\| - \|S(f) - \phi_n(N_n(f))\|$$
$$> 2\,\delta_n\, r(n, \Lambda) - \delta_n\, r(n, \Lambda) = \delta_n\, r(n, \Lambda).$$

Thus, $f_k \notin B_j$. Since $\|h_k\| \leq 6/k$, $\lim_{k \to \infty} f_k = f$, which completes the proof. ∎

3. Asymptotic and Worst Case Settings: Nonlinear Problems

In this section we exhibit relations between the asymptotic and worst case settings for nonlinear problems. That is, we assume that F_1 is a Banach space and G is a normed linear space. The solution operator S, $S : F \to G$, is continuous but in general *nonlinear*. Here, F is a closed subset of F_1. The information about f is provided by, in general, *nonlinear* information $\overline{N}$,

$$\overline{N}(f) = [L_1(f), L_2(f), \ldots, L_n(f), \ldots],$$

where $L_i : F \to \mathbb{R}$ is a nonlinear functional. By N_n we denote the information consisting of the first n functionals of $\overline{N}$, $N_n(f) = [L_1(f), \ldots, L_n(f)]$. Throughout this section we assume that $\overline{N}$ is *smooth* in the following sense:

$$\{\tilde{f} \in F : N_n(\tilde{f}) = N_n(f)\} \quad \text{is closed,} \quad \forall f \in F, \ \forall n = 1, 2 \ldots . \quad (1)$$

Note that adaptive $\overline{N}$ consisting of continuous linear functionals satisfies (1). An algorithm $\overline{\phi}$ that uses $\overline{N}$ is defined as in the previous section.

Notes and Remarks

NR 3:1 All the results of Section 3, except Example 3.3.3, are due to Kacewicz [87a].

3.1. Optimal Algorithms

As before, we wish to find $\overline{\phi}$ such that for any f from F the error $\|S(f) - \phi_n(N_n(f))\|$ goes to zero as fast as possible with n going to infinity. As in the linear case, we show that the best speed of convergence is characterized by how fast

the radii $r(N_n, f)$ tend to zero. As in Section 2.1, $r(N_n, f)$ is the radius of the set $U_n(f)$,

$$U_n(f) = \{S(\tilde{f}) : \tilde{f} \in F, \ N_n(\tilde{f}) = N_n(f), \ \|\tilde{f} - f\| \leq 1\}.$$

Obviously, $r(N_n, f) \in [d(N_n, f)/2, d(N_n, f)]$, where $d(N_n, f)$ is the diameter of $U_n(f)$,

$$d(N_n, f) = \sup \{\|S(\tilde{f}_1) - S(\tilde{f}_2)\| : S(\tilde{f}_1), S(\tilde{f}_2) \in U_n(f)\}.$$

THEOREM 3.1.1. *Suppose that there exists an increasing continuous function $h^* : [0, 1] \to [0, 1]$, $h^*(0) = 0$, such that for any $f \in F$ there exist a positive constant $Q(f)$ and an integer $m(f)$ satisfying*

$$\sup\{\|S(\tilde{f}) - S(f)\| : \tilde{f} \in F, \; \|\tilde{f} - f\| \le q, \; N_n(\tilde{f}) = N_n(f)\} \tag{2}$$
$$\ge h^*(q) \, Q(f) \, d(N_n, f), \qquad \forall q \in [0, 1], \forall n \ge m(f).$$

Then, for any algorithm $\overline{\phi}$ that uses $\overline{N}$ and any positive sequence $\{\delta_n\}$ converging to zero, the set

$$A_1 = \left\{ f \in F : \lim_{n \to \infty} \frac{\|S(f) - \phi_n(N_n(f))\|}{\delta_n \, r(N_n, f)} = 0 \right\}$$

has empty interior in F, i.e., $\overline{F - A_1} = F$.

PROOF: Without loss of generality assume that $r(N_n, f) > 0$, $\forall n$. As in the proof of Theorem 2.1.1, suppose, on the contrary, that for some $\overline{N}, \overline{\phi}$, and $\{\delta_n\}$, there exists a closed ball B in F with center w and radius r, $r \in (0, 1]$, $B = \{f \in F : \|f - w\| \le r\}$, such that

$$\|S(f) - \phi_n(N_n(f))\| = o(\delta_n \, r(N_n, f)), \quad \forall f \in B. \tag{3}$$

We inductively construct a sequence $\{f_k\}$, $f_k \in B$, such that $f^* = \lim_k f_k$ belongs to B and (3) does not hold for f^*.

For large n, choose $\rho_n \in (0, 1]$ such that $\delta_n = (h^*(\rho_n))^2$. Note that $\lim_n \rho_n = 0$. Let $f_0 = w$ be the center of B. Since $f_0 \in A_1$, $\|S(f_0) - \phi_n(N_n(f_0))\|/((h^*(\rho_n))^2 \, d(N_n, f_0))$ tends to zero as n goes to infinity. Continuity of S implies that there exists $r_0 > 0$ such that $\|S(f) - S(f_0)\| \le 1/3$ whenever $\|f - f_0\| \le r_0$. Take an integer $n_0 \ge m(f_0)$ satisfying $\|S(f_0) - \phi_{n_0}(N_{n_0}(f_0))\| \le (h^*(\rho_{n_0}))^2 \, d(N_{n_0}, f_0)/5$, $\rho_{n_0} \le \min\{r_0, r/3\}$, and $h^*(\rho_{n_0}) \le Q(f_0)$. The assumption (2) implies that there exists $f_1 \in B$ such that $\|f_1 - f_0\| \le \rho_{n_0}$, $N_{n_0}(f_1) = N_{n_0}(f_0)$, and

$$\|S(f_1) - S(f_0)\| \ge \tfrac{1}{2} h^*(\rho_{n_0}) \, Q(f_0) \, d(N_{n_0}, f_0)$$
$$\ge \tfrac{1}{2} (h^*(\rho_{n_0}))^2 \, d(N_{n_0}, f_0) > 0.$$

Suppose that $f_0, f_1, \ldots, f_k \in B$ and $n_0 < n_1 < \cdots < n_{k-1}$ are constructed such that

$$\|f_{i+1} - f_i\| \le (r/3)^{i+1}, \quad i = 0, 1, \ldots, k-1,$$
$$\|S(f_k) - S(f_{k-1})\| \ge \tfrac{1}{2} (h^*(\rho_{n_{k-1}}))^2 \, d(N_{n_{k-1}}, f_{k-1}) > 0.$$

To construct f_{k+1}, we proceed as follows. Choose $r_k \in (0,1]$ such that $\|f - f_k\| \le r_k$ implies $\|S(f) - S(f_k)\| \le \|S(f_k) - S(f_{k-1})\|/3$. Choose $n_k \ge \max\{m(f_k), n_{k-1} + 1\}$ such that

$$\|S(f_k) - \phi_{n_k}(N_{n_k}(f_k))\| \le (h^*(\rho_{n_k}))^2 d(N_{n_k}, f_k)/5,$$
$$\rho_{n_k} \le \min\left\{r_k, r\|f_k - f_{k-1}\|/3\right\}, \quad \text{and}$$
$$h^*(\rho_{n_k}) \le Q(f_k).$$

Due to (2), there exists $f_{k+1} \in B$ such that $\|f_{k+1} - f_k\| \le \rho_{n_k}$, $N_{n_k}(f_{k+1}) = N_{n_k}(f_k)$, and

$$\|S(f_{k+1}) - S(f_k)\| \ge \tfrac{1}{2}\left(h^*(\rho_{n_k})\right)^2 d(N_{n_k}, f_k) > 0.$$

As in the proof of Theorem 2.1.1, one can check that $\{f_k\}$ is a Cauchy sequence, and hence $\lim_{k \to \infty} f_k = f^* \in B$. Thus,

$$\lim_{n \to \infty} \frac{\|S(f^*) - \phi_n(N_n(f^*))\|}{(h^*(\rho_n))^2 \, d(N_n, f^*)} = 0. \tag{4}$$

It is easy to verify that $N_{n_k}(f^*) = N_{n_k}(f_k)$ and $\|S(f_{k+1}) - S(f_k)\| \le \|S(f_k) - S(f_{k-1})\|/3$ for all k. Furthermore,

$$\|S(f_{k+p}) - S(f_k)\| \ge \|S(f_{k+1}) - S(f_k)\| - \sum_{i=2}^{p} \|S(f_{k+i}) - S(f_{k+i-1})\|$$

$$\ge \left(1 - \sum_{i=2}^{p} 3^{-(i-1)}\right)\|S(f_{k+1}) - S(f_k)\|.$$

Continuity of S with p tending to infinity yields

$$\|S(f^*) - S(f_k)\| \ge \tfrac{1}{2}\|S(f_{k+1}) - S(f_k)\|.$$

From this we conclude

$$\begin{aligned}
\|S(f^*) &- \phi_{n_k}(N_{n_k}(f^*))\| \\
&\ge \|S(f^*) - S(f_k)\| - \|S(f_k) - \phi_{n_k}(N_{n_k}(f^*))\| \\
&\ge \tfrac{1}{2}\|S(f_{k+1}) - S(f_k)\| - \|S(f_k) - \phi_{n_k}(N_{n_k}(f_k))\| \\
&\ge \tfrac{1}{20}h^*(\rho_{n_k})^2 \, d(N_{n_k}, f_k).
\end{aligned} \tag{5}$$

Furthermore, the assumption (2) for $f = f^*$, $q = 1/2$, and $n_k \ge m(f^*)$ yields that

$$d(N_{n_k}, f^*) \le \sup\left\{ \frac{\|S(\tilde{f}) - S(f^*)\|}{h^*(1/2)\, Q(f^*)} : \right.$$

$$\left. \tilde{f} \in F,\ \|\tilde{f} - f^*\| \le \frac{1}{2},\ N_{n_k}(\tilde{f}) = N_{n_k}(f^*) \right\}.$$

Take $\tilde{f}$ from F such that $\|\tilde{f}-f^*\| \le 1/2$ and $N_{n_k}(\tilde{f}) = N_{n_k}(f^*) = N_{n_k}(f_k)$. Then $\max\left\{\|f^* - f_k\|, \|\tilde{f} - f_k\|\right\} \le \|f^* - f_k\| + \|\tilde{f} - f^*\| \le 1$, whenever k is so large that $\|f^* - f_k\| \le 1/2$. Therefore

$$\|S(\tilde{f}) - S(f^*)\| \le \|S(\tilde{f}) - S(f_k)\| + \|S(f^*) - S(f_k)\| \le 2\,d(N_{n_k}, f_k).$$

This means that for sufficiently large k,

$$d(N_{n_k}, f_k) \ge \tfrac{1}{2}h^*(1/2)\,Q(f^*)\,d(N_{n_k}, f^*).$$

This together with (5) contradicts (4). Hence, the proof is complete. ∎

We now prove that a ρ-spline algorithm, which is defined in Section 2, also enjoys optimality properties for the nonlinear case. For simplicity we assume that $\rho \le 2$.

THEOREM 3.1.2. *Suppose that there exists a nondecreasing function H : $\mathbb{R}_+ \to \mathbb{R}_+$ such that for every $f \in F$ there exist a positive constant $Q_1(f)$ and an integer $m_1(f)$ satisfying*

$$\begin{aligned} \sup\left\{\|S(\tilde{f}) - S(f)\| : \tilde{f} \in F_1,\ \|\tilde{f} - f\| \le q,\ N_n(\tilde{f}) = N_n(f)\right\} \\ \le H(q)\,Q_1(f)\,d(N_n, f), \qquad \forall n \ge m_1(f),\ \forall q \in [0, 3\,\|f\|\,]. \end{aligned} \quad (6)$$

Then the error of a ρ-spline algorithm $\overline{\phi^*}$ that uses $\overline{N}$ satisfies the estimate

$$\|S(f) - \phi_n^*(N_n^*(f))\| \le 2\,H\big((\rho + 1)\|f\|\big)\,Q_1(f)\,r(N_n, f)$$

for any $f \in F$ and any $n \ge m_1(f)$.

PROOF: Note that

$$\|S(f) - \phi_n^*(N_n^*(f))\| = \|S(f) - S(\sigma_n(N_n(f)))\| \le \sup\|S(\tilde{f}) - S(f)\|,$$

where the supremum is taken over all elements $\tilde{f} \in F$, $\|\tilde{f} - f\| \le \|f - \sigma_n\|$, and $N_n(\tilde{f}) = N_n(f)$. Since $\|f - \sigma_n\| \le (1 + \rho)\|f\|$, the needed estimate follows directly from (6). ∎

Theorems 3.1.1 and 3.1.2 yield the following corollary.

COROLLARY 3.1.1. *If (2) and (6) hold then a ρ-spline algorithm $\overline{\phi^*}$ that uses $\overline{N}$ is optimal in the asymptotic setting, i.e., for any algorithm $\overline{\phi}$ that uses $\overline{N}$ and any positive sequence $\{\delta_n\}$ converging to zero, the set*

$$A_2 = \left\{f \in F : \lim_{n\to\infty} \frac{\|S(f) - \phi_n(N_n(f))\|}{\delta_n\,\|S(f) - \phi_n^*\,(N_n(f))\|} = 0\right\}$$

has empty interior in F.

3.2. Optimal Information

In this section we briefly discuss the optimal choice of functionals which form information $\overline{N}$. We state some theorems without proofs since these are similar to the proofs of corresponding theorems from Section 2.2.

For a given class Λ of permissible functionals, let

$$r(n, \Lambda, f) = \inf \left\{ r(N_n, f) : N_n = [L_1, L_2, \ldots, L_n] \text{ with } L_i \in \Lambda \right\}$$

be the nth minimal radius for the element f. We have

THEOREM 3.2.1. *For arbitrary information $\overline{N}$ from the class Λ which satisfies (2) of Section 3.1, for any algorithm $\overline{\phi}$ that uses $\overline{N}$, and for any positive sequence $\{\delta_n\}$ converging to zero, the set*

$$A_3 = \left\{ f \in F : \lim_{n \to \infty} \frac{\|S(f) - \phi_n(N_n(f))\|}{\delta_n \, r(n, \Lambda, f)} = 0 \right\}$$

has empty interior in F.

Suppose now that there exists $N_n = [L_{1,n}, \ldots, L_{n,n}]$ such that $L_{i,n} \in \Lambda$ and the error of a ρ-spline algorithm ϕ_n^* that uses N_n satisfies $\|S(f) - \phi_n^*(N_n(f))\| = O(r(n, \Lambda, f))$. That is, we have

$$\|S(f) - \phi_n^*(N_n(f))\| \le b(f) \, r(n, \Lambda, f), \quad \forall f \in F, \forall n = 1, 2, \ldots,$$

for a positive number $b(f)$. Take

$$\overline{N}^* = [N_1, N_2, \ldots, N_{2^k}, \ldots].$$

LEMMA 3.2.1. *Suppose that $\overline{N}^*$ additionally satisfies (6) of Section 3.1. Then the error of a ρ-spline algorithm $\overline{\phi}^*$ that uses $\overline{N}^*$ satisfies the estimate*

$$\|S(f) - \phi_n^*(N_n^*(f))\| \le H\big((\rho + 1) \, \|f\|\big) \, Q_1(f) \, b(f) \, r\big(\lceil (n+1)/4 \rceil, f\big)$$

for any $f \in F$ and any $n \ge 1$.

THEOREM 3.2.2. *Suppose that the assumptions (2) and (6) of Section 3.1 hold for the information $\overline{N}^*$. Assume additionally that*

$$r\big(\lceil (n+1)/4 \rceil, \Lambda, f\big) = \Theta\big(r(n, \Lambda, f)\big), \quad \forall f \in F.$$

Then the information $\overline{N}^*$ and a ρ-spline algorithm $\overline{\phi}^*$ that uses $\overline{N}^*$ are optimal, i.e., for arbitrary adaptive information $\overline{N}$ from Λ, an arbitrary algorithm $\overline{\phi}$ that uses $\overline{N}$, and an arbitrary positive sequence $\{\delta_n\}$ converging to zero, the set

$$A_4 = \left\{ f \in F : \lim_{n \to \infty} \frac{\|S(f) - \phi_n(N_n(f))\|}{\delta_n \, \|S(f) - \phi_n^*(N_n^*(f))\|} = 0 \right\}$$

has empty interior in F.

3.3. Applications

In this section we give examples of problems for which the assumptions (2) and (6) of Section 3.1 hold.

First of all observe that they hold for continuous linear solution operators S with $F = F_1$ and any adaptive information $\overline{N}$ consisting of continuous linear functionals. Indeed,

$$\sup \left\{ \|S(\tilde{f}) - S(f)\| : N_n(\tilde{f}) = N_n(f), \, \|\tilde{f} - f\| \le q \right\}$$
$$= \sup \left\{ \|S(h)\| : N_n(f + h) = N_n(f), \, \|h\| \le q \right\} = \frac{q}{2} \, d(N_n, f).$$

Hence, (2) and (6) of Section 3.1 hold with $h^*(q) = H(q) = q/2$ and $Q(f) = m(f) = Q_1(f) = m_1(f) = 1$.

These assumptions also hold for some nonlinear problems. We now report without a proof that they hold for the solution of ordinary differential equations, see Kacewicz [87c].

EXAMPLE 3.3.1. Let $F = F_1 = \{f : \mathbb{R}^{d+1} \to \mathbb{R}^d : f^{(r)}$ continuous, $f(x) = 0$ for $x \notin D\}$ for a bounded open convex set $D \subset \mathbb{R}^{d+1}$. Then F_1 is a Banach space when equipped with $\|f\| = \sum_{|\alpha| \le r} \|\partial^{|\alpha|} f / (\partial^{\alpha_1} y_1 \dots \partial^{\alpha_{d+1}} y_{d+1})\|_{\sup}$, where $\alpha = [\alpha_1, \dots, \alpha_{d+1}]$ and $|\alpha| = \sum_{i=1}^{d+1} \alpha_i$. The operator S, $S : F_1 \to G = C[0,1]$, is defined as the solution of the initial value problem, $S(f) = z$ with z being the solution of

$$\begin{cases} z'(x) = f(x, z(x)), & \forall x \in [0,1], \\ z(0) = \eta. \end{cases}$$

Then (2) and (6) of Section 3.1 hold for adaptive information consisting of continuous linear functionals.

For the class $\Lambda = F_1^*$ consisting of all continuous linear functionals, we indicated in Section 11 of Chapter 5 that

$$\inf_{f \in F} r(n, F_1^*, f) = \Theta\left(n^{-(r+1)}\right) \quad \text{as } n \to +\infty.$$

This means that the speed of convergence of any algorithm that uses continuous linear functionals is at most $n^{-(r+1)}$ and there exist algorithms, such as ρ-spline algorithms, for which this speed of convergence is achieved.

For the class $\Lambda = \Lambda^{\text{std}}$ of standard information consisting of only evaluations of the function and partial derivatives, we indicated in Section 11 of Chapter 5 that

$$\inf_{f \in F} \; r(n, \Lambda^{\text{std}}, f) = \Theta(n^{-r}) \quad \text{as } n \to +\infty.$$

This means that the speed of convergence of any algorithm that uses standard information is at most n^{-r}, and again this speed is achievable.

The next example for which the assumptions (2) and (6) hold is provided by a simple optimal control problem recently considered by Kacewicz [87d] (see also Werschulz [87d] who studies optimal properties of finite element methods for this problem).

EXAMPLE 3.3.2. Let $F_1 = C^r([0,1])$ with the norm $\|f\| = \sum_{i=0}^{r} \|f^{(i)}\|_{\infty}$, and let $G = C([0,1])$. For f from the class $F = \{f \in F_1 : f(x) \geq 0 \, \forall x \in [0,1]\}$, define the solution operator S so that $S(f)$ is the function that minimizes the integral

$$\int_0^1 \left[u'(x)^2 + f(x)\, u(x)^2 \right] dx$$

over the set of twice differentiable functions $u : [0,1] \to \mathbb{R}$ with $u(0) = 1$. Equivalently, $S(f)$ is a unique solution of the two boundary value problem,

$$u''(x) = f(x)\, u(x), \; \forall\, x \in (0,1), \quad \text{and} \quad u(0) = 1, \; u'(1) = 0.$$

For the class $\Lambda = \Lambda^{\text{std}}$ of standard information, we have

$$\inf_{f \in F} \; r(n, \Lambda^{\text{std}}, f) = \Theta(n^{-r}) \quad \text{as } n \to +\infty.$$

This means that the best speed of convergence of algorithms that use standard information is roughly n^{-r}. An optimal algorithm is based on a polynomial interpolating spline and a multiple shooting method. It has error $o(n^{-r})$ and the combinatory cost of its nth step is proportional to n. Further properties of this algorithm as well as numerical experiments may be found in Kacewicz [87d].

We end this section by presenting an example of a nonlinear problem for which the results in the worst case and asymptotic settings are quite different.

EXAMPLE 3.3.3. Assume that F_1 is the space $C^\infty([0,1])$ of infinitely-differentiable functions $f : [0,1] \to \mathbb{R}$. Define the set

$$F = \{f \in F_1 : f(0) < 0 < f(1), f \text{ has a unique zero } \alpha, f(\alpha) = 0,$$
$$\text{and } f^{(k)}(\alpha) \neq 0, \text{ for some } k \leq m\}.$$

Here, m is a given integer, $m \geq 1$, which bounds multiplicity of zeros of functions from F. The solution operator is now defined as the solution of nonlinear equation $f(x) = 0$, i.e., $S(f) = \alpha$, where $f(\alpha) = 0$.

Consider for simplicity the class $\Lambda = \Lambda^{\text{std}}$ of standard information. It is well known that bisection information and algorithm are optimal in the worst case setting, see, e.g., Sikorski [82a]. The nth minimal radius is given by

$$\inf_{f \in F} r(n, \Lambda^{\text{std}}, f) = 2^{-(n+1)}.$$

In the asymptotic setting one can do much better. Assume first that $m = 1$. Then one can combine Newton's iteration, $x_{i+1} = x_i - f(x_i)/f'(x_i)$, with bisection to guarantee global and quadratic convergence, see Anderson and Björck [73], Brent [71], and Bus and Dekker [75].

Let m be an arbitrary integer. Knowing that the multiplicity of a zero is at most m, one can recover the actual multiplicity k of a zero and then combine the modified Newton's iteration, $x_{i+1} = x_i - k\, f(x_i)/f'(x_i)$, with bisection to guarantee global and quadratic convergence.

Thus, for finite m we can construct a quadratically convergent sequence $\{x_i\}$ whose error is given by

$$|x_i - \alpha| = O(2^{-2^i}) \quad \text{as } i \to +\infty.$$

Here the constant in the big O-notation essentially depends on the function f. This speed of convergence is much faster than the speed in the worst case setting. For example, to guarantee that the error is at most ε, we have to compute $\lceil \log(1/\varepsilon) - 1 \rceil$ function values in the worst case setting, and only $O(\log\log(1/\varepsilon))$ function and derivative values in the asymptotic setting.

Note that if the set F is redefined by dropping the assumption about the bound on multiplicity of zeros then, as shown by Sikorski and Trojan [87], bisection regains its optimality properties since it is not possible to construct a sequence $\{x_i\}$ whose error goes to zero faster than 2^{-i}.

4. Asymptotic and Average Case Settings

In this section we show relations between the asymptotic and average case settings for linear problems equipped with a Gaussian measure. As in Chapter 6, we assume that F_1 is a separable Banach space and G is a separable Hilbert space both over the real field. The space F_1 is equipped with a Gaussian measure μ with mean zero and correlation operator C_μ, $C_\mu : F_1^* \to F_1$. We assume that C_μ is injective. The solution operator S, $S : F_1 \to G$, is continuous and linear,

and $F = F_1$. As in Section 2 of this chapter, we consider adaptive information,

$$\overline{N}(f) = [L_1(f), L_2(f; y_1), \ldots, L_n(f; y_1, \ldots, y_{n-1}), \ldots]$$

with $y_1 = L_1(f)$ and $y_i = L_i(f; y_1, \ldots, y_{i-1})$ for $i = 2, 3, \ldots$. We assume that $L_{i,y}(\cdot) = L_i(\cdot; y_1, \ldots, y_{i-1})$ is a continuous linear functional for all $y_1, \ldots, y_{i-1}$, and $L_{i,y}$ is measurable with respect to y. Without loss of generality we assume that $L_{i,y}$ are μ-orthonormal, i.e., for every fixed $y = [y_1, y_2, \ldots]$,

$$\langle L_{i,y}, L_{j,y} \rangle_\mu = L_{i,y}(C_\mu L_{j,y}) = \delta_{i,j}, \quad \forall i, j = 1, 2, \ldots.$$

As in Section 2, we write $\overline{N} = \{N_n\}$ and $\overline{\phi} = \{\phi_n\}$, where N_n is information of cardinality n consisting of the first n adaptive functionals from $\overline{N}$, and $\phi_n : N_n(F_1) = \mathbb{R}^n \to G$.

In this section we study three problems:

(i) For a given information operator $\overline{N} = \{N_n\}$, find an *optimal algorithm* $\overline{\phi}^* = \{\phi_n^*\}$ that uses $\overline{N} = \{N_n\}$. That is, find an algorithm $\overline{\phi}^*$ such that

$$\mu\left(\left\{f \in F_1 : \lim_{n \to \infty} \frac{\|S(f) - \phi_n(N_n(f))\|}{\|S(f) - \phi_n^*(N_n(f))\|} = 0\right\}\right) = 0$$

for any algorithm $\overline{\phi} = \{\phi_n\}$ that uses $\overline{N}$.

(ii) Characterize the rate of convergence of an optimal algorithm $\overline{\phi}^*$.

(iii) Find *optimal* information $\overline{N}^*$, i.e., $\overline{N}^*$ for which the rate of convergence of optimal algorithm $\overline{\phi}^*$ that uses $\overline{N}^*$ is the best possible.

Notes and Remarks

NR 4:1 Section 4 is based on Wasilkowski and Woźniakowski [87].

4.1. Optimal Algorithms

In this subsection we deal with the first problem (i) of Section 4. We prove that the μ-spline algorithm is optimal. Recall that the μ-spline algorithm $\overline{\phi}^s = \{\phi_n^s\}$ is defined, as in Section 5.4 of Chapter 6, by

$$\phi_n^s(y) = \sum_{i=1}^n y_i \, S(C_\mu L_{i,y}).$$

As we know, the μ-spline algorithm is the unique algorithm which minimizes the average error.

THEOREM 4.1.1. *The μ-spline algorithm $\overline{\phi}^s$ is optimal. That is, for any algorithm $\overline{\phi} = \{\phi_n\}$ that uses $\overline{N} = \{N_n\}$ we have*

$$\mu\left(\left\{f \in F_1 : \lim_{n\to\infty} \frac{\|S(f) - \phi_n(N_n(f))\|}{\|S(f) - \phi_n^s(N_n(f))\|} = 0\right\}\right) = 0.$$

As before, we use the convention 0/0=1.

PROOF: Given an algorithm $\overline{\phi}$, let

$$A = \left\{f \in F_1 : \lim_{n\to\infty} \frac{\|S(f) - \phi_n(N_n(f))\|}{\|S(f) - \phi_n^s(N_n(f))\|} = 0\right\}.$$

Take a number $q \in (0,1)$ and define

$$A_n = \{f \in F_1 : \|S(f) - \phi_n(N_n(f))\| < q\,\|S(f) - \phi_n^s(N_n(f))\|\}.$$

Then $A \subset \bigcup_{i=1}^\infty \bigcap_{n=i}^\infty A_n$. Note that A and A_n are measurable, and

$$\mu(A) \le \lim_{i\to\infty} \mu\left(\bigcap_{n=i}^\infty A_n\right) \le \overline{\lim_{n\to\infty}}\ \mu(A_n). \tag{1}$$

We estimate $\mu(A_n)$. Decompose the measure μ as in Chapter 6. That is, $\mu_1 = \mu N_n^{-1}$ and $\mu_2(\cdot|y)$ is the conditional measure after $y = N_n(f)$ has been computed. Recall that μ_1 is Gaussian with mean zero and correlation matrix identity, and $\mu_2(\cdot|y)$ is Gaussian with mean element $\sigma_n(y) = \sum_{i=1}^n y_i\, C_\mu L_{i,y}$ and correlation operator $C_{n,y}$ given by

$$C_{n,y}L = C_\mu L - \sum_{i=1}^n \langle L, L_{i,y}\rangle_\mu\, C_\mu L_{i,y}.$$

Furthermore,

$$\mu(A_n) = \int_{\mathbb{R}^n} \mu_2(A_n|y)\,\mu_1(dy). \tag{2}$$

Let $g_n(y) = \phi_n(y) - \phi_n^s(y)$. Then

$$N_n^{-1}(y) \cap A_n = N_n^{-1}(y) \cap A_n(y) + \sigma_n(y),$$

where $A_n(y) = \{h \in F_1 : \|Sh - g_n(y)\| < q\,\|Sh\|\}$. Since $\mu_2(\cdot|y)$ is concentrated on $N_n^{-1}(y)$ and $\sigma_n(y)$ is its mean element, we have

$$\mu_2(A_n|y) = \mu_2\left(N_n^{-1}(y) \cap A_n|y\right) = \mu_{2,y}\left(A_n(y)\right),$$

where $\mu_{2,y}$ is Gaussian with mean element zero and correlation operator $C_{n,y}$. Take now $\nu_y = \mu_{2,y}S^{-1}$. As we know, ν_y is Gaussian with mean element zero and correlation operator $C_{\nu,y}$,

$$C_{\nu,y}g = C_\nu g - \sum_{i=1}^n \langle g, SC_\mu L_{i,y}\rangle SC_\mu L_{i,y}, \quad \forall g \in G,$$

with C_ν being the correlation operator of $\nu = \mu S^{-1}$. For

$$B_n(y) = S(A_n(y)) = \{g \in G : \|g - g_n(y)\| < q\,\|g\|\}$$

we have

$$\mu_{2,y}(A_n(y)) = \nu_y(B_n(y)). \tag{3}$$

Observe that $g_n(y) = 0$ implies that $B_n(y) = \emptyset$. Assume therefore that $g_n(y) \neq 0$. Let $e_1 = g_n(y)/\|g_n(y)\|$. Every element $g \in G$ can be decomposed as $g = \langle g, e_1\rangle e_1 + g_2$, where $\langle g_2, e_1\rangle = 0$. Then for $g \in B_n(y)$ we have

$$\langle g - g_n(y), e_1\rangle^2 + \|g_2\|^2 < q^2 \langle g, e_1\rangle^2 + q^2\|g_2\|^2.$$

This yields $(1 - q^2) \langle g, e_1\rangle^2 - 2\langle g, e_1\rangle\,\|g_n(y)\| + \|g_n(y)\|^2 < 0$, and consequently

$$\frac{\|g_n(y)\|}{1 + q} < \langle g, e_1\rangle < \frac{\|g_n(y)\|}{1 - q}.$$

Since the measure ν_y is Gaussian, the last inequalities yield

$$\nu_y(B_n(y)) \leq \nu_y\left(\left\{g \in G : \frac{1}{1+q} < \frac{\langle g, e_1\rangle}{\|g_n(y)\|} < \frac{1}{1-q}\right\}\right)$$

$$= \begin{cases} 0 & \text{if } \langle C_{\nu,y}(e_1), e_1\rangle = 0, \\ (2\pi)^{-1/2} \int_{a_n}^{b_n} \exp(-t^2/2)\,dt & \text{otherwise}, \end{cases}$$

where

$$a_n = \frac{\|g_n(y)\|}{(1+q)\,\langle C_{\nu,y}(e_1), e_1\rangle} \quad \text{and}$$

$$b_n = \frac{\|g_n(y)\|}{(1-q)\,\langle C_{\nu,y}(e_1), e_1\rangle}.$$

If $\langle C_{\nu,y}(e_1), e_1\rangle \neq 0$, we estimate $\exp(-t^2/2)$ by its value at a_n. Then we get

$$\nu_y(B_n(y)) \leq \frac{1}{\sqrt{2\pi}}(b_n - a_n) \exp\left(\frac{-a_n^2}{2}\right) = \sqrt{\frac{2}{\pi}}\frac{q}{1-q}a_n \exp\left(\frac{-a_n^2}{2}\right).$$

Since $x \exp(-x^2/2) \leq 1/\sqrt{e}$, we finally get

$$\nu_y(B_n(y)) \leq \beta \frac{q}{1-q}, \tag{4}$$

where $\beta = \sqrt{2/(\pi e)} = 0.48394....$

From (2), (3), and (4) we conclude that $\mu(A_n) \leq \beta q/(1-q)$. Then (1) yields

$$\mu(A) \leq \beta \frac{q}{1-q}. \tag{5}$$

Since q is arbitrarily small, $\mu(A) = 0$ as claimed. ∎

Notes and Remarks

NR 4.1:1 Theorem 4.1.1 remains true for more general measures μ. Namely, assume that μ is *elliptically contoured* with mean zero and correlation operator C_μ, see Crawford [77] and **NR 5.4:1** of Chapter 6. That is, μ is of the form

$$\mu(B) = \int_0^\infty \mu_G \left(\frac{1}{\sqrt{t}} B \right) \alpha(dt), \quad \forall B \in \mathcal{B}(F_1),$$

where α is a measure defined on Borel sets of $(0, +\infty)$ such that

$$\int_0^\infty \alpha(dt) = \int_0^\infty t \, \alpha(dt) = 1.$$

Here μ_G denotes the Gaussian measure with mean zero and correlation operator C_μ. Note that $\mu_G(t^{-1/2} \cdot)$ is a Gaussian measure with mean zero and correlation operator $t \, C_\mu$. Since (5) holds for any Gaussian measure with mean zero, then

$$\mu_G \left(\frac{1}{\sqrt{t}} A \right) \leq \frac{\beta q}{1-q}, \quad \beta = \sqrt{\frac{2}{\pi e}},$$

and consequently

$$\mu(A) = \int_0^\infty \mu_G \left(\frac{1}{\sqrt{t}} A \right) \alpha(dt) \leq \frac{\beta q}{1-q}.$$

This implies that $\mu(A) = 0$, as claimed.

NR 4.1:2 The proof of Theorem 4.1.1 supplies a slightly stronger result. Namely, for $q \in (0,1)$ let

$$B = \left\{ f \in F_1 : \varlimsup_{n \to \infty} \frac{\|S(f) - \phi_n(N_n(f))\|}{\|S(f) - \phi_n^s(N_n(f))\|} < q \right\}.$$

Then repeating the proof of Theorem 4.1.1 for the set B instead of A, one can get

$$\mu(B) \leq \min \left\{ \frac{1}{2}, \sqrt{\frac{2}{\pi e}} \frac{q}{1-q} \right\}.$$

Thus, for small q, the measure of B is also small. We do not know whether this estimate is sharp. Due to **NR 4.1:1**, the estimate also holds for an elliptically contoured measure.

4.2. Rate of Convergence

We turn to problem (ii). That is, we characterize the rate of convergence of the μ-spline algorithm $\overline{\phi^s} = \{\phi_n^s\}$ that uses information $\overline{N} = \{N_n\}$. We prove that the sequence of local average radii $r^{\text{avg}}(N_n, N_n(f))$, see Section 2 of Chapter 6, characterizes the rate of convergence.

THEOREM 4.2.1.

$$\mu\left(\left\{f \in F_1 : \lim_{n \to \infty} \frac{\|S(f) - \phi_n^s(N_n(f))\|}{r^{\text{avg}}(N_n, N_n(f))} = 0\right\}\right) = 0.$$

PROOF: Let

$$A = \left\{f \in F_1 : \lim_{n \to \infty} \frac{\|S(f) - \phi_n^s(N_n(f))\|}{r^{\text{avg}}(N_n, N_n(f))} = 0\right\}.$$

Take a number $q \in (0, 1)$ and define

$$A_n = \{f \in F_1 : \|S(f) - \phi_n^s(N_n(f))\| < q\, r^{\text{avg}}(N_n, N_n(f))\}.$$

Then $A \subset \bigcup_{i=1}^{\infty} \bigcap_{n=i}^{\infty} A_n$ and $\mu(A) \leq \overline{\lim}_n \mu(A_n)$. We estimate $\mu(A_n)$. Proceeding as in Section 4.1, we get

$$\mu(A_n) = \int_{\mathbf{R}^n} \mu_2\left(\{f : \|S(f) - \phi_n^s(N_n(f))\| < q\, r^{\text{avg}}(N_n, y)\}|y\right)\mu_1(dy)$$

$$= \int_{\mathbf{R}^n} \nu_y\left(\{g \in G : \|g\| < q\, r^{\text{avg}}(N_n, y)\}\right)\mu_1(dy),$$

where ν_y is the Gaussian measure on G with mean element zero and correlation operator $C_{\nu,y}$ given in Section 4.1.

From Lemma 5.6.1 of Chapter 6 we know that

$$r^{\text{avg}}(N_n, y) = \sqrt{\text{trace}(C_{\nu,y})}.$$

Due to Kwapień's estimate, see Lemma 2.9.1 of the appendix with $a = 2$, we have

$$\nu_y\left(\left\{g \in G : \|g\| \leq q\sqrt{\text{trace}(C_{\nu,y})}\right\}|y\right) \leq \tfrac{4}{3}\psi(2q),$$

where $\psi(x) = \sqrt{2/\pi} \int_0^x \exp(-t^2/2)\, dt$. Thus, $\mu(A) \leq (4/3)\psi(2q)$. Since q can be arbitrarily small and $\psi(2q)$ tends to zero with q, we conclude that $\mu(A) = 0$, as claimed. ∎

It is also true that Theorem 4.2.1 holds for any algorithm $\bar{\phi} = \{\phi_n\}$ that uses $\overline{N} = \{N_n\}$. That is,

$$\mu(B) = 0 \text{ for } B = \left\{ f \in F_1 : \lim_{n \to \infty} \frac{\|S(f) - \phi_n(N_n(f))\|}{r^{\text{avg}}(N_n, N_n(f))} = 0 \right\} = 0. \quad (6)$$

Indeed, repeating the proof of Theorem 4.2.1 we get

$$\mu(B) \leq \overline{\lim_{n \to \infty}} \int_{\mathbf{R}^n} \nu_y \left(\left\{ g \in G : \|g - a\| \leq q \sqrt{\text{trace}(C_{\nu,y})} \right\} \right) \mu_1(dy),$$

where $a = a(y) = \phi(y) - \phi_n^s(y)$. It is known, see Lemma 2.9.3 of the appendix, that a Gaussian measure of the ball $B_r(a)$ of radius r and center a is maximal for $a = 0$. Thus,

$$\nu_y \left(\left\{ g \in G : \|g - a\| \leq q \sqrt{\text{trace}(C_{\nu,y})} \right\} \right)$$
$$\leq \nu_y \left(\left\{ g \in G : \|g\| \leq q \sqrt{\text{trace}(C_{\nu,y})} \right\} \right) \leq \tfrac{4}{3} \psi(2q).$$

Therefore, $\mu(B) \leq (4/3)\psi(2q)$, and since q can be arbitrarily small, $\mu(B) = 0$, as claimed. ∎

Theorem 4.2.1 states that, modulo a set of measure zero, the μ- spline algorithm does not converge *faster* than the sequence of local radii. We now show that the μ-spline algorithm converges no *slower* than the sequence of local radii.

THEOREM 4.2.2.

$$\mu \left(\left\{ f \in F_1 : \lim_{n \to \infty} \frac{r^{\text{avg}}(N_n, N_n(f))}{\|S(f) - \phi_n^s(N_n(f))\|} = 0 \right\} \right) = 0.$$

PROOF: Let

$$A = \left\{ f \in F_1 : \lim_{n \to \infty} \frac{r^{\text{avg}}(N_n, N_n(f))}{\|S(f) - \phi_n^s(N_n(f))\|} = 0 \right\}.$$

Take a number $q \in (0, 1)$ and define

$$A_n = \left\{ f \in F_1 : \|S(f) - \phi_n^s(N_n(f))\| \geq \frac{1}{q} r^{\text{avg}}(N_n, N_n(f)) \right\}.$$

Then $A \subset \bigcup_{i=1}^{\infty} \bigcap_{n=i}^{\infty} A_n$ and $\mu(A) \le \overline{\lim}_n \mu(A_n)$. As in the proof of Theorem 4.2.1, we conclude that

$$\mu(A_n) = 1 - \int_{\mathbb{R}^n} \nu_y \left(\left\{ g \in G : \|g\| < \frac{1}{q} \sqrt{\operatorname{trace}(C_{\nu,y})} \, |y| \right\} \right) \mu_1(dy).$$

For any probability measure ρ with correlation operator C_ρ and for any ball $B_r = \{g \in G : \|g\| < r\}$ we have

$$\operatorname{trace}(C_\rho) = \int_G \|g\|^2 \, \rho(dg) \ge \int_{G - B_r} \|g\|^2 \, \rho(dg) \ge r^2 \, \rho(G - B_r)$$
$$= r^2 \left(1 - \rho(B_r) \right).$$

Thus,

$$\rho(B_r) \ge 1 - \frac{\operatorname{trace}(C_\rho)}{r^2}.$$

In particular,

$$\nu_y \left(\left\{ g \in G : \|g\| < \frac{1}{q} \sqrt{\operatorname{trace}(C_{\mu,y})} \right\} |y| \right) \ge 1 - q^2.$$

Therefore, $\mu(A_n) \le q^2$, and consequently $\mu(A) \le q^2$. Since q can be arbitrarily small, $\mu(A) = 0$, as claimed. $\blacksquare$

Notes and Remarks

NR 4.2:1 Theorem 4.2.1 remains true also for elliptically contoured measures. Then for

$$A = \left\{ f \in F_1 : \lim_{n \to \infty} \frac{\|S(f) - \phi_n(N_n(f))\|}{\sqrt{\operatorname{trace}(C_{\nu, N_n(f)})}} = 0 \right\},$$

we have $\mu(A) = 0$. To prove this, let A_n be defined as in the proof of Theorem 4.2.1. Then

$$\mu(A) \le \overline{\lim_{n \to \infty}} \, \mu(A_n) = \overline{\lim_{n \to \infty}} \int_0^{\infty} \mu_G \left(\frac{1}{\sqrt{t}} A_n \right) \alpha(dt).$$

For every fixed t, $\mu_G(1/\sqrt{t}\,\cdot)$ is a Gaussian measure with mean zero and correlation operator $t \, C_\mu$. Repeating the proof of Theorem 4.2.1, we get that

$$\mu(A_n) \le \frac{4}{3} \int_0^{\infty} \int_{\mathbb{R}^n} \psi \left(\frac{2q}{\sqrt{t}} \right) \mu_1(dy) \, \alpha(dt) = \frac{4}{3} \int_0^{\infty} \psi \left(\frac{2q}{\sqrt{t}} \right) \alpha(dt).$$

From the definition of ψ, we have

$$\int_0^\infty \psi\left(\frac{2q}{\sqrt{t}}\right)\alpha(dt) = \frac{2}{\pi}\int_0^\infty \int_0^{2q/\sqrt{t}} \exp(-x^2/2)\, dx\,\alpha(dt)$$

$$= \frac{2}{\pi}\int_0^q \int_0^{2q/\sqrt{t}} \exp(-x^2/2)\, dx\,\alpha(dt) + \frac{2}{\pi}\int_q^\infty \int_0^{2q/\sqrt{t}} \exp(-x^2/2)\, dx\,\alpha(dt)$$

$$\leq \int_0^q \left(\sqrt{\frac{2}{\pi}}\int_0^\infty \exp(-x^2/2)\, dx\right)\alpha(dt)+$$

$$\sqrt{\frac{2}{\pi}}\int_q^\infty \int_0^{2\sqrt{q}} \exp(-x^2/2)\, dx\,\alpha(dt)$$

$$= \alpha((0,q]) + \sqrt{\frac{2}{\pi}}\int_0^{2\sqrt{q}} \exp(-x^2/2)\, dx =: a(q).$$

Since $0 = \alpha(\emptyset) = \lim_{q\to 0^+} \alpha((0,q])$, we see that $\alpha((0,q])$ and $\sqrt{2/\pi}\int_0^{2\sqrt{q}} \exp(-t^2/2)\, dt$ tend to zero with q. Hence, $\lim_{q\to 0^+} a(q) = 0$. Since $\mu(A) \leq \overline{\lim}_n \mu(A_n) \leq a(q)$ and q can be arbitrarily small, $\mu(A) = 0$, as claimed.

NR 4.2:2 The proof of Theorem 4.2.2 supplies a slightly stronger result. Namely, for $q \in (0,1)$, let

$$B = \left\{ f \in F_1 : \overline{\lim_{n\to\infty}} \frac{r^{\mathrm{avg}}(N_n, N_n(f))}{\|S(f) - \phi_n^s\,(N_n(f))\|} \leq q \right\}.$$

Then repeating the proof of Theorem 4.2.2 we get $\mu(B) \leq q^2$. Thus, for small q, $\mu(B)$ is close to zero. We do not know whether this estimate is sharp.

4.3. Optimal Information

In this section we deal with the third problem (iii) of Section 4 for the class $\Lambda = F_1^*$. That is, we find optimal information $\overline{N}^* = \{N_n^*\}$ for which the rate of convergence of the μ-spline algorithm $\overline{\phi^s} = \{\phi_n^s\}$ that uses $\overline{N}^*$ is best possible. From the results of Section 4.2, this is equivalent to finding information $\overline{N}^*$ for which the sequence of local radii $\{r^{\mathrm{avg}}(N_n^*, N_n^*(f))\}$ goes to zero as fast as possible.

As in Chapter 6, let C_ν be the correlation operator of the a priori measure $\nu = \mu S^{-1}$. Then $C_\nu = C_\nu^* \geq 0$ and C_ν has finite trace. Let m denote the total number of positive eigenvalues of C_ν. Observe that m may be infinite. Let η_i^*, $i < m + 1$, be the orthonormal eigenelements of C_ν,

$$C_\nu \eta_i^* = \lambda_i^*, \qquad \lambda_1^* \geq \lambda_2^* \geq \cdots > 0.$$

For $i < m + 1$ define $L_i^*(f) = \langle S(f), \eta_i^* \rangle / \sqrt{\lambda_i^*}$, and for $n < m + 1$ define

$$N_n^*(f) = [L_1^*(f), L_2^*(f), \ldots, L_n^*(f)].$$

The information N_n^* is nth optimal nonadaptive information in the class of all continuous linear functionals $\Lambda = F_1^*$, see Theorem 5.5.1 of Chapter 6. Its local average radius does not depend on y and is given by

$$r^{\mathrm{avg}}(N_n^*, y) = r^{\mathrm{avg}}(N_n^*) = \sqrt{\sum_{i=n+1}^{m} \lambda_i^*}.$$

Without loss of generality we assume from now on that $m = +\infty$. Define the information

$$\overline{N^*} = \{N_n^*\}.$$

We stress that $\overline{N^*}$ is *nonadaptive* and the μ-spline algorithm $\overline{\phi^s} = \{\phi_n^s\}$ that uses $\overline{N^*}$ consists of linear algorithms ϕ_n^s of the form

$$\phi_n^s(N_n^*(f)) = \sum_{i=1}^{n} \langle S(f), \eta_i^* \rangle \, \eta_i^*.$$

Observe that the sequence of μ-spline algorithms is easily updated since $\phi_{n+1}^s(N_{n+1}^*(f)) = \phi_n^s(N_n^*(f)) + \langle S(f), \eta_{n+1}^* \rangle \, \eta_{n+1}^*$. This enables its efficient implementation.

Theorem 4.2.2 states that the μ-spline algorithm $\overline{\phi^s}$ converges at least as fast as the sequence of radii $\{r^{\mathrm{avg}}(N_n^*)\}$, i.e.,

$$\mu\left(\left\{f \in F_1 : \lim_{n \to \infty} \frac{r^{\mathrm{avg}}(N_n^*)}{\|S(f) - \phi_n^s(N_n^*(f))\|} = 0\right\}\right) = 0.$$

We are ready to prove optimality of $\overline{N^*}$.

THEOREM 4.3.1. *The nonadaptive information $\overline{N^*}$ is optimal in the class $\Lambda = F_1^*$ consisting of continuous linear functionals, i.e., for any adaptive information $\overline{N} = \{N_n\}$ and any algorithm $\overline{\phi} = \{\phi\}$ that uses $\overline{N}$ we have*

$$\mu\left(\left\{f \in F_1 : \lim_{n \to \infty} \frac{\|S(f) - \phi_n(N_n(f))\|}{r^{\mathrm{avg}}(N_n^*)} = 0\right\}\right) = 0.$$

PROOF: The proof follows from (6) and the fact that N_n^* is nth optimal information, i.e., $r^{\mathrm{avg}}(N_n^*) \le r^{\mathrm{avg}}(N_n, N_n(f))$ for any N_n and any $f \in F_1$, see Section 5.5 of Chapter 6. ∎

Theorem 4.3.1 states that adaption does not help for approximation of linear operators in the asymptotic setting. This agrees with the similar result in the worst and average case settings, as explained in Chapters 4 and 6.

The best possible rate of convergence is obtained by the μ-spline algorithm that uses the information $\overline{N}^*$. This rate of convergence is given by $r^{\mathrm{avg}}(N_n^*) = \sqrt{\sum_{i=n+1}^{\infty} \lambda_i^*}$. Thus, it depends on how fast the truncated series of the trace of C_ν goes to zero. For instance, if $\lambda_i^* = i^{-p}$ for some $p > 1$ then

$$r^{\mathrm{avg}}(N_n^*) = (p-1)^{-1/2}\,(n+1)^{-(p-1)/2}\,\left(1+o(1)\right) \quad \text{as } n \to +\infty.$$

If $\lambda_i^* = q^i$ for $q \in (0,1)$ then

$$r^{\mathrm{avg}}(N_n^*) = \sqrt{q^{n+1}/(1-q)}.$$

Chapter 11

Randomization

1. Introduction

In this chapter we study random information and random algorithms. Our main focus is to investigate how much randomization can lower the worst and/or average case complexities.

Randomization has been studied in many papers, see **NR 1:2**. Efficient random algorithms are known for many problems, and their costs provide upper bounds on the complexity. However, tight lower bounds on the complexity are known for only a few problems, such as some optimization problems, see Nemirovsky and Yudin [83]. The main emphasis of this chapter is to obtain tight lower bounds on the complexity when random information and random algorithms are used.

We shall study randomization in the worst and average case settings. Although random information and algorithms seem to be interesting primarily in the worst case setting, we shall, for technical reasons, begin the analysis with the average case setting. More specifically, in Section 2 we give basic definitions and in Section 3 we study random algorithms and random information for linear problems equipped with Gaussian measures. We prove that for such problems randomization does not essentially help. This result will be needed for analyzing randomization in the worst case setting which is the subject of Section 4. We derive lower bounds on complexity for problems such as integration, function approximation and optimization. As we shall see, randomization helps for only some of these problems.

Before starting the formal analysis, we make a general remark. The implementation of random information and/or random algorithms requires a random number generator. There are many different algorithms which simulate random processes, see e.g., Knuth [81]. These algorithms are implemented on *deterministic* computers and obviously they can, at best, generate "pseudo"-random numbers. Not surprisingly, there is a group of researchers, see e.g., Zaremba [68], which is very critical of pseudo-random computation. On the other hand, there is another group which believes that pseudo-random computation may be viewed as a close approximation of random computation, and that randomness is a very powerful tool for computation even if implemented on deterministic computers, see **NR 1:3**. We believe that both groups have important reasons for their approval and/or disapproval of randomization. To avoid taking a specific stance in that philosophical dispute, we will not discuss the simulation of random processes. We shall assume that our permissible operations include generating of random numbers, which may or may not be a practical assumption. We want to know how much can be gained when such an assumption is made.

Notes and Remarks

NR 1:1 This chapter, except Section 4.2, is based on Wasilkowski [87a]. Section 4.2 is based on Novak [87c].

NR 1:2 Although we do not intend to cover the huge literature on randomization, we mention a few papers and books which are especially relevant to the analysis of this chapter. A most popular problem for which randomization is studied is multivariate integration. Also, problems such as function approximation and optimization are analyzed in a number of papers. In most cases, random information of only *fixed* cardinality is studied. The reader may consult the papers and/or books of Brooks [58, 59], Bakhvalov [59, 61, 62], Hammersley and Handscomb [64], Haber [66, 69, 70], Halton [70], Ermakov [75], Granovskii and Ermakov [77], Schwefel [77], Hengartner and Theodorescu [78], Niederreiter [78], Rubinstein [81], Nemirovsky and Yudin [83], Novak [83, 85, 87a,c], Zieliński and Neumann [83], Sobol [85], and Sukharev [88]. The reader is also referred to a recent paper of Packel [87b], where a game-theoretic approach to randomization is discussed.

NR 1:3 The reader may find a mathematical theory which addresses features of randomness and construction of random numbers in, e.g., Coveyou [69], Zvonkin and Levin [70], Schnorr [71, 77], Niederreiter [78, 85], Zieliński [78], Knuth [81], Fishman and Moore [86], and Devroye [86]. See also Novak [87a], where a general discussion of randomization can be found.

2. Random Information and Random Algorithms

In this section we give formal definitions of random information and random algorithms. We also define their errors and cost in both the worst and average case settings. To motivate our approach, we begin with an integration example.

EXAMPLE 2.1. The solution operator S is given by $S(f) = \int_{[0,1]^d} f(x)\, dx$, and the class F consists of functions $f, f : [0,1]^d \to \mathbb{R}$, whose all derivatives up to order r are bounded by 1, say, in the sup-norm. The class Λ consists of function evaluations. It is well known, see Bakhvalov [59], that the worst case complexity for this problem is $\text{comp}^{\text{wor}}(\varepsilon) = \Theta\left(\varepsilon^{-d/r}\right)$. For d large relative to r, it is huge even for modest ε. Thus, for high dimensions, integration is intractable in the worst case setting.

One possible remedy is to permit function evaluations at randomly chosen points. The primary example of this approach is provided by the classical Monte Carlo method. This method relies on random selection of n uniformly distributed points $t_1, \ldots, t_n \in [0,1]^d$. Here n is fixed. Then f is evaluated at these points and

$$U_{\vec{t}}(f) = \frac{1}{n} \sum_{i=1}^{n} f(t_i)$$

is an approximation to the integral $S(f)$. The information about f is random since it depends on the random selection of $\vec{t} = [t_1, \ldots, t_n]$, $N_{\vec{t}}(f) = [f(t_1), \ldots, f(t_n)]$. However, the cardinality n and the algorithm $\phi(y_1, \ldots, y_n) = n^{-1} \sum_{i=1}^{n} y_i$ are deterministic. It is well known that for any f from F, the expected error is at most $n^{-1/2}$. Thus, we can compute an ε-approximation with cost proportional to ε^{-2}. Comparing this with $\text{comp}^{\text{wor}}(\varepsilon)$ we see the superiority of the Monte Carlo method whenever $d > 2r$.

We now present another algorithm for the scalar case, $d = 1$, assuming additionally that the functions f are periodic. For a given k, the cardinality n is selected randomly with uniform distribution from $\{k+1, \ldots, 2k\}$, and then the approximation is provided by

$$U(f) = \frac{1}{n} \sum_{i=1}^{n} f\left(\frac{i}{n+1}\right).$$

Again, information about f is random since it depends on the random selection of the cardinality n. Bakhvalov [61] proved that for every f the expected error is proportional to $k^{-(r+1/2)}$. The expected cardinality is $(3k+1)/2$, and we can compute an ε-approximation with cost proportional to $\varepsilon^{-2/(2r+1)}$. Since the worst case complexity is now proportional to $\varepsilon^{-1/r}$, the improvement due to the random choice of cardinality is obvious.

Although the information and algorithms presented above utilize very simple randomization, they are more efficient than any deterministic information and algorithms. We presented them here to motivate the following general definition of randomization, where information operations, the cardinality of information, and algorithms may all be selected randomly.

As always, we want to approximate $S(f)$ for any $f \in F$ for a given class Λ of permissible information operations.

We begin by defining *random information*. As in the deterministic case, information about f consists of a number of permissible evaluations, the ith depending on all previously computed values. In addition, the ith evaluation may now depend on a number $t_i \in \mathbb{R}$ chosen randomly with some probability ρ_i. This probability may depend on previously computed values $y_1, \ldots, y_{i-1}$ as well as on previously selected $t_0, t_1 \ldots, t_{i-1}$. More precisely, at the zeroth step, we randomly select t_0 and decide if any evaluation is needed by computing the value of the termination function, $\text{ter}_0(t_0)$. At the first step, we choose $L_1(\cdot; t_0) \in \Lambda$, compute $y_1 = y_1(f, t_0) = L_1(f; t_0)$, randomly select t_1, and decide whether to terminate by evaluating $\text{ter}_1(y_1; t_0, t_1)$. At the ith step, we choose $L_i(\cdot; y_1, \ldots, y_{i-1}; t_0, \ldots, t_{i-1}) \in \Lambda$, compute $y_i = L_i(f; y_1, \ldots, y_{i-1}; t_0, \ldots, t_{i-1})$, randomly select t_i, decide whether to terminate by evaluating $\text{ter}_i(y_1, \ldots, y_i; t_0, \ldots, t_i)$, and the process is repeated.

We now define *random algorithms*. After computing the information, we chose an algorithm $\phi_{\vec{t}}(\cdot) = \phi(\cdot; t_0, \ldots, t_{n_{\vec{t}}(f)+1})$ by selecting another $t_{n_{\vec{t}}(f)+1}$, and finally we approximate $S(f)$ by $U_{\vec{t}}(f) = \phi_{\vec{t}}(N_{\vec{t}}(f))$. Here $\vec{t} = [t_0, t_1, \ldots]$,

$$n_{\vec{t}}(f) = \min\{i : \text{ter}_i(y_1, \ldots, y_i; t_0 \ldots, t_i) = 1\}$$

denotes the total number of information evaluations, and

$$N_{\vec{t}}(f) = [y_1, \ldots, y_{n_{\vec{t}}(f)}; \vec{t}]$$

denotes the computed information.

Hence, $U = (\phi, N, \vec{\rho})$, where $\vec{\rho}$ is the product of probability measures ρ_i, and ϕ, N are random mappings with $\phi_{\vec{t}}$ and $N_{\vec{t}}$ denoting realizations of the random choices. Note that any deterministic U may be viewed as random with the probability measures ρ_i being atomic, i.e., concentrated at one point.

We illustrate the above definitions for the Monte Carlo method:

- (▷) $\text{ter}_i \equiv 0$ for $i \leq n-1$, and $\text{ter}_n \equiv 1$. Hence, ter_i is independent of $\vec{t}$ and of computed values, and $n_{\vec{t}}(f) \equiv n$ is fixed,
- (▷) ρ_i is Lebesgue measure restricted to $[0, 1]^d$,

(▷) $L_i(f; y_1, \ldots, y_{i-1}; t_0, \ldots, t_i) = L_i(f; t_i) = f(t_i)$ and

$$N_{\vec{t}}(f) = [f(t_1), \ldots, f(t_n); \vec{t}] \quad \text{with} \quad \vec{t} = [t_1, \ldots, t_n]$$

(▷) $U(f) = \phi_{\vec{t}}(y_1, \ldots, y_n) = n^{-1} \sum_{i=1}^{n} y_i$. Note that $\phi_{\vec{t}}$ does not depend on $\vec{t}$.

The definition of random U given above is quite complicated and sometimes not convenient for analysis. Therefore, we now present another, equivalent way of looking at randomization. Namely, suppose that instead of random selection per step, we perform it once at the beginning. Hence, we randomly select t, which is a member of some space T endowed with a probability measure ρ. Then, based on the selected t, we choose a deterministic $U_t = (\phi_t, N_t)$, and compute $U_t(f) = \phi_t(N_t(f))$ as an approximation to $S(f)$. Such U, denoted by $U = (\phi, N, T, \rho)$, is said to be of *mixed strategy* form due to its analogy with game theory. Nemirovsky and Yudin [83] proved that there exists a *Polish* space (i.e., a complete separable metric space) T such that the class of random U's coincides with the class of mixed strategy U's. In particular, we have the following duality: any random $U = (\phi, N, \vec{\rho})$ can be represented in a mixed strategy form, i.e., $U = (\phi', N', T, \rho')$ for suitably chosen probability measure ρ'. We shall use this duality quite extensively in this chapter, representing U by $(\phi, N, \vec{\rho})$ or by (ϕ, N, T, ρ) interchangeably.

We now define the worst and average case complexities for the class of random information and random algorithms. We begin with the worst case setting, where the error of $U = (\phi, N, T, \rho)$ in its mixed strategy form is defined by

$$e^{\text{wor-ran}}(U) = \sup_{f \in F} \int_T \|S(f) - \phi_t(N_t(f))\| \, \rho(dt),$$

and the cost by

$$\text{cost}^{\text{wor-ran}}(U) = \sup_{f \in F} \int_T \text{cost}(U_t, f) \, \rho(dt).$$

Here $\text{cost}(U_t, f)$ is the cost of using deterministic U_t for f, defined as in Chapter 3. Note that for deterministic U the corresponding distribution $\vec{\rho}$ is atomic, and therefore $e^{\text{wor-ran}}(U)$ and $\text{comp}^{\text{wor-ran}}(U)$ coincide with $e^{\text{wor}}(U)$ and $\text{comp}^{\text{wor}}(U)$, respectively.

The (*worst case*) ε-*complexity with randomization* is defined as in Chapter 3, with the only difference that the class of information and algorithms is expanded to include random ones. Hence,

$$\text{comp}^{\text{wor-ran}}(\varepsilon) = \inf\{\text{cost}^{\text{wor-ran}}(U) : U \text{ such that } e^{\text{wor-ran}}(U) \leq \varepsilon\}.$$

In the average case setting, given an a priori probability measure μ on F, the error of $U = (\phi, N, T, \rho)$ is defined by

$$e^{\text{avg-ran}}(U) = \left(\int_F \int_T \|S(f) - \phi_t(N_t(f))\|^2 \, \rho(dt) \, \mu(df) \right)^{1/2}$$

and the cost by

$$\text{cost}^{\text{avg-ran}}(U) = \int_F \int_T \text{cost}(U_t, f) \, \rho(dt) \, \mu(df).$$

Again, we have the obvious correspondence between these two definitions and the definitions of error and cost for any deterministic U, $e^{\text{avg-ran}}(U) = e^{\text{avg}}(U)$ and $\text{cost}^{\text{avg-ran}}(U) = \text{cost}^{\text{avg}}(U)$.

The (*average case*) ε-*complexity with randomization* is defined by

$$\text{comp}^{\text{avg-ran}}(\varepsilon) = \inf \left\{ \text{cost}^{\text{avg-ran}}(U) : U \text{ such that } e^{\text{avg-ran}}(U) \le \varepsilon \right\}.$$

Optimality of U^* in either setting is defined analogously to Chapter 3. That is, $U^* = (\phi^*, N^*, T^*, \rho^*)$ is *optimal* iff

$$e^{\text{x-ran}}(U^*) \le \varepsilon \qquad \text{and} \qquad \text{cost}^{\text{x-ran}}(U^*) = \text{comp}^{\text{x-ran}}(\varepsilon)$$

for x=wor or x=avg, depending on the setting.

Note that $\text{comp}^{\text{wor-ran}}$ and $\text{comp}^{\text{avg-ran}}$ differ from comp^{wor} and comp^{avg}, respectively, only by enlarging the class of information and algorithms. This is indicated by adding "ran" to the names of both worst and average case complexities. We immediately obtain the following estimates

$$\text{comp}^{\text{wor-ran}}(\varepsilon) \le \text{comp}^{\text{wor}}(\varepsilon) \quad \text{and} \quad \text{comp}^{\text{avg-ran}}(\varepsilon) \le \text{comp}^{\text{avg}}(\varepsilon)$$

for any problem and arbitrary probability measure μ.

3. Average Case Setting

In this section we study linear problems defined as in Chapter 6. That is, the solution operator S is linear, $S : F_1 \to G$, where F_1 is a separable Banach space and G is a separable Hilbert space. The space F_1 is equipped with a Gaussian measure μ, and the class F is either the whole space F_1 with the a priori measure equal to μ or is a ball B_q with the a priori measure equal to μ_q, $\mu_q(\cdot) = \mu(\cdot \cap B_q)/\mu(B_q)$. We prove that for such problems randomization does not help significantly.

3.1. Linear Problems for the Whole Space

In this section we assume that $F = F_1$. Let N_n^* be the nth optimal nonadaptive (deterministic) information in the class Λ, see Section 5.5 of Chapter 6, and let ϕ_n^s be the μ-spline algorithm that uses N_n^*.

Consider arbitrary $U = (\phi, N, T, \rho)$. By the average cardinality of random N we mean

$$\operatorname{card}^{\text{avg-ran}}(N) = \int_F \int_T n_t(f)\, \rho(dt)\, \mu(df).$$

Then the *average ε-cardinality with randomization* is defined by

$$m^{\text{avg-ran}}(\varepsilon) = \inf\left\{\operatorname{card}^{\text{avg-ran}}(N) : e^{\text{avg-ran}}(U) \le \varepsilon \text{ for any } U \text{ using } N\right\}.$$

Let $A_i = \{(t, N(f)) : n_t(f) = i\}$ and let η be the joint probability measure, $\eta = \rho \otimes \mu N_t^{-1}$. Then $\operatorname{card}^{\text{avg-ran}}(N) = \sum_{i=0}^{\infty} i\, \eta(A_i)$ and

$$e^{\text{avg-ran}}(U) = \left(\sum_{i=0}^{\infty} \int_{A_i} e^{\text{avg}}(\phi_t, N_t, y)^2\, \eta(d(t,y))\right)^{1/2},$$

where $e^{\text{avg}}(\phi_t, N_t, y) = \left(\int_F \|S(f) - \phi_t(y)\|^2\, \mu_2(df|y)\right)^{1/2}$ is the local average error defined in Section 3.1 of Chapter 6.

From Chapter 6, we know that for every information N of fixed cardinality i and for every $y = [y_1, \ldots, y_i]$,

$$r^{\text{avg}}(N, y) \ge r^{\text{avg}}(N_i^*, y) = r^{\text{avg}}(N_i^*) = e^{\text{avg}}(\phi_i^s, N_i^*),$$

where N_i^* is ith optimal information and ϕ_i^s is the μ-spline algorithm that uses it. Hence,

$$e^{\text{avg-ran}}(U)^2 \ge \sum_{i=0}^{\infty} r^{\text{avg}}(N_i^*)^2\, \eta(A_i).$$

Proceeding as in Section 5.6.2 of Chapter 6, we conclude that

$$m^{\text{avg-ran}}(\varepsilon)$$
$$\ge \min\left\{a\,i + (1-a)\,j : i \le j,\ a\,r^{\text{avg}}(N_i^*)^2 + (1-a)\,r^{\text{avg}}(N_j^*)^2 \le \varepsilon^2\right\}.$$

In fact, we have equality. To see this, take a^*, i^*, and j^* for which the minimum above is attained. Define the following random U^*,

$$U_t^*(f) = \begin{cases} \phi_{i*}^s(N_{i*}^*(f)) & \text{with probability } a^*, \\ \phi_{j*}^s(N_{j*}^*(f)) & \text{with probability } 1 - a^*. \end{cases}$$

Then $e^{\text{avg-ran}}(U^*) \leq \varepsilon$ and the average cardinality of N^* is equal to $a^* i^* + (1 - a^*) j^*$. This proves that

$$m^{\text{avg-ran}}(\varepsilon)$$
$$= \min \left\{ a\, i + (1 - a)\, j : i \leq j,\ a\, r^{\text{avg}}(N_i^*)^2 + (1 - a)\, r^{\text{avg}}(N_j^*)^2 \leq \varepsilon^2 \right\}.$$

Furthermore, $\text{cost}^{\text{avg-ran}}(U^*) \leq (c + 2)\, m^{\text{avg-ran}}(\varepsilon)$. Since $\text{comp}^{\text{avg-ran}}(\varepsilon) \geq c\, m^{\text{avg-ran}}(\varepsilon)$ holds also for the randomized case, we conclude that U^* is almost optimal and that $\text{comp}^{\text{avg-ran}}(\varepsilon) \leq (c + 2)\, m^{\text{avg-ran}}(\varepsilon)$.

We make another observation. Comparing $m^{\text{avg-ran}}(\varepsilon)$ with Theorem 5.7.2 of Chapter 6, we see that it is almost the same as the average ε-cardinality number (without randomization),

$$m^{\text{avg}}(\varepsilon) - \tfrac{1}{2} \leq m^{\text{avg-ran}}(\varepsilon) \leq m^{\text{avg}}(\varepsilon).$$

These estimates are sharp, as shown in **NR 3.1:2**. We summarize this in the following

THEOREM 3.1.1. *For an arbitrary linear problem,*

(i) *the average ε-complexity with randomization satisfies the following estimates*

$$c\, m^{\text{avg-ran}}(\varepsilon) \leq \text{comp}^{\text{avg-ran}}(\varepsilon) \leq (c + 2)\, m^{\text{avg-ran}}(\varepsilon),$$

where c is the cost of one information operation,
(ii) *U^* defined above is almost optimal,*
(iii) *randomization does not help significantly since*

$$m^{\text{avg}}(\varepsilon) - \tfrac{1}{2} \leq m^{\text{avg-ran}}(\varepsilon) \leq m^{\text{avg}}(\varepsilon)$$
$$-\frac{c}{2} + \frac{c}{c + 2}\, \text{comp}^{\text{avg}}(\varepsilon) \leq \text{comp}^{\text{avg-ran}}(\varepsilon) \leq \text{comp}^{\text{avg}}(\varepsilon).$$

Notes and Remarks

NR 3.1:1 We extend the analysis of this section for more general error criteria. It is done similarly to Section 6.3 of Chapter 6, where we studied the average case setting with an arbitrary error functional ER : $G \to \mathbb{R}_+$. The average error of deterministic $U = (\phi, N)$ was defined by

$$e^{\text{avg}}(U) = \int_{F_1} \text{ER}(S(f) - \phi(N(f)))\, \mu(df).$$

Proceeding similarly for the randomized case, we let

$$e^{\text{avg-ran}}(U) = \int_{F_1} \int_T \text{ER}(S(f) - \phi_t(N_t(f)))\, \rho(dt)\, \mu(df)$$

be the error of $U = (\phi, N, T, \rho)$. The cost of U and the complexity are defined as before. Note that in deriving Theorem 3.1.1 we did not use the fact that the error of U is defined in the $\mathcal{L}_2$ sense. Instead, we relied on the properties of conditional measures and especially on the properties of local radii of deterministic information. These properties hold for a general error functional, as proven in Section 6.3 of Chapter 6. Hence, Theorem 3.1.1 is also true for an arbitrary error functional ER, the only difference being that in the definition of U^*, the μ-spline algorithms should be replaced by the translated μ-spline algorithm, see Section 6.3 of Chapter 6. Hence we have

COROLLARY 3.1.1. *For an arbitrary linear problem and an arbitrary error functional,*
   (i) *the average ε-complexity with randomization satisfies the following estimates*

$$c\, m^{\text{avg-ran}}(\varepsilon) \le \text{comp}^{\text{avg-ran}}(\varepsilon) \le (c+2)\, m^{\text{avg-ran}}(\varepsilon),$$

   (ii) U^* *is almost optimal,*
   (iii) *randomization does not help significantly,*

$$m^{\text{avg}}(\varepsilon) - \tfrac{1}{2} \le m^{\text{avg-ran}}(\varepsilon) \le m^{\text{avg}}(\varepsilon).$$

We illustrate Corollary 3.1.1 for the error functional $\text{ER}(g) = 1$ if $\|g\| \ge \varepsilon$, and $\text{ER}(g) = 0$ otherwise. As we know from Chapter 8, the probabilistic setting corresponds to this error functional. Thus, randomization does not help significantly for linear problems in the probabilistic setting.

NR 3.1:2 To see that the estimates $m^{\text{avg}}(\varepsilon) - 1/2 \le m^{\text{avg-ran}}(\varepsilon) \le m^{\text{avg}}(\varepsilon)$ are sharp, consider the integration problem with the classical Wiener measure, $r = 0$, and with Λ consisting of function evaluations. We claim (the derivation is left to the reader in **E 3.1:1**) that for infinitely many values of ε, the optimal U^* is determined by i^*, j^*, and a^* such that $i^* + 1 = j^*$ and $a^* = 1/2$. Furthermore, $N_{i^*}^*$ and $N_{j^*}^*$ consist of function evaluations at disjoint sets of points. Hence, for such values of ε, we have $m^{\text{avg}}(\varepsilon) - 1/2 = m^{\text{avg-ran}}(\varepsilon)$. On the other hand, taking $\varepsilon = r^{\text{avg}}(N_k^*)$ for arbitrary k, we get $m^{\text{avg}}(\varepsilon) = m^{\text{avg-ran}}(\varepsilon) = k$.

Exercises

E 3.1:1 Prove the claim from **NR 3.1:2**. Hint: Use the fact that $N_n^*(f) = [f(2/(2n + 1)), f(4/(2n + 1)), \dots, f(2n/(2n + 1))]$ is the unique nth optimal information, see **NR 2.1:3** of Chapter 7.

3.2. Linear Problems for Bounded Domains

In this section we assume that $F = B_q$, similarly to Section 5.8 of Chapter 6. Using the results from the previous section and essentially repeating step by step the proof of Theorem 5.8.1 of Chapter 6, one obtains

THEOREM 3.2.1.

(i) *Let* $x = 1 - \mu(B_q)$ *satisfy* $1 - x - \sqrt{3x} > 0$. *Then*

$$\frac{c}{c+2} \frac{1 - x - \sqrt{3x}}{1 - x} \, \mathrm{comp}^{\mathrm{avg\text{-}ran}} \left(\varepsilon \sqrt{\frac{1 - x}{1 - x - \sqrt{3x}}} \right)$$

$$\leq \mathrm{comp}^{\mathrm{avg\text{-}ran}}(\varepsilon, q) \leq \frac{1}{1 - x} \, \mathrm{comp}^{\mathrm{avg\text{-}ran}} \left(\varepsilon \sqrt{1 - x} \right).$$

(ii) *If*

$$\mathrm{comp}^{\mathrm{avg\text{-}ran}}(\varepsilon(1 + \delta)) = \mathrm{comp}^{\mathrm{avg\text{-}ran}}(\varepsilon) \, (1 + O(\delta)) \quad \text{as } \delta \to 0$$

then for any $a < a^*$, a^* *defined in Section 5.8 of Chapter 6,*

$$\mathrm{comp}^{\mathrm{avg\text{-}ran}}(\varepsilon, q) = \mathrm{comp}^{\mathrm{avg\text{-}ran}}(\varepsilon) \, \left(1 + o\big(\exp(-q^2 a/2) \big) \right) \left(1 + O(c^{-1}) \right)$$

as q *and* c *go to infinity.*

Combining Theorems 3.1.1 and 3.2.1, we have

COROLLARY 3.2.1. *Suppose that* $\mathrm{comp}^{\mathrm{avg}} \left(\varepsilon(1 + \delta) \right) = \mathrm{comp}^{\mathrm{avg}} \left(1 + O(\delta) \right)$ *as* $\delta \to 0$. *Then for large* c *and* q, *and small* ε, *we have*

$$\mathrm{comp}^{\mathrm{avg\text{-}ran}}(\varepsilon, q) \simeq \mathrm{comp}^{\mathrm{avg}}(\varepsilon).$$

Notes and Remarks

NR 3.2:1 Theorem 3.2.1 as well as Corollary 3.2.1 can be generalized for a continuous linear functional and different error criteria along the lines of **NR 5.8:2** of Chapter 6. In particular, Corollary 3.2.1 holds for the absolute error criterion defined in the $\mathcal{L}_p$ sense, $p \in [1, +\infty)$.

4. Worst Case Setting

In this section, we study randomization in the worst case setting. In Section 4.1, we prove that randomization does not help for such problems as function approximation, optimization, function inverse, and topological degree. Section 4.2 is based on Novak [87c]. We present there sharp complexity bounds for integration of multivariate functions. In Section 4.3, we study linear problems with an unrestricted class Λ and prove that randomization does not help in this case.

4.1. Function Approximation and Other Problems

In this section we estimate the worst case complexity with randomization for an arbitrary solution operator S, $S : F \to G$, where F is a class of functions,
$$F \subset \{f : D \to \mathbb{R} : f^{(r)} \text{ is continuous on } D\}$$
with $D = [0,1]^d$. Information consists of function and/or derivatives values at some (perhaps randomly chosen) points.

To derive lower bounds, we assume without loss of generality that random information is of the following form
$$N_{\vec{t}}(f) = [f(t_1), \dots, f^{(r)}(t_1), \dots, f(t_k), \dots, f^{(r)}(t_k); \vec{t}\,],$$
where $\vec{t} = [t_0, t_1, \dots]$ and t_i are selected randomly with probability ρ_i. Here, $f^{(r)}$ denotes the Frechet derivative of f and the cardinality of $N_{\vec{t}}$ is equal to $n_{\vec{t}}(f) = k\, d \binom{d+r}{r}$, see **E 4:1** of Chapter 4. Note that $n_{\vec{t}}(f)$ depends linearly on k.

Recall that given $U = (\phi, N, \vec{\rho})$, randomization in the ith step may depend on the already computed values. This means that $\vec{\rho}$ is a function of f. In what follows, we shall write $\vec{\rho}_f$ for the probability measure of randomization when f is fixed. Note that $\vec{\rho}_{f_1} = \vec{\rho}_{f_2}$ if the functions f_1 and f_2 have the same information.

LEMMA 4.1.1. *Suppose that for arbitrary random information there exist a function f^* from F, and sequences $\{A_k\}_{k=1}^{\infty}$ and $\{f_k\}_{k=1}^{\infty}$ such that for each k,*

(i) *$f_k \in F$ and $A_k \subset D$ is Borel measurable,*
(ii) *$f_k|_{D-A_k} = f^*|_{D-A_k}$,*
(iii) *$\vec{\rho}_{f^*}(\{\vec{t} : t_i \notin A_k, \forall i \le k\}) \ge \frac{1}{2}$.*

Then

$$\text{comp}^{\text{wor-ran}}(\varepsilon)$$
$$\ge c \inf \left\{ \sum_{i=1}^{\infty} i\, p_i : p_i \ge 0, \sum_{i=0}^{\infty} p_i = 1, \left| \sum_{i=0}^{k} p_i - \tfrac{1}{2} \right| \le \frac{2\varepsilon}{\|S(f_k) - S(f^*)\|}, \forall k \right\}$$
$$\ge c \sup_{k}\, (k+1) \left[\frac{1}{2} - \frac{2\,\varepsilon}{\|S(f_k) - S(f^*)\|} \right].$$

PROOF: Take an arbitrary $U = (\phi, N, \rho)$ with $e^{\text{wor-ran}}(U) \le \varepsilon$. Let D_i be the set of $\vec{t}$ for which f^* is evaluated at exactly i points. Then

$$\text{cost}^{\text{wor-ran}}(U) \ge c \sum_{i=1}^{\infty} i\, \vec{\rho}_{f^*}(D_i). \tag{1}$$

Note that for every k,

$$e^{\text{wor-ran}}(U) \geq \sum_{i=0}^{k} \int_{D_i} \|S(f_k) - \phi_{\vec{t}}(N_{\vec{t}}(f_k))\| \, \vec{\rho}_{f_k}(d\vec{t})$$

$$\geq \sum_{i=0}^{k} \int_{D_{i,k}} \|S(f_k) - \phi_{\vec{t}}(N_{\vec{t}}(f_k))\| \, \vec{\rho}_{f_k}(d\vec{t}),$$

where $D_{i,k} = \{\vec{t} \in D_i : t_j \notin A_k, \forall j \leq k\}$. Due to (ii), $N_{\vec{t}}(f_k) = N_{\vec{t}}(f^*)$ for $\vec{t} \in D_{i,k}$ and $\vec{\rho}_{f_k} = \vec{\rho}_{f^*}$. Therefore, the above estimate holds also with f_k replaced by f^*. Hence

$$\varepsilon \geq e^{\text{wor-ran}}(U) \geq \tfrac{1}{2} \|S(f_k) - S(f^*)\| \sum_{i=0}^{k} \vec{\rho}_{f^*}(D_{i,k}).$$

Due to (iii),

$$\sum_{i=0}^{k} \vec{\rho}_{f^*}(D_{i,k}) \geq \sum_{i=0}^{k} \vec{\rho}_{f^*}(D_i) - \vec{\rho}_{f^*}(\{\vec{t} : t_i \in A_k \text{ for some } i \leq k\})$$

$$\geq \sum_{i=0}^{k} \vec{\rho}_{f^*}(D_i) - \tfrac{1}{2}.$$

This, together with (1) and the fact that $\sum_{i=0}^{\infty} \vec{\rho}_{f^*}(D_i) = 1$, proves the first inequality. The second one follows from the fact that $\sum_{i=0}^{k} p_i - 1/2 = 1/2 - \sum_{i=k+1}^{\infty} p_i$ and $\sum_{i=1}^{\infty} i\, p_i \geq (k+1) \sum_{i=k+1}^{\infty} p_i$. ∎

LEMMA 4.1.2. *For an arbitrary measure $\vec{\rho}_{f^*}$ and for every k and m, there exists a cube*

$$A_{j^*,m} = \left[\frac{j_1^*}{m}, \frac{j_1^*+1}{m}\right] \times \cdots \times \left[\frac{j_d^*}{m}, \frac{j_d^*+1}{m}\right] \subset D$$

such that

$$\vec{\rho}_{f^*}(\{\vec{t} : t_i \notin A_{j^*,m}, \forall i \leq k\}) \geq 1 - \frac{k}{m^d}.$$

PROOF: There are m^d disjoint (modulo boundaries) cubes $A_{j,m}$ forming the partition of D. Let $p_{i,j}$ be the probability that $t_i \in A_{j,m}$. Then $k = \sum_{i=1}^{k} \sum_{j} p_{i,j}$, which implies that for some j^* we have $\sum_{i=1}^{k} p_{i,j^*} \leq k/m^d$. Since $\sum_{i=1}^{k} p_{i,j^*} \geq \vec{\rho}_{f^*}(\{\vec{t} : t_i \in A_{j^*,m} \text{ for some } i \leq k\})$, the proof is complete. ∎

We now apply Lemmas 4.1.1 and 4.1.2 to a number of solution operators.

4.1.1. Function Approximation

Let $S(f) = f$ and $F = \{f : D \to \mathbb{R} : \|f^{(r)}\|_{\sup} \leq 1\}$. Let G be the space of continuous functions with the sup-norm. We apply Lemma 4.1.1 with $f^* = 0$, and $\{A_k\}$ and $\{f_k\}$ defined as follows.

For given k, let $m = m(k) := \lceil (2k)^{1/d} \rceil$. The set A_k is a cube $A_{j^*,m}$ from Lemma 4.1.2. Obviously, it satisfies (iii). The functions f_k is given by

$$f_k(x) = \alpha \, m^{2d(r+1)-r} \prod_{i=1}^{d} \left[x_i - \frac{j_i^*}{m} \right]_+^{r+1} \left[\frac{j_i^* + 1}{m} - x_i \right]_+^{r+1}.$$

Here $\alpha = \alpha(r, d)$ is a normalizing positive constant so that $\|f_k^{(r)}\|_{\sup} \leq 1$. Observe that α is independent of m. Obviously, f_k belongs to F and vanishes outside A_k. Therefore, (i) and (ii) are satisfied.

Note that $\|S(f^*) - S(f_k)\| = \|f_k\| = \alpha \, 2^{-2d(r+1)} \, m^{-r} = c_1 m^{-r}$. Hence, Lemma 4.1.1 yields

$$\mathrm{comp}^{\mathrm{wor\text{-}ran}}(\varepsilon) \geq c \sup_k (k+1) \left[\frac{1}{2} - \frac{2\varepsilon}{c_1} m(k)^r \right].$$

For given ε, choose $k^* = k^*(\varepsilon) = \lfloor (c_1/8\varepsilon)^{d/r}/2 \rfloor$. Then $1/2 - 2\varepsilon c_1^{-1} m(k^*)^r \geq 1/4$ and

$$\mathrm{comp}^{\mathrm{wor\text{-}ran}}(\varepsilon) \geq \tfrac{1}{4} c \, (k^* + 1) = \Omega\big(c\varepsilon^{-d/r}\big).$$

This bound is sharp (modulo a multiplicative constant) since there are algorithms using $\Theta\left(\varepsilon^{-d/r}\right)$ function values at deterministically chosen points whose error does not exceed ε for any $f \in F$. For instance, one such algorithm is provided by the tensor product of one-dimensional perfect splines interpolating f at the points of a regular grid. We summarize this in

THEOREM 4.1.1. *For the function approximation problem, randomization does not help and*

$$\mathrm{comp}^{\mathrm{wor\text{-}ran}}(\varepsilon) = \Theta\left(\mathrm{comp}^{\mathrm{wor}}(\varepsilon)\right) = \Theta\big(c\varepsilon^{-d/r}\big).$$

4.1.2. Maximum and Extremal Points

We begin with the function maximum problem defined as follows. Let the class F be as in Section 4.1.1. Let $S(f) = \max_{x \in D} f(x)$ and $G = \mathbb{R}$

with $\|g\| = |g|$. This problem has been studied by Nemirovsky and Yudin [78, 83]. They proved that

$$\text{comp}^{\text{wor-ran}}(\varepsilon) = \Omega\big(c\varepsilon^{-d/r}\big). \tag{2}$$

This bound is sharp since there exist deterministic algorithms that use $\Theta\,(\varepsilon^{-d/r})$ function values at deterministically chosen points whose error is at most ε for any $f \in F$. One such algorithm is provided by the search of the maximal value of f at the points of a regular grid. Note that (2) easily follows from Lemma 4.1.1 with f^*, f_k, and A_k constructed as in the function approximation problem since $|S(f^*) - S(f_k)| = c_1 m^{-r}$ also holds for the function maximum problem.

We now discuss the extremal points problem, where an approximation to x_f, $f(x_f) = \max_{x \in D} f(x)$, is sought. Since the result we are going to report is negative, we restrict the class F by assuming additionally that $d = 1$ and that any $f \in F$ has exactly one extremal point x_f. Then $S(f) = x_f$ and $G = \mathbb{R}$ with $|\cdot|$ as its norm.

For small $\delta > 0$, take $f^*(x) = (x(\delta - x))_+^{r+1}$. Instead of cubes from Lemma 4.1.2, consider the sets $A_{j,m} = (0, \delta) \cup [(m + j)/(2m), (m + j + 1)/(2m)]$. Certainly, for any $\vec{\rho}_{f^*}$ there exists a positive δ_0 such that for all δ with $\delta \le \delta_0$, Lemma 4.1.2 holds for one of the sets $A_{j,m}$. This will be the set A_k in Lemma 4.1.1. The function f_k is defined in a similar way as in the function approximation problem. Since $S(f_k) - S(f^*) = x_{f_k} - x_{f^*} \ge (1 - \delta)/2$, Lemma 4.1.1 yields

$$\text{comp}^{\text{wor-ran}}(\varepsilon) = +\infty$$

for $\varepsilon < 1/8$. We summarize this in

THEOREM 4.1.2. *For the maximum problem,*

$$\text{comp}^{\text{wor-ran}}(\varepsilon) = \Theta\,(\text{comp}^{\text{wor}}(\varepsilon)) = \Theta\big(c\varepsilon^{-d/r}\big),$$

and for the extremum point problem with $\varepsilon < 1/8$,

$$\text{comp}^{\text{wor-ran}}(\varepsilon) = \text{comp}^{\text{wor}}(\varepsilon) = +\infty.$$

Hence, randomization does not help for either problem.

4.1.3. Function Inverse

The function inverse problem is to approximate f^{-1}, where f is a one-to-one function. We choose F to be the class of d-dimensional *one-to-one* functions $f = (f_1, \ldots, f_d) : D \to D$ such that $f(D) = D$, $f(0, \ldots, 0) = (0, \ldots, 0)$, $f(1, \ldots, 1) = (1, \ldots, 1)$, and $\max_{i,j} \|\partial f_j / \partial x_i\|_{\sup} \leq 2$. Then $S(f) = f^{-1}$ is a well defined operator with range in G, the space of continuous functions with norm $\|[h_1, \ldots, h_d]\| = \max_i \|h_i\|_{\sup}$.

We apply Lemma 4.1.1 with $f^*(x) = x$, A_k a cube as before, and $f_k(x) = f^*(x) + (g_k(x), \ldots, g_k(x))$. Here

$$g_k(x) = \delta \, (2m)^{4d-1} \prod_{i=1}^{d} \left[x_i - \frac{j_i^*}{m} \right]_+^2 \left[\frac{j_i^* + 1}{m} - x_i \right]_+^2 ,$$

where $m = m(k) = \lceil (2k)^{1/d} \rceil$ as in Section 4.1.1, and $\delta \in (0,1)$ is chosen such that $f_k \in F$. It is easy to check that for small δ, $\|S(f^*) - S(f_k)\| = \Theta(m^{-1}) = \Theta(k^{-1/d})$. Hence, Lemma 4.1.1 yields

$$\mathrm{comp}^{\mathrm{wor\text{-}ran}}(\varepsilon) = \Omega(c\,\varepsilon^{-d}).$$

This bound is sharp since there exists a deterministic algorithm using $\Theta(\varepsilon^{-d})$ function values whose error is at most ε for any $f \in F$. We omit the proof since it is similar to the proof from Wasilkowski [83b], where deterministic methods for inverting scalar functions ($d = 1$) have been studied. We summarize this in

THEOREM 4.1.3. *For the function inverse problem, randomization does not help and*

$$\mathrm{comp}^{\mathrm{wor\text{-}ran}}(\varepsilon) = \Theta\big(\mathrm{comp}^{\mathrm{wor}}(\varepsilon) \big) = \Theta(c\,\varepsilon^{-d}).$$

4.1.4. Topological Degree

We now apply Lemma 4.1.1 to estimate the complexity of computing the topological degree of functions. This problem for the worst case setting without randomization is discussed in Section 13 of Chapter 5. As in that section, let

$$F = \{ f : D \to \mathbb{R}^d : \|f(x) - f(y)\| \leq K \|x - y\|, \ \forall\, x, y \in D, \text{ and}$$
$$\|f(x)\| \geq \kappa, \ \forall\, x \in \partial D \}$$

with $d \geq 2$, $D = [0,1]^d$, K and κ positive numbers, and $\|\cdot\| = \|\cdot\|_\infty$. The solution operator is $S(f) = \deg(f)$ and Λ consists of function evaluations.

As reported in Section 13 of Chapter 5, Boult and Sikorski [85, 86] proved that

$$\mathrm{comp}^{\mathrm{wor}}(0) = \Theta\left(c \left(\frac{K}{8\,\kappa} \right)^{d-1} \right) \quad \text{as} \quad \frac{K}{8\,\kappa} \to +\infty.$$

We now show that the same estimate holds even if randomization is allowed. The proof of Boult and Sikorski [86] is based on the following observation, which will be also used in applying Lemma 4.1.1. Let A be a cube of diameter not exceeding $8\kappa/K$ with one face on the boundary of D. Then there exists a function $\tilde{f} \in F$ with $|S(\tilde{f})| = 1$ and such that $\tilde{f}|_{D-A} = (\kappa, \ldots, \kappa)$.

We are ready to apply Lemma 4.1.1. Take $f^* = (\kappa, \ldots, \kappa)$. Let $m = \lceil K/(8\kappa) \rceil$. For $k \leq (2dm^{d-1} - 1)/2$, we take $A_k = A^*$, where A^* is a cube of diameter $1/m$ with one face on ∂D, and for which (iii) of Lemma 4.1.1 holds. Such a cube exists since one can partition the boundary of D into $2dm^{d-1}$ cubes of dimension $(d-1)$ and with diameter $1/m$. The functions f_k are equal to $\tilde{f}$. For $k > (2dm^{d-1} - 1)/2$, we take $A_k = \emptyset$ and $f_k = f^*$. Since $S(f^*) = 0$ and $|S(\tilde{f})| = 1$, Lemma 4.1.1 yields that $\mathrm{comp}^{\mathrm{wor}\text{-}\mathrm{ran}}(0) = \Omega\left(c\,d\,m^{d-1}\right)$. We summarize this in

THEOREM 4.1.4. *For the topological degree problem, randomization does not help and for large $K/(8\kappa)$ we have*

$$\mathrm{comp}^{\mathrm{wor}\text{-}\mathrm{ran}}(0) = \Theta\left(\mathrm{comp}^{\mathrm{wor}}(0)\right) = \Theta\left(c\left(\frac{K}{8\kappa}\right)^{d-1}\right).$$

Notes and Remarks

NR 4.1:1 Randomization with information of *fixed* cardinality for the function approximation and optimization problems in different classes of functions has been studied in many papers. In particular, Novak [83, 85, 87a] considers the classes $C_d^{r,\alpha}$ and $W_p^{r,d}$, where $r \geq 1$, $\alpha \in (0,1]$ and $p \in [1, +\infty]$, see **NR 2:1** of Chapters 5 and 7. It is known, see Novak [87a], that for Λ consisting of function evaluations, randomization with fixed cardinality of information does not help for the function approximation and optimization problems in the class $C_d^{r,\alpha}$ or $W_p^{r,d}$ with $rp > d$. For both problems in $C_d^{r,\alpha}$, the nth minimal radii are proportional to $n^{-(r+\alpha)/d}$, whereas for the function approximation problem in $W_p^{r,d}$ with $rp > d$, it is proportional to $n^{-(r/d-1/p)}$.

For the function approximation and optimization problems, randomization does not help even if random varying cardinality of information is used. This can be proven using Lemma 4.1.1, and details are left to the reader.

Exercises

E 4.1:1 Let F be the class of regular functions, like in Section 4.1.1, which have a unique zero α_f, $f(\alpha_f) = 0$. Let Λ consist of function and derivatives evaluations, and let $S(f) = \alpha_f$. Here $G = \mathbb{R}^d$ with the $\mathcal{L}_2$-norm. Using Lemmas 4.1.1 and 4.1.2, prove that $\mathrm{comp}^{\mathrm{wor}\text{-}\mathrm{ran}}(\varepsilon) = +\infty$ for small ε.

E 4.1:2 Consider the following function zero problem: F, Λ, and S are as in **E 4.1:1**, but now the error of an approximation $U_t(f)$ is measured in the residual sense, i.e., we want $|f(U_t(f))|$ to be small. Using Lemmas 4.1.1 and 4.1.2, find a tight complexity lower bound for this problem. Hint: Show that this problem is essentially equivalent to the function approximation problem.

E 4.1:3 Consider the following extremal points problem: F, Λ, and S are as in Section 4.1.2 but now the error of an approximation $U_t(f)$ is measured in the residual sense, i.e., we want $\max_{x \in D} f(x) - f(U_t(f))$ to be small. Let $r^{\text{wor}}(n)$ be the worst case nth minimal radius for this problem. Prove that $r^{\text{wor}}(n+1) \geq r^{\text{wor}}(n; I)$, where $r^{\text{wor}}(n; I)$ stands for the worst case nth minimal radius for the function approximation problem. Using this estimate and Lemas 4.1.1 and 4.1.2, derive a tight complexity lower bound for this extremum points problem with randomization.

E 4.1:4 Let $F = C_d^{r,\alpha}$ as in **NR 4.1:1**. Prove that for the function approximation and optimization problems, randomization does not help even if random varying cardinality of information is used.

4.2. Integration

In this section we study the integration problem,

$$S(f) = \int_D f(x)\, dx,$$

for F and Λ defined as

$$F := \left\{ f : D \to \mathbb{R} : f^{(r)} \text{ is continuous and } \|f^{(r)}\|_{\sup} \leq 1 \right\},$$

$D = [0,1]^d$, and Λ consists of function and/or derivatives evaluations.

This problem has been extensively studied, and there are many papers devoted to this subject. We are not in a position to cover the relevant literature. Instead, we recall some results of Bakhvalov [59], and present a recent result of Novak, see Novak [87c]. Bakhvalov exhibited random information of fixed cardinality n and an algorithm with error proportional to $n^{-(r/d+1/2)}$. In terms of complexity this means that

$$\text{comp}^{\text{wor-ran}}(\varepsilon) = O\!\left(c\,\varepsilon^{-2d/(2r+d)}\right).$$

Bakhvalov also proved that no information *of fixed cardinality* and no algorithm can have error smaller that $\Theta\left(n^{-(r/d+1/2)}\right)$. Novak proved that this bound is sharp even among information with *random* cardinality. Namely,

THEOREM 4.2.1. *For the integration problem,*

$$\text{comp}^{\text{wor-ran}}(\varepsilon) = \Theta\!\left(c\,\varepsilon^{-2d/(2r+d)}\right).$$

PROOF: It suffices to show that

$$\text{cost}^{\text{wor-ran}}(U) \leq c\,n \qquad \text{implies} \qquad e^{\text{wor-ran}}(U) \geq \alpha\,n^{-(r/d+1/2)},$$

where α is a positive number independent of n.

Consider therefore any U with $\text{cost}^{\text{wor-ran}}(U) \leq cn$. We first prove that for arbitrary probability measure μ on F,

$$e^{\text{wor-ran}}(U) \geq e^{\text{avg-ran}}(U) \geq \tfrac{1}{2} \inf\{r^{\text{avg}}(N) : \text{card}^{\text{avg}}(N) \leq 2n\},$$

where $r^{\text{avg}}(N)$ is the average radius of N in the $\mathcal{L}_1$ sense and $\text{card}^{\text{avg}}(N)$ is the average cardinality both with respect to μ. Indeed, since

$$\int_T \int_F n_t(f)\,\mu(df)\,\rho(dt) \leq n,$$

we conclude that the set $T' := \{t \in T : \int_F n_t(f)\,\mu(df) \leq 2n\}$ has ρ-measure at least $1/2$. Hence,

$$
\begin{aligned}
e^{\text{avg-ran}}(U) &\geq \int_{T'} \int_F |Sf - \phi_t(N_t(f))|\,\mu(df)\,\rho(dt) \\
&\geq \tfrac{1}{2}\inf\{r^{\text{avg}}(N) : \text{card}^{\text{avg}}(N) \leq 2n\},
\end{aligned}
$$

as claimed.

To complete the proof, we construct a probability measure μ for which

$$\inf\{r^{\text{avg}}(N) : \text{card}^{\text{avg}}(N) \leq 2n\} \geq \alpha_1\, n^{-(r/d+1/2)}$$

with α_1 a positive number which is independent of n. (In what follows, we shall use α_2 and α_3 to denote positive constants independent of n.) Let $f_1, \ldots, f_{8n}$ be nonnegative functions from F with disjoint supports such that $\int_D f_i(x)\,dx = \alpha_2\, n^{-(r/d+1)}$. Obviously, such functions exist, see e.g., Section 4.1.1. Consider

$$F_0 := \left\{ f = \sum_{i=1}^{8n} s_i f_i : s_i \in \{-1, +1\} \right\},$$

and μ concentrated on F_0, $\mu(\{f\}) = 2^{-8n}$ for every $f \in F_0$. Let N be arbitrary information with $\text{card}^{\text{avg}}(N) \leq 2n$. Then with μ-probability at least $1/2$, $n(f) \leq 4n$. Equivalently, with probability at least one half, $f = \sum_{i=1}^{8n} s_i f_i$ is known to within at most $4n$ coefficients s_i. From this, it can be shown that

$$
\begin{aligned}
r^{\text{avg}}(N) &\geq \frac{1}{2}\, n^{-(r/d+1)}\, \alpha_2\, 2^{-4n} \sum_{i=0}^{4n} \binom{4n}{i} |2n - i| \\
&\geq \alpha_3\, n^{-(r/d+1)}\, n^{1/2} = \alpha_3\, n^{-(r/d+1/2)}.
\end{aligned}
$$

This completes the proof. ∎

Notes and Remarks

NR 4.2:1 (Novak [87a,c]) Random information with *fixed* cardinality has been considered for the integration problem for a number of function classes. For example, consider the classes $C_d^{r,\alpha}$ and $W_p^{r,d}$ as in **NR 4.1:1**. Then the nth minimal radius $r^{\text{wor-ran}}(n, F)$ of random information with cardinality n in the class F with the error defined in the $\mathcal{L}_2$ sense is given by

$$r^{\text{wor-ran}}(n, C_d^{r,\alpha}) = \Theta(n^{-((r+\alpha)/d+1/2)})$$

$$r^{\text{wor-ran}}(n, W_p^{r,d}) = \Theta(n^{-(r/d+a)}),$$

where $a = 1/2$ if $p \geq 2$, and $a = 1 - 1/p$ for $p \in [1,2)$ and $r - d/p + d/2 \geq 0$, see Bakhvalov [59, 62] and Novak [87a] for the class $W_p^{r,d}$. Since the proof of Theorem 4.2.1 carries over to the classes mentioned above, we have

$$\text{comp}^{\text{wor-ran}}(\varepsilon, C_d^{r,\alpha}) = \Theta(\varepsilon^{-2d/(2(r+\alpha)+d)})$$

$$\text{comp}^{\text{wor-ran}}(\varepsilon, W_p^{r,d}) = \Theta(\varepsilon^{-d/(r+ad)}).$$

For deterministic information we have

$$r^{\text{wor}}(n, C_d^{r,\alpha}) = \Theta(n^{-(r+\alpha)/d}) \quad \text{and} \quad \text{comp}^{\text{wor}}(\varepsilon, C_d^{r,\alpha}) = \Theta(\varepsilon^{-d/(r+\alpha)}),$$

$$r^{\text{wor}}(n, W_p^{r,d}) = \Theta(n^{-r/d}) \quad \text{and} \quad \text{comp}^{\text{wor}}(\varepsilon, W_p^{r,d}) = \Theta(\varepsilon^{-d/r}),$$

whenever $r\,p > d$ or $p = 1$ and $r = d$, see Bakhvalov [59] for the class $C_d^{r,\alpha}$, and Sobolev [65], Polovinkin [74], and Novak [87a]. Further results may be found in Besov [80, 81].

4.3. Linear Problems with Unrestricted Information

In this section we consider continuous linear solution operators $S : F_1 \to G$ with F_1 and G being separable Hilbert spaces. The class F is the unit ball in F_1. Information may consist of evaluations of arbitrary continuous linear functionals chosen randomly and adaptively. That is, $\Lambda = F_1^*$. To simplify the analysis, we redefine the error of $U = (\phi, N, T, \rho)$ by taking

$$e^{\text{wor-ran}}(U) = \sup_{f \in F} \left(\int_{t \in T} \|S(f) - \phi_t(N_t(f))\|^2 \, \rho(dt) \right)^{1/2}.$$

We first recall some results concerning worst case complexity without randomization. Namely, let $K_1 = S^*S : F_1 \to F_1$, and let λ_i be defined by

$$\lambda_i = \inf \left\{ \sup_{\lambda \in \text{sp}(K_1) - B} \lambda : B \text{ has at most } k \text{ elements} \right\}.$$

Then

$$\text{comp}^{\text{wor}}(\varepsilon) = \Theta(c \, \min\{k : \lambda_k \leq \varepsilon^2\}),$$

see **NR 5.3:2** and **5.3:3** and Theorem 5.8.1 of Chapter 4.

We show now that the sequence $\{\lambda_i\}$ also plays an important role for randomization.

LEMMA 4.3.1.

$$\text{comp}^{\text{wor-ran}}(\varepsilon) = \Omega\left(c \, \min\left\{k : \sum_{i=k+1}^{\infty} \lambda_i \gamma_i \leq \varepsilon^2\right\}\right),$$

where $\{\gamma_i\}$ is an arbitrary sequence of nonincreasing positive numbers such that $\sum_{i=1}^{\infty} \gamma_i < +\infty$.

PROOF: We need the following simple observation. If the bound on $\|f\|$ in the definition of F is replaced by another number, say q, then the complexity $\text{comp}^{\text{wor-ran}}(\varepsilon, q)$ for the new problem equals $\text{comp}^{\text{wor-ran}}(\varepsilon/q)$. Hence, it is enough to bound $\text{comp}^{\text{wor-ran}}(\varepsilon, q)$, or equivalently to assume that the bound 1 in the definition of F is replaced by arbitrary q. This and Corollary 3.2.1 imply that for any Gaussian measure μ on F_1,

$$\text{comp}^{\text{wor-ran}}(\varepsilon) = \Omega(\text{comp}^{\text{avg}}(\varepsilon)).$$

Since $\Lambda = F_1^*$, we know from Chapter 6 that $\text{comp}^{\text{avg}}(\varepsilon) \geq c m^{\text{avg}}(\varepsilon)$ and

$$\lceil m^{\text{avg}}(\varepsilon) \rceil = \min\left\{k : \sum_{i=k+1}^{\infty} \alpha_i \leq \varepsilon^2\right\},$$

where $\{\alpha_i\}$ is a nonincreasing sequence of the eigenvalues of the correlation operator $C_\nu = C_\mu^{1/2} S^* S C_\mu^{1/2}$ of the *a priori* measure $\nu = \mu S^{-1}$. Hence to complete the proof, we need only choose an appropriate measure μ. Recall that for Hilbert spaces, any symmetric operator with finite trace is the correlation operator of some Gaussian measure. Hence, given the sequence $\{\gamma_i\}$, we take μ so that its correlation operator C_μ commutes with $K_1 = S^* S$ and has γ_i's as the eigenvalues. Then C_ν has the eigenvalues $\lambda_i \gamma_i$ which completes the proof. ∎

We illustrate Lemma 4.3.1 by the following examples.

(1) Let $\lambda_i \geq \alpha > 0$. Then for small ε,

$$\text{comp}^{\text{wor}}(\varepsilon) = \text{comp}^{\text{wor-ran}}(\varepsilon) = +\infty.$$

(2) Let $\lambda_i = i^{-p}$ for some positive p. Then setting $\gamma_i = i^{-(1+\delta)}$, $\delta > 0$, we get

$$\text{comp}^{\text{wor}}(\varepsilon) = \Theta(c\varepsilon^{-1/p})$$

and

$$\text{comp}^{\text{wor-ran}}(\varepsilon) = \Omega\left(c\varepsilon^{-(1/p-\delta)}\right), \; \forall \delta > 0.$$

(3) Let $\lambda_i = q^i$ for some positive $q < 1$. Then setting $\gamma_i = q_1^i$, $q_1 < 1$, we get

$$\text{comp}^{\text{wor}}(\varepsilon) = \Theta(\text{comp}^{\text{wor-ran}}(\varepsilon)) = \Theta(c\ln\varepsilon^{-1})$$

These results indicate that randomization does not help significantly for linear problems with unrestricted class of information.

Notes and Remarks

NR 4.3:1 We elaborate on the assumption that $\Lambda = F_1^*$. To indicate which class of permissible functionals is used, we write $\text{comp}^{\text{wor-ran}}(\varepsilon, \Lambda)$ and $\text{comp}^{\text{wor}}(\varepsilon, \Lambda)$ instead of $\text{comp}^{\text{wor-ran}}(\varepsilon)$ and $\text{comp}^{\text{wor}}(\varepsilon)$, respectively. Obviously, $\text{comp}^{\text{wor-ran}}(\varepsilon, \Lambda) \leq \text{comp}^{\text{wor}}(\varepsilon, \Lambda)$ and

$$\text{comp}^{\text{x}}(\varepsilon, \Lambda_1) \leq \text{comp}^{\text{x}}(\varepsilon, \Lambda_2) \quad \text{for} \quad \text{x} = \text{wor, wor-ran} \quad \text{and} \quad \Lambda_2 \subset \Lambda_1.$$

Hence, the results stated above say that $\text{comp}^{\text{wor-ran}}(\varepsilon, F_1^*)$ is essentially the same as $\text{comp}^{\text{wor}}(\varepsilon, F_1^*)$. Due to **NR 5.3:3** of Chapter 4, $\text{comp}^{\text{wor}}(\varepsilon, F_1^*) = \text{comp}^{\text{wor}}(\varepsilon, \Lambda^c)$, where Λ^c is the class of all finitely continuous (in general nonlinear) functionals. This means that for deterministic information, F_1^* is already as powerful as such an extremely large class as Λ^c. This may explain why randomization does not help.

NR 4.3:2 Results of this section can be applied to obtain a lower bound on complexity for restricted classes Λ, $\Lambda \subset F_1^*$. As indicated above, $\text{comp}^{\text{wor-ran}}(\varepsilon, \Lambda) \geq \text{comp}^{\text{wor-ran}}(\varepsilon, F_1^*)$, and $\text{comp}^{\text{wor-ran}}(\varepsilon, F_1^*)$ is insignificantly different from $\text{comp}^{\text{wor}}(\varepsilon, F_1^*)$. If additionally,

$$\text{comp}^{\text{wor}}(\varepsilon, F_1^*) = \Theta(\text{comp}^{\text{wor}}(\varepsilon, \Lambda))$$

then $\text{comp}^{\text{wor}}(\varepsilon, \Lambda)$, $\text{comp}^{\text{wor-ran}}(\varepsilon, \Lambda)$, $\text{comp}^{\text{wor}}(\varepsilon, F_1^*)$, and $\text{comp}^{\text{wor-ran}}(\varepsilon, F_1^*)$ are essentially proportional. To illustrate this, consider the function approximation problem. The solution operator is given by $S(f) = f$, Λ consists of function and/or derivatives evaluations, F is a ball in the Sobolev space $W_2^{r,d}$ defined in **NR 4.1:1**, and $G = \mathcal{L}_2([0,1]^d)$. It is known that

$$\text{comp}^{\text{wor}}(\varepsilon, F_1^*) = \Theta(\text{comp}^{\text{wor}}(\varepsilon, \Lambda)) = \Theta(c\varepsilon^{-d/r}).$$

Hence randomization does not significantly help for the function approximation problem in the class $W_2^{r,d}$ no matter which class Λ is used.

Exercises

E 4.3:1 Prove that randomization does not help for ill-posed problems, i.e., prove that $\text{comp}^{\text{wor-ran}}(\varepsilon) = +\infty$ for unbounded S and $\Lambda = F_1^*$.

Chapter 12

Noisy Information

1. Introduction

In this chapter we report some results concerning noisy information. Such information is much harder to analyze than exact information, and optimality results are quite limited. Therefore, we report only partial results concerning specific issues such as optimal error algorithms and adaption versus nonadaption for linear problems.

In Section 2 we discuss the worst case setting with deterministic noise. In Section 3 we discuss the average case setting assuming that the noise is a random variable. In Section 4 we briefly discuss mixed settings in which, for instance, the worst case setting with random noise is treated.

2. Worst Case Setting with Deterministic Noise

In this section we study the worst case setting with noisy information. As in Chapter 3, let $S : F \to G$ be a solution operator and let Λ be the class of permissible information operations.

2.1. Basic Definitions

Recall that any (exact) information has the following form

$$N(f) = [L_1(f), L_2(f; y_1), \ldots, L_{n(f)}(f; y_1, \ldots, y_{n(f)-1})],$$

where $y_i = L_i(f; y_1, \ldots, y_{i-1})$ is the exact value of the ith information operation, and the cardinality $n(f)$ of N at f is given by $n(f) = \min\{i : \text{ter}_i(y_1, \ldots, y_i) = 1\}$. We now assume that the ith evaluation is erroneously computed and, instead of the exact value y_i, we obtain a perturbed value z_i. For adaptive N, the choice of successive functionals is based on these observed values and not on the unknown exact values. Thus, at the ith step we get

$$z_i = y_i + x_i = L_i(f; z_1, \ldots, z_{i-1}) + x_i,$$

where the noise x_i is unknown. Also the termination decision is now based on the observed values z_i, i.e., we terminate the information computation when $\text{ter}_i(z_1, \ldots, z_i) = 1$. Hence, *noisy information* about f is equal to

$$N(f, \vec{x}) = [L_1(f) + x_1, \ldots, L_{n(f)}(f; z_1, \ldots, z_{n(f,\vec{x})-1}) + x_{n(f,\vec{x})}].$$

Here $\vec{x} = [x_1, x_2, \ldots]$ is noise, and $\vec{z} = [z_1, z_2, \ldots]$ is observed information with z_i given above. The cardinality of N at f depends now on $\vec{x}$ and is equal to

$$n(f, \vec{x}) = \min\left\{i : \text{ter}_i(z_1, \ldots, z_i) = 1\right\}.$$

Observe that for nonadaptive information N we have

$$N(f, \vec{x}) = N(f) + \vec{x}.$$

For adaptive N, this equality is not true in general since the choice of the ith functional as well as the total number of them may depend on the noise. That is, $L_{i,\vec{z}}(\cdot) = L_i(\cdot; z_1, \ldots, z_{i-1})$ may be different than $L_{i,\vec{y}}(\cdot) = L_i(\cdot; y_1, \ldots, y_{i-1})$. Using the notation $N_{\vec{z}} = [L_{1,\vec{z}}, \ldots, L_{n(f,\vec{x}),\vec{z}}]$, we have $N(f, \vec{x}) = N_{\vec{z}}(f) + \vec{x}$ but not necessarily $N(f, \vec{x}) = N(f) + \vec{x}$.

Usually we have some *a priori* knowledge about the possible values of x_i. For instance, we may know that $|x_i| \le \eta$ or $|x_i| \le \eta(|y_i| + \gamma)$ for some positive η and γ. In general, we assume that for every N and f we know a set $E(f, N)$ of all possible values of $\vec{x}$. Formally, this means that we are given a mapping,

$$E : F \times \Psi \to 2^{\mathbb{R}^\infty} - \emptyset,$$

where Ψ is the class of all permissible information operators N.

We give three examples of different operators E:

(i) $E(f, N) \equiv \{0\}$ corresponds to the exact information.

(ii) $E(f, N) = \{\vec{x} : |x_i| \le \eta, \forall i\}$ means that the absolute error of evaluating y_i does not exceed η. In this case, the bound on the noise is independent of f and N.

(iii) $E(f, N) = \{\vec{x} : |x_i| \le \eta |y_i|, \forall i\}$ means that the relative error of evaluating y_i does not exceed η. Here the bound on the noise depends on $y_i = L_i(f; z_1, \ldots, z_{i-1})$.

We now define the radius of noisy information. Although the radius can be defined independently of the concept of algorithm, see **NR 2.1:1**, we define it to be the minimal (worst case) error among all algorithms that use the information. The error of an algorithm ϕ is given now by

$$e^{\mathrm{wor}}(\phi, N, E) = \sup_{f \in F} \; \sup_{\vec{x} \in E(f, N)} \|S(f) - \phi(N(f, \vec{x}))\|.$$

Hence

$$r^{\mathrm{wor}}(N, E) = \inf_{\phi} e^{\mathrm{wor}}(\phi, N, E).$$

Note that if noise is not present, i.e., $E \equiv \{0\}$, then the above definitions coincide with the worst case definitions of Chapter 4,

$$r^{\mathrm{wor}}(N, \{0\}) = r^{\mathrm{wor}}(N) \quad \text{and} \quad e^{\mathrm{wor}}(\phi, N, \{0\}) = e^{\mathrm{wor}}(\phi, N).$$

The (worst case) cost of $U = (\phi, N, E)$ and the (worst case) ε-complexity are defined as in Chapter 3.

As for exact information, it is easy to see that varying cardinality does not help for linear problems with arbitrary E. Hence from now on we shall consider only information of fixed cardinality.

Notes and Remarks

NR 2.1:1 Following IUC we present a definition of the radius of information without using the concept of an algorithm. For a given $\vec{z}$ from $E(F, N)$, $A(\vec{z}) = \{f \in F : \vec{z} - N_{\vec{z}}(f) \in E(f, N)\}$ is the set of problem elements for which $\vec{z}$ could be a value of the noisy information. Hence the local radius of N at $\vec{z}$ is given by

$$r^{\mathrm{wor}}(N, E, \vec{z}) = \mathrm{rad}(S(A(\vec{z}))) = \inf_{g \in G} \sup \{\|S(f) - g\| : f \in F, \; \vec{z} - N_{\vec{z}}(f) \in E(f, N)\}.$$

The (global) radius is then given by $r^{\mathrm{wor}}(N, E) = \sup_{\vec{z}} r^{\mathrm{wor}}(N, E, \vec{z})$. Obviously, the radius defined in such a way is a sharp lower bound on the error of any algorithm that uses N. Hence the two definitions of the radius of information, presented here and in Section 2.1, coincide.

2.2. Uniformly Bounded Noise

In this section we deal with uniformly bounded noise. That is, for any information of cardinality n,

$$E(f, N) = \{\vec{x} \in \mathbb{R}^n : \|\vec{x}\|_E \le \eta\}, \quad \forall f \in F.$$

Here η is a given nonnegative number, and $\|\cdot\|_E$ is a norm. For $\|\cdot\|_E = \|\cdot\|_\infty$ we have the noise discussed in (ii) of Section 2.1.

Every problem defined by S, F, and N with uniformly bounded noise can be translated into an equivalent problem $\tilde{S}$, $\tilde{F}$, and $\tilde{N}$ with exact information. More precisely, for

$$\tilde{F} = F \times \{\vec{x} \in \mathbb{R}^n : \|\vec{x}\|_E \leq \eta\},$$
$$\tilde{S} : \tilde{F} \to G \quad \text{defined by} \quad \tilde{S}([f, \vec{x}]) = S(f),$$
$$\tilde{N}([f, \vec{x}]) = N(f, \vec{x}),$$

we obviously have

$$e^{\text{wor}}(\phi, \tilde{N}, \{0\}) = e^{\text{wor}}(\phi, N, E), \; \forall \phi, \quad \text{and}$$
$$r^{\text{wor}}(\tilde{N}, \{0\}) = r^{\text{wor}}(N, E).$$

This observation is important for a number of reasons. We explain this assuming that our problem is linear, see Section 5.1 of Chapter 4. That is, S is a linear operator, and $F = \{f : \|Tf\| \leq 1\}$ for some linear restriction operator T. Then the equivalent problem is also linear since $\tilde{S}$ is a linear operator, and $\tilde{F} = \{\tilde{f} = [f, \vec{x}] : \|\tilde{T}\tilde{f}\| \leq 1\}$ with a linear restriction operator $\tilde{T}([f, \vec{x}]) = [Tf, \vec{x}]$ and $\|\tilde{T}([f, \vec{x}])\| = \max\{\|Tf\|, \|\vec{x}\|_E/\eta\}$. Hence the analysis for linear problems with exact information can be used here. In particular, for nonadaptive information N with uniformly bounded noise we get

$$r^{\text{wor}}(N, E) = r^{\text{wor}}(\tilde{N}) = \alpha \; \sup\{\|\tilde{S}(\tilde{f})\| : \tilde{N}(\tilde{f}) = 0, \tilde{f} \in \tilde{F}\}$$
$$= \alpha \; \sup\{\|S(f)\| : \|N(f)\|_E \leq \eta, f \in F\},$$

where $\alpha \in [1, 2]$.

Since adaption does not help significantly for linear problems with exact information, see Section 5.2 of Chapter 4, we conclude that it also does not help significantly for linear problems with uniformly bounded noise.

We now discuss optimal algorithms that use nonadaptive information with uniformly bounded noise for linear problems. If S is a functional then there exists a linear optimal error algorithm which follows directly from Smolyak's Theorem 5.5.1 of Chapter 4 applied to $\tilde{S}$ and $\tilde{N}$. The same is true when $S(f)$ is a function and the norm in G is $\|\cdot\|_{\text{sup}}$. Obviously, both statements hold for arbitrary $\|\cdot\|_E$.

Linear optimal error algorithms exist for arbitrary linear S, provided that both $\|T(\cdot)\|$ and $\|\cdot\|_E$ are inner product norms. More precisely, for a given positive λ, let $\sigma_\lambda = \sigma_\lambda(\vec{z})$ be the smoothing spline, i.e., $\sigma_\lambda \in F$ and

$$\|T\sigma_\lambda\|^2 + \lambda\|N(\sigma_\lambda) - \vec{z}\|_E^2 = \inf_{f \in F_1} \left(\|Tf\|^2 + \lambda\|N(f) - \vec{z}\|_E^2\right).$$

Melkman and Micchelli [79] proved that there exists λ^* such that the smoothing spline algorithm $\phi_{\lambda^*}^s$,

$$\phi_{\lambda^*}^s(\vec{z}) = S(\sigma_{\lambda^*}(\vec{z})),$$

is an optimal error algorithm. Obviously, $\phi_{\lambda^*}^s$ is a linear algorithm.

We stress that this result holds when $\|\cdot\|_E$ is an inner product norm. The problem is open for other norms including $\|\cdot\|_E = \|\cdot\|_\infty$, which seems to be the most interesting case for uniformly bounded noise.

We now briefly discuss nth optimal information for a linear problem in which F_1 and G are separable Hilbert spaces with inner products $\langle \cdot, \cdot \rangle_1$ and $\langle \cdot, \cdot \rangle_2$, respectively, F is the unit ball in F_1, and $K_1 = S^*S$ is a compact operator. The class Λ is a subset of F_1^*, i.e., $L \in \Lambda$ implies that $L(f) = \langle f, \zeta \rangle_1$ for some $\zeta \in F_1$. Note that for uniformly bounded noise, one needs to restrict the class of permissible elements ζ. To see this, assume for a moment that $\Lambda = F_1^*$, take any $\zeta \neq 0$ and any number $\alpha \neq 0$, and define $L_\alpha(\cdot) = \langle \cdot, \alpha \zeta \rangle_1$. If $z_\alpha = y_\alpha + x_\alpha$, $|x_\alpha| \leq \eta$, is a noisy value of $y_\alpha = L_\alpha(f)$ then z_α/α tends to the exact value of $y = L(f) = \langle f, \zeta \rangle_1$ as α tends to infinity. Hence, since $\alpha \zeta$ is now permissible for any α, we are able to compute inner products with arbitrarily small error. This contradicts the essence of noisy evaluations.

Therefore, we restrict the class of permissible information operations to

$$\Lambda = \{ \langle \cdot, \zeta \rangle : \zeta \in F_1, \|\zeta\|_1 \leq 1 \} .$$

Recall that for exact information, $E \equiv \{0\}$, the nth minimal radius is equal to $r^{\text{wor}}(n, \{0\}) = \sqrt{\lambda_{n+1}}$, where λ_i are the ordered eigenvalues of $K_1 = S^*S$. The nth optimal information is given by

$$N_n^*(f) = [\langle f, \zeta_1^* \rangle, \dots, \langle f, \zeta_n^* \rangle],$$

where ζ_i^* is the normalized eigenelement of K_1 corresponding to λ_i.

We first discuss the noise for which $\|\cdot\|_E$ is a Euclidean norm, $\|\vec{z}\|_E = \left(\sum_{i=1}^n z_i^2 \right)^{1/2}$, and $\eta \leq 1$. It is easy to see that

$$r^{\text{wor}}(n, E) = \inf \{ r^{\text{wor}}(N, E) : N \text{ nonadaptive with cardinality } n \} \tag{1}$$
$$\geq \max \left\{ \sqrt{\eta^2 \lambda_1}, \sqrt{\lambda_{n+1}} \right\} .$$

Furthermore, for the information N_n^* one can easily show that

$$r^{\text{wor}}(N_n^*, E) = \sup \left\{ \|S(f)\|_2 : \|f\|_1 \leq 1, \sum_{i=1}^n \langle f, \zeta_i^* \rangle_1^2 \leq \eta^2, i = 1, \dots, n \right\}$$
$$= \sqrt{\eta^2 \lambda_1 + (1 - \eta^2) \lambda_{n+1}}.$$

Hence

$$\max\left\{\sqrt{\eta^2 \lambda_1}, \sqrt{\lambda_{n+1}}\right\} \le r^{\text{wor}}(n, E) \le r^{\text{wor}}(N_n^*, E)$$
$$= \sqrt{\eta^2 \lambda_1 + (1 - \eta^2) \lambda_{n+1}}.$$

From this we have $r^{\text{wor}}(N_n^*, E) \le \sqrt{2}\, r^{\text{wor}}(n, E)$. Thus, N_n^* is always close to nth optimal information. For small η, $\eta^2(\lambda_1 - \lambda_{n+1}) << \lambda_{n+1}$, we have

$$r^{\text{wor}}(n, E) \simeq r^{\text{wor}}(N_n^*, E) \simeq \sqrt{\lambda_{n+1}} = r^{\text{wor}}(n, \{0\}).$$

For such η, the effect of noise is negligible.

We now consider the noise in the $\mathcal{L}_\infty$ norm, $\|\cdot\|_E = \|\cdot\|_\infty$ and $\eta < 1$. The estimate (1) also holds for this case. It can be shown that for N_n^*,

$$r^{\text{wor}}(N_n^*, E) = \left(\eta^2 \sum_{i=1}^{k} \lambda_i + \lambda_{n+1}(1 - k\eta^2)\right)^{1/2},$$

where $k = \min\{n, \lfloor 1/\eta^2 \rfloor\}$. Hence,

$$\max\left\{\sqrt{\eta^2 \lambda_1}, \sqrt{\lambda_{n+1}}\right\} \le r^{\text{wor}}(n, E) \le r^{\text{wor}}(N_n^*, E)$$
$$= \left(\eta^2 \sum_{i=1}^{k} \lambda_i + \lambda_{n+1}(1 - k\eta^2)\right)^{1/2}.$$

This estimate is sharp (modulo a multiplicative constant) if, for instance, the eigenvalues of K_1 converge to zero fast enough, $\lambda_i = O(i^{-p})$ for $p > 1$. For small η, $\eta^2 \sum_{i=1}^{k}(\lambda_i - \lambda_{n+1}) << \lambda_{n+1}$, we have

$$r^{\text{wor}}(n, E) \simeq r^{\text{wor}}(N_n^*, E) \simeq \sqrt{\lambda_{n+1}} = r^{\text{wor}}(n, \{0\}),$$

and N_n^* is almost nth optimal also for uniformly bounded noise in the $\mathcal{L}_\infty$ norm, and the effect of the noise is negligible.

On the other hand, if $\eta^2 \sum_{i=1}^{k}(\lambda_i - \lambda_{n+1})$ is comparable to or larger than λ_{n+1}, the nth optimal information is not known.

We finally discuss the ε-complexity $\text{comp}^{\text{wor}}(\varepsilon, \eta)$ with noise bounded by η in the $\mathcal{L}_\infty$ norm. For $\varepsilon < \eta\sqrt{\lambda_1}$, (1) implies that $\text{comp}^{\text{wor}}(\varepsilon, \eta) = +\infty$. On the other hand, if $\varepsilon \ge \eta\sqrt{\lambda_1}$ and $\eta^2 \sum_{i=1}^{k}(\lambda_i - \lambda_{n+1}) << \lambda_{n+1}$ with $n = m^{\text{wor}}(\varepsilon) = \min\{i : \sqrt{\lambda_{i+1}} \le \varepsilon\}$ then the ε-complexity for noisy information is roughly the same as for the exact information. If additionally the cost c of one inner product evaluation is large, then

$$\text{comp}^{\text{wor}}(\varepsilon, \eta) \simeq \text{comp}^{\text{wor}}(\varepsilon) \simeq c\, m^{\text{wor}}(\varepsilon).$$

In this case, the information N_n^* and the spline algorithm are almost optimal and the effect of noise is negligible. If, however, $\eta^2 \sum_{i=1}^k (\lambda_i - \lambda_{n+1})$ is comparable or larger than λ_{n+1} then the $\text{comp}^{\text{wor}}(\varepsilon, \eta)$ is unknown.

Notes and Remarks

NR 2.2:1 Papers on uniformly bounded noise include Chernousko [68], Marchuk and Osipenko [75], Micchelli and Rivlin [77], Melkman and Micchelli [79], Gal and Micchelli [80]. There is also an interesting stream of research on optimal algorithms for uniformly bounded noise and complete information, i.e., N is *one-to-one* and $F = F_1$ is finite dimensional, see Milanese and Belforte [82], Milanese, Tempo, and Vicino [84, 86], Kacewicz, Milanese, Tempo, and Vicino [86], Kacewicz, Milanese, and Tempo [87], Milanese and Tempo [85], and Vicino, Tempo, Genesio, and Milanese [87]. The latter work has practical applications for problems arising in system identification, parameter and state estimation, and prediction.

NR 2.2:2 Micchelli and Rivlin [77] studied uniformly bounded noise for linear problems with nonadaptive information. The idea of replacing S, F, and N by $\tilde{S}$, $\tilde{F}$, and $\tilde{N}$ is due to them. The fact that adaption does not essentially help was observed in IUC.

NR 2.2:3 (Lee, Pavlidis, and Wasilkowski [87]). Consider $S(f) = f$ with $G = C([0,1])$ and $F = \{f : [0,1] \to \mathbb{R} : f^{(r-1)}$ is abs. cont. and $\|f^{(r)}\|_\infty \le 1\}$. The class Λ consists of function and derivatives evaluations. The noise is defined by $\|\cdot\|_E = \|\cdot\|_\infty$. It is easy to see that for any information N,

$$r^{\text{wor}}(N, E) \ge r^{\text{wor}}(N) + \eta.$$

Hence, from Tikhomirov [69], see also **NR 3:1** of Chapter 5, we get that $r^{\text{wor}}(n, E) \ge K_r (\pi n)^{-r} (1 + o(1)) + \eta$, where K_r is the rth Favard constant. This bound is achieved by piecewise Lagrange polynomial interpolation at n equally spaced points for $r = 1$ and 2. For $r \ge 3$, an algorithm based on piecewise Lagrange interpolation polynomial at n "almost" equally spaced points has the error not exceeding

$$\left(\sqrt{2/(r\pi)} \, (2n)^{-r} + \sqrt{r/(2\pi)} \, \eta \right) (1 + O(r^{-1})).$$

This means that

$$r^{\text{wor}}(n, E) = a_1 \, n^{-r} + a_2 \, \eta$$

with

$$K_r \, \pi^{-r} (1 + o(1)) \le a_1 \le \sqrt{\frac{2}{r\pi}} \, 2^{-r} (1 + O(r^{-1})) \quad \text{and} \quad 1 \le a_2 \le \sqrt{\frac{r}{2\pi}} (1 + O(r^{-1})).$$

Hence, we have that $\text{comp}^{\text{wor}}(\varepsilon, E) = +\infty$ if $\varepsilon \le \eta$, and $\text{comp}^{\text{wor}}(\varepsilon, E) = \Theta(c \varepsilon^{-r})$ for $\varepsilon >> \eta$.

NR 2.2:4 Uniformly bounded noise is unrealistic for a number of problems. To see this, consider the following example. Let S and F be as in **NR 2.2:3** with $r \ge 1$. Consider $N(f) = [f(t_1), \ldots, f(t_n)]$. For $r \ge 1$, both z_i and $f(t_i)$ can attain arbitrary large values in the class F, though uniformly bounded noise implies that $|f(t_i) - z_i| \le \eta$ no matter how large z_i is. However, even if we make the idealistic assumption that the only source of noise is the representation of $f(t_i)$ in floating point arithmetic, then, at best, we have $z_i = (1 + \eta_i) f(t_i)$ with $|\eta_i| \leq 2^{-t}$, where t is the number of mantissa bits. Since $f(t_i)$ can be arbitrarily large, $|z_i - f(t_i)|$ is not uniformly bounded.

We hope that this simple example explains the need to study other kinds of noise. Needless to say, general noise is even harder to analyze than uniformly bounded noise. For general noise, one should also study different error criteria, since sometimes the standard absolute error criterion is not appropriate. To illustrate this, let us consider the function approximation problem discussed above, i.e., let S and F be as in **NR 2.2:3**, with noise defined by $E(f, N) = \{\vec{x} : |x_i| \leq \eta(|y_i| + \gamma), \forall i\}$. Then for arbitrary information consisting of function and/or derivative evaluations, $r^{\text{wor}}(N, E) = +\infty$, see IUC.

3. Average Case Setting with Random Noise

In this section we study the average case setting for linear problems with random noise. As in Chapter 6, let F_1 be a separable Banach space equipped with a Gaussian measure μ. The solution operator S is continuous and linear with range in a separable Hilbert space G.

Notes and Remarks

NR 3:1 Section 3 is based on Kadane, Wasilkowski, and Woźniakowski [88].

3.1. Basic Definitions

As in Section 2.1, we observe $N(f, \vec{x})$ instead of $N(f)$. We now assume that the noise is a random variable with a known probability measure.

More specifically, we assume that when attempting to compute $y = L(f)$, $f \in F$ and $L \in \Lambda$, we observe

$$z = y + x = L(f) + x,$$

where the noise x is a random variable with a known probability measure $\eta(\cdot; y, L)$. That is, for any Borel set A of $\mathbb{R}$,

$$\text{Prob}(x \in A) = \int_A \eta(dt; y, L).$$

Hence

$$N(f, \vec{x}) = \vec{z} = [z_1, z_2, \ldots, z_{n(f, \vec{x})}].$$

Here $z_i = z_i(f, \vec{x}) = y_i + x_i = L_i(f; z_1, \ldots, z_{i-1}) + x_i$, where $y_i = y_i(f, \vec{x})$ $=L_i(f; z_1, \ldots, z_{i-1})$ and x_i is a random variable with probability measure $\eta(\cdot; y_i, L_{i,\vec{z}})$. As before, $L_{i,\vec{z}}$ stands for $L_i(\cdot; z_1, \ldots, z_{i-1})$.

Throughout this section we assume that η satisfies two conditions

$$\begin{aligned}
\eta(A;\cdot,\cdot) &= \eta(-A;\cdot,\cdot), &&\forall\, A \in \mathcal{B}(\mathbb{R}), \\
\eta(\cdot;y,\cdot) &= \eta(\cdot;-y,\cdot), &&\forall\, y \in \mathbb{R},
\end{aligned} \tag{1}$$

where $-A = \{f \in \mathbb{R} : -f \in A\}$. Assumption (1) implies that the mean value of the noise is zero and that the probability measure of the noise depends on y only through the absolute value of y.

We illustrate η by three examples of probability measures which are absolutely continuous with respect to Lebesgue measure. The density of $\eta(\cdot;y,L)$ is denoted by $\rho(\cdot;y,L)$.

(i) $\rho(t;y,L) = w(t)$ for some nonnegative w. For instance, $w(t) = \exp\left(-t^2/(2\sigma)\right)/\sqrt{2\pi\sigma}$ corresponds to $\eta(\cdot;y,L)$ being Gaussian (normal $\mathcal{N}(0,\sigma)$). Since w is independent of y and L, the noise x has the same probability whether y and/or $\|L\|$ are large or small. We think that this is an unrealistic assumption for a number of applications.

(ii) $\rho(t;y,L) = \exp\left(-t^2/(2\sigma(y))\right)/\sqrt{2\pi\sigma(y)}$, where, for instance, $\sigma(y) = y^2$. This corresponds to a Gaussian probability whose variance depends on the exact value y.

(iii)

$$\rho(t;y,L) = \begin{cases} \dfrac{1}{2\alpha\|L\|(|y|+\delta)} & \text{if } \dfrac{t}{\|L\|(|y|+\delta)} \in [-\alpha,\alpha], \\ 0 & \text{otherwise.} \end{cases}$$

Here α and δ are positive (small) numbers. This means that the noise x is uniformly distributed in the interval $[-\alpha\|L\|(|y|+\delta),\, \alpha\|L\|(|y|+\delta)]$. If $|y|$ is large relative to δ then the relative error $|z-y|/|y|$ has, roughly, uniform distribution on $[-\alpha\|L\|,\, \alpha\|L\|]$. If $|y|$ is small relative to δ then the absolute error $|z-y|$ has, roughly, uniform distribution on $[-\alpha\|L\|\delta,\, \alpha\|L\|\delta]$. Note that the noise x depends on the norm of L. This means that computing $L_c(f)$ instead of $L(f)$ with $L_c = cL$ for $c \in \mathbb{R}$, corresponds to noise x_c which behaves as cx. This kind of noise may be viewed as an abstraction of rounding errors in floating point arithmetic.

The *average cardinality* of N is defined by

$$\mathrm{card}^{\mathrm{avg}}(N,\eta) = \int_{F_1} \int_{\mathbb{R}^\infty} n(f,\vec{x})\,\eta(d\vec{x};\vec{y},N)\,\mu(df),$$

where μ is the *a priori* measure on F_1 and

$$\eta(A;\vec{y},N) = \int_A \prod_{i=1}^{k} \eta(dx_i;y_i,L_{i,\vec{z}})$$

for any Borel set A of $\mathbb{R}^k$.

The *average error* of an algorithm ϕ is defined by

$$e^{\mathrm{avg}}(\phi, N, \eta) = \left(\int_{F_1} \int_{\mathbb{R}^\infty} \|S(f) - \phi(N(f, \vec{x}))\|^2 \, \eta(d\vec{x}; \vec{y}, N) \, \mu(df) \right)^{1/2},$$

and the *average radius* of N is defined by

$$r^{\mathrm{avg}}(N, \eta) = \inf_\phi e^{\mathrm{avg}}(\phi, N).$$

As in Chapter 6, we assume that ϕ and L_i are measurable.

Notes and Remarks

NR 3.1:1 As in Chapter 6, we can define the radius of noisy information without the concept of an algorithm. Then the restriction to measurable ϕ would not be necessary.

3.2. Normally Distributed Noise

Suppose that each x_i has a normal, $\mathcal{N}(0, \sigma)$, distribution which is independent of y_i and L_i. Similar as in Section 2.2, we let $\tilde{F}_1 = F_1 \times \mathbb{R}^\infty$, $\tilde{S}([f, \vec{x}]) = S(f)$, and $\tilde{L}_i([f, \vec{x}]; z_1, \ldots, z_{i-1}) = L_i([f, \vec{x}]; z_1, \ldots, z_{i-1}) + x_i$. Since the *a priori* measure μ on F_1 is Gaussian, the joint probability on $\tilde{F}_1$ is also Gaussian. Hence, the analysis of Chapter 6 for linear problems with exact information can be easily applied to linear problems with noisy information when the noise is normal. In particular, adaption does not essentially help and piecewise linear algorithms are almost optimal. Obviously, these results also hold for bounded domains and/or different error criteria.

Notes and Remarks

NR 3.2:1 If N is nonadaptive then a smoothing spline algorithm, see Section 2.2, is again the optimal error algorithm. The interested reader is referred to Wahba [84] and papers cited there.

3.3. Does Adaption Help?

In this section we try to analyze the power of adaptive information for general noise. As we shall see in the next section, adaption can generally be much more powerful than nonadaption as exhibited in the following two examples. The distribution of noise in these examples is discrete. We choose this for simplicity. The same result could be achieved with a continuous distribution of noise. In Section 3.3.2 we make an additional assumption on the structure of adaptive information and prove that then adaption does not help.

3.3.1. Examples

EXAMPLE 3.3.1. Let $F_1 = F_2 = \mathbb{R}$, $S = I$ and $\mu = \mathcal{N}(0,1)$. Let $x_i = -1$ or $x_i = +1$, each with probability $1/2$. Consider adaptive N^a which consists of repetitive observations of $L(f) = f$, i.e., $N(f, \vec{x}) = [z_1, \ldots, z_{n(f,\vec{x})}]$, $z_i = f + x_i$, with the following termination rule: $n(f, \vec{x}) = \min\{i \geq 2 : z_{i-1} \neq z_i\}$. As always, $\min \emptyset = +\infty$. Note that for every f, $n(f, \vec{x}) = i$ with probability $2^{-(i-1)}$. Then the algorithm $\phi(N^a(f, \vec{x})) = (z_{i-1} + z_i)/2$ is equal to f, and therefore it has average error zero. Hence

$$r^{avg}(N^a, \eta) = 0.$$

The average cardinality of N^a is given by

$$\text{card}^{avg}(N^a, \eta) = \sum_{i=2}^{\infty} \frac{i}{2^{i-1}} = 3.$$

Consider now nonadaptive N_k^{non} consisting of k repetitive noisy observations of $L(f) = f$. Then f can be recovered exactly only with probability $1 - 2^{-(k-1)}$ (when two observations are different). Hence

$$r^{avg}(N_k^{non}, \eta)^2 = \frac{1}{2^k} \inf_{\phi} \int_{F_1} \left((f - \phi(f+1))^2 + (f - \phi(f-1))^2 \right) \mu(df)$$

$$= \frac{1}{2^k \sqrt{2\pi}} \int_{\mathbb{R}} \inf_{x \in \mathbb{R}} \left((z - 1 - x)^2 \exp\left(\frac{-(z-1)^2}{2} \right) \right.$$

$$\left. + (z + 1 - x)^2 \exp\left(\frac{-(z+1)^2}{2} \right) \right) dz.$$

The last infimum is attained for

$$x = x(z) = \frac{(z-1)\exp\left(\frac{-(z-1)^2}{2}\right) + (z+1)\exp\left(\frac{-(z+1)^2}{2}\right)}{\exp\left(\frac{-(z-1)^2}{2}\right) + \exp\left(\frac{-(z+1)^2}{2}\right)},$$

i.e., the optimal algorithm $\phi^*(z, \ldots, z) = x(z)$, and

$$r^{avg}(N_k^{non}, \eta) = \left(\frac{4}{2^k \sqrt{2\pi}} \int_{-\infty}^{\infty} \frac{\exp\left(\frac{-(z+1)^2}{2}\right)}{1 + \exp(-2z)} dz \right)^{1/2}.$$

Hence, information N_k^{non} of cardinality k has positive average radius, while information N^{a} solves the problem exactly with average cardinality equal to 3.

EXAMPLE 3.3.2. Let $F_1 = F_2 = \mathbb{R}^2$ be equipped with the Euclidean norm, i.e., $f = [f_1, f_2]$ and $\|f\|^2 = f_1^2 + f_2^2$. Consider $S(f) = [f_1, f_2]$. Let $\mu = \mathcal{N}(0, 1)$ and let the noise of observing $G_i(f) = f_i$ be so that $x_i = -1$ or $x_i = +1$, each with probability $1/2$. Consider adaptive N^{a} with fixed cardinality, $n(f, \vec{x}) \equiv n$, such that $L_1 = L_2 = G_1$, $L_i = G_1$ if $z_1 = \cdots = z_{i-1}$ and $L_i = G_2$ otherwise. Similarly to Example 3.3.1, one can show that

$$r^{\mathrm{avg}}(N^{\mathrm{a}}, \eta) = \sqrt{b\, n}\, 2^{-(n-2)}\bigl(1 + o(1)\bigr) \quad \text{as } n \to +\infty,$$

where

$$b = \frac{4}{\sqrt{2\pi}} \int_{-\infty}^{\infty} \frac{\exp\left(\frac{-(z+1)^2}{2}\right)}{1 + \exp(-2z)}\, dz.$$

On the other hand, if N^{non} consists of n_1 noisy observations of G_1 and $(n - n_1)$ noisy observations of G_2, then

$$r^{\mathrm{avg}}(N^{\mathrm{non}}, \eta) \geq \sqrt{b}\, \max\{2^{-n_1/2}, 2^{-(n-n_1)/2}\},$$

which is minimized for $n_1 = n/2$. This means that any nonadaptive information of cardinality n has average radius satisfying

$$r^{\mathrm{avg}}(N^{\mathrm{non}}, \eta) \geq 2^{-n/4}\sqrt{b}.$$

Hence adaption is quadratically more powerful than nonadaption.

In the examples above we exhibited adaptive information N^{a} which was more powerful than any nonadaptive information. In Example 3.3.1, we constructed N^{a} by taking advantage of varying cardinality. In Example 3.3.2, $n(f, \vec{x})$ was fixed; however, we adaptively changed the number of repetitions of the functional G_1. Thus, in both examples adaption was more powerful than nonadaption either because of varying cardinality or varying the number of repetitions of certain nonadaptive functionals. In the next section we show that these are the only causes in which adaption is more powerful than nonadaption.

3.3.2. Adaptive Choice of Observations Does Not Help

In this section we prove that adaption does not help when the cardinality and the numbers of repetitions of the same observation are fixed, even though observations (i.e., functionals) may be chosen adaptively. That is, for given k and $n_1, \ldots, n_k$, let $\sum_{i=1}^{k} n_i = n$ and

$$N(f, \vec{x}) = \vec{z} = [\vec{z}_1, \ldots, \vec{z}_k], \qquad (2)$$

where for $1 \leq i \leq k$ and $1 \leq j \leq n_i$ we have

$$\vec{z}_i = [z_{i,1}, \ldots, z_{i,n_i}] \quad \text{and} \quad z_{i,j} = L_i(f; \vec{z}_1, \ldots, \vec{z}_{i-1}) + x_{i,j},$$

and the functionals $L_{1,\vec{z}}, \ldots, L_{k,\vec{z}}$ are μ-orthonormal for every fixed $\vec{z}$,

$$L_{i,\vec{z}}(C_\mu L_{j,\vec{z}}) = \int_{F_1} L_i(g; \vec{z}_1, \ldots, \vec{z}_{i-1}) L_j(g; \vec{z}_1, \ldots, \vec{z}_{j-1}) \, \mu(dg) = \delta_{i,j}. \quad (3)$$

REMARK 3.3.2.1. The notion of fixed repetition numbers n_i requires us to distinguish between the functionals $L_{i,\vec{z}}$, $i = 1, \ldots, k$. One might hope that it would be enough to assume that $L_{i,\vec{z}} \neq L_{j,\vec{z}}$ for $i \neq j$. This assumption is, however, too weak. Indeed, consider once more adaptive information N^{a} from Example 3.3.2 with L_i replaced by $\tilde{L}_i = L_i + \varepsilon^{i-1} G_2$ for sufficiently small ε. Let $N_\varepsilon^{\mathrm{a}}$ consists of single observations of $\tilde{L}_1, \ldots, \tilde{L}_n$. For small ε, $N_\varepsilon^{\mathrm{a}}$ and N^{a} are practically the same, though the first information has fixed repetition numbers ($n_i = 1$), whereas the second one has varying repetition numbers. Hence the assumption $L_{i,\vec{z}} \neq L_{j,\vec{z}}$ does not lead to a meaningful notion of fixed repetition numbers.

Our definition of fixed repetition numbers requires μ-orthonormality (3) of $L_{i,\vec{z}}$. Observe that this holds for Examples 3.3.1 and 3.3.2. As explained in Chapter 6, μ-orthonormality is not restrictive for exact information. We have chosen this definition for noisy information to simplify further analysis. We stress that this choice is not unique. Furthermore, Theorem 3.3.1, which we present below, need not be true for different notions of fixed repetition numbers.

We are ready to state

THEOREM 3.3.1. *For any adaptive N^{a} of the above form, there exists a vector $\vec{z}^* \in \mathbb{R}^n$ such that*

$$r^{\mathrm{avg}}(N_{\vec{z}^*}^{\mathrm{non}}, \eta) \leq r^{\mathrm{avg}}(N^{\mathrm{a}}, \eta).$$

Here $N_{\vec{z}^*}^{\mathrm{non}}$ *stands for nonadaptive information obtained from N^{a} by replacing $\vec{z} = z(\vec{f}, \vec{x})$ by $\vec{z}^*$ in the functionals used by N^{a}.*

We sketch the proof of Theorem 3.3.1. The detailed proof can be found in Kadane, Wasilkowski, and Woźniakowski [88]. To simplify the notation, we assume that for every $y \in \mathbb{R}$ and every $L \in F_1^*$ the probability of the noise, $\eta(\cdot; y, L)$, is absolutely continuous with respect to Lebesgue measure, and we denote its density by $\rho(\cdot; y, L)$. In the sequel, $\mu_k = \mathcal{N}(0, I)$ on $\mathbb{R}^k$, i.e., for any Borel set $A \subset \mathbb{R}^k$,

$$\mu_k(A) = (2\pi)^{-k/2} \int_A \exp\left(\frac{-\|y\|^2}{2}\right) d_k \vec{y}. \tag{4}$$

Let N be adaptive information of the form (2). We need a few lemmas which we state without proofs.

LEMMA 3.3.1. *For every algorithm ϕ,*

$$e^{\mathrm{avg}}(\phi, N, \eta) = \sqrt{\int_{F_1} \|S(f)\|^2 \, \mu(df) - R(\phi, N)} \tag{5}$$

with

$$R(\phi, N) =$$
$$\int_{\mathbb{R}^n} \int_{\mathbb{R}^k} \left(2 \sum_{i=1}^k y_i \langle S(C_\mu L_{i, \vec{z}}), \phi(\vec{z}) \rangle - \|\phi(\vec{z})\|^2 \right) \rho(\vec{x}; \vec{y}, N) \, \mu_k(d\vec{y}) \, d_n \vec{x}, \tag{6}$$

where $\vec{z} = [\vec{z}_1, \ldots, \vec{z}_k]$ and $\vec{z}_i = [y_i + x_{i,1}, \ldots, y_i + x_{i,n_i}]$.

We now exhibit an *optimal error* algorithm, i.e., an algorithm ϕ^* using noisy information N for which $e^{\mathrm{avg}}(\phi^*, N, \eta) = r^{\mathrm{avg}}(N, \eta)$. Keeping in mind that $\rho(\vec{x}; \vec{y}, N)$ is the density of $\eta(\vec{x}; \vec{y}, N)$ and that μ_k is given by (4), we change variables in (6) by setting $z_{i,j} = y_i + x_{i,j}$. Then

$$R(\phi, N) = (2\pi)^{-k/2} \int_{\mathbb{R}^n} \int_{\mathbb{R}^k} \left(2 \sum_{i=1}^k y_i \langle S(C_\mu L_{i, \vec{z}}), \phi(\vec{z}) \rangle - \|\phi(\vec{z})\|^2 \right)$$
$$\times \prod_{i=1}^k \left(\exp\left(\frac{-y_i^2}{2}\right) \prod_{j=1}^{n_i} \rho(z_{i,j} - y_i; y_i, L_{i, \vec{z}}) \right) d_k \vec{y} \, d_n \vec{z}. \tag{7}$$

Define

$$\nu_i(\vec{z}_i | \vec{z}_1, \ldots, \vec{z}_{i-1})$$
$$= \frac{1}{\sqrt{2\pi}} \int_{\mathbb{R}} \exp\left(\frac{-y_i^2}{2}\right) \prod_{j=1}^{n_i} \rho(z_{i,j} - y_i; y_i, L_i(\cdot; \vec{z}_1, \ldots, \vec{z}_{i-1})) \, dy_i. \tag{8}$$

Then

$$\int_{\mathbf{R}^{n_i}} \nu_i(\vec{z}_i | \vec{z}_1, \ldots, \vec{z}_{i-1}) \, d_{n_i} \vec{z}_i = 1. \tag{9}$$

This means that $\nu_i(\cdot | \vec{z}_1, \ldots, \vec{z}_{i-1})$ is the density function of a probability measure on $\mathbf{R}^{n_i}$. Define

$$\lambda_i(y_i | \vec{z}_1, \ldots, \vec{z}_i)$$

$$= \frac{(2\pi)^{-1/2} \exp\left(\frac{-y_i^2}{2}\right)}{\nu_i(\vec{z}_i | \vec{z}_1, \ldots, \vec{z}_{i-1})} \prod_{j=1}^{n_i} \rho\big(z_{i,j} - y_i; y_i, L_i(\cdot; \vec{z}_1, \ldots, \vec{z}_{i-1})\big). \tag{10}$$

Since $\int_{\mathbf{R}} \lambda_i(y_i | \vec{z}_1, \ldots, \vec{z}_i) \, dy_i = 1$, $\lambda_i(\cdot | \vec{z}_1, \ldots, \vec{z}_i)$ is the density of a probability measure on $\mathbf{R}$. We rewrite (7) using (8) and (10),

$$R(\phi, N) = \int_{\mathbf{R}^n} \left(2 \sum_{i=1}^{k} \langle S(C_\mu L_{i,\vec{z}}), \phi(\vec{z}) \rangle \int_{\mathbf{R}} y_i \lambda_i(y_i | \vec{z}_1, \ldots, \vec{z}_i) \, dy_i \right.$$

$$\left. - \|\phi(\vec{z})\|^2 \right) \prod_{i=1}^{k} \nu_i(\vec{z}_i | \vec{z}_1, \ldots, \vec{z}_{i-1}) \, d_n \vec{z}. \tag{11}$$

Let

$$H_i(\vec{z}) = H_i(\vec{z}_1, \ldots, \vec{z}_i) = \int_{\mathbf{R}} y_i \, \lambda_i(y_i | \vec{z}_1, \ldots, \vec{z}_i) \, dy_i. \tag{12}$$

Then the algorithm ϕ^* is defined by

$$\phi^*(\vec{z}) = \sum_{i=1}^{k} H_i(\vec{z}) \, S(C_\mu L_{i,\vec{z}}). \tag{13}$$

We comment on the implementation of (13). The functionals $L_{i,\vec{z}}$ are given by the noisy adaptive information N. The elements $S(C_\mu L_{i,\vec{z}})$ are determined by the problem being solved. Observe that for nonadaptive information these elements do not depend on $\vec{z}$. In any case, to compute $\phi^*(\vec{z})$ we have to compute $H_i(\vec{z})$ given by (12). The difficulty of computing $H_i(\vec{z})$ depends on the density function ρ of the noise. For some ρ it is relatively easy to compute $H_i(\vec{z})$. Then $\phi^*(\vec{z})$ can also be relatively easy computed.

LEMMA 3.3.2. *The algorithm ϕ^* defined by (13) is optimal, i.e.,*

$$e^{\mathrm{avg}}(\phi^*, N, \eta) = r^{\mathrm{avg}}(N, \eta) = \sqrt{\int_{F_1} \|S(f)\|^2 \, \mu(df) - R(\phi^*, N)}, \tag{14}$$

where

$$R(\phi^*, N) = \int_{\mathbb{R}^n} \|\phi^*(\vec{z})\|^2 \nu(\vec{z}) \, d_n \vec{z} \quad \text{and} \quad \nu(\vec{z}) = \prod_{i=1}^{k} \nu_i(\vec{z}_i | \vec{z}_1, \ldots, \vec{z}_{i-1}).$$

LEMMA 3.3.3. *For* $i = 1, \ldots, k$ *and all vectors* $\vec{z}_1, \ldots, \vec{z}_i$,

$$\nu_i(\vec{z}_i | \vec{z}_1, \ldots, \vec{z}_{i-1}) = \nu_i(-\vec{z}_i | \vec{z}_1, \ldots, \vec{z}_{i-1})$$
$$H_i(\vec{z}_1, \ldots, \vec{z}_{i-1}, \vec{z}_i) = -H_i(\vec{z}_1, \ldots, \vec{z}_{i-1}, -\vec{z}_i).$$

Define

$$
\begin{aligned}
G_i(\vec{z}) &= G_i(\vec{z}_1, \ldots, \vec{z}_{i-1}) \\
&= \int_{\mathbb{R}^{n_i}} H_i^2(\vec{z}_i, \ldots, \vec{z}_i) \, \nu_i(\vec{z}_i | \vec{z}_1, \ldots, \vec{z}_{i-1}) \, d_{n_i} \vec{z}_i.
\end{aligned}
\tag{15}
$$

LEMMA 3.3.4.

$$
\begin{aligned}
R(\phi^*, N) &= \int_{\mathbb{R}^n} \left(\sum_{i=1}^{k} \|S(C_\mu L_{i,\vec{z}})\|^2 G_i(\vec{z}) \right) \left(\prod_{i=1}^{k} \nu_i(\vec{z}_i | \vec{z}_1, \ldots, \vec{z}_{i-1}) \right) d_n \vec{z} \\
&= \sum_{i=1}^{k} \int_{\mathbb{R}^n} \|S(C_\mu L_{i,\vec{z}})\|^2 G_i(\vec{z}) \nu(\vec{z}) \, d_n \vec{z}.
\end{aligned}
$$

We are ready to prove Theorem 3.3.1. From Lemma 3.3.4 we have

$$R(\phi^*, N) = \int_{\mathbb{R}^n} G(\vec{z}) \nu(\vec{z}) \, d_n \vec{z}, \tag{16}$$

where $G(\vec{z}) = \sum_{i=1}^{k} \|S(C_\mu L_{i,\vec{z}})\|^2 G_i(\vec{z})$. From this we conclude that there exists an element $\vec{z}^* = [\vec{z}_1^*, \ldots, \vec{z}_k^*] \in \mathbb{R}^n$ for which

$$R(\phi^*, N) \leq G(\vec{z}^*). \tag{17}$$

Define $L_1^* = L_1$ and $L_i^* = L_i(\cdot; \vec{z}_1^*, \ldots, \vec{z}_{i-1}^*)$. Let

$$
\begin{aligned}
N_{\vec{z}^*}^{\text{non}}(f, \vec{x}) = [L_1^*(f) + x_{1,1}, \ldots, L_1^*(f) + x_{1,n_1}, \\
\ldots, L_k^*(f) + x_{k,1}, \ldots, L_k^*(f) + x_{k,n_k}]
\end{aligned}
$$

be *nonadaptive* noisy information. The $x_{i,j}$ are random variables with density function $\rho(\cdot; y_i, L_i^*)$ for all j. We prove that

$$r^{\text{avg}}(N_{\vec{z}^*}^{\text{non}}, \eta)^2 = \int_{F_1} \|S(f)\|^2 \, \mu(df) - G(\vec{z}^*). \qquad (18)$$

Indeed, let ν_i^*, H_i^*, and G_i^* be defined by (8), (12), and (15) for the non-adaptive information $N_{\vec{z}^*}^{\text{non}}$. Then

$$\nu_i^*(\vec{z}_i | \vec{z}_1, \ldots, \vec{z}_{i-1}) = \nu_i^*(\vec{z}_i | \vec{z}_1^*, \ldots, \vec{z}_{i-1}^*),$$
$$H_i^*(\vec{z}_1, \ldots, \vec{z}_{i-1}, \vec{z}_i) = H_i(\vec{z}_1^*, \ldots, \vec{z}_{i-1}^*, \vec{z}_i),$$
$$G_i^*(\vec{z}_1, \ldots, \vec{z}_{i-1}) = G_i^*(\vec{z}_1^*, \ldots, \vec{z}_{i-1}^*).$$

From (16) we conclude that for an optimal algorithm ϕ^* that uses $N_{\vec{z}^*}^{\text{non}}$, we thus have $R(\phi^*, N_{\vec{z}^*}^{\text{non}}) = G(\vec{z}^*)$. Then (14) of Lemma 3.3.2 yields (18).

We return to (17). Due to (17) and (18), we have

$$r^{\text{avg}}(N, \eta)^2 = \int_{F_1} \|S(f)\|^2 \mu(df) - R(\phi^*, N)$$
$$\geq \int_{F_1} \|S(f)\|^2 \mu(df) - G(\vec{z}^*) = r^{\text{avg}}(N_{\vec{z}^*}^{\text{non}}, \eta).$$

This completes the proof of Theorem 3.3.1.

4. Mixed Setting

In Section 2 we discussed the worst case setting with deterministic noise and in Section 3 the average case setting with stochastic noise. Mixed settings are also of interest, though they seem to be even harder to analyze.

Here we briefly discuss the worst case setting with stochastic noise. The error of an algorithm is defined now by

$$e^{\text{wor}}(\phi, N, \eta) = \sup_{f \in F} \sqrt{\int_{\mathbb{R}^\infty} \|S(f) - \phi(N(f, \vec{x}))\|^2 \, \eta(d\vec{x})},$$

and the radius of N by

$$r^{\text{wor}}(N, \eta) = \inf_\phi e^{\text{wor}}(\phi, N, \eta).$$

Finding an optimal algorithm or estimating $r^{\text{wor}}(N, \eta)$ is a very difficult problem. It corresponds to the so called minimax estimation problem in statistics. Optimal algorithms have not been found even for $F = [a, b] \subset \mathbb{R}$, $S = I$, nonadaptive N, and η independent of f, see **NR 4:1**.

Even finding algorithms which are optimal among linear ones is a nontrivial problem in this mixed setting. The reader interested in this subject is referred to Speckman [79b, 80] and Li [82], where optimal linear algorithms are characterized for linear problems with Hilbert spaces F_1, G, and $T(F_1)$, nonadaptive information N, and with white noise.

Notes and Remarks

NR 4:1 As an example of the mixed setting, consider the following statistical problem. Estimate a number f from a given set F, $F \subset \mathbb{R}$, based on observed values $z_i = f + x_i$, $i = 1, \ldots, n$, where the noise x_i is i.i.d. with a given probability density ρ. This corresponds to $S = I$, $F \subset \mathbb{R}$, $N(f) = [f, \ldots, f]$, and the stochastic noise $\vec{x} = [x_1, \ldots, x_n]$ with joint probability η whose density is $\rho \times \cdots \times \rho$. An optimal error algorithm is known only for special cases, one of them discussed below. Suppose that $F = \mathbb{R}$. Then the optimal error algorithm is provided by the so called *Pitman estimator*,

$$\phi^*(\vec{z}) = z_n - A^*(z_1 - z_n, \ldots, z_{n-1} - z_n)$$

with

$$A^*(t_1, \ldots, t_n) = \frac{\int_{\mathbb{R}} x \prod_{i=1}^{n-1} \rho(t_i + x)\, dx}{\int_{\mathbb{R}} \prod_{i=1}^{n-1} \rho(t_i + x)\, dx},$$

see, e.g., Ferguson [67]. The error of ϕ^* is equal to

$$e^{\mathrm{wor}}(\phi^*, N, \eta) = r^{\mathrm{wor}}(N, \eta) = \left(\int_{\mathbb{R}^n} (\phi^*(\vec{x}))^2\, \eta(d\vec{x}) \right)^{1/2}.$$

NR 4:2 We now discuss an application of Pitman estimators to the clock synchronization problem in distributed networks. This problem can be described as follows. Suppose that we are given a network of k processors, each of them having its own local clock which does not drift. Processors communicate by sending local clocks readings, but the message transmission time is not known. Based on a fixed number n of messages sent, we would like to synchronize the clocks as tightly as possible. Thus, we would like to know how these n messages should be sent and how the processors should shift their clocks to minimize the error.

This problem can be cast as a problem in the worst case setting with noisy information, noise being the messages' transmission times. An algorithm is now a k-tuple of local processors' decisions. This problem has been studied in a number of papers assuming deterministic noise x, $x \in [L, H]$, for *a priori* given L and H. See, e.g., Halpern, Megiddo, and Munshi [85] and papers cited there. The following negative result is due to Lynch and Lundelius [85]. Even for a fully connected network, the error of any algorithm is not smaller than $(H - L)(k - 1)/k$, no matter how large n.

Suppose now that the noise is random i.i.d. with a given probability. Using the results reported in **NR 4:1**, Wasilkowski [87b] established the following. For only two processors, $k = 2$, the optimal information is provided by unidirectional messages, i.e., all n messages are sent by one processor. Then the processor-sender does not update its clock, and the processor-receiver updates its clock by the amount equal to the value of the corresponding Pitman estimator. For an arbitrary network, let T be a minimal diameter tree that spans the network. The information is provided by sending $n' = \lfloor n/k \rfloor$ messages along each edge of T. Each processor, after receiving n' messages, synchronizes its clock by using the corresponding Pitman estimator. This information and algorithm are optimal (modulo a multiplicative constant not exceeding the square root of the diameter of T).

Appendix

To make this book as self-contained as possible, we summarize basic concepts and facts concerning functional analysis and measure theory. Detailed treatment and proofs of concepts discussed here may be found in any advanced text. We recommend Dunford and Schwartz [63] for functional analysis, and Kuo [75], Parthasarathy [67], Skorohod [74], and Vakhania [81] for measure theory.

In what follows, we restrict ourselves to the real numbers as the field of scalars.

1. Functional Analysis

1.1. Linear Spaces and Linear Operators

A *linear space over* $\mathbb{R}$ is any nonempty set X which is closed under *addition* and *scalar multiplication*, i.e., for every $x, y, z \in X$ and every scalars $\alpha, \beta \in \mathbb{R}$ the following hold:

(1) $x + y \in X$ and $x + y = y + x$,
(2) $(x + y) + z = x + (y + z)$,
(3) there exists an element in X, denoted by 0, such that $0 + x = x$,
(4) $\alpha x \in X$ and $\alpha(\beta x) = (\alpha \beta)x$,
(5) $(\alpha + \beta)x = \alpha x + \beta x$,
(6) $\alpha(x + y) = \alpha x + \alpha y$,
(7) $1x = x$.

Let $-x$ denote $(-1)x$. Then $-x \in X$ and $x + (-x) = x - x = 0$. Hence, every element $x \in X$ has its *additive inverse* $-x \in X$.

We now give a few examples of linear spaces.

(a) $X = \mathbb{R}^n$ is a space of vectors $x = [x_1, \ldots, x_n]$ with the operations $x + y = [x_1 + y_1, \ldots, x_n + y_n]$ and $\alpha x = [\alpha x_1, \ldots, \alpha x_n]$.

(b) $X = C(D)$ is the space of continuous functions defined on $D \subseteq \mathbb{R}^n$. Here $f + g$ is defined by $(f + g)(t) = f(t) + g(t)$ and αf by $(\alpha f)(t) = \alpha f(t)$ for $f, g \in X$, $\alpha \in \mathbb{R}$, and $t \in D$.

(c) $X = \mathcal{L}_p(D)$ is the space of functions defined on $D \subset \mathbb{R}^n$ for which the Lebesgue integral $\int_D |f(t)|^p \, dt$ exists and is finite. The addition and multiplication operations are defined as in (b).

Let X, Y be two linear spaces. An operator A, $A : X \to Y$, is *linear* iff

$$A(\alpha x) = \alpha A(x) \quad \text{and} \quad A(x + y) = A(x) + A(y), \quad \forall x, y \in X, \ \forall \alpha \in \mathbb{R}.$$

Note that linearity of A implies that $A(0) = 0$. If A is a linear operator, we sometimes write Ax instead of $A(x)$.

Given two linear operators $A_1, A_2 : X \to Y$, define αA_1 and $A_1 + A_2$ by

$$(\alpha A_1)(x) = \alpha A_1(x) \quad \text{and} \quad (A_1 + A_2)(x) = A_1(x) + A_2(x).$$

Obviously, they are linear. Hence, the set of all linear operators from X to Y is again a linear space. This space is denoted by $\mathcal{L}(X, Y)$.

1.2. Linear Independence, Dimension, and Linear Subspaces

Elements $x_1, \ldots, x_n$ of a linear space X are *linearly independent* iff $\sum_{i=1}^n \alpha_i x_i = 0$ implies that $\alpha_1 = \cdots = \alpha_n = 0$.

A linear space X has *dimension* n, $n < +\infty$, if there exist n elements $x_i \in X$ which are linearly independent, and any $(n + 1)$ elements of X are not. Then $\{x_1, \ldots, x_n\}$ is a *basis* of X and any element $x \in X$ has a unique representation $x = \sum_{i=1}^n \alpha_i x_i$. If such a finite number n does not exist, X is said to have *infinite dimension*. The dimension of X is denoted by $\dim X$.

A subset X_1 of X is a *linear subspace of* X if it is itself a linear space. For instance, for any elements $x_i \in X$, $i = 1, \ldots, n$, the set X_1 of all linear combinations $\sum_{i=1}^n \alpha_i x_i$, $\alpha_i \in \mathbb{R}$, is a linear subspace of X and is denoted by $\text{span}(x_1, \ldots, x_n)$. Then $\dim X_1 = n$ iff $x_1, \ldots, x_n$ are linearly independent.

1.3. Norms and Continuous Linear Operators

A *seminorm* on a linear space X is any function $\|\cdot\| : X \to \mathbb{R}_+$ which satisfies the following properties for every $x, y \in X$ and every scalar $\alpha \in \mathbb{R}$:

(1) $\|\alpha x\| = |\alpha| \, \|x\|$,

(2) $\|x + y\| \leq \|x\| + \|y\|$.

If, in addition, $\|x\| = 0$ only for $x = 0$ then $\|\cdot\|$ is called a *norm*. Whenever X is equipped with a norm, we shall say that X is a *normed linear space*.

We now give a few examples of norms. For $X = \mathbb{R}^n$,

(a) $\|x\| = \left(\sum_{i=1}^{n} |x_i|^p \right)^{1/p}$, denoted by $\|x\|_p$, for $p \in [1, +\infty)$ is the classical ℓ_p-norm.

(b) $\|x\| = \max_i |x_i| = \lim_{p \to \infty} \|x\|_p$, denoted by $\|x\|_\infty$, is the classical ℓ_∞-norm.

For $X = C(D)$, $\|f\| = \sup_{t \in D} |f(t)|$, denoted by $\|f\|_{\text{sup}}$, is the classical sup norm. For $X = \mathcal{L}_p(D)$, $\|f\| = \left(\int_D |f(t)|^p \right)^{1/p}$, denoted by $\|f\|_p$, is the classical $\mathcal{L}_p$-norm. The $\mathcal{L}_\infty$-norm, $\|f\| = \lim_{p \to \infty} \|f\|_p$, is denoted by $\|\cdot\|_\infty$.

For a finite dimensional linear space X all norms are equivalent. More precisely, let $\|\cdot\|$ and $\|\|\cdot\|\|$ be any two norms on X. Then there exist two positive numbers α and β such that

$$\alpha \|x\| \leq \|\|x\|\| \leq \beta \|x\|, \quad \forall x \in X.$$

We now recall the *Hölder inequality* which states that for every $f \in \mathcal{L}_p(D)$ and every $g \in \mathcal{L}_{p'}(D)$ with $p \geq 1$ and $1/p + 1/p' = 1$,

$$\int_D |f(t)g(t)| \, dt \leq \|f\|_p \, \|g\|_{p'}.$$

A norm permits us to define the distance between elements of X. The notion of distance enables us to define limits, open and/or closed sets, and the continuity of operators.

Formally, let X and Y be two linear spaces with norms $\|\cdot\|_X$ and $\|\cdot\|_Y$, respectively. An operator A, $A : X \to Y$, is *continuous* iff for every sequence $\{x_i\}$ converging to x^* in X, the sequence $\{A(x_i)\}$ converges to $y^* = A(x^*)$ in Y. For linear operators, continuity is equivalent to continuity at zero, i.e., A from $\mathcal{L}(X, Y)$ is continuous iff $\lim_i x_i = 0$ implies that $\lim_i A(x_i) = 0$ for every sequence $\{x_i\}$. The space of continuous operators is denoted by $\mathcal{B}(X, Y)$. Obviously, $\mathcal{B}(X, Y)$ is a subset, in general a proper one, of $\mathcal{L}(X, Y)$.

An operator A from $\mathcal{L}(X, Y)$ is *bounded* iff

$$\sup_{\|x\|_X \leq 1} \|A(x)\|_Y < +\infty.$$

A linear operator is continuous iff it is bounded. Furthermore, the mapping $A \mapsto \sup_{\|x\|_X \leq 1} \|A(x)\|_Y$ is a well defined norm on the space $\mathcal{B}(X, Y)$. This norm is called the *induced (operator) norm* of A and is denoted by $\|A\|$.

For a finite dimensional X, every linear operator is continuous, i.e., $\mathcal{L}(X, Y) = \mathcal{B}(X, Y)$.

For $Y = \mathbb{R}$, $\mathcal{L}(X, Y)$ consists of functionals. The class of continuous functionals, $\mathcal{B}(X, \mathbb{R})$ is denoted by X^*.

Let X, Z, Y be normed linear spaces and let $A \in \mathcal{B}(X, Y)$ and $B \in \mathcal{B}(Y, Z)$. Then

$$BA \in \mathcal{B}(X, Z) \quad \text{and} \quad \|BA\| \leq \|A\| \, \|B\|.$$

1.4. Banach Spaces

Let X be a normed linear space. We say that X is a *Banach space* iff it is *complete*, i.e., every sequence $\{x_i\}$ that satisfies the Cauchy condition with respect to the norm of X converges to some element in X. More precisely, X is a Banach space iff for every $\delta > 0$ and for sufficiently large m and n, $\|x_n - x_m\| \leq \delta$ implies that $\lim_i x_i$ exists and belongs to X.

Obviously, $X = \mathbb{R}^n$ with any norm is a Banach space. For function spaces, $X = C(D)$ with $\|\cdot\|_{\text{sup}}$ and $X = \mathcal{L}_p(D)$ with $\|\cdot\|_p$ are Banach spaces.

We say that X is *separable* iff there exists a countable subset X' of X which is *dense* in X, i.e., for every $x \in X$ there exists a sequence $\{x_i\}$, $x_i \in X'$, converging to x. Finite dimensional spaces and all the function spaces mentioned above with the exception of $\mathcal{L}_\infty(D)$ are separable.

1.5. Inner Products and Hilbert Spaces

1.5.1. Inner Products

Let X be a given linear space (over $\mathbb{R}$). We say that a function $\langle \cdot, \cdot \rangle : X \times X \to \mathbb{R}$ is a *semi inner product* on X iff the following properties are satisfied for every $x, y, z \in X$ and $\alpha, \beta \in \mathbb{R}$:

(1) $\langle x, x \rangle \geq 0$,
(2) $\langle x, y \rangle = \langle y, x \rangle$,
(3) $\langle \alpha x + \beta y, z \rangle = \alpha \langle x, z \rangle + \beta \langle y, z \rangle$.

A semi inner product is an *inner product* iff $\langle x, x \rangle = 0$ implies that $x = 0$.

Note that any semi inner product induces the following seminorm on X,

$$\|x\| = \sqrt{\langle x, x \rangle}.$$

This seminorm is a norm iff $\langle \cdot, \cdot \rangle$ is an inner product.

We now give two examples of inner products. For $X = \mathbb{R}^n$, $\langle x, y \rangle = \sum_{i=1}^{n} x_i y_i$ is an inner product, and the corresponding induced norm is equal to the ℓ_2 (or Euclidean) norm. For $X = L_2(D)$, $\langle f, g \rangle = \int_D f(t)g(t)\, dt$ is an inner product, and it induces the $\mathcal{L}_2$-norm.

Spaces equipped with inner products are natural extensions of Euclidean space $\mathbb{R}^n$. They enjoy a number of properties, some of which are listed below.

Linear Independence and Gram Matrix. Elements $x_1, \ldots, x_n$ are linearly independent iff the *Gram matrix* $\left(\langle x_i, x_j \rangle \right)_{i,j}$ is nonsingular.

Orthogonality. We say that two elements $x, y \in X$ are *orthogonal* iff $\langle x, y \rangle = 0$. For orthogonal elements x, y we have the Pythagorean theorem,

$$\|x + y\|^2 = \|x\|^2 + \|y\|^2.$$

For two arbitrary elements x, y (not necessarily orthogonal) we have

$$\|x + y\|^2 = \|x\|^2 + 2\langle x, y \rangle + \|y\|^2.$$

1.5.2. Hilbert Spaces

We say that X is a *Hilbert space* iff it is a Banach space whose norm is induced by an inner product. Examples of Hilbert spaces include $\mathbb{R}^n$ with $\|\cdot\| = \|\cdot\|_2$ and $\mathcal{L}_2(D)$ with $\|\cdot\| = \|\cdot\|_2$. We now list some properties of Hilbert spaces.

Orthogonal Projections. Let X_1 be a closed linear subspace of X. Then every element $x \in X$ has a unique representation

$$x = x_1 + x_2,$$

where $x_1 \in X_1$ and x_2 is orthogonal to X_1, i.e., it is orthogonal to every element of X_1. The element x_1 is called the *orthogonal projection of x onto* X_1.

Orthogonal Complement. If X_1 is a closed linear subspace of X, then the set X_2 of all elements which are orthogonal to X_1 is also a closed linear subspace of X. We denote X_2 by $X_1^\perp$. Furthermore, $X = \{x_1 + x_1^\perp : x_1 \in X_1, x_1^\perp \in X_1^\perp\}$, which is denoted by

$$X = X_1 \oplus X_1^\perp.$$

1.5.3. Separable Hilbert Spaces

A Hilbert space X is *separable* iff it is a separable Banach space. For every separable Hilbert space X there exists a countable set $\{x_i\}$ of elements from X which satisfies the following:

(1) x_i are *orthonormal*, i.e., $\langle x_i, x_j \rangle = \delta_{i,j}$,

(2) for every $x \in X$, $x = \lim_n \sum_{j=1}^{n} \langle x, x_j \rangle x_j$, which is denoted by $x = \sum_{j=1}^{\infty} \langle x, x_j \rangle x_j$.

Such a set $\{x_i\}$ is called an *orthonormal system* of X. Note that then

$$\|x\|^2 = \sum_{i=1}^{\infty} \langle x, x_i \rangle^2, \quad \forall\, x \in X.$$

1.6. Bounded Operators on Hilbert Spaces

In this subsection we summarize some basic properties of bounded linear operators defined on a Hilbert space X into a Hilbert space Y.

1.6.1. Bounded Functionals and Riesz's Theorem

Note that for every $a \in X$, the functional L defined by $L(x) = \langle x, a \rangle$ is continuous and linear, and $\|L\| = \|a\|$. Riesz's Theorem states that the opposite is also true, i.e., for every continuous and linear functional L, there exists an element $a \in X$ such that

$$L(x) = \langle x, a \rangle.$$

The induced norm of L is then equal to the norm of a, $\|L\| = \|a\|$.

If X is separable then for arbitrary orthonormal system $\{x_i\}$ we have the following representation

$$L(x) = \sum_{i=1}^{\infty} \langle x, x_i \rangle \langle x_i, a \rangle, \quad \forall\, x \in X.$$

1.6.2. Adjoint Operators

For every bounded and linear operator A, $A : X \to Y$, there exists a unique operator A^*, $A^* : Y \to X$, such that

$$\langle A(x), y \rangle = \langle x, A^*(y) \rangle, \quad \forall\, x \in X,\, y \in Y.$$

The operator A^*, called *adjoint* to A, is also bounded and linear. Furthermore, we have $(A^*)^* = A$, $\|A\| = \|A^*\|$, and $\|A^*A\| = \|A\|^2$. For every two bounded linear operators A_1 and A_2, $(A_1 + A_2)^* = A_1^* + A_2^*$, and $(A_1 A_2)^* = A_2^* A_1^*$.

An operator A from $B(X,X)$ is *self-adjoint* iff $A^* = A$. Then

$$\|A\| = \sup_{\|x\|\leq 1} |\langle A(x), x\rangle|.$$

A self-adjoint operator A is *nonnegative definite* iff $\langle A(x), x\rangle \geq 0$ for every element x. It is *positive definite* iff $\langle A(x), x\rangle > 0$ for every $x \neq 0$. Note that for every bounded A, A^*A is nonnegative definite, and it is positive definite iff A is nonsingular, i.e., $Ax \neq 0$ for $x \neq 0$.

1.6.3. Orthogonal and Projection Operators

An operator $A \in B(X, X)$ is *orthogonal* iff $A^*A = AA^* = I$, where I is the identity operator, $I(x) = x$ for every $x \in X$. Hence, every orthogonal operator is invertible and $A^{-1} = A^*$. Furthermore, $\|A\| = 1$ and $\|A(x)\| = \|x\|$ for every x. Note that every orthogonal operator A preserves inner products, i.e., $\langle A(x), A(y)\rangle = \langle x, y\rangle$ for all x and y. In particular, $A(x)$ is orthogonal to $A(y)$ iff x is orthogonal to y.

An operator $A \in B(X, X)$ is a *projection operator* iff $AA = A$. Obviously, $\|A\| \geq 1$ for a nonzero projection operator A.

There is an important subclass of projection operators which we now discuss. Let X_1 be a closed linear subspace of X. As we know, $X = X_1 \oplus X_1^\perp$, i.e., every $x \in X$ has a unique representation $x = x_1 + x_2$ with $x_1 \in X_1$ and $x_2 \in X_1^\perp$. Then P_{X_1}, defined by

$$P_{X_1}(x) = x_1, \quad \forall\, x \in X,$$

is a bounded linear operator and $\|P_{X_1}\| = 1$ unless $X_1 = \{0\}$. It is a projection since $P_{X_1}(X) = X_1$ and $P_{X_1}|_{X_1} = I|_{X_1}$, which implies that $P_{X_1} P_{X_1} = P_{X_1}$. Such an operator is called an *orthogonal projection onto* X_1. Note that $I - P_{X_1}$ is an orthogonal projection onto $X_1^\perp$, i.e., $I - P_{X_1} = P_{X_1^\perp}$.

To illustrate this, let X be separable with an orthonormal system $\{z_i\}$. Let $X_1 = \mathrm{span}(z_1, \ldots, z_n)$ be the space of all linear combinations of elements $z_1, \ldots, z_n$. Then

$$P_{X_1}(x) = \sum_{i=1}^{n} \langle x, z_i\rangle z_i, \quad \text{and} \quad P_{X_1^\perp}(x) = \sum_{i=n+1}^{\infty} \langle x, z_i\rangle z_i.$$

Projection operators need not be orthogonal projections. However, for an orthogonal operator A the following statements are equivalent,

(1) A is nonnegative definite,
(2) A self-adjoint,
(3) A is an orthogonal projection on its range $A(X)$, i.e., $A = P_{A(X)}$.

1.6.4. Spectrum

Let $A \in \mathcal{B}(X, X)$ be self-adjoint. A number λ is a *regular value of A* iff the equation

$$A(x) - \lambda x = y$$

has a unique solution for every $y \in X$. Then A_λ, defined by $A_\lambda = A - \lambda I$, is bijective, i.e., *one-to-one* and maps *onto* its codomain, and $A_\lambda^{-1} \in \mathcal{B}(X, X)$.

The *spectrum of A*, denoted by $\mathrm{sp}(A)$, is the complement of the set of all regular values of A, i.e.,

$$\mathrm{sp}(A) = \{\lambda \in \mathbb{R} : \lambda \text{ is not a regular value of } A\}.$$

If the equation

$$A(x) - \lambda x = 0$$

has a nonzero solution x then λ is called an *eigenvalue of A* and x is called an *eigenelement of A corresponding to* λ. Obviously, $\lambda \in \mathrm{sp}(A)$.

The spectrum of every operator A is a closed set and is bounded by $\|A\|$, i.e.,

$$\mathrm{sp}(A) \subseteq [-\|A\|, +\|A\|].$$

Spectrum for Nonnegative Definite Operators. Let $A \in \mathcal{B}(X, X)$ be self-adjoint, $A = A^*$, and nonnegative definite, $\langle A(x), x \rangle \geq 0$ for every $x \in X$. Then $\mathrm{sp}(A) \subset \mathbb{R}_+$, and

$$\sup_{\lambda \in \mathrm{sp}(A)} \lambda = \|A\| = \sup_{\|x\| \leq 1} \langle A(x), x \rangle.$$

Furthermore,

$$\mathrm{sp}(A) = \mathrm{c}(A) \cup \mathrm{p}(A).$$

Here $\mathrm{c}(A)$, called the *continuous spectrum of A*, is the set of all nonnegative numbers λ for which $(A - \lambda I)^{-1}$ is well defined on a dense subspace of X but is unbounded, and $\mathrm{p}(A)$, called the *point spectrum of A*, is the set of all eigenvalues of A.

Spectrum of Compact Operators. An operator A, $A \in \mathcal{B}(X, X)$, is *compact* iff for every bounded subset X' of X, the set $A(X')$ is compact. Equivalently, A is compact iff for every bounded sequence $\{x_i\}$ there exists a convergent subsequence $\{A(x_{i_k})\}$. Observe that the identity operator defined on X is compact iff X is finite dimensional.

Let X be separable and A be an arbitrary compact and nonnegative definite operator. To avoid trivial complications, assume that X has infinite dimension. Then zero is the only attraction point of $\mathrm{sp}(A)$, i.e., there exist eigenvalues λ_i from $\mathrm{sp}(A)$ such that $\lim_i \lambda_i = 0$, and $c(A)$ is either empty or is equal to $\{0\}$, the later holds iff 0 is not an eigenvalue of A. Furthermore, there exists an orthonormal system $\{\zeta_i\}$ consisting of eigenelements of A, i.e., $A(\zeta_i) = \lambda_i \zeta_i$ and

$$A(x) = \sum_{i=1}^{\infty} \lambda_i \langle x, \zeta_i \rangle \zeta_i, \quad \forall x \in X.$$

2. Measure Theory

In this section we review basic facts concerning measure theory. We restrict ourselves only to Borel measures defined on a normed linear space X.

2.1. Borel σ-Field, Measurable Sets and Functions

The *Borel σ-field*, denoted by $\mathcal{B}(X)$, is the smallest family of sets from X which contains all open subsets of X and satisfies the following conditions:

(1) $A \in \mathcal{B}(X)$ implies that $X - A \in \mathcal{B}(X)$,
(2) $A_i \in \mathcal{B}(X)$ for $i = 1, 2, \ldots$ implies that $\bigcup_{i=1}^{\infty} A_i \in \mathcal{B}(X)$.

A subset A of X is *(Borel) measurable* iff $A \in \mathcal{B}(X)$. Since X is open, X and $\emptyset$ are measurable. Furthermore, every closed set is measurable.

Let Y be a normed linear space. A function f, $f : X \to Y$, is *measurable* iff $f^{-1}(A) \in \mathcal{B}(X)$ for any $A \in \mathcal{B}(Y)$. Obviously, every continuous f is measurable. If $Y = \mathbb{R}$ then measurability of f is equivalent to the measurability of $f^{-1}((-\infty, a])$ for every $a \in \mathbb{R}$.

2.2. Measures and Probability Measures

A function μ, $\mu : \mathcal{B}(X) \to \mathbb{R}_+ \cup \{+\infty\}$ is a *measure* iff the following conditions are satisfied:

(1) $\mu(\emptyset) = 0$,

(2) μ is *countably additive*, i.e., for every sequence of disjoint and measurable sets A_i,

$$\mu\left(\bigcup_{i=1}^{\infty} A_i\right) = \sum_{i=1}^{\infty} \mu(A_i).$$

A measure μ is *complete* iff every subset of a measurable set B with measure zero, $\mu(B) = 0$, is also measurable. For a complete measure μ the following is true. Let f and g be two functions. If f is measurable and $\mu(\{x \in X : f(x) \neq g(x)\}) = 0$ then g is also measurable.

A measure μ is a *probability measure* iff $\mu(X) = 1$. We now list some properties of probability measures which follow immediately from (1) and (2). In what follows, A, B, and A_i are measurable sets.

(a) $\mu(A \cup B) = \mu(A) + \mu(B) - \mu(A \cap B)$.
(b) If $A \subset B$ then $\mu(B - A) = \mu(B) - \mu(A)$ and, in particular, $\mu(A) \leq \mu(B)$.
(c) $\mu\left(\bigcup_{i=1}^{\infty} A_i\right) \leq \sum_{i=1}^{\infty} \mu(A_i)$.
(d) If $A_i \subset A_{i+1}$, $\forall i$, then

$$\mu\left(\bigcup_{i=1}^{\infty} A_i\right) = \lim_i \mu(A_i) \quad \text{and} \quad \mu\left(\bigcap_{i=1}^{\infty}(X - A_i)\right) = \lim_i \mu(X - A_i).$$

For $X = \mathbb{R}^n$, the classical *Lebesgue* measure is uniquely defined by $\mu(A) = \prod_{i=1}^{n}(b_i - a_i)$ for any set $A = I_1 \times \cdots \times I_n$ with $I_i = [a_i, b_i]$, $I_i = [a_i, b_i)$, $I_i = (a_i, b_i]$, or $I_i = (a_i, b_i)$, $a_i < b_i$. For any measurable set B from $\mathbb{R}^n$ with finite and nonzero Lebesgue measure, $\mu_B(\cdot)$ defined by $\mu_B(A) = \mu(A \cap B)/\mu(B)$ is a probability measure.

2.3. Integrals

We define the Lebesgue integral with respect to a measure μ, beginning with nonnegative integrands.

Let f be a measurable and nonnegative function, $f(x) \geq 0$, $\forall x \in X$, and let E be a measurable subset of X. Then the *integral of f over E* is defined by

$$\int_E f(x)\,\mu(dx) = \sup_{\{E_i\}} \sum_{i=1}^{\infty} \left(\mu(E_i) \inf_{x \in E_i} f(x)\right).$$

Here, the supremum is taken with respect to all measurable and countable partitions of E, i.e., the sets E_i are measurable, disjoint, and $\bigcup_{i=1}^{\infty} E_i = E$. The function f is *integrable* over E if its integral is finite.

We now list some properties of integrals for nonnegative functions. In what follows, E is a measurable set, and f, f_i, and g are measurable and nonnegative.

(1) If $f \le g$ then $\int_E f(x)\,\mu(dx) \le \int_E g(x)\,\mu(dx)$.

(2) $\mu(E)\inf_{x \in E} f(x) \le \int_E f(x)\,\mu(dx) \le \mu(E)\sup_{x \in E} f(x)$.

(3) LEBESGUE DOMINATED CONVERGENCE THEOREM:
   If $f_i(x) \nearrow f(x)$ for every $x \in E$ then

$$\lim_i \int_E f_i(x)\,\mu(dx) = \int_E f(x)\,\mu(dx).$$

(4) $\sum_{i=1}^{\infty} \int_E f_i(x)\,\mu(dx) = \int_E \sum_{i=1}^{\infty} f_i(x)\,\mu(dx)$.

We now define integrals for arbitrary measurable functions. For a measurable function f, let $f_-(x) = \max\{0, -f(x)\}$ and $f_+(x) = \max\{0, f(x)\}$. Obviously, f_- and f_+ are measurable and nonnegative, and $f = f_+ - f_-$. Then the *integral of f over E* is defined by

$$\int_E f(x)\,\mu(dx) = \int_E f_+(x)\,\mu(dx) - \int_E f_-(x)\,\mu(dx),$$

if either f_- or f_+ is integrable. The function f is *integrable* over E if both functions f_- and f_+ are integrable over E.

We now list some properties of integrable functions. In what follows, E is a measurable set, f and f_i are measurable, and g is integrable over E.

(5) f is integrable iff $|f|$ is integrable. Then

$$\left| \int_E f(x)\,\mu(dx) \right| \le \int_E |f(x)|\,\mu(dx) < +\infty.$$

(6) $\int_A g(x)\,\mu(dx) \to 0$ if $\mu(A) \to 0$ and $A \subset E$.

(7) LEBESGUE THEOREM: Let $\lim_i f_i(x) = f(x)$ for almost all $x \in E$, i.e., $\mu(\{x : \lim_i f_i(x) \ne f(x)\}) = 0$, and let $|f_i(x)| \le g(x)$ for every $x \in E$. Then

$$\lim_i \int_E f_i(x)\,\mu(dx) = \int_E f(x)\,\mu(dx).$$

If μ is a probability measure and f is measurable and bounded almost everywhere in E, i.e., $\mu(\{x \in E : |f(x)| > M\}) = 0$ for some finite M, then f is integrable over E and

$$\int_E |f(x)|\,\mu(dx) \le M\mu(E) \le M.$$

2.4. Characteristic Functional

Let μ be a probability measure. Let X^* be the set of all bounded linear functionals defined on X. The *characteristic functional* $\psi_\mu : X^* \to \mathcal{C}$ is defined by

$$\psi_\mu(L) = \int_X \exp\left(i\,L(x)\right) \mu(dx), \quad i = \sqrt{-1}.$$

Characteristic functionals have a number of important properties. Here we list only two of them.

(a) A probability measure is uniquely determined by its characteristic functional, i.e., if two probability measures have the same characteristic functional then they are equal.

(b) Let ψ be a characteristic functional of a probability measure. Let $\tilde{\psi} : X^* \to \mathcal{C}$ satisfy the following properties: $\tilde{\psi}(0) = 1$, $|1 - \tilde{\psi}(L)| \le |1 - \psi(L)|$ for every $L \in X^*$, and $\tilde{\psi}$ is nonnegative definite, i.e., $\sum_{i,j=1}^n a_i \bar{a}_j \tilde{\psi}(L_i - L_j) \ge 0$ for all n, $a_i \in \mathcal{C}$, and $L_i \in X^*$. Then $\tilde{\psi}$ is a characteristic functional of a probability measure.

2.5. Mean Element

An element m from X is a *mean element* of a probability measure μ iff

$$L(m) = \int_X L(x)\,\mu(dx), \quad \forall L \in X^*.$$

A mean element need not exist. However, if it exists then it is unique. It exists if $\int_X \|x\|\,\mu(dx)$ is finite, and then $\|m\| \le \int_X \|x\|\,\mu(dx)$. We now list some weaker conditions under which a mean element exists.

The following condition is necessary for a mean element to exist,

$$\int_X |L(x)|\,\mu(dx) < +\infty, \quad \forall L \in X^*. \tag{a}$$

Let $X^{**} = (X^*)^*$. If X is *reflexive*, i.e, $X^{**} = X$, then (a) is also a sufficient condition. Note that separable Hilbert spaces are reflexive. However, the space of continuous functions with sup norm is not. For nonreflexive spaces we have the following sufficient conditions (which are, in general, not necessary). A mean element exists if in addition to (a) the following holds

$$\inf_{L \in X^*} \mu\left(\left\{x \in X : |L(x)| \ge \alpha \left| \int_X L(z)\,\mu(dz) \right| \right\}\right) > 0,$$

for some $\alpha > 0$.

2.6. Covariance and Correlation Operators

An operator $\tilde{C}_\mu$, $\tilde{C}_\mu : X^* \to X^{**}$, is a *covariance operator* of the probability measure μ iff

$$\left(\tilde{C}_\mu(L_1)\right)(L_2) = \int_X L_1(x)\, L_2(x)\, \mu(dx), \quad \forall L_1, L_2 \in X^*.$$

It exists if

$$\int_X L^2(x)\, \mu(dx) < +\infty, \quad \forall L \in X^*. \tag{a}$$

Suppose that in addition to (a), μ has a mean element m. Then $\hat{C}_\mu$, $\hat{C}_\mu : X^* \to X^{**}$, is a *correlation operator* of μ iff

$$\left(\hat{C}_\mu(L_1)\right)(L_2) = \int_X L_1(x - m)\, L_2(x - m)\, \mu(dx), \quad \forall L_1, L_2 \in X^*.$$

We now list some properties of a correlation operator.

(b) It is symmetric, $\left(\hat{C}_\mu(L_1)\right)(L_2) = \left(\hat{C}_\mu(L_2)\right)(L_1)$.

(c) It is nonnegative definite, $\left(\hat{C}_\mu(L)\right)(L) \geq 0$ for every $L \in X^*$.

(d) If $m = 0$ then $\hat{C}_\mu = \tilde{C}_\mu$.

Whenever $\hat{C}_\mu(X^*)$ is a subset of X, which is the case for reflexive X, we shall identify $\hat{C}_\mu$ with C_μ, where $\left(\hat{C}_\mu(L_1)\right)(L_2) = L_2(C_\mu(L_1))$, and we shall write $C_\mu = \hat{C}_\mu$.

2.7. Induced and Conditional Measures

Let Y be a normed linear space and let $S : X \to Y$ be a measurable mapping. Let μ be a probability measure on X. Then $\nu = \mu S^{-1}$,

$$\nu(A) = \mu\left(S^{-1}(A)\right) = \mu\left(\{x \in X : S(x) \in A\}\right), \quad \forall A \in \mathcal{B}(Y),$$

is a probability measure. It is called an *induced measure* or *measure induced by S*.

Suppose additionally that Y is separable and that $S(X) = Y$. Then there exists a unique family $\{\mu(\cdot|y, S)\}_{y \in Y}$ of probability measures on $\mathcal{B}(X)$ such that for every $B \in \mathcal{B}(X)$,

(1) the set of $y \in Y$ with $\mu\left(S^{-1}(\{y\})|y, S\right) \neq 1$ has ν-measure zero,

(2) $\mu(B|\cdot, S)$ is ν-integrable,

(3) $\mu(B) = \int_Y \mu(B|y, S)\, \nu(dy)$.

This family is called a *conditional measure*.

2.8. Product Measures and Fubini's Theorem

Although one can define the product of arbitrary measures, here we restrict our attention only to probability measures. Let X_1 and X_2 be equipped with probability measures μ_1 and μ_2, respectively. Let $\mathcal{B}(X_1 \times X_2)$ be the minimal σ-field that contains $\mathcal{B}(X_1) \times \mathcal{B}(X_2)$. Then there exists a unique probability measure on $\mathcal{B}(X_1 \times X_2)$, called the *product* of μ_1 and μ_2 and denoted by $\mu_1 \otimes \mu_2$, such that

$$(\mu_1 \otimes \mu_2)(A_1 \times A_2) = \mu_1(A_1)\,\mu_2(A_2), \quad \forall A_1 \in \mathcal{B}(X_1),\ A_2 \in \mathcal{B}(X_2).$$

Furthermore, it has the following property. For arbitrary $A \in \mathcal{B}(X_1 \times X_2)$, let $A_{x_1} = \{x_2 \in X_2 : (x_1, x_2) \in A\}$ and let $A^{x_2} = \{x_1 \in X_1 : (x_1, x_2) \in A\}$. Then

$$(\mu_1 \otimes \mu_2)(A) = \int_{X_1} \mu_2(A_{x_1})\,\mu_1(dx_1) = \int_{X_2} \mu_1(A^{x_2})\,\mu_2(dx_2).$$

FUBINI'S THEOREM. *Let f be a $(\mu_1 \otimes \mu_2)$-measurable and nonnegative function on $A_1 \times A_2$, $A_i \in \mathcal{B}(X_i)$. Then*

$$\int_{A_1 \times A_2} f(x_1, x_2)\,(\mu_1 \otimes \mu_2)(d(x_1, x_2))$$

$$= \int_{A_1} \left(\int_{A_2} f(x_1, x_2)\,\mu_2(dx_2) \right) \mu_1(dx_1)$$

$$= \int_{A_2} \left(\int_{A_1} f(x_1, x_2)\,\mu_1(dx_1) \right) \mu_2(dx_2).$$

2.9. Gaussian Measures

Let X be a separable Banach space. A probability measure μ defined on Borel sets of X is *Gaussian* iff its characteristic functional ψ_μ is of the following form

$$\psi_\mu(L) = \exp\{i\,L(a) - \tfrac{1}{2} L(V(L))\}, \qquad \forall L \in X^*,\ i = \sqrt{-1},$$

for some $a \in X$ and a linear operator $V : X^* \to X$.

The Gaussian measure μ has mean element $m_\mu = a$. It has also correlation operator $\tilde{C}_\mu$ with $\tilde{C}_\mu(X^*) \subset X$. Thus, C_μ exists and $C_\mu = \tilde{C}_\mu$. Furthermore, $C_\mu = V$. Not every operator V is the correlation operator of a Gaussian measure. The characterization of the correlation operators of the Gaussian measures for a Banach space X is an open problem. For a separable Hilbert space X, V is a correlation operator of a Gaussian measure iff V is symmetric, nonnegative definite, and has a finite trace. Then $\text{trace}(V) = \int_X \|x\|^2 \, \mu(dx)$.

An example of Gaussian measures on Banach spaces is provided by the classical Wiener measure which is defined as follows. Let X be the space of continuous functions f defined on $[0,1]$ such that $f(0) = 0$. The space X is equipped with the sup norm. The Wiener measure w is uniquely defined by the following property

$$w\left(\{f \in X : (f(t_1), \ldots, f(t_n)) \in B\}\right)$$
$$= \prod_{j=1}^{n} \frac{1}{\sqrt{2\pi(t_j - t_{j-1})}} \int_B \exp\left(\sum_{j=1}^{n} \frac{-(u_j - u_{j-1})^2}{2\,(t_j - t_{j-1})}\right) du_1 \ldots du_n$$

for every $n \geq 1$, $B \in \mathcal{B}(\mathbb{R}^n)$, and $0 = t_0 < t_1 < \cdots < t_n \leq 1$ with $u_0 = 0$. Its mean is zero and its correlation operator C_w is given by $L_{x_1}(C_w L_{x_2}) = \min\{x_1, x_2\}$ for $L_{x_i}(f) = f(x_i)$.

We now state some special results concerning Gaussian measures which were used in the book. For completeness we present them with proofs.

Notes and Remarks

NR 2.9:1 Lemma 2.9.1 is due to Kwapień [85] and can be found in Wasilkowski and Woźniakowski [87]. Lemmas 2.9.3 and 2.9.4 are due to Wasilkowski [86b]. Lemmas 2.9.5, 2.9.6, and 2.9.7 are due to Lee and Wasilkowski [86].

2.9.1. Measure of a Ball

In this subsection we assume that X is a separable Hilbert space equipped with a Gaussian measure μ with mean element zero.

LEMMA 2.9.1. *Let* $B_q = \{x \in X : \|x\| \leq q\}$. *Then*

$$\mu(B_q) \leq \frac{a^2}{a^2 - 1} \psi\left(\frac{aq}{\sqrt{\text{trace}(C_\mu)}}\right), \quad \forall a > 1, \tag{1}$$

where $\psi(x) = \sqrt{2/\pi} \int_0^x \exp\left(-t^2/2\right) dt$ *is the probability integral.*

PROOF: Assume first that C_μ is positive definite. Let $\{\zeta_j\}$ be the orthonormal system of X consisting of the eigenelements of C_μ, i.e., $C_\mu \zeta_j = \lambda_j \zeta_j$, $\lambda_j > 0$ and $\text{trace}(C_\mu) = \sum_{j=1}^{\infty} \lambda_j$. Consider $\xi_j(x) = \langle x, \zeta_j \rangle / \sqrt{\lambda_j}$ for $x \in X$ and $j = 1, 2, \ldots$. Then $\{\xi_j\}$ is a sequence of independent random variables, each of them with Gaussian distribution with mean zero and variance one. Note that

$$\mu(B_q) = \mu\left(\left\{x \in X : \sum_{j=1}^{\infty} \lambda_j\, \xi_j^2(x) \leq q^2\right\}\right).$$

Let ℓ denote the Lebesgue measure on $[0, 1]$. Let $\{r_j\}$ be the Radamacher system on $[0, 1]$, i.e., $r_j : [0, 1] \to \mathbb{R}$ and $\{r_j\}$ is a sequence of independent random variables, each of them with distribution $\ell(\{t : r_j(t) = -1\}) = \ell(\{t : r_j(t) = +1\}) = 1/2$. For $x \in B_q$ and $\alpha > 0$ we have

$$\ell\left(\left\{t : \left|\sum_{j=1}^{\infty} \sqrt{\lambda_j}\, \xi_j(x)\, r_j(t)\right| \leq \alpha\right\}\right) \geq R\left(\frac{\alpha}{q}\right),$$

where

$$R(u) = \inf_{\sum_{j=1}^{\infty} c_j^2 \leq 1} \ell\left(\left\{t : \left|\sum_{j=1}^{\infty} c_j\, r_j(t)\right| \leq u\right\}\right).$$

This and Fubini's theorem yield that

$$(\mu \otimes \ell)\left(\left\{(x, t) : \left|\sum_{j=1}^{\infty} \sqrt{\lambda_j}\, \xi_j(x)\, r_j(t)\right| \leq \alpha\right\}\right)$$

$$\geq \int_{B_q} \ell\left(\left\{t : \left|\sum_{j=1}^{\infty} \sqrt{\lambda_j}\, \xi_j(x)\, r_j(t)\right| \leq \alpha\right\}\right)\mu(dx) \qquad (2)$$

$$\geq R\left(\frac{\alpha}{q}\right)\mu(B_q).$$

On the other hand, let $\eta_j(x, t) = \xi_j(x)\, r_j(t)$ for $x \in X$, $t \in [0, 1]$ and $j = 1, 2, \ldots$. Then $\{\eta_j\}$ is a sequence of independent random variables, each of them with Gaussian distribution with mean zero and variance one. Therefore, $\sum_{j=1}^{\infty} \sqrt{\lambda_j}\, \eta_j$ has Gaussian distribution with mean zero and variance $\sigma = \text{trace}(C_\mu)$. Hence, the left-hand side of (2) is equal to

$$\frac{1}{\sqrt{2\pi\sigma}} \int_{-\alpha}^{+\alpha} \exp\left(\frac{-t^2}{2\sigma}\right) dt = \sqrt{\frac{2}{\pi}} \int_0^{\alpha/\sqrt{\sigma}} \exp\left(\frac{-t^2}{2}\right) dt = \psi\left(\frac{\alpha}{\sqrt{\sigma}}\right),$$

and therefore

$$\mu(B_q) \leq \frac{\psi\left(\frac{\alpha}{\sqrt{\sigma}}\right)}{R\left(\frac{\alpha}{q}\right)}. \qquad (3)$$

Take $\alpha = a\,q$, where $a > 1$. To estimate $R(a)$, we use Chebyshev's inequality which states that

$$\ell\left(\left\{t : \left|\sum_{j=1}^{\infty} c_j\, r_j(t)\right| > a\right\}\right) \leq \frac{1}{a^2} \int_0^1 \left(\sum_{j=1}^{\infty} c_j\, r_j(t)\right)^2 dt.$$

Since r_j are independent with mean zero,

$$\int_0^1 \left(\sum_{j=1}^{\infty} c_j\, r_j(t)\right)^2 dt = \sum_{j=1}^{\infty} c_j^2 \leq 1.$$

Hence $R(a) \geq 1 - 1/a^2$, and (3) implies (1) in the nonsingular case.

Assume now that C_μ is singular. Let $\tilde{X}$ be the orthogonal complement of $\ker C_\mu$, and let $\tilde{\mu}$ be the Gaussian measure on $\mathcal{B}(\tilde{X})$ with mean element zero and covariance operator $\tilde{C}_\mu = C_\mu|_{\tilde{X}}$. Since $\mu(B_q) = \tilde{\mu}(\{x \in \tilde{X} : \|x\| \leq q\})$ and $\text{trace}(\tilde{C}_\mu) = \text{trace}(C_\mu)$, from the first part of the proof we get (1) for singular C_μ as well. ∎

LEMMA 2.9.2. *Let $B_q = \{x \in X : \|x\| \leq q\}$. Then*

$$\mu(B_q) \geq 1 - 5\exp\left(\frac{-q^2}{2\,\text{trace}(C_\mu)}\right).$$

PROOF: Let $a = q^2/(2\,\text{trace}(C_\mu))$. For $a \leq 1.5$, Lemma 2.9.2 is trivially true since $1 - 5\exp(-a) \leq 1 - 5\exp(-1.5) \leq 0$.

Assume then that $a > 1.5$. From Vakhania [81, p. 40], we know that $x = 1 - \mu(B_q)$ satisfies the inequality

$$x \leq \sqrt{\frac{2}{e}}\, \exp\left(-n\left(1 - \ln\frac{n+0.5}{a}\right)\right)$$

for any integer n. Take $n \in [a - 1.5, a - 0.5]$. Then $\ln\big((n+0.5)/a\big) \leq 0$ and $x \leq \sqrt{2/e}\,\exp(1.5 - a) \leq 5\exp(-a)$. This completes the proof. ∎

LEMMA 2.9.3. *For every balanced and convex set B,*

$$\mu(B) \geq \mu(B + h), \quad \forall h \in X. \tag{4}$$

PROOF: We prove that (4) can be reduced to a problem with a finite dimensional Gaussian measure. Then the well-known Anderson's inequality will complete the proof.

Let $\{\zeta_j\}$ be the orthonormal system consisting of eigenelements of C_μ, $C_\mu \zeta_j = \lambda_j \zeta_j$. Let $X_1 = \ker C_\mu$ and $X_2 = X_1^\perp$. Let $\mu^\perp$ be the Gaussian measure on $\mathcal{B}(X_2)$ with mean zero and correlation operator $C_{\mu^\perp} = C_\mu|_{X_2}$. Then for every $A \in \mathcal{B}(X)$,

$$\mu(A) = \mu^\perp(A \cap X_2). \tag{5}$$

Note that $B \cap X_2$ is convex and balanced and that $(B + h) \cap X_2 \subset (B \cap X_2) + h_2$, where $h = h_1 + h_2$ and h_2 is the orthogonal projection of h onto X_2. Hence, due to (5),

$$\mu(B) = \mu^\perp(B \cap X_2) \text{ and } \mu(B+h) = \mu^\perp((B+h)\cap X_2) \leq \mu^\perp((B\cap X_2)+h_2).$$

This means that to prove (4) we can assume without loss of generality that $\ker C_\mu = \{0\}$, i.e., that all eigenvalues of C_μ are positive.

For $k = 1, 2, \ldots$, define $P_k : X \to \mathbb{R}^k$,

$$P_k(x) = [\langle x, \zeta_1 \rangle / \sqrt{\lambda_1}, \ldots, \langle x, \zeta_k \rangle / \sqrt{\lambda_k}].$$

Note that for every set $A \in \mathcal{B}(X)$, we have $P_k^{-1}(P_k(A)) \supset P_{k+1}^{-1}(P_{k+1}(A))$ and also $A = \bigcap_{k=1}^\infty P_k^{-1}(P_k(A))$. Hence

$$\mu(A) = \lim_k \mu\big(P_k^{-1}(P_k(A))\big), \quad \forall A \in \mathcal{B}(X). \tag{6}$$

Let $\nu_k = \mu P_k^{-1}$ be the induced measure. Then (5) can be rewritten as

$$\mu(A) = \lim_k \nu_k\big(P_k(A)\big), \quad \forall A \in \mathcal{B}(X).$$

As we shall see in the next subsection, ν_k is a Gaussian measure on $\mathcal{B}(\mathbb{R}^k)$ whose mean is zero and whose correlation matrix is the identity. Observe also that $P_k(B)$ is convex and balanced and that $P_k(B + h) = P_k(B) + P_k(h)$. Then Anderson's inequality, see Anderson [55], yields that

$$\nu_k\big(P_k(B)\big) \geq \nu_k\big(P_k(B + h)\big), \quad \forall k = 1, 2, \ldots.$$

This implies that $\mu(B) \geq \mu(B + h)$. ∎

LEMMA 2.9.4. *Let μ_1 and μ_2 be two Gaussian measures with mean elements zero and correlation operators C_{μ_1} and C_{μ_2}, respectively. Let $\alpha_{1,j} \geq \alpha_{2,j} \geq \cdots \geq 0$ be the eigenvalues of C_{μ_j}, $j = 1$ and 2. If $\alpha_{k,1} \leq \alpha_{k,2}$, $\forall k = 1, 2, \ldots$, then*

$$\mu_1(B_q) \geq \mu_2(B_q), \quad \forall q \geq 0,$$

where $B_q = \{x \in X : \|x\| \leq q\}$.

PROOF: As in the proof of Lemma 2.9.3, we can assume that $\alpha_{k,j} > 0$. Then

$$\mu_j(B_q) = \lim_k A_{j,k}, \quad j = 1, 2,$$

where

$$A_{j,k} = (2\pi)^{-k/2} \int_{B_{j,k}} \exp\left(-\sum_{i=1}^{k} \frac{y_i^2}{2}\right) dy$$

and

$$B_{j,k} = \left\{y \in \mathbb{R}^k : \sum_{i=1}^{k} \alpha_{i,j}\, y_i^2 \leq q^2\right\}.$$

Since $\alpha_{i,1} \leq \alpha_{i,2}$, $B_{2,k} \subset B_{1,k}$ for all k. This implies that $A_{1,k} \geq A_{2,k}$ and completes the proof. ∎

2.9.2. Induced and Conditional Measures

We begin with the following simple observation. Let X be a separable Banach space equipped with a Gaussian measure μ whose mean element is m_μ and whose correlation operator is C_μ. Then for a continuous linear functional L, the induced measure μL^{-1} is a Gaussian measure on $\mathcal{B}(\mathbb{R})$ with mean $L(m_\mu)$ and variance $\langle L, L\rangle_\mu = L(C_\mu(L))$.

We now derive the induced and conditional measures for nonadaptive information N, $N(x) = [L_1(x), \ldots, L_n(x)]$. For simplicity we assume that μ has mean element zero and that the functionals L_j are μ-orthonormal, $\langle L_j, L_k\rangle_\mu = L_j(C_\mu(L_k)) = \delta_{j,k}$.

LEMMA 2.9.5. *The measure μN^{-1} is Gaussian with mean element zero and correlation matrix equal to the identity.*

PROOF: For the characteristic functional of the measure $\lambda = \mu N^{-1}$ we have

$$\psi_\lambda(z) = \int_{\mathbb{R}^n} \exp\left(i \sum_{j=1}^{n} y_j\, z_j\right) \lambda(dy) = \int_{\mathbb{R}^n} \exp\left(i \sum_{j=1}^{n} z_j\, L_j(x)\right) \mu(dx)$$

$$= \psi_\mu\left(\sum_{j=1}^{n} z_j\, L_j\right) = \exp\left(-\sum_{j=1}^{n} \frac{z_j^2}{2}\right), \quad \forall\, z \in \mathbb{R}^n.$$

This completes the proof. ∎

From Section 2.7 we know that a conditional measure $\mu(\cdot|y, N)$ exists. Its form is given in the following

LEMMA 2.9.6. *The conditional measure $\mu(\cdot|y, N)$ is Gaussian with mean element $m_y = \sum_{j=1}^{n} y_j\, C_\mu(L_j)$ and correlation operator*

$$C_N = C_\mu - \sum_{j=1}^{n} \left(L_j\big(C_\mu(\cdot)\big)\right) C_\mu(L_j).$$

PROOF: We first prove that for every y there exists a Gaussian measure with mean element m_y and correlation operator C_N. To do this, consider the function $\psi : X^* \to \mathcal{C}$ given by

$$\psi(L) = \exp\left(\frac{-L(C_N(L))}{2}\right), \quad \forall\, L \in X^*.$$

Note that

$$\psi(L) = \exp\left(\frac{-L(C_\mu(L))}{2}\right) \exp\left(\sum_{j=1}^{n} \frac{\langle L, L_j\rangle_\mu^2}{2}\right)$$

$$\geq \exp\left(\frac{-L(C_\mu(L))}{2}\right) = \psi_\mu(L).$$

Thus, $0 \leq 1 - \psi(L) \leq 1 - \psi_\mu(L)$, $\forall\, L \in X^*$. It is easy to check that the remaining assumptions of (b) of Section 2.4 hold. Since ψ_μ is the characteristic functional of the measure μ, (b) of Section 2.4 yields that ψ is the characteristic functional of some probability measure on $\mathcal{B}(X)$. Similarly, one shows that $\exp\big(i\,L(m_y) - L(C_N(L))/2\big)$ is also the characteristic functional of some probability measure on $\mathcal{B}(X)$. Hence, there exists a family of probability measures β_y with the characteristic functional

$$\psi_{\beta_y}(L) = \exp\left(i\,L(m_y) - \frac{L(C_N(L))}{2}\right), \quad \forall\, L \in X^*.$$

Obviously, β_y is Gaussian with mean element m_y and correlation operator C_N.

We now prove that $\mu(\cdot|y, N) = \beta_y$. To prove this we only need to show that β_y satisfies conditions (1)–(3) from Section 2.7. Note that β_y is a translation of β_0,

$$\beta_y(B) = \beta_0(B - m_y), \quad \forall\, B \in \mathcal{B}(X).$$

Since $N(m_y) = y$, to prove that $\beta_y(N^{-1}(\{y\})) = 1$ for all y it is enough to show that $\beta_0(N^{-1}(\{0\})) = 1$. Let $G(x) = \sum_{j=1}^{n} L_j^2(x)$. Then

$$\int_X G(x)\,\beta_0(dx) = \sum_{j=1}^{n} \int_X L_j^2(x)\,\beta_0(dx) = \sum_{j=1}^{n} L_j(C_N(L_j)).$$

A simple calculation yields that $L_j(C_N(L_j)) = 0$, $j = 1, 2, \ldots, n$. Thus, $\int_X G(x)\,\beta_0(dx) = 0$. Since G is nonnegative and $G(x) > 0$ iff $x \notin N^{-1}(\{0\})$, this proves that $\beta_0(X - N^{-1}(\{0\})) = 0$, and hence $\beta_0(N^{-1}(\{0\})) = 1$.

It is easy to observe that $\beta_y(B)$, as a function of y, is ν-integrable for every $B \in \mathcal{B}(X)$, $\nu = \mu N^{-1}$. To complete the proof, we need only to show that the last condition from Section 2.7 holds. Let

$$\tilde{\mu}(B) = \int_{\mathbf{R}^n} \beta_y(B)\,\nu(dy), \quad \forall\, B \in \mathcal{B}(X).$$

Of course, $\tilde{\mu}$ is a probability measure on $\mathcal{B}(X)$ whose characteristic functional is given by

$$\psi_{\tilde{\mu}}(L) = (2\pi)^{-n/2} \int_{\mathbf{R}^n} \left[\int_X \exp(i\,L(x))\,\beta_y(dx) \right] \exp\left(-\sum_{j=1}^{n} \frac{y_j^2}{2} \right) dy$$

$$= (2\pi)^{-n/2} \int_{\mathbf{R}^n} \exp\left(i\,L(m_y) - \frac{L(C_N(L))}{2} \right) \exp\left(-\sum_{j=1}^{n} \frac{y_j^2}{2} \right) dy$$

$$= \exp\left(\frac{-L(C_N(L))}{2} \right)$$

$$\times \int_{\mathbf{R}^n} (2\pi)^{-n/2} \exp\left(i\,L(m_y) \right) \exp\left(-\sum_{j=1}^{n} \frac{y_j^2}{2} \right) dy.$$

The last integral is equal to

$$(2\pi)^{-n/2} \int_{\mathbf{R}^n} \exp\left(i \sum_{j=1}^{n} y_j \left\langle L, L_j \right\rangle_\mu \right) \exp\left(-\sum_{j=1}^{n} \frac{y_j^2}{2} \right) dy$$

$$= \exp\left(-\sum_{j=1}^{n} \frac{\left\langle L, L_j \right\rangle_\mu^2}{2} \right) = \exp\left(-\frac{\left\langle L, L \right\rangle_\mu}{2} + \frac{L(C_N(L))}{2} \right).$$

Thus, $\psi_{\tilde{\mu}}(L) = \exp\left(-\left\langle L, L \right\rangle_\mu \right) = \psi_\mu(L)$, and the uniqueness of conditional measures completes the proof. ∎

We now present the induced and conditional measures for measurable adaptive information N with fixed cardinality. That is,

$$N(x) = [y_1, \ldots, y_n]$$

with $y_1 = L_1(x)$ and $y_j = L_{j,y}(x) = L(x; y_1, \ldots, y_{j-1})$. We assume that for every fixed $y \in \mathbb{R}^n$, $L_{j,y}$ are μ-orthonormal. For $k = 1, \ldots, n$ and fixed $y \in \mathbb{R}^n$, define the following nonadaptive information,

$$N^{\text{non}}_{k,y} = [L_1, L_{2,y}, \ldots, L_{k,y}].$$

LEMMA 2.9.7.

(i) *The induced measure μN^{-1} is Gaussian on $\mathcal{B}(\mathbb{R}^n)$ with mean zero and correlation matrix identity. Hence, $\mu N^{-1} = \mu(N^{\text{non}}_{n,y})^{-1}$ for every $y \in \mathbb{R}^n$.*

(ii) *For every $y \in \mathbb{R}^n$, the conditional measure $\mu(\cdot|y, N)$ for adaptive N is equal to the conditional measure $\mu(\cdot|y, N^{\text{non}}_{n,y})$ for nonadaptive $N^{\text{non}}_{n,y}$.*

PROOF: (induction on n) For $n = 1$, N is nonadaptive and (i) and (ii) follow from Lemmas 2.9.5 and 2.9.6. Suppose therefore that (i) and (ii) hold for adaptive information of cardinality $\leq n-1$. We prove that (i) and (ii) hold for adaptive information of cardinality n.

To show (i), take a Borel set $C \in \mathbb{R}^n$ of the form $C = A \times B$, where $A \in \mathcal{B}(\mathbb{R}^{n-1})$ and $B \in \mathcal{B}(\mathbb{R})$. Let N_{n-1} be the adaptive information consisting of the first $n - 1$ evaluations of N. Then

$$(\mu N^{-1})(C) = \mu\big(\{x \in X : N_{n-1}(x) \in A \text{ and } L_{n,N_{n-1}(x)}(x) \in B\}\big)$$

$$= \int_A \mu\big(\{x \in X : L_{n,y}(x) \in B\}|y, N_{n-1}\big)\,(\mu N^{-1}_{n-1})(dy).$$

Since N_{n-1} has cardinality $n - 1$, the inductive assumptions yield that μN^{-1}_{n-1} is Gaussian on $\mathcal{B}(\mathbb{R}^{n-1})$ with mean zero and correlation matrix identity. Furthermore, $\mu(\cdot|y, N_{n-1,y}) = \mu(\cdot|y, N^{\text{non}}_{n-1})$. Hence, it is Gaussian on $\mathcal{B}(X)$ with mean $m_{n-1,y} = \sum_{j=1}^{n-1} y_j\, C_\mu(L_{j,y})$ and correlation operator $C_{N_{n-1}}$. Since $L_{j,y}$ are orthonormal, we have $L_{n,y}(m_{n-1,y}) = 0$ and $L_{n-1,y}(C_{N_{n-1}}(L_{n-1,y})) = 1$. The observation from the beginning of this subsection yields that $\mu(\{x \in X : L_{n,y}(x) \in B\}|y, N_{n-1}) = \lambda(B)$, where $\lambda = \mu(L^{-1}_{n,y}(\cdot)|y.N_{n-1})$ is Gaussian with mean zero and variance 1. Therefore

$$(\mu N^{-1})(C) = (2\pi)^{-n/2} \int_{A \times B} \exp\left(-\sum_{j=1}^n \frac{y_j^2}{2}\right) dy,$$

which completes the proof of (i). Since (ii) can be proven in a similar way, we skip the proof. ∎

Bibliography

ADLER, I., KARP, R. M., AND SHAMIR, R.

[87]   A simplex variant solving an $m \times d$ linear program in $O(\min(m^2, d^2))$ expected number of pivot steps, to appear in *J. Complexity* **3** (1987).

ADLER, I. AND MEGIDDO, N.

[85]   A simplex algorithm whose average number of steps is bounded between two quadratic functions of the smaller dimension, *J. Assoc. Comput. Mach.* **32** (1985), 871–895.

ADLER, S. J.

[81]   "The Geometry of Random Fields." Wiley Ser. in Prob. and Math. Stat., New York, 1981.

AIRD, T. J. AND RICE, J. R.

[77]   Systematic search in high dimensional sets, *SIAM J. Numer. Anal.* **172** (1977), 296–312.

AKSEN, M. B. AND TURECKIJ, A. H.

[66]   Best quadrature formulas for certain classes of functions (in Russian), *Dokl. Akad. Nauk SSSR* **166** (1966), 1019–1021 [*English transl.: Soviet Math. Dokl.* **7** (1966), 203–205].

ALOIMONOS, J. Y.

[86]   Detection of surface orientation from texture, i: the case of planes, *in* "Proc. of the IEEE Comput. Soc. Conf. on Computer Vision and Pattern Recognition", pp. 584–593, 1986.

ANDERSON, N. AND BJÖRCK, A.

[73]   A new high order method of regula falsi type for computing a root of an equation, *BIT* **13** (1973), 253–264.

ANDERSON, T. W.

[55]   The integral of symmetric unimodal function over a symmetric convex set and some probability inequalities, *Proc. Amer. Math. Soc.* **6** (1955), 170–175.

ANDERSSON, J. E.

[80]   Optimal quadrature of H^p functions, *Math. Z.* **172** (1980), 55–62.

ANDERSSON, J. E. AND BOJANOV, B. D.

[84]   A note on the optimal quadrature in H^p, *Numer. Math.* **44** (1984), 301–308.

ANSELONE, P. M. AND LAURENT, P. J.

[68]   A general method for the construction of interpolating or smoothing spline functions. *Numer. Math.* **12** (1968), 66–82.

ARAUJO, A. AND GINÉ, E.

[80]   "The Central Limit Theorem for Real and Banach Valued Random Variables." Wiley, New York, 1980.

ATTEIA, M.

[65]   Fonctions-spline généralisées. *C. R. Acad. Sci. Paris* **216** (1965), 2149–2152.

[66]   Etude de certains noyaux et théorie des fonctions "spline" en analyse numérique, Ph.D. thesis, De L'institut de Mathématiques Appliquées de Grenoble, 1966.

BABENKO, K. I.

[79]   "Theoretical Background and Constructing of Computational Algorithms for Mathematical-Physical Problems" (in Russian). Nauka, Moscow, 1979.

BABENKO, V. F.

[76]   Asymptotically sharp bounds for the reminder for the best quadrature formulas for several classes of functions. *Mat. Zametki* **19** (1976), 313–322 [*English transl.: Math. Notes* **19**, 187–193].

BABUŠKA, I. AND AZIZ, A. K.

[72]   Survey lectures on the mathematical foundations of the finite element method, *in* "The Mathematical Foundations of the Finite Element Method with Applications to Partial Differential Equations" (A. K. Aziz, ed.), pp. 3–358. Academic Press, New York, 1972.

BABUŠKA, I. AND SOBOLEV, S. L.

[65] Optimization of numerical methods (in Russian), *Apl. Mat.* **1** (1965), 96-130.

BAKHVALOV, N. S.

[59] On approximate calculation of integrals (in Russian), *Vestnik MGV, Ser. Mat. Mekh. Astron. Fiz. Khim.* **4** (1959), 3-18.

[61] An estimate of the mean remainder in quadrature formulas (in Russian), *Zh. Vychisl. Mat. Mat. Fiz.* **1** (1961), 64-77 [*English transl.: U.S.S.R. Comput. Math. and Math. Phys.* **1** (1961), 68-82].

[62] On optimal methods of specifying information in the solution of differential equations (in Russian), *Zh. Vychisl. Mat. Mat. Fiz.* **2** (1962), 569-592 [*English transl.: U.S.S.R. Comput. Math. and Math. Phys.* **2** (1962), 608-640].

[64] On optimal bounds for the convergence of quadrature formulas and Monte-Carlo type integration methods for classes of functions, *in* "Numerical Methods for the Solution of Differential and Integral Equations and Quadrature Formulas" (in Russian), pp. 5-63. Nauka, Moscow, 1964.

[67] On the optimal speed of integrating analytic functions (in Russian), *Zh. Mat. Mat. Mat. Fiz.* **7** (1967), 1011-1020 [*English transl.: USSR Comput. Math. Math. Phys.* **7**, 63-75].

[68] On optimal methods for the solution of problems (in Russian), *Apl. Mat.* **1** (1968), 27-38.

[70] Properities of optimal methods for the solution of problems of mathematical physics (in Russian), *Zh. Vychisl. Mat. Mat. Fiz.* **10** (1970), 555-568 [*English transl.: USSR Comp. Math. Math. Phys.* **10** (1970), 1-20].

[71] On the optimality of linear methods for operator approximation in convex classes of functions (in Russian), *Zh. Vychisl. Mat. Mat. Fiz.* **11** (1971), 1014-1018 [*English transl.: USSR Comput. Math. Math. Phys.* **11** (1971), 244-249].

[72] A lower bound for the asymptotic characteristics of classes of functions with dominating mixed derivative (in Russian), *Mat. Zametki* **12** (1972), 655-664.

[77] "Numerical Methods." Mir, Moscow, 1977.

BARNHILL, R. E.

[67] Optimal quadratures in $L^2(E_\zeta)$, I and II, *SIAM J. Numer. Anal.* **4** (1967), 390-397, 534-541.

[68] Asymptotic properties of minimum norm and optimal quadratures, *Numer. Math.* **12** (1968), 384-393.

BARNHILL, R. E. AND WIXOM, A.

[67] Quadratures with remainders of minimum norm, I and II, *Math. Comput.* **21** (1967), 66–75, 382–387.

[68] An error analysis for interpolation of analytic functions, *SIAM J. Numer. Anal.* **5** (1968), 522–528.

BARRAR, R. B. AND LOEB, H. L.

[76] On a nonlinear characterization problem for monosplines, *J. Approx. Theory* **18** (1976), 220–240.

BARRAR, R. B., LOEB, H. L., AND WERNER, M.

[74] On the existence of optimal integration formulas for analytic functions, *Numer. Math.* **23** (1974), 105–117.

BESOV, O. V.

[80] Intercellular averages and an error estimate for cubature formulas in Sobolev spaces and their generalizations (in Russian), *Proc. Steklov Inst. of Math.* **1** (1980), 45–60.

[81] Error estimates for cubature formulas in terms of smoothness of functions (in Russian), *Proc. Steklov Inst. of Math.* **4** (1981), 11–23.

BLACKWELL, D. AND GIRSHICK, M. A.

[59] "Theory of Games and Statistical Decisions." Wiley, New York, 1959.

BLUM, L. AND SHUB, M.

[86] Evaluating rational functions: infinite precision is finite cost and tractable on average, *SIAM J. Comput.* **15** (1986), 384–398.

BOJAŃCZYK, A.

[84] Complexity of solving linear systems in different models of computation, *SIAM J. Comput.* **21** (1984), 591–603.

BOJANOV, B. D.

[73] Optimal rate of integration and ε-entropy of a class of analytic functions (in Russian), *Mat. Zametki* **14** (1973), 3–10 [*English transl.: Math. Notes* **19** (1973), 551–556].

[74] Best quadrature formula for a certain class of analytic functions, *Zastosow. Mat.* **14** (1974), 441–447.

[75] Best methods of interpolation for certain classes of differentiable functions (in Russian), *Mat. Zametki* **17** (1975), 511–524 [*English transl.: Math. Notes* **17** (1975), 301–309].

[77] Existence of extended monosplines of least deviation, *Serdica* **3** (1977), 261–272.

[78] Existence of optimal quadrature formulas with given multiplicity of points (in Russian), *Mat. Sb.* **105** (1978), 342–370.

[80] Existence and characterization of monosplines of least L_p deviation, *in* "Constructive Function Theory '77," pp. 249–268. BAN, Sofia, 1980.

[86] Comparison theorems in optimal recovery, *in* "Optimal Algorithms, Proc. Intern. Symp." pp. 15–50. BAN, Sofia, 1986.

BOLLEN, J. A. M.

[84] Numerical stability of descent methods for solving linear equations, *Numer. Math.* **43** (1984), 361–377.

BOOTH, R. S.

[67] Location of zeros of derivatives, *SIAM J. Appl. Math.* **15** (1967), 1495–1501.

BORELL, C.

[75] The Brunn-Minkowski Inequality in Gauss Space, *Invent. Math.* **30** (1975), 207–216.

[76] Gaussian Radon Measures on Locally Convex Spaces, *Math. Scand.* **38** (1976), 265–284.

BORODIN, A.

[72] Complexity classes of recursive functions and the existence of complexity gaps, *J. Assoc. Comput. Math.* **19** (1972) 158–174, 576.

BORGWARDT, K-H.

[82] The average number of steps required by the simplex method is polynomial, *Zeitschrift für Operations Research* **26** (1982), 157–177.

BÖRGERS, CH. AND WIDLUND, O. B.

[86] Finite element capacitance matrix methods, Technical Report 261, Courant Institute of Mathematical Sciences, New York, 1986.

BOULT, T. E.

[86] Information-based complexity in nonlinear equations and computer vision, Ph.D. thesis, Columbia University Computer Science Department, 1986.

[87] What is regular in regularization?, to appear in "Proc. of the First IEEE Comput. Soc. Intern. Conf. on Computer Vision", 1987.

BOULT, T. E. AND SIKORSKI, K.

[84] Can we approximate zeros of functions with non-zero topological degree?, Report, Columbia University Computer Science Department, 1984, to appear in *J. Complexity*.

[85] Complexity of computing topological degree of Lipschitz functions in two dimensions, Report, Columbia University Computer Science Department, 1985, to appear in *SIAM Scientific and Statistical Computation*.

[86] Complexity of computing topological degree of Lipschitz functions in n dimensions, *J. Complexity* **2** (1986), 44–59.

[87] A Fortran Subroutine for Computing Topological Degree of Lipschitz Functions, in progress.

BRENT, R. P.

[71] An algorithm with guaranteed convergence for finding a zero of a function, *Comput. J.* **14** (1971), 422–425.

[73] "Algorithms for Minimization Without Derivatives." Prentice-Hall, Englewood Cliffs, N.J., 1973.

[76a] A class of optimal-order zero-finding methods using derivatives evaluations, *in* "Analytic Computational Complexity" (J. F. Traub, ed.), pp. 59–73. Academic Press, New York, 1976.

[76b] Multiple precision zero-finding methods and the complexity of elementary function evaluation, *in* "Analytic Computational Complexity" (J. F. Traub, ed.), pp. 151–176. Academic Press, New York, 1976.

BRENT, R. P., WINOGRAD, S., AND WOLFE, P.

[73] Optimal iterative processes for root finding, *Numer. Math.* **20** (1973), 327–341.

BROOKS, S. H.

[58] A discussion of random methods for seeking maxima, *Oper. Research* **6** (1958), 244–251.

[59] A comparison of maximum-seeking methods, *Oper. Research* **7** (1959), 430–457.

BUS, J. C. P. AND DEKKER, T. J.

[75] Two efficient algorithms with guaranteed convergence for finding a zero of a function, *ACM Trans, Math. Software* **1** (1975), 330–345.

CARASSO, A. AND STONE, A.

[75] "Improperly Posed Boundary Value Problems." Pitnam, London, 1975.

CHAWLA, M. M.

[68] Asymptotic estimates for the error in the Gauss-Legendre quadrature formula, *Comput. J.* **11** (1968), 339–340.

CHAWLA, M. M. AND JAIN, M. K.

[68a] Error estimates for Gauss quadrature formulas for analytic functions, *Math. Comput.* **22** (1968), 82–90.

[68b] Asymptotic error estimates for the Gauss quadrature formula, *Math. Comput* **22** (1968), 91–97.

CHAWLA, M. M. AND KAUL, V.

[73]   Optimal rules for numerical integration round the unit circle, *BIT* **13** (1973), 145–152.

CHERNOUSKO, F. L.

[68]   An optimal algorithm for finding the roots of an approximately computed function (in Russian), *Zh. Vychisl. Mat. Mat. Fiz.* **8** (1968), 705–724 [*English transl.: U.S.S.R. Comput. Math. and Math. Phys.* **8** (1968),1–24].

CHOU, A. W.

[87]   On the Optimality of Krylov Information, *J. Complexity* **3** (1987), 26–40.

CHZHAN GUAN-TSZYUAN.

[62]   On the minimum number of interpolation points in the numerical integration of the heat-conduction equation (in Russian), *Zh. Vychisl. Mat. Mat. Fiz.* **2** (1962), 80–88 [*English transl.: U.S.S.R. Comput. Math. and Math. Phys.* **2** (1962), 78–87].

CIARLET, P. G.

[78]   "The Finite Element Method for Elliptic Problems." North-Holland, Amsterdam, 1978.

CIARLET, P. G. AND RAVIART, P. A.

[72]   Interpolation theory over curved elements, *Comput. Methods Appl. Mech. Engrg.* **1** (1972), 217–249.

COPPERSMITH, D. AND WINOGRAD, S.

[87]   Matrix multiplication via arithmetic progression, *in* "Proc. of the Nineteenth ACM Symp. on Theor. of Comp.", 1987, New York, pp. 1–6.

COVEYOU, R. R.

[69]   Random number generation is too important to be left to chance, *Studies Appl. Math.* **3** (1969), 70–111.

CRAWFORD, J. J.

[77]   Elliptically contoured measures on infinite dimensional Banach spaces, *Stud. Math.* **60** (1977), 15–32.

DARLING, D.

[72]   When is a fixed number of observations optimal?, *in* "Proc. Sixth Berkeley Symp. Math. Stat. and Probab.," **IV** (1972), pp. 33–35.

DAVENPORT, H.

[51]   Note on a principle of Lipschitz, *J. London Math. Soc.* **26** (1951), 179–183.

DeGroot, M. H.

[70]   "Optimal Statistical Decisions." McGraw-Hill, New York, 1970.

Diaconis, P. and Freedman, D.

[83]   Frequency properties of Bayes rules, *Sci. Inference, Data Anal. and Robustness* (1980), 105–115.

Devroye, L.

[86]   "Non-Uniform Random Variate Generation." Springer-Verlag, New York, 1986.

Dryja, M.

[84]   A finite element-capacitance method for elliptic problems on regions partitioned into subregions, *Numer. Math.* **44** (1984), 153–168.

Duchon, J.

[76]   Interpolation de fonctions de deux variables suivant le principe de la flexion des plaques minces, *Revue Francaise d'Automatique, Informatique et Recherche Operationelle*, (1976), 5–12.

Dunford, N. and Schwartz, J. T.

[63]   "Linear Operators—Part I: General Theory." Wiley-Interscience, New York, 1963.

Dunn, H. S.

[67]   A generalization of the Laplace transform, *Proc. Camb. Phil. Soc.* **63** (1967), 155–160.

Dyn, N., Micchelli, C. A., and Rivlin, T. J.

[86]   Blaschke products and optimal recovery in H^∞, Report, IBM, 1986.

Edwards, R. E.

[65]   "Functional Analysis." Holt, New York, 1965.

Eichhorn, B. H.

[68]   On sequential search, selected statistical papers, *Math. Cent. Amsterdam* **1** (1968), 81–85.

Eiger, A., Sikorski, K., and Stenger, F.

[84]   A bisection method for systems of nonlinear equations, *ACM TOMS* **10** (1984), 367–377.

Emelyanov, K. V. and Ilin, A. M.

[67]   Number of arithmetic operations necessary for the approximate solution of Fredholm integral equations (in Russian) *Zh. Vychisl. Mat. Mat. Fiz.* **7** (1967), 905–910 [*English transl.: USSR Comput. Math. and Math. Phys.* **7** (1967), 259–267].

ERMAKOV, S. M.

[75] "Die Monte-Carlo-Methode und verwandte Fragen." Oldenbourg Verlag, München, 1975.

FERGUSON, T. S.

[67] "Mathematical Statistics. A Decision Theoretic Approach." Academic Press, New York, 1967.

FISHMAN, G. S. AND MOORE, L. R.

[86] An exhaustive analysis of multiplicative congruential random number generator with modulus $2^{31} - 1$, *SIAM J. Sci. Stat. Comput.* **7** (1986), 24–45.

FRIED, I.

[73] Boundary and interior approximation errors in the finite-element method, *J. Appl. Mech.* **40** (1973), 1113–1117.

GAL, S. AND MICCHELLI, C. A.

[80] Optimal sequential and non-sequential procedures for evaluating a functional, *Appl. Anal.* **10** (1980), 105–120.

GAUTSCHI, W. AND VARGA, R. S.

[83] Error bounds for Gaussian quadrature of analytic functions, *SIAM J. Numer. Anal.* **29** (1983), 1170–1186.

GEHATIA, M. AND WIFF, D. R.

[70] Solution of Fujita's equation for equilibrium sedimentation by applying Tikhonov's regularizing functions, *J. Polymer Science* (Part A-2) **8** (1970), 2039–2049.

GELFAND, I. M. AND VILENKIN, N. YA.

[64] "Generalized Functions. Volume 4: Generalized Functions." Academic Press, New York, 1964.

GEORGE, A. AND LIU, J. W.-H.

[81] "Computer Solution of Large Sparse Positive Definite Systems." Prentice-Hall, Inc., Englewood Cliffs, N.J., 1981.

GIRSCHOVICH, J.

[78] Extremal properties of Euler-Maclaurin and Gregory quadrature formulas, (in Russian) *Izv. AN Est. SSR, Ser. Fiz.-Mat.* **27** (1978), 259–265.

GLINKIN, I. A.

[81] On optimal integration of monotonic functions (in Russian), *in* "Mathematical Methods in Operations Research." (P. S. Krasnoshekov and N. N. Moisseev, eds.), pp. 37–46. Moscow State University, Moscow, 1981.

GLINKIN, I. A. AND SUKHAREV, A. G.

[85]   Efficiency analysis of some algorithms of numerical integration and
       their applications to the solution of extremal problems (in Russian),
       in "Issues of Cybernetics. Models and Methods of Global Optimiza-
       tion." (V. V. Fedorov, ed.), pp. 23–37, Nauka, Moscow, 1985.

GOLOMB, M.

[77]   Interpolation operators as optimal recovery schemes for classes of
       analytic functions, *in* "Optimal Estimation in Approximation The-
       ory" (C. A. Micchelli and T. J. Rivlin, eds.), pp. 93–138. Plenum,
       New York, 1977.

GOLOMB, M. AND WEINBERGER, H. F.

[59]   Optimal approximation and error bounds, *in* "On Numerical Ap-
       proximation" (R. E. Langer, ed.), pp. 117–190, Univ. of Wisconsin
       Press, Madison, 1959.

GRADSHTEYN, I. S. AND RYZHIK, I.

[80]   "Table of Integrals, Series and Products." Academic Press, New
       York, 1980.

GRANOVSKII, B. L. AND ERMAKOV, S. M.

[77]   The Monte Carlo method (in Russian), *J. of Soviet Math.* **7** (1977),
       161–192.

GRIMSON, W. E. L.

[79]   From images to surfaces: A computational study of the human visual
       system, Ph.D. thesis, MIT, 1979.

[81]   From Images to Surfaces: A Computational Study of the Human
       Visual System, MIT Press, Cambridge, MA. 1981.

GROSS, O. AND JOHNSON, S. M.

[59]   Sequential minimax search for a zero of a convex function, *MTAC*
       (now *Math. Comput.*) **13** (1959), 44–51.

GTOA see Traub and Woźniakowski [80a].

HABER, S.

[66]   A modified Monte-Carlo quadrature, *Math. Comput.* **20** (1966), 361–
       368.

[69]   Stochastic quadrature formulas, *Math. Comput.* **23** (1969), 751–764.

[70]   Numerical evaluation of multiple integrals, *SIAM Rev.* **12** (1970),
       481–526.

[71]   The error in numerical integration of analytic functions, *Q. Appl.
       Math.* **29** (1971), 411–420.

HACKBUSH, W.

[85]   "Multi-grid Methods and Applications." Springer-Verlag, Berlin, 1985.

HADAMARD, J.

[52]   "Lectures on the Cauchy Problem in Linear Partial Differential Equations." Dover, New York, 1952.

HALPERN, J. Y., MEGIDDO, N., AND MUNSHI, A. A.

[85]   Optimal precision in the presence of uncertainty, *J. Complexity* **1** (1985), 170–196.

HALTON, J. H.

[70]   A retrospective and prospective survey of the Monte Carlo method, *SIAM Rev.* **12** (1970), 1–63.

HÄMMERLIN, C. AND HOFFMANN, K.

[83]   "Improperly Posed Problems and Their Numerical Treatment." International Series of Numerical Mathematics **63**, Birkhäuser-Verlag, Basel, 1983.

HAMMERSLEY, J. M. AND HANDSCOMB, D. C.

[64]   "Monte-Carlo-Methods." Methuen, London, 1964.

HARVEY, C. AND STENGER, F.

[76]   A two dimensional analogue to the method of bisections for solving nonlinear equations, *Q. Appl. Math.* **33** (1976), 351–368.

HENGARTNER, W. AND THEODORESCU, R.

[78]   "Eineführung in die Monte-Carlo-Methode." Hanser Verlag, München, 1987.

HESTENES, M. R. AND STIEFEL, E.

[52]   Methods of Conjugate Gradients for Solving Linear Systems, *J. Res. Nat. Bur. Standards* **49** (1952), 409–436.

HIRSCH, M. AND SMALE, S.

[79]   On algorithms for solving $f(x) = 0$, *Commun. Pure Appl. Math.* **2** (1979),281–312.

HÖLLIG, K.

[79]   Approximationszahlen von Sobolev-Einbettungen, *Math. Ann.* **242** (1979), 237–281.

[80]   Diameters of classes of smooth functions, *in* "Quantitive Approximation: Proc. Symp., 1979" (R. A. DeVore and K. Scherer, eds.), pp. 163–175, Academic Press, NewYork, 1980.

HOLMES, R.

[72]   R-splines in Banach spaces: I. Interpolation of linear manifolds, J. Math. Anal. Appl. **40** (1972), 574–593.

HUERTA, I.

[86]   Adaption helps for some nonconvex classes, J. Complexity **2** (1986), 333–352.

HYAFIL, L.

[77]   Optimal search for the zero of the $(n - 1)$st derivative, Report, IRIA/LABORIA, No. 247.

IBRAGIMOV, I. I. AND ALIEV, R. M.

[65]   Best quadrature formulas for certain classes of functions (in Russian), Dokl. Akad. Nauk SSSR **162** (1965), 23–25 [English transl.: Soviet Math. Dokl. **6** (1965), 621–623].

IKEUCHI, K.

[80]   Numerical shape from shading and occluding contours in a single view, AI Lab Memo 566, MIT, 1980.

IUC see Traub, Wasilkowski and Woźniakowski [83].

IVANOV, V. V.

[72]   On optimal algorithms for minimizing functions of a certain class, Kibernetika **4** (1972), 81–94.

JACKOWSKI, T. AND WOŹNIAKOWSKI, H.

[87]   Complexity of approximation with relative error criterion in worst, average and probabilistic settings, to appear in J. Complexity **3** (1987).

JANKOWSKA, J.

[79]   Multivariate secant method, SIAM J. Numer. Anal. **16** (1979), 547–562.

JANKOWSKI, M., SMOKTUNOWICZ, A., AND WOŹNIAKOWSKI, H.

[83]   A note on floating-point summation of very many terms, J. Inf. Processing and Cybernetics-EIK **19** (1983), 435–440.

JANKOWSKI, M. AND WOŹNIAKOWSKI, H.

[77]   Iterative refinement implies numerical stability, BIT **17** (1977), 303–311.

[85]   The accurate solution of certain continuous problems using only single precision arithmetic, BIT **25** (1985), 635–651.

JETTER, K. AND LANGE, G.

[78]   Die Eindeutigkeit $\mathcal{L}_2$-optimaler polynomialer Monosplines, Math. Z. **158** (1978), 23–34.

JOHNSON, R. S.

[60] On monosplines of least deviation, *Trans. Amer. Soc.* **96** (1960), 458–477

KACEWICZ, B. Z.

[76a] The use of integrals in the solution of nonlinear equations in n dimensions, *in* "Analytic Computational Complexity" (J. F. Traub, ed.), pp. 127–141. Academic Press, New York, 1976.

[76b] An integral interpolation iterative method for the solution of scalar equations, *Numer. Math.* **26** (1976), 355–365.

[79] Integrals with a kernel in the solution of nonlinear equations in n dimensions, *J. Assoc. Comput. Mach.* **26** (1979), 233–249.

[82] On the optimal error of algorithms for solving a scalar autonomous ODE, *BIT* **22** (1982), 503–518.

[83] Optimality of Euler-integral information for solving a scalar autonomous ODE, *BIT* **23** (1983), 217–230.

[84] How to increase the order to get minimal-error algorithms for systems of ODE, *Numer. Math.* **45** (1984), 93–104.

[87a] Asymptotic error of algorithms for solving nonlinear problems, *J. Complexity* **3** (1987), 41–56.

[87b] Optimal solution of ordinary differential equations, to appear in *J. Complexity* **3** (1987).

[87c] Minimum asymptotic error of algorithms for solving ODE, to appear in *J. Complexity* **4** (1988).

[87d] A spline algorithm with best convergence properties and almost minimal cost for the numerical solution of a simple optimal control problem, Report, University of Warsaw Institute of Informatics, 1987.

KACEWICZ, B. Z., MILANESE, M., AND VICINO, A.

[87] Conditionally optimal algorithms and estimation of reduced order models, to appear in *J. Complexity* **3** (1987).

KACEWICZ, B. Z., MILANESE, M., TEMPO, R., AND VICINO, A.

[86] Optimality of central and projection algorithms for bounded uncertainty, *Systems and Control Letters* **8** (1986), 161–171.

KACEWICZ, B. Z. AND WASILKOWSKI, G. W.

[86] How powerful is continuous nonlinear information for linear problems?, *J. Complexity* **2** (1986), 306–316.

KADANE, J. B. AND WASILKOWSKI, G. W.

[85] Average case ε-complexity in computer science – a Bayesian view, *in* "Bayesian Statistics 2, Proc. 2nd Valencia Intern. Meeting, 1983" (J. M. Bernardo et al., eds.), pp. 361–374. Elsevier Science Publisher B. V. (North-Holland), 1985.

KADANE, J. B., WASILKOWSKI, G. W., AND WOŹNIAKOWSKI, H.

[88]   On adaption with noisy information, to appear in *J. Complexity* **4** (1988).

KARLIN, S.

[69]   Best quadrature formulas and interpolation by splines satisfying boundary conditions, and the fundamental theorem of algebra for monosplines satisfying certain boundary conditions and applications to optimal quadrature formulas, *in* "Approximations with Special Emphasis on Spline Functions" (I. J. Schoenberg, ed.), pp. 447–466, 467–484. Academic Press, New York, 1969.

KARP, R. M.

[76]   The probabilistic analysis of some combinatorial search algorithms, *in* "Algorithms and Complexity: New Directions and Recent Results" (J. F. Traub, ed.), 1–19. Academic Press, New York, 1976.

[79]   Recent advances in the probabilistic analysis of graph-theoretic algorithms, *Proc. 6th Colloq. Autom. Lang. Program, Lect. Notes Comput. Sci.* **71** (1979), 338–339.

[80]   An algorithm to solve the $m \times n$ assignment problem in expected time $O(mn \log n)$, *Networks* **10** (1980), 143–152.

KARP, R. M. AND LUBY, M.

[83]   Monte-Carlo algorithms for enumeration and reliability problems, *Proc. 24th Ann. Symp. Found. Comput. Sci.* (1983), 56–60.

[85]   A Monte-Carlo algorithm for the multiterminal reliability problem, *J. Complexity* **1** (1985), 45–64.

KASHIN, B. S.

[77]   Diameters of some finite-dimensional sets and classes of smooth functions, *Math. USSR-Izv.* **11** (1977), 317–333.

[80]   On estimates of diameters, *in* "Quantitative Approximation", Proc. Symp. 1979" (R. A. DeVore and K. Scherer, eds.). Academic Press, New York, 1980.

KAUTSKY, J.

[70]   Optimal quadrature formulas and minimal monosplines in L_q, *J. Austral. Math. Soc.* **11** (1970), 48–56.

KEARFOTT, R. B.

[77]   Computing the degree of maps and a generalized method of bisection, Ph.D. thesis, Univ. of Utah, 1977.

[79]   An efficient degree-computation method for a generalized method of bisection, *Numer. Math.* **32** (1979), 109–127.

KEAST, P.

[73] Optimal parameters for multidimensional integration, *SIAM J. Numer. Anal.* **10** (1973), 831–838.

KENDER, J. R.

[86] "Shape from Texture," AI Research Notes, Pitman, London, 1986.

KIEFER, J.

[53] Sequential minimax search for a maximum, *Proc. Amer. Math. Soc.* **4** (1953), 502–505.

[57] Optimum sequential search and approximation methods under regularity assumptions, *J. Soc. Indust. Appl. Math.* **5** (1957), 105–136.

KIEŁBASIŃSKI, A.

[73] Summation algorithm with corrections and some of its applications (in Polish), *Mat. Stos.* **1** (1973), 22–41.

[81] Iterative refinement for linear systems in variable-precision arithmetic, *BIT* **21** (1981), 97–103.

KIM, M. H.

[85] Computational complexity of the Euler type algorithms for the roots of complex polynomials, Ph.D. thesis, CUNY Grad. School, New York, 1985.

KIMELDORF, G. S. AND WAHBA, G.

[70a] A correspondence between Bayesian estimation on stochastic processes and smoothing by splines, *Ann. Math. Stat.* **41** (1970), 495–502.

[70b] Spline functions and stochastic processes, *Sankhya Ser. A* **32** (1970), 173–180.

KNUTH, D. E.

[76] Big omicron and big omega and big theta, *SIGACT News*, Association for Computing Machinery, April, 1976.

[81] "The Art of Computer Science, Vol. 2: Seminumerical Algorithms," 2nd ed. Addison-Wesley, Reading, MA., 1981.

KO, KER-I.

[86] Applying techniques of discrete complexity theory to numerical computation, *in* "Studies in Complexity Theory" (R. V. Book, ed.), pp. 1–62. Research Notes in Theoretical Computer Science, Pitman, London, 1986.

KON, M. A. AND TEMPO, R.

[87] On linearity of spline algorithms, Report, Boston University Department of Mathematics, 1987.

KORNEJČUK, N. P.

[68]   Best cubature formulas for some classes of functions of many vari-
       ables, (in Russian), *Mat. Zametki* **3** (1968), 565–576 [*English transl.:
       Math. Notes* **3** (1968), 360–367].

KOROBOV, N. M.

[63]   "Number Theory Methods in Approximation Analysis" (in Rus-
       sian), Fizmatgiz, Moscow, 1963.

KOROTKOV, V. B.

[77]   A lower bound on cubature formulas (in Russian), *Sib. Mat. Zh.* **17**
       (1977), 1188–1191.

KOSTLAN, E.

[86]   "Statistical Complexity of Numerical Linear Algebra." Ph. D. thesis,
       Univ. Calif., Berkeley, 1986.

KOWALSKI, M. A. AND SIELSKI, W.

[87]   Approximation of smooth periodic functions in several variables, to
       appear in *J. Complexity* **3** (1987).

KOWALSKI, M. A., WERSCHULZ, A. G., AND WOŹNIAKOWSKI, H.

[85]   Is Gauss quadrature optimal for analytic functions?, *Numer. Math.*
       47 (1985), 89–98.

KUCZYŃSKI, J.

[85]   Implementation of the gmr algorithm for large symmetric eigenprob-
       lems, Report, Columbia University Computer Science Department,
       1985.

[86]   On the optimal solution of large eigenpair problems, *J. Complexity*
       2 (1986), 131–162.

KUNG, H. T.

[76]   The complexity of obtaining starting points for solving operator
       equations by Newton's method, *in* "Analytic Computational Com-
       plexity" (J. F. Traub, ed.), pp. 35–57. Academic Press, New York,
       1976.

KUNG, H. T. AND TRAUB, J. F.

[74]   Optimal order of one-point and multipoint iterations, *J. Assoc.
       Comput. Mach.* **21** (1974), 643–651.

[76]   Optimal order and efficiency for iterations with two evaluations,
       SIAM J. Numer. Anal. **13** (1976), 84–99.

KUO, H.-H.

[75]   "Gaussian Measures in Banach Spaces." Lecture Notes in Mathe-
       matics **463**, Springer-Verlag, Berlin, 1975.

KWAPIEŃ, S.

[85]   Private communication.

[87]   Private communication.

LARKIN, F. M.

[70]   Optimal approximation in Hilbert space with reproducing kernel
       functions, *Math. Comput.* **24** (1970), 911–921.

[72]   Gaussian measure in Hilbert space and application in numerical
       analysis, *Rocky Mount. J. Math.* **2** (1972), 372–421.

LATTES, R. AND LIONS, J. L.

[69]   "The Method of Quasi-Reversibility, Applications to Partial Differ-
       ential Equations." American Elsevier, New York, 1969.

LEE, D.

[86]   Approximation of linear operators on a Wiener space, *Rocky Mount.
       J. Math* **16** (1986), 641–659.

LEE, D., PAVLIDIS, T., AND WASILKOWSKI, G. W.

[87]   A note on the trade-off between sampling and quantization in signal
       processing, to appear in *J. Complexity* **3** (1987).

LEE, D. AND WASILKOWSKI, G. W.

[86]   Approximation of linear functionals on a Banach space with a Gaus-
       sian measure, *J. Complexity* **2** (1986), 12–43.

LEVIN, L. A.

[73]   Universal sorting problems (in Russian), *Problemy Peredachi Infor-
       matsiya* **9** (1973), 115–116.

LI, KER-CHAO

[82]   Minimaxity of the method of regularization on stochastic processes,
       Ann. Stat. **10** (1982), 937–942.

LIGUN, A. A.

[76]   Exact inequalities for splines and best quadrature formulas for cer-
       tain classes of functions (in Russian), *Mat. Zametki* **19** (1976), 913–
       926 [*English transl.: Math. Notes* **19** (1976), 533–544].

[78]   On best quadrature formulas for some classes of periodic functions,
       (in Russian), *Mat. Zametki* **24** (1978), 661–669.

LOEB, H. L.

[74]   A note on optimal integration in H_∞, *C. R. Acad. Bulg. Sci.* **27**
       (1974), 615–619.

LOEB, H. L. AND WERNER, M.

[74]   Optimal numerical quadrature in H_p spaces, *Math. Z.* **139** (1974),
       111–117.

LUŠPAJ, N. E.

[66]   Best quadrature formulas for some classes of functions (in Russian),
       Proc. Intern. Conf. Young Res. Math., Charkov (1966), 58–62.

LYNCH, N. A. AND LUNDELIUS, J.

[85]   An upper and lower bound for clock synchronization, Information
       and Control 62 (1985), 190–204.

MAJSTROVSKIJ, G. D.

[72]   On the optimality of Newton's method (in Russian), Dokl. Akad.
       Nauk SSSR 204 (1972), 1313–1315 [English transl.: Soviet Math.
       Dokl. 13 (1972), 838–840].

MARCHUK, A. G. AND OSIPENKO, K. YU.

[75]   Best approximation of functions specified with an error at a finite
       number of points, Math. Notes 17 (1975), 207-212.

MARCUS, M. AND MINC, H.

[64]   "A Survey of Matrix Theory and Matrix Inequalities." Allyn & Ba-
       con, Boston, 1964.

MEERSMAN, R.E.

[76a] On maximal order of families of iterations for nonlinear equations,
       Ph.D. thesis, Vrije Univ., Brussels, 1976.
[76b] Optimal use of information in certain iterative processes, in "Ana-
       lytic Computational Complexity" (J. F. Traub, ed.), pp. 109–125.
       Academic Press, New York, 1976.

MEINGUET, J.

[79]   Multivariate interpolation at arbitrary points made simple, J. Appl.
       Math. Phys. (ZAMP) 30 (1979), 292–304.

MCMULLEN, C.

[85]   Families of rational maps and iterative root-finding algorithms,
       Ph.D. thesis, Harvard Univ., Cambridge., Mass., 1985.

MELKMAN, A. A.

[77] n-widths and optimal interpolation of time- and band-limited func-
       tions, in "Optimal Estimation in Approximation Theory" (C. A.
       Micchelli and T. J. Rivlin, eds.), pp. 55–68. Plenum, New York,
       1977.

MELKMAN, A. A. AND MICCHELLI, C. A.

[79]   Optimal estimation of linear operators in Hilbert spaces from inac-
       curate data, SIAM J. Numer. Anal. 16 (1979), 87–105.

MICCHELLI, C. A.

[84] Orthogonal projections are optimal algorithms, *J. Approx. Theory* **40** (1984), 101–110.

MICCHELLI, C. A. AND MIRANKER, W. L.

[75] High order search methods for finding roots, *J. Assoc. Comput. Mach.* **22** (1975), 52–60.

MICCHELLI, C. A. AND PINKUS, A.

[77] On a best estimator for the class M^r using only function values, *Indiana Univ. Math. J.* **26** (1977), 751–759.

MICCHELLI, C. A. AND RIVLIN, T. J.

[77] A survey of optimal recovery, *in* "Optimal Estimation in Approximation Theory" (C. A. Micchelli and T. J. Rivlin, eds.), pp. 1–54, Plenum, New York, 1977.

[85] Lectures on optimal recovery, *in* "Numerical Analysis Lancaster 1984" (P. R. Turner, ed.), pp. 21–93, Lectures Notes in Math., Springer-Verlag, Berlin, 1985.

MICCHELLI, C. A. AND WAHBA, G.

[81] Design problems for optimal surface interpolation, *in* "Approximation Theory and Applications." (Z. Ziegler, ed.), pp. 329–347. Academic Press, New York, 1981.

MILANESE, M. AND BELFORTE, G.

[82] Estimation theory and uncertainty interval evaluation in presence of unknown but bounded errors: Linear families of models and estimators, *IEEE Trans. Automat. Contr.* **AC-27** (1982), 408-414.

MILANESE, M. AND TEMPO, R.

[85] Optimal algorithms theory for robust estimation and prediction, *IEEE Trans. Automat. Contr.* **AC-30** (1984), 730–738.

MILANESE, M., TEMPO, R., AND VICINO, A.

[84] Robust time series prediction by optimal algorithms theory, *Proc. 23rd IEEE Conf. Decision Control*, Las Vegas, NV, 1984.

[86] Strongly optimal algorithms and optimal information in estimation problems, *J. Complexity* **2** (1986), 78–94.

MILLER, W.

[75] Computational complexity and numerical stability, *SIAM J. Comput.* **4** (1975), 97–107.

MØLLER, O.

[65] Quasi-double precision in floating-point addition, *BIT* **5** (1965), 37–50, 251–255.

MOROZOV, V. A.

[85]   "Methods for Solving Incorrectly Posed Problems." Springer-Verlag,
       New York, 1985.

MOTORNYJ, V. P.

[73]   On the best quadrature formula of the form $\sum_{k=1}^{n} p_k f(x_k)$ for the
       classes of periodic differentiable functions (in Russian), *Dokl. Akad.
       Nauk SSSR* **211** (1973), 1060–1062 [*English transl.: Soviet Math.
       Dokl.* **14** (1973), 1180–1183].
[74]   On the best quadrature formula of the form $\sum_{k=1}^{n} p_k f(x_k)$ for the
       classes of periodic differentiable functions (in Russian), *Dokl. Akad.
       Nauk SSSR Ser. Math.* **38** (1974), 583–614.

MUROTA, K.

[82]   Global convergence of a modified Newton iteration for algebraic
       equations, *SIAM J. Numer. Anal.* **19** (1982), 793–799.

NEMIROVSKY, A. S. AND YUDIN, D. B.

[78]   Efficiency of randomization of control (in Russian), in the miscel-
       lany: *Problems of Random Search*, Zinate, No. 7, Riga.
[83]   "Problem Complexity and Method Efficiency in Optimization,"
       Wiley-Interscience, New York, 1983.

NEWMAN, D. J.

[79]   Quadrature formulas for H^p functions, *Math. Z.* **166** (1979), 111–
       115.

NIEDERREITER, H.

[78]   Quasi-Monte Carlo methods and pseudo-random numbers, *Bull.
       Amer. Math. Soc.* **84** (1978), 957–1041.
[85]   Quasi-Monte Carlo methods for global optimization, *in* Math. Stat.
       and Appl., 4th Pannonian Symp. on Math. Stat., pp. 251–267. (W.
       Grossmann et al., eds.), Reidel, 1985.

NIKOLSKIJ, S. M.

[50]   On the problem of approximation estimate by quadrature formulas
       (in Russian), *Usp. Mat. Nauk* **5** (1950), 165–177.
[79]   "Integration Formulas" (in Russian). Nauka, Moscow, 1979.

NOVAK, E.

[83]   Zur unteren Fehlergrenze von Quadraturverfahren, Ph.D. thesis,
       Universität Erlangen-Nürnberg, Erlangen, 1983.
[85]   Eingeschränkte Monte Carlo-Verfahren zur numerischen Integra-
       tion, *in* "Math. Stat. and Appl., 4th Pannonian Symp. on Math.
       Stat.," (W Grossmann et al., eds.), pp. 269–282, Reidel, 1985.

[86a] Quadrature and widths, *J. Approx. Theory* **47** (1986), 195–202.

[86b] On average case errors in numerical analysis, *J. Complexity* **2** (1986), 229–238.

[86c] The average a posteriori error of numerical methods, *Numer. Math* **50** (1986), 245–252.

[87a] Deterministic, stochastic, and average error bounds in optimal recovery, submitted for publication, 1987.

[87b] Adaption may help for linear problems in the worst case, submitted for publication, 1987.

[87c] Stochastic properties of quadrature formulas, submitted for publication, 1987.

ODEN, J. T. AND REDDY, J. N.

[76] "An Introduction to the Mathematical Theory of Finite Elements." Wiley-Interscience, New York, 1976.

ORTEGA, J. M. AND RHEINBOLDT, W. C.

[70] "Iterative Solution of Nonlinear Equations in Several Variables." Academic Press, New York, 1970.

OSIPENKO, K. YU.

[72] Optimal interpolation of analytic functions (in Russian), *Mat. Zametki* **12** (1972), 465–476 [*English transl.: Math. Notes* **12** (1972), 712–719].

[76] Best approximation of analytic functions from information about their values at a finite number of points (in Russian), *Mat. Zametki* **19** (1976), 29–40 [*English transl.: Math. Notes* **19** (1976), 17–23].

PACKEL, E. W.

[86] Linear problems (with extended range) have linear optimal algorithms, *Aequationes Math.* **30** (1986), 18–25.

[87a] Do linear problems have linear optimal algorithms?, to appear in *SIAM Rev.* (1987).

[87b] The algorithm designer versus nature: A game-theoretic approach to information-based complexity, to appear in *J. Complexity* **3** (1987).

PACKEL, E. W. AND TRAUB, J. F.

[87] Information-based complexity, *Nature* **328** (1987), 29–33.

PACKEL, E. W., TRAUB, J. F., AND WOŹNIAKOWSKI, H.

[87] Measures of uncertainty and information in computation, Report, Columbia University Computer Science Department, 1987.

PACKEL, E. W. AND WOŹNIAKOWSKI, H.

[87] Recent developments in information-based complexity, *Bull. Amer. Math. Soc.* **17** (1987), 9–36.

PAN, V. YA.

[84] "How to Multiply Matrices Faster." Lectures Notes in Computer Science, **179**, Springer-Verlag, Berlin, 1984.

PAPADIMITRIOU, C. H. AND TSITSIKLIS, J.

[86] Intractable problems in control theory, *SIAM J. Control Optim.* **24** (1986), 639–654.

PAPAGEORGIOU, A. AND WASILKOWSKI, G. W.

[86] Average complexity of multivariate problems, Report, Columbia University Computer Science Department, 1986.

PARLETT, B. N.

[80] "The Symmetric Eigenvalue Problem," Prentice-Hall, Inc., Englewood Cliffs, N.J., 1980.

PARTHASARATHY, K. R.

[67] "Probability Measures on Metric Spaces." Academic Press, New York, 1967.

PAULIK, A.

[77] Zur existenz optimaler quadraturformeln mit freien knoten bei integration analytischer funktionen, *Numer. Math.* **27** (1977), 395–405.

PENTLAND, A.

[84] Shading into texture, *in* "Proc. of the Nat. Conf. on Artificial Intelligence," pp. 269–273, Austin, TX, 1984.

PETROV, V. V.

[75] "Sums of Independent Random Variables." Springer-Verlag, Berlin, 1975.

PEVNYJ, A. B.

[82] On optimal search strategies for the maximum of a function with bounded highest derivative (in Russian), *Zh. Vychisl. Mat. Mat. Fiz.* **22** (1982), 1061–1066 [*English transl.: U.S.S.R. Comput. Math. and Math. Phys.* **22** (1982), 38–44].

PINKUS, A.

[75] Asymptotic minimum norm quadrature formulas, *Numer. Math.* **24** (1975), 163–175.

[85] "*n*-Widths in Approximation Theory." Springer-Verlag, Berlin, 1985.

PLASKOTA, L.

[86] Optimal linear information for the search for the maximum of real functions (in Russian), *Zh. Vychisl. Mat. Mat. Fiz.* **26** (1986), 934–938.

POGGIO, T., TORRE, V., AND KOCH, C.

[85] Computational vision and regularization theory, *Nature* **317** (1985), 314–319.

POLOVINKIN, V. I.

[74] Sequences of functionals with boundary layer (in Russian), *Siberian Math. J.* **15** (1974), 296–308.

POUR-EL, M. B. AND RICHARDS, I.

[83] Noncomputability in analysis and physics: a complete determination of the class of noncomputable linear operators, *Adv. in Math.* **48** (1983), 44–74.

POWELL, M. J. D.

[68] On the best L_2 spline approximations, *in* "Numerische Mathematik, Differentialeichungen, Approximationstheorie", ISNM **9**, pp. 317–339. Birkhäuser Verlag, Basel, 1968.

PRÜFER, M. AND SIEGBERG, H.

[80] On Computational Aspects of Topologigal Degree in $\mathbb{R}^n$, Sonderforschungsbereich 72, Approximation und Optimierung, Univ. Bonn, Preprint No. 252, 1980.

RABIN, M. O.

[72] Solving linear equations by means of scalar products, *in* "Complexity of Computer Computations" (R. E. Miller and J. W. Thatcher), pp. 11–20. Plenum, New York, 1972.

[76] Probabilistic algorithms, *in* "Algorithms and Complexity: New Directions and Recent Results" (J. F. Traub, ed.), pp. 21–39. Academic Press, New York, 1976.

[83] Randomized Byzantine generals, *Proc. 24th Ann. Symp. Found. Comp. Sci.* (1983).

RENEGAR, J.

[85a] On the complexity of a piecewise linear algorithm for approximating roots of complex polynomials, *Math. Programming* **32** (1985), 301 318.

[85b] On the cost of approximating all roots of a complex polynomial, *Math. Programming* **32** (1985), 319–336.

[85c] On the efficiency of a piecewise linear homotopy algorithm in approximating all zeros of a system of complex polynomials, Report, Colorado State University, Fort Collins, 1985.

[87a] On the efficiency of Newton's method in approximating all zeros of a system of complex polynomials, *Math. Op. Res.* **12** (1987), 121–148.

[87b]   On the worst-case arithmetic complexity of approximating zeros of
        polynomials, to appear in *J. Complexity* **3** (1987).

[87c]   On the worst case arithmetic complexity of approximating zeros of
        systems of polynomials, Report, Cornell University, Ithaca, 1987.

RIVEST, R. L., MEYER, A. R., KLEITMAN, D. J., WINKLMANN, K., AND
SPENCER, J.

[80]   Coping with errors in binary search procedures, *J. Comput. System
        Sci.* **20** (1980), 396–404.

ROKHLIN, V.

[86]   Private communication.

RUBINSTEIN, R. Y.

[81]   "Simulation and the Monte Carlo Method." Wiley and Sons, New
        York, 1981.

RUDIN, W.

[74]   "Real and complex analysis." 2d ed., McGraw-Hill, New York, 1974.

RUDIN, W. AND SMITH, K. T.

[61]   Linearity of best approximation: A characterization of ellipsoids,
        Proc. Nederl. Akad. Wet. Ser. A. **64** (1961), 97–103.

SAARI, D. G.

[87]   Some informational requirements for convergence, to appear in *J.
        Complexity* **3** (1987).

SAARI, D. G. AND SIMON, C. P.

[78]   Effective price mechanisms, *Econometrica* **46** (1978), 1097–1125.

SAARI, D. G. AND URENKO, J.

[84]   Newton's method, circle maps, and chaotic motion, *Amer. Math.
        Monthly* **91** (1984), 3-17.

SACKS, J. AND YLVISAKER, D.

[66]   Designs for regression with correlated errors, *Ann. Math. Stat.* **37**
        (1966), 68–89.

[68]   Designs for regression problems with correlated errors; many param-
        eters, *Ann. Math. Stat.* **39** (1968), 49–69.

[70a]   Designs for regression problems with correlated errors III, *Ann.
        Math. Stat.* **41** (1970), 2057–2074.

[70b]   Statistical design and integral approximation, *Proc. 12th Bienn.
        Semin. Can. Math. Congr.* (1970), 115–136.

SARD, A.

[49]   Best approximate integration formulas; best approximation formu-
        las, *Amer. J. Math.* **71** (1949), 80–91.

[63] "Linear Approximation," Amer. Math. Soc., Providence, Rhode Island, 1963.

SCHNORR, C. P.

[71] "Zufälligkeit und Wahrscheinlichkeit. Eine Algorithmische Begründung der Wahrscheinlichkeitstheorie." Lecture Notes in Math. **218**, Springer-Verlag, Berlin, 1971.

[77] A survey of the theory of random sequences, in "Basic Problems in methodology and Linguistics," (R. Butts and J. Hintikka, eds.), pp. 193–211. Reidel, Dordrecht, 1977.

SCHOENBERG, I. J.

[64a] On best approximations of linear operators, *Nederl. Akad. Wetensch. Indag. Math.* **67** (1964), 155–163.

[64b] Spline interpolation and best quadrature formulas, *Bull. Amer. Math. Soc.* **70** (1964), 143–148.

SCHÖNHAGE, A.

[86] Equation solving in terms of computational complexity, in *Proc. Intern. Congress Math.*, Berkeley, 1986.

SCHÖNHAGE, A. AND STRASSEN, V.

[71] Schnelle multiplikation grosser zahlen, *Computing* **7** (1971), 281–292.

SCHULZ, M. H.

[74] The complexity of linear approximation algorithms, in "Complexity of Computation," (R. M. Karp, ed.), pp. 135–148. Amer. Math. Soc., Providence, Rhode Island, 1974.

SCHWEFEL, H. P.

[77] "Numerische Optimierung von Computer Modellen Mittels der Evolutionsstrategie." Birkhäuser Verlag, Stuttgart, 1977.

SCHWING, J., SIKORSKI, K., AND STENGER, F.

[84] A Fortran subroutine for numerical integration in H_p, *ACM TOMS* **10** (1984), 152–160.

SHARYGIN, I. F.

[63] A lower estimate for the error of quadrature formulas for certain classes of functions (in Russian), *Zh. Vychisl. Mat. Mat. Fiz.* **3** (1963), 370–376 [*English transl.: U.S.S.R. Comput. Math. and Math. Phys.* **3** (1963), 489–497].

[77] A lower bound for the error of a formula for approximation summation in the class $E_{s,p}(C)$ (in Russian), *Mat. Zametki* **21** (1977), 371–375 [*English transl.: Math. Notes* **21** (1977), 207–210].

SHILOV, G. E. AND FAN DYK TIN

[67]   "Integral measure and derivative on linear spaces" (in Russian).
        Nauka, Moscow, 1967.

SHUB, M. AND SMALE, S.

[85]   Computational complexity: On the geometry of of polynomials and
        a theory of cost, Part I, *Ann. Scient. Ec. Norm. Sup.*, **18** (1985).
[86]   Computational complexity: On the geometry of of polynomials and
        a theory of cost, Part II, *SIAM J. Comput.* **15** (1986), 145–161.

SIERPIŃSKI, W.

[68]   "Elementary Theory of Numbers." PWN, Warszawa, 1968.

SIKORSKI, K.

[79]   A three dimensional analogue to the method of bisection for solving
        nonlinear equations, *Math. Comput.* **33** (1979), 722–738.
[82a]   Bisection is optimal, *Numer. Math.* **40** (1982), 111–117.
[82b]   Optimal quadrature algorithms in H_p spaces, *Numer. Math.* **39**
        (1982), 405–410.
[84a]   Optimal solution of nonlinear equations satisfying a Lipschitz con-
        dition, *Numer. Math.* **43** (1984), 225–240.
[84b]   Study of linear information for classes of polynomial equations, Re-
        port, Columbia University Computer Science Department, 1984.
[84c]   Minimal number of function evaluations for computing topological
        degree in two dimensions, Report, Columbia University Computer
        Science Department, 1984.
[85]   Optimal solution of nonlinear equations, *J. Complexity* **1** (1985),
        197–209.

SIKORSKI, K. AND STENGER, F.

[84]   Optimal quadratures in H_p spaces, *ACM TOMS* **10** (1984), 140–
        151.

SIKORSKI, K. AND TROJAN, G. M.

[87]   Asymptotic optimality of the bisection method, to appear in *Numer.
        Math.*.

SIKORSKI, K. AND WOŹNIAKOWSKI, H.

[86]   For which error criteria can we solve nonlinear equations?, *J. Com-
        plexity* **2** (1986), 163–178.
[87]   Complexity of fixed points: I, to appear in *J. Complexity* **3** (1987).

SKEEL, R. D.

[80]   Iterative refinement implies numerical stability for Gaussian elimi-
        nation, *Math. Comput.* **35** (1980), 817–832.

SKOROHOD, A. V.

[74]   "Integration in Hilbert Space." Springer-Verlag, New York, 1974.

SMALE, S.

[81]   The fundamental theorem of algebra and complexity theory, *Bull. Amer. Math. Soc.* **4** (1981), 1–36.

[82]   The problem of the average speed of the simplex method, *in* "Mathematical Programming, the State of the Art" (Bachem et al., eds.). Bonn, 1982.

[83]   On the average number of steps in the simplex method of linear programming, *Math. Program.* **27** (1983), 241–262.

[85]   On the efficiency of algorithms of analysis, *Bull. Amer. Math. Soc.* **13** (1985), 87–121.

[86]   Algorithms for solving equations, to appear in *Proc. Intern. Congress Math.*, Berkeley, 1986.

[87]   On the topology of algorithms, to appear in *J. Complexity* **3** (1987).

SMOLYAK, S. A.

[60]   Interpolation and quadrature formulas for the class W_s^α and $E_{s,p}(C)$ (in Russian), *Dokl. Akad. Nauk SSSR* **131** (1960), 1028–1031 [*English transl.: Soviet Math. Dokl.* **1** (1960), 384–387].

[65]   On optimal restoration of functions and functionals of them (in Russian), Candidate Dissertation, Moscow State University, 1965.

SOBOL, I. M.

[69]   "Multivariate Quadrature Formulas and Haar Functions" (in Russian). Nauka, Moscow, 1969.

[85]   "Die Monte-Carlo Methode." Deutsch Verlag, Frankfurt, 1985.

SOBOLEV, S. L.

[65]   On the order of convergence of cubature formulas (in Russian), *Dokl. Akad. Nauk SSSR* **162** (1965), 1005–1008 [*English transl.: Soviet Math. Dokl.* (1965), 808–812].

SOLOVAY, R. AND STRASSEN, V.

[77]   A fast Monte-Carlo test for primality, *SIAM J. Comput.* **6** (1977), 84–85; erratum **7** (1978), 118.

SPECKMAN, P.

[79a] $\mathcal{L}_p$ approximation of autoregressive Gaussian processes, Report, University of Oregon Department of Statistics, Eugene, Oregon, 1979.

[79b]   Minimax estimates of linear functionals in a Hilbert space, Report, University of Oregon Department of Statistics, Eugene, Oregon, 1979.

[80]   On minimax estimation of linear operators in Hilbert spaces from noisy data, Report, University of Oregon Department of Statistics, Eugene, Oregon, 1980.

STENGER, F.

[66]   Bounds on the error of Gauss-type quadratures, *Numer. Math.* **8** (1966), 150–160.

[75]   Computing the topological degree of a mapping in $\mathbb{R}^n$, *Numer. Math.* **25** (1975), 23–38.

[78]   Convergence of minimum norm approximations in H_p, *Numer. Math.* **29** (1978), 345–362.

STETTER, F.

[69]   On best quadrature of analytic functions, *Q. Appl. Math.* **27** (1969), 270–272.

STEVENS, K. A.

[79]   Surface perception from local analysis of texture and contour, Ph.D. thesis, MIT, 1979.

STRASSEN, V.

[69]   Gaussian elimination is not optimal, *Numer. Math.* **13** (1969), 354–356.

STYNES, M.

[79a]   An algorithm for numerical calculation of topological degree, *Appl. Anal.* **9** (1979), 63–77.

[79b]   A simplification of Stenger's topological degree formula, *Numer. Math.* **33** (1979), 147–156.

[81]   On the construction of sufficient refinements for computation of topological degree, *Numer. Math.* **37** (1981), 453–462.

SUKHAREV, A. G.

[71]   Optimal strategies of the search for an extremum (in Russian), *Zh. Vychisl. Mat. Mat. Fiz.* **11** (1971), 910–924 [*English transl.: U.S.S.R. Comput. Math. and Math. Phys.* **11** (1971), 119–137].

[72]   Best sequential search strategies for finding an extremum (in Russian), *Zh. Vychisl. Mat. Mat. Fiz.* **12** (1972), 35–50 [*English transl.: U.S.S.R. Comput. Math. and Math. Phys.* **12** (1972), 39–59].

[76]   Optimal search for a zero of function satisfying Lipschitz's condition (in Russian), *Zh. Vychisl. Mat. Mat. Fiz.* **16** (1976), 20–30 [*English transl.: U.S.S.R. Comput. Math. and Math. Phys.* **16** (1976), 17–26].

[79a]   Optimal numerical integration formulas for some classes of functions of several variables (in Russian), *Dokl. Akad. Nauk SSSR* **246** (1979), 282–285 [*English transl.: Sov. Math. Dokl.* **20** (1979), 472–475].

[79b] A sequentially optimal algorithm for numerical integration, *J. Optim. Theor. Appl.* **28** (1979), 363–373.

[86] On the concept of optimal error algorithm, *J. Complexity* **2** (1986), 317–322.

[87] Sequentially-optimal algorithms for problems in numerical analysis, to appear in *J. Complexity* **3** (1987).

[88] "Min-Max Algorithms in Problems of Numerical Analysis" (in Russian), Nauka, Moscow, to appear, 1988.

SULDIN, A. V.

[59] Wiener measure and its applications to approximation methods, I (in Russian), *Izv. Vyssh. Ucheb. Zaved. Mat.* **13** (1959) 145–158.

[60] Wiener measure and its applications to approximation methods, II (in Russian), *Izv. Vyssh. Ucheb. Zaved. Mat.* **18** (1960) 165–179.

SWARZTRAUBER, P. N.

[77] The methods of cyclic reduction, Fourier analysis and the FACR algorithm for discrete solution of Poisson's equation on a rectangle, *SIAM Review* **199** (1977), 490–501.

TERZOPOULOS, D.

[83] Multi-level reconstruction of visual surfaces: Variational principles and finite element representation, *in* "Multiresolution Image Processing and Analysis," (A. Rosenfeld, ed.), Springer-Verlag, New York, 1983.

[84] Multiresolution computation of visible-surface representations, Ph. D. thesis, MIT, 1984.

THUE, A.

[18] Berechnung aller Losungen gewisser Gleichungen von der Form $ax^r - by^r = f$, *Vid.-Selsk. Skrifter, I. Math.-naturv. KL.*, Christiania, **4** (1918).

TIKHOMIROV, V. M.

[60] Diameters of sets in function spaces and the theory of best approximation (in Russian), *Usp. Mat. Nauk* **15** (3) (1960), 81–112 [*English transl.: Russ. Math. Surveys* **15** (3) (1960), 75–111].

[69] Best methods of approximating and interpolating differentiable functions in the space $C[0, 1]$ (in Russian), *Mat. Sb.* **80** (1969), 290–304 [*English transl.: Math. U.S.S.R. Sb.* **9** (1969), 275–289.

[76] "Some Problems in Approximation Theory" (in Russian). Moscow State University, Moscow, 1976.

TIKHONOV, A. N.

[63] Solution of incorrectly formulated problems and the regularization method, *Sov. Math. Dokl.* **4** (1963), 1036–1038.

TIKHONOV, A. N. AND ARSENIN, V. Y.

[77] "Solutions of Ill-Posed Problems." V. H. Winston and Sons, Washington, D. C., 1977.

TODD, M. J.

[78] Optimal dissection of simplices, *SIAM J. Appl. Math.* **34** (1978), 792–803.

TRAUB, J. F.

[61] On functional iteration and the calculation of roots, *Preprints of papers, 16th Natl. ACM Conf. Session 5A-1* (1961), 1-4, Los Angeles, Ca.

[64] "Iterative Methods for the Solution of Equations." Englewood Cliffs, N.J., 1964. Reissued: Chelsea Press, New York, 1982.

[72] Computational complexity of iterative processes, *SIAM J. Comput.* **1** (1972), 167–179.

TRAUB, J. F., WASILKOWSKI, G. W., AND WOŹNIAKOWSKI, H.

[83] "Information, Uncertainty, Complexity." Addison-Wesley, Reading, Mass., 1983.

[84a] Average case optimality for linear problems, *J. Theor. Comput. Sci.* **29** (1984), 1–25.

[84b] When is nonadaptive information as powerful as adaptive information?, *Proc. 23rd IEEE Conf. Decis. Control, Las Vegas*, (1984), 1536–1540.

TRAUB, J. F. AND WOŹNIAKOWSKI, H.

[76a] Strict lower and upper bounds on iterative computational complexity, *in* "Analytic Computational Complexity," (J. F. Traub, ed.), pp. 15–34. Academic Press, New York, 1976.

[76b] Optimal linear information for the solution of nonlinear operator equations, *in* "Algorithms and Complexity: New Directions and Recent Results," (J. F. Traub, ed.), pp. 103–109. Academic Press, New York, 1976.

[79] Convergence and complexity of Newton's iteration for operator equations, *J. Assoc. Comput. Mach.* **26** (1979), 250–258.

[80a] "A General Theory of Optimal Algorithms." Academic Press, New York, 1980.

[80b] Convergence and complexity of interpolatory Newton iteration in a Banach space, *Comput. Math. Appl.* **6** (1980), 385–400.

[80c] Optimal radius of convergence of interpolatory iterations for operator equations, *Aequationes Math.* **21** (1980), 159–172.

[82] Complexity of linear programming, *Oper. Res. Lett.* **1** (1982), 59–62.

[84a] Information and computation, *in* "Advances in Computers **23**," (M. C. Yovits, ed.), pp. 35–92. Academic Press, New York, 1984.

[84b] On the optimal solution of large linear systems, *J. Assoc. Comput. Mach.* **31** (1984), 545–559.

TROJAN, G. M.

[80a] Optimal iterative methods for the solution of nonlinear equations, (in Polish), Ph.D. thesis, Univ. Warsaw, 1980.

[80b] Tight bounds on the complexity index of one point iteration, *Comput. Math. Appl.* **6** (1980), 431–433.

[83] Asymptotic setting for linear problems, unpublished manuscript.

TWOMEY, S.

[77] "Introduction to the Mathematics of Inversion in Remote Sensing and Indirect Measurement." Developments in Geomathematics **3**, Elsevier Scientific Publ., Amsterdam, 1977.

VAKHANIA, N. N.

[81] "Probability Distributions on Linear Spaces." North-Holland, New York, 1981.

VICINO, A., TEMPO, R., GENESIO R., AND MILANESE, M.

[87] Optimal error and GMDH predictors: A comparison with some statistical techniques, to appear in *Intern. J. Forecasting* (1987).

VEROY, B. S.

[86] An optimal algorithm for search of extrema of a bimodal function, *J. Complexity* **2** (1986), 323–332.

WAHBA, G.

[71] On the regression design problem of Sacks and Ylvisaker, *Ann. Math. Stat.* **42** (1971), 1035–1043.

[78] Improper priors, spline smoothing and the problem of guarding against model errors in regression, *J. R. Stat. Soc. Ser. B* **40** (1978), 364–372.

[84] Cross-validated spline methods for the estimation of multivariate functions from data on functionals, *in* "Statistics: An appraisal, Proc. 50th Anniversary Confer., Iowa State Stat. Lab." (H. A. David and H. T. David, eds.), pp. 205–235. The Iowa State Univ. Press, 1984.

WASILKOWSKI, G. W.

[80] Can any stationary iteration using linear information be globally convergent?, *J. Assoc. Comput. Mach.* **27** (1980), 263–269.

[81a] *n*-evaluations conjecture for multipoint iterations for the solution of scalar nonlinear equations, *J. Assoc. Comput. Mach.* **28** (1981),

71–80.

[81b]   The strength of nonstationary iteration, *Aequationes Math.* **24** (1981), 243–260.

[83a]   Any iteration for polynomial equations using linear information has infinite complexity, *J. Theor. Comput. Sci.* **22** (1983), 195–208.

[83b]   Inverse function problem, *J. Inf. Process. Cybern.* **19** (1983), 491–496.

[83c]   Local average error, Report, Columbia University Computer Science Department, 1983.

[84]   Some nonlinear problems are as easy as the approximation problem, *Comput. Math. Appl.* **10** (1984), 351–363.

[85]   Average case optimality, *J. Complexity* **1** (1985), 107–117.

[86a]   Information of varying cardinality, *J. Complexity* **2** (1986), 204–228.

[86b]   Optimal algorithms for linear problems with Gaussian measures, *Rocky Mount. J. Math.* **16** (1986), 727–749.

[87a]   Randomization for continuous problems, to appear in *J. Complexity* **3** (1987).

[87b]   Clock synchronization problem with random delays, Report, Columbia University Computer Science Department, 1987.

WASILKOWSKI, G. W. AND WOŹNIAKOWSKI, H.

[78]   Optimality of spline algorithms, Report, Carnegie-Mellon University Computer Science Department, 1987. Also Chapter 4 in GTOA.

[84]   Can adaption help on the average?, *Numer. Math.* **44** (1984), 169–190.

[86]   Average case optimal algorithms in Hilbert spaces, *J. Approx. Theory* **47** (1986), 17–25.

[87]   On optimal algorithms in an asymptotic model with Gaussian measure, to appear in *SIAM J. Math. Anal.* (1987).

WERSCHULZ, A. G.

[79a]   Maximal order and order of information for numerical quadratures, *J. Assoc. Comput. Mach.* **26** (1979), 527–537.

[79b]   Maximal order for approximation of derivatives, *J. of Comput. and Syst. Sci.* **18** (1979), 213–217.

[80]   Maximal order for quadratures using n evaluations, *Aequationes Math.* **21** (1980), 68–97.

[81a]   On maximal order for local and global numerical problems, *J. Comput. Syst. Sci.* **23** (1981), 38–48.

[81b]   Maximal order for multipoint methods with memory using Hermitian information, *Intern. Journal of Computer Mathematics, Section B* **9** (1981), 223–241.

[82]   Optimal error properties of finite element methods for second order

elliptic Dirichlet problems, *Math. Comput.* **38** (1982), 401–413.

[83]   Measuring uncertainty without a norm, *Aequationes Math.* **26** (1983), 74–82.

[85]   What is the complexity of the Fredholm problem of the second kind?, *J. Integral Equations* **9** (1985), 213–241.

[86a] Complexity of indefinite elliptic problems, *Math. Comput.* **46** (1986), 457–477.

[86b] What is the complexity of ill-posed problems?, Report, Columbia University Computer Science Department, 1986, to appear in *Numer. Funct. Analy. Opt.*

[87a] An information-based approach to ill-posed problems, to appear in *J. Complexity* **3** (1987).

[87b] Finite elements are not always optimal, *Advances in Applied Mathematics* **8** (1987), 354–375.

[87c] Optimal residual algorithms for linear operator equations, in progress.

[87d] Optimal algorithms for a problem of optimal control, Report, Columbia University Computer Science Department, 1987.

WERSCHULZ, A. G. AND WOŹNIAKOWSKI, H.

[86]   Are linear algorithms always good for linear problems?, *Aequationes Math.* **31** (1986), 202–212.

WILANSKY, A.

[78]   "Modern Methods in Topological Vector Spaces." McGraw-Hill, New York, 1978.

WILF, H. S.

[64]   Exactness conditions in numerical quadrature, *Numer. Math.* **6** (1964), 315–319.

WILKINSON, J. H.

[63]   "Rounding Errors in Algebraic Processes." Prentice-Hall, Engelwood Cliffs, N.J., 1963.

[65]   "The Algebraic Eigenvalue Problem." Oxford Univ. Press, London and New York, 1965.

WINOGRAD, S.

[76]   Some remarks on proof techniques in analytic complexity, *in* "Analytic Computational Complexity" (J. F. Traub, ed.), pp. 5–15. Academic Press, New York, 1976.

WOLFF, L.

[87a] Spectral and polarization stereo methods using a single light source, *in* "Proc. of the first IEEE Intern. Conf. on Computer Vision," 1987.

[87b]   Surface curvature and contour from photometric stereo, *in* "Proc. of the SPIE Symp. on Advances in Intelligent Robotics Systems, 1987.

WONGKEW, R.

[85]   The complexity of finding zeros, Ph.D. thesis, Univ. Calif., Berkeley, CA., 1985.

WOŹNIAKOWSKI, H.

[72]   On nonlinear iterative processes in numerical methods (in Polish), Ph.D. thesis, University of Warsaw, Poland.

[74]   Maximal stationary iterative methods for the solution of operator equations, *SIAM J. Numer. Anal.* **11** (1974), 934–949.

[75a]   Generalized information and maximal order of iteration for operator equations, *SIAM J. Numer. Anal.* **12** (1975), 121–135.

[75b]   Properties of maximal order methods for the solution of nonlinear equations, *Z. Angew. Math. Mech.* **55** (1975), 268–271.

[76]   Maximal order of multipoint iterations using n evaluations, *in* "Analytic Computational Complexity," (J. F. Traub, ed.), pp. 75–107. Academic Press, New York, 1976.

[77]   Numerical stability of the Chebyshev method for the solution of large linear systems, *Numer. Math.* **28** (1977), 191–209.

[78]   Round-off error analysis of iterations for large linear systems, *Numer. Math.* **30** (1978), 301–314.

[80]   Roundoff-error analysis of a new class of conjugate-gradient algorithms, *Linear Algebra and Appl.* **29** (1980), 507–529.

[85]   A survey of information based-complexity, *J. Complexity* **1** (1985), 11–44.

[86a]   Information-based complexity, *in* "Annual Review of Computer Science," pp. 319–380. Annual Reviews Inc., William Kaufman, Inc., Palo Alto, Ca., 1986.

[86b]   Probabilistic setting of information-based complexity, *J. Complexity* **2** (1986), 255– 269.

[87]   Average complexity for linear operators over bounded domains, *J. Complexity* **3** (1987), 57–80.

ZALIZNYAK, N. F. AND LIGUN, A. A.

[78]   On optimum strategy in search of global maximum of function (in Russian), *Zh. Vychisl. Mat. Mat. Fiz.* **18** (1978), 314–321.

ZAREMBA, S. K.

[68]   The mathematical basis of Monte Carlo and quasi Monte Carlo methods, *SIAM Rev.* **10**, 303–314.

ŽENSYKBAEV, A. A.

[76]   On the best quadrature formula on the class $W^r L_p$ (in Russian),

Dokl. Akad. Nauk SSSR **227** (1976), 277–279 [*English transl.: Soviet Math. Dokl.* **17** (1976), 377–380].

[77a] Optimal quadrature formulas for some classes of periodic differentiable functions (in Russian), *Izv. An. SSSR, ser. mat.* **41** (1977), 1110–1124.

[77b] On optimal quadrature formulas for some classes of nonperiodic functions (in Russian), *DAN SSSR* **286** (1977), 531–534.

[78] On a property of optimal quadrature formulas (in Russian), *Mat. Zametki* **23** (1978), 551–562.

[79] Characteristic properties of optimal quadrature formulas, *Sibir. Mat. Zh.* **20** (1979).

[81] Monosplines of minimal norm and the best quadrature formulas (in Russian), *Usp. Mat. Nauk* **36** (1981), 107–159 [*English transl.: Russ. Math. Surveys* **36** (1981),121– 180].

[82] Extremality of monosplines of minimal deficiency (in Russian), *Izv. Akad. Nauk SSSR Ser. Mat.* **46** (1982), 1175–1198 [*English transl.: Math. USSR Izv.* **21** (1983), 461–482].

ZIELIŃSKI, R.

[78] "Erzugung von Zufallszahlen." Deutsch Verlag, Thun, 1978.

ZIELIŃSKI, R. AND NEUMANN, P.

[83] "Stochastische Verfahren zur Suche nach dem Minimum einer Funktion." Akademie Verlag, Berlin, 1983.

ZVONKIN, A. K. AND LEVIN, L. A.

[70] The complexity of finite objects and the development of the concept of information and randomness by means of the theory of algorithms (in Russian), *Usp. Mat. Nauk* **6** (1970), 85–127 [*English transl.: Russ. Math. Surveys* **15** (1970), 83–124].

Author Index

Subject Index

A

a posteriori measure, 199, 211, 222, 224, 227, 301

a priori measure, 196–198, 206, 216, 220, 221, 223, 224, 227, 233, 236, 312, 317, 330, 339, 372, 374, 411, 418, 432, 435, 442, 443, 451

absolute error, 5, 7, 24, 43, 105, 107, 109, 113, 115, 174, 175, 177, 316, 319, 325, 326, 331, 333, 335, 346, 355, 364, 366, 367, 371, 374, 422, 435, 442

adaptive information, 28–30, 42, 53, 57–67, 70–72, 75, 82, 88, 91, 94, 101, 106, 108, 126, 174, 184, 196, 216, 217, 236, 237, 239, 240, 242, 244–246, 248, 259, 260, 264, 267–269, 276, 278, 282–286, 294, 316, 320, 328, 347, 350, 381, 383, 389, 391, 392, 400,

401, 443–448, 474

algorithm, 34, 204

asymptotic setting, 24, 38, 375–381, 383, 387, 392, 393, 399, 402, 412

average ε-cardinality number, 213, 214, 248, 300, 310, 313, 420

average complexity, 217, 297, 309, 315, 344

average cardinality, 196, 214–217, 240, 244, 247, 251, 252, 260, 270, 284, 419, 420, 442, 444, 445

average case complexity, 24, 36, 296, 325, 367, 368, 371, 413, 417, 418

average case setting, 3, 5, 7, 10, 15, 23, 35–37, 39, 42, 63, 64, 70, 105, 107, 115, 195–198, 200, 201, 203, 204, 207, 212, 215, 217, 218, 226, 227, 236, 237, 239, 254, 257, 268, 278, 279, 281, 292, 297, 303, 304,